T0320902

A Quiet Revolution?

An irreversible transformation is taking place in the lives of many thousands of university-educated working women in the United Arab Emirates, Oman and the Kingdom of Saudi Arabia. Drawing on eight years' participative research and extensive secondary sources, Nick Forster introduces the first extensive study to describe this development in the Middle East. This book documents the emerging economic and political power of women in these countries, and how they are beginning to challenge ancient and deeply held beliefs about the 'correct' roles of men and women in these conservative Islamic societies, as well as in public- and private-sector organisations. It also describes the vital role that women could play in the economic development and diversification of these countries, and the broader MENA region, in the future. It is an essential read for professionals, scholars and students in fields as diverse as economic development, politics, gender studies, international management, human resource management and Middle Eastern studies.

NICK FORSTER is a writer, business consultant and facilitator based in New South Wales, Australia. Before leaving academia in 2014, he had worked in business faculties at universities in the United Kingdom, Australia, the United Arab Emirates and Oman. He also worked at Al Faisal University in the KSA, where he was a professor of management, director of the MBA program and, occasionally, the acting dean. He has authored or co-authored five books, published more than 130 academic and professional articles, book chapters and conference papers and written numerous research and consulting reports for businesses in the United Kingdom, Australia, Singapore, the United Arab Emirates and Saudi Arabia. He is currently working on a new book, *Why Psychopaths Rule the World*.

A Quiet Revolution?

The Rise of Women Managers,
Business Owners and Leaders
in the Arabian Gulf States

NICK FORSTER

CAMBRIDGE
UNIVERSITY PRESS

CAMBRIDGE
UNIVERSITY PRESS

University Printing House, Cambridge CB2 8BS, United Kingdom

One Liberty Plaza, 20th Floor, New York, NY 10006, USA

477 Williamstown Road, Port Melbourne, VIC 3207, Australia

4843/24, 2nd Floor, Ansari Road, Daryaganj, Delhi – 110002, India

79 Anson Road, #06–04/06, Singapore 079906

Cambridge University Press is part of the University of Cambridge.

It furthers the University's mission by disseminating knowledge in the pursuit of education, learning, and research at the highest international levels of excellence.

www.cambridge.org
Information on this title: www.cambridge.org/9781107143463
DOI: 10.1017/9781316534601

First published 2017

Printed in the United Kingdom by Clays, St Ives plc

A catalogue record for this publication is available from the British Library.

Library of Congress Cataloging-in-Publication Data
Names: Forster, Nick, author.
Title: A quiet revolution? : the rise of women managers, business owners and leaders in the Arabian Gulf States / Nick Forster.
Description: Cambridge, United Kingdom : New York, NY : Cambridge University Press, 2017. | Includes bibliographical references and index.
Identifiers: LCCN 2017007088| ISBN 9781107143463 (Hardback : alk. paper) | ISBN 9781316507780 (pbk. : alk. paper)
Subjects: LCSH: Women executives–Persian Gulf States. | Businesswomen–Persian Gulf States. | Women-owned business enterprises–Persian Gulf States. | Women–Persian Gulf States. | Feminism–Persian Gulf States.
Classification: LCC HD6054.4.P35 F67 2017 | DDC 338.09536082–dc23
LC record available at https://lccn.loc.gov/2017007088

ISBN 978-1-107-14346-3 Hardback
ISBN 978-1-316-50778-0 Paperback

Contents

v

Tables

Preface

This book describes a transformation that is taking place in the lives of tens of thousands of university-educated Arabic-Muslim women in three Arabian Gulf States.[1] These are a small but well-known country, the United Arab Emirates (UAE); one that few Western readers may be familiar with, Oman; and a large, wealthy but much-criticised country, the Kingdom of Saudi Arabia (KSA). It documents the growing economic power and civic influence of these women, the effects of this on ancient and deeply held Islamic religious and cultural beliefs, and how attitudes towards the 'correct' roles of women and men in society and in business and management roles are beginning to change and evolve in these countries in unexpected and surprising ways. It also describes the major contribution that women could make to the economic development and diversification of these countries and the broader Middle East and North Africa (MENA) region in the future. However, this book is not a study of all women in the Middle East or the broader gender sociology and politics of the entire MENA region; it is a study of a relatively privileged but potentially very influential group of university-educated working women in three countries in this region. The implications of this study, however, are relevant to all Islamic countries in the MENA region, and these are described in Chapters 1, 8 and 9 and the Postscript.

In the UAE, for example, over a relatively short period of time (just two generations) the lives of many Emirati women have been transformed. They now enjoy economic, social and personal freedoms that their grandmothers could not have imagined, and life-choices that many of their peers in most other MENA countries can still only dream about. Although it is still very much a 'work in progress,' in some respects the UAE can be regarded as a model for women's economic and social empowerment in a Middle Eastern context. Even in the KSA – a country whose reputation for human rights abuses, judicial cruelty, religious conservatism, corruption and a repressive patriarchal culture is fully merited – there are many brave and resourceful women who are now openly challenging the hegemony of the ruling male elites in the political and legal domains and in public- and private-sector organisations. They have begun to question the oppressive control of the very powerful conservative male clerics and defy deeply ingrained cultural and religious assumptions about the 'correct' roles of women (and men) in this country. There is also, at least among younger, well-educated and more liberal Emiratis, Omanis and Saudis, a growing belief that the emancipation and economic empowerment of women is essential to ensure the long-term economic, political and social futures of their countries. However, as will become apparent in subsequent chapters, there is still a considerable gulf between the 'pro-women' rhetoric of some political rulers, business leaders and media commentators in these countries and what Emirati, Omani and Saudi women actually experience 'at the coal face' in the organisations they work for and as entrepreneurs and business owners.

Although I had an interest in the lives of women in the Middle East before I moved to Dubai in August 2007 and had read some books on the history and cultures of the MENA region, I soon realised that my views about the women and men I first encountered in the UAE in 2007 and in the KSA and Oman between 2011 and 2015 were, to say the least, simplistic and shaped by a largely Western-centric point of view. Over the next eight years, I encountered a very eclectic group of women and men, ranging in age from twenty-one to eighty-five years, who challenged several of the assumptions I had about the people who live, work and raise families in this part of the world. The women I met were very committed to the general development of their respective countries, but they also wanted to fully exploit the new opportunities they had to pursue the careers of their choice and, in some cases, to become leaders in business and politics in the future. They share these hopes and aspirations with many of their female contemporaries in other countries in the MENA region but, unlike previous generations of women in this region, they are uniquely positioned to take advantage of their growing wealth and financial independence.

Drawing on eight years research, this book provides an overview of the many new opportunities that are now available to women in the labour markets of the UAE, Oman and the KSA, but it also highlights the systemic inequalities that still hamper ambitious and talented women in public- and private-sector organisations in these countries.[2] The research presented in this book demonstrates that while women have made remarkable advances over the past two decades in many occupations and professions, particularly in the UAE, deeply ingrained cultural, attitudinal and structural barriers still prevail that will have to be dismantled before a true 'level playing field' is created for women in these countries and the broader MENA region. Having said this, the signs of real change in all three countries are already evident, and these are highlighted throughout this book.

This book adds to an extensive literature on trends and developments in international business and management but it is, to the best of my knowledge, the first one to explain why the growing economic power of women may be a significant catalyst for broader political and social change in the still largely male-dominated and patriarchal societies of these countries over the next ten to twenty years. While several non-governmental organisations, consulting companies and think tanks have examined the possible broader medium- to long-term effects of these significant economic, demographic and socio-cultural changes in the region, very few business and management scholars have addressed these. Furthermore, while many publications have described how organisations can create a more 'level playing field' for women, how this process can be managed in a conservative and patriarchal Arabic-Islamic context is only now being considered by some political and

business and leaders in this part of the world. Hence, I hope this book
may be of interest to anyone who is concerned about the lives of
women in the Middle East and why their emancipation and
empowerment may play an essential role in the economic and
political development of the entire MENA region in the future.

A GUIDE TO THIS BOOK

Chapter 1 begins with a description of a period of time which has
often been portrayed as the 'Golden Age' of Arabic civilisation,
during the Abbasid Caliphate of the eighth to thirteenth centuries.
This provides a stark contrast with the many economic, political,
religious and social challenges facing every country in the
contemporary MENA region, including the UAE, Oman and the KSA.
Some of the material in this chapter makes for uncomfortable
reading, but it would not be possible to write about the lives of
women and men in these countries without referring to these
important contextual issues. Indeed, as we will see in Chapter 8, it is
the existential nature of the many challenges that do confront the
Arabian Gulf States and the broader MENA region today that makes
the economic empowerment and legal emancipation of women one of
the most important national priorities for governments in the region.
This chapter also explores the practical implications of this research
for public-sector and business organisations in the Gulf States and
describes its broader relevance for the medium- to long-term
development of the economies of the MENA region.

Although the contents of Chapters 2, 4 and 6 vary to some
extent, they all provide a brief history of the UAE, Oman and the KSA
and also describe the immense impact of the discovery of oil and gas
on their societies over the last four to five decades. These countries do
have one major advantage when compared to much of the
contemporary MENA region: they are relatively stable and still have
revenues derived from oil and gas that can be used to build the
diversified economies that can support their rapidly growing, young
and increasingly restive populations in the future – but only if their

political and business leaders choose to do this. These chapters also describe the unique challenges facing each country, the changing status and roles of women in these countries over the last twenty to thirty years, the emergence of the first wave of female business and political leaders and the cultural, attitudinal and structural barriers facing Emirati, Omani and Saudi women in the labour markets of their countries. Chapter 3 also features a section on the influence of Islamic theology on gender inequality and segregation in Muslim countries, and Chapters 4 and 6 contain sections on the influence of Ibadism (in Oman) and Wahhabism (in Saudi Arabia) on the lives of women. These chapters also contain evaluations by the World Economic Forum and the United Nations Committee of the Convention on the Elimination of All Forms of Discrimination against Women of the progress that each of these countries has made towards legal and economic equality for women.

Chapters 3, 5 and 7 look at the opinions that Emiratis, Omanis and Saudis have about women in the workplace and their beliefs about the leadership abilities and competencies of women. We evaluate their opinions about the degree of equality that women enjoy in the national labour markets of these countries, describe the cultural and attitudinal barriers they encounter in organisations, summarise the very mixed opinions that men have about a woman's right to work and examine the emerging issues of work–life balance and work–life conflict. These chapters also contain case study sections which look at the experiences of women in two sectors of the labour markets of these countries: information technology (in the UAE), and entrepreneurs and small and medium-sized business owners (in Oman and the KSA). Chapter 5 also contains two contextual sections on the generic challenges facing female entrepreneurs in mature economies and in the MENA region.

Chapter 8 presents the *overwhelming* economic and business cases for creating greater opportunities for women in all professions and occupations in these Arabian Gulf States and the broader MENA region. It proposes that this transformation is one that must be endorsed and encouraged by the governments and business communities of every country in this part of the world. If it is not, almost all countries in this region will struggle to build the sustainable, diversified and internationally competitive economies that can support much larger populations in the future.

Chapter 9 presents a series of policy recommendations for improving the participation of women in public- and private-sector organisations in these countries and the broader MENA region, strategies for increasing their involvement in science, information technology and engineering professions and policies that may need to be enacted to help busy working women cope with work-family conflicts in the future. It also describes a range of national strategies that could be implemented to encourage more women to embrace careers in the private sector and to become entrepreneurs and small business owners.

The Postscript to the book reconsiders the regional economic, political, religious and social challenges first described in Chapter 1 and also describes how the changes and trends identified in Chapters 2 through 7 may affect the lives of millions of women in the Arabian Gulf States and the MENA region in the future. It concludes by asking whether what is being proposed in this book is in harmony with the teachings of Islam and whether the ruling elites and governments of the Gulf States and other countries in the MENA region are likely to embrace these changes and reforms over the next five to ten years.

It is, of course, common knowledge that all Islamic countries in this part of the world are characterised by conservative and patriarchal national cultures. They are also, as we will see in Chapter 1, collectively ranked in the bottom quartile of all international surveys of women's job opportunities, rates of labour force participation, health, education and legal equality. Women are still almost entirely absent from the official religious domain and largely absent from the official political domain but they do have a limited (but growing) role in the economic and civic domains.

Nevertheless, as we will see in Chapters 1 and 8, all countries in this region face significant economic and demographic challenges; ones that will eventually compel them to improve job opportunities for women and greatly increase their participation in their national economies, particularly in the private sector. This, in turn, may lead to greater legal and social equality for women, as it has done in many Western countries over the last thirty to forty years. As noted earlier, the UAE has already realised this need, and Emirati women have made remarkable advances into the national workforce in recent years and now work in almost all professions and occupations. There are similarly encouraging signs in Oman and, surprisingly, even in the KSA. Both economic necessity and demographic trends will eventually compel even oil-rich Saudi Arabia to reform its current labour laws in order to create more job opportunities for the tens of thousands of young women who are now graduating from the country's universities every year and to help more of them become entrepreneurs and business owners in the future.

The greatest pressure for change in the Arabian Gulf States and the broader MENA region may well come from their business communities and business leaders, not from the political (or religious) leadership of countries in the region. This is because many business-people already know that even the oil- and gas-rich countries in the region will face significant economic, political and social problems in the future unless they can create resilient 'post-hydrocarbon' economies within one or, at most, two generations. As this book was being completed in June 2016, it was very evident that the precipitous fall in oil and gas prices between the end of 2014 and mid-2016 was already having a serious impact on the economies and national revenues of the UAE, Oman, the KSA and the other Gulf States. During 2015–2016, with the exception of Kuwait, all countries in the Arabian Gulf ran substantial budget deficits. As we will see in later chapters, this has created much greater pressures on the governments of these countries to accelerate the dual-process of labour market reforms and economic modernisation. The main purpose of this book is to show why this transition can only be accomplished with the active participation of a much greater number of women in the economies and political systems of these countries, and why regional governments will need to make the changes that will be required to achieve this as soon as possible. This transition, however, will be a very difficult one for the political and business leaders of the UAE, Oman, the KSA and every other country in the MENA region to manage, and the reasons for this are described in Chapter 1.

Acknowledgements

This book is the culmination of the time I spent working in the business faculties of three universities in the United Arab Emirates (UAE), Oman and the Kingdom of Saudi Arabia (KSA) from September 2007 to June 2015, and many people have contributed to the themes, ideas and policy recommendations it contains. I'd like to thank Khadija Alarkoubi, Lynda Moore and Carole Spiers for their helpful suggestions about the initial book proposal, Khadija for reviewing some chapters before the book was published and Daniel Lund, a colleague and friend at Al Faisal University, for listening to my half-baked ideas for this book during 2013–2014. I'd particularly like to thank the nine women who attended Master of Business Administration courses in the UAE and the KSA during 2008–2014, who reviewed several chapters of the book during the first half of 2016. It is a sad indictment of the constraints on freedom of expression in these countries that they all requested that I should not mention them by name in this book, as did three former academic colleagues who still work in the Gulf States.

This book would not have been possible without the help and assistance of several postgraduate and undergraduate students in these countries. They helped me gain access to many local public- and private-sector organisations to conduct questionnaire surveys, and also provided helpful personal introductions to female Omani and Saudi business owners. Many women and men in these countries also gave generously of their time for interviews and, in the process, taught me a great deal about their lives, their cultural and religious beliefs and their hopes for the future of their countries. I'd also like to say a special thank you to the group of female undergraduates at Zayed University who first enlightened me about the intricacies of their lives in the UAE during 2008 and also helped me understand why they, and their peers in Oman and the KSA, may play a major role in transforming the lives of women in their countries, the Arabian Gulf States and the broader MENA region in the future. Three of the award-winning final-year Capstone Projects written by some of these young Emiratis are included in the bibliography of this book. This book is dedicated to all of you and your hopes for a secure and prosperous future for yourselves, your families, your children and your countries. Last, but not least, I'd like to thank Paula Parish, Valerie Appelby, Daniel Brown, James Gregory, Stephen Acerra, Isawariya Lakshmi, Fred Goykhman, Yassar Arafat, Divya Arjunan and the marketing team at Cambridge University Press for their invaluable help and advice during the writing, editing and publication of this book.

I The Contemporary Middle East and North Africa

I.I INTRODUCTION

Any study of the experiences of women in the contemporary MENA region has to consider both the volatile history of this part of the world and the cultural characteristics of the countries in which the Emiratis, Omanis and Saudis who are featured in this book live and work. This chapter begins with a brief description of a period of time that has often been called the 'Golden Age' of Arabic civilisation during the Abbasid Caliphate of 762–1258 CE. This provides a bleak contrast with the economic, political and social challenges that confront the entire MENA region today. Section 1.3 describes these in some detail and also considers the impact of the 2011 Arab Spring on the MENA region and the emergence of fundamentalist Islamic groups such as the Islamic State of Iraq and Greater Syria (ISIS). Drawing on recent reports by the United Nations, the World Bank, the World Economic Forum and the world's leading consulting companies, it also examines the economic, political and social status of women in countries in the MENA region. Section 1.4 explores the practical implications of this book for public- and private-sector organisations in the region and describes the economic and business case for improving the economic participation of women in regional labour markets – an issue we return to in greater depth in Chapter 8. It also outlines the broader potential implications of this transformation for the medium- to long-term development of all the national economies of this deeply troubled part of the world.

I.2 THE MENA REGION IN THE PAST

We Arabs used to be at the centre of world culture. We invented mathematics. We were the scholars and scientists. The world used to

1

turn to Arabia for its knowledge and books. And now look at us. We are the poorest people in the world, backwards, tribal and illiterate. Why? Because we have let ourselves be led around like dogs by our leaders, by thieves. Now, with our revolution, we are saying no. We are saying we are dignified. We are proud.

Anwar Hamady, a Yemeni academic (Fleishman, 2011)

Today, the MENA region consists of nineteen countries, stretching from Morocco on the Atlantic coast of Africa to the borders of India and Pakistan in the East. In 2016, it was home to approximately 350 million people (more than three times the population in 1970) and contained about 20 per cent of the global Islamic population of approximately one billion people. Within this region we find Arabia which was, between the eighth and thirteenth centuries, part of one of the most extensive and advanced civilisations in the world: the Abbasid Caliphate. In 1000 CE, the cities of Baghdad, Cairo and Damascus were major hubs of free trade and international commerce, open markets, technological and industrial innovation and major centres of intellectual enquiry and learning. This region was, by the standards of the time, home to one of the most affluent civilisations in the world, the other being China (Morris, 2011: 331–384). In the words of one scholar of Islamic science:

> Proximity to Indian trade routes, a vibrant multi-ethnic culture and safe distance from the traditional military dangers posed by the Byzantine Greeks helped establish Baghdad for centuries as the world's most prosperous nexus of trade, commerce, and intellectual and scientific exchange ... Urban merchants and traders generated the surpluses of cash and leisure time that made the scholarly life possible in the first place. In the division of labour that characterised Arab city life, there was ample room for the thinker, the teacher and the writer
>
> *(Lyons, 2010: 60 and 160).*

What is arguably the oldest multi-faculty higher education institution in the world was founded in the ninth century at Fez in Morocco, and between the ninth and thirteenth centuries the *Bayt al-Hikma* in Baghdad (or, as some Islamic scholars call it, the *Medinat al-Hikma* – 'City of Wisdom') was not only the epicentre of scholarship and research in the Muslim world; it was the leading centre of learning for the entire occidental world at this time. It was supported by generous financial endowments from a succession of Abbasid caliphs and 'it came to comprise a translation bureau, a library and book repository, and an academy of scholars and intellectuals from across the empire' (Lyons, 2010: 63). Here and at other scholarly centres and schools, such as those at the Al Azhar mosque complex in Cairo and at Al Andalus in Spain, many theoretical advances and practical innovations were made in architecture, agriculture and horticulture, algebra, anatomy and medicine, astronomy, cartography, ceramics and glass making, chemistry, economic theory, engineering, mathematics, numerology and optics (including the first known *camera obscura*, later used by Roger Bacon to study solar eclipses) and in psychology and psychotherapy, by the scholars who worked together in what was, by the standards of that time, a generally tolerant, liberal, multi-cultural and multi-ethnic environment.

While Europeans struggled until at least the twelfth century with the most rudimentary mathematical and philosophical concepts, the Abbasid caliphs who reigned from the eighth to the thirteenth century promoted and encouraged an open, enquiring and more rationalistic version of Islam. The ideas of earlier Persian, Roman, Egyptian and Hindu scholars (particularly their numerical system which we know today as 'Arabic' numerals), as well as the works of Aristotle, Archimedes, Euclid, Galen, Hippocrates, Plato, Ptolemy, Pythagoras and many others were retrieved, recorded, studied and further developed by the Islamic and Nestorian Christian *ulama* [1] who worked at the *Bayt al-Hikma*, while Europe endured the Dark Ages following the collapse of the Roman Empire in the fifth century CE. Muslim scientists, such as Avicenna and Averroes, were mapping the heavens and wondering about the origins of the cosmos, while their European contemporaries could only gaze at the complex movements of the solar system and the stars with little more than baffled bewilderment. More than 100 of the most visible stars in the night sky owe their names to astronomers from this time.

Astronomy is just one example of the enormous debt that Europe owed to Islamic proto-science. Many scientific and mathematical words that we now take for granted can be traced back to this time, including *alchemy, algebra, alcohol, alkali, azimuth, elixir, sine, zenith* and *zero* (al-Khalili, 2012: 241). The dissemination of this know-ledge was increased exponentially by using a revolutionary new writing material called paper – invented by the Chinese between the second and third centuries BCE. Without the dissemination of the accumulated knowledge of the *Bayt al-Hikma*, as several scholars have recently demonstrated, the later innovative work of luminaries such as Copernicus, Brahe, Kepler or Galileo might never have happened, and there may have been no European Renaissance ('rebirth') during the sixteenth century and, later, an industrial revolution in England in the mid- to late eighteenth century (al-Khalili, 2012; Lyons, 2010; Masood, 2009; Saliba, 2007).

The destruction of Baghdad and the *Bayt al-Hikma* in 1258 by the Mongol warlord Hulagu Khan marked the end of what is now widely recognised as the Golden Period of the Arabic civilisation and Islamic proto-science, and as increasingly conservative and other-worldly rulers and *imams* came to dominate the different regions of the Caliphate, support and sponsorship for scholarly and scientific pursuits declined markedly during the fourteenth and fifteenth centuries. However, the knowledge generated at the *Bayt al-Hikma* and other centres of learning in the Caliphate would soon find fertile ground in which to germinate and grow in Europe during the fifteenth and sixteenth centuries, particularly after the invention of the printing press by Johannes Gutenberg (Diner, 2009: 71–95). The eventual triumph of the more strict and doctrinaire caliphs that super-seded the Abbasid rulers of the thirteenth century meant that very few rulers in the MENA region re-embraced the proto-science their predecessors had pioneered and simply ignored many of the new technologies generated by the first industrial revolution in Europe during the eighteenth and nineteenth centuries until it was too late (al-Hassan, 1996; al-Khalili, 2012). Furthermore, even in the extensive and long-lasting Ottoman Empire, its rulers failed to understand the economic and military threat posed by the new European powers that began to emerge during the eighteenth century until it had become far too late to counter their global military and economic expansion during the nineteenth century; as a result, the Ottoman Empire was 'gradually overtaken by the dynamism of Europe' (Rogan, 2015: xviii).

Hence, when Napoleon invaded Egypt in 1798, 'he might almost have come from Mars', so great was the economic and technological gulf between the emerging European powers and the countries of the MENA region; and 'by the time that Sadik Rifat Pasha, the Ottoman ambassador to Vienna warned that the Europeans were flourishing thanks to a combination of science, technology and, "the necessary rights of freedom", it was already too late' (Ferris, 2010: 268). By 1920, all of the MENA region was either directly controlled or encircled by European imperial powers, and by the middle of the twentieth century, the discovery of oil in several locations ensured that many of those would be drawn into the political and military affairs of the region from that time to the present day (Diner, 2009; Saliba, 2007).[2] And, as Ferris has observed, those states that possessed oil (and gas) wealth were transformed from small fishing, herding and trading communities 'into economically more vertical societies where the few who controlled the oil became rich and the rest stayed poor. Such inequities were offensive to Islam – which, like Christianity had originated a religion centred on the poor and devoted to social justice – but the attempts of Muslim leaders to redress them by resorting to wealth distribution through state socialism failed' (Ferris, 2010: 269).

It would be fairer to say that this strategy has 'largely failed', because while it has led to rapid GDP growth, extensive infrastructure development and some economic diversification over the past thirty years, we will see in subsequent chapters that it is no longer a sustainable medium- to long-term strategy for any country in the Gulf States and the broader MENA region. We return to look at the lessons that can be learned from this 'Golden Age' of Arabic trade, culture and learning for the future of the region and the prospects for the millions of women who live there at the end of Chapter 9 and in the Postscript to the book.

I.3 THE ECONOMIC, POLITICAL AND SOCIAL CHALLENGES FACING THE MENA REGION TODAY

The problem of modern Islam, in a nutshell, is that we are totally dependent on the West – for our dishwashers, our clothes, our cars, our education, everything. It is humiliating and every Muslim feels it. We were once the most sophisticated civilisation in the world. Now we are backward. We can't even fight our wars without using our enemies' weapons.

Omar Nasiri, a former Moroccan *jihadist* (Ferris, 2010: 272)

Making the leap from the thirteenth century to the second decade of the current century, we find that the MENA region, overall, lags behind most of the rest of the world on many key metrics and indicators of economic, political, social, scientific and educational development, even though many countries in this region have bene-fitted greatly from the wealth derived from their oil and gas industries over the past half century. These metrics and indicators include:

The low average per-capita income growth for the citizens of most countries in the MENA region over the past five decades, combined with a marked concentration of wealth among the ruling political elites of all countries in the region (*The Economist*, 2016e, 2014a and 2013; United Nations, 2015a, 2009, 2005 and 2004).

Endemic national, civil, ethnic and religious conflicts in every Muslim country in the MENA region. In 2016, the most notable examples of this were Iraq, Syria, Libya and Yemen, with growing civil unrest in several other countries such as Lebanon, Oman and even the KSA. Some 10 million people have been rendered homeless by these conflicts and more than 230,000 have been killed (including at least 30,000 children). About two million people have fled these conflict zones, and this, in turn, has led to a major refugee crisis in several North African countries and the European Union.

The prevalence of autocratic governments and non-democratic political systems across the entire MENA region. Countries in this region are also characterised by the lowest political freedom scores of any region of the world, as measured by the existence of participative and open political processes, accountable and equitable legal systems, freedom of speech and expression of thought, independent news media and unrestricted Internet access, and established political rights and freedoms such as the right to vote in transparent democratic elections and the freedom to take part in civil activism (Freedom House, 2016b; Human Rights Watch, 2015; United Nations, 2009, 2005 and 2004).

A notable lack of legal accountability, transparency and governance standards among the ruling political and business elites of many countries in the MENA region, as well as high levels of corruption and fraud. For example, of the 19 countries in the MENA region just 2 were ranked in the top 50 'least corrupt' countries in the world in 2016 (Bahrain and the UAE), and 84 per cent were ranked in the top 50 of 175 countries in Transparency International's 2015 Corruption Perceptions Index. Only six countries in the region had scores above 50/100; anything below this score and corruption is deemed to be 'a serious problem' (Transparency International, 2016).

Even the most stable countries in the region – primarily those that have benefitted greatly from an abundance of oil and gas, such as the UAE, Oman, the KSA, Kuwait, Qatar and Bahrain – have not yet built economies or stable political and civic institutions that would survive for long if their natural resource pipelines were switched off tomorrow. It is true, however, that the members of the Gulf Cooperation Council (GCC) have all made efforts to use their resource wealth to begin the long process of building more diversified, knowledge-based economies, and a handful of their largest companies are internationally competitive (Hertog, 2010a; Hvidt, 2013).

Other indicators of regional under-development include the comparatively low amount of capital spent on research and development (R&D) in both basic and applied scientific research in the region. In 2013, the fifty-seven member countries of the Organisation of the Islamic Conference invested just 0.81 per cent of their combined annual GDPs on R&D. The Muslim world as a whole spends less than 0.5 per cent of their cumulative GDP on R&D, compared to an average of about 5 per cent in countries affiliated with the Organisation for Economic Co-Operation and Development (OECD). In the MENA region, Israel is the clear leader, spending about 4.4 per cent of its GDP on R&D and invests a significant proportion of this in research at its national universities. In addition, countries in the MENA region have fewer than 10 scientists, engineers and technicians per 1,000 people, compared to an average of 40 in emerging economies and 140 per 1,000 in the industrialised world (*The Economist*, 2014a and 2014b; al-Khalili, 2012: 283). There are a few signs of increased spending on scientific research in a few countries, albeit from a very low base. Qatar, for example, increased annual funding on R&D from 0.8 per cent of GDP to 2.8 per cent in the early 2010s. Turkey, which is not part of the MENA region but is a predominantly Islamic country, increased its funding by an average of 10 per cent a year from 2005 to 2010, and its output of scientific papers rose from 5,000 to 22,000 a year between 2002 and 2009. Moreover, countries in the MENA region register very few scientific or industrial patents – approximately one per million of their population each year. In 2013, the ratio was 77.6 per million in Canada and 123.2 per million in Singapore (*The Economist*, 2014a and 2013b).

The 2005 United Nations Arab Human Development Report (AHDR) had noted that the entire MENA region imported fewer scientific and academic books than the United Kingdom alone imported in 2004, and Cambridge University Press published more academic books that year than the *entire* MENA region (United Nations 2005: 34). In 2012, Harvard University alone produced more scientific papers than the combined output of all the universities in seventeen Muslim countries in this region (*The Economist*, 2013b); a situation that was largely unchanged from both the early 2000s (*The Economist*, 2002) and the mid-1990s (Segal, 1996). Between them, universities in the MENA region – excluding Israel – contribute less than 1 per cent of the world's published scientific papers (*The Economist*, 2014a: 9). Furthermore, while the MENA region has produced just 3 Nobel Laureates in Science since 1901 there have been 193 Jewish Nobel Laureates (out of a total of 855 honourees) and a single Cambridge College (Trinity) has produced 32 Nobel Laureates during this period of time (Jewish Virtual Library, 2015).

It is also evident that there are very few elite, world-class universities in the MENA region. There were, for example, only five universities in the entire MENA region ranked in the Times Higher Education and Webometrics top 500 global universities in 2016 and 2015, and four of those were in Israel (Times Higher Education, 2016 and 2015; Webometrics, 2015). An examination of the distribution of world-class universities by country of origin reveals a similar picture: the United States has 142 universities ranked in the top 500, followed by China and Germany with 40 each, the United Kingdom with 34, Spain with 27, Canada with 24 and Australia with 16. The nineteen countries of the MENA region, excluding Israel, had just one university ranked in the global top 500 in 2016 and 2015. There are more than 1,000 universities in the MENA region, with the highest-ranked ones being the Hebrew University of Jerusalem and Tel Aviv University, and both are in the Times Higher Education and Webometrics top 300. Israel is also the highest-ranked regional nation-state, with four universities ranked in the top 500. Saudi Arabia, with approximately fifty accredited universities and colleges of further education, was the only Arabic country that had a university ranked in either the Times Higher Education or the Webometrics top 500 global universities in 2016 and 2015, the King Fahd University of Petroleum and Minerals (Times Higher Education, 2016 and 2015; Webometrics, 2015). However, with this single exception, the higher education (HE) sector of the predominantly Muslim countries of the MENA region is notable primarily for the absence of world-class universities (Forster, 2017).

In addition to these metrics and indicators, the low economic, political, educational and legal status (EPELS) of women in MENA countries has been extensively documented. Globally, only Sub-Saharan Africa countries have a lower EPELS score than Middle Eastern countries on measures of the participation of women in political, economic, professional and social activities and their legal and social rights. These gaps have been and remain particularly acute for millions of uneducated women in the region (Kelly and Breslin, 2014; United Nations, 2016 and 2015a: 107–116; United Nations Economic and Social Commission for Western Asia, 2014a; World Economic Forum, 2015b). In the political domain, for example, even in those countries that have held political 'elections' of some description over the past twenty years, less than 10 per cent of those elected were women. 'Women in power', the United Nations AHDR noted in 2005, 'are often selected from the ranks of the elite or appointed from the ruling party as window-dressing for the ruling regime.' And efforts to address this deficit 'have often been limited to cosmetic empowerment in the sense of enabling notable women to occupy leadership positions in the structure of the existing regime without extending empowerment to the broad base of women; a process that automatically entails the empowerment of all citizens' (United Nations, 2005: 9 and 51). This report also noted that:

> The traditional view that the man is the breadwinner blocks the employment of women and contributes to an increase in women's employment relative to men. Women thus encounter significant obstacles outside family life that reduce their potential. Most limiting of these are the terms and conditions of work: women do not enjoy equality of opportunity with men in job opportunities, conditions, or wages; yet alone in promotion to decision-making positions
>
> *(United Nations, 2005: 8).*

While there are considerable variations in the EPELS of women in individual countries in the MENA region, the average rate of participation by women in paid employment is lower than any other region of the world, including Sub-Saharan Africa, and the overall gender gap between the participation rates of men and women in the labour markets of this region is very wide when compared to almost every other part of the world. For example, the participation rate of women in the 19 national labour markets of the MENA region in 2005 was 33 per cent, compared to an OECD average of 55.6 per cent and more than 70 per cent in Nordic countries such as Norway and Sweden (United Nations, 2005: 8 and 88). This, as we will see in later chapters, has not changed significantly in most countries in the MENA region over the last decade (United Nations, 2015a: 107–116; World Economic Forum, 2015b).

One of the small number of studies that has looked at the attitudes of men towards women's right to work in Islamic societies found what can only be described as 'mixed' viewpoints about this (Telhami, 2013). This study summarised the findings of national opinion polls from Egypt, Jordan, Lebanon, Morocco, Saudi Arabia and the UAE, as well as polls of those of Middle Eastern origin resident in the United States; and Israeli Arab and Palestinian opinion polls from 2003–2012. It found that one fifth of Arabs believed that women should 'never have the right to work outside the house', whereas around one third believed that 'women should always have the right to work outside the home.' However, the largest group felt that 'women should have the right to work only when economically needed.' Between 40 and 50 per cent of respondents in five countries and, perhaps surprisingly, 70 per cent in the UAE agreed with this statement (Telhami, 2013: 167 and 168). A survey of 1,450 women and men in Egypt, Morocco and the KSA in 2012 revealed that 80 per cent of men believed that women should be limited to housekeeping and childcare roles, rising to 97 per cent in the KSA. However, suggesting something of a generational shift in attitudes, this fell to 59 per cent among men aged 15–24 and to 22 per cent among the young women in this group (Shediac et al, 2012: 27). In Chapters 2 through 7 we will look at the foundations of these beliefs and the cultural, attitudinal and structural barriers that continue to inhibit the full participation of women in the national labour markets of the Gulf States and the broader MENA region.

Female enrolment in education, particularly in the Gulf States, has increased exponentially over the past twenty years, and they generally perform better than males do at the secondary and tertiary levels. However, if they are allowed by their fathers or husbands to attend university, they are still concentrated in fields such as education, literature, languages, human resource management and the social sciences. Very few Arab women study for degrees in computer science and information technology (CSIT) and women in the MENA region are noticeably under-represented in science, technology, engineering and mathematics (STEM) professions (Forster and al-Marzouqi, 2011; Kelly and Breslin, 2014; *The Economist* Intelligence Unit, 2014). Many young Arab women continue to avoid educational, career or entrepreneurial opportunities in CSIT, and most of the handful of Arab women who first graduated with science doctorates in the late 1990s and early 2000s chose to work at Western universities (Kandaswamy, 2003). Women in the MENA region are also much more likely to work in the public sector than in wealth-generating private-sector businesses, and few are entrepreneurs and small business owners, and the reasons for these structural imbalances are explained in Chapters 2 through 7 (United Nations, 2004: 80–84 and 108; World Economic Forum, 2015b).

Last, but not least, is the well-documented dearth of women's legal rights in the MENA region, including the restrictions imposed by the 'male guardianship' rules in most MENA countries, the absence of equal legal rights in both the public and private domain and a lack of protection against violence by men. The 2005 UN AHDR noted that 'the forms of violence practiced against women confirm that Arab legislators and government, together with Arab social movements, face a large task in achieving security and development in its comprehensive sense. The mere discussion of violence against women arouses strong resistance in some Arab countries' (United Nations, 2005: 10). In fact, as several female Islamic scholars have noted, 'strong resistance' to such discussions occurs in *all* Arab countries particularly in those that have fallen prey to the most virulent forms of Islamic 'purification' in, for example, Afghanistan in the 1990s, Sudan in the 1990s and 2000s or the ISIS-controlled areas of Iraq and Syria during the 2000s and 2010s. Such forms of violence include 'honour' killings, forced female circumcisions, acid attacks on young girls who attend school and the stoning of alleged 'adulterers' and women who have been the *victims* of rape, domestic violence and so forth (Ali, 2015; 2010 and 2007; Bennoune, 2013; Eltahawy, 2005). This is not to imply that acts of violence against women, either in the domestic sphere or as part of more systemic atrocities committed against women during civil, sectarian or national wars (e.g. gang rapes, forced marriages and so forth), are unique to the MENA region. Such abuses have been perpetrated by men against women in every culture throughout human history.

The popular uprisings in Morocco, Libya, Iran, Tunisia, Bahrain, Egypt and Syria during the Arab Spring were clear evidence that these systemic and endemic economic, political and social problems (and, of course, the relatively low status of women) had not been addressed or resolved by the autocratic governments of these countries. As one Arabic commentator has observed:

> The uprisings were in the first place about *karamah* [dignity] and about ending a pervasive sense of humiliation. The dignity they hoped to restore was not simply in the relationship between rulers and ruled, but also in their relationship between their nations and the outside world ... Fundamentally, most Arab citizens across the region were hungry for freedom, economic opportunity, dignity and individual rights and liberty
>
> *(Talhami, 2013: 17 and 18).*

Many women became involved in these political protests, taking to the streets, being arrested and sometimes being beaten up or suffering humiliating sexual abuse by the police and army (as occurred in Egypt with the military's disgraceful 'virginity tests' in 2013 and in Sudan during 2011) (Khalil, 2011). These protests provided them with an opportunity to demand greater legal, economic, social and human rights and to also show their opposition to the growing tide of Islamic fundamentalism in the MENA region (Bennoune, 2013; Cole, 2014: 271–272). The bravery and resilience of these women were recognised, at least symbolically, when Tawakkol Karman, a Yemeni political activist, was awarded one of three 2011 Nobel Peace Prizes and the Pakistani teenager Malala Yousafzai received the 2014 International Children's Peace Prize. Predictably, both were quickly denounced as 'pawns of the Great Satan' and 'whores' on several fundamentalist Islamic websites (Muhanna-Matar, 2014). We will see in Chapters 2 through 7 that similar hopes and aspirations were expressed by many of the women and men who are featured in this study; above all else, their desire for *karamah*.[2]

The wave of protests in the region in the late 2000s and early 2010s did lead to the overthrow of one set of dictators in Tunisia, Egypt, Libya and Yemen and to growing demands for fundamental reforms in several other countries such as Iraq, Bahrain, the UAE, Oman and the KSA. However, despite the hopes of many people in the MENA region and elsewhere, the Arab Spring had stalled by the end of 2013, and there were few signs that a systemic process of political and social change was likely to occur. In a review of the situation in the MENA region in early 2016, *The Economist* concluded that:

> Arabs have rarely lived in bleaker times. The hopes raised by the Arab Spring – for more inclusive politics and more responsive government, for more jobs and fewer presidential cronies carving up the economy – have been dashed. The wells of despair are overflowing ... Rent-seeking remains rampant and standards in both public education and the administration of justice are still dismal. Economic growth is slow or stagnant; the hand of the security forces weigh heavier than ever, more or less everywhere. Sectarian divisions and class rivalries have deepened, providing fertile ground for radicals who posit their own brutal visions of Islamic Utopia as the only solution
>
> *(The Economist, 2016e: 35–36).*

Moreover, it soon became clear that these protests and uprisings had not led to greater freedoms and rights for women in the region. In fact, in those MENA countries characterised by civil, sectarian, tribal and religious conflicts, the situation for women became noticeably worse during 2012–2016. This prompted *The Economist* to ask, in a lead editorial article in July 2014, 'Why Arab countries have so miserably failed to create democracy, happiness or (aside from the windfall of oil) wealth for its 350 million people is one of the great questions of our time. What makes Arab society so susceptible to vile regimes and fanatics bent on destroying them and their perceived allies in the West?' (*The Economist*, 2014a: 9). While detailed answers to that question are beyond the scope of this book and this topic has been addressed by many commentators in recent times, a summary of some of the main reasons that have been presented to account for the economic, political and social problems facing the MENA region is necessary. This is because these define the sociological contexts in which the women and men who are the primary focus of this study live and help us better understand how they make sense of their societies and their lives in Chapters 2 through 7. Although there are considerable variations given to their relative significance and importance, all commentators on the MENA region claim that the endemic instability of the region today has a number of interrelated causes. These include:

The long-term residual effects of the arbitrary 'carve-up' of the MENA region and the Ottoman Empire as a result of the Sykes-Picot agreement of 1916. The national frontiers created at this time did not reflect the ethnic, cultural and religious make-up of this region; merely the strategic whims of the imperialist powers that created these. This coincided with the installation in power of privileged 'Westernised' ruling elites by European colonial powers after World War I in most MENA countries, which also happened in many countries in sub-Saharan Africa and South-East Asia after World War II (Acemoglu and Robinson, 2012; Rogan, 2015).

The creation of a Jewish state in Palestine in 1948 and the largely unconditional support given to this country by the United States and many of its allies since, combined with regular military incursions by the USA in the MENA region in furtherance of its global military, strategic and energy interests and its support of a succession of autocratic and repressive regimes in the region over the last seven decades. It is probable that the invasion and occupation of Iraq in 2003, engineered by Bush, Cheney, Wolfowitz, Abrams, Libby and the former British Prime Minister Tony Blair, will be judged by future historians as one of the most poorly thought-out, ineptly executed and expensive debacles in military history (Bugliosi, 2008).

A notable lack of legal accountability, transparency and governance standards among the ruling political and business elites of many countries in the MENA region, as well as high levels of corruption and fraud. For example, of the 19 countries in the MENA region just 2 were ranked in the top 50 'least corrupt' countries in the world in 2016 (Bahrain and the UAE), and 84 per cent were ranked in the top 50 of 175 countries in Transparency International's 2015 Corruption Perceptions Index. Only six countries in the region had scores above 50/100; anything below this score and corruption is deemed to be 'a serious problem' (Transparency International, 2016).

The deeply tribal and patriarchal cultures of the entire region, in which deference and loyalty to one's dynastic elders, family, clan and tribe (*sabiyya qabaliyya*), and to local concerns and personal connections (*wasta*), are still paramount. These loyalties may often be at odds with national economic, political and social interests (Diner, 2009).

The significant economic and social pressures generated by the rapid growth of the populations of all MENA countries during the 1990s and 2000s and very high average youth unemployment levels of between 25 and 40 per cent (and more than 50 per cent, on average, for young women in the region)(International Labour Organisation, 2015; United Nations, 2009, 2005 and 2004).

The failure of almost all countries in the MENA region to develop the societal and institutional prerequisites for stable nation-states including representative and non-corrupt political institutions and administrative systems, transparent and inclusive electoral processes, independent legal systems, free and independent news and media organisations, protection for religious and cultural minorities, independent, high-quality schools and universities teaching modern non-Islamic curricula, autonomous civic associations and trade unions and the unwillingness of any country in the MENA region to separate 'mosque and state' (Morris, 2011; Stark, 2014; Telhami, 2013; *The Economist*, 2016e; 2014a, 2014b and 2002).

Almost all Western and some Arabic commentators believe that the pervasive influence of Islam (or, to be more accurate, how this is interpreted and practiced by many Muslims) is one of the principal reasons this region is still characterised by so many endemic and deep-seated problems. The distinction that exists in many non-Islamic countries between religion and the state has no provenance in Islamic theology and law, and so many adherents believe not only that spiritual and secular authority are inseparable but that the latter must – in all circumstances and at all times – be subservient to the former. This means that there can be no separation of religion from the state (*fasl al-dinn wa al-dawla*), and in every Arabic country this means Islam (Ali, 2015; Zakaria, 2004: 119–160). As Ali has observed:

> The leading Muslim clerics have come to the consensus that Islam is more than a mere religion, but rather the one and only comprehensive system that embraces, explains, integrates, and dictates all aspects of human life: personal, cultural, political, as well as religious. In short, Islam handles everything. Any cleric who advocates the separation of mosque and state is instantly anathematized. He is declared a heretic and his work is removed from the bookshelves. This is what makes Islam fundamentally different from other twenty first-century monotheistic religions ... It is not simply that the boundaries between religion and politics are porous. There scarcely are any boundaries ... In countries like Saudi Arabia and Iran, or within mounting insurgent movements such as Islamic State and Boko Haram, the boundaries between religion and politics do not exist at all
>
> *(Ali, 2015: 56–57).*

It is this largely unquestioned religious hegemony that has prevented the development of modern secular political and civic institutions in almost all MENA countries in contrast to, for example, the protracted and difficult process of political change and secularisation experienced by Europe and North America during the nineteenth and twentieth centuries. All countries in those regions witnessed, among other significant societal changes, the gradual separation of church and state, the dismantling of the 'divine right' of monarchs and the power of the landed aristocracy, the industrial and scientific revolutions, the spread of democracy, universal suffrage and greater governmental accountability, the gradual acceptance of the principle of religious diversity and tolerance, the establishment of the right of *habeas corpus*, protection of intellectual freedom and expression of ideas and, more recently, the principal of legal equality for women, ethnic minority and gay and lesbian groups. Furthermore, as many writers have demonstrated, none of these societal, cultural and social transformations would have been possible unless the hegemony of institutionalised religion in Europe and North America had been progressively challenged and then dismantled during the nineteenth and twentieth centuries. In contrast, the predominantly Islamic countries of the MENA region have barely started to even *discuss* these existential political, cultural and social issues (Ali, 2015; Dawkins, 2006; Diner, 2009; Morris, 2011; Stark, 2014).

There is also little disagreement among commentators on the MENA region that an increasing number of alienated younger Muslims are advocating more fanatical interpretations of Islam. This trend was first identified during the early 2000s (Burgot, 2003; Fadl, 2005; Kepel, 2004), and a more recent report by the Tony Blair Faith Foundation has described the very close relationship between Islamic beliefs and jihadist ideology (Badawy et al, 2015). The endemic instability of the MENA region has led to the emergence of revolutionary Sunni and Shiite jihadist groups, such as the militant ISIS (also known as ISIL – the Islamic State of Iraq and the Levant – and Daesh). In early 2014, this group declared that its leader, Abu Bakr al-Baghdadi, was the Caliph of all Muslims and that its intention was to wage a holy war on all 'non-believers' (which, of course, included all Muslims who did not accept his legitimacy). Its long-term goal is to destroy the al-Saud dynasty in the KSA and create a modern-day Caliphate that will – they believe – eventually encompass a region stretching from Spain in the West, all of the MENA region, two thirds of India, the western region of China and all of Malaysia and Indonesia (*The Economist*, 2014a and b).[3] Concurrently, the bloody suppression by President Assad of Syria (a member of the minority Sunni Alawite sect), a similar crackdown by Nuri Al-Maliki on Sunnis in Iraq, the abuses perpetrated against members of the Muslim Brotherhood in Egypt during 2013–2015 and the repression of Shia Muslims in Saudi Arabia and Bahrain during 2012–2016 were all symptomatic of escalating national, ethnic, religious and tribal tensions in the MENA region during the present decade (The Economist, 2016e, l and m).

These continuing and apparently irreconcilable conflicts, combined with the absence of what can broadly be described as 'liberal', strong and independent political and civil institutions in all MENA countries, has meant that very few of them have been able to build modern, diversified, internationally competitive economies. Even the most stable countries in the region – primarily those that have benefitted greatly from bonanzas of oil and gas, such as Bahrain, the KSA, Kuwait, Oman, Qatar and the UAE – have not yet built economies or stable political and civic institutions that would survive for more than a few months if their oil and gas pipelines were switched off tomorrow. While all of these countries have made some efforts to diversify their economies, two reports on the economic and political future of the MENA region have noted that:

> Without deep economic change, the MENA region will be unable to realize the benefits that come from having a young, energetic and aspiring population. The current demographic bulge (in which more than half the population is younger than 25) means that the Middle-East will need to create millions of jobs just to stand still ... Prosperity depends on having a reinforcing virtuous circle in which economic growth, robust and relevant education and creative opportunities come together
>
> *(Saddi et al, 2012: 3).*

The effects of the recent global economic crisis were all-pervasive and have demonstrated that no economy is safe from destabilising external events. Resource-dependent countries with their narrow base of economic activity, are particularly vulnerable ... Not only must countries' GDP be balanced among sectors, but key elements of its economy must be varied, flexible, and readily applicable to a variety of economic opportunities, and areas of over-concentration must be continually identified and mitigated. Policymakers should work to achieve greater economic diversification, in order to reduce the impact of external events and foster more robust, resilient growth over the long-term ... For resource rich developing nations, sector diversification is still the first priority; a failure to achieve this first step in diversification will undermine these countries' strong growth potential

(Shediac et al, 2011: 1–2).

This is sensible advice, but there are three reasons all countries in the MENA region will struggle to build stable and diversified economies in the future, including the three that are the primary focus of this study. First, they are all characterised either by widespread economic, political and social instability or – at best – a *repressive stability*, maintained and supported by oil and gas wealth. Second, they are not what are described by political economists as 'inclusive states', where the use and distribution of the resources and state revenues of each country are subject to independent scrutiny and accountability and are, at least nominally, 'owned' by the people through their elected representatives. Rather, they are predominantly 'extractive', 'rentier' or 'clientilist' societies, ruled over by intransigent and often repres-sive oligarchies. Third, they still exclude many of their female citi-zens and ethnic/religious minorities from active and equal participation in their political systems and do not allow these groups equal access to civic society, to their labour markets and to all occupations and professions, particularly at the most senior levels (Beblawi, 1990; Diner, 2009: 11–37; Hertog, 2010a: 9–10, 37–38 and 264–275; Wenar, 2016). As *The Economist* has remarked:

All too many of the Arab world's 350 million people are caught between rotten governments and often violent oppositions. Its would-be-reformers have retreated to the conditions described by the late Syrian playwright Saadallah Wannous as 'condemned to hope', trapped either in stagnant repression or cycles of strife they are unable to make progress. This stasis has heightened long-standing concerns that Arab countries are in some fundamental way unsuited to the modern world, concerns which have spawned a gaggle of grand theories. But, it is a particular pattern of twentieth-century modernisation, rather than its absence, that lies behind the region's political failure . . . It takes openness for society to progress. Closed politics may be tempered by an openness to ideas and to an open economy, as in China. Open politics can make up for poverty and a paucity of human resources too. But to have closed politics and closed minds together is a recipe for disaster; for proof, consider the current fate of all the Arab states

(The Economist, 2014b: 21).

This report and other recent studies that have documented the progress being made towards economic diversification during the 2010s indicate that all countries in the MENA region are confronted with several major challenges. These include the need to develop more open regional markets to increase trade – while protecting national sovereignty, balancing internal political stability with the economic openness and institutional accountability required to build internationally competitive 'post-oil' national economies and reducing the economic distortions caused by lavish government spending on subsidies for energy, food, education, healthcare and so forth. In 2014, these amounted to approximately $150 billion or 12.8 per cent of the GCC's total GDP according to The Economist (2014b: 21).[4] Other challenges include coping with the privatisation of subsidised and protected nationalised industries, creating inclusive economies that benefit all citizens – not just the region's elites – improving educational provision at the primary, secondary and tertiary levels, building their middle-classes and encouraging more women into their labour markets (Hvidt, 2013). As one study has noted, 'by providing policy stability governments can unleash the region's considerable human promise: its increasingly educated and ambitious youth, its budding middle-class, and its aspiring women' (Shediac et al: 1). However, despite some improvements in their fortunes in recent times in some countries in the region, women are still the largest of the excluded, repressed and 'condemned to hope' groups in all MENA countries.

Globally, economically excluded women constitute a group that the consulting company Price Waterhouse Coopers has called 'the Third Billion', the first and second billion being the people of India and China (Aguirre et al, 2013). Citing data from the United Nations International Labour Organisation, Aguirre and her colleagues noted that:

Roughly 865 million women will be of working age (20–65) by 2020, yet will still lack the fundamental prerequisites to contribute to their national economies. Either they don't have the necessary education and training to work, or – more frequently – they simply can't work, owing to legal, familial, logistical and financial constraints. Of these 865 million people, 812 million live in emerging and developing nations. We call this group the Third Billion, because their economic impact will be just as significant as that of the billion plus populations of China and India. Yet the women of the Third Billion have been largely overlooked in many countries, and actively held back in others

(Aguirre et al, 2013: 1).

An earlier report on women in the MENA region by another team of consultants at Booz&Co suggested that:

These women have the potential to become middle-class entrepreneurs, employees and consumers, but whose economic lives have previously been stunted, underleveraged or suppressed. As they enter the economic mainstream, they will have a huge impact around the world. This will probably affect the Middle-East dramatically, especially given its high levels of female education. For example, women in Kuwait, Qatar and Saudi Arabia constitute 67 per cent, 63 per cent, and 57 per cent respectively, of university graduates. Yet, in many countries, only a minority of women participate in the labour force, and comparatively few in the private sector. Bringing educated women and properly skilled youth into the economy will fuel growth, enterprise creation, and employment. Ultimately, that will provide the bedrock of stability that the MENA region has lacked: a stable middle-class

(Saddi et al, 2012: 9).

In the UAE, Oman and the KSA, the first generation of university-educated women began to enter the labour market in large numbers during the 2000s. Most young university-educated Emirati, Omani and Saudi women now pursue some kind of professional career, and a small but growing number are creating their own businesses. Consequently, their disposable wealth and economic power are growing. If, as other research data indicates, men are now lagging well behind women in educational attainment at both secondary and tertiary levels in these three countries, it is probable that they will lose out to well-educated, highly motivated and ambitious women in the future. For example, a study by the Dubai Women Centre found that 93 per cent of Emirati women described themselves as 'very ambitious', and 75 per cent aspired to senior positions in their chosen careers (Dubai Women Centre, 2008); and 52 per cent of Arabic women surveyed by the UAE recruitment and job search agency Bayt.com in 2010 believed that they were 'much more ambitious than their male counterparts' (Bayt.com, 2010). This shift in the self-belief and self-confidence of women has the potential – if actively supported and encouraged – to create a transformative growth engine that will assist in the lengthy process of creating stable and growing economies in the region. They also have the potential to have profound effects on the status and economic power of women in both the Gulf States and the broader MENA region in the future. Whether the countries of this region will embrace this opportunity is, of course, a question we will address in later chapters.

1.4 THE PRACTICAL IMPLICATIONS OF THIS BOOK

This book has three objectives. The first, as noted in the Preface, is to explain why the Islamic countries of the Gulf States and the broader

MENA region cannot hope to build stable and internationally competitive economies in the future unless a much greater number of women are allowed to participate in their national economies. Second, to demonstrate that the medium- to long-term commercial success of many of the indigenous companies that operate in this region will depend on how well they deal with the issue of women's participation in their workforces during the 2020s and beyond. Third, to present the compelling economic rationale and business case for encouraging a much higher level of participation by women in the labour markets of the MENA region in the future. Although we look at these propositions in greater depth in Chapters 8 and 9, a few examples of the general impact of equal opportunities on the bottom-line results of companies and national economic performance are presented here.

For example, the evidence compiled by the 1995 United States Federal Glass Ceiling Commission showed that the average annual return on investment of those companies that did not discriminate against women was more than double that of companies with poor records of hiring and promoting women (Federal Glass Ceiling Commission, 1995). In 2000, Alan Greenspan, the former United States Federal Reserve Chairman, argued that discrimination was bad for both business profitability and national economic performance, and he also suggested that ending discrimination against women and ethnic minorities had to be achieved immediately, not at some indeterminate point in the future: 'By removing the non-economic distortions that arise as a result of discrimination, we can generate higher returns on both human and physical capital. Discrimination is against the interest of business. Yet, business people often practice it. In the end the costs are higher, less real output is produced and the nation's wealth-accumulation is reduced' (Greenspan, 2000).

Several subsequent studies have indicated that parity between men and women is also likely to contribute to the bottom-line results of companies. For example, one study rated the performance of the

Standard and Poor's 500 companies on equal-opportunity factors, including the recruitment and promotion of women and minorities and the companies' policies on discrimination. It found that companies rated in the bottom 100 for equal opportunities had an average of 8 per cent return on investment. Companies ranked in the top 100 had an average return of 18 per cent (Sussmuth-Dykerhoff et al, 2012). Furthermore, research on 'high-performance' companies and 'employers of choice' during the 1990s and 2000s showed that many of these had made early commitments to gender (and ethnic) diversity and to promoting women into senior management positions. These were and are among the most visionary, successful, resilient, adaptable and profitable companies in the world (see, for example, Collins, 2001; Corporate Leadership Council, 2004; Katzenbach, 2000; Martel, 2002; O'Reilly and Pfeffer, 2000). And, while there has been no research by business and management scholars on the direct impact of female employees on the bottom-line performance of companies in the MENA region, a survey by McKinsey in 2010 reported that 34 per cent of companies in the Middle East who had made genuine efforts to empower female employees 'reported increased profits; and 38 per cent said that they expected to see improved profits as a result of these initiatives' (Barta et al, 2012).

A 2011 Booz&Co report, citing data from the World Bank, indicated that some countries in the MENA region could improve their annual GDPs *by an average of 34 per cent* if women were employed in their national labour markets at the same rates as men are (Hoteit et al, 2011). A more recent comprehensive global report by the McKinsey Global Institute has examined how economic, legal and social gender inequality is distributed across the world and the impact of this on national economic growth and development Using fifteen standardised gender-parity indicators across ninety-five countries that are home to 93 per cent of the world's female population, McKinsey analysts found that North America and Oceania had the highest average equality score of 0.74 and Western Europe 0.71 (a score of 1 represents perfect economic, legal and social parity between men and women). They noted that the MENA region had an overall score of 0.48, South Asia (excluding India) had the lowest score of 0.44 and the UAE, Oman and the KSA were three of the twenty-one countries that had 'high' or 'extremely high' gender equality gaps (Dobbs et al, 2015 ix, 9 and 15). They also estimated the loss of national economic output that accompanies large gender inequalities. Globally, the world economy could be $28 trillion (26%) richer, if the gaps in labour-force participation, hours worked and productivity of women and men were bridged. Even reducing these gender gaps to the level of the most gender-egalitarian countries in each region would add $12 trillion to global output by 2025. India could add more than 55 per cent a year to its GDP, South Asia nearly 50 per cent, Latin America 38 per cent, East and South East Asia and Sub-Saharan Africa more than 30 per cent, and the MENA region could add *more than 50 per cent* to its cumulative annual GDP. Their report also noted that 'In India and the MENA region, boosting female labour-force participation would contribute 90 and 85 per cent, respectively, to the total additional economic opportunity', or $2.7 trillion in total GDP by 2025 (Dobbs et al., 2015: 4).

The message from these and other similar studies that are reviewed in Chapter 8 is very clear: to be more competitive, now and in the future, organisations in this part of the world must utilise the full range of talents of all their staff, regardless of their gender (or, indeed, national and cultural backgrounds), and robust gender diversity policies make very good business sense (Ellis et al, 2015; Hunt et al, 2015; International Finance Corporation, 2013b). There are many reasons to believe that this has to – eventually – happen in public- and private-sector organisations in the MENA region, if these countries are to transform the rhetoric of creating competitive economies into a reality in the future.

Consequently, there are three principal reasons the ideas presented in this book may be of interest to business and political leaders in this part of the world. First, the unrest in many MENA countries during the 2000s and early 2010s was and is a reaction to US military incursions in the region, autocratic and repressive dictatorships, corruption, inequality, poverty and dwindling economic opportunities for the rapidly growing number of indigenous young people in this region of the world. This unrest, as noted earlier, was also characterised by the active participation of tens of thousands of women, demanding greater economic, political and social rights (Bennoune, 2013; Coleman, 2010). Second, there is a growing realisation – at least among more liberal, educated and well-informed groups in the MENA region – that their countries have to come to terms with an inescapable economic reality (even those with substantial oil and gas reserves): *there are no examples of advanced, diversified, industrial economies in which a substantial proportion of women are not economically active in their labour markets and where barriers to their entry into all professions and occupations have been dismantled over the last 30 to 40 years* (Aguirre et al, 2013; Dobbs et al, 2015; Saddi et al, 2012; Shediac et al, 2011).

These are, as we will see, inescapable economic realities, and if the nation-states of the MENA region are to rise from their generally low ranking among the world's leading economies and on other many other indexes of national development, can they continue to hold back the dreams, aspirations and ambitions of women in this region for much longer? Of course, similar arguments have been made repeatedly by *The Economist* (2016e; 2016c; 2016b; 2015e; 2015c; 2014b; 2014a and 2002), by the United Nations in all of its reports on the MENA region and in the other studies cited in this chapter. For example, in his foreword to the 2005 AHDR, the Chairman of the United Nations Development Program observed that:

> The situation for women in Arab countries has been changing over time, often for the better, yet many continue to struggle for fair treatment. Compared to their sisters elsewhere in the world, they enjoy the least political participation. Conservative authorities, discriminatory laws, chauvinist male peers and tradition-minded

kinsfolk watchfully regulate their aspirations, activities and conduct. Employers limit their access to income and independence. In the majority of cases, poverty shackles the development and use of women's potential. High rates of illiteracy and the world's lowest levels of labour participation are compounding to create serious challenges. Although a growing number of individual women, supported by men, have succeeded in achieving greater equality in society, and more reciprocity in their family and personal relationships, many remain victims of legalized discrimination and enshrined male dominance.

This year's report presents a compelling argument as to why realising the full potential of Arab women is an indispensable prerequisite for development in all Arab states. It argues persuasively that the long hoped-for Arab 'renaissance' cannot and will not be accomplished unless the obstacles preventing women from enjoying their human rights and contributing more fully to development are eliminated and replaced with greater access to the tools of development [and by] placing Arab women firmly at the centre of social, economic and political development in the entire region

(United Nations, 2005iii and i).

Third, as documented earlier, on almost every metric of economic development most countries in the MENA region lag behind the leading economies of the world and, with the notable exception of their oil and gas sectors, they have very few world-class companies. Consequently, as noted in the Preface, if real change is to occur in the most conservative countries of this region, such as the KSA, the main impetus for this will probably not come from their political or religious leaders. Rather, it will come from their business leaders, because they know (or, at least, they *should* know) what will happen to economic growth and living standards in their countries if they do not use their remaining oil and gas wealth to develop their economies and to reform their commercial, educational, civic and governmental institutions over the next two decades. This belief is supported by numerous reports and studies published between 2000 and 2016 which have also argued that there is and will continue to be a direct causal link between the economic development of all nation-states in the MENA region and the emancipation of women in these countries. Indeed, as this book will endeavour to show, neither can come to pass without the other. The recent reports by the World Bank, the World Economic Forum, the United Nations, McKinsey, Booz&Co and others cited in this chapter have all highlighted the need for countries in the MENA region to improve educational opportunities for women – particularly at the tertiary level – increase the participation of women in regional labour markets and in all professions and occupations and create legal and regulatory frameworks that can promote equal-opportunity principles. Implicitly, these reports also indicate that the cultural, attitudinal and structural barriers that prevent women from playing a much fuller role in public- and private-sector organisations must be challenged and dismantled. If they are not, the long-term economic and political future of most countries in the MENA region looks bleak. The fact that all Arab countries had, by 2010, signed the United Nations Convention on all Forms of Discrimination against Women signifies very little unless they can initiate the long and complex process of implementing its many key recommendations and policies.

A few countries in this region have already woken up to these realities. For example, even before the UAE experienced the sobering economic downturn of the late 2000s and early 2010s, this small country was already facing a variety of economic, social and environmental challenges. The UAE government's 2015 and 2008 national strategic plans had both made it clear that the country had to continue to focus on industrial and business development in order to safeguard the country's economic growth and prosperity in the future, an issue that we return to look at in Chapters 2 and 3 (Dubai Strategic Plan 2015; United Arab Emirates Government,

2008). Similar challenges confront all countries in the Gulf States and the broader MENA region. The KSA, for example, has one significant advantage and one significant disadvantage when compared to the UAE. Its advantage is that the country has oil reserves that may last for another 20 to 30 years at current and anticipated rates of consumption. Its great disadvantage is that, on all measures and metrics of economic, social and political advancement for women, it now lags at least fifteen years behind the UAE and decades behind the leading industrial economies of the OECD. Oman is in a similar position to the UAE because, while its oil and gas revenues are declining year by year, it does have a more liberal approach to both women's education and their employment rights when compared to the KSA.

As noted in the Preface, this book also describes how public- and private-sector organisations in this part of the world can create a level playing-field for women and also ensure that their best female employees are given the opportunity to rise to leadership positions in the future. These processes have been documented in an extensive academic and practitioner literature that has described the introduction of equal-opportunity policies in many Western public- and private-sector organisations during the 1990s, 2000s and 2010s. Many of these have already been implemented, to varying degrees, in almost all businesses operating in North America, Europe, Oceania and other regions of the world. A question that will, of course, be asked is 'Can these be implemented in an Arabic/Islamic context?', and we will address this in Chapter 9 and also describe other policy initiatives that could be implemented at the national level in MENA countries in order to promote the interests of women employees in their national labour markets.

Over time, these initiatives could create an environment that will encourage more women into professional, business and management roles and to become entrepreneurs and small business owners. In turn, if encouraged, these women could make a significant contribution to the lengthy process of building the economies that will be required to sustain the countries of the MENA region – with much larger populations – during the 2020s and beyond. Furthermore, companies operating in this part of the world do not have to wait for legislative changes to be enacted by national governments to make these changes. Providing they do not violate existing *shari'a* laws, indigenous companies can introduce policies and practices that will encourage talented and ambitious women to work for them. They can create working environments and organisational cultures in which women employees are judged on competence, character and performance, not their gender, and are empowered to rise to leadership positions in the future.

They could be implemented – with a high level of commitment and adequate resources – by any group of senior managers in companies that can see the need for change and who are committed to the transformation that would be required in the operational cultures of their companies, in their recruitment and employment practices and in the career and promotion opportunities they provide for female employees. They can learn how to do this from best-practice examples of 'women-friendly' companies in the West, which have made this a strategic human resource management (HRM) priority over the last ten to fifteen years. They can also benefit from advice about the implementation of strategic equal-opportunity policies and how to create working cultures and HRM policies that support the interests of their women employees within generally conservative Islamic contexts. The well-established equal-opportunity principles described in Chapter 9 are now integral elements of business and management practices in many countries, and we will see that these ideas and principles are now beginning to gain some traction in a few companies that operate in the Gulf States and the broader MENA region. These would benefit any companies that are concerned about their long-term futures, winning the local and global 'war for talent', maximizing their growth prospects and enhancing their competitive abilities in the MENA region and globally in the future.

1.5 CONCLUSION

It is possible that some readers of this book may believe that it is not appropriate for a Western man to write about these issues or suggest what countries in the MENA region 'should do' vis-à-vis their womenfolk, while others may suggest that it is yet another example of a Western-centric interpretation of a part of the world that only Arabs can truly understand (al-Barwani, 2011). While these concerns are understandable, it can also be said that enhancing the economic and legal rights of women in this region is, as all of the female and some of the male interviewees in this book believed, consistent with the teachings of the Prophet. It is also in harmony with Islamic teachings which emphasise the intrinsic worth and dignity of all human beings and the principle of hisbah (doing good). It is consistent with the Islamic principles of hadith – of being true to the teachings of the Prophet and his belief that improving our knowledge about the world was a noble activity in itself – and also ijtihad, the need to reinterpret Islamic teachings and laws in the light of changes and developments in Islamic societies, a principle endorsed by all of the Arab women and men who contributed to the first United Nations AHDR in 2005 (United Nations, 2005: 147, 222–223). It is also consistent with the core principles and recommendations laid down in the Convention on all Forms of Discrimination Against Women which, as noted earlier, all countries in the MENA region are now signatories to (even if they have done this, in all cases, with significant qualifications). And, in the words of one very brave female Saudi Arabian activist, writer and journalist:

> The rigid interpretations of Islamic law by hard-liners no longer provide solutions to the problems facing the Arabic world today . . . we cannot continue to allow only one legal authority on the interpretation of shari'a laws or recognize only one absolute judgement on judicial issues . . . fundamentalists must understand that no one has absolute authority on the truth . . . We need to make better judgments and formulate new legislation on issues

related to the status of women, Muslim lifestyles, Islamic
economies, the situation of Muslims in non-Muslim societies,
the relationships between Muslims and the West, and so on
(Fatany, 2011b).

Moreover, this book is essentially a narrative account of university-
educated, professional Emiratis, Omanis and Saudis describing their
experiences (good and bad) of the societies they have grown up in, the
roles of women and men in their societies and workplaces and, most
importantly, their hopes and fears for their countries and their dreams
and aspirations for their children's and grandchildren's futures. It is
their story and one that their rulers may wish to listen to. Readers of
this book will also know that history is littered with examples of
what has invariably happened to human societies when their political
and religious leaders have been unable to relinquish and share power,
who have failed to adapt to new circumstances and challenges and
have lost touch with their citizens. In every case, they have struggled
to survive and most of them have ceased to exist (Acemoglu and
Robinson, 2012, Beinhocker, 2007; Diamond, 2005; Morris, 2011;
Tainter, 2006).

Hence, although it may not be easy for some readers of this
book to accept this proposition, the people and governments of the
entire MENA region are confronted with a range of existential economic, political and social challenges, including one that I now consider to be an irreversible 'quiet revolution' in the aspirations and
hopes of a rapidly growing number of educated, ambitious and
increasingly independent women in the UAE, Oman and the KSA.
The potential of this demographic and social change is enormous and,
if nurtured and encouraged, could have many beneficial and transformational effects both within and beyond the borders of these three
countries in the future. While the challenge of transforming
entrenched conservative social attitudes and overcoming institutional inertia to allow women to become more equal partners in the
political systems and economies of the MENA region is formidable,

I hope that the political and business leaders of all countries in the MENA region might respond in a positive way to the ideas and recommendations contained in this book. They may also resonate with anyone who has an interest in the future of the MENA region, because if the many challenges that confront this part of the world are not resolved soon, this will have a direct impact on all of us in the future.

2 The United Arab Emirates

2.1 INTRODUCTION

This chapter begins with a description of the recent history of the UAE and how this small and unknown desert country has made a remarkable transition from being a protectorate of Great Britain for 162 years to become an international hub of trade and commerce during the 1980s, 1990s and 2000s. We then look at the economic, political and social challenges facing the UAE and the progress it has made towards building a resilient and stable national economy. We examine the changing life experiences of Emirati women since the establishment of the UAE as an independent state in 1971 and their progress in the national workforce over the last twenty years. This is followed, with reference to recent World Economic Forum (WEF) Global Gender Gap (GGG) and Convention on the Elimination of all Forms of Discrimination Against Women (CEDAW) reports, by an analysis of claims made by the national government of the UAE that it now ensures equality of access for women to the UAE labour market and equality of opportunity in the workplace. We then look at the cultural, attitudinal and structural barriers that women still encounter in the labour market of the UAE. This section contains a contextual analysis of the omnipresent influence of Islam in the MENA region and the effects of this on perceptions of the 'appropriate' roles of women and men in Emirati society and in the workplace. In the conclusion, we evaluate the progress that Emirati women have made in the national workforce within the context of the development and diversification of the UAE's national economy and the effects of the steep fall in global oil and gas prices on the country's finances during 2014–2016.

2.2 A BRIEF HISTORY OF THE UAE

Any description of the recent economic and political history of the UAE has to include the words 'astonishing', 'rapid' and 'transformational'. Over the last forty years this country has quickly evolved into a thriving and modern nation–state, a place of employment for millions of nationals from many other countries and a popular holiday destination for thousands of tourists. In the 1990s, for example, very few people outside the MENA region would have had heard of its 'second city' Dubai, but by the mid-2000s most people knew something about 'the story of a small Arab village that grew into a big city ... the most luxurious city the world has ever known: the City of Gold' (Krane, 2009: vii–viii). Suddenly, everyone seemed to know about this desert metropolis with its indoor ski centre, its plans for the highest skyscraper in the world, the multi-million dollar properties being built on 'Palm Islands' constructed in the sea, very conspicuous consumption and a place where even some of the high-rise office buildings were covered in bling.

The lands that eventually became the UAE did not constitute a recognisable state until December 1971, when six of the Emirates (*imara*) – Abu Dhabi, Dubai, Sharjah, Ajman, Umm al-Quwain and Fujairah – embraced federation under the visionary leadership of the first president of the UAE, Sheikh Zayed bin Sultan al-Nahyan (Ras al-Khaima joined in 1972). Until that time, the Emiratis had been protectorates of the United Kingdom with a largely subsistence economy. Before the discovery of oil in the late 1950s, while Emiratis were part of a rich and ancient Arabic cultural heritage, there was little government infrastructure, no currency other than gold or silver, no tarmac roads, no tradition of private property ownership and no agreed body of statute law. For centuries the tribes that inhabited the region had spent alternating periods as villagers, traders and semi-nomadic Bedouins and, before the English started taking an interest in the southern and south-eastern coasts of the Arabian Peninsula as an important strategic region during the early nineteenth century, there was often open conflict between these groups. However, the leaders (*sheikhs*) of these tribes did agree to sign a treaty with Britain in 1819, and the region became part of a regional protectorate known as the Trucial States (or 'Trucial Oman' or 'Trucial Coast States'), a treaty that lasted until the formation of the UAE (Davidson, 2005: 5–103; Lacey, 2009: 1–62).

The political structures of the Trucial States were decentralised and fluid, which was a natural by-product of the region's geography, very limited natural resources and its age–old tribal social system. All social groups were organised into patrilineal (*al-taraf*) tribes where the authority and status of tribal leaders was based solely on their claimed descent from esteemed ancestors, 'whether real or fictional' (Davidson, 2005: 11). The primary allegiance of all members of the original Bedu tribes in the region (many of which still exist today in the UAE) was to their tribal leaders (*asabiyya qabaliyya*), a state of affairs that persists in the seven *imara* of the UAE and, with local variations, in every other Gulf state to the present day. The sheikhs who led these tribes did not enjoy the hereditary rights of today's royal sheikhs; they earned this by proving that they were more intelligent, more generous or braver than their rivals. Cooperative labour was the norm, within broader kinship and tribal networks, enabling moderation over disputed pasturelands and cooperation in small-scale agriculture areas. And, as Davidson has noted, 'a crucial aspect of the traditional administrative structure was its ability to subsidise the population. This was an important manifestation of the ruler's authority and in many ways the precursor to the system of wealth distribution practiced during the oil era. Indeed, during this period, the rulers frequently used heavy subsidies to buy influence from other tribes, thereby keeping the peace' (Davidson, 2005: 19). This widespread practice, known as 'patrimonialism' or 'clientelism' has continued to the present day in the UAE and the other Arabian Gulf States.

Before the wealth generated by the discovery of oil and gas began to transform the living standards of the people of the region we now know as the UAE, life was tough. The region had very few natural resources and was located in one of the hottest, most arid and driest areas of the planet. Except for some artisans and merchants who lived in better-constructed houses of two or three floors, most homes were simple mud and palm or thatch *barasti*. Very few had access to electricity, and everyone drew their water from communal wells. Standards of living were generally low, with an economy based largely on localised maritime trading (particularly with Iran and India), pearl-diving and fishing, limited agriculture around the country's oases, pottery manufacturing and woodwork, tailoring and weaving and sheep and camel herding, with a little additional income for some tribal leaders derived from the landing fees for planes that had to stop in the area to refuel. Until 1963, wealthier Emirati families may also have owned slaves, who were themselves often the children of former slaves stretching back for generations (Davidson, 2005: 5–64).[1] In 1950, the population of the area was about 80,000, and any visitors to Abu-Dhabi or Dubai would have encountered small coastal towns that had changed little over the preceding 200 years:

> Much of Dubai was a clamorous Arabian *souk*. Alleys shaded by straw roofs let tiny beams of sunlight poke through the murk. The lanes were too narrow for cars, but donkey carts, camels and even stray herds of goats could get inside, and it was by all accounts cacophonous. Shop owners sat cross-legged on the ground offering customers a stool and tea. Men with rifles and daggers wandered, Iranians in their suit jackets and Omanis in their coloured scarves, roguish Bedouin from the desert, overconfident in their ragged clothes, strutted like they owned the place. The Bedouin were the poorest of them all, but held themselves above town folks. Butchers hacked at stringy goat carcasses and kicked up cascades of flies. Vendors piled dented cans of sardines and beans into pyramids. Meat scraps sizzled on the grill. Carpenters cobbled furniture from Indian lumber. Halfway down the *souk*, a bright passageway offered stairs to the creek, where the *abras* sat – just

like today – with pilots yelling for passengers to choose a boat. Nearby, men built wooden *dhows* on the creek banks, sealing their hulls with fish oil

(Krane, 2009: 41).

At this time, Emirati women would have all led segregated lives, conformed to traditional dress codes, and they would have been generally deferential to their fathers or husbands. However, it is a misconception that Emirati women played no role in the economic life of the UAE before the 1970s, for the simple reason that most Emirati families were poor and they had to rely on several sources of income to make ends meet throughout the year. While their role was primarily domestic, some Emirati women owned commercial trading, fishing and pearling boats and there are several examples of female merchants at this time. However, as Soffan has observed, while many Emirati women did work, this was largely behind the scenes. Typically, UAE business women were represented in the public domain by male relatives in most business transactions – a practice that is no longer a legal requirement in the UAE but one that persists in countries like Saudi Arabia and Yemen. If they wanted to sell their houses, or to buy a new farm, they had to use their fathers' or husbands' names for these transactions. However, UAE women did make decisions affecting the running and management of their homes, and they were often involved in home-based businesses, such as growing fruit and vegetables, raising chickens, selling goats' cheese and milk and weaving cloth and embroidering fabrics. A few women even raised bees and sold honey. Moreover, women who inherited money often invested this in buying land and small farms to pass on to their children (Soffan, 1980).

One interview, conducted with the feisty seventy-five-year-old grandmother of a Zayed University student in 2010, reveals something of the persistence of UAE business women in the face of cultural and religious constraints at this time:

> When I was a girl, my family always told me that a woman should not work outside her house in fishing or in selling any product,

because they thought that women should work at home and serve her husband. However, I proved the opposite. When my husband divorced me and went to India for trading, I had no choice but to open a small shop to provide a living for my five sons. I sold fish and clothes ... In the beginning of my journey in business I faced many difficulties, like rumours about breaking our cultural norms. But soon, other women began to open their own shops and businesses.

An eighty-five-year-old Emirati woman, who lived in Ras al-Khaimah before the discovery of oil in the UAE, commented that:

Women were important members of the society with crucial roles. They did not just stay at home as some might think ... when I was young you could see many women in the mountains and oases working on agriculture and in coastal areas some were fishing as well. There were even a few women from the coastal area of Abu-Dhabi who were involved in pearl-diving, whether to pay back family debts or to provide for their family's livelihood when their husbands or fathers had died or after a divorce.

Nevertheless, the division of labour at home at this time reflected the conservative Islamic culture that had prevailed throughout the Gulf region for centuries. In general, women did not take part in public activities, and although they did enjoy certain legal rights the law was heavily weighted in favour of men in matters relating to marriage, divorce (khula) and inheritance. According to one Arabic historian:

The social order was based upon the superior power and rights of men; the veil and the harim were visible signs of this. A view of the relations between men and women which was deeply rooted in the culture of the Middle East, which had existed long before the coming of Islam, and was preserved in the countryside by immemorial custom but also changed in the city by the development of the shari'a ... a system of law and ideal social morality, the *shari'a*, gave formal expression to the rights of women, but also laid down their limits. According to the *shari'a*, every woman should have a male guardian – her father, brother or some other male member of her family

(Hourani, 1991: 120–121).

The education system at this time was also based on traditional beliefs, and school (*madrassa*) facilities were often rudimentary. Although everyone was taught to read the Qur'an, many people could not write and education did not extend beyond basic mathematics and some history in the small number of schools that operated at this time. Religious education formed a significant part of primary-school curricula during the students' morning classes. This was usually followed by classes in the afternoon in which a group of students formed a semi-circle (*halqat al-elmya*), and discussed different subjects with their teachers (Fakhro, 1990). In an interview with a seventy-two-year-old Emirati woman in April 2009, whose father had been a religious teacher, she observed that most women had no automatic right to even a basic level of education before the 1970s: 'We were not allowed to study outside our homes. We mainly studied the Holy Qur'an and Arabic reading and writing. There were almost no opportunities for us to study science or mathematics because these were not considered to be suitable subjects for young girls.' Anyone wanting to study beyond primary school had to travel to India, Pakistan or Iran, and this opportunity was restricted to men. Higher education was limited to the sons of those who occupied the highest positions in Emirati society until the early 1980s (Krane, 2009: 39–46). Thus, until the discovery of large reservoirs of oil and gas in the late 1950s and early 1960, this region was sparsely populated, and most of the population lived in very basic housing. Many of the tribes that inherited these lands lived a semi-nomadic life, and general standards of living were, at the time, very low in comparison to some countries in the Middle East, such as Egypt, and many other countries outside this region. The economy was, for all practical purposes, pre-industrial and based largely on herding, a limited amount of farming, craft manufacturing, fishing and pearling. This was, of course, all about to change in ways that no one at this time could have imagined.

In August 1958, a drilling barge called *The Enterprise* dropped anchor off Das Island close to Abu Dhabi, an event that was noticed by very few people at the time. In what was an oil geologist's equivalent of a golfer's hole-in-one, soon after starting the first test drill, a black scum started bubbling to the surface. Sample testing revealed this to be 'sweet, light crude', the best-quality crude oil that it is possible to find. Two months later, drillers located the Murban reservoir in the desert to the west of Abu-Dhabi, which turned out to be one of the biggest oil reservoirs in the Middle East. The first cargo of crude oil left Abu Dhabi in 1962, and by 1963 oil was being pumped from twenty-three wells. In 1965 the Zakhum field was located – the third-largest ever found in the Middle East. By 1968, Abu-Dhabi was exporting 24 million tons of petroleum a year. In Dubai, major fields were located in 1966, 1970, 1972 and 1973. Although no commercially viable oil deposits were found in any of the other *imara*, it is the fabulous wealth that was generated by this oil bounty that not only drove the process of unification that culminated in the establishment of the UAE on 2 December 1971 but also kick-started the remarkable economic and social transformation of the entire country (Hawley, 1971; Heard-Bey, 2005: 152).

The discovery of some of the biggest oil reserves on the planet during the 1960s soon turned the UAE into a more prosperous nation. However, it was not until the 1973 oil crisis that the country benefited from the steep rise in global crude-oil prices, and rapid economic growth and infrastructure development soon followed. Gross domestic product (GDP) grew from $30 billion in 1972 to $120 billion in 1980. Over the next two decades annual GDP fluctuated between a low of approximately $80 billion in 1986 and a high of $124 billion in 1996. By 2000, this had increased to $141.5 billion, surging to $200.1 billion in 2008 on the back of $150-per-barrel crude-oil prices, falling back to $194.7 billion in 2009 in the aftermath of the global economic downturn of the late 2000s. By the mid-2000s, the combined value of the assets of the UAE's sovereign wealth fund and government-owned companies were estimated to be in excess of $1 trillion and, until 2009, generating annual returns of more than 10 per cent (Davidson, 2009: 62). As Davidson has noted:

> This compares very favourably with the world's other sovereign wealth-managing countries, notably Singapore and Norway, with $490 billion and $390 billion respectively. It places Abu Dhabi far ahead of other Gulf investors such as Kuwait with $260 billion, Dubai with about $100 billion and Qatar, with a modest $60 billion. By far the most prominent of Abu Dhabi's sovereign wealth funds is the Abu Dhabi Investment Authority (ADIA). Founded in 1976, it had reached about $100 billion in overseas assets and about $360 billion by 2005 ... it is likely that ADIA is still the world's largest sovereign wealth fund
>
> *(Davidson, 2005: 62).*

> With acquisitions across Asia, Africa and increasingly in Western Europe and North America, the Emirates' plethora of government-backed investment vehicles are already in control of funds several times greater than those of other prominent asset-managing states ... With astute management and strong government backing, Abu Dhabi should be able to weather the looming global recession and morph steadily over the next decade into one of the most impressively innovative economies in the Arab world
>
> *(Davidson, 2009: 75–76).*

By 2012, annual GDP had risen to $392 billion, to $399.45 billion in 2013 and to $419 billion by the end of 2014 (Countryeconomy.com, 2015). In 2015, the UAE was the second-largest Arab economy after Saudi Arabia and had the sixth-highest level of per-capita GDP in the world behind Qatar, Luxembourg, Singapore, Norway and Brunei (Countryeconomy.com, 2016). In 2010, on six measures of human development, the UAE was ranked at number 30 globally, and at number 1 in the MENA region. In 2015, it was ranked 41 and 1 respectively (United Nations, 2015a and 2010a). The income from oil revenues led directly to major investments in several sectors throughout the 1970s, 1980s, 1990s and 2000s, including ports, cargo transport hubs, airports and airlines, commercial and residential building construction, new roads, a light railway in Dubai and several new hospitals and universities; and it also allowed the government to create a very generous cradle-to-grave welfare support system for Emirati nationals. This welfare system included social security benefits, free land for housing, a well-developed healthcare system and free primary and secondary education. In 2014, the government allocated 51 per cent of its total domestic budget for social services and social benefits and pensions for Emirati citizens; and salaries for federal employees in sectors such as education, health, defence and the judiciary were increased by 100 per cent. As Bertelsmann Stiftung has observed, 'In this context, the ruling families have been very successful in promoting patron-client relationships in which the stability of the polity is directly related to the preservation of social status and economic privileges among UAE nationals' (Bertelsmann Stiftung, 2015a: 11 and 16–17).

2.3 ECONOMIC, POLITICAL AND SOCIAL CHALLENGES FACING THE UAE

While the economic growth of the UAE was certainly spectacular during much of the 2000s (averaging 13.4 per cent a year from 2000–2008), this helter-skelter growth stalled in early 2009, as the price of oil fell from more than $150 a barrel to around $60 in the aftermath of the global recession. This coincided with the collapse of the country's construction and property bubbles and a 50 per cent fall in the value of real estate in Dubai during the next twenty-four months. This left Dubai, which was heavily reliant on these two sectors, saddled with outstanding debts of $80 billion. To use an old but appropriate cliché, the straw that finally broke this camel's back was excessive borrowing by Nakeel, the property-development arm of Dubai World, and an announcement in November 2009 that it would be unable to pay back a $4 billion Islamic bond (*sukuk*). Its entire business strategy during the 2000s had been based on ever-increasing property prices – a strategy that would implode after the sub-prime mortgage market collapsed in the United States during 2007. This coincided with several very unfavourable commentaries on the UAE, which focused not only on the lack of transparency and rule of law in several of the country's major financial institutions but also on the exploitation and high death, injury and suicide rates of labourers on building sites, the high incidence of human trafficking and the abuse of domestic servants in the country (Krane, 2009: 207 and 216–219).

On 14 December 2009, the government of Abu Dhabi stepped in to rescue Dubai from the brink of default, providing a $10 billion loan to cover the costs of the *sukuk* owed to investors by Nakeel. Three weeks earlier, the Dubai government had requested a delay in repayments of $26 billion, a move that panicked local and international financial markets (*The Economist*, 2009). These events, combined with a 50 per cent fall in the value of real estate in Dubai and a general loss of faith in local standards of corporate governance and legal redress, led to a widespread fall in investor confidence, with economic growth shrinking to less than 2 per cent during 2010–2011. Dubai emerged from these difficulties in part because Nakeel, Dubai World and other companies were able to agree debt-restructuring agreements with their major creditors but mainly because the more conservative oil-rich Abu Dhabi could not have allowed Dubai to fail.[2] However, it did emerge from this uncertain period in a more resilient state, if less brash and confident than it was during much of the 2000s. A new regulatory framework was introduced to monitor excessive borrowing and opaque business practices, particularly in the finance, property and construction sectors, and some local companies also started to take issues such as corporate governance and corporate social responsibility more seriously (Krane, 2009: 315–319). In the longer term, these reforms will be a good thing for the economic and social development of this remarkable city during the 2020s and 2030s.

In 2015, the UAE had the world's seventh-largest reserves of oil and gas in the world and was the world's sixth-largest producer of petroleum. The bulk of the country's oil and gas reserves are located in the emirate of Abu Dhabi. Oil production policies are determined by the Supreme Petroleum Council (SPC), the state-owned Abu Dhabi National Oil Company (ADNOC) and the Abu Dhabi Gas Industries Limited Company (GASCO), which together control sixteen subsidiaries in the oil, natural gas and petrochemical sectors. The much smaller oil and gas sectors of Dubai are managed by the Dubai Supreme Energy Council (DSCE). Some of the other Emirates also have very small oil and natural gas sectors, but information about these is limited (United States Energy Information Agency, 2015a: 1–2). Despite an extensive program of economic diversification, which began in the early 1990s, oil and gas revenues still underpinned approximately 42 per cent of the country's annual GDP in 2015. The government has claimed that it has oil and gas reserves that will last for about fifty years at current levels of production and consumption, although some agencies have estimated that this may only last for another twenty years (Aleklett et al, 2010; Smith, 2014; United States Energy Information Agency, 2015a: 1).

Sheikh Zayed bin Sultan Al Nahyan and the leaders of the other *imara* knew by the early 1990s that their resource wealth would not last forever, and they had also concluded that the only way that the UAE could survive in the future was to create a modern, diversified and competitive national economy long before the country's oil and gas were depleted. This led to their decision to join the World Trade Organisation in 1996 and to embark on a more intensive and strategic process of economic diversification during the early 2000s. To achieve this objective, the UAE had to accelerate the growth of its economy, expand the private sector and also ensure that leading international companies regarded the UAE as a good place to do business. The UAE Government Strategy Document 2008, for example, made it very clear that the country had to continue to focus on industrial and commercial diversification in order to safeguard the country's economic growth and prosperity in the future, a message that was reinforced in the UAE Government Strategy Document 2013. This report and all previous five-year strategic economic development plans have emphasised the need for continuing economic development at the macro level and business diversification at the meso- and micro-levels as key strategic priorities for the country and each of the *imara* during the 2010s and beyond. The 2013 and 2008 strategy documents have identified the following key economic, business and human resource challenges facing the UAE:

Promoting economic development and diversification and modernising all government organisations.

Creating a regulatory and legal environment conducive for sustainable, long-term growth and prosperity.

Achieving comprehensive national development and building national human resources.

Expanding existing sectors of strength – domestically and internationally (construction, storage and transportation, tourism, emerging technologies and financial/professional services).

Creating new sectors of strength in the UAE with sustainable competitive advantage in new and emerging technologies, solar and nuclear power, the knowledge economy, off-shore agricultural developments and broadening the country's manufacturing and business bases.

Building a first-class education system and ensuring world-class healthcare for all Emiratis.

Promoting creativity and innovation and encouraging more entrepreneurship among Emiratis in order to develop new businesses and encourage the development of the country's small and medium enterprise (SME) sector.

Creating a sustainable and balanced infrastructure including electricity, water, roads, transportation and waste management while protecting the environment.[3]

Ensuring the presence of a sound, transparent and fair judiciary.

Protecting Emirati nationals' interests and well-being, maintaining a
cohesive society and preserving a strong national Emirati identity
(United Arab Emirates Government, 2013 and 2008).

The process of economic diversification was and remains particularly
important for Dubai because less than 10 per cent of its annual
income is now derived from hydrocarbon revenues, and even more
so for the other five *imara*, who are almost entirely reliant on Abu
Dhabi for energy and food subsidies, their social welfare systems,
investment in infrastructure and the development of new industrial
and business zones. In order to meet the manpower demands of the
rapidly growing and diversifying UAE economy during the 1990s and
2000s, expatriate workers were hired in increasing numbers. In 2016,
some four million expatriates were working in the UAE – almost
entirely in the private sector – and Emiratis make up just 13 per cent
(851,164) of the 8.3 million people who live in the UAE (United Arab
Emirates National Bureau of Statistics, 2016: 19; World Population
Review, 2016). This means that while the country will continue to
rely on expatriate workers for the foreseeable future, it will have to
encourage more nationals into the high-value business, commercial,
industrial and technology sectors that can sustain the country in the
future – particularly those that have been identified in its most recent
national economic development plans. This will, inevitably, also
mean that more Emirati women will have to be encouraged to work,
and a good proportion of these will have to consider working in the
private sector and as entrepreneurs and SME owners.

However, despite a countrywide program of 'Emiratisation'
being established in the 1970s (which was enhanced and extended
during the 1990s and mid- to -late 2000s), few Emirati women were
working in the UAE private sector in 2016 despite being granted
special salary guarantees and employment rights. And, while there
have been numerous public exhortations by the country's political
leaders over the last decade about the need for more Emiratis to work
in the private sector, these have not had the impact they would have

hoped for. In 2013 the UAE government announced that '2013 will be the year of Emiratisation' when it launched the Ashber Initiative to encourage more Emiratis to work in the private sector and 'to encourage entrepreneurship among young UAE nationals to further strengthen their participation in leading the national economy' (Emiratisation.org, 2015). Even so, several commentators had already noted during the late 2000s that the makeup of the UAE's economy was not well suited to the changing needs of university-educated and ambitious young Emiratis, male or female. Davidson, for example, believed that 'only a limited number of jobs is likely to be available in government departments, oil companies or investment vehicles; and those nationals with alternative aspirations, abilities and qualifications will remain frustrated' (Davidson, 2009: 65). And, as predicted higher-education enrolment trends materialised during the 2000s, the number of female Emirati graduates applying for positions in the public sector grew exponentially. As a result, the public sector in the United Arab Emirates had already reached saturation point by the early 2010s, and more than 60 per cent of those employed there were Emirati women. We will look again at these structural imbalances in the UAE's labour market later in this chapter and in Chapter 3 (United Arab Emirates Government, 2014).

Political and Social Challenges

The UAE can be best described as a 'quasi-participative repressive autocracy', and there are, in all practical terms, no restrictions on the political powers of the president of the UAE (Sheikh Khalifa bin Zayed al-Nahyan, the ruler of Abu Dhabi), the prime minister (Mohammed bin Rashid al-Maktoum, the ruler of Dubai), the Supreme Federal Council (SFC) and the rulers of the other five *imara*. It has been estimated that the president and his family have a personal fortune of $15 billion, and the al-Maktoum family has about $4 billion. In common with the other Arabian Gulf States, power and influence flows top-down in the rentier political system of the UAE from the ruling elite to the rest of Emirati society, and the outcome of this has been:

> An awkward hybrid form of neo-patrimonial government of seemingly modern institutions astride much older traditional [power structures] which allows the hereditary rulers, and their closest relatives, to dominate directly the highest levels of the federal decision-making process and, through the use of carefully selected representatives, to control the UAE's token legislature . . . Policy implementation takes place within a large number of ministries, parastatals and other bureaucracies . . . Managed almost exclusively by non-elected appointees with close ties to the traditional polity, the majority of the UAE's Chambers of Commerce, judicial bodies and financial organisations are firmly fixed into the neo-patrimonial network. In many cases, the rigidity of these institutions has been compounded by a number of other pathologies, including bureaucratic self-interest, opaqueness and, of course, a complete lack of impartiality
>
> *(Davidson, 2005: 298).*

The SFC is the highest executive body in the UAE, and this is comprised of the president (who is elected by the SFC), the prime minister, the hereditary rulers of the other six *imara* and others who may be appointed to this body on an ad hoc basis. The national assembly is known as the Federal National Council (FNC), but, as with the equivalent assemblies in Oman and the KSA, its powers were at first limited to offering suggestions on legislation created by the SFC. Restricted elections were held for the country's forty-person FNC in 2006, 2011 and 2015 for half of the seats, with the other representatives being nominated by the rulers of the seven *imara*. Today, this half-elected body can advise on and propose amendments to draft legislation and also submit questions to the SFC. In 2011, 129,274 adult Emiratis were eligible to vote in national elections in 2011 and only 25 per cent did so, when one woman was elected to the FNC. In the October 2015 elections, voter turnout increased to 35 per cent

(79,000 Emiratis out of an electoral college of 224,279 voters), and 252 men and 78 women stood for election for the twenty available seats in the FNC. One woman, Naama al-Shahran, was elected, and eight women were appointed to this body by sheik Khalifa al-Nahyan (Wikipedia, 2016). This and similar recent initiatives in the KSA, Oman and Bahrain was an acknowledgment by some Gulf rulers that they needed to be seen doing more to broaden political participation among their citizens following the uprisings and widespread civil unrest across the MENA region during 2011–2012. However, while the UAE government has promised to increase the franchise to 50 per cent of the Emirati population 'in due course', it has ignored a 2011 petition, signed by 133 prominent Emiratis, to introduce direct elections to the FNC that all Emiratis can participate in (Bertelsmann Stiftung, 2015a: 6; *The Economist*, 2015a).

The UAE has a federal court system with three main branches (civil, criminal and *shari'a*), and the legal system retains many 'traditional' penalties for crimes such as flogging, beheading, amputation, crucifixion and stoning. While flogging is used routinely, the other four punishments are hardly ever used. Homosexuality and apostasy are still punishable by death. The constitution of the UAE permits the right of assembly, freedom of opinion, freedom of worship and freedom of communication, but opportunities to establish independent political or civic associations are severely restricted. This means that there is no (official) political opposition or alternative political parties, all planned public gatherings, ceremonies, forums and conferences require prior approval, the national media is tightly controlled and joining any overseas NGO or association requires official permission. Several NGOs, including the UAE Jurists, the local branches of the U.S. National Democratic Institute and the Adenauer Foundation, have been closed down in recent times. This means that 'the public space between the nuclear family and the state is sparsely populated [and] exchange of an associational nature remains largely confined to the family or tribal affiliation, while other forms of engagement are largely discouraged' (Bertelsmann

Stiftung, 2015a: 11). Trade unions are also banned, and occasional strikes among the exploited itinerant migrant workers of the UAE have been dealt with harshly. Several human rights organisations have described the plight of many migrant workers in the country as 'modern-day slavery'. Criticism of the president, prime minister, royal family members or any of the rulers of the *imara* are forbidden by law and the government often censors foreign media reports that are critical of the UAE and its rulers (Human Rights Watch, 2016).

The UAE also ranks poorly in international indices of freedom, civil liberties and human rights. In 2015, *The Economist* rated the UAE at 148 out of 185 countries on its 'Democracy Index', Freedom House gave the country its second-lowest freedom rating (6/7, where 1 is the highest freedom rating) and the UAE was ranked 118/180 countries in the 2015 Press Freedom Index, a fall of thirty-one places since 2010 (The Economist Intelligence Unit, 2015b; Freedom House, 2016; Reporters Without Borders, 2015a). The government of the UAE has not responded positively during the 2000s to petitions asking for broader political rights, and some of those who have been active in calling for further political reforms have been forced to recant their support. In 2013, ninety-four members of the banned *al-Islah* (Muslim Brotherhood) group were given prison sentences of up to fifteen years and were also stripped of their UAE citizenship. It has been estimated that at least 100 other activist Emirati citizens have been imprisoned without trial and some have been tortured, and an unknown number of Shiites have also been expelled from the UAE during the 2000s (Bertelsmann Stiftung, 2015a: 7–8; Human Rights Watch, 2016). A new anti-terrorism law passed in August 2014 contained clauses that imposed further restrictions on civil liberties. These developments prompted Bertelsmann Stiftung to conclude that 'tolerance for freedom of expression in the UAE saw a continued decline in the reporting period [and] the authorities have broadened surveillance capabilities to the point of becoming a Big Brother state'(Bertelsmann Stiftung, 2015a: 31). Moreover, the country's military alliance with the KSA and the USA in the war in Yemen and the struggle to defeat ISIS have all increased the potential for domestic terrorist activities to increase and the radicalisation of disaffected younger Emiratis.

However, while both religious conservatives and liberals have questioned the legitimacy of the ruling political elite in the UAE during the 2010s, the overwhelming majority of the secure and comfortable Emirati population trusts and supports their rulers, and there has been no widespread backing for further political liberalisation up to this point in time. In addition, the major government bureaucracies are generally efficient and responsive, and the administrative systems of the country work reasonably well (Buhumaid et al, 2016). Consequently, the UAE has not experienced the widespread protests that Oman, the KSA and many other MENA countries did after the 2011 Arab Spring. The country was not faced with any dynastic succession issues during 2016–2017, unlike Oman, and it has not had to cope with a regime change, as the KSA did during 2015–2016. Although falling oil and gas revenues during 2015–2016 have had a significant effect on the national economy, the ruling elite of the UAE appears to be stable and secure for now.

2.4 THE CHANGING STATUS AND ROLES OF WOMEN IN THE UAE

I call upon my sisters and daughters all over the country to recognize that their responsibilities are great and are not less than those of men in this society. The achievements of women in the United Arab Emirates (UAE) in such a short time have made me happy and convinced me that what we planted yesterday will today start to bear fruit. Nothing could delight me more than to see a woman taking up her distinctive position in society. Nothing should hinder her progress. Like men, women deserve the right to occupy high positions, according to their capabilities and qualifications.

What women have achieved in the UAE during a short period of time makes me happy and confident that what we planted yesterday has begun to bear fruit. The role of UAE women in society has started to emerge and to materialize into something that will be of benefit for the welfare of our present and future generations.

The first president of the UAE, HRH Sheikh Zayed bin Sultan al-Nahyan, 2000

Over the last two decades, the UAE has witnessed what can only be described as a revolution in the economic power and social freedom of Emirati women. Today, they have opportunities that their mothers and grandmothers could have only dreamed about and the freedoms they now have are very different to those of young women in more conservative Middle Eastern countries, such as Saudi Arabia or Yemen. These changes would have been impossible without the active support of successive UAE presidents and the governments and local authorities of the seven *imara*. Forty years ago, as we saw earlier in this chapter, there were few educational opportunities beyond a very basic primary school education for young female Emiratis, and none had access to higher education. However, Sheikh Zayed bin Sultan al-Nahyan believed that if the country was serious about national economic development it had to allow women full access to secondary and tertiary education and this became a government priority in the UAE during the 1980s and 1990s. With the rapid expansion of the university sector over the last two decades and the establishment of Zayed University in 1998 and other government universities and vocational colleges, many more young Emirati women have since received a tertiary education. By 2015, 37,417 Emirati women were enrolled in private universities and 29,803 in government universities. The figures for men were 39,492 and 11,848 (United Arab Emirates National Bureau of Statistics, 2016: 61). University education is free for Emirati women, and they receive full grants for postgraduate courses in the UAE and can also apply for scholarships to study abroad. In government universities, which mainly educate Emiratis, more than 70 per cent of the graduates are women and about 80 per cent of these pursue professional careers after graduating. In common with many other countries, females have also been outperforming males at the primary, secondary and tertiary sectors since the mid-2000s (Ghafour, 2016; The Ministry of Higher Education, 2010).

In addition to the rapid expansion of higher education in the UAE over the last two decades, numerous government-funded women's organisations and associations have been created to promote the economic and social interests of Emirati women under the umbrella of the UAE Women's Federation (UAEWF). This was established on 27 August 1975, by HRH Sheikha Fatima bint Mubarak, wife of the late Sheikh Zayed. She worked tirelessly to promote the role of women after the creation of the UAE and established the first women's society in the country, the Abu Dhabi Women Society, in 1973. The primary role of the UAEWF in the early days of the UAE was to promote education, health and social welfare for Emirati women. Today it has a more strategic role in helping UAE women to achieve their professional ambitions, realise their leadership potential and to represent them collectively in discussions with government departments involved in women's development in the UAE. It is also responsible for suggesting new laws or changing existing legislation that affect women at work and in the community. Many women's societies are linked together under the aegis of the UAEWF, including the Abu-Dhabi Women's Society, Dubai Women's Development Society, Dubai Women Establishment, Family Development Foundation, General Women's Union, Sharjah Women Association, Ajman Um al-Mo'mineen Women's Association, Umm al-Qaiwain Women Association, Ra al-Khaimah Women Association and the UAE General Women Union. Government support has also enabled these societies to publish three Arabic-language women's magazines and to allow their members to participate in international women's conferences (General Women's Union, 2008; Mubarak, 2007; Salloum, 2003). The UAEWF is also a member of the League of Arab Women.

Other examples of initiatives for Emirati women include the launch of the UAE Women Leadership Development Program in

2008 and the Dubai School of Government (DSG), who held their Second Arab Women Leadership Forum in 2010 on the theme of 'Women's Leadership in Organisations: Towards New Conceptions of Work–Life Balance'. This forum explored the issue of work–life balance in the UAE, the lack of provision of childcare facilities in both public- and private-sector organisations in the country, the obstacles and challenges faced by working women who have families and organisational policies that could be introduced to improve work–family balance in the UAE (Trade Arabia, 2010); an issue we will look at again in Chapters 3 and 9. The Dubai Women Establishment (DWE) has also convened several leadership forums and symposia for women over the last decade and, in February 2016, held a two-day conference that attracted more than 2,000 participants and 200 speakers (Dubai Women Establishment, 2016). In addition to these, the UAE also held four *Women as Global Leaders* conferences during the 2000s and early 2010s, hosted by Zayed University, which included many well-known international female business and political leaders as keynote speakers.

Two other recent initiatives in the UAE were the launch of the National Strategy for the Empowerment of Emirati Women (NSEEW) 2015–2021 by HRH Shaikha Fatima bint Mubarak, the chairwoman of the General Women's Union in March 2015, and the establishment of the UAE Gender Balance Council (UAEGBC) in early 2015, chaired by Shaikha Manal bint Mohammed bin Rashid al-Maktoum, the president of the DWE (*Gulf News*, 2015b). The NSEEW is an updated version of an earlier national plan for women launched in 2002. The unveiling of this strategy, which coincided with celebrations for the 2015 International Women's Day, was intended to provide an institutional framework for all federal and local government private-sector and civic organisations to enable Emirati women 'to contribute fully to the modernisation and development of the UAE' (*Gulf News*, 2015a). The mission of the UAEGBC is to 'boost the UAE's efforts to evolve and enhance the role of women as key partners in building the future of the nation'. At the launch of this initiative, Sheikha

Manal commented that 'the impact of a significant female presence in leadership roles has wide ranging benefits on the economy, on governance, and on society at large. The UAE has always worked to dismantle barriers that create tensions between the genders. We have a great opportunity to uncover new paths that we may walk on together' (Leaders Middle East, 2015). Dubai was also host to the first *Global Women's Forum* to be held in the MENA region on 22 February 2016 (Redvers, 2015a).

As a result of these initiatives and several major legislative changes affecting access to higher education and the workplace over the last twenty years, many more Emirati women now work in jobs in almost all professions, and some have reached leadership positions in both public- and private-sector organisations. The proportion of female employees in the UAE workforce quadrupled between 1980 and 1990, and the number of Emirati women in the national workforce grew from 18,144 in 1995 to 38,657 in 2000 to more than 100,000 in 2010, when women comprised 27.95 per cent of the Emirati national workforce (Bitar, 2010), a figure that according to government sources at the time 'will increase substantially over the next decade' (Ministry of State for Federal National Council Affairs, 2009). This prediction proved to be correct: by 2015, 46.5 per cent of Emirati women were working full time compared to 92.0 per cent of male Emiratis (Majdalani et al, 2015: 16; United Nations, 2015a). The figure for women, it should be noted, is still rather low when compared to the labour-force participation rates of women in the world's leading developed economies, which is now, on average, about 70 per cent (United Nations, 2015a: 224).

Younger Emirati women have also begun to 'break the mould' by branching out of traditional work roles, such as teaching, and becoming commercial airline pilots and joining the UAE military, the police and the national customs service. A Women's Corps within the Armed Forces and a women's military training college were established in Abu Dhabi in the early 2010s, bearing the name of one of the great heroines of Arab history, Khawla bint al-Azwar. The country's first female fighter pilot joined the UAE Air Force in early 2014 and was later involved in airstrikes against ISIS groups in Yemen and Syria (*The National*, 2010). Three more women have since graduated as fighter pilots and at least thirty serve with the country's special security services (Embassy of the United Arab Emirates, 2015). More than 100 Emirati women now enrol as trainees in the police service each year (about 20 per cent of the total intake). They are represented across all sectors of the service, including traffic, VIP protection and forensic pathology and also, in a culture that does not generally approve of canines, dog handling (Powell, 2009). Several Emirati women now work in senior positions in the executive offices of the governments of Dubai and Abu Dhabi, and when I visited two interviewees at the Dubai Executive Council offices on the thirty-seventh floor of the Emirates Tower in May 2011, most of the employees I encountered that day were women.

Women have been appointed to key political and national cabinet positions in the judiciary and diplomatic corps. Jawan al-Dhaheri became the country's first female judge in 2007, and by January 2016, four more women had been appointed as judges (*qadi*) and two as public prosecutors, and seventeen had been promoted to assistant public prosecutors and marriage officials. Shaikha Lubna al-Qasimi was the first Emirati woman to become a minister of state (for International Cooperation and Development, then Economy and Planning and, most recently, Minister for Tolerance). Three are ambassadors, one is a consul general, and Lana Nusseibeh became the country's first female permanent representative to the United Nations in September 2013 (Embassy of the United Arab Emirates, 2015). In June 2016, nearly one-quarter of the members of the country's national assembly were women, nine were members of the FNC and five have served in the UAE federal cabinet. However, as noted, only one woman has ever been directly elected to the FNC – the others were all government appointees. In November 2015, the FNC elected its first female speaker, Amal al-Qubaisi, who was the first woman to be elected to this position in the MENA region (Dubai Women Establishment, 2016; Middle East Online, 2015).

Examples of high-profile UAE women business and public-sector leaders, and also some who can be regarded as pioneers for other Emirati women, include Reem al-Hashimi, Minister of State and CEO for Expo 2020 in the UAE; Amina al-Rustamani, CEO of TECOM Investments; Zainab Mohammed, Property Management, Marketing and Communications Manager at Wasl Properties; Majida Ali Rashid, Assistant Director General, Dubai Land Department; Raja al-Gurg, Managing Director of the Easa Saleh Al Gurg Group and Chair of the Dubai Women Business Council; Futaim al-Falasi, the very popular radio presenter of The Taim Show; Noura al-Kaabi, CEO of Abu Dhabi's media free zone, TwoFour54, and a member of the FNC; Maryam Matar, founder of the UAE Genetic Diseases Association; Salma Hareb, CEO of the Jebel Ali Free Zone Authority and Economic Zones World; Mona al-Marri, Director General of the Dubai Media Office; Sarah Shuhail, founder of the Centre for Women and Children; Nashwa al-Ruwaini, known as 'the Oprah of the Middle East', founder and CEO of Pyramedia; Maha al-Farhan, founder and CEO of medical and clinical testing company ClinArt; Amal al-Qubaisi, General Manager of the Abu Dhabi Educational Council and the first woman to be appointed to the Federal National Council; Ingie Chalhoub, President and Managing Director of the Etoile Group; Elissa Freiha, founder and director of WOMENA (an investment fund for female entrepreneurs); Hind Siddiqi, vice president of Ahmed Siddiqi and Sons; Nisreen Shocair, CEO of Virgin Megastores Middle East; Amal al-Marri, founder of the SAL restaurant chain; Nayla al-Khaja, the UAE's first female film director and founder of the D-SEVEN production company; Muna Harib al-Muhairi, founder of several charitable organisation such as Seeds of Change and Breathing Numbers; and Mona Ataya, CEO of Mumzworld (CEO Middle East, 2015). Other notable examples in 2015 included Khulood Ahmad, the Vice President of Distribution at Dubai Bank, Marwan Abdulaziz Janahi, Executive Director of the Dubai Biotechnology and Research Park and Hamda al-Huraizi, the CEO of the Caviar International Company, which operates in the

Middle East and Europe. Several others are in senior positions in the real estate and construction sectors, such as Samira Abdulrazzak, a Zayed University graduate, who is CEO of Dubai Infinity Holdings, and Noor Sweid, who is Director of Strategy at the Depa Group.

However, the proportion of Emirati women working in the private sector, as either employers or employees, is small – less than 5 per cent of the total number of Emiratis in the UAE labour force – despite much greater efforts having been made by both government organisations and private-sector companies to encourage female Emiratis to consider careers outside the public sector in recent years (United Arab Emirates Government, 2014). By 2015, as noted above, Emirati women comprised more than 60 per cent of the workforce in the public sector, of which nearly one third were in middle and senior management positions (Dubai Women Establishment, 2015; Embassy of the United Arab Emirates, 2015). The strong preference that many female (and male) Emiratis still have for employment in this sector will be very difficult to change. It is a very attractive option for Emirati women, combining perhaps the best public-sector pay rates and benefits in the world with a working environment that respects women and local cultural values and which also allows most of them to enjoy a harmonious work–family balance.

The only policy initiative that could change this is to make the public sector less attractive to them. While there were few indications that this was likely to happen in the early- to mid-2010s, we will see in the conclusion to this chapter that this may change in the future. With a persistent employment rate of 15 to 20 per cent among younger Emiratis, it is becoming evident that UAE nationals must become more willing to embrace careers in the private sector and as entrepreneurs. This seems to be particularly true of male Emiratis, who, according to some commentators, have often been content just to finish high school and take well-paid and secure jobs in government organisations, the police and the military (Khan, 2009: 267–270). The challenge for the UAE and other countries in the MENA region is how to encourage more women (and men) to move from the 'safety blanket' of the public sector and government-owned commercial organisations and to become more significant contributors to high-value, creative and innovative entrepreneurial activities in the future. We will look at how this could be achieved in Chapter 9.

In 2002, the UAE National Strategy for the Advancement of Women established business women's councils for each of the seven Chambers of Commerce and Industry in the UAE and also created the Dubai Business Women Council (DBWC) and Abu Dhabi Business Women Group (ADBW). These have provided training on entrepreneurship and consulting services for establishing new businesses (including seed funding) since the mid-2000s. Other organisations such as the Khalifa Fund, Dubai SME, the Arab Business Angels Network, the Ruwad Establishment in Sharjah, the Estihara Scheme in the Western Region and the Mohammed bin Rashid Establishment for Young Business Leaders also provide support for entrepreneurs. The overall level of entrepreneurial activity among Emirati nationals is high by international standards, with 9.3 per cent of Emiratis involved in some form of entrepreneurial activity compared to 13.5 per cent in the number-one-ranked country, Sweden (Sokari et al, 2013: 18).

In 2007, there were about 12,000 self-employed female Emirati members of the UAE Business Women's Council, a total that appears to have changed little from the early to mid-2000s (Haan, 2004; Nasr et al, 2005). Their economic contribution to the UAE economy was estimated to be about 10 billion dirhams in 2009 (about $3 billion), a very small part of the country's national GDP (Abouzied, 2008; Ministry of State for Federal National Council Affairs, 2009: 3). The total number of self-employed Emirati women increased to about 18,000 by December 2015, although there was no reliable information available at this time on the net contribution of this group to the country's annual GDP. The UAE was also ranked at number 27 in the 2015 Global Entrepreneurship and Development Institute's female entrepreneurship index ranking of seventy-seven countries and was the number-one country for female entrepreneurship in the MENA region (Terjesen and Lloyd, 2015: 11 and 15).

However, Emirati entrepreneurs and SME owners are still predominantly male and women still encounter cultural, religious and institutional barriers when creating new businesses. Although there have been some notable entrepreneurial ventures launched by Emirati women, the evidence suggests that would-be female entrepreneurs during the 2000s and early 2010s were handicapped by limited networking opportunities, a lack of support from fathers, male relatives and husbands, a lack of confidence and 'fear of failure', restricted access to sources of start-up capital, a higher rate of initial funding rejections by banks, negative (male and female) attitudes towards female entrepreneurs and even something of a backlash against women becoming more financially independent of men (Erogul and McCrohan, 2008, 2007a and 2007b; Kargwell, 2012; Preiss and McGrohan, 2006; Sokari et al, 2013). It also appears that the female Emirati business women who have been featured in media reports over the last few years are almost entirely those from wealthy families who have inherited all or part of an existing family-owned business. Most female business start-ups in the UAE are much more likely to be home-based micro-enterprises and concentrated in a limited but socially acceptable range of service businesses such as tailoring, hairdressing and beauty salons, human resource management, retail, fashion and interior decoration (Gallant and Pounder, 2008). It is also apparent that female Emirati entrepreneurs remain more risk averse than men and are much less likely to create innovative high-value enterprises and, disappointingly, their enterprises are more likely than those run by men to go out of business within the first three years of operation (Sokari et al, 2013: 30; Madichie and Gallant, 2012). And, more than half of the women in one study of female Emirati entrepreneurs believed that most male Emiratis did not think that the entrepreneurial abilities of women were equivalent to those of men (Kargwell, 2012: 53). For Houda Abu Jamra, founding partner at the private equity firm TVM Capital MENA, the reasons so few Emirati women were becoming entrepreneurs a few years ago were self-evident:

The reality is there are few women in the workplace, especially in the private sector, so it follows that there are few women-owned enterprises that private equity can invest in. There is also something deeper at play – there are lots of social and cultural reasons why there are so few women owning businesses, and gender equality has been identified as one of the seven major challenges facing the MENA region … There is certainly a need for banks and other service providers to embark on dedicated programs to support women getting into business. There is some movement in the GCC, but not enough is being done at the moment …
A factor that, in my mind, surely plays a big role here is the issue of combining family and business and how to make it work. This is no different from the West, where it is still one of the biggest challenges for working women … I am personally convinced that women run businesses have the same chances to succeed if given the same support by family, friends and society. They might be slower, but I think they are also much more careful than men in their approach to taking risks

(Nair, 2011: 32).

It would appear that Emirati women have made good progress in the national labour market over the last twenty years, but how does the UAE compare to other societies in terms of economic opportunities and gender equality? To answer this question, we can compare the progress that the UAE has made with the WEF's GGG reports, the comprehensive annual studies of global gender inequalities that have been published since 2006. These utilise fourteen indicators of female inequality clustered into four categories: economic participation and opportunities for work, educational attainment, political empowerment and health and survival. The GGG reports focus on gender gaps and differentials in countries, not on their absolute levels of economic development. This enables them to identify where significant gender inequalities may exist, even if general standards of living and per-capita GDP may be quite high in any particular country (as it is in the

UAE, Oman, the KSA and the other Arabian Gulf States). The WEF recognises that 'the advancement of women is an important economic, business and societal issue with a significant impact on the growth of nations' (World Economic Forum, 2011: 3), and also hopes that its reports 'will act as a catalyst for change by providing policy makers with a snapshot of the relative strengths and weaknesses of their country's performance compared to that of other nations [and] to serve as a basis for designing effective measures for reducing gender gaps' (World Economic Forum, 2007: vii).

The twenty countries of the MENA region had the worst cumulative global score for female inequality in 2007, 2011, 2013 and 2015, and not one has ever been ranked in the top 100 countries for female equality. For comparative purposes, the top-five-ranked countries for women's equality in 2011 were Iceland, Norway, Finland, Sweden and Ireland; in 2013, Iceland, Finland, Norway, Sweden and – surprisingly – the Philippines; and in 2015, Iceland, Norway, Finland, Sweden and Ireland. In 2011, the UAE was ranked 103 out of 135 countries. In 2013, it was ranked 109/136 countries and in 2015, 119/145. The UAE's ranking for 'economic participation and opportunity' for women was 119/135 in 2011, 122/136 in 2013 and had fallen to 128/145 countries by 2015. However, the UAE has been rated as being either the number-one or number-two country in the Gulf region for female equality in the ten GGG reports published since 2006 (World Economic Forum, 2015b: 8, 9, and 10; 2013: 12, 13 and 18; 2011: 9, 10 and 15).

There are several reasons why the UAE continues to have this low ranking. The first is that the WEF and the United Nations have always taken a rather dim view of countries that may be signatories to international treaties that affect the lives and well-being of women but who do not then behave in accordance with either the letter or the spirit of these. In 2005, the UAE became a signatory to CEDAW (United Nations, 2015b) and the United Nations Convention on Women's Rights, and a permanent federal government committee – the Commission on the Status of Women – reports each year to the

Federal National Assembly. In addition, 'in principle' equal rights between men and women are also enshrined in the UAE constitution in Articles 14 and 25 and also in Article 32 of the UAE Federal Labour Laws(al-Abed, 2007: 244–249). The UAE was also the first country in the MENA region to enforce quotas for women on company boards in 2015 and it is also a member of the United Nations Entity for Gender Equality and the Empowerment of Women.

However, the UAE government only signed up to the CEDAW agreement with several major reservations in relation to Article 2(f): 'the obligation to eliminate or abolish discriminatory laws, regulations, customs and practices', Article 9: 'the right to nationality', Article 15(2): 'legal capacity', Article 15(4): 'freedom of movement and choice of domicile' Article 16: 'on equal rights in marriage and family relations', Article 29: 'arbitration of conflicts arising from the convention' and other provisions that the government of the UAE regards as contradictory to *shari'a* laws (International Federation for Human Rights, 2010). To date, with the notable exception of extending nationality rights to the children of Emirati women who are married to non-UAE nationals, the national government has not taken any steps to either review these reservations or work towards removing them from its legal statutes. Furthermore, as noted above, while 'in principle' equal rights for all citizens of the UAE are enshrined in the UAE constitution these do not specifically mention women: 'All persons are equal before the law, without distinction between citizens of the UAE in regard to race, nationality, religion or social status', and 'Equality, social justice, ensuring safety, and security, and equality of opportunity for all citizens shall be the pillars of our society' (al-Abed, 2007: 119).

Furthermore, while Article 32 of the UAE Federal Labour laws states that 'A woman shall be paid the same wage as a man if she performs the same work', there are no systems in place in the UAE to monitor if wage equality between men and women is practiced or, if it is not, what might be done to remove wage differentials (Constitute Project, 2012: 5 and 7; Dubai Women Establishment, 2009: 43–44). The

United Nations has also been unable to provide any statistical data on wage inequalities between men and women in the UAE in any of its recent human development reports (United Nations, 2015a: 216). In addition, there are no national laws or policies that explicitly outlaw gender-based discrimination either at work or in the domestic sphere.[4] Consequently, women in the UAE still have no direct legal redress for gender discrimination at work, fathers and husbands still have the legal right to prevent their wives and daughters from working outside the home and women still require the written authorisation of their male 'guardians' (*mahram*) to travel abroad, regardless of their seniority. And in 2016, Emirati men still had the legal right to seize the passports of their wives or daughters or request that the immigration authorities prevent their departure from the UAE.

The second reason these reports have consistently awarded the UAE a low international ranking is the lack of information about its compliance with other international labour conventions (such as the UN's Equal Remuneration Convention or the ILO's Discrimination – Employment and Occupation – Convention), as well as the lack of adequate data on the distribution of women in the national labour market and how many have reached leadership and executive positions in organisations. One report that has examined this issue indicates that a mere 1 per cent of the members of the boards of publicly listed Emirati-owned companies are women and only 14 per cent are in senior management roles in private-sector companies (Majdalani et al, 2015: 5); and we will see how this compares to a selection of OECD countries in Chapter 8. In addition, independent women's associations that might be able to advocate for improved women's rights are not permitted in the UAE and a group of women who tried to create a women's advocacy group in 2013 were arrested by the police (Bertelsmann Stiftung, 2016a: 6). While the UAE federal government and many of the women's organisations mentioned earlier may sincerely claim that women now enjoy equality of opportunity in the workplace, including pay equity with men, there is – to the best of my knowledge – no reliable independent research that could validate this claim.

The third reason for the low global ranking of the UAE stems from the very heavy concentration of Emirati women in public-sector employment (Holdsworth, 2010), the under-representation of Emirati women in some sectors (e.g. science, technology, engineering, mathematics and academia) combined with the very small number of Emirati women who are self-starting entrepreneurs and SME owners. Only about 4 per cent of Emirati women were employed in science, technology, engineering or mathematics (STEM) professions during the 2000s, mainly in the public sector (Dubai Women Establishment, 2008d: 3), a situation that was unchanged by the early 2000s (Forster and al-Marzouqi, 2011) but which may be improving to some extent today. Consequently, for those who compile the WEF's GGG reports, this evidence indicates that the progress that the UAE is making towards gender equality across all sectors of its economy and labour market is patchy, and this has prevented the UAE from being placed higher in its annual GGG rankings up to this point in time. Having said this, it may well be that the UAE's current ranking is a harsh one, certainly when compared to those of other Gulf States such as the KSA and Bahrain with whom it has always been closely bracketed in the GGG reports.

For example, Raja al-Gurg, a well-known Emirati businesswoman who has lived through the changes described in this chapter, believes that while 'UAE society is still patriarchal, we have already seen moderate changes from the previous restrictive attitudes towards women in the workplace. Work is increasingly being seen not merely as a source of income [for Emirati women] but as an important part of establishing a personal and professional identity' (Nagraj, 2012: 46). And while Emirati women are still concentrated in the public sector or in marketing, retail and HRM functions in the private sector, they are moving incrementally into finance, the media, the oil sector, healthcare and science, technology and engineering roles. We will also see in Chapter 3 that many of the working Emirati women I interviewed for this book did not agree with these generally negative external assessments of the status of women in the UAE.

Nevertheless, significant gender inequities do persist in the UAE because it remains in many ways a very traditional Muslim society, with all the implicit cultural assumptions that naturally follow from this about the 'correct' public and private roles of Emirati women and their responsibilities to their community, their extended families, their husbands and their children. However, as noted in Chapter 1, gender equality has been identified as one of the key factors that have driven economic growth in world's leading economies over the last four decades in numerous reports published by the United Nations and the World Economic Forum. To cite one more illustrative example, the extensive global development studies carried out by the Culture Matters Research Project in the United States during the 2000s identified twenty-five clusters of cultural factors that characterise 'progress-prone' and 'progress-resistant' societies. These include religious beliefs, ethical codes, education, work motivation, private property, innovation, entrepreneurship, competitive markets, the rule of law, democracy, future orientation and several other factors including, at number 24, 'gender equality'. In progress-resistant cultures, 'women are subordinated to men in most dimensions of life' (Harrison, 2006: 36–37; see also Harrison and Huntington, 2000). Consequently, it may well be – notwithstanding the undeniable progress made by Emirati women in higher education and the national labour market over the last twenty years – that the UAE is in several important respects still 'progress-resistant' in terms of gender equality for women.

2.5 THE CULTURAL, ATTITUDINAL AND STRUCTURAL BARRIERS FACING WOMEN IN THE UAE

'Better the voice of the she-devil than that of a girl'; 'If your wife gives birth to girls you shall suffer until the day you die'; 'A maiden is a calamity but marriage is a protection'; 'A girl belongs to her husband or the grave.'

'Paradise lies at the feet of mothers'; 'He who has not fathered girls has not really lived.'

Old – and contradictory – Arabic proverbs (United Nations, 2005: 148)

As noted in the preface, a discussion of the status of women in the countries of the MENA region, and the cultural, attitudinal and structural barriers they still routinely encounter in their societies, must take into account the sociological characteristics of the Islamic culture(s) in which they live. This requires some discussion of what the Qur'an says about the rights, roles and responsibilities of women in Islamic societies, although it has to be said that there will (inevitably) be those who will not agree with my interpretation of this. However, it is reasonable to say at the outset that those who have addressed this contentious issue fall into two distinct camps. On the one hand, we have Islamic intellectuals like Abdulla al-Qasemi, Farah Antun, Qasim Amin, Tahir al-Haddad and Nazira Zayn al-Din. They have highlighted sections of the Qur'an and the accumulated body of Islamic theology in the *Hadith, Sunnah* and *Qiyas* that emphasise a degree of equality between men and women, where 'the root principle in Islamic statutes is equality between men and women, apart from those areas in which the text explicitly assign a prerogative or a distinction to one of the genders, for reasons pertaining not so much to gender as to social responsibility and legal status' (Fahami Howeidy, quoted by the United Nations, 2005: 144).

They have also argued that early Islamic laws granted women many new legal rights that had never previously existed in the spheres of family life, marriage, education, participation in political affairs, inheritance, control over their wealth and the right to work outside the home. They did not have these rights before the time of the Prophet Muhammed and these 'lent support to basic equality between men and women by giving women equal (but not necessarily identical) rights with men, be they personal, civil, social or political rights' (al-Munajjed, 1997: 13). Some of these scholars have also documented and described the lives of thousands of Muslim women who actively participated in their societies in civic, military and legal roles in the past (al-Barwani, 2011; Fadl, 2005). Two often-cited examples of what most educated Emirati, Omani and Saudi women consider to be the Prophet's true beliefs about women are his first wife, Khadija, a successful businesswoman who is still regarded as a role model for many Muslim women and one of his other wives, Aisha, who participated in politics and the compiling of the *Hadith* after the Prophet's death. She also became a leader in the fight against Ali bin Abi Taleb (who modern-day Shiites regard as the first true *imam* of the Islamic faith). Fadl, Nasr and several other liberal Islamic scholars believe that where inequalities have existed in Islamic societies, these have been created by cultural and social forces not the Islamic faith itself (Fadl, 2005: 250–274; Nasr, 2009: 250–275).

Consequently, because of (mis)interpretations by conservative male religious scholars and the influence of local traditions and cultures, Muslim women have often had significant restrictions imposed upon them. The Qur'an, for example, states that women should be protected and taken care of by men as the heads of the household (the *qawwamuna* principle), but this evolved over time into edicts that explicitly forbade women to work outside the home or speak to a man who was not a member of their family. In a similar fashion, two *suras* in the Qur'an (7.26 and 33.59), indicating that women (and men) should cover their bodies and be modest in their attire, regressed into strictly applied cultural practices and legal edicts which mandated that women should always cover their entire bodies and faces in public. As al-Munajjed, Bennoune and other scholars have noted, the practice of veiling was *not* mandated in early Islamic law and a similar trend can be observed in the practice of gender segregation in public spaces in conservative Islamic societies. This prohibition was unknown in the Prophet's time and only became established as a widespread cultural practice after semi-nomadic Arabs started to settle in urban centres during the seventh and eighth century CE (Bennoune, 2013: 118; al-Munajjed, 1997: 25, 41–43, 47–57). The Malaysian organisation Sisters in Islam in their analysis of the *suras* of the Qur'an that specifically mention the roles and obligations of women in Islamic societies emphasise this point:

Islam was a liberating religion that uplifted the status of women and gave them rights that were considered revolutionary 1400 years ago. In spite of this founding spirit, Muslim practices today often oppress women and deny them the equality and human dignity granted in the Qur'an. *Our research has shown that oppressive interpretations of the Qur'an are influenced mostly by cultural practices and values that regard women as inferior and subordinate to men*

(Sisters in Islam, 2015: 1; my emphasis).

On the other hand, most scholars – citing other *suras* from the Qur'an that emphasise the fundamentally *unequal* natures of men and women – have concluded that it is both the edicts contained in the Qur'an and, more importantly, the cultural and institutional practices of Islam historically and today that are the main impediments to the full emancipation of women in Muslim countries and their hopes for achieving economic, legal, political and social equality with men. For example, 'Men have authority over women because God has made the one superior to the other, and because they spend their wealth to maintain them. Good women are obedient. They guard their unseen parts because God has guarded them. As those from whom you fear disobedience, admonish them, forsake them in beds apart and beat them. Then if they obey you, take no further action against them.' A second *sura* suggests that 'Women shall with justice have rights similar to those exercised against them, although men have a status above women' (The Qur'an: al-Nisa 4.34 and al-Baqarah 2.226; the Koran, 2005: 64 and 33). A variant on this edict is: 'Men are the protectors and maintainers of women, because God has given the one more strength than the other and because they support them from their means' (The Qur'an: al-Nisa 4.34; as presented by al-Munajjed, 1997: 83). A third *sura* suggests that 'women [should] turn their eyes away from temptation and to preserve their chastity: not to display their adornments (except such as are normally revealed); to draw their veils over their bosoms and not to display their finery except to their husbands, their fathers, their husband's fathers, their sons, their step-sons, their brothers, their brothers' sons, their women servants and their slave-girls; male attendants lacking in natural vigour and children who have no carnal knowledge of women' (The Qur'an: *al-Nur* 24.30; the Koran, 2005: 248).

Consequently, those Muslim women who have written commentaries on this issue are generally scathing about recent attempts to emphasise the 'moderate' nature of Qur'anic decrees about women and also deeply sceptical about any notions of an 'Islamic feminism' (Ali, 2015, 2010 and 2007; Eltahawy, 2015; Tucker, 2008). Ali, for example, believes that:

> In the text of the Qur'an and in Shari'a law, men and women are self-evidently not equal. Muslim women are considered to be physically, emotionally, intellectually and morally inferior to men, and they have fewer legal rights. The Qur'an decrees that daughters inherit half a son's share: 'Allah prescribes with regard to your children: to one of the masculine sex falls (in the division of an estate) just as much as two of the feminine sex.' The value of their testimony in a court of law is fixed as half that of a man's. Even in the case of rape, the victim's testimony is worth half that of her rapist.
>
> Women living under Islamic law cannot travel, study, marry, sign most legal documents or even leave their home without their father's permission. They may not be permitted to participate in public life, and their freedom to make decisions regarding their private life is severely, often brutally, curtailed. They may not choose with whom they have sex nor, when they are married, when or whether to have sex. They may not choose what to wear, whether to work, to walk down the street. In Iran you may be legally married at nine; on the order of a judge, you may be lashed ninety-nine times with a whip for committing adultery. Then, on

the order of a second judge, you may be sentenced later to death by stoning, a terrible fate which has befallen several Iranian women in recent times

(Ali, 2010: 163–4 and 229).

Currently, apostate non-Muslims are not permitted to visit the holy cities of Mecca and Medina but, if they were, he or she could buy a 1,265-page souvenir book (in Arabic); a kind of 'best of' compilation of edicts (*fatwa*)by Saudi clerics about, well, pretty much everything you can possibly imagine. To most non-Muslims, these edicts and the thousands of both draconian and petty *fatwa* that have been issued to help people navigate their daily lives, hygiene ('Should water, toilet paper or both be employed after using the toilet?'), appropriate sexual behaviour between spouses and dress/appearance issues ('Is plucking my eyebrows or dyeing my hair okay?'), would be intolerable. As Macfarquhar has observed, 'if you expand all the institutions as well as the services issuing religious rulings across more than two dozen countries in the Middle East, you begin to get the sense that the raft of daily life floats on a veritable sea of religious pronouncements' (Macfarquhar, 2009: 129–130). And, even to many Muslims, some of these are absurd. For example, for Muslim women to maintain their appearance of *fadila* (modesty), it is considered to be inappropriate and even indecent (*tabaruf*) not to wear an *abaya* in the presence of non-family men. Hence, not so long ago:

A working woman asked her imam, or cleric, whether she had to veil her hair around the one male colleague with whom she had worked with every day for years and years. The cleric ruled that if she suckled her colleague on her breast five times, a traditional Islamic prescription for becoming a sanctioned surrogate mother, then he could be considered to be family and she could remove her headscarf at work. Naturally, the idea of a grown, hirsute man slurping a colleague's bared breast so that she could discard the

most modest part of her dress, while certainly breaking new
ground, defied logic and the fatwa was shouted down

(Macfarquhar, 2009: 127–128; the cleric mentioned in this quote was
Abdul Mohsen al-Obeikan who we will encounter again in Chapter 6).

The arbitrary and subjective nature of the religious edicts issued in
the different countries of the MENA region can be highlighted with
reference to three examples from the 2000s. In Bahrain, the well-
known Sunni cleric Sheikh Yusuf al-Qaradawi pronounced that
women could run for elected positions on the national assembly in
2002, providing they were suitably qualified and if their duties did not
conflict with their roles as wives and mothers. He did, however,
instruct women to avoid eye contact with men in the assembly if
they were elected. An unidentified Bahraini man sought another
ruling from a Wahhabist Saudi cleric, who, presumably using exactly
the same sacred texts, pronounced that women should be prohibited
from standing for office in his country because 'men are supposed to
control women and handle their affairs'. In 2005, another (unnamed)
Saudi religious scholar decreed that not only should women not stand
for elected office, no one could vote for any man whose platform
included advocating rights for women (i.e. being allowed to
drive, working outside the home, traveling alone and so forth)
(Macfarquhar, 2009: 129–130 and 144–146). And yet in 2015, Saudi
clerics did not formally oppose women voting and standing in municipal elections in the KSA. The one provision to this ruling was that
no candidates (male or female) could propose any policies that vio-
lated the Qur'an or *shari'a* law. This practice of obtaining edicts that
suit individual preferences and prejudices has been described as
'*fatwa* shopping' and '*fatwa* chaos' and, in the definitive words of
the United Nations, 'there is no consistent interpretation or definitive concepts acceptable to all the Arab States for applying *shari'a*
laws' (United Nations, 2005: 181).

Within the scope of this book, it is not possible to address these
debates in further depth or to include further examples of liberal

Islamic theologians who have championed greater legal and social equality for Muslim women.[5] But it is important to reiterate the point that several prominent Muslim scholars have been very critical of the status of women in contemporary Islamic societies and they have also called for both greater *ijtihad* and a renaissance (*al-nahda*) in Islamic theology in recent times (Ali, 2015: 53–76 and 223–238; Bennoune, 2013; Eltahawy, 2015; Fadl, 2005: 250–274; al-Rasheed, 2010; Wadud, 2006). It should also not be forgotten that restrictions on the legal and social rights of women have been a notable characteristic of other patriarchal religions such as Roman Catholicism, Judaism and Evangelical Protestantism which, historically, excluded most women from any participation in the public sphere. And it is important to note that none of the women that I interviewed in the UAE and Oman, and only some in the KSA, would agree with Ali's depiction of Islam and the largely negative effects that she believes it has on their lives or how they think about and deal with women's issues (*qadiyyat al-mara*) in their countries. Similar opinions were also expressed by many of the ninety-four female Arab leaders who were interviewed for the *Arab Women: Leadership Outlook 2009–2011* report (Dubai Women Establishment, 2009: 32).

However, having noted this continuing debate, all the historical evidence indicates that women throughout the early, middle and later Islamic periods were segregated and largely excluded from the economic sphere and public life in the major cities of the Caliphate. This state of affairs continued, with local variations, throughout the Muslim diaspora in the centuries that followed, and it persists today, to a greater or lesser extent, in all countries in the MENA region. For example, the contributors to the United Nations 2005 AHDR report concluded that:

> Juristic interpretations, formulated in the schools of Islamic
> jurisprudence, contributed to the establishment of norms
> sanctioning the principle of discrimination between the sexes. The
> contents of the *suras* were transformed into fundamental and

general tenets, although they are not so ... They were broadened to include the relationships between men and women in different situations, and in general to bolster discrimination between the two sexes. The authority of such subsidiary *suras* was reinforced by invoking the Prophet's *sunnah*, a long list of unconfirmed sayings of the prophet that was used to diminish women's humanity

(United Nations 2005: 145).

The strategy of interpretation that led to laws affirming the inferiority of women centred on two principles: first, a disregard of the fundamental Qur'anic verses that recognize equality and honour human beings and, second, the use of subsidiary verses and other arguments for a hierarchy of the sexes, to justify inequality. [Consequently], men have always been given priority and preference in jurisprudential studies relating to women ... whose function is to support men in a position higher than women in society, since the man is always the father, the husband or some other male among the woman's agnates

(United Nations 2005: 146–147).

It is no secret that women remain subject to domination, both spiritual and material, directly and indirectly. The degree and strength of this domination vary from one environment to the other, depending on the stage of life through which the woman is passing ... Relations within the family have continued to be governed by the father's authority over his wife under the sway of the patriarchal order ... Studies of the Arab world point out that Arab women are largely absent from the political domain, only thinly present in the social welfare sector, shadowy in the civil and cultural spheres, insignificant in the economic domain, and almost completely missing from the official religious domain

(United Nations 2005: 167–169).

Consequently, it would have been normal for almost all Emirati girls and boys to have been taught to believe in the value of male superiority from earliest childhood. As they grew up and were, for the most part, educated in male- or female-only schools this belief would have been reinforced over time. Their teachers may have directed them to sections of the Qur'an that encouraged this conviction and played down or even ignored sections which suggested greater equality between men and women. Young men were taught that they were responsible for the conduct of their wives, sisters and mothers, that they were their natural guardians and protectors, and the behaviour of 'their' women would reflect on them throughout their lives. These beliefs are deeply rooted in Arabic cultures and so not only would the Western idea of 'gender equality' have been alien to many Emiratis, it would have been regarded as a direct threat to a male Emirati's identity and his deeply held and sincere belief that he was the head of the family and responsible for the welfare of his womenfolk. In fact, any man who did not accept these responsibilities would have been regarded by his peers as *dayooth* (rough translation: an irresponsible wimp). Naturally, these beliefs had a powerful influence on the status and roles of Emirati women in the past and this is how one group of smart, socially aware and ambitious young Emirati women at Zayed University described this in 2008:

> The UAE's culture was very conservative before the discovery of oil and the union of the seven Emirates – in terms of a woman's education, her role in the family or the society in general. At that time, the seven Emirates consisted of a group of tribes that were strongly associated with their cultural values and historical traditions. These tribes were headed by dominant male members and, consequently, some women were treated as feeble human beings by their families. Emirati girls were rarely allowed to have a proper education and were often married when they were very young. In the past, families rarely allowed their daughters to see much of the outside world or to even consider a professional career. Instead, girls were obliged to stay at home and learn cooking and other household responsibilities from their mothers. These

traditional views hindered many women from achieving wider participation and involvement in professional careers or as business entrepreneurs

(abridged from Ebrahim et al, 2008: 9–10).

Although there has been considerable change in Emirati society over the last two decades, it is still characterised by a patriarchal Islamic culture. Fathers still exert a great deal of control over their daughters' lives, and they continue to make many of the important decisions that affect their education, their jobs and careers and their choice of marriage partner. Most marriages are still 'arranged', even if many younger Emirati women now have more freedom when choosing marriage partners and they are now more likely to delay marriage until their late twenties or early thirties. Some Emirati fathers still do not allow their daughters to pursue certain careers, and others do not allow them to work in mixed-gender workplaces. Consequently, one career that fathers have traditionally preferred was teaching Emirati women in girls-only schools or employment in the 'safer' public sector so that their daughters would not have to work in mixed-gender environments. Some Emirati families continue to be very reluctant to let their daughters study abroad or work overseas on their own. This lack of mobility can be an impediment to those women who might choose to work for large private-sector companies, where international mobility is often an essential prerequisite for career advancement (Forster, 2000; Hewlett and Rashid, 2010). In addition, some young Emirati women believe that their pre-ordained role in life is to be mothers, to support their husbands and to raise their children, roles that socially conservative women of other religious faiths also subscribe to (Kaufmann, 2010). And, as in the West, a minority of young, well-educated Emirati women may choose not to pursue careers, either because they come from wealthy families and do not need to work for a living or because they are marrying wealthy husbands. These deeply held beliefs and practices reflect the fact that the Emiratis were – until very recent times – part of a very traditional and semi-nomadic tribal culture, deeply imbued in the beliefs and practices of Islam. And inevitably, the deeply ingrained cultural and religious beliefs that permeate Emirati society continue to have a strong influence on the gender self-perceptions and self-attributions of young women (and men) in the UAE.

Clearly then, 'masculinity' is one of the most dominant and deeply ingrained cultural attributes of the UAE and every other country in the MENA region. Consequently, men living in very masculine cultures who have very conservative and traditional views about the nature of women will – probably – believe that they are 'intuitive', 'caring', 'submissive', 'irrational' and 'emotional' and should be 'supporters' or 'followers' of men. They will – probably – believe that men are more 'logical', 'strategic', 'competitive', 'rational', 'unemotional' and 'better decision makers' and 'leaders'. However, there can only be one possible consequence of these stereotypical beliefs among men: the creation of mind-sets that results in their societies and the organisations that operate within them creating overt and covert attitudinal and structural barriers to women's advancement. Attitudinal barriers include beliefs that discriminate against women or negatively stereotype women simply because they are women. These attitudes are expressed in phrases such as: 'women are indecisive, inconsistent and constantly changing their minds', 'women use their sexuality to get what they want', 'women are too emotional', 'women aren't good team players', 'women fall apart when the going gets tough', 'women love to gossip and natter', 'women are too soft to make the really hard decisions', 'women take things too personally', 'women can't take a good joke', 'women complain too much about discrimination', 'women let their families get in the way of their jobs' and so forth (adapted from Manning and Haddock, 1995; see also Simmons, 1996: 83–95).

The consequence of these traditional stereotypes is that, over time, negative attitudes and beliefs about women become deeply embedded in the mind-sets of men. They become an integral part of their masculine identities and operate at a largely unconscious level, and this is the main reason it is so difficult to change these after they have become established. In turn, these become part of taken-for-granted cultural beliefs about the intrinsic natures of men and women. These can then lead to the creation of structural barriers which prevent them from doing certain kinds of jobs or bar them from rising to leadership positions in organisations. Here is a rather disquieting example of all three barriers in operation at the same time:

> Since the prettier candidate has already been blessed by God, it is only right that we should hire the uglier one', said Nik Abdul Aziz during a lecture to all government employees in the Malaysian state of Kelantan. 'After all, if we do not choose the ugly candidate, who will?' Aziz, Chief Minister of Kelantan (one of Malaysia's most fervent Islamic states), explained the thinking behind his latest decree: 'There are far too many pretty women in government offices at the moment, distracting male workers and lowering business efficiency with their pert and yielding tightness. But, when ugly women are employed in an office, then the work rate increases wondrously. Besides, we must be ever watchful for possible immoral activities. It is well known that pretty women cause unhealthy activities that lead to insanity, blindness, sickness and the bends. That is why, from now on, thorough ugliness must be considered a deciding factor at all job interviews
>
> *(Private Eye, 1996: 23)*.

When positions became vacant in government departments in Kelantan, the Malaysian state controlled by a fundamentalist Islamic party, attractive women need not apply. The ban on women with good looks was announced by the State's Chief Minister, Nik Abdul Aziz. His announcement attracted widespread criticism but he said that he was only trying to be fair to women who were not attractive 'Normally, women who are blessed by Allah with good looks are married to rich husbands', he said. Since they would not need to work, there would be more job opportunities for women who were less 'comely'. In March 1999, Aziz had upset women's groups when he said that his government was considering a ban on women working. He later said that the ban would only apply to women whose husbands could not afford to support their family. He was condemned for his latest stand by Zainah Anwar, a member of Sisters in Islam, whose leaders are authorities on the Koran and regularly challenge decisions made by the all-male religious officials (*ulama*), that discriminate against women: 'Beauty, or lack of it, should not be used as a basis of hiring or firing. This is a discriminatory practice that has no place in a modern democratic society

(Stewart, 2002).

A more recent example of similarly conservative attitudes occurred on the Sama Dubai TV program *The Successful Woman* in May 2008. During her interview, the CEO of Black Pearl Caviar International, Hamda al-Huraizi, narrated this anecdote:

> After attending some presentations from women entrepreneurs at the first UAE Entrepreneurs Forum in Dubai Press Club, I asked a famous Emirati businessman, who is known in the UAE for his investment in young entrepreneurs' projects, 'What do you think about these businesses?' He leaned back and said: 'It's just terrific. But, I would never invest in a women-led business. Don't get me wrong, women are great for running day-care centres and have done a lot for customer service, but as an investor, you cannot take that risk as they might leave to get married or pregnant. They might not be committed to their work because of their family responsibilities
>
> *(Sama Dubai broadcast, 8.00 p.m., 3 May 2008; quote provided by a female Zayed University management student).*

This example demonstrates that while women in the UAE have achieved much over the last two decades, traditional cultural and attitudinal stereotypes have persisted (as they do in many non-Islamic countries). And as we will see in Chapter 3, they continue to be expressed by some university-educated Emirati men today. Nevertheless, many Emirati women now choose to work and build careers, some have created successful businesses, and there are many women in leadership roles in the public-sector of the UAE and a small but growing number in the private-sector. More and more Emirati fathers support the education of their daughters and provide active support and encouragement for them to pursue careers and, in some cases, start their own businesses. As more women have entered the UAE labour market and succeeded in their professions and careers, it is apparent that traditional views about the 'correct' roles of women in UAE society and the workforce have been evolving and changing for a while, as have the gender self-perceptions and self-beliefs of young Emirati women (Marmenout, 2009; Moore and Forster, 2009). These changing beliefs were also expressed by the female undergraduates I interviewed at Zayed University during 2008–2011. Although they needed some gentle encouragement to talk openly and freely about these issues, it was apparent that almost all of them were:

Confident, ambitious and fully committed to pursuing careers in their chosen professions.

Planning to marry men who would allow them to work and also provide support for their careers.

Delaying marriage and pregnancy for a few years while they made some progress in their jobs and careers.

And, in two cases, planning to insert clauses in marriage contracts which would allow them to work throughout their lives.

This shift in attitudes is reflected in the confidence that this group had about their future prospects in 2010:

I would like to be very successful in finance and also be the first Emirati woman to become the Minister of the Economy or be in any other ministerial positions [laughs]! I would like to be part of the changes that are going on in our government, our society and our economy. I want to be an effective ambassador for the UAE.

I would like to be an inspirational business leader and inspire other young women in the future ... And, I also want to marry a handsome man and be the mother of three children!

(22-year-old finance major; Dean's List award winner in 2010).

Our leaders often say that they want the UAE to be the number one in everything. So, in the future when I travel outside the UAE, whenever I say to people I'm from the UAE, they know about the UAE and they see that our country is one of the first Gulf countries and their image of our country is very positive, and that we are successful and a country of creativity and innovation ... I want foreigners to think of the UAE as one country, not just 'Dubai and Abu Dhabi'. I want them to think we have smart and visionary leaders and I want us to be a country that respects different religions and cultures. I also want us to be a modern and tolerant Islamic country ... We, as Emirati women, we always like to be proud of our identity and we want to make our parents proud of whatever we do. And this is very important because we sometimes say our parents have done half the job but it is up to us to finish the job!

(22-year-old project management major).

I believe that there are wide opportunities. There are fantastic opportunities for every Emirati national, especially the females. It will take time, but we can see the changes and even some men are changing nowadays [laughs]. We now have four female ministers and female judges and seats on the FNC. But, we don't want people just to say 'you have opportunities' just for the sake of saying that. We want them to choose us because we are hard-working and effective and efficient

(23-year-old accounting major).

However, all of these recently graduated students did recognise that there would be some barriers and challenges to overcome:

There are still some jobs, occupations that are basically just for men. Like, when I was doing my internship, I was the first female in [this company] and they were not used to this and some of the men treated me like I had come from another planet. This is one of the obstacles, because some Emirati men are still not used to working with women, but I think this has been changing and will change even more in the future ... I also think that the higher you go there are more obstacles, but I think this is true in every culture. The higher you go, the harder it is

(22-year-old marketing major).

I would like to see the cultural barriers go away. The attitudes of some men also need to change. I think that some, particularly the older ones, still do not want women to work. I remember my father saying when he used to work for [a large construction company] that the CEO of that company often used to say that he did not want women working for him and as long as he was in that position he would make sure that no women would work for him, or would even be allowed into the building. We need to get rid of men who still have this attitude, that don't want women working

(22-year-old management major).

They also believed that they would play a very important role in changing the attitudes of Emirati men:

There is this perception that Emirati women are lazy and that all they think about is money and fashion and beauty. There are some women who are like this, but this is not true of most of us. Life is not just about having a Gucci bag and expensive shoes [laughs]. We want to work hard and make a contribution to our country. We are ambitious and many of us will work hard and we want to be successful. I want to change the way other people view Emirati women, to show them that we want to get ahead and we want to be noticed. I also want to change the view that we should just follow men and we want to be recognised as people who can also make changes ... I want to change this negative perception of Emirati women in the work environment, that we can be hard working and be successful ... But, it is up to us to do this and to beat this challenge.

(23-year-old finance major).

2.6 CONCLUSION

The UAE has clearly made significant progress towards its national strategic objective of creating an open, modern and diversified national economy based on an acceptance of the realities of globalisation combined with legal, regulatory and fiduciary reforms that have encouraged and supported business growth, an open economic environment and market liberalisation. In 2016, for example, the UAE was ranked at number 22 in the World Bank's 'Ease of doing business' report and a very creditable 12/144 countries in the World Economic Forum's ranking of international competitiveness in 2015 (World Bank, 2016a; World Economic Forum, 2015a: 13). The Heritage Foundation Index of Economic Freedom placed the UAE at 25/178 countries, with high scores for 'rule of law', 'open markets', 'regulatory efficiency', 'investment freedom' and 'financial freedom' (Heritage Foundation, 2016) and, while there is certainly a lack of transparency in public procurement processes, there is little evidence of widespread corruption. Data from the World Bank Knowledge Economy Index, which looks at the extent to which the cultural, legal, business, innovation, educational and scientific environments of countries are conducive for sustainable long-term economic development, placed the UAE at number 42 out of 146 countries in 2012 (World Bank, 2013; this index has not been updated since). The government has made substantial investments in high-tech manufacturing, biotechnologies, pharmaceuticals, telecommunications, tourism, healthcare, education, aerospace and several other growth sectors in recent years (United Arab Emirates Government, 2014). In October 2014, the government launched a National Innovation Strategy with the aim of making the UAE 'one of the most innovative nations in the world within seven years', with $1.2 billion in additional funding. It also created a permanent *Museum of the Future* in Dubai and announced that a 'CEO of Innovation' would be appointed at every government department in the Emirates (*Gulf News*, 2015c; United Arab Emirates Cabinet, 2014).

Most of its citizens enjoy very high standards of living and the UAE is a stable and peaceful country, despite some internal protests and a clampdown on political dissent in the aftermath of the Arab Spring and the rise of ISIS. It is often promoted as a positive role model for other Gulf countries and the broader MENA region, with only Qatar having made comparable economic and social progress over the last two decades, and it has also become a haven for many professional people escaping from violence and instability in other Middle Eastern countries. It remains a popular work destination for millions of expatriate professionals. As noted earlier, the UAE has the second-largest economy in the Gulf after Saudi Arabia and it accounts for more than one quarter of the GDP of the countries in the Gulf Cooperation Council (GCC). It still has the seventh-largest reserves of oil and gas in the world, which in 2015 accounted for 42 per cent of the country's GDP (United States Energy Information Agency, 2015b: 4). This suggests that the UAE may be able to achieve its ambitious economic goals but, as we will see in Chapter 8, there is still a lot of work to do to transform a national economy that is still very dependent on oil and gas to one that is diverse, innovative and knowledge based; and this may be further hampered by fluctuations in global oil and gas prices over the next five to ten years.

The price of oil fell from about $110 a barrel in mid-2014 to $36 at the end of 2015 and fluctuated between $25 and $53 a barrel during 2016 (The Financial Forecast Centre, 2016). This will have a significant impact on the UAE's revenues and GDP during 2016–2017 and beyond unless the price for crude oil increases significantly. Perhaps as an indicator of things to come, the UAE government announced in July 2015 that it was ending all gasoline subsidies and would set consumer prices in accordance with global petroleum prices in the future. In early 2016, it also put on hold the construction of the $11 billion national railway network. These actions followed a reduction in electricity subsidies for domestic, business and industrial users in 2014 (*The Economist*, 2016g: 46; Kerr and Clark, 2015). The 2015 Bertelsmann Stiftung report on the UAE has also warned that:

> Advances on the market economy are tempered by less progress on the democracy and state management front, where the past two years have witnessed a level of regression. Instead of promoting a degree of political reform that maintains momentum with societal developments, the rulers have increasingly closed access for citizens to the political arena ... Moreover, UAE rulers have begun to significantly curtail freedoms of assembly and expression, and other civil rights. The most dramatic consequence has been a crackdown on civil society ... Regression on the political front is all the more disappointing given the fact that no structural constraints prevent the government from pursuing a comprehensive reform process.
>
> It has become clear that, as far as prioritisation of policy goals and their implementation the core emphasis is on the consolidation of existing ruling arrangements and the prevention of power devolution through decentralisation and the sharing of responsibilities. This approach works for the moment as the rulers are able to use the tremendous financial resources at their disposal to buy societal compliance but, at the same time, it is beginning to threaten the overall consensus on goals that have defined the UAE's stability up to this point ... *The government will find it difficult to maintain such a two-pronged approach, as the economic and political dimensions of development cannot remain mutually exclusive*
>
> (Bertelsmann Stiftung, 2015a: 1–2; my emphasis).

As we have seen, the UAE has made good progress in increasing the participation of women in its labour market and most of the young women who graduate from the country's universities each year choose to work full time. The entry of large numbers of Emirati women into the UAE labour market since the early 2000s has been a very significant change in a society which was, in living memory, sparsely populated, semi-nomadic and economically underdeveloped. However, while the life experiences of most Emirati women have been transformed over the last three decades, they are still restricted to certain sectors of the UAE labour market (such as the public sector); not many work in the private sector and only a few are self-starting entrepreneurs and business owners. In addition, as we will see in the next chapter, barriers do persist which are preventing women from achieving full equality with men in UAE society and in the workplace. Having said this, if present trends continue, it is likely that attitudes towards the 'correct' roles of women in the UAE will continue to evolve in the future given the relatively young age of most Emiratis, and several interviewees mentioned that there were clear signs of a generational shift in attitudes towards working women:

> My parents were of a very moderate family, they were not of the
> extreme religious kind. They were not as we say in Arabic, *ghulat*
> [extremists]. But, like all Emirati families, they did care about
> accepted social norms – and these things come before religion – not
> just for the girls but also for my brothers … but, for my father, he
> cared about us and so when I decided to work he did not impose any
> limits on me. My mother didn't work, and I think my father did not
> want her to be independent and when I was growing up we were
> always taught to be a good sister, a good wife and someone who
> satisfies the service of males. It was always about fitting into how
> our society thinks women should be, so you just go with the crowd,
> the herd … I once asked my father about this, and he was very
> honest. He said, 'I was afraid. I did not want her to be better than
> me and if she was working, she might leave me at any minute if she
> had financial independence. I wanted her purpose, or her meaning

in life, to be so attached to me that she did not want to leave me';
and so I asked him, 'Would you do the same thing now?', and he
said, 'No I wouldn't, because now I have daughters and I see how
their husbands treat them and I don't agree with this anymore.'
I have to say that I see that many things have changed in this
regard. Our roles have shifted and my sisters work even though
they are all married

> *(37-year-old private-sector bank manager, married with two children;*
> *studied for an MBA during 2009–2011).*

In conclusion, it is reasonable to say that the broader cultural changes
that are required to encourage a more level playing field for women
in all sectors of the UAE labour market are lagging behind the significant economic changes that have occurred in this country over the
last thirty years, an issue that has been identified in earlier studies of
this country (Davidson, 2005; Gallant and Pounder, 2008). Having
said this, it seems likely that Emirati women will make a significant
contribution to the development and diversification of the country's
economy in the future, an important theme we return to look at in
Chapter 8. It should also be emphasised that many other countries
have gone through similar economic and social transformations in
recent decades. Until the late 1980s, for example, the labour force
participation rate of women in the United States, Australia, New
Zealand, Spain and Ireland was less than 30 per cent. This has since
increased to nearly 70 per cent in all of these countries, and if the
UAE can increase the participation rate of Emirati women to similar
levels, it has been estimated that it could increase its annual GDP by
12 per cent a year, which would more than offset the decline in oil and
gas revenues in the future (Aguirre et al, 2012; Dobbs et al, 2015).
How the UAE government and its public- and private-sector organisations can encourage greater participation by women in all sectors and
at all levels of its national economy is described in Chapter 9.

3 The Experiences of Women in Public- and Private-Sector Organisations in the United Arab Emirates

3.1 INTRODUCTION

In this chapter, we first describe the attitudes of Emiratis towards female bosses and women in leadership positions. We then examine the cultural and attitudinal barriers that women encounter in their workplaces, summarise the very mixed opinions that men have about a woman's right to work in the UAE and evaluate their opinions about the degree of equality that Emirati women enjoy in the national labour market. We then look at their views about the likelihood that more women will become leaders in public- and private-sector organisations in the UAE in the future. Next, we focus on one area of the UAE labour market where Emirati women have been, until very recently, noticeably under-represented – the UAE information technology (IT) sector. We look at the challenges and barriers they have encountered in this sector and their explanations for why so few young Emirati women were choosing to work in IT during the late 1990s and early 2010s and also ask if this state of affairs has changed since this time. We then examine an issue that is of growing concern to some working Emirati women (particularly those employed in the private sector): how to balance the competing demands of their work and home lives. The chapter concludes by evaluating the significant progress that national women have made in the UAE labour market and the emergence of Emirati women business leaders; but it also highlights areas in which they are still underrepresented – particularly in the private sector and as entrepreneurs and business owners.

3.2 THE ATTITUDES OF EMIRATIS TOWARDS WOMEN IN THE WORKPLACE AND IN LEADERSHIP ROLES

The material presented in this section is based on questionnaires completed by 337 Emirati employees at twelve public and nine private-sector organisations. This survey was supplemented by forty interviews with working Emirati women and men who were attending the Zayed University (ZU) Executive MBA program and twenty final-year undergraduate female business and management students. The questionnaire survey and interviews were conducted in Dubai, Sharjah and Abu Dhabi between February 2008 and June 2011.[1] Some of the tables in this section also include data from other surveys that have examined the attitudes of women and men towards women in business leadership roles in the United States in order to provide comparisons between these and the results of the UAE employee surveys. Our respondents were employed in a variety of medium to large organisations in the UAE (twelve public and semi-government organisations and nine private-sector companies); 57.9 per cent of the sample was female. The age profiles of the respondents reflect the relatively youthful working population of the UAE, with 50.4 per cent of the sample being aged twenty to twenty-nine, 31.2 per cent thirty to thirty-nine, 15.4 per cent forty to forty-nine, and just 3.0 per cent were more than fifty years of age. Most of them worked in supervisory or middle-management roles: 30.3 per cent had less than five years' work experience; 27.0 per cent had six to ten years' experience and 26.1 per cent had eleven to fifteen years' work experience. Only 16.6 per cent of these women and men had worked full time for more than fifteen years.

The first four sets of data, presented in Table 3.1, provide a summary of the attitudes that these women and men have about working for a female leader. The results indicate that most Emirati women were comfortable with the prospect of working for a female boss, although a noticeable minority were only 'sometimes' comfortable about this. Most also believed that it is acceptable for a man to work for a female boss, but more than a third were not comfortable with this idea. More than 40 per cent of the men did not appear to have difficulties working for a female boss, but around one quarter were personally 'not comfortable' about this prospect, and nearly a third of this group did not find the idea of Emirati men working for a female boss to be acceptable.

At first glance, these responses may appear to be symptomatic of somewhat conservative attitudes among Emirati men about the prospect of working for female bosses, but the comparative data included in Table 3.1 indicates that these were very similar to those of male and female managers in the United States in the mid-1960s. Researchers at the Harvard Business School have documented the changing attitudes of male and female business leaders in the United States towards women managers and executives in 'Are women executives people?' (1965), 'Executive women – 20 years on' (1985) and 'What men think they know about executive women' in 2005 (Carlson et al, 2006). In 1965, only 35 per cent of 2,000 male executives had a 'favourable attitude' towards women in management, and less than 27 per cent felt 'comfortable' working for a women. The respective figures for women in 1965 were 82 per cent and 78 per cent. Forty years later, in 2005, more than 80 per cent of male executives had 'a favourable attitude' towards women in management, and more than three quarters felt 'comfortable' working for a woman. The figures for women in 2005 were 85 per cent and 78 per cent respectively – very little change from 1965 (Carlson, et al: 28). This means that while male attitudes about working for a woman did indeed become more positive in the United States during this period of time, *it took two generations for this to happen* and for conservative and negative attitudes towards female employees to evolve to the point where four out of five male employees could say that they were 'comfortable working for a woman' and had a generally favourable attitude towards women in management roles. This also indicates that it will be some time before most Emirati men become 'comfortable' with this idea. Because it is beyond the remit of this book, we

TABLE 3.1 *The attitudes of Emiratis towards working for a female boss* (N = *195 women and 142 men*)

Women
'I am comfortable with the idea of working for a female boss'
Always: 32.3
Often: 29.2
Sometimes: 28.2
Rarely: 5.1
Never: 5.2
'The idea that men can work for a female boss is acceptable to me'
Always: 18.5
Often: 24.1
Sometimes: 27.2
Rarely: 15.4
Never: 14.8
Men
'I am comfortable with the idea of working for a female boss'
Always: 19.0
Often: 21.8
Sometimes: 31.0
Rarely: 14.1
Never: 14.1
'The idea that men can work for a female boss is acceptable to me'
Always: 19.7
Often: 18.3
Sometimes: 31.0
Rarely: 15.5
Never: 15.5

Comparative data (Carlson et al, 2006)
'I would feel comfortable working for a woman'

	1965	*2005*
Women	*78.0*	*78.0*
Men	*27.0*	*75.0*

1965, N = *2,000; 2005,* N = *286 executives*
(*% that agreed with this statement*)
All data in this and subsequent tables are in percentages and rounded to
   the nearest decimal point

can only speculate about the reasons one in five female American executives were not positive about the prospect of working for another woman in either 1965 or, more surprisingly, in 2005.

There were also somewhat mixed results when we asked these women and men, 'Do you think that male Emiratis still have difficulties accepting decisions made by a female boss?', with nearly half the men and more than half of the women indicating that male Emirati employees still have some 'issues' with this (Table 3.2).

TABLE 3.2 *Do you think that male Emirati employees still have difficulties accepting decisions made by a female boss?*

Women	Men
Always: 16.9	*Always: 14.1*
Often: 34.4	*Often: 32.4*
Sometimes: 31.3	*Sometimes: 29.5*
Rarely: 10.8	*Rarely: 11.3*
Never: 6.6	*Never: 12.7*

Most of the female interviewees, and even some of the men, felt that women in managerial and leadership roles were sometimes not taken as seriously as male leaders. A twenty-five-year-old woman, who worked for an Emirati bank, observed that:

> I think we need to get rid of some of the laws that hold women back in the workplace. Some Emirati men need to take women more seriously, that they have views and opinions that matter, and they should be considered as being as important as those of men. There's still this view that if you're a woman and you have strong opinions that somehow you were not 'well-raised. So, even if you have a valid opinion about something, some men will either ignore you or think you're some kind of trouble-maker
> *(25-year-old marketing manager; studied for an MBA during 2008–2009).*

And one of only five indigenous female engineers I encountered during the eight years I worked in the Arabian Gulf made some comments that reflect the experiences of many women working in male-dominated environments, not just in the UAE but in many other MENA countries:

> There are a lot of barriers. For me, I have definitely encountered discrimination, but you have to be strong. For example, it is the law here that any female who wants to work has to obtain the written permission of their male guardian, and that authorisation cannot be faked or counterfeited, and it has to be verified by the authorities. This has to be done every time you start work at a new organisation ... At work, I still get the feeling that top management sometimes still prefer not to have contact with female employees, but this is changing I think. In the past, they always seemed to limit opportunities to meet with them and to discuss your work face-to-face, under the excuse that, 'You are a female'. But, for me, I have always tried to do this and then they got the idea that I was going to do this, so some of them have become more flexible and so I get to see most senior managers now ... I say that men who don't like working with women should be segregated into male-only working sectors [laughs] where they can enforce their beliefs. I don't mind if they impose their religious views with their families, but this should not happen in the workplace
>
> *(38-year-old manager at a construction company; married with two children; studied for an MBA during 2009–2011).*

Another interviewee commented that:

> It is true that many Emirati women now work, but I think that most Emirati men are still not aware how important work is to many women in the society and so I think that these attitudes need to change. And of course, there is also, 'the guardian' problem. Everything still has to be signed by a man, including many financial transactions, what we call *ahliyya*. Whether you want to study, whether you want to work, whether you want to travel abroad, always the father or the husband has to approve this. Even

to enter university. This is a huge, huge barrier for all women. You literally can't do anything if your father or husband does not agree. I don't know any of my female friends who do not believe that this has to change

> (37-year-old manager, tourism; married with three children; studied for an MBA during 2010–2012).

Several male interviewees were quite critical of the more conservative attitudes that some Emirati men still exhibit towards female employees. A thirty-nine-year-old senior manager at a telecommunication company who had more than sixteen years' work experience commented:

I think attitudes have definitely changed. I mean, when I first started working here, there were hardly any women employees and they all worked in separate offices and mainly in clerical roles. All the middle and senior managers were men ... But, now maybe more than 30 per cent of our employees are women and they work in all the different departments. But, we still have very few in senior positions because I think there is still the opinion that Emirati women aren't ready for leadership positions and that some men, maybe many of our expatriate employees*, won't accept the authority of a woman ... I think this will change, but we need a more concerted effort to develop our younger female employees for leadership roles and to maybe make the culture of the company more accepting. I think this will happen, but it will take time

> (* This was in reference to the large number of male employees from Pakistan and India who worked at this company).

We then asked a series of questions to elicit their attitudes towards women in leadership roles and as leaders of organisations and their beliefs about the leadership abilities and competencies of Emirati women (Table 3.3).

It was perhaps predictable that women expressed more confidence in the ability of women to succeed in leadership positions and to be the leaders of organisations when compared to male Emiratis.

TABLE 3.3 *The attitudes of Emiratis towards female leaders and their beliefs about the leadership abilities and competencies of Emirati women*

'Do you think that Emirati women can be successful in business leadership positions?'

Women	Men
Always: 14.4	*Always: 11.3*
Often: 32.3	*Often: 23.2*
Sometimes: 39.0	*Sometimes: 35.9*
Rarely: 10.8	*Rarely: 24.0*
Never: 3.5	*Never: 5.6*

'Do you think that it is acceptable for an Emirati woman to be the leader of an organisation?'

Women	Men
Very much so: 54.4	*Very much so: 28.9*
Maybe: 37.4	*Maybe: 57.0*
Never: 8.2	*Never: 14.1*

'Do Emirati women have the same leadership abilities and competencies as men?'

Women	Men
Always: 8.2	*Always: 7.7*
Often: 42.6	*Often: 26.1*
Sometimes: 29.2	*Sometimes: 29.6*
Rarely: 11.8	*Rarely: 21.1*
Never: 8.2	*Never: 15.5*

'Do you think that Emirati women have the ability to succeed in leadership positions?'

Women	Men
Very much so: 64.1	*Very much so: 28.2*
Maybe: 24.6	*Maybe: 50.0*
Never: 11.3	*Never: 21.8*

And, while a majority of them believed that women had the same leadership abilities as men, only a third of male Emiratis thought that this was true. Having said this, we might also conjecture that the more interesting data lies in the number of responses in the 'sometimes' and 'maybe' categories in Table 3.3. These suggest that a significant number of women and men are not making *pre-emptive* generic assumptions about the leadership potential or abilities of all Emirati women. Rather, they are indicating that while some women (but not all) can indeed be successful in leadership roles, and some of them do have the same leadership abilities and competencies as men, not all women have 'the right stuff' to succeed as leaders. It was also very evident that while most Emirati men were not opposed to women working, a large minority still had concerns about this. The twenty Emirati men I interviewed (who were all university educated) fell into three distinct groups, which I came to think of as the 'Yes' group ($N = 4$), the 'Yes, but ...' group ($N = 12$) and, the 'No' group ($N =4$). The extracts from three of these interviews illustrate the very different attitudes that these men had about working Emirati women:

> I know that I'm probably not typical, but I do now believe that women should be allowed to hold any jobs for which they are qualified, and we need to encourage more Emirati women to be well-educated and to work ... This was not what I was taught to believe when I was growing up and at first I did not want to work with women, and there were many reasons for this ... But, I have seen what women can do and I have changed my beliefs a lot in this regard. Both of my daughters have graduated from your university and work, and now that my children are adults my wife also works in her own business ... I accept this idea now because as a Muslim man, I do not have the right to interfere negatively with my wife or daughters' ambitions, as long as this does not affect their responsibilities to their families. On the other hand, this applies to the responsibilities of the husband as well today, so it is a double-edged sword ... This will also support our nation's move towards sustainable development because we need more women to work and to contribute more to this
>
> *(46-year-old executive at a finance company; married with five children; studied for an MBA between 2009–2011).*

For me it depends. I think it is okay for some women to work, but I do not believe that Islamic principles should be changed and shifted to help women to do this and our traditions and culture do not allow this. I think women should be allowed to work, and can hold any job and can study anything, as long as they do not compromise their families. For example, a woman in engineering has to accept the fact that she will deal mostly with males, and may have to work on a factory site and wear a safety uniform, so this may not be acceptable to her family … The principles of Islam are that women should cover themselves properly and adhere to Islamic rules in the workplace …
She must also not neglect her responsibilities as a mother and a wife. If the family suffers, a woman should not have the right to work

> *(33-year-old public-sector middle manager; married with two children; studied for an MBA during 2009–2011).*

Actually, I do fear the growing power of Emirati women because they may forget our Islamic principles and guidelines, and these women will reflect badly on the image of UAE as an Islamic country. I will not accept this idea because everything in the world has specific requirements and most women will never be able to satisfy these requirements … I also fear the neglect of Islamic rules and applications in our society. Specifically speaking, I mean that women in power in any Islamic community should never forget the teachings of Islam, and that Islam is not only praying and fasting, it is a way of life and in the end we were created only to worship Allah … This attitude is directly linked to Islam in the sense that women should not mix with men. I believe that it is the responsibility of the man to be the guardian of the woman and to ensure that she does not divert from the right path in any way

> *(38-year-old manager, construction company; married with four children; his wife had never worked outside the home; studied for an MBA between 2008–2010).*

These mixed opinions about the roles of Emirati women in the UAE labour market and their leadership abilities are reflected in the data in Table 3.4, which indicate that women were generally more optimistic about the possibility that the UAE business community will accept more female Emirati executives in the future when compared to men. Male Emiratis were more likely to be neutral about or disagree that this is likely to happen any time soon, and they were much more pessimistic about the chances of this happening when compared to male executives in the United States in 2005.

TABLE 3.4 *Will the UAE business community ever wholly accept female executives?*

Women	Men
Strongly agree: 15.4	Strongly agree: 12.0
Agree: 26.7	Agree: 21.1
Neutral: 19.0	Neutral: 23.9
Disagree: 25.1	Disagree: 22.6
Strongly disagree: 13.8	Strongly disagree: 20.4

Comparative data (Carlson et al, 2006)
'The business community will never wholly accept female executives'

	1965	2005
Women	47.0	39.0
Men	67.0	20.0

1965, N = 2,000 American executives; 2005, N = 286 executives
(% that agreed with this statement)

At first glance, these results may appear to reflect considerable pessimism among a significant minority of both women (38.9%) and men (43.0%) about the likelihood that this will happen in the future. However, the comparative data in Table 3.4 indicate that the beliefs that Emirati women have about this are quite similar to those of female American executives in 2005. And, to repeat a point made earlier about the data in Table 3.1, while attitudes towards female business leaders did become more positive in the United States during this period of time, it took two generations for these to evolve to the point that most men believed that there was a greater probability that the US business community would 'wholly accept' female executives.

In the next section of the questionnaire, we asked our respondents a series of questions about equality of opportunity for Emirati women and if they thought that there were still barriers and challenges for Emirati women to overcome in the workplace (Table 3.5).

TABLE 3.5 *Beliefs about equality of opportunity for Emirati women and the challenges and barriers they encounter in the workplace*

'Is there now full equality of opportunity for Emirati women in the workplace?'	
Women	*Men*
Strongly agree: 7.2	*Strongly agree: 15.5*
Agree: 11.3	*Agree: 26.8*
Neutral: 19.1	*Neutral: 33.8*
Disagree: 41.5	*Disagree: 19.0*
Strongly disagree: 20.9	*Strongly disagree: 4.9*
'Are there still challenges and barriers for Emirati women to overcome in the workplace?'	
Women	*Men*
Strongly agree: 14.9	*Strongly agree: 14.1*
Agree: 60.5	*Agree: 38.7*
Neutral: 17.4	*Neutral: 18.3*
Disagree: 6.2	*Disagree: 18.3*
Strongly disagree: 1.0	*Strongly disagree: 10.6*

It is evident from these results that while female Emiratis know that there are now more opportunities for gainful employment, only a small number of them believed that there was full equality of opportunity for women in the workplace when compared to men, although more than a third of Emirati men were 'neutral' about this and more than 20 per cent of them did not agree that this was the case. A majority of the men agreed that there were 'still challenges and barriers for Emirati women to overcome in the workplace', and three-quarters of the women agreed with this statement. More significantly, it was apparent that both women and men believed that female Emiratis are much less likely to be in leadership positions in the private sector in the future when compared to the public sector (Tables 3.6 and 3.7). This suggests that they believed that the barriers to women's career advancement in private-sector organisations were more significant than those in public-sector organisations, where, it appears, there is now a reasonable degree of parity between men and women. However, the data from Pew Research in Table 3.6 suggest that their opinions about the prospects for female Emirati executives in the private sector were quite similar to those of men and women in the United States in 2015.

TABLE 3.6 *At this moment in time, do you think that it is easier for Emirati men to become leaders in private-sector organisations than it is for women?*

Women	Men
73.3	81.0

Comparative data (Parker et al, 2015: 32)
'It is easier for men to get top executive positions in business'

Women	Men
61.0	74.0

N = *921 women and 914 men in the United States*
(% that agreed with this statement)

TABLE 3.7 *Do you think we will see more Emirati women in leadership positions in the public sector and in business organisations in the future?*

In public-sector organisations:	
Women	*Men*
Definitely: 77.4	*Definitely: 57.1*
Maybe: 22.1	*Maybe: 38.8*
Unlikely: 0.5	*Unlikely: 4.1*
In business organisations:	
Women	*Men*
Definitely: 55.4	*Definitely: 43.0*
Maybe: 42.0	*Maybe: 42.2*
Unlikely: 2.6	*Unlikely: 14.8*

These women and men were also asked about some possible future scenarios for Emirati women in leadership positions in public- and private-sector organisations in 2030 (Table 3.8).

The data in Table 3.8 add credence to one of the suggestions made in Chapter 2 about the continuing underrepresentation of Emirati

TABLE 3.8 *Possible scenarios for Emirati women in leadership positions in public and private-sector organisations by 2030*

'By 2030, Emirati men will continue to hold more leadership positions in public-sector organisations than women do'

Women	Men
33.3	62.0

'By 2030, Emirati women will hold as many leadership positions as men in public-sector organisations'

Women	Men
66.7	38.0

'By 2030, Emirati men will continue to hold more of the top positions in business organisations than women'

Women	Men
58.4	76.8

'By 2030, Emirati women will hold as many top positions in business organisations as men'

Women	Men
41.6	23.2

(% that 'strongly agreed' or agreed' with these statements)

Comparative data (Parker et al, 2015: 5)

'Men will continue to hold more top executive positions in business in the future'

Women	Men
55.0	52.0

'It's only a matter of time before there are as many women as men in top executive positions in business'

Women	Men
44.0	45.0

N = 921 women and 914 men in the United States
(% that agreed with these statements)

women in the private sector and their overrepresentation in public-sector employment. They show that while more than three quarters of the women and two in five men believed that there will be more women in public-sector leadership roles by 2030, only 41.6 per cent of women and 23.2 per cent of men agreed that Emirati women will hold as many top positions in business organisations as men by then. While there is no comparative data about the prospects for more female public-sector leaders in the United States, the comparative data by Pew Research in Table 3.8 also indicates that there are not major differences in the beliefs that American employees and female Emiratis have about the likelihood that there will be as many women as men in executive positions in business in the future. While Emirati men are more than twice as likely as American men to believe that this will not happen, it is encouraging that nearly a quarter believed that this will come to pass by 2030. The similarity of the results for American and Emirati women are also rather surprising, because it is only in the last two decades that women have entered the UAE labour market in significant numbers. While this transition began in the United States during the 1960s and 1970s, picked up speed during the 1980s and 1990s, and then accelerated during the 2000s, it is apparent that attitudes towards women in leadership roles in the United States have changed slowly and incrementally and they are not significantly different to those of educated professional Emirati women today.

This suggests that attitudes towards working professional women (and women in leadership roles) may be evolving faster in the UAE than they did in the United States and many other countries over the last four to five decades. To illustrate this, one of the first female Emiratis to be promoted to a senior management position in the organisation she worked for observed that:

> *Alhamdulillah*, things have definitely changed. I was one of the
> first women to work in [this organisation], and at first it was very

hard working with so many men. It was a segregated work environment and all the managers were men when I joined. It used to be *haram* for men and women to work together, and some women do still prefer this, but young men and women are more comfortable with this idea today. I can also say that I haven't personally faced discrimination in my job ... I was trusted with loads of work, and was one of the first women to represent our organisation abroad, and they gave me lots of options. I did realise early on that there weren't any laws that said I couldn't do certain things, so it was about showing them that I could do a really good job ... I also have to give credit to some of the men in my organisation, who decided that we should employ more women, because they realised that they stay longer, they are more punctual and their productivity is better! So, when there are job openings today they often prefer to hire women because there are many motivated and bright young Emirati women who want to work these days

(44-year-old bank executive; married with three children).

In conclusion, we can say with some confidence that attitudes towards Emirati women in the workplace and in leadership roles have been evolving quickly in the UAE over the last ten to fifteen years and more than 90 per cent of these women *and* men agreed that 'prospects for working women have generally improved in the UAE over the last ten years'. It is also possible, to emphasise this point, that attitudes towards working women may be changing more quickly than they did in many Western countries during the 1960s, 1970s, 1980s and 1990s. However, while all our respondents agreed that there were good employment opportunities for women, it was evident that many women still encountered barriers in the workplace, and some Emirati men still have very conservative attitudes towards working women. More than a third of the female private-sector employees also believed that 'women are not able to progress beyond a certain level in my organisation', although only one in seven female public-sector employees agreed with this statement. In addition, as we have seen, only a small minority of women believed that 'there is now full equality of opportunity for Emirati women in the workplace' and more than two thirds agreed that 'there are still challenges and barriers for Emirati women to overcome in the workplace.' In spite of these difficulties, all of these women were fully committed to their careers and professions and they work for exactly the same reasons that women in the West do. When they were asked to provide three or four reasons they chose to work, more than 80 per cent of the group indicated that 'achieving my personal goals in life' was important to them; more than two thirds mentioned 'financial independence' and 'personal growth and development'; and almost half said 'interest in/challenges of/love of my vocation or profession' were important to them. In other words, they choose to work for the same reasons that women in many other countries do – for fulfilment, independence and personal growth.

3.3 WOMEN IN THE UAE INFORMATION TECHNOLOGY SECTOR

In Chapter 1 we highlighted the lack of investment by MENA countries in basic science and research, and in Chapter 2 we noted the underrepresentation of women in science, technology, engineering and mathematics (STEM) professions in the MENA region. In Chapter 2, we also described the cultural, attitudinal and structural barriers that women still encounter in the UAE labour market, and in the previous section we looked at how these continue to affect Emirati women in the workplace. We now explore these issues in more depth by looking at the reasons Emirati women continue to be underrepresented in the computer science and information technology (CSIT) sectors of the UAE, particularly in the private sector, and the challenges and barriers encountered by those few women who have worked in IT jobs. It is divided into two parts. The first explains why women are under-represented in CSIT in all countries and highlights the lack of research on women in CSIT in the UAE and other countries in the MENA region. The second describes the principal findings of twenty in-depth interviews conducted with Emirati women who were working in the UAE IT sector during 2010.[2] We then compare this research with a more recent study of several hundred Emirati under-graduates studying STEM disciplines at UAE universities (The Economist Intelligence Unit, 2014). Strategies for improving the participation rates of Emirati women in this sector and in science, engineering and mathematics occupations are described in Chapter 9.

The Challenges Facing Women in STEM and CSIT Occupations

It has been well documented that women, historically and globally, have been under-represented in STEM occupations, and many young women continue to steer clear of educational, employment or entre-preneurial opportunities in these fields. Despite general increases in women's participation in STEM subjects at universities, their repre-sentation in CSIT jobs in the workplace has not approached parity with men in any country, and, in the MENA region, very few women work in CSIT fields. There is an extensive international research literature that has documented the reasons women have been under-represented in these sectors. Computer manufacturing and IT, in all their diverse forms, have been among the fastest-growing industries in the world over the last three decades, and technology job opportunities are predicted to grow at a faster rate than jobs in most other business and industrial sectors over the next decade (The Economist Intelligence Unit, 2014). However, research during the mid-late 2000s showed that while qualified women should have been well-positioned to move into these new jobs, the IT industry as a whole was failing to attract them in large numbers, and a significant number of women employed in the IT industry were choosing to leave it (Hewlett et al, 2008a).

For example, according to a study by the Centre for Work-Life Policy in the United States, while 74 per cent of women in technol-ogy reported 'loving their work', 41 per cent of women left technology companies after ten years' employment, compared to just 17 per cent of men (Ashcraft and Blithe, 2009). And more than half of the women employed by technology companies were leaving their organisations at the mid-level point in their careers after gaining ten to twenty years of experience, often before reaching leadership positions. Although there have been a few well-known examples of women leaders in the IT sector, such as Carly Fiorina (former CEO of Hewlett-Packard), Sheryl Sandberg (Facebook), Meg Whitman (former CEO of eBay and current CEO of Hewlett-Packard) and Donna Dubinsky (Palm and Handspring), just 11 per cent of the senior management positions in IT companies were occupied by women in the mid-late 2000s (i.e. CEO, CIO, CTO, VP, director, IT strategist or architect; Ashcraft and Blithe, 2009). In addition, while many more women have become small-business owners over the last two decades, own 40 per cent of all SMEs in the United States, generate $US 1.4 trillion in annual sales and employ 7.9 million people, female technology entrepreneurs have been and continue to be very uncommon (National Association of Women Business Owners, 2015;).

A variety of reasons have been identified by researchers for the under-representation of women in CSIT. These include national education policies (Cohoon and Aspray, 2007 and 2006); the lack of female science and IT teachers at primary, secondary and tertiary levels and the quality of the interactions between (invariably male) teachers and female students (Jenson and Rose, 2003; Kock and Upitis, 1996); and the differential use of computers at school and home by boys and girls (Lupart and Cannon, 2002). Some research studies have also identified differences between boys and girls, with girls, generally, having less positive attitudes towards and interest in computers when compared to boys (Cohoon and Aspray, 2007 and 2006). Other reasons that have been identified include the differential use of computer games – most were designed for and bought by boys and young men – and the content of these was often violent and also reinforced negative gender stereotypes (Cohoon and Aspray, 2006: 23; Jenson and Rose, 2003). Family and community influences on girls' educational and academic choices and career aspirations can also have a negative effect. Even when parents value education highly, there can be gender biases in the way they influence, consciously or unconsciously, their children's educational choices. They might not encourage their daughters, for example, to pursue science and engineering degrees or believe that these are inappropriate occupations – unless one or both of the parents work in these (Cohoon and Aspray, 2006).

Several factors that may inhibit women from realising their full potential in IT occupations have also been identified. These include the cultural stereotyping of women (Hewlett, et al, 2008a and Hewlett, et al, 2008b; Ramsey and McCorduck, 2005; Samulewicz et al, 2010); cultural and attitudinal stereotypes about the 'nature' of women who work in IT (Kandaswamy, 2003); women being less willing than men to promote themselves and their interests at work when compared to men (Ramsey and McCorduck, 2005); a lack of role models, mentors or sponsors – many women have identified isolation and an absence of appropriate mentoring or sponsorship as one of the key barriers to their advancement in IT companies (Hewlett, et al, 2008a; Hewlett, et al, 2008b) and perceived inequities in promotion/performance review processes (Simard et al, 2005). Other factors include a lack of networking opportunities, which may play a role in rendering women in technology 'invisible' and issues to do with work/family balance. Women in IT report significantly more pressure to put in 'face time' and to be 'available 24/7' when compared to women in other employment sectors (Hewlett et al, 2008b). Many women working in mid-level positions in IT have commented that the 'motherhood assumption' was a barrier to career success in IT, and some men also believe that motherhood can be a barrier for women in IT (Simard et al, 2005). As we will see, many of these factors were prevalent in the UAE IT sector during the late 2000s and early 2010s, although there are some indications that attitudes towards young Emirati women working in IT are changing for the better.

Case Study

Unfortunately, the research literature on women working in CSIT in the MENA region and the UAE was (and continues to be) limited. The one notable exception to this was a report by three researchers at the Masdar Institute for Science and Technology in Abu Dhabi (Samulewicz et al, 2010). However, this focused on the attitudes of undergraduate and postgraduate students towards careers in science, technology and engineering and their generally negative perceptions of these professions, not the experiences of Emirati women who were working in these sectors. Although we contacted a number of local women's organisations, we were unable to locate a sufficient number of Emirati women working in IT to conduct a valid questionnaire survey. We were, however, able to locate twenty Emirati women who were employed in the local IT sector during January and February 2010, and sixteen research questions were addressed during the interviews that followed. Our analysis followed a standard three-stage process for editing and analysing the data gathered during these interviews.[3] This generated rich textual accounts of their experiences of working in IT and how they accounted for the under-representation of Emirati women in the UAE IT sector during the early 2010s.

They worked in a variety of public- and private-sector companies in a range of IT occupations. The ages of our interviewees ranged from twenty-five to forty-seven, and eighteen of the group were married with children. They all started to work in IT in their early twenties, seven of the group had worked for more than ten years in this field and four were in senior management positions. Seven of the women in our interview group can be described as 'IT pioneers' because they were among the first Emirati women to pursue careers in this sector during the mid- to late 1990s. They were attracted to IT for a variety of reasons: an intrinsic interest in mathematics and science subjects at school and an early interest in computers; the attractions of a new and rapidly evolving business sector; the creative challenges associated with programming and developing computer systems for businesses; and, for a few, opportunities to travel abroad on work assignments. However, all of them observed that they were in a very small minority at the schools they attended and almost all of their peers had gravitated to more 'acceptable' female professions such as healthcare, education and human resource management.

Our interviewees identified several reasons IT can be an attractive option for Emirati women. First, it plays a pivotal role in all businesses and industries in general, and is constantly changing and evolving. The acquisition of new knowledge is an integral part of the IT profession and this can be appealing to women who don't like their work to be routine and unchanging. Second, Emirati women are becoming more independent and have started to look for other challenges and opportunities rather than choosing 'safer' career options such as education or healthcare. Third, there are many career opportunities available in IT, including knowledge management, multimedia, software development, network design, graphic design, gaming, cloud computing and so forth. Fourth, there has been a growing need for qualified women in these fields because there are significant skills gaps in the local IT labour market, currently filled largely by male expatriates, not Emirati nationals. Fifth, it can (paradoxically) be an attractive career option for more conservative Emirati women who may prefer to remain veiled or work in women-only environments; in some 'back-room' IT roles they may not have to engage in regular interactions with men at work. However, in response to the question 'Why do so few Emirati women choose careers in the IT sector?', our interviewees were unanimous that while IT was an attractive career choice for them, they did not believe this was the case for most young Emirati women. For example, Interviewees 8 and 12 made these comments:

> I don't think it is an attractive career option for many young Emirati women. Well, if it is attractive, then it's because of the high salaries – salaries in the IT sector are often much better than the salaries in other sectors ... Girls get into IT because they like to

interact with their PCs, perhaps more than interacting with people – like in communication and media jobs. I think you have to have a love for mathematics, programming, and web design from an early age, and many Emirati girls just aren't that interested in these. But, I don't think this is just a problem for the UAE. I mean, I think girls generally are not that interested in scientific and technical subjects ... I also think that there is an image problem as well – we don't have any really high-profile Arabic women working in IT, or creating their own IT businesses. So, I think Emirati girls are not attracted to IT because they think it is a boring field, and you have to be a geek or a nerd [laughs]. I hope – *inshallah* – that will change in the future

(35-year-old head of enterprise portal team, private-sector IT company).

It is true that it's more like a man's job in IT. Women in these fields face many issues: they have to be able to work 24/7; sometimes they often have to work with men who are strangers, and sometimes have to physically move things around when trying to solve network problems in a business. I think for some areas, like networking, IT is not a good field for a girl. For example, my brother works at [a local telecommunication company]. There, they don't have any female employees in their networking section because they are not convinced that a woman should be working in that section, even if they have the right qualifications and are interested in doing it ... Also, some Emirati men don't like this. When there are local males with you, they normally find this wrong, they will normally say 'She is a woman, and not expected to do this kind of physical work.' Men think that if a woman is doing this kind of job, they feel offended, so they try to keep her away, and start doing this and that and interfering with her work

(34-year-old senior marketing and IT manager, private-sector
tourism company).

Several other interviewees also commented that IT can be a very *physical* occupation, which may be another factor that deters some Emirati women from embracing IT careers. For example, Interviewee 17 observed that:

> We have lots of student trainees from local universities and colleges. I won't say all of them, but many female students won't do the cabling work, for example, when we take them to the data centre, they show interest in how it works but they are not willing to do the cabling themselves. Another example is that the students show interest in configuring the routers but they don't want to install it because of their fancy *abayas*. They can't even move freely in it and if you enter the data centre you should not wear high heels otherwise you could break your legs, but most of them still do. When the students are here, I keep telling them 'Go to the data centre and do the cabling, and wear comfortable shoes and your *abaya* should be normal and not fancy'; but all the students come as if they are not expecting to work in this environment. They want office work! This is one reason that makes any organisation ask, 'How we are going to employ these students if they are not willing to change?'
>
> *(34-year-old IT systems analyst, local government organisation).*

All our interviewees believed that young Emirati women are strongly influenced by their peers and families when choosing which subjects to study at school and university, and they often commented on the lack of female role models in the IT sector, in the Middle East generally and particularly in the UAE and the other Gulf States. The female role models that young Emiratis are exposed to in media portrayals and local business publications invariably work in real estate, construction, import–export companies, the media, fashion and design, the financial sector or the public sector. Several interviewees also observed that there was a lack of suitably qualified Emirati women teaching science and IT subjects at primary and secondary schools in the UAE, another factor that may well contribute to the lack of female school students choosing to study CSIT subjects at university. And, as noted in Chapter 2, the UAE is still a patriarchal society, and careers that fathers (and mothers) have traditionally preferred include teaching – in girls-only Emirati schools – and those that are available in the 'safer' Emirati-dominated public sector, where their daughters do not have to work in mixed-gender environments. The IT sector in the UAE is still heavily dominated by men – particularly in the private sector – and this is something that still acts as a deterrent to some Emirati parents.

All of our interviewees also believed that IT required a very specific character, including a willingness to work long hours and to interact with men in what is still a very male-dominated profession. Several of the older interviewees (those over forty years) also felt that many of the current generation of young women Emiratis were simply not willing to put in the hard work that is required to be successful in an IT career, particularly in the private sector. To quote Interviewee 8 again:

> The majority of the new generation of Emirati girls are looking for easy degrees and easy cash and many students avoid IT because they think it is hard work, which it is. But, I don't think this is just an IT problem. Most young Emiratis, men or women, whatever their profession is, they choose to work in the public sector, because they are not prepared to work longer hours, for less pay, in the private sector in their early years ... This is the reality, and I don't see how that will change but until it does, very few young Emirati women will work in IT in the private sector.

Although more young Emirati women may want to work in the private sector, it can be very difficult if they have to work very long hours and travel home alone late at night or if they are expected to work in other countries and if they also have young children. For most Emirati women, as we noted in Chapter 2, the longer working hours expected in private-sector organisations remain a significant deterrent and can have a profound influence on their choice of careers. It is, along with the issue of mixed-gender working environments, one of the main reasons why most young Emirati women continue to opt for employment in public-sector organisations and why so few choose to work in CSIT professions, particularly in the private sector.

The collective response of our twenty interviewees to the questions 'Do Emirati women face discrimination in IT because of their gender?' and 'Are there cultural or attitudinal barriers that women encounter in this sector that they would not find in other business sectors?' can be summarised as 'Yes' and 'Yes, but with several qualifications.' For example, Interviewee 6 made these comments:

> *Iwah!* Most of our team leaders are male. If my manager wants to send me to work for projects with other companies, we should meet their IT team and cooperate with them to complete that project. If they are male and local, they often refuse to be with any female because their culture doesn't accept an Emirati woman to be in a room full of local men. It is acceptable if they are Indian or American women or men from other cultures; but with local women that still can't happen. For example, a few weeks ago, they wanted to send me to work with an IT team in [another company], but then they called me back and said 'No, we can't have a female working with them.' There were seven local males, and they said 'How can we work with her?' Sometimes it's really a very big problem
>
> *(27-year-old technical consultant, private-sector IT company).*

However, according to Interviewee 11:

> It is internationally recognised that the IT remains a male-dominated industry and many studies have been made in this regard. I think the female contribution varies from one country to another, and we need to increase the female contribution in the UAE. But, I think it can be too easy to blame discrimination for the lack of women in the IT field ... When I first came into [this company] there were hardly any women but more have joined recently and proved they can do a good job. I can say that I've

not faced any discrimination and have managed to get into this senior job, while raising a family ... I've felt always that the most important thing was to deliver good results and when that started happening even the older more traditional Emirati men began to accept me

(32-year-old senior IT project team leader, private-sector IT company).

While almost all of our interviewees did acknowledge that cultural, attitudinal and structural barriers existed in their workplaces, they were – without exception – very indignant about the assumption that Islam or the teachings of the Qur'an are the primary causes of women's inequality in the UAE IT sector. For example, interviewees 11 and 6 commented that:

Well, if there is an Islamic barrier, it exists in all business sectors not just in IT. Despite the culture, most UAE ladies are more open now, more free, and most don't mind working in a mixed environment. But we still have some families who won't allow their daughters to work in a place that is full of men; they would not allow them to work night shifts or to travel alone and our traditional dress can be uncomfortable in a busy IT working environment. But that is not our religion, it's our culture. Until this changes and it becomes more acceptable for Emirati women to work with men, to perhaps not wear traditional dress all the time and to work away from home then there'll be problems for women working in IT

(32-year-old senior IT project team leader, private-sector IT company).

I don't think it is Islam that creates any kind of obstacles that prevent women from working in IT, as the UAE government and our leaders support and encourage the women in all occupations and jobs. It's our culture not our religion that creates some problems ... For example, if you are a lady, staying late outside the home is often regarded as wrong and also I think that some men still do not take women as seriously as they should. Many Emirati men still think that they know more than the women do.

Even if they know that women now are very well educated and know more than they do they will never admit this. Emirati men can be very insecure about this and prefer to think that a girl always has less knowledge than they do. They even make fun of what she knows and they don't take her seriously, which is something strange and annoying for women these days! In their eyes, she's still a *bint*, which means 'girl' not 'woman'

> *(27-year-old technical consultant, private-sector IT company).*

Interviewee 10 made the following comments about the impact of UAE cultural values and mores on women working in this sector:

This is not an Islamic issue. Islam has encouraged women historically to be in all fields and there is nothing in the Qur'an that prevents women from being in the workforce. Women by themselves are putting limitations on themselves, because of the UAE's cultural traditions, not just in IT but in other jobs too. For example, it's still quite rare for an Emirati woman to choose engineering or science, because of her mind-set or – more likely – her family's mind-set … But, Islam has not created these limitations, it is our ancient traditions and the limitations we impose on ourselves, because it is how some people in this society still think … I am an Emirati mother, and I work in IT but I still have these traditions in my mind! I have a daughter, and I can't imagine allowing my daughter to work long hours on her own in the office until 10 pm in the evening. This is not acceptable to me. I will not allow her to travel alone, if this means she has to travel with a group of men. I would not be comfortable if I let her do that, I need to protect her and this is the idea behind doing these things … Being protective of our daughters is a very normal thing in the UAE and Arab countries. Most UAE families are like this, which is something good in one way but it can be an obstacle in other ways if Emirati families place limitations on their daughters' ambitions

> *(41-year-old IT analyst, semi-government energy company).*

We observed in Chapter 1 that the UAE is a unique country in the MENA region in terms of the legal rights, freedoms and opportunities it offers to both national and expatriate women and in its comparatively moderate interpretations of Islam and *shari'a* law. However, cultural, structural and attitudinal barriers were still deterring young Emirati women from pursuing careers in the UAE IT sector in the early 2010s. We conclude this section with another quote from Interviewee 8, which illustrates their pervasive nature:

> I have been working now for 12 years in the IT sector, and three years in a management position. When I was a young network engineer, no one thought that an Emirati lady could do that job. My role was to configure and to build a network setup, and within that I had to physically install some devices. I needed to take the routers and physically carry and install them at the customer's site or in our data centres. We were serving several customers, so we needed to install devices at their sites and build and establish the connections. I had to do cabling as well from scratch. As a lady, I don't mind working on such tasks and I got used to dealing with it ... Also, as an IT person, I have to be available after working hours and during the weekends in case there were any incidents or tasks because most of the outages or service interruption happens after working hours and should be fixed immediately to not inconvenience the customer. Sometimes, I used to stay until one or two in the morning at the office in the data centre and my family was strongly against that, but it was happening and they couldn't stop me doing the job that I really wanted to do.

Four conclusions can be drawn from this case study. First, Emirati women were clearly lagging behind in the local IT sector when compared to the significant inroads they had been making into many other professional occupations in the UAE during the 2000s and early 2010s. Second, the reasons young Emirati women were not attracted to careers in IT and were under-represented in this sector at this time, were very similar to those identified in many other countries; but there were also some deterrent factors that were unique to the UAE. Third, national women working in IT have faced distinctive barriers in this sector arising from the conservative male cultural *mores* exhibited by some of the men they had to deal with at work and the unique and demanding challenges of IT work. Fourth, all our interviewees believed that these factors were having a negative effect on the decisions that young Emirati women were making about pursuing careers in IT in the early 2010s.

Has this state of affairs changed since this study was completed? A 2014 report on 394 Emirati undergraduates studying STEM disciplines at UAE universities suggests that attitudes towards women in these occupations 'are changing rapidly', and an increasing number of Emirati parents were encouraging their daughters to study STEM subjects at universities and embrace careers in these occupations after they graduate. In addition, 87 per cent of the participants in this survey believed that 'greater opportunities are opening up to females wanting to study in this area' (*The Economist* Intelligence Unit, 2014: 10). However, this report also indicated that '34 per cent of families had discouraged their daughters from choosing STEM [courses]' and 'females still face an array of obstacles in the workplace including managing a work–life balance, cultural obstacles, such as society seeing women as family caretakers rather than engineers or scientists, a lack of female role models and mentors and gender discrimination. More proactive measures from both the public and private sector are needed to tackle these obstacles' (*The Economist* Intelligence Unit, 2014: 4). This report also noted that:

UAE–based women who come from rich backgrounds tend to be less likely to engage in science, technology and engineering compared with those with a lower socioeconomic status. The well-off among Emirati society have easier access to managerial professions through personal or family contacts, or *wasta*, and expectations of the type of jobs they would be engaged with are different

(The Economist Intelligence Unit, 2014: 14).

Furthermore, and this confirms one of the main findings of our study of women in the UAE IT sector:

Pupils are currently forced to choose either science or art streams at the age of 15. Teenagers often choose arts because they perceive it as easier than science, resulting in an oversupply of arts and humanities graduates, which in turn exacerbates unemployment among nationals later in life. Plans are afoot to change the system, but the specifics of what will replace it are yet to be announced

(The Economist Intelligence Unit, 2014: 12).[4]

Hence, while attitudes towards young women in CSIT occupations are becoming more positive, there are still barriers that are preventing more of them from pursuing careers in this sector of the UAE labour market. In Chapter 9, we describe three generic strategies that could be implemented in order to encourage young Emirati women to work in STEM and CSIT professions and help them rise into managerial and leadership positions in these fast-growing sectors of the UAE economy in the future.

3.4 BALANCING WORK AND FAMILY LIFE

The issues of work–life balance and work–family conflict have been the subject of hundreds of research articles and dozens of books over the last two decades, including some well-known recent examples such as Sheryl Sandberg's *Lean In* (2013). This section presents a conceptual framework for understanding work–life balance and work–family conflict issues in the UAE, describes the results of a questionnaire survey of more than one hundred working married Emirati women and also considers the broader implications of the data results. 'Work–life balance' is defined here as 'the ability to harmonise and cope effectively with the competing demands of work and family life', and work–family conflict is defined as 'situations where people find it difficult to balance the demands encountered in one domain (family) due to their involvement in the other domain (work)' (adapted from Aycan, 2008). Four broad causes of work–family conflict have been identified in the international research literature, and these formed the basic framework for this study (adapted from Aycan, 2008; Aycan et al, 2004; Drago, 2007; Halpern and Cheung, 2008; Joplin et al, 2003; Lewis, 2010; Lewis et al, 2007; Yang, 2005):

> *Role or Strain Overload:* arising from multiple demands at work that may affect an employee's ability to cope with family responsibilities. Several studies have found that work overload is strongly correlated with work–life imbalance in many countries, reducing the amount of time that employees can spend with families and negatively affecting other non-work personal relationships.
>
> *Work-to-family interference:* when work responsibilities interfere with family life and make it difficult to perform household tasks or spend adequate time with children.
>
> *Family-to-work interference:* when family responsibilities interfere with work demands, which may make it difficult or impossible to perform efficiently and effectively at work.
>
> *Cultural (gendered) assumptions and expectations:* the belief that women, even if they work outside the home, are still primarily responsible for management of the domestic unit, housework and childcare, even in dual-income households.

In addition to these, three clusters of gender, organisational and cultural norms have been identified in this literature which influence the way that work–life balance and work–family conflict issues are interpreted by women, men and public- and private-sector organisations across different national cultures. These are the *Motherhood Norm*, the *Ideal Worker Norm* and the *Individualism Norm*:

> *The Motherhood Norm:* the ancient and deeply held beliefs that women should be, primarily, mothers and managers of their households. This

may discourage them from being fully committed to demanding full-time professional jobs which, in turn, may prevent them from reaching senior positions in their careers because they are not regarded by their employers as 'ideal workers'.

The Ideal Worker Norm: the belief that employees must be totally committed to their employers and available '24/7/365' in order to gain promotions, earn higher salaries and – if they have the ambition – to serve in leadership positions. This widely prevalent norm will affect the amount of time that employees have to spend with their families – unless they have other support systems in place such as stay-at-home spouses, extended families or paid domestic help.

The Individualism Norm: the assumption that employers (and governments) should not, as a general rule, interfere in the private lives of their citizens unless their behaviour poses a threat to their employer, their colleagues, themselves, their families or others. While there are considerable variations in the amount of help and support given by national governments and employers to help women employees balance their work and family responsibilities, the literature is very consistent about one matter: most organisations, public or private, still view work and personal life as competing priorities in a zero-sum game, in which a gain in one area invariably means a loss in the other. In their view, every time an employee's personal interests win, the organisation pays the price, and so they may often regard work–life programs as little more than an unwelcome form of 'employee welfare' (Aycan, 2008; Drago, 2007; Forster, 1999; Lewis, 2010; Lewis et al, 2007; Thomas, 2004).

One of the themes that emerged in the IT case study was the issue of work–family balance. However, very little attention has been paid to this issue in the MENA region by business and management scholars, and so the research on which this section is based was one of the first to describe the emergence of work–life balance and work–family conflict issues in the UAE and the growing challenges that Emirati women may face in balancing their busy work and family lives (Forster et al, 2014).[5] The sample consisted of 119 married Emirati women: 21.1 per cent were aged 20–25 years, 25.6 per cent twenty-five to thirty, 40.0 per cent thirty to thirty-five and just 13.3 per cent were older than thirty-five. Again, these data reflect the relatively youthful female working population of the UAE following the national baby boom of the 1980s and 1990s and the employment opportunities that became available to Emirati women during the 2000s. As noted, all of these women were married, and fifty-eight had one child, thirty-five had two, eighteen had three and seven had four or more children; 93.5 per cent of our respondents had husbands who were also working full time or managing their own businesses. They worked in a variety of public and semi-government (N = 79) and private-sector organisations (N = 40) and included national and local government employees, airline employees, bank officers and branch managers, customs officials, financial officers, human resource managers, import–export managers, a few women working in IT, marketing managers, medical professionals, media employees, police officers, research analysts, schoolteachers and university employees. Most of them worked in supervisory or middle-management roles: 38.5 per cent of our respondents had less than five years' work experience, 26.7 per cent had six to ten years' work experience and 22.6 per cent had eleven to fifteen years' experience. Only 12.2 per cent of these women had worked for more than fifteen years.

On average, women in the private sector reported that they worked longer weeks than their peers in the public sector (5.4 versus 5.0 days per week), and there were noticeable differences in their average daily working hours (Table 3.9). In the public-sector sub-sample, a majority of respondents reported being 'neutral' about the amount of time they spend at work, with 30.6 per cent of respondents reporting that they were 'happy' and 11.9 per cent 'very happy' with their working hours. However, more respondents in the private-sector sub-sample felt 'unhappy' or 'very unhappy' about the amount of time they spend at work (37.4 per cent compared to 11.4 per cent among public-sector employees). Furthermore, 61.2 per cent of private-sector employees reported that work pressures 'sometimes make me feel very tired', and only 10.5 per cent reported that their work never left them feeling tired. And while 31.8 per cent of public-sector

TABLE 3.9 *Daily hours worked by women in public,*
semi-government and private-sector organisations in the UAE
(N = 119 women)

	Daily average working hours			
	7–8	*9–10*	*11–12*	*12 or more*
Public sector and semi-government	65.6	30.8	3.6	0.0
Private sector	33.6	45.4	21.0	0.0

(This includes 'time spent on work-related duties while at home' and
'commuting hours' in order to assess the total number of hours engaged
in these activities by these women each week. 66.6 percent of our
respondents reported that they took '30 minutes or less' to travel to
work, 28.6 reported '30–60 minutes' and the remainder reported 'more
than 60 minutes')

employees indicated that they had 'sometimes' dealt with work
during weekends and holidays, this figure rose to 71.2 per cent among
those working in the private sector. To develop a clearer picture of
how our respondents cope with the competing demands of work and
family life, we asked them a general question: 'Do you feel that you
are able to balance your work responsibilities and family life?' The
results are presented in Table 3.10.

TABLE 3.10 *Do you feel that you are able to balance your work*
responsibilities and family life?

	Never	*Rarely*	*Sometimes*	*Often*	*Always*
Public sector and semi-government	2.1	8.7	30.3	37.4	21.5
Private sector	7.2	24.1	35.9	20.0	12.8

The responses to this question show that most of the women who
work in the public and semi-government sectors felt that they were
able to balance their work responsibilities and family life, although

nearly 30 per cent reported that it was sometimes difficult to balance the competing responsibilities of work and family. The situation for those working in the private sector was rather different, with nearly one third reporting that they were 'never' or 'rarely' able to balance the demands of their jobs and families. There was also clear evidence of negative spill-over between work and our respondents' leisure time, with noticeable differences in the responses of the private-sector employees when compared to public and semi-government employees (Tables 3.11 and 3.12).

TABLE 3.11 *How often do you think about work when you are not actually at work or when traveling to work?*

	Never	Rarely	Sometimes	Often	Always
Public sector and semi-government	0.0	30.8	62.1	7.1	0.0
Private sector	0.0	8.7	47.2	37.9	6.2

TABLE 3.12 *Do you ever miss out on quality time with your families and friends because of work pressures?*

	Never	Rarely	Sometimes	Often	Always
Public sector and semi-government	0.0	28.7	55.9	15.4	0.0
Private sector	0.0	8.4	65.5	26.1	0.0

The data also suggested that work responsibilities had few negative effects on the amount of time that our public-sector respondents had to spend with their children. However, once again, the longer working hours required of those working in private-sector companies in the UAE was having a discernible effect on the time they could spend with their children during the week and at weekends (Tables 3.13 and 3.14).

In order to evaluate how Emirati women coped with the competing demands of work and family, we also asked them about the childcare arrangements in their households. The data showed that most working

TABLE 3.13 *On an average working day, how much time do you have to spend with your children?*

	< 2 hours	2–3 hours	3–4 hours	> 4 hours
Public sector and semi-government	12.6	29.4	38.6	19.4
Private sector	49.6	28.6	21.8	1.0

TABLE 3.14 *During an average weekend, how much time do you spend with your children?*

	< 4 hours	4–5 hours	5–6 hours	> 6 hours
Public sector and semi-government	3.3	12.6	26.9	57.2
Private sector	19.4	35.3	25.2	20.1

TABLE 3.15 *Who – primarily – takes care of your children while you are at work?*

	Spouse	Parents, in-laws or close relatives	Servant or Nanny
Public sector and semi-government	0.0	52.9	47.1
Private sector	0.0	56.3	43.7

Emirati women – regardless of the employment sector that they work in – were still heavily dependent on extended families and older relatives for child care and support from nannies and servants who, by Western standards, are extremely cheap to employ (Table 3.15).

Only a minority of our respondents felt overwhelmed by the competing demands of their home and work lives, but there was evidence of some strains and stresses being created by this across the entire sample (Table 3.16). These findings confirm the results of other studies on work–life balance and work–family conflict and

TABLE 3.16 *What is the impact of home life on your work performance?*

	Public sector and semi-government	Private sector
Impact		
My home life has no impact on my work performance	*33.4*	*27.7*
Family responsibilities can reduce the time I have to work on job- related tasks	*9.3*	*14.7*
Family responsibilities can distract me from work-tasks	*8.4*	*21.7*
Problems at home can make me feel irritable at work	*12.1*	*17.8*
At times, work pressures and family responsibilities can overwhelm me	*4.1*	*15.4*
(% that 'strongly agreed' or 'agreed' with each statement)		

suggest that there is a 'high-pressure' subgroup of about one in six Emirati women working in the private sector who, at times, were struggling to balance the competing demands of high-pressure jobs and busy family lives.

In the final section of the survey, we examined the work–life balance support provided by our respondents' employers. The data portray a very mixed picture of both the general availability of work–life balance support in UAE organisations and the provision of specific services or HR policies that are known to help with balancing work and family responsibilities (Table 3.17).

In an open-ended question, we asked those respondents who had reported conflicts between their jobs and family lives to indicate five factors that they believed to be the greatest hindrances to achieving better work–life balance. In order of importance, these were 'Negative/patriarchal/conservative attitudes of (male) senior

TABLE 3.17 *Work–life balance support and services provided by employers*

'Does your company have any specific services or HR policies to help with work–life balance?'			
	Yes	No	Not sure/don't know
Public sector and semi-government	*32.0*	*52.1*	*15.9*
Private sector	*22.7*	*57.2*	*20.1*

'What support does your company provide to help with WLB?'		
	Public sector and semi-government	Private sector
Policy		
Flexible starting and finishing times	*19.4*	*27.2*
Option to work part-time or job share	*19.2*	*4.8*
Crèche, day-care or nursery at your workplace	*0.0*	*0.0*
Career breaks or sabbaticals	*17.4*	*0.0*
Parental or family advice	*15.6*	*0.0*
Paid maternity leave*	*100.0*	*100.0*

*(This excludes 'Not sure/don't know' responses. * On 30 September 2012, forty-five days of paid maternity leave became mandatory for all full-time female Emirati employees. Additional discretionary maternity leave/salary is provided by some international private-sector companies in the UAE.)*

managers, bosses or supervisors' (N = 35); 'Inadequate maternity leave provisions' (N = 33); 'Lack of childcare facilities at work' (N = 27); 'Negative attitudes of family members' (N = 25); 'culture and religion' (i.e. social pressures to put family and their husband's career before their jobs; N = 25); and, 'technology' (i.e. being accessible 24/7 for work-related matters; N = 24). The final question we asked our respondents in the questionnaire was 'Do you think that if employees enjoy a good balance between their work and family lives, then their work performance will improve?, 77.1 per cent replied 'Yes', 21.1 per cent replied 'Not Sure' and 1.8 per cent replied 'No'.

In conclusion, there were noticeable and consistent differences in the responses of Emirati women who worked in the private sector when compared to those in the public sector. Women in the former group reported longer working hours, had less time to spend with their children and families and experienced greater difficulties in balancing work and family commitments. There was also clear evidence of role and strain overload, work-to-family interference and family-to-work interference among this group. However, most of the women in both groups had the support of extended families and kin who routinely helped out with childcare or they could afford nannies and, in some cases, servants. This meant that work–family conflict appeared to be a less significant and stressful issue than it continues to be for many working women in Western societies. Having said this, one of the few studies that has looked at the attitudes of female Emiratis towards work and how satisfied they are with their jobs concluded that:

> Married women were significantly dissatisfied with their jobs [which] may be attributed to several factors. First, it is obvious that women still have a defined role in UAE society and are expected to carry out domestic responsibilities, bearing children and looking after their families' needs and homes. Second, workplaces do not offer sufficient childcare centres for working mothers. More than seventy per cent of respondents reported that they lacked childcare services in their workplace. Third, the prevailing culture considers motherly care to be more beneficial for children than professional day-care centres. Fourth, to avoid work–family conflict, Middle Eastern women have a defined role: to be obedient and respectful to men and to be

efficient in carrying out day-to-day house responsibilities
and bearing children

(Shallal, 2011: 124).

At the time of this research in 2011, the issues of work–life balance
and work–family conflict were not a noticeable part of mainstream
public discourse in the UAE. However, as we will see in Chapter 9,
these have become more widely discussed topics in the Emirati community since. Moreover, as noted earlier, it seems very likely that a
growing number of working Emirati women will not be able to rely on
their extended families for support in the future to the extent that
they may have been able to in the past, largely because of increasing
occupational and geographical job mobility among Emirati women.
As a result of this, work–life balance and work–family conflict are
likely to become more significant issues in the UAE in the future
particularly for private-sector employees, where both the 'ideal
worker' and 'individualism' norms described earlier in this section
are very prevalent. Ameliorating these will require positive and creative solutions from business organisations and the UAE federal government if they are not to become impediments to the active
participation of more Emirati women in the private sector during
the 2020s and beyond. Most of the women in this study felt that the
organisations they worked for could be more sympathetic to work–life
balance and work–family conflict issues and they suggested a range of
HRM initiatives that could be implemented to help with these (flexi-
hours and longer maternity leave allowances, for example). These,
they believed, would also enhance their prospects of becoming leaders
in the future – particularly in the private sector. Their suggestions and
the implications of these for the advancement of women in the UAE
labour market are discussed further in Chapter 9.

3.5 CONCLUSION

Over the last two decades, the UAE has been witness to a transformation that was described towards the end of Chapter 1 as a 'quiet

revolution', and the freedoms and opportunities now enjoyed by many Emirati women are very different to those of their mothers and grandmothers and those of most young women in other MENA countries. As we saw in Chapter 2, their labour force participation rate has increased exponentially over the last decade, and while women are still under-represented among the ruling political elites of the seven *imara*, there have been significant changes in their representation at the senior levels of public-sector organisations. A growing number of Emirati women have moved into senior positions in this sector, they are increasingly involved in the political administration of the country and a small but growing number are becoming successful business owners. As the number of upwardly mobile young Emirati female professionals grows, some will inevitably overtake their less able male peers in status, power, wealth and influence. Emirati men are lagging behind in educational attainment at the tertiary level and, as suggested earlier, it is probable that some of them will lose out to their well-educated, highly motivated and ambitious female peers in the future. As economic gender equality increases, the female professional middle-class of the UAE will also grow and Emirati women will not only help their nation to create a resilient economy; this process will in all probability have an irreversible effect on their independence, economic power and social status in the future.

However, the traditional view that women 'take care' and men 'take charge' is still embedded in the culture of Emirati society today, and some men still believe that women should not be allowed to work and should not be senior politicians, public-sector leaders, engineers, fighter pilots or chief executives or, indeed, become *imams* or serve as the *sheikha* of any of the *imara*. They still think that the most suitable role for women is to be wives and mothers and if women do reach senior positions in the UAE these men still think that they will either fail, will not be able to handle the demands of their jobs and will neglect their families. But it must be remembered that these traditional and conservative attitudes are not unique to men in the UAE; *they are universal.* In North America, the United Kingdom and Australia, the first wave of ambitious career women who entered male-dominated organisations during the 1980s and 1990s and who also had children and family responsibilities were also generally regarded by most men as being less committed to their work, less productive, less competent, less successful in their careers and 'not good mothers' (see, for example, Sinclair, 1998; Sinclair and Wilson, 2002; White, Cox and Cooper, 1994; Wilson, 1995).

Two barriers to equality that still confront women in the UAE are ones that are, to some extent, self-imposed. The first concerns their personal beliefs about what they want, what they are capable of achieving and what they need to do to realise their dreams and ambitions. Their self-belief and self-confidence continue to be affected by the influences they are exposed to when they are young, and in a male-dominated culture some may continue to believe that they do not have what it takes to succeed in professional careers or as leaders. The second, as we have seen, are the difficulties that a growing number of working Emirati women have in managing highly demanding jobs (particularly in the private sector) while coping with childcare and domestic responsibilities. But if more Emirati women are to become leaders in the UAE in the future, they must develop greater self-confidence and belief in their abilities and, when required, renegotiate their domestic and childcare responsibilities with their husbands, extended families and employers. In fact, these may well be two of the biggest challenges that young Emirati women will have to deal with in their career and life-journeys in the future.

Two short stories can illustrate how these personal challenges were overcome by two prominent (and married) Emirati business women. The first is Raja al-Gurg, who is the president of the UAE Business Women Council and managing director of the Easa al-Gurg Group, where her sisters Muna and Maryam also work. However, she has acknowledged that she was quite shy before she started her career, lacked confidence in her ability to work and to interact effectively with men in business and was genuinely concerned about what others might say about her if she took this step. However, with her father's support and his insistence that she complete her education, she developed the confidence to follow her dreams. She started her professional life as a teacher and became headmistress of Zabeel Secondary School for Girls and, after working in several other jobs, started working in her father's business (Majdalani et al, 2015: 19). When she was asked about the reason for entering the business world, she said:

> At first I never thought I wanted to go into business. But when
> I took a role in my father's company, I had to prove that I could be
> successful regardless of the fact that I was a woman. It is crucial
> that all women push their own boundaries and have the will to
> succeed. We must let our achievements be known. Getting to the
> top of the mountain is easy but to reside there involves much more
> work. With the UAE's rapid development, now it is a great time for
> women to start businesses and to move up in the professional and
> business world
>
> *(AME Info, 2005).*

A contemporary of Raja al-Gurg is Fatima al-Jaber, who is one of the best known female business leaders in the UAE. As chief operating officer of the Al Jaber Group (ALG), she shares the responsibility of managing more than 50,000 staff and more than US$5 billion in assets. After a successful career in the Public Works department of Abu Dhabi Municipality, in 2006 she joined the company founded by her father. In addition to guiding the diversified construction company through a very difficult debt restructuring process after the worst financial crisis that the UAE had ever faced in the late 2000s, a process that was not completed until June 2014(Arabian Business, 2014). She has been a regular speaker at business conferences across the Middle East as well as acting as a high-profile ambassador for working Emirati women. Fatima is also an active member of the Abu Dhabi Chamber of Commerce (ADCC) and was the first woman to be elected to the board of directors of the ADCC in December 2009. She has said that she was 'amazed by this outcome. I didn't think a lot of men would elect me. For me it is a personal success, because I could represent women and be elected by men' (CEO Middle-East, 2011: 23). She is regularly voted among the most powerful Arab business women, being ranked the twenty-third 'Most powerful Arab woman' in 2015 by CEO Middle-East (2015: 46), and believes that attitudes towards Emirati women in the UAE workforce were changing fast during the early 2010s:

> The UAE is miles and miles ahead of other Gulf countries in terms of equality [and you] now see female ministers in all areas of government and in our parliaments ... My mother and mothers of the previous generation were not working mothers, they were all housewives. Now I'm a working mother and I see the majority of my colleagues and friends are working mothers, so it's exactly the opposite
>
> *(CEO Middle-East, 2011: 26).*

In conclusion, women have made significant progress in the public sector, there are several well-known and successful female Emirati leaders in government and in the FNC and some are now prominent business leaders. However, while much progress has been made over the last decade, there is still some way to go before traditional cultural and attitudinal barriers are no longer prevalent in public- and private-sector organisations in the UAE. We know that while most Emirati women would agree that they have good opportunities to pursue careers and to work, they still believe that there are barriers and impediments to their career progression in most organisations, particularly in the private sector, and many of them remain pessimistic that a significant number of women will ascend to leadership positions in private-sector companies in the near future. We also know that a sizeable proportion of Emirati men still have traditional and conservative opinions about working Emirati women and also question their ability to succeed in leadership roles. Moreover, for most university-educated Emirati women, the longer working hours, lower salaries and mixed working environments in private-sector organisations remain significant deterrents. They remain underrepresented in this sector, not many are self-made entrepreneurs and business owners and, even today, few work in STEM professions. Many Emirati women still prefer to work in public-sector organisations because these generally offer better pay, more security, better holiday entitlements and shorter working hours when compared to equivalent jobs in the private sector, particularly for younger employees. Nevertheless, there are many reasons to be optimistic about both the future for women in the UAE and the long-term economic development and security of this small but dynamic, innovative and (at least in economic terms) successful country, providing it can also liberalise its highly centralised and repressive political system. However, as we have seen, the advancement of women in the UAE labour market is still, in in several respects, a work in progress and we will return to re-examine this and its significance for the future growth and diversification of the UAE economy in Chapter 8.

4 The Sultanate of Oman

This chapter begins with a description of the recent history of modern Oman and its economic development since Sultan Qaboos bin Said became the ruler of the country in 1970. This is followed by an evaluation of the systemic economic, political and social challenges facing Oman and the progress this country has made towards its ambitious economic development goals. We then examine the changing life experiences of Omani women, their progress in the national workforce over the last two decades and the emergence of a few female leaders in the country's public and private sectors. This is followed, with reference to recent World Economic Forum Global Gender Gap (GGG) and Convention on the Elimination of all Forms of Discrimination Against Women (CEDAW) reports by an analysis of the economic and legal status of women in Oman. Next, we describe the cultural, attitudinal and structural barriers that women still encounter in the national labour market and how Islamic beliefs continue to shape perceptions of the 'correct' roles of women and men in Omani society and in the workplace. In the conclusion we evaluate the progress that women have made in the national workforce, the short-term effects of the steep fall in global oil prices on the country's economy during 2014–2016 and the likely longer-term effects of the rapid depletion of Oman's hydrocarbon resources over the next two decades.

4.2 A BRIEF HISTORY OF OMAN

Oman is a country that most people who live outside the MENA region are unlikely to be familiar with and not only has its recent history been more turbulent than that of its better-known northern GCC neighbour, the UAE, it faces more serious short- to medium-term economic, political and social problems. The first impression that all visitors to Oman have is of a modern, successful country with an excellent infrastructure, busy highways and many new buildings and malls with brand-name shops stocked with consumer goods. But, like all the Arabian Gulf States, Oman remains a traditional and patriarchal society with a hierarchical and tribal social system and strict devotion to the Islamic faith. Omanis have always had a strong sense of tribal identity, with names like al-Wahaibi and al-Balushi clearly indicating the areas of the country from which they originated. Some tribes, such as the al-Abris from Sahten, can be pinpointed to specific *wadis* in the Hajar Mountains. More than thirty-five tribes are known to have inhabited Oman during the nineteenth and twentieth centuries, with each of these further sub-divided into clans and extended families. Each tribe had its own unique traditions, beliefs and dialects and there has always been a distinct hierarchical tribal 'pecking-order' in Oman. The Al bu Said tribe, for example, has a preeminent economic and political position among the other tribes in Oman because of its close links with the royal family, while the Jibbali people of the Dhofar region still form a somewhat marginalised ethnic and cultural group. And, as in the UAE and the KSA, the primary allegiance of all members of these tribes was to their tribal leaders, a state of affairs that persists in Oman today. This means that communal interests and grievances were invariably expressed through family, clan and tribal connections to those in positions of power in the regional administrative centres of the country (*muhafadhat*) and the national government in Muscat.

Until comparatively recently Oman was a sparsely populated country, divided between the patrilineal descendants of 'free' Arabs and the descendants of client groups and slaves – a division which, according to some commentators, persists to this day. Until the mid-1960s, there was limited government infrastructure, no tarmac roads, no established tradition of private property ownership, no agreed body of statute law and no national currency (the Indian rupee was used until 1970). Cooperative labour was the norm, within broader kinship and tribal networks, enabling local disputes to be resolved quickly and better cooperation over small-scale agriculture areas. Most Omanis lived in simple *barasti* made of clay and palm fronds. There were just three non-Qur'anic primary schools in Oman, serving 900 boys, and no secondary schools in the country before the mid-1960s. In 1970, there was just one hospital in Oman. Like the UAE, the country's economy revolved primarily around agriculture, fishing, camel and livestock herding, subsistence agriculture, textile manufacturing and small-scale bartering and trading. Additional income was also derived from male Omanis who worked in East African countries and other Gulf states. Oman was also, for many centuries, a source of frankincense – the aromatic gum extracted from a species of tree which grows only in the south of the country at Hadhramaut, and also in Yemen and parts of Somalia (Janzen, 1986; Wikan, 1982).

Little is known about the lives of women in Oman before the 1970s, because there are very few English-language studies on the history and sociology of this country, and even these devote very little attention to this topic (e.g. a recent study by Jones and Ridout published in 2015 dedicates fewer than 10 of 290 pages to Omani women). The limited information we do have indicates that Omani women would have conformed to traditional dress codes, and they would have been generally deferential to their fathers or husbands. They would have also clearly understood what it meant 'to be a female from the roles expected of married, divorced, or widowed women, to the forms of comportment they were to embody' (Limbert, 2010: 15–16). However, this did not mean that women remained isolated in their homes, and they enjoyed rich social lives with other local women in their towns, villages and neighbourhoods. And, as in the UAE, women did play some part in the economic life of Oman before the 1970s, because most Omani families had to rely on several sources of income to sustain themselves throughout the year.

In agricultural areas, women worked in the fields, tending alfalfa and wheat, grazing animals, collecting well water, grinding flour for bread and chopping wood. Like their contemporaries in the UAE, women also were involved in the management of their homes and household budgets and were often involved in home-based businesses such as raising livestock, growing fruit (particularly dates) and vegetables, selling chickens and goats' cheese and milk, and weaving cloth and embroidering fabrics. Moreover, when widowed women inherited money, they were allowed to invest this in land and small farms to pass on to their children. There were also a few isolated examples of female business owners in the 1950s and 1960s, but while some Omani women did work in the cities and larger towns, this was largely behind the scenes. Typically, Omani business women would have been represented in the public domain by male relatives in business transactions, and if they wanted to sell or buy property their male guardians would have signed any legal documents on their behalf (Limbert, 2010; Skeet; 1992).

Although geologists from American, French and British oil companies had begun searching for oil in Oman in the 1920s, the first commercially viable reservoir in the country was not discovered until 1962 in Yibal, in the Dhahira region, followed by further discoveries of large reserves in Natih in 1963 and Fahud in 1964. In August 1967, the state-owned Petroleum Development Oman Company (PDOC) began production and started exporting crude oil. The Omani government took a 60 per cent stake in PDOC with the remainder held by British Petroleum, known then as the Anglo-Persian Oil Company, and Compagnie Francaise des Petroles. Today, Shell, Total and Partex now own most of this 40 per cent stake. Production of oil fluctuated during the 1970s, 1980s and 1990s. By 1973 Oman was producing 293,000 barrels per day (BPD) and had produced 106 million barrels of oil at the end of that year. Production then climbed to a peak of 970,000 BPD in 2000, and PDOC produced 945,000 BPD in 2013. The country's gas sector is controlled by the Oman Gas Company, and gas reserves stood at approximately 510 km^3 in 2014 (United States Energy Information Agency, 2015b: 3).[1] The rapid increase in oil prices, following the oil embargo imposed by the oil-producing states of the Gulf after the Arab–Israeli conflict of the early 1970s, quadrupled the funds that Sultan Qaboos had at his disposal to develop Oman's economy and set in process many economic, educational, cultural and social changes that have continued to the present day. These were first articulated in detail in the First Five Year Plan (1976–1980) and these plans have been published every five years since this time.

All visitors to Oman soon realise that most of the credit for the stabilisation of Oman and the economic modernisation of this country that has occurred since the early 1970s is attributed to the 'wisdom and determination' of Sultan Qaboos bin Said, whose portrait can be seen in all government buildings, universities and hospitals and on large billboards throughout Muscat (Limbert, 2010: 4). When he ascended to the throne, after a bloodless coup on 23 July 1970, Oman had been in a period of protracted civil war and unrest whose complex origins stretch back for decades. This ended a period of isolation, economic decline and social dislocation under the divisive rule of the previous ruler, Sultan Said bin Taimur. By the end of the 1960s, his subjects and many powerful tribal leaders who had been marginalised, imprisoned or exiled by Said bin Taimur finally rebelled against him, leading to the coup and his replacement by his twenty-nine-year-old son, Qaboos bin Said (formally, Qaboos bin Sa'id al-Bu Sa'id). His father was then exiled and moved into a suite at the Dorchester hotel in London, where he died in 1972.[2]

Sultan Qaboos was appointed as the country's new ruler on 2 August 1970 and immediately abolished many of his father's draconian social restrictions, established a new government administration in Muscat, and also created several new ministries including education, health, interior and justice. For the first time, the interior regions of Oman (the Imamate of Oman) and the coastal regions (the Sultanate of Muscat) were unified in a single territory known as the Sultanate of Oman. He also spent much of his early time in power visiting the regions to present himself to the people and consolidate relationships with local tribal leaders, a tradition which has continued throughout his reign with annual 'meet-the-people' tours (Jones and Ridout, 2015: 145–150). While Sultan Qaboos did not start the process of national economic development, he and his coterie of national and local leaders have created a modern government infrastructure and started to build the kind of diversified national economy that can sustain the country when its oil and gas reserves are depleted. Substantial investments in infrastructure were made throughout the 1970s, 1980s, 1990s and 2000s including ports, cargo transport hubs, power stations, new airports (and a national airline), commercial and residential building construction, an extensive network of roads and many new schools, hospitals and universities (Jones and Ridout, 2015: chapters 6–7; Limbert, 2010: chapter 1).

The country's total population grew from 2,018,074 in 1993, of which approximately 1,500,000 were Omanis, to 2,773,479 in 2005. Between 1993 and 2014 the proportion of expatriates working in the country increased from 23.90 to 44.00 per cent of the total population. By 2015, the population of Oman had increased to 4,296,830, of which 2,378,936 (55.40%) were Omanis and 1,917,894 (44.60%) were expatriates. The government of Oman has never been in a position from which it could provide the lavish public welfare provisions of countries like the UAE, the KSA, Bahrain and Qatar or provide completely free education at the tertiary level. This has meant that most Omani families have tended to have fewer children than their wealthier Gulf neighbours over the last two decades. Nevertheless, in common with all MENA countries, Oman experienced a baby boom during the 1990s and 2000s and so it has a very young population with a median age of twenty-three in 2015; 70 per cent of the population is under thirty years of age. Approximately one fifth of the national population is younger than fifteen, 47 per cent are aged fifteen to thirty-four, 28 per cent are aged thirty-five to sixty-four and only about 5 per cent of Omanis are more than sixty-five years old (National Centre for Statistical Information, 2016a: 4). These demographic realities, combined with high unemployment levels among young Omanis, internal political unrest between 2011 and 2014 and the growing risk of political radicalisation prompted the establishment of the National Youth Commission (NYC), which was given the task of 'engaging the youth of Oman with the growth and development of the nation' (*Times of Oman*, 2015b). It has been estimated that the total population of Oman, including expatriates, could increase to more than eight million by 2035, when the Omani population may exceed four million and the average age of the Omani population will have risen to forty-five (National Centre for Statistics and Information, 2016a; United Nations Economic and Social Commission for Western Asia, 2015). This forecast, however, is based on the Oman government's projected rates of economic growth over the next twenty years, which most analysts now believe to be unrealistic.

In June 1995, the pivotal Oman 2020 Conference was held in Muscat, which involved the national and regional leaders of Oman, members of the two assemblies of the country's bicameral national parliament, the Oman Chamber of Commerce and Industry, the heads of the country's ministries, a vice president of the World Bank, economic advisors and development experts from several countries and, to make the conference as visible as possible, several journalists from outside the Gulf region. Building on a report commissioned from the World Bank in 1991 (World Bank, 1994) and recognising the country's over-dependence on its two finite hydrocarbon resources, the Vision 2020 document articulated an ambitious national strategic development plan that encompassed economic diversification, the development of the country's human resources and the expansion of the private-sector and the privatisation of some government owned assets and organisations (Strolla and Peri, 2013; Sultanate of Oman, 1995). Implicitly, this report also called for a liberalisation of the country's business regulatory framework to boost inward capital investment and to encourage the growth of Oman's small private sector.

While acknowledging the 'wise leadership of His Majesty Sultan Qaboos bin Said', 'the political stability, social harmony and security of Oman' and 'the strategic geographical location' of the country, this report was candid about the many challenges facing the country and the importance of addressing these. At this time, the government of Oman planned to reduce Oman's reliance on oil and gas; finite resources which were expected, at that time, to run out by the early 2010s (oil) and the 2040s (gas). The Vision 2020 document noted that 'the achievement of sustainable development requires, primarily, the diversification of the production base of the Omani economy. This is in order to reduce our reliance on oil and increase dependence on other production activities. The national income sources will thus diversify from a single non-renewable resource to many renewable resources' (Sultanate of Oman, 1995: 137). In 1995, the Oman government aimed to reduce the country's dependence on oil from 37.2 per cent of GDP to 26.1 per cent in 2000 and to less than 10 per cent by 2020, while increasing the share of gas production to the country's annual GDP from 0.9 per cent in 1995 to 10 per cent by 2020. It also wanted to raise the contribution of the private sector to 'not less than 60 per cent of gross revenues by 2020' and, pretty much from scratch, create a thriving manufacturing sector in Oman (Sultanate of Oman, 1995: 129 and 131).

The government planned to substantially reduce the direct economic role of the government and its involvement in several key sectors of the economy including electricity and water, sewerage, postal services, roads and freeways and telecommunications (Sultanate of Oman, 1995: 131); and expand the private sector to become 'the main source of employment opportunities for the Omani people' by developing new capital-intensive and export-oriented businesses and industries and by creating a thriving entrepreneurial and SME sector supported by a state-controlled Venture Capital Fund (VCF) and other new agencies (Sultanate of Oman, 1995: 139-140). Other initiatives included planned improvements to the management, quality and efficiency of the government sector and state-controlled business entities and other services such as the judiciary, education, health and social security; as well as reforms of the country's business regulatory frameworks to encourage greater foreign investment and facilitate the entry of more overseas businesses (Sultanate of Oman, 1995: 131 and 134).

The Oman government hoped to reduce unemployment levels among Omanis, by first implementing and then expanding the national 'Omanisation' program, lowering the number of Omanis in the public sector and increasing their role in wealth generation in private-sector enterprises, while reducing the country's heavy dependence on expatriate workers (Sultanate of Oman, 1995: 136–137). This was also the first public-policy document that specifically mentioned the need to increase the participation rate of women in the national labour market, 'especially in occupations that suit their capabilities, together with the provision of appropriate support for establishing their economic projects' and 'to promote policies and mechanisms which realise equal opportunities for all individuals in the community'(Sultanate of Oman, 1995: 155). Last, but not least, the government indicated that it wanted to manage this complex transition 'in a way that ensures the maintenance of Omani customs and traditions' and 'in an ecologically sound way'(Sultanate of Oman, 1995: 127).[3]

The government also planned to 'intensify the linkage between the Omani and the global economy', join the World Trade Organisation (WTO) and also strengthen economic relations with other GCC states (Sultanate of Oman, 1995: 141). Oman became a member of the WTO in October 2000 and also signed a free trade agreement with the United States. It had also begun discussions with the International Labour Organisation in the late 1990s to implement its 'Decent Work Program' across Oman's labour market; a lengthy process of reform that is still in progress (International Labour Organisation, 2010; Strolla and Peri, 2013: 19). Concurrent with the publication of Vision 2020 the government also published a quasi-constitutional document, the Oman Basic Statute of the State (OBSS) in 1995 (Sultanate of Oman, 1996) which:

Created new institutions, formalised a number of political conventions, and created a fairly open framework to permit future developments. In this respect it may be seen, historically, as being of a piece with the politics of Oman Vision 2020. The two processes effectively yoked together the extension of political participation (on the basis of *shari'a*) and the liberalisation of the economy, a process that would also depend for its success upon a much higher level of citizen participation ... While new challenges would emerge on the international front in the first decade of the twenty-first century, the question of the relationship between economic participation on the part of Omani citizens would continue to be the most pressing concern for Oman's government and, increasingly, for its citizens too

(Jones and Ridout, 2015: 230–231).

The economic transformation of this country, like those of the other oil-rich Gulf States, has been very rapid, and one of the first Omani women I interviewed in 2015 introduced me to the Arabic word *sa'b al-tasdiq* when describing the speed of this process. Towards the end of this chapter, we assess the extent to which Oman has coped with this 'unbelievable' transformation and how it is currently dealing with the economic, political and social challenges identified by Jones and Ridout and other scholars. In the next section, we evaluate how much progress Oman has made towards achieving the original objectives of Vision 2020 and the ambitious national economic goals that have been set out in the five-year plans that followed this.

4.3 ECONOMIC, POLITICAL AND SOCIAL CHALLENGES FACING OMAN

Addictions are never easy to overcome. Economic ones are no different. Oman's dual-dependence on hydrocarbon revenue and foreign labour has beleaguered development planning in the Sultanate since its first Five Year Development Plan was released in 1976. This over reliance continues to challenge labour market reform and private sector development. Despite being the first Gulf country to develop a long-term development vision (in 1995), Oman continues to circle back to old patterns, demonstrating a preoccupation with short-term goals over long-term planning and survival over sustainability ... the state, constrained by historically acquired dependencies, perpetuates unsustainable economic patterns through its habit of tackling symptoms rather than underlying conditions.

Ennis and al-Jamali (2014: 3 and 4–5)

It is very noticeable that while Oman has undergone a period of rapid infrastructure development over the last four decades, this has not (generally) taken the form of the more garish high-rise developments of Dubai or Riyadh. Omanis are proud of their history and culture which is reflected in both the architectural design of the new buildings in Muscat and in the way they have faithfully restored many old buildings and historical monuments. Muscat is full of well-designed buildings, particularly those which house many of its ministries and the national embassies of other countries and the city's mosques are recognised as being among some of the most elegantly designed examples of these in the Middle East. Although there were a few exceptions, my overall impression of Muscat in 2015 was of a well-designed city with generally good urban infrastructure and a blend of sand-coloured or whitewashed buildings which reflect a respect for Oman's traditions and culture.

Of course, the rapid urban development of Muscat and other cities and towns in Oman over the last three decades was only made possible because of the revenues generated by its oil and gas industries and the rapid growth of the nation's economy since the late 1970s. In 1980 the country's GDP was $6,342 billion. By 1990, this had risen to $11,686 billion and to $19,450 billion by 2000. It reached $30,905 billion in 2005 and, in the immediate aftermath of the global recession, had risen to $58,814 billion in 2010. In December 2014, Oman's GDP was $81,699 billion, which means that it was classified as a 'high-income' economy by the World Bank (Oman Development

Bank, 2015: 9; World Bank, 2016b). Oman's economy was ranked at number 52 globally and at number 7 in the MENA region in 2015 and ranked 47/144 countries in the World Economic Forum's 2015 international competitiveness rankings (World Economic Forum, 2015a: 13). In 2014, Oman had a per-capita GDP of $20,832, a fall from a peak of $22,923 in 2012 – 43.3 per cent of the United States' per capita GDP (Countryeconomy.com, 2016).

Three core objectives of the Oman Vision 2020 strategic plan were self-sufficiency in food production, extensive infrastructure development and the expansion of key industrial and business sectors. Despite the creation of intensive agricultural zones along the Batinah coast and other similar developments, the first objective has not been achieved. The second and third objectives have been partially realised. There have been extensive and ongoing expansions of the country's port facilities, new industrial and manufacturing hubs were established at Salalah, Duqm, Raysut and Sohar during the 1980s, 1990s, 2000s and 2010s, and two extensive oil and gas refineries have been completed at Sur and Duqm. In 2013, the Oman government also announced plans to build the world's largest crude oil storage facility at Duqm (*Gulf Business*, 2013). A planned national rail system, costing $13 billion, will cover 2,244 km of tracks and will eventually connect Oman's three major port cities, the UAE and, possibly, the KSA. New industrial estates have been developed at several locations, including Sur, Nizwa and Buraimi, and the Duqm area has been developed extensively in recent times, with a growing port, a ship repair yard and dry dock and several new industrial zones (The Public Establishment for Industrial Estates, 2015a and 2015b). Notable growth areas of the economy during the 2000s and 2010s include agriculture, copper, fibre-optics, steel, chemicals, textiles, general manufacturing, re-exported goods and livestock. The country's mining sector may also grow, and several recent new finds of zinc, limestone, gypsum and silicon have raised hopes that this sector could make a significant contribution to the country's GDP in the future. New trade agreements with several emerging south-east Asian

countries agreed during 2015–2016 should also increase export opportunities for Omani companies (Oxford Business Group, 2015b: 7;
Strolla and Peri, 2013: 18).

In a part of the world that has very little rain or cloud cover,
there is also great potential for the development of a substantial solar
industry in Oman. Approximately $2.5 billion has already been ear-
marked for new solar projects in the country, and it has been estimated that solar generation and the manufacture of solar panels and
ancillary equipment such as batteries could contribute $12 billion to
Oman's annual GDP by 2023 (Bioenergy Consult, 2015; *Times of
Oman*, 2015a). With significant new investments in hotels and overseas marketing, tourism is expected to grow from 2.4 per cent of GDP
to 3.0 per cent by 2020 (Strolla and Peri, 2013: 20) or, possibly, '6.0 per
cent' according to another source (*Gulf Business*, 2013). A large new
resort area was opened in Bandar Jissah in 2005, and the Wave Sea-
front residential development there allowed expatriates the opportunity to buy properties in Oman for the first time. Another very
ambitious project, Blue City – a massive residential and commercial
coastal development – was put on hold in the aftermath of the real
estate slump of the late 2000s (Hall and Fattah, 2010). The 2015
budget also committed new funds for further tourism and hotel projects and the construction of the Oman Convention and Exhibition
Centre in Muscat (Oman Development Bank, 2015).

In its comprehensive review of Oman's economic performance
to the end of 2014, the Oxford Business Group concluded that the
non-oil sector of the Oman economy had achieved 'strong and consistent growth'. However, this continued to be 'largely driven by
hydrocarbons' with 47 per cent of the country's GDP being derived
from the oil and gas sector, 35 per cent from services, 17 per cent from
industrial and manufacturing activities and 2 per cent from agriculture. Between 2000 and 2012, Oman's non-oil/gas sectors grew by an
average of 10 per cent a year, albeit from a very low base, but this had
slowed to 7.6 per cent by 2013. This report also noted that much of
this growth was generated by strong demand for oil and gas and high

global prices for both commodities between 2010 and 2014 (Oxford Business Group, 2015b). However, as noted in Chapter 2, the price of crude oil fell from about $110 a barrel in mid-2014 to $36 at the end of 2015 and fluctuated between $25 and $53 a barrel during 2016. For gas, the price dropped from about US$5.00 per normal cubic metre (NCM) to $2.20 during the same period (Nasdaq, 2016). Because Oman's production break-even price for oil is $105 a barrel, this had a severe effect on Oman's GDP during 2015–2016. And, if the price for these commodities does not increase appreciably, this will also have a significant impact on Oman's national revenues and economic growth during 2016 and beyond (United States Energy Information Agency, 2015b: 1).

The Eighth Five Year Plan (2011–2015) indicated that public expenditure would be OMR 42.71 billion ($111.046 billion) during this period, at an average of OMR 8.54 billion a year, with OMR 8.1 billion to be spent on infrastructure projects, primarily on airports, seaports, roads and the further development of new and existing industrial zones. While 75 per cent of total government revenues would be derived from oil and gas during this period, the government expected to see 'a growth rate of 10 per cent in non-oil economic activities' during 2011–2015 and the creation of 200,000–275,000 new jobs for Omanis (177,000 new jobs had been created during 2006–2010); 22.6 per cent of government expenditure was to be allocated to defence and national security and 54.2 per cent to civil ministries and 'development expenditure' for civil ministries. Thirty-five per cent of the remaining civil budget was allocated to health, 34 per cent to education and 1 per cent to vocational training. There was no indication in this plan of financial resources that were to be allocated to the development of the country's private, entrepreneurial or SME sectors (Mathew, et al, 2011: 3–5, 8, 11 and 13).

It is notable that this plan also repeated many of the objectives specified in the seven previous national economic plans. The Fifth Five Year Plan 2001–2005, for example, had indicated that a particular emphasis would be placed 'on increasing national participation in both the public and private sectors to replace expatriate labour' (Mathew, et al, 2011: 3). It had also identified the importance of diversifying the economy as oil and gas reserves declined, creating more job opportunities for Omanis in the private sector, improving its human resource capabilities, further infrastructure development, the economic development of the country's poorer inner regions, the development of new industrial zones, encouraging the growth of 'an efficient and competitive private sector', further investments in primary, secondary and tertiary education and liberalisation of the country's fiduciary regulations to encourage more foreign investment (Mathew, et al, 2011: 3). Many of these were repeated in the Eighth Five Year Plan 2011–2015:

> Oman is striving to create job opportunities for its nationals in various economic sectors. The Sultanate is striving to best use its human resources, seeking to secure job opportunities, increase economic growth and maintain equilibrium between supply and demand in the labour market. Human resource development is high on the Government's agenda, where employment of nationals is a national objective, as made explicit in the Omanisation policy. Broadening of the labour market, increasing national labour force participation, and expanding and enhancing the role of the private sector to create more jobs for Omanis, continue to be at the top of the government's priorities
>
> (International Labour Organisation, 2010: 2–3).

However, the Oxford Business Group has demonstrated that the progress Oman has made towards its original Vision 2020 goals has been slow. For example, it had been envisaged in 1995 that less than 10 per cent of the country's GDP should be dependent on oil and gas proceeds by 2020. However, in 2011 more than 50 per cent of government revenues were still derived from these and this had only fallen to 44 per cent by early 2016. It had also been envisaged that the country's industrial and manufacturing sectors would contribute 29 per cent of GDP by 2020 and services 47 per cent. The planned figure for agriculture was 5 per cent of non-oil/gas GDP by 2020 but, as noted, this had reached just 2 per cent by 2016 (Oxford Business Group, 2015b: 1; Trading Economics, 2016). While increased gas production will make up for some of this shortfall, it is difficult to see how non-oil and gas revenues can close these gaps within such a short period of time. In 2012, Sultan Qaboos had warned that the government's generous social subsidies and public-sector job creation schemes were not sustainable in the medium to long term, a statement that was serendipitous coming before the steep drop in global oil prices during 2014–2016. This led to a flurry of public announcements about selling off non-essential government assets to the private sector, encouraging greater entrepreneurship among Emiratis and providing more logistical and financial support for new businesses (Al Monitor, 2014). What effect all of this has had on the level of new business start-ups is difficult to discern at this moment in time, but we will return to look at this issue in Chapter 5 and at the experiences of ten female SME owners in Muscat.

One of the other major long-term goals of the Vision 2020 document was to build a larger economy, while at the same time reduce Oman's over-dependence on expatriate workers and also increase employment opportunities for its rapidly growing population. An outcome of its Second Five-Year Plan (1981–1985) was the country's first 'Omanisation' program, introduced in 1988. This comprised a series of policies, which have been supplemented and refined several times since, to promote employment among Omani nationals through quota systems and by enhancing their education and training. In 1995, for example, the Vision 2020 document had stipulated that by 2020, 95 per cent of employees in the public sector and 75 per cent of employees in the private sector would be Omanis. It also specified that certain employment categories were to be reserved for Omanis including accountants' clerks, civil engineers, nurses, primary school teachers and other occupational groups. The government also set fixed targets for the employment of Omanis in six sectors of the country's private sector and, to cite one example, by

1999 nearly 80 per cent of all positions in the banking sector were occupied by nationals and 30 per cent of those were held by women. By 1999, the number of Omani employees working in the country's well-funded and fast-growing public sector had exceeded 70 per cent and in some departments exceeded 90 per cent. By 2005, more than 80 per cent of the employees in the public sector were Omanis, but they only made up 15 per cent of the private-sector workforce. In the Seventh Five-Year Plan (2006–2010), the government had stipulated that transport, storage and telecommunication companies were to have a minimum of 60 per cent national employees; finance, insurance and real estate, 45 per cent; hotels and restaurants, 30 per cent; wholesale and retail trading, 20 per cent; and contracting companies, 15 per cent (Ennis and al-Jamali, 2014; Strolla and Peri, 2013: 4).

By 2011, just 12 per cent of the 1.4 million employees working in the private sector were Omanis, and nearly 157,000 new jobs created that year were filled by expatriates, an increase of 14 per cent from 2010. In response to internal political unrest during the Arab Spring, 45,000–50,000 new public-sector jobs were created by the government in 2011 (*Gulf Business*, 2013; Ennis and al-Jamali, 2014: 12), prompting several thousand Omanis to resign from private-sector positions and join the public sector. The Omanisation level fell from 16 to 12 per cent between 2011 and 2013, while the number of expatriates working in the private sector increased to fill these new vacancies (Bertelsmann Stiftung, 2014b: 24; Ennis and Al Jamali, 2014: 5 and 13). This structural imbalance is one that has long been recognised by observers of Oman:

> It illuminates the presence of a disjointed two-tiered labour market in which nationals and non-nationals have disparate wage expectations and compete for different categories of jobs ... The Omani labour force remains unbalanced, primarily in the public sector, where supply outstrips demand because Omanis tend to resort to public service with the perception that it provides better incentives such as high earnings, better working conditions and

pensions benefits at the end of service ... The inability of the public sector to absorb the Oman labour supply has led to a real problem of unemployment

(Ennis and al-Jamali, 2014: 5 and 3).

And yet, not only does the national labour market remain 'disjointed', 'two-tiered' and 'unbalanced', it also consumes a significant proportion of the country's revenues, with the country's public-sector wage bill soaking up an astonishing $50 of every barrel of oil produced in Oman (Rajab and al-Mahrizi, 2013). As Jones and Ridout have discerned:

> The problem appears to be both supply and demand
> simultaneously. There are not enough Omanis with the right
> education for the kind of work that the economy might demand
> from them, while at the same time there is a shortage of
> employment opportunities for the expanding number of Omani
> students seeking work. The results of this mismatch can be seen
> in the protests of 2011, which clearly demonstrated the existence
> of aspirations frustrated and in the government response, which
> was to create more public sector jobs (which are, of course,
> unlikely to be wealth-producing). Thus, the initial response
> appears to only compound the problem it seeks to solve
>
> *(Jones and Ridout, 2015: 264).*

Omanis, like Emiratis and Saudis, still have a marked preference for employment in the public sector and for very similar reasons. Despite numerous government initiatives during the 2000s and 2010s and several public appeals by Sultan Qaboos, only about one third of Omanis work in the private-sector workforce, and their distribution within this is heavily skewed towards three sectors: finance, oil and gas utilities and minerals. Just 10 per cent of the biggest Omani-owned businesses were responsible for hiring nearly 80 per cent of all nationals employed in the private sector, because the largest companies still contribute the most to employment in the non-government sector of the national economy and they are also the least likely to employ expatriates because of Omanisation requirements. Moreover, a disproportionate number of Omanis continue to be employed in protected low-paying clerical jobs which make only a minimal contribution to the national economy. In addition, the unemployment rate amongst Omanis remained stubbornly high during the first part of this decade at 15 per cent, with 100,000 registered job seekers in 2014 and almost one third of those aged fifteen to twenty-four were unemployed at this time (Ennis and al-Jamali, 2014: 8 and 10).

While the government would clearly like more Omanis to work in the private sector, there are few indications that they are willing to do this. A survey of 300 sixteen- to twenty-nine-year-old Omanis in 2015 revealed that 70 per cent of this group would prefer to work in the public sector or a government or municipal organisation, and 52 per cent of those working in the private sector said they would prefer to have a public-sector job. This choice was followed by banking and finance (32%), oil and gas (21%), aviation (17%), real estate (12%) and computers/IT (11%). However, when asked what their ideal role in the future would be, 34 per cent indicated 'running my own business' (39% of men and 27% of women), while 18 per cent of the young women in this sample indicated that their ideal job was human resource management. Another surprising result of this survey was that only 44 per cent of this group considered the country's private sector to be 'very' or 'extremely' important for the employment of Omani nationals, suggesting that government appeals to younger citizens to participate in the growth of the country's underdeveloped private sector are not being heeded (Benchiba-Savenius et al, 2016: 10, 13–14 and 19).

Political and Social Challenges

Not only does Oman have rapidly declining oil reserves, major structural imbalances in its national economy and labour market, a continuing over-reliance on expatriate workers, a lack of engagement by its nationals in the private sector and high unemployment rates among younger Omanis, it also has some very challenging political waters to navigate through during the late 2010s and early 2020s. Oman is a hereditary monarchy, and Sultan Qaboos is both the supreme ruler of the country and its head of state. In December 1996, the Council of Oman was created and a bicameral legislature established. This consisted of the State Council (*Majlis al-Dawla*) with members nominated by the Sultan, and a few prominent Omani women have been appointed to this body by Sultan Qaboos since its creation. In 1997, a royal decree (No. 86/97) was issued that established an upper chamber – the Consultative Council (*Majlis al-Shura*) – and members of this body have been elected by universal suffrage since 2003 for four-year terms. In the most recent national elections in October 2015, 570 men and 20 women stood for election and one woman, Nemah bint Jamiel bin Farhan al-Busaidiya, was elected to this body (Trabelsi, 2015). The country's national cabinet, the Council of Ministers (*Majlis al-Wuzara*), is not an elected body and membership of this is entirely dependent on the Sultan's patronage. While Sultan Qaboos has generally sought to accommodate the country's diverse tribal, regional and ethnic interests by ensuring a balance of these groups among his senior ministers and advisers, all meaningful political power in Oman resides with him and his inner circle of senior ministers and advisers in Muscat.

The powers of both houses of the national assembly are limited to offering advice on economic, cultural and social issues, investment decisions and administrative reforms. They have no oversight of national military, security or financial matters, no legislative powers and their members may only comment on and suggest amendments to legislation proposed by the Sultan's Council of Ministers. In 2011, municipal councils were established in the eleven administrative regions of Oman whose members are also elected by universal suffrage for four-year terms (Bertelsmann Stiftung, 2015b: 5–6 and 11). While Article 33 of the OBSS permits 'the freedom to form associations on national bases, for lawful causes and with peaceful means in compliance with the Basic Statute' (Sultanate of Oman, 1996: 11), the right of assembly and opportunities to establish independent political or civic associations are severely restricted. In common with the UAE and the KSA, this means that there is no (official) political opposition, alternative political parties are banned, all planned public gatherings, ceremonies, forums and conferences require prior approval, and joining any overseas NGO or association also requires official permission. In 2015, the Economist rated Oman as being the twenty-fifth-most-authoritarian country in the world, 142/167countries, and Freedom House gave the country its second-lowest freedom rating (6/7; where 1 is the highest freedom rating) in 2016 (Freedom House, 2016; *The Economist* Intelligence Unit, 2015b: 8).

The combination of political stability, plentiful oil and gas revenues, rising standards of living and ample job opportunities meant that the lack of executive power among their elected representatives would not have concerned most Omanis during the 1990s and 2000s. However, there are now growing worries about what will happen to Oman after Sultan Qaboos dies and the direction the country will take when this transpires. He was absent for much of 2014 and early 2015 for cancer treatment in Germany, and speculation about his declining health continued during 2016 when he returned to Germany for further cancer therapy (Al Monitor, 2015, 2014; *The Economist*, 2016i: 43). Hence, it is likely that a new monarch and head of state will have to be found soon, but he has no male heirs.[4] This uncertainty is adding to the worries that many Omanis now have about the long-term future of their country in the absence of the all-pervasive presence of the only national leader that most of its young population has ever known. Some Omanis told me that Sultan Qaboos has two preferred successors, whose names are contained in secure documents that he has already signed, while others suggested that his position may pass to one of the three sons of his chief advisor, HH Sayyid Assad bin Tariq al Said, whose official title is Representative of his Majesty. How this process is handled and who is eventually picked as his successor will matter a great deal, because this person will not have the popular support or legitimacy of Sultan Qaboos. He (it cannot be a she) will have to tread a very fine line between honouring Oman's military alliances and preserving its relatively stable relationship with Iran while maintaining a high level of expenditure on its armed services. He will have to deal with growing internal pressures for further political reform and greater participation in decision making by Omanis, and also continue the very complex process of developing the national economy as its brief window of oil and gas-generated wealth closes.

There have also been numerous internal protests over the last ten years, many instances of the arbitrary arrest and imprisonment of protesters, allegations of beatings and torture and even some deaths. Throughout the first half of 2011, during the Arab Spring, there were widespread and sometimes violent protests across the country with Omanis demanding further economic, political and social reforms (including the creation of a constitutional monarchy), an end to corruption among senior government officials and wage increases in some public-sector occupations. Some of these protests involved Omani women. These were soon followed by employee strikes at Omantel, PDO, WJ Towell, Oman Air and at several hotels in Oman. In 2014, the government spent $60 million on buying anti-riot vehicles and equipment from South Korean firms and also initiated a massive recruitment drive for its police and security services after the internal protests of 2011–2013. There have also been several demonstrations against Oman's friendly diplomatic and economic relationships with the United States during the 2000s and 2010s. However, although small-scale pro-reform protests continued throughout 2014, none of the protesters and strikers appeared to be calling for the overthrow of the Oman government or questioned the legitimacy of Sultan Qaboos' rule, and these protests did eventually lead to several senior government officials and ministers being imprisoned or fined for bribery and corruption (Human Rights Watch, 2014; Jones and Ridout, 2015: 257–258). Nevertheless, as Jones and Ridout have cautioned:

Many of the grievances expressed [at that time] had been expressed before, in muted and sporadic ways, for some time. The emergence in Oman of social media and, in particular, blogs and discussion forums such as the *Sablah* had allowed for a level of public conversation about social and political problems not previously available in print and broadcast media ... Among the participants in such forums were relatively young and well-educated adults and students, some of whom expressed frustration at the lack of personal freedoms and a sense of political stasis ... it is clear enough that the formal conditions are in place for the development of a much more representative political system. It is much less clear, however, to what extent the underlying social and economic situation makes such development possible or likely

(Jones and Ridout, 2015: 252–253).

As these scholars have also suggested:

The economic situation today – and this situation will become more acute in future years – is such that governments whose members are also involved in a competitive and representative political system will find it just as difficult (in not more so) to resist the temptation to address economic demands from their constituents by falling back on the familiar tactics of subsidies and welfare provision

(Jones and Ridout, 2015: 261).

In other words, if Oman is to have a secure future it cannot rely on the short-term and generally *ad hoc* economic and social strategies that have been implemented by the national government up to this point in time. Most analysts have concluded that there must be further significant economic, political and social reforms, and these will have to include a transformation of the roles that Omani women currently play in the national economy– in all sectors and at all levels.

4.4 THE CHANGING STATUS AND ROLES OF OMANI WOMEN

Many years ago, I said that if the energy, capability and enthusiasm of women were excluded from a country's active life, then that country

would be depriving itself of 50 per cent of its genius. I have taken very
good care that this should not happen to Oman, and I look forward to
the further progress of women in my country with the greatest pleasure
and confidence.

Sultan Qaboos, ruler of Oman, 2006

Today, like their peers in the UAE, some Omani women have greater opportunities and more wealth, independence and life options than their mothers and grandmothers did. Until the 1970s, there were few educational opportunities beyond a basic primary school education for most young female Omanis, and very few had access to higher education at that time. However, the political elite of Oman has known since the 1970s that if the country was to grow and diversify its economy it had to allow women full access to primary, secondary and tertiary education and also increase their participation in the country's labour market. Consequently, education became a key national priority in Oman during the 1980s and 1990s, as it was in the UAE at that time. Between 1970 (when a universal education policy for boys and girls was introduced) and 2011, 1,400 new primary and secondary schools were built in Oman. With the establishment of Sultan Qaboos University in 1982 and twenty-seven other government and private-sector universities and colleges, many more young Omani women now receive a tertiary education (al-Barwani: 2011:225).

Female enrolment in the tertiary sector increased from zero in 1970 to 49 per cent in 2007. In 2014, women made up 58 per cent of total enrolments at public and private universities and foreign universities and at technical, health and scientific colleges and nearly 70 per cent of the students enrolled at private universities and colleges. In 2014, out of a total of 29,258 students at these institutions, 16,958 were women and 12,300 were men, and about 10 per cent of Omani females were studying at overseas universities. In common with the UAE and many other countries, Omani females are also outperforming males at the secondary and tertiary levels and tend to have lower dropout rates from university degree courses (Bertelsmann Stiftung, 2015b: 21; Goveas and Aslam, 2011: 233–234).

During the 1990s, as Omanisation policies took effect across the national labour market, women began to fill more of the positions that had been filled largely by expatriate men, particularly in the public sector, which 'had a particularly positive effect on poor, less educated women, who were increasingly able to obtain jobs as cleaners, hospital orderlies, and kitchen help, allowing them to support themselves in the face of hardship and giving them a new role in the community' (Talei, 2010: 347). By 2003, women made up 17.2 per cent of the national labour force, by 2010 24.7 per cent and nearly 30 per cent by early 2016, and they now work in most professions and occupations – particularly in the large and well-funded Oman public sector. However, just 50,817 were working in the private sector in March 2016 compared to 158,719 men (National Centre for Statistical Information, 2016a: 16). Before the collapse in oil and gas prices during 2014–2016, the participation of women in the national workforce had been expected to continue to grow throughout the 2010s and early 2020s as more women completed tertiary education and delayed marriage until later in life (Talei, 2010: 357).

The Omani Women's Association (OWA) was the first official women's group recognised by the Oman government in 1971 and control of this was transferred to the male-led Ministry of Social Affairs in 1984 when a new body, the Directorate General for Women's and Children's Affairs, was established. At first, this organisation was primarily concerned with the health and welfare of women living in urban and rural areas and improving literacy and family care programs but, more recently, has turned its focus to supporting the advancement of women in the national labour market and offering training courses for women entrepreneurs (Goveas and Aslam, 2011: 233; Omani Women's Association, 2016 and 2014). A separate organisation, the Rural Women's Development Centre, operates under the supervision of the OWA. There is also a National Strategy for the Advancement of Women which has four principal goals:

To promote the full participation and involvement of women in the economic and social development process.

To design strategies and policies to enhance the situation of women in all spheres of national development.

To expand the representation of women in decision-making positions and enable them to effectively participate in national decision-making and planning.

To review legislation to ensure equal rights between men and women with the goal of eliminating all forms of discrimination against women (United Nations, 2011: 4).

In principle, equal rights between all citizens of Oman are enshrined in the OBSS. Article 12 guarantees 'justice, equality and equal opportunities for Omanis', Article 17 prohibits discrimination on the basis of 'gender, origin, colour, language, religion, sect, domicile, or social status', and sexual harassment in the workplace is a criminal offence (Sultanate of Oman, 1996: 6 and 8). These stipulations, however, only apply to Omani citizens. They do not cover the country's large population of female expatriate workers. In addition, the OBSS contains no commitment to promoting equality of opportunity for Omani women in the national labour market. Moreover, existing national labour laws do not specify that men and women should receive 'equal pay for equal work' and the Oman government has not yet ratified the Equal Remuneration Convention of the International Labour Organisation. To the best of my knowledge, no independent studies have been conducted in Oman to evaluate if wage equality between men and women is practiced or, if it isn't, what might be done to remove salary differentials in the workplace and the United Nations has been unable to provide any statistical data on wage inequalities between men and women in Oman in any of its recent human development reports (United Nations, 2015a: 216). In addition, there are no national laws or policies that explicitly outlaw gender-based discrimination either at work or in the domestic sphere. In 2016, women were still prohibited from working from 7.00 p.m. to 8.00 a.m. unless they obtain approval from the Ministry of Labour, which may inhibit their ability to work in occupations where shift or night work may be required (in some IT jobs or in hospitals, for example).

The lack of systemic legal protection for women, in both the occupational and domestic spheres, is reflected in Oman's recent rankings in the WEF's Global GGG reports. In 2011, Oman was ranked 127 out of 135 countries, in 2013, 122/136 and in 2015 its ranking had fallen to 135/145. Oman's ranking for 'economic participation and opportunity' for women was 130/135 in 2011, 123/136 in 2013 and this had fallen to 134/145 countries in 2015. In 2015, it was the fourth-ranked country in the Gulf region for female equality. To repeat a comment made in Chapter 2, the nineteen countries of the MENA region had the worst cumulative global score for female inequality in 2011, 2013 and 2015, and not one has ever been ranked in the top 100 countries for female equality. As noted in Chapter 3, the five top-ranked countries for women's equality in 2011were Iceland, Norway, Finland, Sweden and Ireland; in 2013, Iceland, Finland, Norway, Sweden and the Philippines and in 2015, Iceland, Norway, Finland, Sweden and Ireland (World Economic Forum 2015b: 8, 9 and 10; 2013: 12, 13 and 18; 2011: 9, 10 and 15).

The first reason that Oman has this low ranking is that while it has been a signatory to the CEDAW since 2006 and is also a member of the United Nations Convention on Women's Rights, the national government signed this convention with several major reservations in relation to Article 2(f): 'the obligation to eliminate or abolish discriminatory laws, regulations, customs and practices', Article 9: 'the right to nationality', Article 15(2): 'legal capacity', Article 15(4): 'freedom of movement and choice of domicile', Article 16: 'on equal rights in marriage and family relations', Article 29: 'arbitration of conflicts arising from the convention' and other provisions that the government of Oman considers to be in violation of *shari'a* laws (United Nations, 2011). To date, the national government has not taken any steps to remove these from its legal statutes, and, as a result, progress in implementing the Convention has been patchy and slow. In its detailed review of Oman's compliance with this, CEDAW noted that 'the Convention has not been directly invoked in national courts and there is a lack of awareness about the Convention and its provisions amongst the judiciary', and 'in national legislation, there is no explicit prohibition of *de jure* and *de facto* discrimination against women in all areas of life as required by article 2 of the Convention'. The CEDAW committee also documented the absence of 'any comprehensive and effective complaints mechanism, accessible especially to women, including women migrant workers' (United Nations, 2011: 2–3).

While acknowledging the importance of the General Directorate for Women, CEDAW expressed reservations about its 'inadequate' financial and human resources and the lack of integration between its activities and public- and private-sector organisations in Oman. The CEDAW committee also noted the very low representation of women in the *Majlis al-Shura* and the *Majlis al-Dawla* and in the government, the judiciary and diplomatic corps (United Nations, 2011: 4 and 6). However, perhaps the most significant comment made by CEDAW in this report was as follows:

> The committee notes with concern the very low participation rate of women in the labour force, as well as the fact that women's labour force participation is concentrated in younger age groups and declines with age, indicating a tendency for women to become exclusively responsible for care [domestic] work as they get married. Also, the Committee is concerned that working women are concentrated in education and health sectors, which indicates a clear gender-based segregation of the labour-force
>
> *(United Nations, 2011: 8).*

Hence, the second reason for the low gender-equality ranking of Oman arises from the participation rate of women in the national labour market. According to the United Nations Children's Fund (UNICEF), 'the labour force participation rate among women aged 15 and above is only 25 per cent [in 2013] while the corresponding figure for men is 77 per cent ... The labour force participation rate of young men is more than twice as high as that of young women, 49 per cent – 23 per cent respectively, despite the fact that boys and girls net enrolment rates in secondary education are about the same and literacy rates are high' (United Nations Children's Fund, 2014: 4). In December 2015, 29.0 per cent of Omani women were working full-time compared to 82.6 per cent of men. This is still low when compared to women in the UAE (46.5 per cent) and very low when compared to the labour-force participation rates of women in the world's leading industrial economies, which is now – on average – 70 per cent among members of the OECD (United Nations, 2015a: 224).

The third reason for Oman's low GGG report ranking stems from the heavy concentration of Omani women in public-sector employment. In 2010, for example, nearly 40 per cent of employees in the Oman public sector were women but they constituted only 17.10 per cent of the private-sector workforce (Talei, 2010: 349), a figure that had changed little by 2014 or 2016 (National Centre for Statistical Information, 2016a, 2016b: 16; *The Week Oman*, 2014a). Young Omani women have a marked preference for employment in the public sector, 'which combined with social stigmas related to certain occupations and sectors deemed inappropriate for female labour, results in a private sector that is often an unwelcoming place for female employees' (Ennis and al-Jamali, 2014: 8). In addition, data from Ministry of National Economy in 2010 indicated that only 2 per cent of women in Oman were classified as 'self-employed' and they constituted less than 1 per cent of Omani employers (International Labour Organisation, 2010: 5). We will see in the next chapter that these very low figures changed little between 2010 and 2016.

Another indicator of continuing gender inequality in the Oman labour market is the very small number of Omani women who have held senior and ministerial positions in the public sector and in the country's political system. In 2016, there were some notable examples of women who had risen to senior ranks such as Hunaina al-Mughairy, Ambassador of the Sultanate of Oman to the United

States; Asila al-Harthi, the first female member of the Oman Chamber of Commerce and Industry and the first female executive at the Oman Oil Company; Dr. Rawiyah bint Saud al-Busaidiyah, the Minister of Higher Education; Dr. Rajiha bint Abdulamir bint Ali, the Minister of Tourism; Dr. Shariffa bint Khalfan al-Yahya, the Minister of Social Development; Saada bint Salim bin Mohammed al-Ismail, Director of the Women's Sport Department, Ministry of Sports Affairs; and HH Dr. Mona bint Fahad al-Said, the Assistant VC of Sultan Qaboos University, but their numbers were still small in 2016.

While there has been steady growth in the number of Omani women holding senior and executive positions in the public sector (774 in 2015 versus 510 in 2008), they are still underrepresented in executive positions in the private sector, and only a handful sit on the boards of directors of publicly listed companies in Oman (*The Week Oman*, 2015a). In the 2015 CEO Middle-East annual ranking of 'The world's 100 most powerful Arab women', not one Omani woman was included, in stark contrast to the examples of women from the UAE, the KSA and other MENA countries who were on this list (CEO Middle-East, 2015). They continue to be underrepresented in many private-sector companies, and few are choosing to become entrepreneurs and SME owners or work in STEM professions. Last but not least, and this is something that differentiates Oman from the UAE, there is some anecdotal evidence that women who are the descendants of servant tribes and slave groups in Oman (who, while Muslims, are not considered to be of 'Arab blood') still face discrimination in the national labour market (Reality in Oman, 2010). While I was unable to find any reliable independent verification of these claims, it should be remembered that slavery was not formally abolished in Oman or neighbouring Yemen until 1970.

The fourth reason the WEF's GGG reports have consistently awarded Oman a very low international ranking for gender equality is the lack of data on the distribution of women in the public and private sectors of the Oman economy and sufficient information about how many may have reached leadership and executive positions in organisations. While the Oman government and the women's organ-isations mentioned earlier may sincerely claim that women enjoy equality of opportunity in the workplace and pay equity with men, there was (writing in June 2016) still no publicly available independ-ent research that could validate these claims. In the absence of such verification, the World Economic Forum judges that the progress that Oman – like the UAE and the KSA – is making towards gender equality across all sectors and at all levels of its national labour market is, at best, limited. Another issue highlighted by CEDAW is the absence of fully independent women's associations or human rights organisations in Oman. One example of this was when a group of women attempted to organise an independent business forum for Oman women in 2004. They tried to obtain approval to register this as an NGO, as they were legally required to do, but their application was denied and all further meetings were prohibited. Although the first Women in Business Conference was approved in 2008 and was a great success (Women in Business Conference, 2008), Omani women are still not allowed to create independent organisations to represent their collective interests. Furthermore, no international women's rights organisations are allowed to operate in Oman. Consequently:

> Such restrictions impede the ability of women to organise
> independently and lobby effectively for the expansion of their
> rights. The OWA, which is closely supervised by the Ministry of
> Social Development, does not address sensitive issues such as
> civil and political rights or women's autonomy and security ...
> The OWA, and the local organisations it controls, do not have
> the authority to address more sensitive issues regarding women's
> rights and lack the proper training and knowledge necessary
> to do so
>
> (United Nations, 2011: 16 and 19).

And, while Omani men have been allowed to establish labour and workers' unions since 2006 and also have the legal right to complain about working conditions and even organise strikes, no unions specifically address women's issues in Oman today. Hence, while traditional attitudes towards women are slowly changing:

> Oman's patriarchal culture, in combination with conservative religious norms, continues to have a profound impact on women. Despite progress, women face discrimination in almost all areas of life, and men are traditionally and legally seen as heads of the household. Women remain underrepresented in the judiciary and government structures, and do not have full freedom to make decisions about their health and reproductive rights. Moreover, they are afforded unequal rights under the personal status law which governs inheritance, marriage divorce, and child custody
>
> *(United Nations, 2011: 2).*

All of these considerations have prevented Oman from being placed higher in the WEF's annual gender-equality rankings, and the CEDAW report demonstrated that there was still much work to be done in order to enhance the legal rights of women and increase their participation in Oman's economy and political system. While the government and some business leaders have tried to encourage a more liberal interpretation of the country's labour laws and have improved women's legal rights to some extent, these efforts have only been partially successful in changing traditional attitudes towards women in decision-making and leadership roles. Oman is still, like the UAE and the KSA, a very 'masculine' culture and – notwithstanding the undeniable progress made by women in higher education and the national labour market over the last twenty years – remains, in many respects, 'progress-resistant' in terms of gender equality (Harrison, 2006: 36–37; Harrison and Huntington, 2000). But, as we will see in Chapter 5, most of the working Omani women who were interviewed for this book did not agree with these very negative assessments of the status of women in their country and it may well be that the WEF's ranking of Oman (like the UAE's) is a harsh one. Nevertheless, it cannot be denied that significant gender inequities persist in Oman because it remains a conservative Islamic society, with all the implicit beliefs that follow from this about the public and private roles of Omani women and their responsibilities to their community, their extended families, their husbands and their children.

4.5 THE CULTURAL, ATTITUDINAL AND STRUCTURAL BARRIERS FACING WOMEN IN OMAN

It has been estimated that approximately 75 per cent of Omanis are members of the Sunni Ibadi branch of Islam although other estimates have put this as low as 40–45 per cent, with the remainder being predominantly Sunnis (Katz, 2004: 5). This originated during the eighth century CE, when the first attempt was made to establish an imamate in the lands that now constitute Oman based on Ibadi religious, political and legal principles. The most notable of these principles were 'the equality of all Muslims and the opposition to tyrannical power, both of which were to be sustained through the leader of the Muslim community being chosen through a process of *shura*. The specific Ibadi emphasis on *shura* ... is one of the principle ways in which Ibadis are conventionally distinguished from Sunnis and Shias' (Jones and Ridout, 2015: 9). While a few Ibadis can be found in other MENA countries, such as Libya and Tunisia, Oman is home to the largest number of adherents to this branch of Sunni Islam in the world. As Jones and Ridout have noted:

> The consolidation of Al bu Said rule has depended substantially on the dynasty's capacity to conduct the business of government with appropriate regard for Ibadi principles and sensibilities. The government risks opposition when its policies can be portrayed as out of touch with principles to which Imamate leaders, or others seeking to reaffirm the centrality of Ibadism, might lay claim ... The Omani government has been largely successful in drawing on Ibadi cultural values while avoiding any major Islamist mobilisation based on them. In this respect, modern Oman seems to have found a much more comfortable accommodation

between religious practice and institutions, on the one hand, and the modern largely secular institutions of government, on the other, than have many states in the region

(Jones and Ridout, 2015: 10–11).

Consequently, like the UAE, the rulers of Oman have been fairly pragmatic in their interpretation and practice of their faith and also tolerant of other forms of Islamic worship and the varied religious beliefs and practices of their large expatriate populations (although proselytising is strictly forbidden). This may be because Ibadis are more likely to agree that individual reason and intellect have a role to play in interpreting discrepancies and contradictions in Islamic texts (Limbert, 2010: 84), something that all doctrinaire Wahhabists in the KSA would not accept. Nevertheless, Oman is an orthodox Islamic country that obeys *shari'a* laws and its legal system is entirely subordinate to the doctrinaire Ministry of Justice and, ultimately, to Sultan Qaboos. These realities are reflected in the legal rights of women in Oman. Despite changes to some national laws in 2008 and educated women advocating for greater awareness of legal rights, female Omanis still face discrimination in the legal system and, as we have seen, certain provisions of the country's laws continue to subject women to gender-based discrimination in the workplace and in the domestic sphere.[5] In part, this is a consequence of the very small number of women who have qualified to practice as lawyers in Oman. In 2010, for example, only 5 women served as general prosecutors, just 2 (of 117) lawyers who can present cases to the Oman High Court were women and there were no female judges at this time (Talei, 2010: 341). I did hear, anecdotally, that more Omani women have qualified as lawyers in recent years but could find no independent confirmation of this.

Oman's Personal Status Law (PSL) assigns differential rights and responsibilities to women and men. Men, for example, are assigned 'financial responsibility for the family', while women have no such obligation, and the PSL also tends to favour men in marriage, divorce, child-custody and inheritance disputes (Talei, 2010: 343). While women can conduct their own business affairs and enter into business contracts, the freedom to do so is always constrained by family pressures and it is still very difficult for most Omani women to ignore the wishes of their male guardians. Marriage is still a defining moment in the lives of most Omani women and men and although the legal right to choose marriage partners was extended to both males and females in 1971, fathers are still responsible for vetting potential marriage partners and giving their final blessing to the betrothal. As in the UAE and the KSA, Omani women are forbidden by law from marrying non-Muslim men while men are free to marry non-Omani women, although very few ever do this. Women also have to obtain official permission to marry non-Omani Muslims. While women are legally entitled to choose what subjects they might study at university and have some freedom over their career choices, these decisions cannot be made without prior discussion and approval from their male guardians. Hence, most Omani women will face personal problems and familial disapproval if they decide to ignore the wishes of their fathers and husbands. Notwithstanding the constitutional assurances in the OBSS cited earlier in this section, Omani women still face routine gender-based discrimination in the workplace and at home and, in the view of Human Rights Watch, 'despite such constitutional guarantees, women still continue to face discrimination in law and in practice' (Human Rights Watch, 2014: 3).

The CEDAW report, while noting 'the State party's efforts to exclude gender-role stereotypes in school books and curricula, and the positive role played by NGOs to promote a change in the stereotypical roles of women', was 'concerned by the pervasive patriarchal attitudes and deep-rooted stereotypes on the State party regarding the roles and responsibilities of women and men in all spheres of life' (United Nations, 2011: 5). According to one of the few studies on women in Oman, 'negative attitudes and traditional stereotypes about women in Arab/Islamic societies have been, and still are, a major resisting force to progress for professional working women';

and the lack of child-care services, professional day-care centres, kindergartens and inadequate maternity leave also create considerable difficulties for many working Omani women (Goveas and Aslam, 2011: 236 and 237). A more recent report on Oman has commented that 'Women and children face discrimination in many areas. In the patriarchal society of Oman, women are excluded from certain state benefits, such as housing loans, and are refused equal rights under the personal status law. Women also experience restrictions of their self-determination in respect to health and reproductive rights' (Bertelsmann Stiftung, 2015b: 9).

Consequently, as described in the UAE in Chapter 2, it would also have been customary for almost all Omani girls and boys to have been taught to believe in the value of male superiority from earliest childhood, and this belief would have been reinforced as they grew up. Young men would have been told over and over again that they were responsible for the conduct of their wives, sisters and mothers and were their guardians and protectors, and the behaviour of 'their' women would reflect on them throughout their lives. Such beliefs would also have been reinforced at the female-only and male-only government schools that most Omanis would have attended (Limbert, 2010: 86–98). As a result, not only are Western notions of 'gender equality' still alien to many Omanis, they are regarded as a threat to their sincere beliefs that they are responsible for the welfare of the women in their immediate and extended families. Fathers in Oman still have a strong influence on their daughters' lives, and they play an instrumental role in the decisions that affect their education, their choice of jobs and careers and the selection of marriage partners.

Most marriages are still 'arranged', even if Omani women in their twenties now have more freedom when choosing their life partners and are more likely to delay marriage until their mid-to late twenties if they are in full-time employment. Like family patriarchs in the UAE, some Omani fathers still do not allow their daughters to pursue certain careers, and others will not allow them to work in mixed-gender workplaces. Many Omani families continue to be very reluctant to let their daughters study or work overseas on their own. In addition, some Omani women continue to believe that their primary role in life is to be mothers, to support their husbands and to raise their children. And, as in the West, a minority of young, well-educated Omani women may choose not to pursue careers, either because they come from wealthy families and do not need to work for a living or because they are marrying wealthy husbands.

Nevertheless, it is apparent that attitudes towards what women are 'allowed' to do are changing in Oman. With the opening of higher education to Omani women in the 1990s, many more women have earned tertiary degrees and have chosen to work and build careers, some have started their own companies and a few have become business leaders. Many Omani fathers now support the education of their daughters and provide support and encouragement for them to pursue professional careers. Traditional views about the 'correct' roles of women in Omani society and the workforce are also evolving and changing, as are the gender self-perceptions and beliefs of young Omani women, and it was clear that the hopes and aspirations of the management students I interviewed at Sultan Qaboos University in 2015 were very similar to those of their peers at Zayed University in the UAE. They were:

> Fully committed to pursuing careers in their chosen professions and, generally, quite confident and ambitious.
>
> Intending to marry only those men who will allow them to work and who would provide some support for their careers.
>
> Delaying marriage and pregnancy for a few years while they made some progress in their jobs and careers, although none of this group was planning to insert clauses in marriage contracts which would allow them to work throughout their lives.

The trend towards later marriages in Oman is a notable one. In the early 1980s, female Omanis were married, on average, at the age of seventeen, but this had risen to twenty-five by 2007 (Talei, 2010:

340). Among the group of Omani students I interviewed, two had been married during their undergraduate studies and two were getting married immediately after graduation, but the other six indicated that they planned to wait until their late twenties before doing this. This shift in attitudes and later marriages are also reflected in the confidence that this group had about their future prospects in 2015. For example:

> I really want to be able to have the freedom to do what I want to do in marketing. I don't want to live with any regrets when I'm older and so I want to take my chances and not be afraid of responsibility. I heard Sultan Qaboos talking about the opportunities that there are for women in Oman two or three years ago and I thought, 'My God, that's true'. I want to make my parents proud, especially my mum because she sacrificed so much for us when we were growing up . . . I want to be very successful in marketing and, maybe, one day, start up my own marketing business. It is not that easy at the moment, but I think that more women will start their own businesses in the future and they will prefer to deal with a woman, who is maybe more sensitive to their needs
>
> *(22-year-old marketing major).*

> I have a few dreams. I want to be the master of whatever I do, *yanni*, by that I mean I don't want to be mediocre, I want to be successful. Whatever job I have I want to do my best. Career wise and family wise, I want to be the best I can be and in whatever I do. I want to be a good worker, a good mother and a good wife. I want to aim high and then be a role-model for others . . . The main thing for me is that I don't want people, men [laughs], to say I can't do certain things just because I am a woman. I want to be judged by what I do and my achievements not because I'm a young woman
>
> *(22-year-old finance major).*

Marriage! Obviously, my parents want me to marry and have children, *wallah*! But, there is not the pressure, well at least not in my family, to do this immediately. My father has always been supportive of what I wanted to do at university and my mother even more so. She had a university degree, which was unusual for that time, but she did not work after she got married and I think she was sometimes frustrated by this ... I plan to work, and have a successful career and I would expect whoever is lucky enough to marry me [laughs] to support me in this. I do not think I can marry a man who thinks I should just be 'a housewife'. And what's the point? I mean, why go to university and work hard for four years not to use that? I want to have both, a good career and a good family

(23-year-old management major).

However, all of these students did recognise that there are still barriers and challenges for many Omani women to overcome. For example:

Many Omani women do not have the freedoms we have to pursue our education and then work. The majority of women here are oppressed, they don't get the chance to maybe go to college and then have a career. When they graduate from high-school they just get married and that's it. That's her life. But, we have the option now to get married or not, but they don't. We have the option to become educated, they don't. We can work, they can't ... Many Omani families are still very conservative about these things and I think that's very sad

(23-year-old accounting major).

I think there are still barriers in Omani society. Of course they exist, but that has changed a lot in the last ten years or so. Everyone knows this. But, we need to be less reliant on men. I mean many of my friends have got degrees, but all they do is just stay at home. What's the point of getting a good education and then not use it?

I would guess that at least 30 per cent of the women who graduate from this university will never work in the future. They'll just get married and have children ... But, this doesn't apply to my friends from school. All of them are planning to work in the future because our education encouraged us to be more independent and to maybe not accept a more traditional role ... I hope that many more Omani women will work and will own their own businesses. There is so much potential here and a lot of this is wasted at the moment. But, I think we need better mentoring and more support from men

(23-year-old management major).

Obviously we would like to see change but it's also going to take a long time. But, I think we are heading in that direction. When I think about Islam, it's about equality between men and women but I believe sometimes we are not really applying Islam here. I believe very much in my religion, and in our traditions and culture, but sometimes these can limit opportunities for women ... In fact my grandmother is always saying, 'We don't apply Islam here!' That's something I don't like here, because we often hear that things are done 'Because this is what Islam says' but it's not really. To me, it's about what we see as *al-wasatiyya*, being moderate in our beliefs and being true to the teachings of the Prophet, not believing what some old men say about these things

(22-year-old finance major).

4.6 CONCLUSION

Oman is increasingly calling upon women to shape its future and the future of the region. While social and legal challenges remain for Omani women, as they do for women across the globe, an estimated one-third of all civil servants in Oman are women, and more Omani women than men pursue a university education. In March 2004, Oman's first woman minister was appointed to head the Ministry of Education. Today women in Oman are free to drive, work, own land, vote and hold office. Women's empowerment enhances educational achievement and economic productivity, reduces infant mortality, and contributes to improved health and nutrition. The organisers of this conference hold that increasing the participation of women in all manner of decision making is crucial to human development.

Sultan Qaboos Cultural Centre (2014)

It is reasonable to describe Oman, in the context of the broader MENA region, as a qualified success story, but it is still (like the UAE) a work in progress. While consciously maintaining its customs, traditions and Islamic values, it has made some progress towards the original objectives of its ambitious Oman Vision 2020 document and its long-term goal of creating a diversified national economy that can sustain the country when its oil and gas reserves are depleted. Oman also appears to be a reasonably attractive destination for foreign companies, with the Heritage Foundation Index of Economic Freedom placing the KSA at 52/178 countries in 2016, with good scores for 'open markets', 'regulatory efficiency', 'investment freedom' and 'financial freedom', but with somewhat lower scores for 'rule of law' and 'open markets' (Heritage Foundation, 2016). However, in a review of the economic, political and social challenges facing Oman in 2004, Katz observed that:

> Compared to neighbouring Saudi Arabia, there is very little press coverage in Oman, And, unlike many stories about how bad things are in the Kingdom, the little reporting done on the Sultanate is generally positive. It would be a mistake, however, to conclude from Oman's glowing press coverage that all is well there. Oman, in fact, is experiencing some very difficult problems that are likely to get worse in coming years
>
> *(Katz, 2004: 1).*

He could have written the same words twelve years later because many of the problems he identified in 2004 were still prevalent in 2016. Katz had also pointed out that much of Oman's predicted economic growth had been dependent on consistently high oil prices throughout the 2000s and 2010s, which have been on a roller-coaster ride over the last ten years and which fell by more than 75 per cent between September 2014 and January 2016. Oman is not yet even close to reducing the country's dependence on oil and gas revenues from 41 per cent in 1996 to less than 10 per cent by 2020 or to creating the diversified economy that could replace Oman's reliance on these by 2020. Moreover, the 2015 Bertelsmann Stiftung report on Oman made the following critical comments about the government's rhetoric about 'economic diversification' and the reality of the patchy progress it has made towards this goal:

> The dismantlement of Ministry of National Economy in 2011, which prepared and monitored the five-year plans, illustrates the dilemma in which the Oman leadership finds itself. Initial actions by the new Supreme Council for Planning, apart from frequent arbitrary royal directives addressing short-term issues among specific sectors of the population, *have yet to demonstrate a coherent development framework or allay considerable uncertainties related to the country's long-term economic and social priorities* [and] *lack the ability to set and maintain strategic priorities in a coherent manner* ... From this point of view, *the official challenges of Omanisation and economic diversification go far beyond the issue of employment and call into question the whole political and economic structure which Oman has relied on for the past 44 years*
> (*Bertelsmann Stiftung, 2015b: 23 and 29; my emphases*).

Rules that regulate the employment of expatriate labour (such as the Kafala sponsorship system) and policies for the 'Omanisation' of the private sector are still in force. Since 2010, however, emergency social and economic measures adopted in response to the Arab spring (such as the creation of tens of thousands of public sector jobs for nationals, the sharp increase in public benefits and salaries in the public and private sector) in a sense contradict privatisation and deregulation policies implemented over the last decade [and] politically strategic segments of the economy remain controlled by business actors who are loyal allies of the regime. Because most members of the governing elite are directly or indirectly involved in business, privatisation and economic liberalisation policies have mainly benefitted those who are already leading business actors … Despite the return of many Omanis to the country since the 1970s, and the growing expatriate workforce, *one of the main constraints for management performance remains the lack of a skilled national workforce that can meet the demands of the new economic sectors that the government wishes to develop in the post-oil era*

(Bertelsmann Stiftung, 2015b: 14–15; my emphasis).

According to Transparency International, nepotism and corruption certainly exist in Oman with the country being ranked 64/174 countries in 2015 with a score of 45/100, where a score below 50 signifies that corruption is 'a serious problem' (Transparency International, 2016). This, combined with the many vested economic and business interests of the ruling elite of Oman, may well act as impediments to further necessary reforms of the country's economy and political system in the short to medium term. Moreover, data from the World Bank Knowledge Economy Index, which looks at the extent to which the cultural, legal, business, educational and scientific environments of countries are conducive for sustainable long-term economic development, placed Oman at number 42 out of 146 countries in 2013 – a surprisingly high ranking (World Bank, 2013). In addition, according to a report from Chatham House, 'the relative share of GDP attributed to hydrocarbon related activities has not declined significantly in the last decade; hovering between 44 and 54 per cent in Oman …

Oman's failure to diversify is a palpable problem that confronts the nation's millennial generation and their children' (Ennis and al-Jamali, 2014: 22).

This, combined with a state-led rentier developmental model and rapidly depleting oil resources will make it very difficult for Oman to manage a rapid and smooth transition from an economy still heavily dependent on gas and oil to one that is highly diversified and production oriented, and this will be further hampered by fluctuations in global oil and gas prices over the next five to ten years. It is, therefore, not easy to square these critical observations about the erratic progress that Oman is making towards economic diversification and political reform with either Strolla and Peri's belief that 'Oman's economy is set on the right path of sustainable growth, development, diversification and progress' (2013: 19), or the comments made by the Chairman of the National Bank of Oman, Mohammed Mahfoodh al-Ardhi, in May 2015. In a lead article in the *Times of Oman* in 2015, he suggested that:

> Oman is steadily moving towards achieving its long-term strategic and development goals, largely in line with Vision 2020 ... the forward thinking approach implemented by our government over the past decades has led to a well-organised strategy that will support and protect Omanis for generations to come ... will reduce the dependence on a foreign workforce, and encourage the development of Omanis so that they could take over the reins of the economy
>
> *(al-Ardhi, 2015).*

Unfortunately, every rigorous analysis of Oman's progress towards its original Vision 2020 goals indicates that these comments, while understandable, were both overly optimistic and not supported by the government's own economic data. Al-Ardhi suggested in this article that the non-oil and gas sectors now contributed 'more than half' of the country's annual GDP. However, the country's oil and gas sectors still accounted for more than 80 per cent of total export and state revenues at the end of 2015. And, while he pointed out that Oman's GDP growth would be 'five per cent in 2015 which exceeds initial targets that were fixed at three per cent growth', he did not mention that the original Vision 2020 plan had predicted average annual GDP growth rates of more than 7 per cent a year by 2020 and he did not consider the potential effects of the collapse in global oil and gas prices on economic growth during 2015–2016.

The remainder of his article merely repeated the wish lists that have appeared in every five-year economic plan going back to 1980 about the need to develop the country's infrastructure, ports, water and sewerage, roads, IT infrastructure, healthcare, schools, hospitals, education, agriculture, tourism, manufacturing capabilities and so forth (al-Ardhi, 2015). Last, but by no means least, no information was provided in this article about the substantive progress that Oman has made in any of these domains since either 2006 or 1996 or the extent to which the country's private sector has developed over the past two decades. To highlight just one example of a mismatch between the original goals of the Vision 2020 document and the present-day reality, it had been planned that the ratios of Omanis working in the public sector (68%) and private sector (15%) should become 95 per cent and 75 per cent respectively by 2015. While 82.7 per cent of public-sector jobs were filled by nationals in 2013, just 22.5 per cent of Omanis were employed in the private sector (Ennis and al-Jamali, 2014: 7).

In fact, the original objectives of Vision 2020 remain far from realisation, there are still relatively high levels of unemployment particularly among young Omanis, and the demand for expatriate workers has never been greater. The majority of Omanis are still employed in the public sector and those in private-sector employment 'are concentrated in specific economic sectors and occupations. At the same time, the single occupational category where affirmative action for Omanis succeeded – lower-skilled middle-class clerical jobs – is also the one most at risk of technological obsolescence'

(Ennis and al-Jamali, 2014: 2). The very ambitious goals of the original Vision 2020 strategic document are a long way from being fully realised, in part because significant economic diversification requires far more Omanis to become involved in wealth-generating ventures in the private sector and this has to include more Omani women. This has not yet happened for the same reasons that it has not occurred in the KSA and, to a lesser extent, in the UAE. In all three countries most nationals still work in the public sector and, accustomed to the largesse provided by oil and gas wealth over the last three decades, still tend to view employment in very traditional and largely transactional terms. Most female (and male) Omanis, as we have seen, continue to avoid working in the private sector, and only a few choose to become entrepreneurs and SME owners. The consequence of this is the perpetuation of an over-dependence on expatriate workers in the private sectors of the national economy and the use of valuable oil and gas revenues to allow Omanis to continue working in the public sector.

In 2015, for the first time in six years, Oman had a deficit of 7.8 per cent of GDP, which represented a marked deterioration in the state's finances since 2013, when Oman had a budget surplus of 8.1 per cent of GDP, and this deficit rose sharply to 16 per cent of GDP during 2016. This led to government announcements of a range of austerity measures, including a reduction in fuel subsidies, a doubling of gas prices for industrial users, an increase in corporate tax rates from 12 to 15 per cent, the removal of some public-sector employment perks and the issuing of a $520 million sovereign Islamic bond (sukuk)(The Economist, 2016i: 43–44). These short-term measures suggest that Oman's ruling elite was treading water during 2016, in part because of uncertainties about who would succeed Sultan Qaboos but also because the country's leaders did not appear to be able to agree on the deeper reforms that the country would need to introduce to ensure its long-term economic future. Oman will also confront the harsh reality of a post-hydrocarbon economy much sooner than its wealthier northern GCC neighbours.

According to the most recent estimates, existing oil and gas reserves will run out completely by 2026 and 2040 respectively (United States Energy Information Agency, 2015b: 4), and as several Omanis told me when discussing these issues with them in 2015, their country may well be running out of time to deal with these challenges.[6] The 'old' solutions – maintaining a very large public sector, job-creation schemes, subsidies for staple foods, price controls, generous social welfare provisions, no personal income tax and so forth – are not viable medium- to long-term options for Oman, and if the country does have to deal with other economic crises in the next ten years it appears to have a very limited capacity to cope with these. These realities have led Jones and Ridout to conclude that in the future:

> Life in Oman after all will not be wholly unfamiliar. It is unlikely that the oft-cited and somewhat fatalistic Arab Gulf prediction that future generations will live a desert lifestyle similar to that of the Bedouin before the advent of oil will prove to be accurate. In some respects, there will be a great deal of continuity between the pre- and post-oil periods. But this is not because things will return to how they were before, but rather because so many aspects of the way things are now are already a continuation of the way things were before, rather than a radical departure from the past
>
> (Jones and Ridout, 2015: 269).

As regards women, we noted earlier that the WEF's ranking for 'economic participation and opportunity' for Omani women did improve significantly from 123/136 countries in 2013 to 92/145 in 2015. However, all the evidence indicates that while some Omani women now have the opportunity to attend university, to work and pursue careers, the majority do not. As is the case with the UAE and the KSA, most Omani women who do choose to work continue to opt for employment in the public sector, and while some have risen to middle and senior management positions the government sector is still led predominantly by men. Few women are members of either the *Majlis al-Dawla* or the *Majlis al-Shura* and they are largely absent from Sultan Qaboos' inner group of senior ministers and advisers. Only a small number of Omani women work in the expatriate-dominated private sector and even fewer are entrepreneurs or self-starting small business owners. Only a tiny number can be described as 'business leaders' and all studies of Omani women indicate that most of them still encounter ingrained cultural, attitudinal and structural barriers in the national labour market. Hence, while the Dean of the College of Education at Sultan Qaboos University may believe that Oman's five-year development plans have achieved the objective of ensuring gender equality for women in the labour market, all external reports indicate that while this may be true of female education and health, they are a long way from achieving full equality with men in all sectors of the national economy (al-Barwani, 2011: 218).

There is, without any doubt, a long and uncertain road to travel before there is a level playing field for women in public and private-sector organisations in Oman and in all professions and occupations. But many other countries have gone through similar economic and social transformations in recent decades. Until the late 1980s, as noted earlier, the average labour force participation rate of women in Western countries was less than 30 per cent. This has since increased to more than 50 per cent, on average and 70 per cent in OECD countries. And, if Oman can increase the labour market participation rate of national women to more than half, this could add 12 per cent to its annual GDP (Aguirre, et al, 2012; Dobbs, et al, 2015) which would go some way to making up for the inevitable and steep decline in the country's oil and gas revenues during the 2020s. To do this, however, Oman must find other new and innovative ways to support its growing and increasingly restive young population as soon as possible rather than pursue old strategies that have largely served the vested interests of its ruling elite and maintained the political status quo since 1971. It also has to encourage more of its women and men to work in new wealth-generating businesses in the private sector, and this, it now appears, must become a national priority. How the government of Oman and its public- and private-sector organisations can promote greater participation by women in all sectors and at all levels of its economy is described in Chapter 9.

5 The Experiences of Women in Public- and Private-Sector Organisations in Oman

5.1 INTRODUCTION

In Chapter 4 we described the limited progress that women have made in public- and private-sector organisations in Oman and in this chapter we focus on their mixed experiences in the workplace. It has a similar structure to Chapter 3, with the exception of the case-study section. We first review the attitudes of Omanis towards female bosses and women in leadership positions. We then examine the cultural and attitudinal barriers that women encounter in their workplaces, summarise the opinions that men have about a woman's right to work in Oman and evaluate their opinions about the degree of equality that women enjoy in the national labour market. We also look at their beliefs about the likelihood that more women will become leaders in public- and private-sector organisations in the future. This is followed by an analysis of the experiences of 10 female entrepreneurs and small and medium-sized enterprise (SME) owners in Oman. We then examine an issue that is of growing concern to some Omani women (particularly those employed in the private sector): how to balance the competing demands of their work and home lives. In the conclusion we evaluate the progress that women have made in the national labour market and also ask if they are likely to make a bigger contribution to the economic development of Oman in the future.

5.2 THE ATTITUDES OF OMANIS TOWARDS WOMEN IN THE WORKPLACE AND IN LEADERSHIP ROLES

The material presented in this section is based on a questionnaire survey of 104 female and 76 male employees at 10 public- and 6 private-sector organisations in Muscat. This survey was supplemented by twenty interviews with working Omani women and men and a group of ten of final-year female undergraduate students at Sultan Qaboos University (SQU) in Muscat during 2015.[1] As in Chapter 3, some of the tables in this section also include data from other surveys that have examined the attitudes of women and men towards women in business leadership roles in the United States in order to provide comparisons between these and the results of the Oman employee survey. The majority of those who responded to the questionnaire survey were female and the age profile of the respondents reflects the relatively youthful working population of Oman, with 53.3 per cent of the sample being aged twenty to twenty-nine, 29.5 per cent thirty to thirty-nine, 13.3 per cent forty to forty-nine and just 3.9 per cent more than fifty years of age. Most of these women and men worked in supervisory or middle-management roles: 31.1 per cent had fewer than five years' work experience; 26.1 per cent had six to ten years' experience, and 25.0 per cent had eleven to fifteen years' work experience. Only 17.8 per cent of these women and men had worked full time for more than fifteen years.

The four sets of data, presented in Table 5.1, provide a summary of the attitudes that these women and men have about working for a female boss. The results indicate that while a clear majority of Omani women were comfortable with the prospect of working for a female boss and half of them also believed that it is acceptable for a man to work for a female boss, one quarter of them were not comfortable with this idea. Two out of five men did not appear to have difficulties working for a female boss, but more than 40 per cent were not comfortable about this prospect and more than one third of this group did not find the idea of Omani men working for a female boss to be acceptable.

As with the UAE men, these results may appear to indicate that male Omanis have very conservative attitudes about the prospect of working for a female boss, but the comparative data included in Table 5.1 indicates that these responses were not too dissimilar to

TABLE 5.1 *The attitudes of Omanis towards working for a female boss* (N = *104 women and 76 men*)

Women
'I am comfortable with the idea of working for a female boss'
Always: 33.6
Often: 27.9
Sometimes: 30.8
Rarely: 5.8
Never: 1.9
'The idea that men can work for a female boss is acceptable to me'
Always: 22.1
Often: 31.7
Sometimes: 21.2
Rarely: 16.4
Never: 8.6
Men
'I am comfortable with the idea of working for a female boss'
Always: 17.2
Often: 22.5
Sometimes: 31.6
Rarely: 18.3
Never: 10.4
'The idea that men can work for a female boss is acceptable to me'
Always: 17.2
Often: 19.8
Sometimes: 30.3
Rarely: 18.3
Never: 14.4

Comparative data (Carlson et al, 2006)
'I would feel comfortable working for a woman'

	1965	*2005*
Women	*78.0*	*78.0*
Men	*27.0*	*75.0*

1965, N = *2,000 executives; 2005,* N = *286 executives*
(% that agreed with this statement)

those of male and female managers in the United States in the mid-1960s. We noted in Section 3.2 of Chapter 3 that researchers at the Harvard Business School have documented the changing attitudes of male and female business leaders in the United States towards women managers and executives between 1965 and 2005 and also commented on the significant change that had occurred in male attitudes towards women in management roles. In 1965, only 35 per cent of 2,000 male executives had a 'favourable attitude' towards women in management, and fewer than 30 per cent felt 'comfortable working for a woman' (the respective figures for women in 1965 were 82 per cent and 78 per cent).

Forty years later, in 2005, more than 80 per cent of male executives had 'a favourable attitude' towards women in management and three quarters felt 'comfortable working for a woman'. The figures for women in 2005 were 85 per cent and 78 per cent respectively (i.e. very little change from 1965; Carlson et al, 2006: 28). To reiterate the point, it took two generations for largely negative male attitudes to evolve to the point where three quarters of male American executives expressed a generally favourable attitude towards women in leadership roles and were also 'comfortable' with the idea of working for a woman. Hence, in the context of the conservative Islamic culture of Oman, it is encouraging that two out of five of these relatively young men do not seem to mind working for a female boss, although it is likely to be a long time before most Omani men are 'comfortable' with this.

There were somewhat mixed results when we asked these women and men, 'Do you think that male Omanis still have difficulties accepting decisions made by a female boss?', with more than half of these women and men indicating that most male employees still have problems with this (Table 5.2). During the interviews with Omani employees, it quickly became apparent that almost all of the female interviewees and some of the men felt that women in managerial and leadership roles were sometimes not taken as seriously as men:

TABLE 5.2 *Do you think that Omani employees still have difficulties accepting decisions made by a female boss?*

Women	Men
Always: 17.3	Always: 22.3
Often: 33.7	Often: 30.2
Sometimes: 33.6	Sometimes: 34.3
Rarely: 8.6	Rarely: 10.5
Never: 6.8	Never: 2.7

I have to say that I do feel that some men still do make negative judgments about me just because I am a woman. For example, I remember a few years ago that even though I had excellent work appraisals, they waited for nine months before they appointed me to my current job because they were trying to find a man to fill my role! I think if they had been able to find a man who was ten or twenty per cent less good than me they would have appointed him ... I sometimes think I have to work two or three times better than a man, just to prove I'm the best person for this job ... Here, it's still about male dominance and some men still do not want women to be successful and independent

(35-year-old middle manager, private-sector organisation).

We know that there are more opportunities for women to work these days, and this is good, but when you look around it is still mainly men who are in the leadership positions. When I first started working here there were very few women and, how do you say, we were invisible and I think it was much harder for me to get promotions at first and to be taken seriously by many of the men ... This is much better now, because many women work at [a government ministry], maybe a third of the employees now and so there are more women in middle-management and senior positions ... I have also noticed that young women are more confident than we were and I think we will see more of them in senior roles in the future

(38-year-old public-sector finance manager).

A thirty-three-year-old woman, who worked in a marketing role for a private-sector company, observed that:

Organisations should do more for women, but I'm not too optimistic because there are factors that are preventing this. One reason is that women are not the decision-makers here. At all levels the decision makers are still male, in government and in business. So, for them, it's not in their interests to let half the power go to women. They believe that 'If we share things with women, then our power and authority will diminish.' So they may say this in words that they encourage this but in reality they do not accept this. They do not encourage women and they still prefer to have males in the decision-making roles and women are not doing enough, they do not stand up for themselves and they do not stand up for each other ... But, maybe if I was a man I'd think the same way [laughs]!

And, while they acknowledged that there had been substantial changes in Omani society over the last fifteen to twenty years, all agreed that there were still significant barriers for them to overcome. For example:

This is a very difficult question to answer! I can say that I did not experience any prejudice when I was studying for my degree although there were very few girls who studied IT when I did. The Basic Law says that we cannot be discriminated against just because we are women, but how shari'a law is interpreted here, by men of course, does discriminate against women in marriage, divorce, who gets custody of the children and inheritance. That is what we must deal with. But, at work it is more complicated. I cannot say that I have personally felt negative attitudes but I can say that some of my friends say that they have ... I think it is also different depending where you work and in the government sector there are many more women, so I think it is easier for a woman there if you compare this to a woman who might be working in a business where there are usually only a few Omani women

(35-year-old IT manager, public-sector organisation).

I'd like to see more laws that protect women in the workplace, that ensure that they can't be discriminated against because they are women and also have some legal protections if they do face discrimination. At the moment these don't exist and so even if we feel that there is some discrimination there is really nothing we can do about this. For example, it's well known that men are usually paid more than women because their employers say that they have *qawwamuna*, and so should be paid more than women. This is wrong. I have children so what is the difference! If a woman does the same job as a man she should be paid the same!

(28-year-old bank employee, private sector).

We then asked a series of questions to elicit their attitudes towards women in leadership roles, as leaders of organisations, and their beliefs about the leadership abilities and competencies of Omani women (Table 5.3).

Predictably, the data indicate that women had much more confidence in the ability of women to succeed in leadership positions and to be the leaders of organisations when compared to male Omanis. And while nearly half of the women believed that women had the same leadership abilities as men, fewer than 40 per cent of male Omanis thought that this was true. Having said this, we can reiterate the conjecture proposed in Chapter 3 that the more interesting data lies in the number of responses in the 'sometimes' and 'maybe' categories in Table 5.3. These suggest, as the results for the UAE employees did in Chapter 3, that a significant number of these Omanis are not making pre-emptive generic assumptions about the leadership potential or abilities of all women. They are indicating

TABLE 5.3 *The attitudes of Omanis towards female leaders and their beliefs about the leadership abilities and competencies of Omani women*

'Do you think that Omani women can be successful in business leadership positions?'

Women	Men
Always: 13.4	*Always: 9.5*
Often: 33.6	*Often: 22.8*
Sometimes: 39.4	*Sometimes: 33.3*
Rarely: 10.6	*Rarely: 23.3*
Never: 3.0	*Never: 11.1*

'Do you think that it is acceptable for an Omani woman to be the leader of an organisation?'

Women	Men
Very much so: 56.7	*Very much so: 29.2*
Maybe: 37.5	*Maybe: 57.3*
Never: 5.8	*Never: 13.5*

'Do Omani women have the same leadership abilities and competencies as men?'

Women	Men
Always: 15.4	*Always: 7.9*
Often: 29.8	*Often: 21.1*
Sometimes: 37.5	*Sometimes: 30.3*
Rarely: 11.5	*Rarely: 23.7*
Never: 5.8	*Never: 17.0*

'Do you think that Omani women have the ability to succeed in leadership positions?'

Women	Men
Very much so: 59.6	*Very much so: 22.6*
Maybe: 27.9	*Maybe: 51.3*
Never: 12.5	*Never: 26.1*

that while some women can be successful in leadership roles and some of them do have the same leadership abilities as men, not all women can succeed as leaders. Having said this, it was evident that Omani men have very mixed views about working women and their leadership abilities and the ten university-educated men I interviewed during October 2015 again fell into three distinct groups, a 'Yes' group who were broadly supportive of women in management and leadership roles ($N = 2$), a 'Yes, but ...' group ($N = 5$) and a 'No' group who were strongly opposed to this idea ($N = 3$). The extracts from three of these interviews illustrate the continuum of attitudes that these men had about working Omani women and their potential as leaders:

> Women are capable of being leaders as long as they take the job seriously with passion and strongly believe in what they are doing. With the great availability of information, knowledge and education it has become no problem to improve one's ability to lead a team or an organisation.. Women are now proving that they can be very successful, therefore I would have no problem if one would lead an organisation that I work for. Sometimes it is rather good to have women in leadership roles who recognise employees' rights and encourage their good efforts ... Women in the past didn't get this encouragement and support from the government. But, women nowadays get a lot more encouragement and they are succeeding in many different jobs and responsibilities ... To me this is more than just about being nice to women. I now believe this will be important for the future because they must help us to build a stronger economy and society
>
> *(43-year-old public-sector executive; married with two children).*

In principle I am not opposed to a woman who works, providing she holds her family to be the most important part of her life. I believe that this is the primary role of women, but she should not be prevented from working if that is her wish ... You must understand that we have different beliefs about these matters and our traditions and culture impose some restrictions on what women are allowed to do ... Many Omanis believe that while women should be allowed to work, this must not compromise their families and children ...

I also am not sure if all professions should be open to women, for example on building sites and in construction because of the dress restrictions and this would cause problems in my company if more women did work for us ... For now, I also believe that men will be the leaders in our politics and in business organisations because I believe they have the better aptitudes for this. I mean there may be more women leaders in these areas in the future but men are better suited to these positions*

> (36-year-old manager at a construction company; married with three children. His wife had never worked outside the home; *I had asked him if he thought there would be more Omani women in leadership positions in the future).

No, I do not believe that women have the automatic right to work, providing their families or husbands provide for their needs. If they do not have a husband, or a family to support them, they may be permitted to work. I will explain this. In the West, you believe that women have this right but we believe that it is the role of the man to provide for his wife's and children's needs. This does not mean we do not respect women but we also must not forget the teachings of Islam. We believe that Allah has given men and women their special abilities and talents ... women are gentler and weaker than men who have more strength and authority so it is his natural role to be the guardian of women ... It is a question of two halves, men are one half and women are the other half. This allows men to provide for the families and to be the leaders, and for roles such as politics and military service, and women to be mothers and wives ... This is a way of life for us and means that men are the maintainers and protectors of women

> (39-year-old manager at an oil refinery; married with five children; his wife had never worked outside the home).

These mixed opinions about working Omani women and their leadership abilities are reflected in the data in Table 5.4, which indicate that women, when compared to men, were generally more optimistic about the possibility that Oman's business community will accept

TABLE 5.4 *Will the Oman business community ever wholly accept female executives?*

Women	Men
Strongly agree: 15.4	*Strongly agree: 9.3*
Agree: 24.1	*Agree: 14.6*
Neutral: 19.2	*Neutral: 26.9*
Disagree: 25.0	*Disagree: 27.1*
Strongly disagree: 16.3	*Strongly disagree: 22.1*

Comparative data (Carlson et al, 2006)
'The business community will never wholly accept female executives'

	1965	*2005*
Women	*47.0*	*39.0*
Men	*67.0*	*20.0*

1965, N = 2,000 executives; 2005, N = 286 executives
(% that agreed with this statement)

more female executives in the future. Male Omanis were much more likely to be neutral about or disagree that this is likely to happen any time soon, and almost half felt that this was unlikely to happen. At first glance, these results may appear to reflect considerable pessimism among a significant minority of both women and men about the likelihood of this happening. However, the comparative data in Table 5.4 also indicate that the beliefs that Omani women have about this are very similar to those of female American executives in 2005 (Carlson 2006: 28). And, to repeat a point made earlier about the comparative data in Table 5.1, while attitudes towards female business leaders did become more positive in the United States during this period of time, it took nearly two generations for these to evolve to the point that most men believed that there was a greater probability that the US business community would 'wholly accept' female executives.

We then asked our respondents a series of questions about equality of opportunity for Omani women and if they believed that there were still barriers and challenges for Omani women to overcome in the workplace (Table 5.5).

TABLE 5.5 *Beliefs about equality of opportunity for Omani women and the challenges and barriers they encounter in the workplace*

'Is there now full equality of opportunity for Omani women in the
   workplace?'

Women	Men
Strongly agree: 0.0	Strongly agree: 8.0
Agree: 7.7	Agree: 17.1
Neutral: 25.0	Neutral: 38.2
Disagree: 44.2	Disagree: 23.6
Strongly disagree: 23.1	Strongly disagree: 13.1

'Are there still challenges and barriers for Omani women to overcome in
   the workplace?'

Women	Men
Strongly agree: 26.0	Strongly agree: 17.0
Agree: 50.9	Agree: 23.6
Neutral: 19.3	Neutral: 28.9
Disagree: 3.8	Disagree: 18.4
Strongly disagree: 0.0	Strongly disagree: 12.1

It is evident that while Omanis know that there are now more opportunities for women to work, only a small number of these women agreed that there was equality of opportunity for women in the workplace. Nearly 40 per cent of men were 'neutral' about this and more than one third did not agree that this was the case. Two out of five men also believed that there were 'still challenges and barriers for Omani women to overcome in the workplace' and more than three quarters of the women agreed with this statement. More significantly, both women and men believed that female Omanis are much less likely to be in leadership positions in the private sector in the future when compared to the public sector (Tables 5.6 and 5.7). However, the comparative data from Pew Research suggest that their opinions about the prospects for female executives in private-sector organisations were not markedly different to those of men and women in the United States in 2015 (Table 5.6).

TABLE 5.6 *At this moment in time, do you think that it is easier for Omani men to become leaders in private-sector organisations than women?*

Women	Men
87.5	83.0

(% that agreed with this statement)

Comparative data (Parker et al, 2015: 32)
'It is easier for men to get into top executive positions in business'

Women	Men
61.0	74.0

N = 921 women and 914 men in the United States
(% that agreed with this statement)

TABLE 5.7 *Do you think we will see more Omani women in leadership positions in the public sector and in business organisations in the future?*

In public-sector organisations:

Women	Men
Definitely: 74.1	*Definitely: 56.7*
Maybe: 23.1	*Maybe: 39.4*
Unlikely: 2.8	*Unlikely: 3.9*

In business organisations:

Women	Men
Definitely: 41.2	*Definitely: 51.1*
Maybe: 61.6	*Maybe: 63.1*
Unlikely: 2.8	*Unlikely: 14.2*

We also asked our respondents about some possible future scenarios for Omani women in leadership positions in public- and private-sector organisations in 2030 (Table 5.8).

These data add credence to the evidence presented in Chapter 4 about the continuing underrepresentation of Omani women in the private sector and their overrepresentation in public-sector

TABLE 5.8 *Possible scenarios for Omani women in leadership positions in public and private-sector organisations by 2030*

'By 2030, Omani men will continue to hold more leadership positions in public-sector organisations than women do'

Women	Men
44.2	*61.9*

'By 2030, Omani women will hold as many leadership positions as men in public-sector organisations'

Women	Men
55.8	*38.1*

'By 2030, Omani men will continue to hold more of the top positions in business organisations than women'

Women	Men
79.9	*84.1*

'By 2030, Omani women will hold as many top positions in business organisations as men'

Women	Men
12.1	*15.9*

(% that 'strongly agreed' or agreed' with these statements)

Comparative data (Parker et al, 2015: 5)

'Men will continue to hold more top executive positions in business in the future'

Women	Men
55.0	*52.0*

'It's only a matter of time before there are as many women as men in top executive positions in business'

Women	Men
44.0	*45.0*

N = 921 women and 914 men in the United States
(% that agreed with these statements)

employment. They show that while more than half of the women and two in five men believed that there will be more women in public-sector leadership roles by 2030, only 12.1 per cent of women and 15.9 per cent of men agreed that Omani women will hold as many senior positions in business organisations as men by 2030. It could be argued that even this group of women and men may be over-optimistic about this possibility given the slow pace at which women have been rising to executive and board-level positions in most non-Islamic countries and the relative lack of women in middle-management positions in Omani private-sector companies today. While there is no comparative data about the prospects for more female public-sector leaders in the United States, the comparative data by Pew Research in Table 5.8 does indicate that there are notable differences between the beliefs that Omanis have about the likelihood that there will be as many women as men in executive positions in business in the future and those of American men and women in 2015. This also suggests that male attitudes towards women in leadership roles have been evolving at a rather slower pace in Oman when compared to the UAE.

In conclusion, we can say that attitudes towards Omani women in the workplace and in leadership roles have changed to some extent in Oman over the last ten to fifteen years and more than two thirds of the women and the men agreed that 'prospects for working women have generally improved in Oman' over the last ten years. However, while all our respondents agreed that there were much better employment opportunities for women, it was evident that most of them still encountered barriers in the workplace and some Omani men still have very conservative attitudes towards working women and female leaders. More than a third of the female private-sector employees believed that 'women are not able to progress beyond a certain level in my organisation', although only one in six female public-sector employees agreed with this statement. In addition, as we have seen, only a small minority of women believe that there is now 'full equality of opportunity for Omani women in the workplace' and nearly three quarters agreed that 'there are still challenges and barriers for Omani women to overcome' in the workplace. In spite of these difficulties, all of these women were fully committed to their careers and professions, and they work for exactly the same reasons that women in many other countries do: for fulfilment, independence and personal growth. When they were asked to provide three or four reasons why they chose to work, three quarters of the group indicated that 'achieving my personal goals in life' was important to them, two thirds mentioned that 'financial independence' and 'personal growth and development' were important and just over half indicated their intrinsic interest in their vocation or profession.

5.3   FEMALE ENTREPRENEURS AND SMALL BUSINESS OWNERS

It is nearly four decades since the first studies of female entrepreneurs appeared in the United States and the United Kingdom.[2] However, in a comprehensive review of 630 research articles, Jennings and Brush concluded that the sub-area of female entrepreneurship research did not really 'come of age' until the early 2000s when there was a proliferation of articles on this topic, with 'at least twenty' literature review articles being published on this topic between 2000 and 2013. Between 1976 and 2000, 138 scholarly articles on women entrepreneurs were published. From 2000 to 2012, 492 articles were published, an increase from an average of less than 6 to about 38 articles a year. This research has focused on the processes by which women become entrepreneurs, the psychological and contextual factors that facilitate or impede their entrepreneurial activities and the personal consequences of becoming entrepreneurs. It has also examined whether these are different or similar to those encountered and experienced by male entrepreneurs (Jennings and Brush, 2013: 664–666). Jennings and Brush draw several general conclusions about female entrepreneurs from this extensive literature:

> Although there are considerable local and regional variations, women are less likely than men to be engaged in entrepreneurial activities, less likely to be self-employed and less likely to be involved in 'academic entrepreneurship' (i.e. the commercialisation of scientific research and patents). It also appears that women, from a young age, have lower levels of

'entrepreneurial self-efficacy' and less desire to become entrepreneurs in adulthood when compared to men. When they have established their businesses, women are more likely to be satisfied by running micro-businesses (rather than going for growth), more likely to keep their companies in private ownership and much less likely than men to issue initial public offerings (Jennings and Brush, 2013: 668).

Broadly speaking, women start businesses for the same reasons that men do. However, entrepreneurial activity is 'embedded in family systems', meaning that many female entrepreneurs do not regard their business activities as being separate from other aspects of their lives, as men are more liable to do. Consequently, women are more likely than men to start a small business in the hope that this will help them achieve a better work–family balance. However, most research studies have indicated that women entrepreneurs usually struggle to achieve this (Jennings and Brush, 2013: 687–691).

Women, in general, launch new businesses with less capital than men and also 'tend to operate with lower levels of both debt and equity beyond the start-up stage ... are less likely than male entrepreneurs to utilise financing by formal, external sources during start-up; and less likely to use debt financing, in particular to finance ongoing operations'. Some research studies have also concluded that there was evidence of discrimination against would-be women entrepreneurs by banks and other financial institutions in the 1980s and 1990s, although other studies have suggested that there was little evidence of gender-based discrimination against women by these organisations (Jennings and Brush, 2013: 669–670).

The evidence concerning differences between the strategic, organisational and managerial practices of women and men is mixed. Women are much more likely to run home-based business when compared to men. They are over-represented in consumer retail and personal services' businesses and under-represented in manufacturing, extractive industries and business services (Jennings and Brush, 2013: 685–686).

As noted in Chapter 3, female technology entrepreneurs are extremely rare. In contrast to the generic organisational behaviour literature, which has suggested that there are fundamental differences between the leadership and management styles of women and men, 'few differences have been reported with respect to the organisational and managerial practices of female and male entrepreneurs', and female and male entrepreneurs may 'organise and manage their forms with a mix of stereotypically feminine and masculine approaches'. However, they note that 'surprisingly little systematic empirical work has examined whether women and men tend to manage their firms differently' (Jennings and Brush, 2013: 670–671).

Several studies have suggested that businesses created by women do not perform as well over the medium to long term as those headed by men and with respect to many standard economic indicators 'female-led firms tend to exhibit inferior performance'. On average, according to these studies, female-led companies tend to be smaller, grow less quickly, have fewer total assets and employ fewer people. Other studies, however, have questioned these results and concluded that there are no significant differences in the performance of female/male-led businesses and, in some cases, women-owned SMEs out-perform those owned by men when measured on financial metrics such as return on sales, assets and common equity. And, in general, women tend to be slightly more contented and satisfied with the performance of their (perhaps smaller) businesses when compared to men (Jennings and Brush, 2013: 671–673).

Entrepreneurship is not a 'gender-neutral' phenomenon. It 'occurs within – and is thus impacted by – a system of socially-constructed and widely shared beliefs about the characteristics typically associated with women and men and the behaviours and roles deemed appropriate for members of each sex.' Several studies have suggested that entrepreneurship tends to be perceived and portrayed as a stereotypically masculine endeavour, and many people 'typically associate the entrepreneurial role with masculine traits such as, self-reliance, competitiveness and assertiveness'. We will see that these assumptions also have an effect on female entrepreneurs in Oman and the KSA (Jennings and Brush, 2013: 683–684).

It is only very recently that researchers have begun to consider how regional, national, cultural, religious and familial factors may encourage or inhibit female entrepreneurial activity. As we have seen in Chapters 2, 3 and 4, cultural and religious beliefs in Islamic countries have a powerful influence on attitudes about the roles of women and men in society and in the workplace. We will see that these are also prevalent in the entrepreneurial sectors of Oman and, in Chapter 7, the KSA.

Comprehensive global data on female entrepreneurship and SME activity is not yet available, but it has been estimated that approximately 130 million women in eighty-three countries were managing their own businesses in 2015 (Kelley et al, 2015: 1). Moreover, numerous reports have been published over the last decade that have emphasised the need to encourage higher levels of female entrepreneurship and business ownership in order to encourage greater female participation in national labour markets and to boost economic growth in emerging economies (Bosma et al, 2007; Ernst & Young, 2009; Organisation for Economic Cooperation and Development, 2014, 2012 and 2004; Singer et al, 2014). However, the United Nations has noted that 'in all regions, women are less likely than men to initiate their own enterprises' and identified four major barriers to their participation in entrepreneurship: unequal access to finance, legal restrictions, gender discrimination and unequal access to technology (United Nations, 2015a: 112). More than a decade ago, the OECD Working Party on SMEs and Entrepreneurship (2004) had observed that while women's entrepreneurship was an important and untapped source of economic growth in emerging markets, women represented a very small minority of all entrepreneurs in the MENA region, a comment that was repeated in its 2014 and 2012 reports. This, the 2004 report concluded, was a major market failure that needed to be addressed by governments and policy makers in many countries (Organisation for Economic Cooperation and Development, 2004).

This report had also noted the concentration of women in specific entrepreneurial sectors (primarily education, service industries, retail and home-based micro-businesses) and their under-representation in high-value business sectors. Citing evidence from several regional and global studies, the report noted that there were, on average, much higher levels of female business ownership and entrepreneurship in the world's leading industrial economies and that the rate of female business start-ups in these countries had begun to accelerate significantly during the mid-1990s and early 2000s (Organisation for Economic Cooperation and Development, 2004: 5, 7, 15–17), a trend also highlighted by Ernst & Young in 2009 and the 2015 Global Entrepreneurship Monitor (GEM) report (Ernst & Young, 2009; Kelley et al, 2015: 6–9). In the United States, for example, the number of female-owned small companies quadrupled from two million to eight million between 1982 and 1997. In 1997, for the first time, women-owned SMEs employed more people than the Fortune 500 companies did. By 2015, women owned nearly 40 per cent of all SMEs operating in the United States and generated nearly $2 trillion in revenue (National Association of Women Business Owners, 2015).

The 2004 OECD report also highlighted a definitive 'chicken-and-egg' problem. Several studies have shown that there is a strong positive correlation between levels of female participation in the workforce of national economies and the number of female entrepreneurs and SME owners that are active in any particular country. This suggests that women had to first enter the national labour markets of many Western countries in significant numbers in the 1970s and 1980s before more conducive legal and cultural environments emerged, *which then enabled more women to become self-employed and create their own businesses during the 1990s and 2000s*. These countries also progressively enacted laws and regulatory frameworks that outlawed gender and other forms of discrimination in their labour markets and workplaces, which helped to facilitate this process (Organisation for Economic Cooperation and Development, 2004: 22).

This, as we will see in Chapters 8 and 9, means that it is very unlikely that there will be a substantial growth in female entrepreneurs (*albaseeta*) and SME ownership in countries in the Gulf and MENA region unless national governments can first improve the general education levels of women, increase the number of women employed in their national workforces, particularly in the private sector, and also introduce legislation that outlaws gender discrimination in their labour-markets. The 2004 OECD report also observed that the opportunities that women have to become entrepreneurs 'reflect societal conditions at a particular historical juncture, and thus certain kinds of firms cannot be founded (by certain types of persons) before their time. Thus, both the firms created, and the persons creating them, resemble each other within a specific historical era' (Organisation for Economic Cooperation and Development, 2004: 30). We will ask if Oman, the UAE, the KSA and the other countries of the MENA region are approaching their 'particular historical juncture' in Chapter 8 and the Postscript to this book.

Female Entrepreneurship in the MENA Region

The primary non-governmental agency for promoting female entrepreneurship and small business ownership in the region is the MENA-OECD Women's Business Forum (WBF). Established in 2007, its mission is to 'help governments and the private sector make concrete improvements to the business environment for women entrepreneurs [and] to help identify areas where targeted intervention is needed to support women led businesses' (MENA-OECD Investment Program, 2007: 3). This original mission was augmented in 2011 by the establishment of national task forces for the eighteen MENA countries that were participants in the WBF program (MENA-OECD Investment Program, 2011). A report by the OECD Investment Program in 2009 noted that levels of women's entrepreneurship in the region were the lowest in the world and less than 10 per cent of women started their own businesses, compared to 19 per cent of men, and only 20 per cent held ownership positions in businesses, primarily in family-owned companies. Consequently, 'stronger and more targeted efforts are needed to support businesses, in particular women- led firms [and] strong leadership and targeted policies are needed to support the development of women led businesses.' This report also called on national governments to 'tap into the great potential of an increasingly well-educated youth and female population, who can contribute to economic diversification in sectors that are internationally competitive, knowledge-driven and labour intensive, support women's economic empowerment, take concrete policy actions to promote women's entrepreneurship and level the playing field for women' (MENA-OECD Investment Program, 2009: 2).

This report, to no-one's great surprise, concluded that there were 'significant gender-specific barriers' to women, which was preventing more of them from becoming entrepreneurs and SME owners in the MENA region. These barriers included cultural and religious norms, difficulties in obtaining business financing loans, complex and time-consuming approval processes, status of ownership and other collateral legal requirements and, in many countries, the requirement to obtain legal permission from male guardians to establish new businesses. The OECD called on all governments in the region to 'reduce these barriers and help adopt policy responses and solutions that encourage women's employment and business development'. It also called for targeted policies to encourage women's entrepreneurship including 'the removal of 'gender related obstacles to entrepreneurship', 'fostering greater awareness of the benefits of entrepreneurship among women and placing higher value on the role of women in the economy and society' and 'to develop programs specifically designed to support women's entrepreneurship and involvement in micro, small and medium-sized enterprises' (MENA-OECD Investment Program, 2009: 2–3, 4 and 9).

A subsequent and much more detailed report by the OECD concluded that levels of female entrepreneurship in the MENA region 'are well below those of comparably developed regions [which is] in part due to the low levels of participation of women in the formal economic sphere, as both employees and business leaders.' This report also noted that most businesses owned by women in the MENA region tended to be very small; nine out of ten were sole-proprietorship micro-businesses, and many of these were home-based enterprises operating in the informal economy (Organisation for Economic Cooperation and Development, 2012: 15 and 31). Among the many policy recommendations advocated by the OECD in this report were a call for regional governments to promote coordinated labour-market policies that would increase women's participation in entrepreneurship, establish ministries dedicated to promoting female entrepreneurship and SME ownership and improve 'fragmented' institutional support frameworks for women entrepreneurs. It also called for changes to existing business cultures to become more supportive of entrepreneurial activity among women, creating a more level playing-field for women entrepreneurs, improving business development services and entrepreneurship training, developing female entrepreneurship networks and associations and significantly improving women's access to credit and start-up finance (Organisation for Economic Cooperation and Development, 2012: 15–19). Very similar observations, criticisms and policy recommendations for improving the participation of women in the entrepreneurial and SME sectors of countries in the MENA region can be found in the 2009 MENA-OECD study (Organisation for Economic Cooperation and Development, 2009: 36–37), and in a more recent report on 1,228 female SME owners in five MENA countries (Brush, 2014: 5).

5.4 FEMALE ENTREPRENEURS AND SMALL BUSINESS OWNERS IN OMAN

We saw in Chapter 4 that the government of Oman has been trying – as part of its long-term economic diversification strategy – to encourage more nationals to work in the country's expatriate-dominated private sector and to become entrepreneurs and business owners. This, as one scholar has noted, has been 'one of the most vogue regional policy trends' in the Gulf States over the past few years as their populations continue to grow and tens of thousands of young people graduate from local universities every year, seeking employment opportunities (Ennis, 2015: 117). Over the last fifteen years, the Oman government has set up several organisations to facilitate and accelerate this process, including:

The Directorate General of SME Development. This has three departments: the Department of Guidance, the Business Pioneers Department and the Business Development Department.

The Oman Development Bank (OMD). This was founded in 1977, with a specific remit to invest in new and emerging sectors of the Oman economy and to be the leading investor in the Omani SME sector. The OMD's 2014 annual report indicated that it had issued 4,632 loans to the Oman SME sector worth 42.4 million Oman riyals (OMR) in 2014 and 5,213 loans worth OMR 51.3 million in 2013 ($110,148,000 and $133,269,000) (Oman Development Bank, 2015: 8).

The Self-Employment and National Autonomous Development (SANAD) program. SANAD was launched in 2001 to develop small-business projects among male and female Omanis aged eighteen to forty, provide advice and consulting services for start-ups and provide seed funding for individual and group entrepreneurial projects. It has more than 160 local offices in all of the governates of Oman, and a total of 42,740 Omanis had registered on this program from its inception to the end of December 2014, of whom 38 per cent were women (Gulf News, 2015d and 2010; SANAD Fund for Supporting and Developing Small Projects, 2015).

The National Business Centre (NBC). This was created by the Public Establishment for Industrial Estates in 2012 to 'facilitate and support the growth of investable ideas into business; building entrepreneurial skills through dedicated and focused training, coaching and mentoring; and providing business support facilities from office space, administrative support, financial support and consultancy services that are crucial in ensuring the success and survival of new ventures.' This organisation also acts as an incubator for new business ideas and concepts and acts as a link between large companies in Oman, entrepreneurs and the country's SME sector and it will also 'target budding entrepreneurs from universities' (Muscat Daily, 2015 and 2014).

The government of Oman would also like smaller companies to be able to 'piggy-back' off large-scale infrastructure and industrial programs in the country and has mandated that 10 per cent of all sub-contracts awarded by large companies must be awarded to SMEs (National Business Centre, 2015). The government also decreed, in May 2014, that 5 per cent of all annual business lending by Oman banks should be directed to Omani nationals – approximately 1 billion OMR ($2.6 billion) a year (Oxford Business Group, 2014: 1). Because of the shortage of suitably qualified Omani nationals it also exempted start-up companies from the general restrictions on private-sector companies employing expatriates in 2014 (Visa Reporter, 2014).

The Public Authority for Small and Medium Enterprises Development (PASMED). This was established in 2013, under the control of the Ministry for Commerce and Industry, to provide logistical and financial support for start-up firms in Oman. It also provides financial, technical, marketing and management courses for entrepreneurs (Buckley and Rynhart, 2011: 43–45). A number of other government-sanctioned initiatives have also been launched to support start-ups and assist established SMEs in both urban and rural areas of Oman. These include the Fund for the Development of Youth, Initilaaqah (part of the Shell group's worldwide LiveWire program), Sharakah and the Al Raffd Fund (which offer loans of up to OMR 100,000, about $260,000), Knowledge Oasis Muscat, the Information Technology Authority Incubation Centre, the Startup Oman program, the Cisco Entrepreneur Institute, the Muscat Entrepreneurs Conclave, the Oman Women's Entrepreneurship Network and the Women's Entrepreneurship Day (Oman) (Muscat Daily, 2014; Strolla and Peri, 2013: 20; Women's Entrepreneurship Day, 2014).

As part of its negotiations to introduce the International Labour Organisation's (ILO) Decent Work Country Programme to Oman, the government made a commitment in 2010 to 'foster an entrepreneurship culture in the Sultanate' and to review and consolidate the Know About Business (KAB) program, which had been introduced into all vocational training centres and technical colleges in the late 2000s (International Labour Organisation, 2010: 16). It committed to establishing a training centre and follow-up unit at the self-employment centre of SANAD and also announced that 'a program for SMEs (including women's entrepreneurship development) will be adapted to the Omani context and a training of trainers will be conducted.' The government also reiterated its commitment to promoting a more entrepreneurial culture 'through the creation of an enabling environment and the provision of SME support for youth, men and women.' This report also emphasised the urgent need for Oman to put much more effort into developing a thriving entrepreneurial and SME sector and to provide more resources and better training and education for female and male entrepreneurs (International Labour Organisation, 2010: 11 and 16–17).

Given that most government, MENA-OECD Investment Program and private-sector initiatives to encourage higher levels of entrepreneurial activity were initiated fairly recently, it is too early to judge if these have had any effect on the participation of Omani women (and men) in business start-ups over the last two to three years or if they are going to have any appreciable medium-term impact on an under-developed and over-regulated national SME sector (Buckley and Rynhart, 2011: 89–94 and 97–99). According to one recent report, for example, while more than 90 per cent of all firms registered in Oman fall into the SME category their net contribution to Oman's annual GDP is small – less than 15 per cent per annum. In the European Union, SMEs contributed 55 per cent to its member states' total GDP in 2013 (Ennis, 2014: 135). Four out of five SMEs in Oman have fewer than five employees, they employ only ten per cent of the national workforce and two thirds of start-ups fail within three years (Oxford Business Group, 2014: 1). Consequently, 'the thousands of micro-businesses that serve the ever-growing consumption and services needs of Omanis and expatriates, hardly contribute to the active employment of Omanis' (Ennis and al-Jamali, 2014: 15). In 2010, just 2 per cent of these often small and marginal businesses were owned and managed by Omani women, and half of those were sole-proprietorship micro-businesses. It is also worth noting that Oman was not included in either the 2015 Global Entrepreneurship and Development Institute's Female Entrepreneurship Index of seventy-seven countries or the 2015 GEM report on global female entrepreneurship (Kelley et al, 2015; Terjesen and Lloyd, 2015: 11).

Case Study

Given the lack of publicly available information on Omani women entrepreneurs, it proved to be difficult to locate a suitable sample of female-owned self-starting businesses that were not part of a larger family-owned enterprise, or home based micro-enterprises, and which also had at least five employees. However, after being provided with the name of one female Omani entrepreneur by an undergraduate student at Sultan Qaboos University (her older sister), seventeen more were identified by early April 2015.[3] The owners of these businesses were contacted and ten of them agreed to be interviewed, either at their businesses or at SQU during May or by video calls during July, August and September 2015. It should be noted that this case study was not a definitive analysis of all female entrepreneurs in Oman. It was an exploratory investigation – within the framework of the broader research literature on women entrepreneurs globally, in the MENA region and in Oman – of the experiences that a small group of Omani women entrepreneurs had while trying to establish and grow their businesses.

It has been noted in several reports that reliable information on the participation of self-employed women in MENA countries is not available, partly because of the way that 'participation' is defined and because of the under-counting of workers in the informal sector (International Labour Organisation, 2010: 5), an issue that has also been highlighted by the MENA-OECD Investment Program (MENA-OECD Investment Program, 2009: 9). While acknowledging the lack of reliable labour-market data on female entrepreneurs in Oman, it is reasonable to conclude that few Omani women are either self-starting entrepreneurs or own their own businesses. The few research studies that have documented the experiences of Omani women entrepreneurs from the early 2000s to 2015 confirm these findings. A study in 2002, for example, noted that the very small number of businesses owned by Omani women were mainly micro-businesses, employed very few staff and did not make a significant contribution to the country's annual GDP. These businesses were largely restricted to 'female' business sectors such as beauty salons and hairdressing, food and catering, education, restaurants, consulting and HR, tourism and retail (al-Riyami et al, 2002).

This mix has changed to some extent, but the proportion of women starting businesses and becoming business owners has only increased slightly over the last fifteen years, and a web search for 'female entrepreneurs in Oman' and 'notable Omani women entrepreneurs' during March 2015 revealed very few companies, such as Shadya al-Ismaily (Deema Oman), Ghada al-Harthya (G Patisserie and Cafe G Catering), Etab Zadjali (Cake Gallery) and Hilal al-Salama (Al Salama Fire Engineering Consultancy). More recent studies have also suggested that there is a big gap between 'entrepreneurial intentions' and starting a business: for every Omani woman who does create a new business, there are probably six or seven women who would like to do this but don't take the plunge. They have also highlighted the absence of an organic 'bottom-up' innovation and entrepreneurial ecosystem in Oman (and other oil-rich Arabian Gulf States) to support female entrepreneurship, as opposed to the entirely 'top-down', rentier frameworks and loan-systems that the government has been trying to implement through its various ministries (Bastian, 2015; Belwal et al, 2014; Ennis, 2014).

The interviewees ranged in age from twenty-eight to forty-nine and, on average, started their businesses when they were thirty years old. Six were married, two were divorced and two of the women were single. Eight of these women had children. Eight had university degrees, two also had MBAs, one had a PhD and two had college diplomas. All of these women had worked for at least five years prior to establishing their own businesses, seven in the public sector and three in the private sector, of whom two had worked for their families' businesses before creating their own firms and four mentioned that other members of their extended families were also involved in business ventures. Seven of the women had worked in jobs that were related to the businesses they created, and three indicated that these had grown out of hobbies or pastimes that had interested them during their teenage years and twenties. The main sources of financing for their businesses were personal or family savings (four), business loans from a commercial bank (three) and business loans from the OMD (two) and SANAD (two). None of these women reported that they had difficulties obtaining loans although their experiences were, almost certainly, atypical.

They managed several types of small companies: food and catering (three), retail (two), women's tailoring and fashion (two), printing and publishing (one), women's beauty and hairdressing salon (one) and consulting, recruitment and HR training (one). On average, they had been in business for 5.25 years. The average number of employees in these businesses was nine, the smallest number of employees was six and the largest number was thirty-seven. None of these businesses was involved in manufacturing; they were all service companies, and two of them had expanded their businesses to the UAE. Eight of these women were sole-owners of their business, one was in a partnership with another woman and one was owned jointly with her husband. Only three had plans to expand their businesses within the next five years. Seven had no plans to do this, and none of these women were planning to publicly list their companies in the future. When I asked them what were the main reasons they had decided to becoming entrepreneurs all of them mentioned 'independence' or 'autonomy' as being the most important factors, followed by 'dissatisfaction' or 'frustration' with the jobs they had been doing in large public- or private-sector organisations. Three of these women had also worked in family-run enterprises during their twenties but, thwarted by a lack of opportunities, had decided to create their own businesses:

> I and my two sisters tried to play a more active role in [my father's] business when I worked for him, but he and my brothers always had some concerns about us dealing with expatriate employees and representing the company in places like Riyadh. Instead of sending me or one of my sisters to negotiate with Saudi companies he would send a male manager. This caused many arguments! My father still thinks I should spend more time with my children

and husband, but they are now more supportive of what I'm doing. One day my daughters will come and work for me and the boys can go and work for my brothers!

(35-year-old; food and catering business).

Only one of these women expressed some bemusement about being a business owner. I had asked her, 'Did you think you would ever have your own business when you were growing up?' and she replied:

La! No, I didn't! I mean my mother didn't even attend school after she was 14, so even the idea that I would eventually go to a university and work was crazy when I was young. But I did, because I wanted a different life to hers and the other women who lived in my village. Even then, my father and mother would have preferred me just to marry and have children and not work … I think I've always had a, how do you say, a rebellious streak, and even though I worked for many years and did get married and had three children, I always had this hope that one day I could create my own business … I know that this is unusual for a woman in this country because most women are still very controlled by their families, and they are expected to submit their wishes and aspirations to their family. What I did clashes with these beliefs … Luckily, my husband is what you would call more liberal and he was very supportive of this ... I also hope that my two daughters will also see me as a role model and be successful business women when they graduate from their university courses!

(44-year-old from a rural family; retail business).

'Personal fulfilment' and 'personal growth' came next, followed by 'the challenge of creating my own business' and 'identifying a new market opportunity'. All of the women indicated that 'making money' was a motivation, but it was not the most important one for any of them. All of these women also mentioned the greater visibility of Arabic women business leaders and business owners, particularly in the UAE, as something that had also influenced their decision to create their own companies. Only one woman, a divorcee, said that 'economic necessity' was a motivating factor, in order to support herself and her children after an acrimonious separation from her husband, who had then moved abroad with his second wife. Six of these women acknowledged the support that their families and husbands had given them when establishing their businesses. As this forty-year-old woman who established her consulting, recruitment and HR training business in 2011 observed:

> You are familiar with our laws and you know about our rules which mean that without approval from a male guardian it can be very difficult to start a business in Oman, for a woman I mean. But my husband is a good man and he always supported me in my ambitions and he said, 'If you want to do it, do it!' Except when our children were young he has never prevented me from working and he helped me find a loan from a bank, and from SANAD, and also with the preparation of all the forms – there are a lot of those – for the Ministry of Commerce and Industry, the Licensing Department, the Ministry of Health, the Labour Department and so on ... I'm not sure I could have done this without his help ... I would also like to add that I don't think I could have done this when I was in my twenties, because the society was not so accepting of these things, *yanni*, for a woman to do this, to be her own boss, but I think it is easier now for a woman to become a business owner.

Later in the interview, she made these comments:

> It is very noticeable that Oman women mainly create businesses that are 'acceptable' to men, in fashion, retail, beauty salons, education, HR training and so on. A lot of these businesses are only for women clients, not men ... I mean where are the women technology entrepreneurs and how many women own factories on the industrial estates? Hardly any at all! I think if we are really

serious about involving more women in creating new businesses, we have to include an element of this in all courses that students do, at school and at universities and we have to encourage them to do this. They should not just expect to work for a big company or a government department which I think too many young Omanis still expect to do.

However, all of these women felt that conservative attitudes in Oman created problems and difficulties for women entrepreneurs, although these were changing:

> I think the most important issue for Omani women to understand is that the law and our religion do not prevent us from becoming business-women. I mean that Islam does not prevent us from doing this but the attitudes of some men can be a problem, because they will use this as an excuse to stop their wives or daughters from running a business ... Another issue is if I hire expatriate men to work for me which I have often done. The laws of our country do not prevent me from doing this but there may be some disapproval of this because they are not members of my family, so my strategy was to employ expatriate women who could interact with the male employees. I also hired one of my younger brothers last year which also helps
>
> *(39-year-old; retail business).*

> Obviously, it is not so easy for a woman to create a business in Oman, when compared to America or Australia. People are still not used to this idea. But, being an entrepreneur is hard, whether you're a man or a woman. For me, I always had a very clear idea about what I wanted to create and I was confident that I could do this ... So, yes, Oman is conservative with regard to gender, but things are changing, and if you have a good product and care about your customers you can be successful if you are willing to work hard and learn from your mistakes ... It is good that our leaders talk more about this matter, for us to be more self-

sufficient, but everyone needs to do much more to encourage this in families, in the media, in university and college courses – everywhere ... It is also still an annoyance to me that men are surprised to find that they are talking to a woman when they call and ask to speak to the owner about something. Or, if they call by and see me sitting in the Managing Director's office and think I am a secretary!

(36-year-old; retail business).

The three women who had been in business since the mid-2000s were very critical of the complex bureaucratic processes they had to endure in several different government ministries when establishing their businesses. Among the difficulties they identified were the plethora of forms and certificates that had to be completed, the number of separate licenses they had to obtain and difficulties in complying with the country's strict Omanisation policies after they had opened their businesses (a policy, as noted earlier, has been recently waived for start-up companies in Oman). These difficulties have also been highlighted by the World Bank Group, who ranked Oman 149 out of 189 countries for 'ease of starting a business', a fall from 121/189 in 2015 (World Bank, 2016b).

These women also commented on the lack of women's entre-preneur networks when establishing their businesses and they had to rely primarily on informal female networks, their own research or on advice from family members who had experience of creating and managing SMEs. Eight of these women also felt that the official support systems that are supposed to help Omani women establish small businesses were still 'inadequate' and 'underdeveloped' in 2015. Even those who had established businesses within the last two to three years were critical of the bureaucratic hurdles involved in setting up new businesses. On a more positive note, none of these women mentioned that they had major problems balancing their work and family commitments, and only two indicated they experi-enced 'some' work–life conflict. In fact, most of them felt that they had more time to spend with their families and children when compared to the time they had been working as employees in large organisations. Moreover, all of the women observed that the situation was better for young women entrepreneurs today and several mentioned that the government and private-sector initiatives described earlier *should* have a beneficial effect on the rate of business start-ups among women in Oman. Hence, these women also believed that it would gradually become easier and more acceptable for Omani women to become entrepreneurs. For example:

> The biggest problem is that we still do not have an environment that is very friendly to women who want to be independent and manage their own businesses, and there are still many restrictions on how we can interact with men when we are trying to manage a business ... but, I do not see how the government can call for Omanis to create new businesses, and then not support us when we are trying to do this. I think many women would consider doing this if there were not so many obstacles and difficulties to deal with and I think the government has to provide more support for women ... and they really need to take away the male-guardianship rules! I think they understand this better now but these things will take time to change
>
> *(37-year-old; women's beauty and hairdressing business).*

> As I have explained, it was very difficult for me to start my business and there were many obstacles that were overcome at the beginning. But, this was always my dream and I have succeeded in doing this ... I have also noticed that there are more Omani women who are starting their own businesses and I think this is a very encouraging sign, but there are also many things that the government could do to make it easier for women to do this and to encourage them ... I think that this will improve in the future because everyone knows that we have to develop all of our business sectors and we can't do that unless we are creating a lot more new businesses
>
> *(38-year-old; printing and publishing business).*

The outcomes of this exploratory study correspond with those of other studies on women entrepreneurs and SME owners in Oman, the UAE, the KSA and the broader MENA region. For instance, the generic factors that inhibit many Omani women from becoming entrepreneurs and SME owners are not unique to their country. The traditional gender stereotypes and negative attitudes towards female entrepreneurs and business owners that prevail in many other Islamic countries, including the UAE and the KSA, are also widespread in Oman. It is also apparent that while Omani women are being exhorted by government authorities and the media to become entrepreneurs, it cannot be said that there is a 'female-friendly' small business culture in Oman.

There was also evidence from the interviews that families played a pivotally important role in the decisions that these women made about creating their own businesses. Six of the women, for example, indicated that their families (and husbands) were very supportive of their decision to become entrepreneurs, but they also believed that this level of support was not typical of most Omani families. They all confirmed that most Omani women are still prevented from 'doing their own thing' by their families and/or husbands, and there was still some social stigma associated with Omani women becoming entrepreneurs. Four of these women also felt that young women were not willing to work hard enough to create new businesses, eight of them felt that young Omani women were still too 'risk averse' and, without exception, believed that the continuing availability of well-paid and secure employment in the public sector was a major disincentive for most Omani women to become entrepreneurs and SME owners.

They also believed that existing registration and licensing law procedures were still too complex, repetitive and time consuming, and that the Omani Chamber of Commerce and Industry did not understand the unique problems faced by female entrepreneurs and did not work effectively to support small-business start-ups among women. They also said that there was a lack of suitably qualified and motivated Omanis to satisfy their human resource needs, citing both the lower salaries they were able to offer and longer and more flexible working hours they required from employees as also being deterrents for many Omanis. All of them wanted the recently introduced waiver on employing expatriate employees in new start-up companies to be extended to existing SMEs because, as one of these ladies observed, 'The biggest problem I have faced, and I know this is a widespread problem, is finding good staff. Many Omanis do not want to do this kind of work and so we are very reliant on expatriate workers.' Last but not least, eighteen of these women indicated that the provision of subsidised day-care services would be one of the most important changes that the government could introduce to help working Omani women.

I asked these women what else could be done to encourage more Omani women to become entrepreneurs and SME owners. They all suggested that public- and private-sector universities should offer more major programs or specialisation courses in innovation, entrepreneurship and small-business management, and they should also set up business incubators to encourage more undergraduates to become entrepreneurs. This is something that Sultan Qaboos University, regarded as the top national university in Oman, is aware of. A proposal to introduce a new undergraduate degree specialisation in Innovation and Entrepreneurship at the Sultan Qaboos University College of Economics and Political Science (CEPS) was submitted to the University Council in November 2013. This proposal noted that more than half of the top fifteen universities in the world offered entrepreneurship programs, and 30 per cent of senior-year undergraduate students wanted a specialisation in innovation and entrepreneurship at CEPS (al-Hashemi et al, 2013: 9 and 12). However, while the authors of this proposal showed that its curriculum was in alignment with national initiatives to develop entrepreneurial and SME management skills among young educated people in Oman, this new program had not been introduced to the CEPS curriculum by June 2016.[4] An analysis of the business and management programs offered by the top ten universities in Oman, during January 2016, revealed that only one of these offered a specialisation in entrepreneurship (Majan University College, where five of twenty-three core courses on their undergraduate management program had 'small business' or 'entrepreneurship' in their titles). One university (Dhofar) had established a Centre of Entrepreneurship in October 2014, but it did not appear to offer specialist undergraduate or postgraduate courses in this subject.[5]

Even if an entrepreneurship specialisation is to be introduced at CEPS in the near future, there will be an uphill battle to 'sell' the idea of entrepreneurship to new intakes of students at SQU (and other local universities). This would then be followed by a time-lag of three to four years before they enter what is likely to be a depressed national labour market in the late 2010s and early 2020s, and it would be several more years before any businesses they create become established. During the spring semester of 2015, for example, I asked fifty final-year students who were attending an organisational development and change course how many of them were thinking about creating their own businesses. About one fifth of the group raised their hands. When I then asked if they could describe their business concept or if any of them had started to prepare a business plan, only three students were able to do this. Only one of the ten final-year female undergraduates interviewed in May 2015 indicated that she was 'thinking seriously' about creating her own business, had discussed this with her parents and also done some preliminary research on the logistics of turning her business concept into a commercial reality.

A recent study of entrepreneurship initiatives in Oman in 2014 concluded that government initiatives to encourage entrepreneurship are '*ad hoc* and rife with inconsistencies', and the promotion of SME growth in Oman is:

> Wedged between an international neo-liberal policy agenda
> and a regional economy circumscribed by two interrelated

path-dependencies that are difficult to correct – national addictions to hydrocarbon revenue and foreign labour. Entrepreneurship promotion, although cast in the language of private sector development, has thus far become another vehicle for state patronage. In fact the mechanisation of SME support by familiar rentier patterns may only be delaying a day of reckoning while in fact compounding existing fiscal and social challenges ... *the embedded structure of the regional political economy has resulted in entrepreneurship promotion policies which will not unleash the transformative economic processes necessary for reform. It has merely marked the continuation of business as usual with a new façade* ... Chambers of Commerce and Industry in Oman claim to be promoting entrepreneurship [but their] primary constituencies remain the family business empires whose interests, more often than not, conflict with those of new, smaller start-ups

(Ennis, 2015:116 and 126; my emphasis).

Ennis's conclusions match up with those of other reports on the continuing structural imbalances that exist in the Oman labour market, most notably its over-reliance on expatriate workers, its continuing 'addiction' to oil and gas revenues and the country's 'top-down' political, administrative and business systems. In Chapter 1 we had also commented on the lack of investment in basic research and development and the low levels of industrial innovation and patent registrations in Oman and all other countries in the MENA region. Consequently, much entrepreneurial and small business activity in Oman is still not concentrated in high-value and high-growth sectors such as bio, nano and quantum technologies, IT and software development, renewable energy technologies, high-tech engineering, cutting-edge manufacturing and so forth. Efforts to encourage entrepreneurship and SME ownership have been almost entirely top-down and it appears that the new businesses that are being created continue to be in low-value-added sectors and employ few staff. Would-be-entrepreneurs in Oman also continue to complain about 'nepotism and favouritism within the ministries', steep registration fees, the lack of procedural clarity, burdensome bureaucratic processes and difficulties obtaining start up financing from Omani banks (Ennis, 2015: 132).

While all the women I interviewed were running solvent businesses, none of these were in high-value markets, only three had modest plans to expand their companies, and they did not employ many Omanis (in fact, with one exception, most of their employees were expatriates). And, as noted earlier, just 2 per cent of SMEs in Oman are owned and managed by national women, and half of those are sole-proprietorship micro-businesses. There also appears to be a significant disconnect between the government's appeals for more Omanis to become entrepreneurs and the courses that are currently being offered to their 'best and brightest' at the country's top public and private universities. This indicates that there is still a very large gap between government- and state-controlled media rhetoric and the reality of establishing the kind of thriving entrepreneurial and SME sector in Oman that its young people will readily participate in. In Chapter 9, we will review some strategies that could be implemented by government and private-sector organisations to increase the participation of Omani women (and men) in high-value entrepreneurial ventures in the future.

However, as noted earlier, this small sample of women entrepreneurs is not representative of all Omani women entrepreneurs and SME owners, and so we still have no idea how many Omani women may be *thinking* about creating their own businesses but choose not to do this because of family pressures, because their male guardians refuse to sign the various legal documents that are required to establish a new firm or because the hurdles to achieving this goal appear to be too high. As in the UAE and the KSA, there are probably a significant number of women in Oman who aspire to create new businesses but choose not to because of these barriers, but additional research would be required to confirm this. We also know very little about the roles and responsibilities of women in established family-owned businesses in Oman and how their experiences may differ from those of self-starting female entrepreneurs.

5.5 BALANCING WORK AND FAMILY LIFE

As noted in Chapter 3, the issues of work–life balance and work–family conflict have been the subject of hundreds of research articles and dozens of books over the past three decades. However, in common with the UAE, it is only recently that dual-career couples have emerged in Oman and, concurrently, growing concerns about the impact of work on family life, the traditional roles of Omani women and Islamic beliefs and values. Although there are one or two passing references to work–life balance and work–family conflict issues in the few articles that have been written about women in Oman, no systematic research has been conducted on these issues (Goveas and Aslam, 2011: 237). Hence, what follows is one of the first accounts of the emergence of work–life balance and work–family conflict issues in this country and the growing challenges that some Omani women face in balancing their work and family lives. It describes the results of a questionnaire survey of ninety-one married working Omani women conducted during April 2015 and the work–life balance support provided by their employers and also discusses the broader implications of the data results.[6]

The demographic data reflect the relatively youthful working population of Oman, following the national baby boom of the 1980s and 1990s: 21.1 per cent of this group were aged twenty to twenty-five years, 25.6 per cent twenty-five to thirty, 40.0 per cent thirty to thirty-five, and just 13.3 per cent were older than thirty-five; thirty-five of these women had one child, twenty-eight had two, twenty-one had three and seven had four or more children. Of our respondents, 93.4 per cent had husbands who were also working full time or managing their own businesses. Most of these women worked in supervisory or middle management roles and 35.2 per cent had less than five years' work experience; 28.5 per cent had six to ten years' work experience and 23.1 per cent had eleven to fifteen years' experience. Only 13.2 per cent of these women had worked for more than fifteen years. On average, women in the private sector reported that they worked slightly longer weeks than their peers in the public sector (5.1 versus 5.0 days per week), and there were also some differences in their average daily working hours (Table 5.9).

In the public-sector sub-sample, a majority of respondents reported being 'neutral' about the amount of time they spend at work, with 33.6 per cent of respondents reporting that they were 'happy' and 13.1 per cent 'very happy' with their working hours. However, more respondents in the private-sector sub-sample felt 'unhappy' or 'very unhappy' about the amount of time they were spending at work (32.2 per cent compared to 12.1 per cent among public-sector employees). Furthermore, 33.2 per cent of the private-sector employees reported that work pressures 'sometimes make me feel very tired' and only 12.8 per cent reported that their job never left them feeling tired. And while 26.8 per cent of public- and semi-government-sector employees indicated that they had 'sometimes' dealt with work

TABLE 5.9 *Daily hours worked by women in public, semi-government and private-sector organisations in Oman (N = 91 women)*

| | Daily average working hours | | | |
	7–8	9–10	11–12	12 or more
Public sector and Semi-government	*73.6*	*27.4*	*0.0*	*0.0*
Private sector	*28.6*	*62.7*	*8.7*	*0.0*

(This includes 'time spent on work-related duties while at home' and 'commuting hours' in order to assess the total number of hours engaged in these activities by these women each week. 62.9 per cent of our respondents reported that they took '30 minutes or less' to travel to work, 28.6 reported '30–60 minutes' and the remainder reported 'more than 60 minutes)

during weekends and holidays, this figure rose to 67.2 per cent among those working in the private sector. To develop a clearer picture of how our respondents cope with the competing demands of work and family life, we asked them a general question: 'Do you feel that you are able to balance your work responsibilities and family life?' The results are presented in Table 5.10.

TABLE 5.10 *Do you feel that you are able to balance your work responsibilities and family life?*

	Never	Rarely	Sometimes	Often	Always
Public sector and Semi-government	2.2	12.1	30.8	32.9	22.0
Private sector	11.0	24.2	36.2	14.3	14.3

The responses to this question show that a majority of the women who work in the public and semi-government sectors feel that they are able to balance their work responsibilities and family life, although nearly one third of them reported that it was 'sometimes' difficult to balance these competing responsibilities. The situation for those working in the private sector is rather different, with one third reporting that they were 'never' or 'rarely' able to balance the demands of their jobs and families. There is also evidence of negative spill-over between work and our respondents' leisure time, with noticeable differences in the responses of the private-sector employees when compared to public and semi-government employees (Tables 5.11 and 5.12).

TABLE 5.11 *How often do you think about work when you are not actually at work or when travelling to work?*

	Never	Rarely	Sometimes	Often	Always
Public sector and semi-government	0.0	27.5	65.9	6.6	0.0
Private sector	0.0	16.4	50.5	27.5	5.6

TABLE 5.12 *Do you ever miss out on quality time with your families and friends because of work pressures?*

	Never	Rarely	Sometimes	Often	Always
Public sector and semi-government	4.3	29.6	59.4	6.7	0.0
Private sector	0.0	12.1	59.3	28.6	0.0

The data also suggested that work responsibilities had few negative effects on the amount of time that our public-sector respondents had to spend with their children. However, once again, the longer working hours required of those working in private-sector companies in Oman was having an effect on the time they could spend with their children during the week and at weekends (Tables 5.13 and 5.14).

TABLE 5.13 *On an average working day, how much time do you have to spend with your children?*

	< 2 hours	2–3 hours	3–4 hours	> 4 hours
Public sector and semi-government	6.6	34.1	44.0	15.3
Private sector	47.3	29.6	21.9	1.2

TABLE 5.14 *During an average weekend, how much time do you spend with your children?*

	< 4 hours	4–5 hours	5–6 hours	> 6 hours
Public sector and semi-government	4.4	10.9	31.8	52.9
Private sector	19.6	31.8	27.5	21.1

In order to evaluate how Emirati women coped with the competing demands of work and family, we also asked them about the childcare arrangements in their households. The data showed that most working Omani women – regardless of the sector that they work in – were still heavily dependent on extended families and older relatives for child care and support or a combination of family support, nannies and servants (Table 5.15). Only a small minority of our respondents felt overwhelmed by the competing demands of their home and work lives, but there was evidence of some strains and stresses among this group of women (Table 5.16).

TABLE 5.15 *Who – primarily – takes care of your children while you are at work?*

	Spouse	Parents, in-laws or close relatives	Servant or Nanny
Public sector and semi-government	*2.1*	*55.0*	*42.9*
Private sector	*0.0*	*57.1*	*42.9*

TABLE 5.16 *What is the impact of home life on your work performance?*

	Public sector and semi-government	Private sector
Impact		
My home life has no impact on my work performance	*74.8*	*44.0*
Family responsibilities can reduce the time I have to work on job- related tasks	*8.9*	*14.2*
Family responsibilities can distract me from work-tasks	*7.7*	*24.2*
Problems at home can make me feel irritable at work	*8.6*	*17.6*
At times, work pressures and family responsibilities can overwhelm me	*0.0*	*13.4*
(% that 'strongly agreed' or 'agreed' with each statement)		

These findings confirm the results of other studies on work–life balance and work–family conflict, indicating the existence of a 'high-pressure' subgroup of some one in four Omani women working in the private sector who, at times, may have been struggling to balance the competing demands of high-pressure jobs and busy family lives.

In the final section of this survey, we examined the support provided by our respondents' employers to help them balance their work and family lives. The data portray a clear picture of both the lack of work–life balance support in public- and private-sector organisations in Oman and specific services or HR policies that are known to help with balancing work and family responsibilities (Table 5.17).

In an open-ended question, we asked those respondents who had reported conflicts between their jobs and family lives, to indicate five factors that they believed to be the greatest hindrance to achieving better work-life balance. In order of importance, these were 'Negative/patriarchal/conservative attitudes of (male) senior managers, bosses or supervisors' (N = 23); 'Inadequate maternity leave provisions' (N = 18); 'Lack of childcare facilities at work' (N = 19); 'Negative attitudes of family members' (N = 17); 'culture and religion' (i.e. social pressures to put family before work and their husband's career; N = 14); and 'technology' (i.e. being accessible 24/7 for work-related matters; N = 11). The final question we asked our respondents in the questionnaire was, 'Do you think that if employees enjoy a good balance between their work and family lives, then their work-performance will improve?' Four out of five of these women replied 'Yes', one in five were 'not sure' and none of them replied 'No'.

At the time this research was conducted during 2015, work–life balance and work–family conflict were not a noticeable part of public discourse or media commentary in Oman. However, as we noted in Chapter 3 in the context of the UAE, these may become more significant issues in the future, and they are already a source of concern to some of the small number of Omani women who work in the private sector. There were consistent differences in the responses of Omani women who worked in the private sector when compared to those in the public sector. Women in the former group reported longer

TABLE 5.17 *Work–life balance support and services provided by employers*

'Does your company have any specific services or HR policies to help with work–life balance?'			
	Yes	No	Not sure/don't know
Public sector and semi-government	14.3	71.4	14.3
Private sector	18.6	77.0	4.4

'What support does your company provide to help with WLB?'		
	Public sector and semi government	Private sector
Policy		
Flexible starting and finishing times	16.4	21.9
Option to work part-time or job share	15.3	4.3
Crèche, day-care or nursery at your workplace	0.0	0.0
Career breaks or sabbaticals	7.6	0.0
Parental or family advice	0.0	0.0
*Paid maternity leave**	100.0	100.0

*(This excludes 'Not sure/don't know' responses. * Omani women are eligible to receive 60 days paid maternity leave and can take also 12 months unpaid leave in addition to this. Additional discretionary maternity leave/salary is also provided by some international private-sector companies in Oman)*

working hours, had less time to spend with their children and families and experienced greater difficulties in balancing work and family commitments. There was also some evidence of work overload and of conflicts between their home and work lives. However, most of the women in both groups did have the support of extended families who routinely helped out with childcare, or they could afford nannies and, in some cases, servants. This meant that work–family conflict appeared to be a less significant and stressful issue than it is for many working women in Western societies.

However, it seems likely that a growing number of working Omani women will not be able to rely on their extended families for support in the future to the extent that they may have been able to in the past. Of course, this is based on the assumption that their participation rate in the national labour market will increase significantly over the next five to ten years. If this does happen, then work–life balance and work–family conflict will become more significant issues in Oman in the future particularly for private-sector employees, where working hours are generally longer and there are generally much greater pressures on employees to put in whatever hours are required by their employers. Ameliorating these potential conflicts will require positive and creative solutions from the government of Oman and employer organisations if they are not to become impediments to the participation of more women in the private sector during the 2020s and beyond. Most of the women in this study felt that the organisations they worked for could be more sympathetic to work–life balance and work–family conflict issues and, as their peers in the UAE did, they also suggested a range of HR initiatives that could be implemented to ameliorate these. They also believed that these would also enhance their prospects of becoming leaders in the future, particularly in the private sector. Their suggestions and the implications of these for the advancement of women in the national labour market and the growth and development of Oman's economy in the future are discussed further in Chapters 8–9.

5.6 CONCLUSION

We observed in Chapter 4 that while the labour-force participation rate of women in Oman has increased over the last decade it is still – *pro rata* – much lower than the participation rate of women in the UAE. More Omani women have moved into senior positions in the public sector and they are increasingly involved in the administration of the country, but they are still under-represented among the ruling political elite and there were just two women ministers in a national cabinet of thirty in 2016 (in the education and higher-education portfolios). The studies that have looked at the aspirations of working Omani women have concluded that while they were very ambitious and highly motivated they were often very frustrated by traditional male expectations of their roles in society and in the workplace (Goveas and Aslam, 2011; al-Lamki, 2007). Many thousands of young Emirati women are now graduating from the country's universities every year, many of them want to work and be successful in their careers and a growing number are probably nurturing ambitions to create their own businesses. If they are encouraged in their endeavours, then women could make a much bigger contribution to the development of an economy that can sustain all Omanis in the future, and this, in turn, could have an irreversible effect on their independence, economic power and social status in the future.

However, as in the UAE, the traditional view that women 'take care' and men 'take charge' is still entrenched in the culture of Omani society today. There are a sizeable number of men who still believe that women should not work and that the most suitable role for a woman is to be a good wife and a mother. Many of them still have doubts about how well women might perform in leadership roles and possible effects of this on their families and children. My research during the five months I spent in Oman confirms Jones and Ridout's belief that Omani women continue to face significant cultural and social barriers which are impeding their full participation in the national labour market, in particular the types of jobs and entrepreneurial activities that can generate new and diverse sources of national wealth in the future (Jones and Ridout, 2015: 264).

While university-educated working Omani women would agree that they now have much better opportunities to pursue careers, they still believe that there are barriers and impediments to their career progression in organisations and in their professional careers and most men and women remain pessimistic that a significant number of Omani women will ascend to leadership positions in private-sector companies in the future. Moreover, for most university-educated Omani women, the longer working hours, lower salaries and mixed working environments in private-sector organisations remain significant deterrents to a career move outside the public-sector. These factors continue to influence their choice of careers and explain why many young Omani women still prefer to work in public and semi-government organisations. As in the UAE, these generally offer much better employment conditions when compared to equivalent jobs in the private sector, particularly for younger employees. Women continue to be underrepresented in the private sector, and very few are self-made entrepreneurs and business owners.

At the same time, there are two 'self-imposed' barriers to equality that confront women in Oman, ones they share with their peers in the UAE and the KSA: their beliefs about their own capabilities and what they need to do to achieve their life goals. Their self-efficacy continue to be affected by the influences they are exposed to when they are young and, in male-dominated Oman, some may continue to believe that they do not have what it takes to succeed in professional careers, as business owners and as leaders. The second, as we have seen, are the difficulties that some professional women have in managing highly demanding jobs – particularly in the private sector – while coping with childcare and domestic responsibilities.

Although the Decent Country Program (2010–2013) made several references to the urgent need to develop new policies and strategies to empower women in the national labour force, and the Takatuf program was established in 2013 to enhance the country's human resource capabilities, there were – to the best of my knowledge – no country-wide, integrated national programs in place in 2015 to facilitate the advancement of women in public- and private-sector organisations in Oman (al-Jashmi, 2015; Takatuf HR Academy, 2015). Nevertheless, there are some reasons to be cautiously optimistic about the future for women in Oman and the long-term development and security of this country, providing the political and business leadership of the country makes wise decisions about the economic, political and social reforms that will be required to achieve this. Women have made significant progress in the public sector, there are several well-known female Omanis in the national assembly and a few have become business leaders. And, at least anecdotally, all the Omanis I discussed these issues with during my time in Oman believed that the economic empowerment of women will play a vital role in the development of their country in the future. However, as we have seen, the general advancement of women in the national labour market of Oman has been patchy and we will return to re-examine this issue and the indispensable role they could play in Oman's economy during the 2020s and beyond in Chapter 8.

6   The Kingdom of Saudi Arabia

6.1   INTRODUCTION

In this chapter, we first describe the recent history of the KSA and its strategic importance as the world's largest producer of oil. We look at the economic, political and social challenges facing this country, the progress it has made towards its long-term objective of building a diversified post-hydrocarbon economy and then review the changing life experiences of Saudi women and their entry to the national workforce over the last twenty years. This is followed by an account of the symbolic significance of this country for Islam and the global Muslim diaspora (*umma*) and an analysis of the pervasive influence of Wahhabist Islamic beliefs in the KSA. We look at how these shape perceptions of the intrinsic natures of women and men, their roles in Saudi society and their responsibilities to their families. This is followed, with reference to recent World Economic Forum (WEF) Global Gender Gap (GGG) reports and a review of the KSA's observance of the Convention on the Elimination of All Forms of Discrimination against Women (CEDAW), by an analysis of the status of women in Saudi society, the labour market and the workplace. Towards the end of this chapter, we evaluate the limited progress that women have made in the Saudi labour market and workforce and ask if recent economic and legal reforms are likely to have a beneficial effect on the legal rights of women in the KSA and increase their very low levels of participation in the country's workforce.

6.2   A BRIEF HISTORY OF THE KSA

In theory, Saudi Arabia should not exist – its survival defies the laws of logic and history. Look at its princely rulers, dressed in funny clothes, *trusting in God rather than man, and running their country on principles that most of the world has abandoned with relief. Shops are closed for prayers five times a day, executions take place in the street – and let's not even get started on the status of women. Saudi Arabia is one of the planet's enduring – and for some – quite offensive enigmas ... It is a dramatic and important story, and as I set out to tell it, I cannot help wondering: will they ban this book* like the last one!*

Lacey (2009: xxiii; *they did)

On first impression, the major cities of the KSA look much like many others in the Arabian Gulf region with numerous high-rise office and apartment buildings, a cornucopia of large malls selling consumer goods of every description, fast-food outlets (McDonald's, Burger King, Dunkin' Donuts, KFC and so on), multi-lane freeways, car parks crammed full of large and expensive German, American and Japanese four-wheel vehicles and dealerships selling all the best-known luxury automobile brands. But one soon notices that all shops and offices close down several times during the day and evening for prayers, and during the holy month of Ramadan everything slows down to a very leisurely pace. There are no cinemas showing English-language films, no theatres, bars and nightclubs or venues for live music – although both music and dance have always been an important part of Saudi life. Then you become aware of the ubiquitous signs posted in all the malls, public buildings and universities in Riyadh: 'Family area – no single men allowed!', 'No men allowed in this shop!', 'Female only bank!' and 'Women only section/prayer room/library/lift/seating area!' One quickly realises that beneath a thin veneer of modernity, the people of this country live in a very traditional, deeply conservative and male-dominated society. It is also a country where 'young women are guarded like crown jewels until their wedding' and almost every decision they make throughout their lives has to be approved by their fathers, husbands or brothers (Haidar, 2015: 5).

Even before I left the UAE and moving to Riyadh in August 2011, the all-encompassing influence of the country's austere religious authorities was very evident. The lengthy customs' form I was required to complete indicated that there were many forbidden (*haram*) items that could not be brought into the KSA. These included some obvious ones such as pork, alcohol and any images of the naked body, but also all non-Islamic religious texts and any books that were critical of Islam, the KSA or the Saudi royal family. Books on human evolution and atheism were also prohibited. Religious icons, Christmas decorations and stuffed animal toys were not allowed, nor were DVDs or CDs with 'anti-Islamic' or 'profane' images. Consequently, four boxes of prohibited items were sent back to my home in Australia before my move to Riyadh. Another forbidden item, I later discovered, was the *Toy Story* movie series, which was confiscated from my household container by Saudi Customs in October 2011, although the nature of the subversive threat Woody, Buzz Lightyear and the rest of the gang posed to the KSA was never explained. Hence, anyone with a curious mind who visits the KSA is bound to ask 'Why is this country the way it is?' and also perhaps wonder, as one long-term observer of this country has done, why 'there is a 1400 year gap between what the place looks like and how it functions' (Macfarquhar, 2009: 246). To answer these questions, we need to look at the turbulent history of the KSA and, in the following sections, unravel the complex political, legal, cultural, religious and social characteristics of this country.

For many centuries, the Arabian Peninsula served as an important trading and commercial link between the Occidental and Oriental worlds. It is also the birthplace of the Prophet Muhammed in 570 CE (year 0 in the Islamic faith), and the location of the two holiest sites in the Muslim world at *Al Masjid al-Haram* (Mecca) and *Al Masjid al-Nabawi* (Medina). For more than six centuries after the death of the Prophet, the region that would later become Saudi Arabia was ruled over by a succession of foreign empires and, by the early eighteenth-century, had become an isolated country, populated by fragmented, semi-feudal, nomadic tribes and known by Saudis as the period of *jahiliyya* (ignorance of the true faith). In 1744, Muhammad ibn Saud, the ruler of Diriyah and an *imam*, Muhammad bin Abd al-Wahhab, united some of these tribes and created the first Saudi proto-state. They also promoted a very strict and literalist interpretation of Islam, based on the Hanbali school of Islamic theology. In 1818, the Ottoman Empire destroyed Diriyah, but the al-Saud family later regained control of central Arabia and established a new government. This eventually collapsed in 1891 after a long period of tribal infighting. The al-Saud family then fled to Kuwait until Abdul Aziz bin Saud (known as ibn-Saud or al-Saud in the West and formally as Abdal Aziz ibn al-Rahman al-Saud) returned to capture Riyadh in 1902 (al-Rasheed, 2010: 1–2; 13–35).

After the collapse of the Ottoman Empire after World War I and the carve-up of the MENA region under the Sykes-Picot agreement of 1916, Saudi Arabia did not become a European colony but fell within the British sphere of influence in the region and Lloyd George's government gave its support to al-Saud's rule over the nascent Saudi state at the end of World War I. After a protracted period of internal conflict, fifty-two documented battles and the defeat of several rivals, al-Saud became king in 1932 and established the Kingdom of Saudi Arabia, *al-Mamlakah al-Arabiyah as-Su'diyah* (the Arab Saudi Kingdom), with the Qur'an forming the basis of its first constitution. He was also proclaimed as the official Guardian of the Two Holy Mosques at Mecca and Medina and the head of the *umma*. Originally separated into four distinct tribal regions, the KSA was organised into five major provinces, al-Hijaz, Najd, al-Ahsa, Asir and Taboouk (the western, central, eastern, southern and northern provinces) and Riyadh, located in Najd, became the official political and administrative capital of the country (al-Munajjed, 1997: 1–6; al-Rasheed, 2010: 1–2 and 37–66).[1]

Before the discovery of oil in the 1930s, Arabian society was divided between those who lived in the interior such as the Sharif, Rashid and Najd tribes, those who inhabited other small towns and villages in the provinces and semi-nomadic Bedouin tribes who had ancient ancestral roots in the region. Communities were based around tribal, clan and extended families. As in the UAE and Oman, allegiances to these were paramount and tribes were associated with specific regions of the KSA, and these were only incorporated into al-Saud's realm after he had overcome the resistance of several local tribal leaders. There is, as in other Gulf States, a tribal hierarchy – with the Najds from the central province at the top, followed by the Hijazis and eastern-province Sunnis and the rest below these. Tribal identity and loyalty were strong and this has continued to the present day, with political and social influence still deeply affected by tribal affiliation and *wasta*. The country's main sources of income came from trading and some agriculture, as well as exports such as camels, horses, wool and dates. However, the biggest source of national revenue was the tax paid by pilgrims attending the annual *hajj* (pilgrimage) in Mecca. Oil prospecting began in the eastern provinces in 1933, and the first significant oil discoveries were made in 1938. The KSA initially granted a sixty-year concession for oil exploration to California (later Standard) Oil in 1933 in exchange for $50,000 in gold. Five years later, the country's first commercially viable oil wells near Riyadh and in Dammam were discovered. While al-Saud did not live to see the transformation of the KSA's economy, as the supreme ruler he controlled all of these resources and so he, his family and their descendants eventually became not only fabulously wealthy but also the source of all the largesse distributed by the Saudi state to its citizens since this time (al-Rasheed, 2010: 69–101).

Although some economic and infrastructure development occurred during the next forty years, it was not until King Faisal bin Abdulaziz and the Arab members of OPEC imposed an oil embargo on the United States and the West in 1973, in protest at the United States' involvement in the Yom Kippur War, that rapid economic development began and the KSA moved from the margins to the centre of Arab and world politics. The global oil crisis which followed led to a swift rise in global crude-oil prices and annual GDP surged during the 1970s, and the KSA became the largest oil producer in the world in 1976. As a result, GDP grew from $9.23 billion a year in

1972 to $164.31 billion in 1980, and between 1973 and 1980 the KSA also gradually assumed full control of its national oil sector and the company that had managed this, renaming it the Saudi Arabian Oil Company (Saudi Aramco). However, while some infrastructure development did occur during the 1980s and 1990s the economic wealth of the first oil boom of the 1970s was squandered and, in the view of all commentators, the economic development plans created by the KSA's government during this time were not executed effectively. A combination of lower oil prices, several poorly implemented five-year development plans, mismanagement of the national economy, the costs incurred by funding the Iraqi side during the Iran–Iraq War (1980–1988) and the support provided to the United States during the liberation of Kuwait in 1991 led to much slower economic growth during the 1980s and 1990s, rising unemployment and a domestic debt level of 97 per cent of GDP by the end of 2002 (al-Rasheed, 2010: 130–154).

However, as oil prices rose from $24 a barrel in 2002 to $149 by July 2008 and oil production rose from 4,310 million BPD in 2002 to 9,225 million BPD, state revenues more than doubled and the stagnation of the Saudi economy came to an end. This allowed the Saudi state to cancel proposals to limit spending on social welfare and subsidies and announce a new program of major infrastructure projects, including the creation of six new industrial cities and the construction of eight new hospitals, 250 primary care centres, more than 2,000 schools, forty-one vocational colleges and several new universities such as the King Abdullah University of Science and Technology. Significant budget allocations were also set aside for improvements to water supplies, agriculture, municipal services, transport, telecommunications, industrial development and credit banks (al-Rasheed, 2015: 216–217, 219 and 260). In 2000, GDP was $188.9 billion, which then surged to $475.09 billion by 2008 and fell back to $369.12 billion in 2009 during the global recession. By the end of 2014, this had risen to $805 billion and per-capita GDP was approximately $26,000 a year, compared to $43,000 in the United

States (Index Mundi, 2016; World Bank, 2015). In 2016, the KSA had the largest proven oil reserves in the world, some 266 billion barrels or about one quarter of the world's oil reserves, and more than 95 per cent of the country's oil production was controlled by Saudi Aramco, easily the world's biggest company with combined assets of about $36 trillion. The largest petrochemical plant in the world at Jubail Industrial City, Ras Tanura, came on stream in 2016 and will eventually employ more than 150,000 technicians and engineers from Saudi Aramco and Dow Chemicals. The country also had the sixth-largest gas reserves in the world in 2016 (*The Economist*, 2016d).

The rapid increase in national wealth during the 1970s also led to swift growth in the country's population. In 1974, the first year the national population statistics were gathered, the country's total population was about seven million, of whom 791,000 were non-Saudis. This grew from 16.53 million in 2004 to 28.37 million in 2011 to 30,886,545 at the end of 2014. Of this total, 13,823,584 were Saudis (6,984,215 men and 6,839,215 women), and the remainder were expatriates and their dependents (Kingdom of Saudi Arabia Central Department of Statistics, 2015: 26; Kingdom of Saudi Arabia Monetary Agency, 2015: 24, 36–37). The KSA's total indigenous population may grow to more than 20 million by 2035, an increase of 30 per cent from 2014. The fertility rate during the 1980s and 1990s was seven children per Saudi woman, which had declined to three by the early 2000s (United Nations Economic and Social Commission for Western Asia, 2014b: 2). Such a youthful population, as we will see, brings with it enormous potential for economic growth in the KSA but also a significant risk of civil and social unrest if they are not provided with adequate employment opportunities in the future.

The wealth generated by oil and gas has funded the implementation of ten economic development plans in the kingdom. The first four plans, from 1970 to 1990, focused on infrastructure development, education and training, private enterprise, increasing foreign investment and joint ventures and improvements to healthcare and social services. The fifth plan (1990–1995) emphasised defence, government social services, regional development, a significant expansion of the KSA's university sector, the development of the country's private sector and improving private-sector employment opportunities for Saudi nationals. It was also the first national economic plan to specifically mention the need to increase the participation of women in the national labour force and to provide better administrative and financial support to encourage them to start new businesses. The sixth plan (1995–2000) focused on improving the efficiency and quality of government services, which had expanded tenfold in size over the preceding fifteen years, the diversification of the economy away from oil-dependent industries and the continuing expansion of tertiary education. The seventh plan (2000–2005) again focused on economic diversification and the expansion of the nation's private sector. However, although rapid development across multiple sectors of the economy followed, between 1985 and 2000 the KSA's GDP grew at an average of no more than 1.2 per cent a year while the population was growing by more than 4 per cent a year, and it was not until 1998 that significant economic reforms were instituted and the Saudi economy began to recover with the support of rising oil prices during the early 2000s (Hertog, 2015: 97–124).

After oil prices had fallen below $10 a barrel in 1998, the KSA government introduced a series of programs designed to diversify the national economy, develop the country's private sector and begin reducing the state's heavy reliance on oil revenues. In 1999, the Supreme Economic Council (SEC) was created to oversee the KSA's economic, industrial, agricultural and employment policies and a privatisation program. Other reforms, following the establishment of the Saudi Arabian General Investment Authority (SAGIA) in 2000, included the further privatisation of large state-owned companies (such as telecommunications), opening up previously closed sectors of the economy to private investment, the removal of barriers to foreign investment, the creation of support services for new foreign investors and changes to the national business regulatory framework. The KSA applied for membership of the World Trade Organisation

(WTO) in 1992 and was admitted to this in 2005 after responding to 3,400 questions and providing 7,000 pages of supporting documentation Vietor and White, 2015: 9; World Trade Organisation, 2005).

The eighth plan (2005–2010) emphasised the diversification of the country's economic base (particularly in manufacturing, energy, healthcare, natural gas, mining, tourism and information technology), the expansion of education and training, creating more job opportunities for Saudi nationals in the private sector, the creation of six new 'economic cities' such as the King Abdullah Economic City north of Jeddah and the Economic Knowledge City located near Medina, increased funding for applied and technical sciences and the 'furtherance of initiative and creativity in all spheres' (Vietor and White, 2015: 10). This plan also repeated the call for more Saudi women to work and play a greater role in the economic development of the KSA:

> Particular stress is placed on the increased participation of women in the economy; providing greater employment opportunities for women; and strengthening the role of the family in society through upgrading the capabilities of Saudi women and the removal of constraints on their increased participation in economic and development activities
>
> *(Kingdom of Saudi Arabia Ministry of Economy and Planning, 2005: iii).*

In order to reduce the KSA's reliance on oil, King Abdullah also approved other economic reforms at this time including further deregulation of business, the continuing privatisation of state assets and the creation of a more conducive regulatory framework to encourage foreign investment. A number of changes were also instituted at most of the major government ministries, including the judiciary, the state security agencies, the military and the *al-mutawwa'a* (religious police) where several very conservative senior officials were replaced with more moderate ones. The ninth plan (2010–2015), pragmatically, focused on 'maintaining Islamic values and teachings, boosting national security, safeguarding human rights, enhancing social stability, and reinforcing the country's Islamic and Arab identity.' It also emphasised sustainable economic diversification and social development, human development and health services 'moving towards a knowledge-based economy', enhancing the role of the private sector and SMEs in the economy, improving transparency and accountability in the public and private sectors and protecting the country's environment and natural resources (Kingdom of Saudi Arabia Ministry of Economy and Planning, 2010).[2] Plans were also announced for work to begin on a $22 billion metro and light railway system in Riyadh in 2012 with 176 km of train lines and eighty-five stations. This was expected to open in 2019, although how many car-owning Saudis might use this remains uncertain (Corby, 2015: 13; Railway Technology Market and Customer Insight, 2012).

The tenth and most recent economic plan repeated much that had appeared in earlier economic plans and covered the importance of 'consolidating national unity', sustainable economic and social development, 'a transition to a knowledge-based economy and a knowledge society', 'raising the productivity of human resources and labour', 'reducing the unemployment rate among Saudis', improving public services, 'diversifying resources and ensuring their sustainability', enhancing the role of the private sector and SMEs in the economy, scientific and technological development, improving transparency and accountability in the public and private sectors, improving the quality of general and higher education, protecting the environment and natural resources and 'improving the entrepreneurial, cognitive and physical capacities of the youth to participate efficiently in the development process.' There were three very minor references to Saudi women in this twenty-nine-page document (Kingdom of Saudi Arabia Ministry of Economy and Planning, 2015). The government also identified five key manufacturing sectors for further development and expansion – general industrial development, automotive, minerals and metals, plastics, solar energy and home appliances – and also announced plans to expand the country's tourism industry (Kingdom of Saudi Arabia Ministry of Commerce and Industry, 2015). While opportunities to do this are limited (because of the prohibition on alcohol and strict dress codes throughout the KSA), the government can probably triple the number of 'Islamic tourists' in the future. It is investing significantly in the tourism infrastructure of Jeddah, Mecca and Medina for visitors to the annual *hajj* (Smith, 2013).

The national stock market (*Tadawul*), regulated by the Capital Markets Authority since 2003, was opened to foreign investors in 2014 when it had an estimated capital value of SAR 1,1812 billion ($483 billion) and 169 registered companies (*The Economist* Middle East and Africa, 2014: 4). In conjunction with the four most recent national economic plans, several specialised credit, funding and advisory institutions have also been created by the government over the last two decades to 'contribute to the achievement of the development objectives of the Kingdom.' These include the Saudi Industrial Development Fund, the Saudi Arabia General Investment Fund, the Real Estate Development Fund, the Agricultural Development Fund, the Saudi Fund for Development, the Public Investment Fund, the Saudi Credit and Savings Bank, the Domestic Loan and Subsidy Program, the Abdul Latif Jameel Community Service Program and the Human Resource Development Fund. Other agencies have also been established to create more economic opportunities for poor and uneducated women in urban and rural areas (al-Munajjed, 2010a: 7–8; Kingdom of Saudi Arabia Monetary Agency, 2015: 40).

The country's economy grew by more than 6 per cent a year between 2011–2013 and in 2014 the IMF declared that the KSA was 'one of the best performing G-20 countries' during the 2010s (Vietor and White, 2015: 1). By 2015, the KSA was ranked at number 35 of 185 countries in the United Nations Human Development report, two places ahead of the UAE (United Nations, 2015a: 208). It was also ranked 24/144 countries in the WEF's ranking of international competitiveness – a decline from eleventh place in 2011 – and 49/189 countries for 'ease of doing business' (World Economic Forum, 2015a). The Saudi state routinely trumpets its achievements in these fields, particularly on the KSA's National Day in September, when the media is saturated with reports and advertisements informing Saudis about the country's economic achievements and the infrastructure projects created by the al-Sauds. While al-Rasheed has observed that 'in terms of material affluence, technology, modern health facilities and education, the achievements of the state are abundant and visible to people inside and outside Saudi Arabia', she has also cautioned that 'this official narrative is the dominant official wisdom' and 'submerged with propaganda' (al-Rasheed, 2015: 12). The KSA also faces several internal and external pressures and threats that may present a significant challenge to this official wisdom, the long-term political future of the al-Saud dynasty and the legitimacy of the entire rentier Saudi state in the near future.

6.3 ECONOMIC, POLITICAL AND SOCIAL CHALLENGES FACING THE KSA

As noted earlier, the KSA had the world's largest proven oil reserves in 2016 (estimated to be approximately 266 billion barrels) and the fifth-largest natural gas reserves in the world, which accounted for 86 per cent of the country's total exports in 2014. It was also the world's largest exporter of petroleum and the second-largest producer of petroleum after the United States. The country's oil and gas sectors are dominated by the state-owned Saudi Aramco, under the oversight of the Ministry for Petroleum and Mineral Resources (MPMR) and the Supreme Council for Petroleum and Minerals (SCPM). After terrorist attacks on some oil-installations during the 2000s, and unrest in the Shiite-dominated east of the country during 2012–2016, some 20,000 National Guard and military security plus an additional 5,000 security personnel employed by Saudi Aramco now guard these facilities. With almost all of its major oil production and infrastructure projects now completed, the KSA is expanding its refining, petrochemicals, power generation and natural gas sectors.

Currently, however, approximately 60 per cent of daily oil production is not available for export, because nearly one million barrels of oil are consumed every day in the country's power stations to meet the country's rapidly growing domestic and industrial power needs, including several large and energy-intensive desalination plants. During the 2000s, national energy consumption grew at about 7 per cent a year (Vietor and White, 2015: 7). In 2013, 292.2 billion kilowatt hours (kwh) of electricity were generated to meet this demand, which was more than twice as much as in 2000, and this was expected to quadruple to 1.2 billion kwh a year by 2032. Many external commentators have criticised the KSA for this policy because it encourages wasteful consumption by domestic, business and industrial users and has squandered vast quantities of oil that could have been used to generate additional export revenues. Moreover, this has reduced incentives for business and industry to be more productive and energy efficient. In 2010, King Abdullah ordered the creation of the King Abdullah City for Atomic and Renewable Energy to conduct feasibility studies on creating solar, wind and nuclear energy industries in the KSA and also stepped up exploration for new sources of natural gas (Vietor and White, 2015: 8). The government has also said that it is committed to deriving half of its domestic electricity requirements from solar, nuclear and other renewable resources 'by 2032'; and recent actions by the KSA to significantly expand its renewable energy sector and reduce energy and fuel subsidies indicate that the rulers of the kingdom are already planning for the advent of a 'post-oil' economy (Eye of Riyadh, 2016; United States Energy Information Agency, 2015c: 1–3, 13 and 15).

Although the Saudi government avoids open discussions about or independent scrutiny of its oil and gas reserves, several studies have suggested that the kingdom has already passed peak oil extraction capabilities. On the basis of current use, these reports have all suggested that Saudi Arabia could become a net *importer* of oil by the early 2030s unless it can significantly lower its wasteful domestic use of oil, improve household, commercial and industrial energy efficiency and also significantly expand its renewable energy sector (Aluwaisheg, 2012; Daya and el-Baltaji, 2012; Vidal, 2011). Other more recent reports have indicated that Saudi estimates about their reserves may be over-optimistic, because domestic annual oil consumption has accelerated alarmingly over the last fifteen years (at 5% to 8% a year) to about forty barrels per person, up from thirty per person in 2000. This rate of consumption is the highest per capita in the world – four times the rate of consumption in the United States and eight times the rate in Japan. These reports also cited claims made by the US government that the kingdom's oil reserves could be 40 per cent less than official government figures claim and, after they were made, the KSA government did not dispute them in any public forum (Ahmed, 2016; al-Khatteeb, 2015: 1; United States Energy Information Agency, 2015c: 4).

On the basis of the information that is available and the secrecy that Saudi Aramco and the Saudi government impose on data about its oil reserves, it is not possible to be absolutely certain about these claims. However, there is no disagreement that the steep fall in global oil prices during 2014–2016 did lead to a substantial fall in government revenues. The KSA also had a growing budget deficit during this period, one that was expected to grow to 13.5 per cent of GDP during 2016. As a result, it was forced to draw on its foreign reserves and also issue government bonds and burned through about one fifth of its national and foreign cash reserves to prop up its public finances and spending commitments between the end of 2014 and June 2016. Although the country had approximately $732 billion of central bank and foreign reserves at the end of 2014, these had fallen to $623 billion by December 2015 (al-Khatteeb, 2015: 2; *The Economist*, 2016b: 7). The country's credit rating was cut from 'positive' to 'negative' by Standard and Poors in October 2015 and it has been estimated that the KSA could use up $450 billion of these cash reserves by the end of 2018. At this rate, the KSA would use up all of its financial reserves by 2021 if oil and gas prices were to remain low (Ahmed, 2016: 23; *The Economist*, 2016j and 2016a).

The problem for the al-Sauds and the KSA's ruling elite is that their national economy, the country's expensive public-sector infrastructure, the state's growing military and security budget and the largesse it provides for its citizens and ever-expanding royal family are all largely dependent on oil and gas revenues. In 2016, these still accounted for 90 per cent of all government revenues and more than 40 per cent of total annual GDP. The KSA needs oil to be priced at around $80 a barrel to finance its lavish spending commitments, but as noted in Chapters 2 and 4, the price of oil fell from about $110 a barrel in mid-2014 to $36 at the end of 2015 and fluctuated between $25 and $53 a barrel during the 2016. Oil and gas prices were also expected to remain subdued during 2017–2020 for three reasons. The first is the resilience shown by shale-oil producers in other parts of the world; most of these were still in business in 2016. The precipitous fall in oil prices during 2014–2015 was a direct consequence of the decision of the MENA members of OPEC to increase oil production in order to put weaker producers – primarily in the shale-oil sector – out of business. This has proven to be a costly gamble, with American and Canadian shale-oil producers maintaining production levels during 2015–2016, even though several smaller operators went under as oil prices fell below $60 a barrel (the break-even figure for most companies who obtain crude oil by fracking). The second reason is the effect of the additional output that will be generated by Iran after economic sanctions were lifted in late 2015 and, potentially, Iraq if it becomes more stable. Third, in many other countries there has been an inexorable shift to renewable sources of energy as national governments introduced energy policies designed to reduce their reliance on oil, gas and coal. These developments had a significant impact on the KSA's revenues and GDP during 2015–2016 and will have a severe effect on economic growth and diversification well into the 2020s unless the price for crude oil increases significantly (The Financial Forecast Centre, 2015; Spindle, 2013).

While the al-Sauds and the ruling elite of the KSA have always found ways to survive slumps in oil prices in the past, circumstances have changed – perhaps forever. This is not just because of the recent sharp decline in oil and gas prices, political, sectarian and religious conflicts in the MENA region, the regional wars that the

KSA is involved in and its crippling levels of military and security spending. The biggest challenge it now faces is accommodating its growing population and providing jobs for the millions of young people who will be flooding into the country's labour market between now and 2030. Half of the KSA's population is under twenty-five and two thirds is under thirty, and a measure of the challenges that now confront the rulers of the KSA is that they will have to find a way to *double* the country's current GDP over the next two decades. They will also have to create at least two million new jobs by 2020 and as many as six million by 2030 (al-Khatteeb, 2015: 3; al-Kibsi et al, 2015: 5). This represents a very large ticking time-bomb that is counting down quickly and the KSA, in common with Oman, may be running out of time to deal with these challenges. Hence, if the al-Sauds and the business and public-sector leaders of the KSA cannot initiate essential economic, political, legal and social reforms quickly, even this bastion of 'stability' in the MENA region may be threatened by darker and more reactionary forces in the near future.

Another problem for the KSA is the major structural imbalances in its national workforce. In 2014, there were 10,192,208 million workers employed in the national labour market, of which 3,718,561 were Saudis. Of these, 2,854,531 were male and 864,030 were female employees meaning that Saudi women, pro rata, made up less than 10 per cent of the national labour force and, overall, only about one third of all Saudis of working age are in paid employment. More than three million Saudis and about 72,000 non-Saudis were employed in the public sector of the KSA in 2015 (al-Kibsi et al, 2015: 4, 88 and 91; Kingdom of Saudi Arabia Central Department of Statistics, 2015: 15–16 and 23). And, as noted earlier, while the official male Saudi unemployment rate was estimated to be around 12 per cent and nearly 30 per cent for those aged eighteen to twenty-four, about 34 per cent of Saudi women of working age were officially registered as 'unemployed' in 2014 (Jiffry, 2014). These unemployment levels are expected to rise significantly before the end of this decade as more young Saudis enter the labour market (Kingdom of Saudi Arabia Monetary Agency, 2015: 39; United Nations, 2015a: 25).

Although 'Saudisation' laws have been in place since the 1990s, these have only been partially successful in increasing the participation of Saudis in the private sector. As a result, the Ministry of Labour introduced a new Saudi Employment Strategy in 2009 to enhance the scope of these policies and address the continuing structural imbalances in the national labour market. This consisted of two programs with a twenty-five-year timeline: *Nitaqat*, to allocate quotas for nationalisation rates according to the size and industrial sector of companies and to impose fines and penalties for non-compliance and *Hafiz*, which provided all Saudi nationals with a 'job-seeker allowance' of SAR 2,000 (about $550) a month for one year and, to encourage private-sector employment, also shared salary costs with employers for up to two years. However, while this has been successful in reducing the large number of expatriate workers in the public sector, it is not known what effect (if any) these initiatives have had on reducing unemployment among Saudis or if it has encouraged greater participation in the private sector. For example, the detailed 2010 Global Entrepreneurship Monitor report for the KSA concluded that 'the Saudisation program, while well intentioned, has a somewhat limited potential to make a significant contribution to the country's employment needs and economic development' (Skoko et al, 2010: 43).

Moreover, in 2013, the Ministry of Labour revealed that 87 per cent of private-sector companies (mainly SMEs) were to be exempted from the Saudi job quota requirement category, as they employed fewer than ten employees (*Arab News*, 2014c; Kingdom of Saudi Arabia Ministry of Labour, 2013; Kingdom of Saudi Arabia Monetary Agency, 2015: 38–39). And, in what may well be a sign of the private thoughts of the country's leadership about the imbalances in its national workforce, the government announced in March 2013 that all illegal foreign workers would be deported unless they left voluntarily or obtained legitimate work visas. In December 2013, the government claimed that three million migrant workers had obtained visas and one million had left the KSA. Ostensibly, this policy was introduced to discourage employers from employing non-registered workers and also to create more job opportunities for Saudis, although no information has been provided since to indicate how many Saudis may have obtained jobs as badly paid domestic servants, taxi drivers, factory workers, cleaners or labourers (*Saudi Gazette*, 2013a).

In October 2015, the KSA Oil Minister announced that government was considering an increase in domestic energy prices in an attempt to reduce a budget deficit that was approaching 20 per cent of GDP in 2015, or about SAR 367 billion ($98 billion) (al-Khatteeb, 2015: 1; Kingdom of Saudi Arabia Monetary Agency, 2015: 23). During the last week of December, this decision was ratified and subsidies on electricity, gas and water were slashed in January 2016, with an additional pledge to move to market pricing for all utilities by 2020.[3] Saudis and expatriate workers also witnessed the very unusual sight of motorists queuing for petrol before prices were hiked by 50 per cent on 1 January 2016. Additional measures included the introduction of a value-added tax of 5 per cent on some consumer goods, 'sin' taxes on cigarettes and sugary drinks and levies on unused vacant land (*The Economist*, 2016b).

The Deputy Crown Prince, Muhammad bin Salman, told *The Economist* that under the aegis of the government's Transformation Plan 2020, 'no economic reform is taboo', and his goals were 'to eliminate the budget deficit in the next five years even if the oil price stays low', 'to reduce dependence on oil', 'increase non-oil revenue by $100 billion within five years', 'achieve maximum efficiency for ministries and departments and combat corruption' and 'to create six million new jobs by 2030' (*The Economist* Middle East and Africa, 2016). Following significant public-sector restructuring initiatives announced in late 2014 and early 2015, the Council of Economic and Development Affairs also approved plans for the privatisation of more than two dozen government agencies and state-owned companies, including the national airline and the world's most valuable firm,

Saudi Aramco and the sale of millions of hectares of state-owned land for commercial and industrial development (*The Economist*, 2016d). It was also planning to allow private companies to tender for the delivery of public services, introducing charter schools and, for the first time, creating an insurance-based healthcare system (al-Harthi, 2015; Kingdom of Saudi Arabia Monetary Agency, 2015: 41–43).

However, *The Economist* has noted several times in a series of articles it has published about the KSA during the 2010s that every economic plan from the Third Plan (1980–1985) onwards has talked about the need to reduce the country's dependence on hydrocarbons, diversify the national economy and expand the private sector, shrink its large expatriate workforce and increase employment opportunities for Saudis. And yet, apart from creating many public-sector jobs for Saudis, every five-year plan has failed to deliver on its promises. As *The Economist* suggested in early January 2016:

> Words are cheap and the obstacles huge. Saudi Arabia has promised reform before, only for its efforts to fizzle into insignificance. Its capital markets are thin and the capacity of its bureaucracy even thinner. The investment that it needs in its young people, its non-oil industries, its tourism infrastructure and much else will not happen unless investors believe in the country's future. That confidence will be hard to build
>
> (*The Economist*, 2016c: 16).

In spite of all the economic initiatives announced in the KSA's ten five-year plans and the recent reforms announced by Crown Prince Muhammad bin Salman during the second half of 2015 and in January and April 2016, the petroleum and gas sectors still accounted for 86 per cent of export earnings, 90 per cent of government revenues and 40 per cent of total GDP during 2016 (*The Economist*, 2016k: 14). The extensive social welfare networks established by the al-Sauds has created an economy in which the overwhelming majority of Saudis (male and female) are still employed by the government in large and well-funded public-sector bureaucracies, while the private sector remains underdeveloped and reliant on a large and still-growing expatriate workforce. There are also significant mismatches between the skills and knowledge required to build a more diversified economy and what is currently being provided by the country's tertiary education sector, an issue we will return to in Chapter 7 (Forster, 2017).

While the government of the KSA is keen to increase the contribution made by the private sector in order to offset the steep decline in oil and gas revenues during 2015–2016 and to increase employment opportunities for Saudi nationals in the private sector, there are still few indications that this is happening. While it does have several global businesses including Saudi Aramco, the Saudi Arabian Basic Industries Corporation (SABIC), National Commercial Bank (NCB), the Olayan Group and the joint-stock mineral development company Maadan, it does not have a well-developed and internationally competitive private sector. In addition, while the Saudi economy and social welfare systems have been heavily subsidised by oil and gas wealth for a long time, no one outside the KSA believes that this is sustainable in the medium- to long-term. The number of Saudis of working age is projected to double by 2030, and many of the tens of thousands of young women and men graduating from the country's universities will also be seeking employment. Accommodating their needs will require turning a top-down, rentier, statist economy on its head, boosting entrepreneurship and private business, introducing more market-driven efficiencies and making a much more concerted effort to diversify the national economy away from oil and gas (International Monetary Fund, 2013; *The Economist*, 2016b; Vietor and White, 2015: 9). We will ask if the ruling elite of the KSA is likely to do this in the conclusion to this chapter.

Political and Social Challenges

Is Saudi Arabia a freak case of oil and patrimonialism that defies generalisation?

Hertog (2010b: 259)

The KSA has been an absolute monarchy since 1932, and although it has recently allowed limited national and local elections it is one of the least democratic countries in the world; and no official opposition is permitted, formally or informally (al-Rasheed, 2015: 261–262). In 2015, *The Economist* rated the KSA as the fifth-most-authoritarian country in the world, out of 185 countries, and Freedom House gave the country its lowest freedom rating (7/7) in 2016, where 1 represents the highest freedom rating (*The Economist* Intelligence Unit, 2015b; Freedom House, 2016a). The media is heavily controlled and censored. The KSA was ranked 164/180 countries for 'press freedom' in 2015 and has also been designated 'An Enemy of the Internet' (Reporters without Borders, 2015b). The Qur'an and *shari'a* law form the bedrock of the Saudi constitution, there is no distinction in the country's legal system between the secular (*almani*) and the sacred (*moqaddas*) domains and the Saudi state and Wahhabist Islam are deeply bound together. Although the late King Abdullah reorganised the judicial system in 2007 to create specialised courts (commercial, labour, family and so forth) this remains entirely subservient to *shari'a* laws.

King Fahd, who preceded King Abdullah, created a Council of Ministers in 1992 (*Majlis al-Wuzara*), with representatives from the twenty-two major government ministries, and this holds all legislative and executive power. A sixty-member, all-male, non-elected Consultative Council (*Majlis al-Shura*) was also created (later expanded to 151) to replace the original Consultative Assembly, which can comment on policy proposals and the national budget but cannot draft new legislation. In common with the rulers of the UAE and Oman, his successor, King Abdullah, tried to balance the many regional and tribal interests in his kingdom in the appointments he made to this body during his reign. However, because no official opposition is permitted, political and economic decision making in the KSA is controlled by the 200 or so male descendants of King Abdul Aziz bin Saud, the *diwan* (senior advisers) and other members of the extensive royal family, the *ulama*, the heads of government ministries, leading business families, the thirteen regional governors and tribal sheikhs. It has been estimated that there are now 'at least' 15,000 royal princes and princesses in the very extensive al-Saud clan, all of whom benefit from state handouts estimated to be a minimum of $120,000 a year (tax free). Hundreds of these princes and a few princesses are employed by the state's national security services and major government ministries, and most of the country's senior political and ministerial positions are, in all practical terms, fiefdoms controlled by this group (Bertelsmann Stiftung, 2015c: 3; *The Economist* Middle-East and Africa, 2014; Macfarquhar, 2009: 254).

In January 2013, King Abdullah appointed thirty women to the *Majlis al-Shura* for the first time, a number that has not increased since. They sit in a segregated 'women-only' area in the Great Council Chamber (Inter-Parliamentary Union, 2016). In the thirteen provinces of the KSA, there is a municipal council system, which was also established in 1992, and the first elections to these were held in 2005, although women were excluded from voting or standing as candidates until 2015. Municipal councils are also only advisory bodies – they have no legislative or oversight powers and must submit all budgets to the central government for approval. In 2011, King Abdullah – who often expressed public support for legal and social reforms for women – announced that they would be allowed to run in municipal elections for the first time in 2015. In September 2014, they were permitted to register as electoral candidates and to vote, an event that the country's Grand Mufti condemned as 'opening the door to evil'. This followed many years of campaigning for this basic human right by activist Saudi women, most notably Hatoon al-Fassi and Nailah Attar who had established the *Baladi* (My Country) Initiative to train female candidates and their campaign managers. However, the government put a stop to Ms Fassi's initial attempts to teach women how to register to vote and conduct election campaigns because this would have given female candidates 'an unfair advantage'. Women were further hampered by only being allowed to address male voters by video because of the ban on unrelated men and women interacting in public places. In December 2015, about 119,000 Saudi women registered to vote (less than 10% of those deemed eligible to do this), and

900 women stood for election out of a field of 3,150 candidates for 2,100 council seats. For the first time in the KSA's history, twenty-one women were elected to public office – about 1 per cent of the country's council members (Australian Broadcasting Corporation, 2016; *The Economist*, 2015a: 49 and 2016g: 45).

On 23 January 2015, the eighty-year-old King Salman bin Abdulaziz al-Saud was crowned as the new monarch of the KSA, succeeding his half-brother King Abdullah.[4] The Saudi people were, with the notable exception of the Shiite minorities in the south-west and east of the country, generally supportive of his accession and the appointment of his energetic thirty-year-old son Muhammad bin Salman as the Deputy Crown Prince and Defence Minister. Although King Abdullah initiated several economic, political and social reforms during his reign, at a time of violent chaos in much of the MENA region, King Salman inherited many political challenges from his predecessor. He would also have been well aware that the al-Sauds have survived for nearly eight decades, through several regional wars, internal rebellions and terrorist incidents, civic unrest and economic downturns by maintaining three compacts:

> With the Wahhabist clerical establishment for religious legitimacy and to burnish the king's role as the official custodian of the holy sites of Mecca and Medina. It has been pointed out by many commentators that the relationship between the al-Sauds and the KSA's clerics, while deeply rooted, is often a bi-polar one. On the one hand, it promotes what both parties regard as the virtues and benefits of the Wahhabist religious narrative for the country while, on the other, being the primary source of the doctrinaire theological and political teachings which encourage the radicalisation of alienated young Saudi men (and some women). However, neither party would want to see an end to this mutually beneficial compact in the foreseeable future.

> With most of its citizens by delivering an extensive system of cheap land and housing, social welfare, free education and medical

care, subsidies for many basic foodstuffs and utilities and by providing well-paid and secure public-sector employment for Saudi nationals. This compact can only continue for as long as the Saudi state is willing and able to expend much of its oil and gas wealth on sustaining it.

With the United States, since 1945, to defend its territory and interests in exchange for oil and gas supplies and preserving stability in global oil-markets. Despite some periods of fragility in this relationship, every American administration has maintained close political, economic and business links with the al-Sauds. For the last seventy years they have also generally refrained from any criticism of the internal domestic politics of the KSA and its appalling human rights record [5]

(al-Rasheed, 2010: chapters 6–9; Wenar, 2016: 89–95).

However, this tripartite compact is under threat. For decades, the rulers of the KSA have been involved in a very delicate and complex double game of internal and external diplomacy. Internally, it has had to balance the demands of its young, fast-growing, educated and increasingly restive population and its deeply conservative religious authorities and their antipathy towards the 'corrupting' influence of Western culture. It has also had to find some kind of accommodation between those who want to see more economic, political and social reforms – primarily the growing educated, professional middle class – and the *ulama*, doctrinaire Wahhabists and non-urban groups, who are strongly opposed to these changes. Externally, it has had to balance its close geo-political, military and economic relationships with the United States and many other western nations with the hostility that many of its citizens, and those of other MENA countries, have towards American military incursions in the region and American government policies towards Israel, Palestine, Libya, Syria, Iran and Iraq (al-Rasheed, 2015: 233–237). In 2013, for example, in a very public protest at these policies, Saudi Arabia rejected a seat on the UN Security Council, even though it had been petitioning for this for years (Baird, 2016: 13). Moreover, there is a growing feeling among several governments in the West that the KSA is not a reliable ally, is incapable of maintaining stability in the Middle East and will be unable to deal effectively with terrorism in the region in the future.

The Saudi regime has consistently demonstrated a very hard-line policy towards *al-sahwa* (religious opposition) and jihadism, and it has ruthlessly crushed small-scale uprisings and rebellions whenever they have occurred. It has generally dealt quickly with internal terrorist attacks such as the siege of the Mecca mosque in 1979 and the attacks on the US consulate in Jeddah, expatriate compounds, oil refineries, the Ministry of the Interior and the headquarters of the security services during the early to mid-2000s which resulted in about 200 deaths (Hegghamer, 2010: 207–230). Notwithstanding the continuing and growing threat of internal opposition and growing resentment at the profligacy of the Saudi royal family, the main security threats to the KSA come from outside the country: from Yemen and Iran, from radicals who return home after fighting overseas and, of course, from ISIS whose ultimate goal is to destroy the al-Sauds and take over the KSA and the holy sites of Mecca and Medina. In 2015, there were fifteen documented 'incidents' involving ISIS militants in the KSA (Baird, 2016: 13). In 2014, the KSA also became involved in a poorly planned military incursion into Yemen and had an increasingly fractious relationship with the United States over Iran, the handling of the crisis in Syria, and the perennial Israeli-Palestinian conflict.

During 2015–2016 the kingdom was also dealing with increasing civil unrest among its Shiite minority in the south-west and east of the country after the execution of a senior Shiite cleric, Nimr al-Nimr, and forty-six other Shiites in January 2015. His seventeen-year-old nephew was sentenced to death by crucifixion and beheading in 2015. Many of the country's biggest oil reservoirs are located in the east where Shiites make up 40 to 50 per cent of the local population, and the ruling elite of the KSA has not forgotten the Shiite uprising of 1980 which was ruthlessly suppressed and clashes between Shiite protesters and security forces in 2011 led to twenty deaths. New anti-terror laws introduced in 2014 make virtually all forms of dissent and civil disobedience 'terrorist' offences, and more people have been executed during King Salman's first year in office than in the preceding ten years. It has also been estimated that there are about 30,000 political prisoners in the KSA (*The Economist*, 2016b, 2016c; *New Internationalist*, 2016; al-Rasheed, 2016).

It is possible that some younger women and men in the KSA may become more vocal in their demands for greater political and social rights as a generation gap grows between the increasingly educated, more aware and very young population of the KSA and the elderly, conservative political and religious elites of the country. Through the Internet and satellite providers such as OSN, they now have access to most of the world's news and entertainment channels and, with some exceptions, can watch pretty much anything they choose to. In addition, tens of thousands of young men and women have studied abroad and since returned to the KSA with (perhaps) a different world-view and beliefs about how their country is governed. There are also an increasing number of university-educated women entering the labour market, who will also have been exposed to political and social perspectives that they would not have encountered while at school or in their homes. While difficult to measure quantitatively, it seems reasonable to assume that this exposure will have some kind of transformative effect on social attitudes among younger Saudis, particularly if the KSA fails to create adequate employment opportunities for them in the future.

It has also been suggested that the explosion of social media is providing alternative channels for young people to express their dissatisfaction with aspects of life in the KSA; the kingdom has the highest per capita rate of Twitter users in the world and at least 40 per cent of Saudis are members of social networks (*Arab News*, 2014a). However, even if younger Saudis are becoming more cosmopolitan and (in Western terms) more 'liberal' in their social attitudes, they still have no legitimate public forums in which they can express their grievances. And, as we have seen, the ruling elite of the KSA has always taken a very dim view of any public displays of opposition to their rule in the past. As al-Rasheed has cautioned, 'Whether new communication technologies will foster serious political change remains doubtful. So far, it has allowed Saudis to express themselves without incurring the wrath of a political system that remains closed to serious and real democratisation [and] has contributed to the increased polarisation of Saudi society along ideological, regional, tribal and sectarian lines' (al-Rasheed, 2010: 274).

There is certainly anecdotal evidence that the marginalisation and alienation of young Saudis has been growing and also becoming more polarised between those who want to see more political and social reforms and those who want to see a return to 'true Islam', as is the case in several other MENA countries. One survey of 3,500 young Arabs showed that the proportion of those who believed that their country 'was heading in the right direction' fell from 98 per cent to 57 per cent between 2005 and 2015, and most of the Saudi respondents indicated that they would prefer to live and work in the UAE if they could (ASSDA'A Burson-Marsteller, 2015). However, this is an issue that has received scant attention in the KSA, other than the government introducing remedial strategies to limit the engagement of young people with radical Islam and organisations such as ISIS and al-Qaeda. Nevertheless, the evidence for this has been apparent for some time in books like *Joyriding in Riyadh* (Menoret, 2014), *The Girls of Riyadh* (Alsanea, 2008) and *Princess* (Sassoon, 2004), among others. In *Joyriding*, Menoret's fascinating ethnographic account of the sub-culture of illegal drag racing (*tafheet*) and intimate liaisons between young Saudi men, he quotes one young man who captured the frustration and disaffection of many young males in Saudi society:

> It's hard for me to say I'm a reformist, you know why? Because it's useless to fix a wreck. Are you going to dive in the ocean to fix the *Titanic*? It's not possible ... it's useless, it's a wreck. Whereas if you're aboard a ship that has a few problems, like, I'm ready to cut

my arms and legs off to fix it. I'm even ready to sacrifice my life so that twenty thousand can live, no problem. Our problem here is that our ship is lost, reform is impossible [and] there will be a possibility for reform only if we launch a new ship … Because I really think that this ship of ours, now, is lost. I mean we are a society with no politics, and that oppresses me, really, we have become a society with no state

(Menoret, 2014: 41).[6]

However, although there is growing disenchantment among some young people in the KSA, most Saudis (young or old) are conservative and few openly question the legitimacy of the al-Sauds. If they were asked by their rulers, a large majority would still choose to have the solidity and permanence of an autocratic monarchy and put up with inefficient government bureaucracies, corruption, religious busybodies and the ubiquitous *al-mabahith* (secret police) rather than experiment with the uncertainties of greater democracy and political participation or, indeed, improved women's rights. This does not mean that they are gullible, naïve or ill informed, as some Western commentators may have implied (Wenar, 2016: 235–236), but it does mean that so long as the state's largesse towards its citizens endures most Saudis will put their current high standards of living ($52,300 per capita in 2016) and the relative security and stability of their country first.

This is not to say that the rulers of the KSA are unaware that some of their population wants greater political freedom and the potential for greater civic unrest if their demands continue to be thwarted. In response to the potential for internal disorder posed by the 2011 Arab Spring, King Abdullah announced in 2012 that an additional $36 billion would be spent on social benefits, including the creation of 400,000 public-sector jobs, the introduction of additional unemployment benefits for Saudis and the building of half a million new houses (Bertelsmann Stiftung Index, 2015c: 1). This was later increased to $US 100 billion (although another source says this was '$130 billion': Wenar, 2016: 94). In addition, every Saudi citizen also received a two-month tax-free salary 'bonus' on the accession of King Salman in 2015 (Oxford Business Group, 2015a: 2). The question that remains, however, is for how long would this largesse, loyalty and acquiescence last if the country's oil taps were turned off tomorrow, and would the Saudi state and the kingdom's economy be able to cope with this?

6.4 THE CHANGING STATUS AND ROLES OF SAUDI WOMEN

Considering the significant human capital represented by Saudi women and the large pool of wealth in their hands, Saudi women could and should become a major growth driver for the country's diversification policy, and reduce the Kingdom's overdependence on oil. By tapping into this large potential, the Saudi public and private sectors have a new tool through which to develop and grow social and economic policies that transcend generations ... The true potential lies in this development happening in parallel with positive growth in the mind-set of the society. Only then will we see the real impact of the Saudi woman.

Almasah Capital (2010: 2)

In 1997, in one of the first books published in the West that portrayed the lives of women in the KSA, al-Munajjed suggested that:

> Misconceptions about the status of Saudi women have distorted their true social image and depicted them as second class citizens. It is true that traditional norms and patriarchal values have shaped the role of women in Saudi Arabia; however this should not be seen as an impediment to Saudi women taking part in the process of national development ... Today, Saudi women are contributing to and participating actively in the growth of the kingdom. Professional, educated women are eagerly seeking new opportunities in the labour-market and are keen to play more responsible roles at the community level. Indeed, education and

work outside the home have provided new horizons for Saudi
women beyond the traditional confines of marriage and
motherhood, and this has had a positive effect on their behavior,
self-esteem, aspirations and relations with others

(al-Munajjed, 1997: 6).

While acknowledging that her sample of fifty university-educated and
fifty uneducated women could not be representative of all Saudi
women, she was convinced that the lives of Saudi women were
improving for the better and were likely to change significantly over
the following two decades. It is true that some Saudi women today
have greater opportunities and freedoms and, compared to the situation that prevailed twenty years ago, greater independence and life
options and more personal disposable income. Four decades ago there
were few educational opportunities beyond a basic primary school
education for most young female Saudis and very few had access to
higher education or opportunities for independent employment.
However, in common with the UAE and Oman, some of the rulers
of the KSA knew in the 1970s that they had to improve women's
access to primary, secondary and tertiary education and also increase
their participation in the country's labour market.

The country's education sectors had evolved very slowly
between the 1930s and 1960s and it was only in the 1970s that their
development became a national priority. Girls were first allowed to
attend these in 1970 but, at first, this was not compulsory. The
number of girls attending primary and secondary school grew from
nearly 50,000 in 1965 to more than 284,000 in 1975. By 1986, this had
risen to nearly 650,000 out of a total enrolment of 1.78 million
students (al-Munajjed, 1997: 64–65). By 2014, 99 per cent of Saudi
girls were attending primary and secondary school. Although the
number of schools in the KSA reached 26,934 in 2014 and all girls
are now required to attend primary and secondary schools (Gorney,
2016: 124), education remains strictly segregated along gender lines,
an issue we revisit in the discussion that follows and in Section 6.5.

As more girls began to graduate from high schools during the 1980s there were growing demands from some middle-class families, who had been sending their daughters to foreign universities for tertiary education, to open up the KSA university sector to women. While there were a few places available for women at the University of Riyadh (established in 1957), it was only when a separate female campus was created at the King Faisal University (opened in 1967) that more women could attend university. In 1975, of 26,347 students enrolled at universities in the KSA, 5,310 were women. This had risen to 50,434 women out of a total enrolment of 130,924 by 1986 (al-Munajjed, 1997: 69). Seven more public universities were built and opened during the 1980s and 1990s and today there are about thirty-five public and private universities and many tertiary colleges in the KSA that graduate about 250,000 students a year; and more than half of those are women. An awareness of the lack of scientific and technology skills in the KSA prompted the government to create the co-educational King Abdullah University for Science and Technology in 2009, which became known as 'the Arab MIT', and to establish the Technical and Vocational Training Corporation (TVTC). By 2014, the TVTC had established ten new colleges and enrolled 5,000 students and planned to create twenty-seven more with a total enrolment of 300,000 students by 2020 (Technical and Vocational Training Corporation, 2016). Some 300 agreements have also been signed with universities in the United States, Europe and China to allow their faculty to teach in Saudi universities, design joint curricula and encourage research collaboration (*Chronicle of Higher Education*, 2010: 10). In 2015, approximately 1.5 million students were attending these institutions, and 170,000 were studying at overseas universities. In 2015, approximately one quarter of the national budget was allocated to primary, secondary, tertiary and vocational education ($36.5 billion), an increase of 15 per cent since 2009 (Bertelsmann Stiftung, 2015c: 20).

In the KSA, *shari'a* laws are integrated into all education programs including those taught at the nation's universities and vocational colleges. A large part of the primary school curriculum is dedicated to Islam, while at secondary schools, students can follow a 'religious' (i.e. Islamic) or 'technical' track, and Islamic studies remain an important part of the foundation-year studies of university undergraduates. Education at all levels is also strictly segregated in government schools from the age of five and at mixed universities. There are several women-only universities, while all mixed universities and vocational colleges have women-only entrances, lifts and study areas, and all classrooms have separate entrances and sections for men and women. The one exception to this is the King Abdullah University of Science and Technology (KAUST), established in 2009, which is the only non-segregated co-educational institution in the country. All Saudi women still have to obtain the written permission of their male guardian (father, husband or brother) to attend a university or vocational college.

Several studies have been very critical of the general quality of education in the KSA and the dated curricula, the rote learning pedagogies and the lack of critical and creative thinking that students are exposed to at primary and secondary schools. These studies have also criticised the academic standards at many Saudi universities and the mismatches between the courses they deliver and the practical skills, competencies and knowledge that employers in the KSA now expect from the graduates they recruit. In 2014, more than 60 per cent of female students graduated with degrees in religious studies, social studies, history and literature despite the labour market already being swamped with social science and humanities graduates, although there have been some recent efforts to increase the number of STEM and medical graduates in the country's public universities (Islam, 2014). It is apparent that there is still a significant mismatch between the skills required in the private sector of the Saudi labour market and those that are being acquired by most young female Saudis at the country's tertiary institutions (*Arab News*; 2014b; Bertelsmann Stiftung, 2015c: 20; Forster, 2017).

Despite the shortcomings of the KSA's education system, the number of Saudi women who work full time has grown over the last ten to fifteen years. In 2015, women made up 17.6 per cent of the Saudi component of the national workforce and most of them (about 85%) work in the public sector, particularly in education. All Saudis have a strong preference for public-sector employment, where salaries are, on average, 70 per cent higher than those in the private sector. As noted earlier, at least 34 per cent of Saudi women of working age were officially registered as unemployed in 2014 compared to 12 per cent of men (Jiffry, 2014). In addition, 1.2 million women were in the state welfare program and not counted in these unemployment statistics. Including these raises their unemployment rate to more than 50 per cent. Of those, 78.3 per cent are university graduates, and at least 1,000 Saudi women with doctorates are also unemployed, a significant loss to the national economy and the country's higher education sector (al-Kibsi et al, 2015: 10; Oxford Business Group, 2015a: 6).

While most Saudi women still do not work, some women who are members of powerful families did benefit from the opening up of the Saudi economy and the economic boom that ensued between 2003 and 2014. Examples of high-profile women business and public-sector leaders in the KSA, and also some who can be regarded as pioneers for other Saudi women in 2015, included Loujain al-Hathloul, a women's right's activist who became an international *cause celebre* after being arrested for trying to drive from the UAE into the KSA in December 2014 and being imprisoned for three months; Lubna al-Olayan, Director of the Olayan Group and CEO of the Olayan Financing Company; Haifa al-Mansour, film director, whose film *Wadjda* about a rebellious young Saudi girl who dreams of owning a bicycle won several international awards in 2015; Bayan Mahmoud al-Azahran, who opened the first-ever all-female law practice in the KSA in 2014; Hayat Sindi, investor, scientist, entrepreneur and UNESCO Goodwill Ambassador for the Sciences and one of the first women to be appointed to the *Majlis al-Shura*; Huda al-Ghoson, Executive Director of Human Resources, Saudi Aramco; Somaya Jabarti, Editor-in-Chief, *Saudi Gazette*; Samia al-Amoudi, obstetrician, gynaecologist, breast cancer campaigner and author of thirteen books; Samira Islam, the first Saudi woman to gain both bachelor and doctoral degrees, the first Saudi professor of pharmacology, the first female vice dean at a Saudi university and the first Arab woman to be nominated as a UNESCO Scientist of the Year; Khawla al-Kuraya, a cancer expert at King Faisal Specialist Hospital and Research Centre and the first Saudi woman to receive a King Abdulaziz Award of Excellence; Muna abu Sulayman, fashion, media and CSR entrepreneur, humanitarian activist and philanthropist; Summer Nasief, Executive of Healthcare and Lifesciences, IBM Saudi Arabia, and advocate for increasing the participation of women in the KSA labour market; Rajah Moharrak, graphic designer and the first Saudi woman to climb Mount Everest in 2013; Thoraya Obaid, a member of the Shura Council; until 2014 she was the Executive Director of the United Nation Population Fund and an under-secretary general at the United Nations; Nayed Taher, CEO and co-founder, Gulf One Investment Bank; Dima Ikhwan, accountant, an associate at KPMG Advisory and a comedy writer; Nermin Saad, an engineer by training who, unable to find work as an engineer in the KSA, established the virtual engineering company Handasiyat; Badreya al-Bishr, novelist, journalist and TV presenter; Manal al-Sharif, social activist and repeat driving offender;[7] and Mishaal Ashemimry, aerospace engineer and founder of MISHAAL Aerospace (CEO Middle-East, 2015). Other notable Saudi women in 2016 include Princess Ameera al-Taweel, who chairs several charitable foundations and supports a wide range of humanitarian causes; Sara al-Suhaimi, the MD & CIO of Asset Management at Jadwa Investment and Dr. Salwa al-Hazzaa, who was Head of the Ophthalmology Department at King Faisal Specialist Hospital.

While the achievements of these Saudi women must be applauded, it is evident that most of them do not wield much real economic or political power, and an odd omission from this list are any of the small number of Saudi women who are in senior public-sector positions. It is also noticeable that hardly any of these women (and, of course, Saudi women in general), were the CEOs of private-sector companies in the KSA. Moreover, the success and high profile enjoyed by these women disguises the problems that most Saudi women still have in finding salaried employment in an environment of strict gender segregation in all public- and private-sector organisations. Although a few high-profile women have appeared at international economic forums and conferences and a few have become senior public sector officials and business leaders, they have only been granted a presence in areas that do not challenge the authority of the Saudi state or entrenched male business interests. This is a privileged group that al-Rasheed has described as the 'elite women of the KSA', and she believes that the handful of women who have succeeded in business only managed to do this with the prior approval of their (very wealthy) families and the patronage of the state. This privileged and unrepresentative group of women 'had already escaped the general restrictions imposed on the majority of Saudi women' and:

> While princes still dominate the business world, their daughters and sisters have also achieved a high level of economic activity, especially in owning and managing business that cater to women – beauty parlours, all-women hotels, fashion companies, sports' centres and other such ventures. They are joined by women from the newly emerging entrepreneurial classes that are tied to the state either as loyal coteries or as partners in business ventures. Neither extremist religious views nor conservative cultural values have hindered the integration of such business women into the general economy
>
> (al-Rasheed, 2015: 306).

Consequently, it is not surprising that all the reports that have been published on gender equality in the KSA have been very critical of the lack of systemic legal protection for women in both the occupational and domestic spheres. This is reflected in the KSA's rankings in the WEF's annual GGG reports. In 2011, the KSA was ranked 131 out of 135 countries, in 2013, 127/136 and 134/145 in 2015; and the country's ranking for 'economic participation and opportunity' for women was 132/135 in 2011, 134/136 in 2013 and 138/145 in 2015. In 2015, it was the fourteenth-ranked country in the Gulf region for female equality. As also noted in the corresponding sections of Chapter 2 and Chapter 4, the twenty countries of the MENA region had the worst cumulative global score for female inequality in 2011, 2013 and 2015 and not one has ever been ranked in the top 100 countries for female equality (World Economic Forum, 2015b: 8, 9 and 10; 2013: 12, 13 and 18; 2011: 9, 10 and 15).

There are several reasons the KSA has this low ranking. The first concerns the KSA's non-compliance with the international gender-equality conventions and treaties it has signed over the last two decades. While the KSA has been a signatory to the CEDAW treaty since 2000, in its most recent report on the KSA the CEDAW Committee noted, as it did with the UAE and Oman, that the government of the KSA had signed this convention with several major reservations. These were in relation to Article 1: 'the principle of equality between men and women', Article 2(a): 'extending state responsibility to outlaw acts of discrimination by public and private actors, Article 2(f): 'the obligation to eliminate or abolish discriminatory laws, regulations, customs and practices', Article 5(a): 'to promote women's full enjoyment of their human rights', Article 9: 'the right to nationality', Article 15(2): 'legal capacity', Article 15(4): 'freedom of movement and choice of domicile', Article 16: 'on equal rights in marriage and family relations', Article 29: 'arbitration of conflicts arising from the convention' and several other provisions. The CEDAW committee commented that it was very concerned 'about the general reservations made upon ratification of the Convention by the State Party, which is drawn so widely that it is contrary to the object and purpose of the convention' (United Nations, 2008: 2). It is also noteworthy, if not a great surprise, that CEDAW has not conducted a follow-up review of the KSA's compliance with this convention since 2008.[8]

CEDAW also expressed its concern 'about the lack of awareness of the Convention and its implementation in practice' and that 'the Convention has not been made fully operational in the State party, as relevant laws remain to be adopted.' The Committee also noted 'with concern' that the KSA government had not provided any information on cases in which the provisions of the Convention had ever been invoked in any court proceedings. The Committee called on the government of the KSA to amend its domestic laws to conform with all of the international treaties it had signed and 'to enact a comprehensive gender equality law and to raise awareness about the Convention among the general public'. It also called on the government to create 'a legal culture supportive of women's equality with men and non-discrimination on the basis of sex', to allow the development of independent women's associations and organisations and to provide 'a clearer and more detailed picture' of what steps (if any) it was taking to ratify the provisions of the Convention (United Nations, 2008: 2–3, 4, 5 and 8). Nearly a decade after this critical report was published, there is no evidence that the government of the KSA or, indeed, its Orwellian 'Human Rights Commission' has taken any steps towards either reviewing the criticisms and reservations it contained or if it they have been working towards implementing any of its principle recommendations. In a report published in the same year as the CEDAW report, Human Rights Watch (HRW) observed that:

> There appear to be no written legal provisions or official decrees explicitly mandating male guardianship and sex segregation, yet both practices are essentially universal inside Saudi Arabia. It is certainly the case that the government has done little to end these discriminatory practices and thus plays a central role in enforcing them. In doing so, *the Saudi government continues to ignore not only international law, but even elements of the Islamic legal tradition that support equality between men and women. The religious establishment has consistently paralyzed any efforts to advance women's rights by applying only the most restrictive provisions of Islamic law while disregarding more progressive interpretations and the evolving needs of a modern society* ... For as long as it fails to take steps to eliminate the

discriminatory practices of male guardianship and sex segregation,
the Saudi government is scorning its international commitment
to guarantee women and girls the right to education, freedom of
movement, marriage with their free and full consent and
their right to health, including protection from and redress for
family violence

(Human Rights Watch, 2008: 4; my emphasis).

It is the case that the government of the KSA, with a few minor
exceptions, has continued to uphold these practices since this report
was published, and almost all of the country's clerics remain resolutely opposed to the principle of legal equality for Saudi women.[9]
Although official Saudi employment laws and regulations do not
explicitly discriminate against women, regulations covering discrimination against women in the labour market are very limited. For
example, Saudi labour regulations consist of 245 articles, but only
12 of these mention 'women's issues' such as child care, breastfeed-
ing, maternity and sick leave and there is no mention of the principle
of equal pay for men and women or any provisions that explicitly
outlaw gender discrimination in the workplace. Where limited rights
have been introduced, there have been delays in implementing these,
and so they remain largely unenforced. For example, the male guardian (*wakeel*) requirement for public-sector employment was modified
by the Council of Ministers and approved by the Ministry of Commerce several years ago, but this ruling has largely been ignored in
practice. Consequently:

Discrimination, both *de facto* and *de jure* is rampant. Women
are strongly disadvantaged in public life and in the judicial system.
The ultra-conservative Wahhabi version of Sunni Islam in Saudi
Arabia requires strict segregation of the sexes, including in
government office, workplaces and public spaces. Women also
face disadvantages relating to the requirement for male
guardianship, limitations of freedom of movement, a lack of laws
defining a minimum age for marriage, and inequalities in family law

(Bertelsmann Stiftung, 2015c: 9–10).

Gender segregation is strictly enforced in the KSA, and the law prohibits women from mixing with unrelated men in public spaces in the KSA and Article 160 of the KSA's labour laws still stipulates that 'In no cases may men and women co-mingle in places of work or in accessory facilities' (a prohibition, it should be noted, that is increasingly ignored in practice). All government buildings, hotels and restaurants, malls, banks, hospitals, schools, universities and so forth have separate male-only and female-only areas and the Riyadh Zoo sets aside three visiting days for women and three days for men. Although it is simplifying things somewhat, public spaces are considered to be the domain of men while the private space of the home is considered to be the female domain. The private domain is regarded as a sanctuary, and it is the duty of all Saudi males to defend the sanctity of this space. On the few occasions I was invited into a Saudi family home, I was not introduced to the host's wife or daughters and even at dinner parties women and men were served in separate parts of the house, and this segregation included any expatriate women who were attending. At Al Faisal University, where I worked for three years, women and men had separate entrances, lifts, eating areas and libraries. Women entered lecture rooms via separate entrances and sat on a raised platform behind an opaque screen. About 20 per cent of the women I taught on the MBA program there would only meet face to face in my office with either a female administrative staff member or a male guardian in attendance. It was also very apparent that Saudi males only socialised with other men and Saudi women spent almost all of their leisure time with either female friends or their children. Unrelated men and women do not, as a general rule, ever freely mix or socialise in public spaces in the KSA.

The second reason for the very low gender-equality ranking of the KSA is a consequence of both the limited participation rate of Saudi women in the country's political system and their unequal distribution across the national labour market. While the political representation of women has improved a little after the municipal elections in December 2015, of those Saudi women of working age just one in seven is in full-time employment although more than half of all university graduates are female. More significantly, as we have seen, while the female participation rate in the national labour market increased from 12.2 per cent in 2009 to 17.6 per cent by 2015 to just over 18 per cent in 2016, more than one third of Saudi women of working age were officially registered as unemployed, compared to about 12 per cent of men (and, as noted earlier, this may be more than 50%). Saudi women also work in a very limited range of professional occupations, principally in human resource management, education and banking, although from 2013 they were also allowed to work in retail and grocery stores.

It also appears that the preference that women have for public-sector employment is unlikely to diminish any time soon. In a 2011 survey of 2,400 Saudi university graduates, 61 per cent of female graduates expressed a preference for employment in this sector, compared to 24 per cent of men. And, while 67 per cent of male and 33 per cent of female graduates were keen to work for international companies operating in the KSA, only 6 per cent of females and 9 per cent of males wanted to work in a Saudi private-sector company, a remarkable finding. Of the twenty most popular 'employers of choice' identified in this survey by men, sixteen were North American or European companies, while women chose twelve KSA public-sector organisations, five Saudi private-sector and three multinational companies as their preferred employers (Gulf Talent, 2011: 14 and 26). This does not bode well for the KSA government's stated ambition to encourage more of its nationals to work in the country's private sector. Moreover, very few of the small number of female Saudis who are employed in the private sector can be classified as business leaders. One study that has examined this indicates that less than one tenth of 1 per cent of the members of the boards of publicly listed KSA-owned companies were women in 2010, and it could not provide any data on the number of women in senior management or executive positions in the private sector (Almasah Capital, 2010: 5). We will see how this low figures compares to a selection of OECD countries in Chapter 9.

The third reason the WEF's GGG reports have consistently awarded the KSA a low international ranking is the lack of information about its compliance with international labour and gender-equality conventions, such as the UN's Equal Remuneration Convention, the ILO's Discrimination (Employment and Occupation) Convention and CEDAW. There is also a lack of detailed and up-to-date gender-disaggregated data on the status of Saudi women in the national labour market or adequate information about the proportion of Saudi women who are in senior management or leadership roles in either public- or private-sector organisations. This lack of evidentiary data has been noted in several studies, for example:

> The Saudi labor market lacks up-to-date, gender-specific statistical data on the role of Saudi women in the economy. Statistical techniques, indicators, definitions, methodologies, processes and concepts in the area of women and work need to be much more developed. The absence of complete and updated sociodemographic and employment data on women hinders socioeconomic planning and future labor market policies
>
> *(al-Munajjed, 2010a: 12).*

It appears that there has been no progress in these areas since 2010 and, as a result, there is very little information available in the public domain which describes what initiatives or active steps (if any) have been taken, either by the Saudi government or by private-sector organisations, to promote the interests of Saudi women or increase their participation in the national labour market. For example, in September 2013, Tata Consultancy Services and General Electric announced that they were going to create the first all-female business processing centre in Saudi Arabia, which would eventually employ 3,000 women (Crabtree and Allam, 2014), but this is one of just a few isolated examples of such initiatives.

In the absence of any visible commitment to gender equality and the lack of detailed statistical information on women in the national labour market, the WEF judges that the progress the KSA has made towards gender equality across all sectors of its national labour market has been extremely limited and slow, and this has prevented the KSA from being placed higher in the its annual gender-equality rankings. This indicates that there is a great deal of work to be done to improve the legal rights of women and increase their participation in the wealth-generating sectors of the national economy and in the country's political system. The KSA has one of the most 'masculine' national cultures in the world and – notwithstanding the progress made by young Saudi females in higher education and by some women in the national labour market over the last twenty years – it remains, in most respects, extremely 'progress-resistant' in terms of gender equality (Harrison, 2006: 36–37; Harrison and Huntington, 2000). However, we will see in Chapter 7 that most of the university-educated working women who were interviewed for this book did not agree with these extremely negative assessments of the status of women in the KSA and they were also, generally, quite optimistic about their futures.

6.5 THE CULTURAL, ATTITUDINAL AND STRUCTURAL BARRIERS FACING WOMEN IN THE KSA

Here, we understand human nature as static. We think that women can do certain things, but not others.
You're faced with being humiliated every day. We do not really have an identity.

Professor A. al-Abdulhai, King Saud University and an anonymous female university professor, Riyadh (Human Rights Watch, 2008: 7 and 23)

No, we are not free in this country and that to me is unacceptable. I no longer accept that men can define what 'I am' and dictate what I can and cannot do with my life. I hope to leave Saudi Arabia and achieve my dreams abroad.

(30-year-old HR manager; unmarried; studying part time for an MBA at Al Faisal University, Riyadh; interviewed in May 2013. In 2016, she was a PhD student at a Canadian university)

Understanding the lives of women in the KSA and their low level of engagement in the country's workforce requires some understanding of the variant of Islam that is practiced by the majority Sunni population of the KSA (khususiya). It is well known that the kingdom is one of the most fundamentalist Islamic countries in the world and its Wahhabist theology is rigorously enforced throughout Saudi society. Visitors to the KSA will notice, for example, that many more women wear *niqabs* when compared to the UAE, Oman and most other MENA countries and even expatriate women must always wear an *abaya* when in public places. Saudi women are faced with many restrictions on free movement, independent travel and, to the bemusement of most people outside the KSA, are still prohibited from driving. Most Saudis (about 85–90%) are Sunnis, who follow the Hanbali school of Islamic jurisprudence, although most Saudis would not generally describe themselves as 'Wahhabist', preferring to identify themselves only as true Sunnis or Salifis. As we have seen, Muhammad bin Abd al-Wahhab's reform movement of the mid-eighteenth century had been based on a revival of Hanbali's doctrinaire and conservative interpretations of the Qur'an. Consequently, when al-Saud became the first ruler of a unified Saudi state in 1932, Wahhabism became the only officially sanctioned form of Islamic belief. Since that time, there has been an enduring relationship between the al-Saud dynasty and senior Wahhabist clerics (hay'at kibal al-ulama) and, while it continues to be a mutually beneficial relationship, it has not been without tensions and, on occasions, open conflict.

A detailed discussion of the reasons why the KSA is dominated by this ultra-conservative variant of Islam, and the long-standing Sunni-Shia religious schism in this country and the MENA region is beyond the scope of this book but these have been described by several other authors (Badawy et al, 2015; Holland, 2012; Lacey, 2009, 2001; al-Rasheed, 2010; Vassiliev, 1998). However, to understand why Wahhabism did become the dominant form of Islamic belief after the establishment of the KSA in 1932, it is helpful to look at the explanation given by Fukuyama in the first volume of his analysis of the emergence of the modern global system of independent nation states. He observed that in the Arab world:

> The traditional monarchs put in place by the British, French and Italian colonial authorities in countries including Egypt, Libya, Syria and Iraq were quickly replaced by secular nationalist military officers who proceeded to centralize authority in powerful executives that were limited by neither legislatures nor courts. The traditional role of the *ulama* was abolished in all of these regimes, and was replaced with a 'modernized' law that emanated solely from the executive. The only exception to this was Saudi Arabia, which had not been colonized and maintained a neo-fundamentalist regime whose executive authority was balanced by a *Wahhabi* religious establishment. Many of the executive-dominated Arab regimes turned into oppressive dictatorships that failed to produce either economic growth or personal freedom for their people. The legal scholar Noah Freedman argues that the rise of Islamism in the early twenty first-century and the widespread demand for a return to the *shari'a* throughout the Arab world reflect a grave dissatisfaction with the lawless authoritarianism in the region and nostalgia for a time when executive power was limited by a genuine respect for the law
>
> *(Fukuyama, 2011: 285–286).*

Hence, Saudi Arabia – a deeply tribal society imbued with an extremely conservative religious and patriarchal culture – did not experience the 'taste' of modernity that many other countries in the MENA region did. Consequently, its largely illiterate people had no exposure to *any* of the ideas that had fuelled the renaissance, the reformation and the industrial and scientific revolutions in the West prior to the creation of the kingdom in 1932. This played a critical role both in the maintenance of the al-Saud dynastic monarchy and in establishing the Wahhabists as the preeminent religious power in the country. Their suffocating grip on national life was further strengthened after the discovery of oil and this has only been challenged very occasionally since this time. The main point of difference between Wahhabist Islam and the more moderate variants of the Muslim faith practiced in the UAE and Oman lies in its denunciation of all forms of 'mediation' between Allah and the *umma*. For Wahhabists, the *Hadith*, *Sunnah* and *Qiyas* are the only legitimate sources of Islamic knowledge and individual reason or intellect has no role to play in 'reinterpreting' the inviolable and ageless edicts of the Prophet. Hence, when they say *'la 'illaha illa allah'* and *'Muhammed rasoou-allah'* they mean this without the slightest equivocation or doubt.

Consequently, although many Muslims respect Christians and Jews as *Ahl al-Kitab* (People of the Book), adherents of this variant of Islam are very hostile to any deviation from what they regard as the only legitimate religious faith or any form of religious change or innovation *(bid'a)*, and they also see the world as being starkly divided between *dar al-Islam* (the Islamic world) and *dar al-Harb* (the realm of Islam's enemies). In their eyes, such 'deviations' include the adherents of all other religious faiths and minority groups within Islam – particularly Shiites – and, of course, anyone who is *mulhid* (atheist). It should also be remembered that the Saudi state – in order to maintain the support of its clerics – has spent at least $70 billion supporting the spread of Wahhabism abroad and funding the construction of mosques in many other countries. As we now know, some of these have been directly responsible for radicalising alienated young Muslims who live in those countries in recent times (Badawy et al, 2015; Baird, 2016; *The Guardian*, 2010; Wenar, 2016: 91).

Since 1971, senior clerics in the KSA have been appointed to the powerful and influential Council of Higher Ulama, and they advise the monarch on all religious matters, *shari'a* laws and *fatwas*. Their edicts are implemented with considerable zeal by the civil police and the feared *al-mutawwa'a*. To say that Saudi clerics are very conservative would be something of an understatement. They have, at various times, opposed the introduction of the telegraph, paper money, cars, television and many other technological innovations that they consider to be symbols of westernisation (*tagrib*). They have issued *fatwas* against American soap operas, clothing made of silk, coloured *abayas*, all-you-can-eat buffets, funeral headstones, owning dogs as domestic pets – because they are 'unclean' – and women's sports. They also once declared, in an echo of my *Toy Story* experience, that Mickey Mouse was 'a soldier of Satan'. They resisted the abolition of slavery, the introduction of primary, secondary and tertiary education for girls, women's right to work, and to vote and then stand in local elections. After young Saudis persisted in buying red presents for the objects of their affections on St Valentine's Day a few years ago, all red consumer products and all advertising featuring the colour red were prohibited during the days leading up to St Valentine's Day (Haidar, 2015: 79–80; Withnall, 2014). While many Saudis and some Islamic religious scholars are very critical of the power of the *al-mutawwa'a* and the clerics, their grip on public life is unlikely to be weakened significantly in the foreseeable future. As Macfarquhar has observed:

> Since the KSA is the birthplace of Islam, the ruling al-Saud princes and the myriad theological institutions that help to maintain their rule like to present the kingdom as a perfect society. The religious establishment determines the parameters of any public debate, evaluating everything through the Wahhabi teachings unique to the Arabian peninsula, and vehemently rejecting any alternative. For them, the Wahhabi school is Islam, all the others are wrong ... Conservatives consider Saudi Arabia to be the main bastion of civilisation, and so they battle anything which they fear might diminish its status
>
> (Macfarquhar, 2009: 248–249 and 260).

As a result, for several decades, there has been a permanent state of tension between Saudis and the conservative religious authorities, with the royal family acting as the final – and sometimes very reluctant – arbiter between these two groups:

The balance tips one way or the other depending on where the leading princes sense their best interests lie. A pious king can push the religious establishment around rather more than an impious one [but] the modern tragedy in Saudi Arabia, as elsewhere is that the rulers keep such discussions bottled up in the private sphere [and] in that restricted environment, problems tend to fester rather than slouch towards resolution ... There are so many competing voices, all claiming legitimacy, that it is difficult for anyone to separate *fatwas* rooted in a genuine desire to interpret the faith from those formulated to achieve political goals. The cacophony hampers singling out any one ruling as authentic ... critics say that far more *fatwas* are rooted in ideology, in the desire to push a particular policy, than in weighty religious wisdom

(*Macfarquhar, 2009: 100, 101–102 and 126*).

In the KSA, a multiplicity of *fatwas* is enforced with vigour by the all-pervasive *al-mutawwa'a*. Religiously schooled young Saudi men (and a few women) are recruited to this organisation which has been described as 'an employment agency for tens of thousands of Saudi men [who are] unfit to work anywhere else'. These officials 'infuriate and intimidate the non-zealous segment of the population. It doesn't take much to get a well-educated Saudi seething in frustration at the waste of time and invasion of privacy entailed by any encounter with the *al-mutawwa'a'* (Macfarquhar, 2009: 269 and 124). Popular stories of the problems that Saudi women have encountered by not being allowed to drive, arrogant and unfaithful husbands, not being permitted to go out to a local video shop without a male relative to hire a video of *Cinderella* for their young daughters and calling the police to apprehend burglars who then refused to enter the house if no male relatives were at home were all ridiculed in the popular satirical TV comedy *Tash Ma Tash* during the 2000s. This program was condemned by Saudi clerics (as was the very popular Turkish series *Noor* which featured a handsome, kind, emancipated husband and his wife), but it was allowed to stay on the air because it made both King Fahd and King Abdullah laugh (Macfarquhar, 2009: 99–103). As

Macfarquhar has wryly observed, 'while domineering, control-freak husbands can be found in every culture, Saudi Arabia is one of a handful of societies whose legal system actually endorses these attitudes and behaviours' (Macfarquhar, 2009: 102).

In some instances, the behaviour of the religious police has caused international outrage. One of the most infamous examples of this was the unnecessary deaths of fifteen young girls in a school fire in Mecca during March 2002. As the fire broke out and spread, the officials of the *al-mutawwa'a* refused to let the girls out and barred the exits because, in their haste to escape, they had not donned their *abayas* and *niqabs* and were thus 'indecently' dressed; and there were reliable reports that they had also beaten these young girls with sticks to force them back into the building. They also prevented fire fighters from entering the building because it fell under the jurisdiction of the male-dominated Directorate of Girl's Education, and men were forbidden by law to enter this 'female-only' building. After hearing in person from the Governor of Mecca, who had visited the school and interviewed the fire fighters, King Abdullah summarily removed all girls' schools from the supervision of the religious authorities. He also took the opportunity to appoint the first female minister in the KSA's history, promoting Nora bin Abdullah al-Fayez to the position of Deputy Minister of Education. However, even this tragic incident was not enough to provoke the al-Sauds or any government ministers into criticising the religious police and their inhumane behaviour. And, as Macfarquhar and others have attested, the *al-mutawwa'a* have since been involved in hundreds of other disgraceful incidents involving Saudi and expatriate women (Fadl, 2005; 250–253; Macfarquhar, 2009: 259–268). It was, therefore, little surprise when several of the women and men I interviewed in the KSA made several critical comments about the *al-mutawwa'a* and also introduced me to a new Arabic word: *zlayeb* (morons).

Al-Rasheed, who has written about women in the KSA for nearly three decades, believes that while the roles of Saudi women have changed to some extent over the last two decades their lives are still largely controlled by men, in every sphere and in every domain. Whether they work in 'caregiver' or 'supporter' roles as teachers, nurses and social workers or as scientists, doctors, entrepreneurs or journalists, they are only allowed to do this with the prior approval of men. The subordination and exclusion of women in the KSA is, she believes, not primarily a religious or social issue but a political one, driven by the state's own 'legitimacy narrative'. Hence, while it often refers to religious legitimation to justify segregated gender roles:

> Its ultimate objective is control and surveillance practiced under the guise of protecting the moral order. From its early history, the state has projected an image of itself as a moral agent, guarding the chastity of women. Women are a frontier zone, a fixed boundary requiring protection against deviance, transgression and violation – violation not of the female body, but of the body of the state ... Their invisibility in the public sphere is, ironically, a visible token of state piety and its commitment to Islam
>
> (al-Rasheed, 2015: 293–294 and 296).

This theme has been highlighted by other scholars, such as al-Dabbagh, who has observed that 'the gender ideology promoted in the political culture idealises women's domesticity [and] elevates gender segregation ... women become the symbol of national identity; their appearance, behavior and role in society at large symbolise the leadership's commitment to protecting its "tribal family" from Western influences and challenges to patriarchal control during times of social change' (al-Dabbagh, 2009: 9). These beliefs are reflected in the many social restrictions and *fatwas* that govern the daily lives of all women in the KSA. Since 1971, the clerics of the Saudi Council of Higher Ulama have produced more than 30,000 rulings governing the behaviour and conduct of women and *qadiyyat al-mara* (women's issues). These now constitute several volumes and 'the contents and sheer amount of their *fatwas* reflect a fetishism amounting to an obsession with all things feminine [and] hardly any aspect of the female body, behaviour or life is left unregulated by a *fatwa*' (al-

Rasheed, 2015: 295). She also presents a convincing case that their obsession with the regulation and control of women is not just a reflection of their conservative beliefs; it is also an expression of their marginalisation from mainstream political and economic matters since the mid-2000s. Since then, their domain has been restricted largely to the social arena and issues relevant to women.

However, the outcome of the unrestricted power they do have in this domain has been the creation of 'detailed religiously sanctioned opinions that fix women in a particular framework, the purpose of which is to guard the symbolism of gender politics in the kingdom' (al-Rasheed, 2015: 296). For example, Saudi clerics have often decreed that women are not eligible to be religious, political or legal leaders because they are, by nature, weak, hesitant, emotional and 'lacking full control' of their bodies and minds. And because the 'seductive and dangerous sexuality' of women must be controlled and hidden, they are opposed to any relaxation in the country's strict clothing codes and any proposals to introduce mixed-gender workplaces, and they have also advocated that all-female hospitals, banks and businesses must be maintained *forever*. Consequently, al-Rasheed is very sceptical about the public statements made by some high-ranking government officials and the late King Abdullah about women's education, employment and emancipation. She believes that this is just 'an upgrade to Saudi authoritarianism by playing the gender card', even if there are few notable examples of more liberal clerics who are advocates of a 'moderate emancipation agenda' (al-Rasheed, 2015: 269 and 302).

In the highly conformist culture of the KSA, many Saudi women naturally acquiesce in their subordinate roles, while others find ways to fight back in the private domain and by small acts of rebellion (such as driving cars). But as al-Rasheed has said, 'whether women choose conformity or silent rebellion, they live their lives in a country that has not yet resolved big questions about its identity [and] those women who "rebel" are defining themselves in new ways that challenge old perceptions of Saudi society and the state' (al-Rasheed,

2015: 301–302), and we will encounter several examples of women who are trying to redefine and loosen their 'social boundaries' in Chapter 7. However, even if some women are trying to change things, even those from extremely wealthy and comfortable backgrounds have had to endure repressed and constrained lives, as this member of the Saudi royal family recalled:

> Since I was a young girl, unloved by my father, and tortured by a cruel older brother, I longed for the opportunity to tell the entire world how too many young Saudi girls live lives clouded by sadness or anger that their brothers are greatly loved while they, as females, are merely endured. I have lived my life as a princess, and still I have had few options ... I can scarcely imagine how other young Saudi girls abide their lives. I know of young girls forced to become the third or fourth wife of old men. I know of women who have been instantly divorced when diagnosed with serious illness. Some of these women are mothers and their terrorised children are taken from their arms to be raised by another woman. I know of young girls who have been put to death by members of their own family, often for nothing more than perceived misconduct ... My father was a merciless man; as a predictable result, my mother was a melancholy woman. Their tragic union eventually produced sixteen children, of whom eleven survived perilous childhoods. Today, their ten female offspring live their lives controlled by the men to whom they are married. Their only surviving son, a prominent Saudi prince and business man with four wives and numerous mistresses leads a life of great promise and pleasure ... We Saudi women have few possibilities for genuine change. We Saudi women need your help. Many of you live in countries where you can insist that your governments demand change from one of their economic and social partners, Saudi Arabia.

> The authority of a Saudi male is unlimited; his wife and children survive only if he desires. In our homes, he is the state. This

complex situation begins with the rearing of our young boys.
From an early age, the male child is taught that women are of
little value: they exist only for his comfort and convenience. The
child witnesses the disdain shown for his mothers and sisters;
this open contempt leads to his scorn of all females, and makes
it impossible for him to enjoy friendship with anyone of the
opposite sex. Taught only the role of master and slave, it is little
wonder that by the time he is old enough to take a mate he
considers her his chattel, not his partner. And so it comes to be
that women in my land are ignored by their fathers, scorned by
their brothers and abused by their husbands ... By treating
women as slaves, as property, men have made themselves as
unhappy as the women they rule, and have made love and true
companionship unattainable to both sexes

(abridged from Sassoon, 2004: 19–20 and 29–30).[10]

In recent years, the highly regulated state and commercial media –
such as Al Watan, Al Sarq, Al Wasat and the Al Arabiya television
station – have broadly welcomed proposals for reforms that would
address the problem of domestic violence, enhance the legal rights of
women, reduce the very strict *ikhtilat* prohibitions between unrelated women and men and improve their participation in the national
labour market. However, al-Rasheed is very doubtful that this 'pro-
women' rhetoric will be translated into concrete legal and social
policy reforms anytime soon, and she is not particularly hopeful that
most women are ready to challenge either the Saudi state or the
country's *imams*:

It is clear that many women realise the limitations of their small
[acts of] resistance, and many others prefer to place themselves
under state patriarchy, as they see it as an escape from tradition and
the social conservatism of their families and tribal groups. As weak
subjects vis-à-vis the state and its religious institutions, women
resort to 'weak' weapons that have so far resulted in more
prosecution, arrest and harassment by society, the state and its

religious law-enforcing agencies. Whether women will be able to negotiate a better deal with the state remains unclear in the foreseeable future, given that women remain professionally unorganised

(al-Rasheed, 2015: 312).

The lack of significant change in the KSA up to this point in time indicates that al-Rasheed may well be right. Although numerous reports, cited in this and earlier chapters, have argued that economic modernisation and diversification cannot happen without the active participation of much greater numbers of Saudi women in the national labour market, the government has taken no steps to introduce equal-opportunity legislation, there is no ministry for women's affairs and there are no independent NGOs which can promote women's rights in the KSA. It can also be mentioned that during his lengthy interview with *The Economist* in January 2016, Crown Prince Muhammad made just two minor references to the status of Saudi women and even those were in the context of what he described as the KSA's 'scary population figures' (*The Economist* Middle East and Africa, 2016). It was also noticeable during my time in the KSA that while government officials made several public statements in support of greater female emancipation, they invariably added the caveat that they had to proceed slowly in order not to alienate the more traditional and conservative elements in Saudi society. The only notable difference between today and the 2000s is that the KSA's *ulama* have been less vociferous about women's issues. During that decade they had dispensed numerous *fatwas*, banning women from appearing in the media, mixing with men at book fairs, engaging in sporting activities, watching Western TV programs, driving (again), standing in municipal elections and so forth.

Another significant impediment is the lack of women who can defend the interests of female Saudis in the country's legal system. Although women have attended university law courses since 2005 and several hundred have since graduated, the first Saudi woman – Arwa al-Hujaili – was not allowed to practice until 2013, after graduating in 2010 and petitioning the Ministry of Justice for three years for permission to do this. In 2012, after receiving a petition from 3,000 law graduates, King Abdullah issued a Royal Decree allowing women to register as lawyers, but it was not until al-Hujaili began working as a lawyer in the United States and had publicised her predicament that the Ministry of Justice granted her application and those of four other Saudi women. In 2014, the first women's law practice was opened in Riyadh by Bayan Mahmoud al-Azahran, representing women and men. However, in 2016, there were just sixty-seven female lawyers out of a total of 3,400, and there were still no female public prosecutors or judges in the KSA (*Al Arabiya News*; 2014; Carrington, 2013; Pollard, 2013). Judge Faisal Orani, who opposes the introduction of female judges and 'fresh from sentencing a whisky-drinker to 80 lashes', commented that 'women are better at representing other women because women natter more than men and so women understand them better.' However, even this old-school traditionalist admitted that 'over time, anything can change. Maybe I'll change too' (*The Economist*, 2016g: 45). Sheikh Abdullah al-Manie – a religious adviser at the Saudi royal court – had suggested in 2011 that women with legal qualifications should be allowed to become judges and also qualify as *muftia* (female religious scholars) and become members of the General Presidency of Scholarly Research and Ifta. This proposal was strongly opposed and declared as prohibited by a zealous Ministry of Justice official, Sheikh al-Obeikan, who we first encountered in Chapter 2. He was later dismissed by King Abdullah after he had publicly condemned draft proposals to improve women's legal rights (al-Shihri, 2012).

Several conferences and symposia in the KSA over the last decade have highlighted the need for more women to enter the labour force, and yet few steps have been taken by the Saudi government to facilitate this process or to openly discuss the main impediments to this: conservative Islamic beliefs about the roles of women in society, strict gender segregation in the workplace and public spaces, the absence of gender-equality legislation, the unwillingness of 'educated but idle' women to work and strong resistance from conservative families who will not allow their wives and daughters to work (al-Rasheed and Azzam, 2012: 7). As al-Rasheed has suggested:

> The status of Saudi women will not change when tribalism disappears, the religious scholars develop progressive interpretations of Islam, or Saudi society becomes less conservative, but when the state ceases to measure its legitimacy using a constructed gendered moral order in which women are symbols of piety, debauchery, or modernity ... A complete disengagement between women and the state's civic myths is a prerequisite for the emancipation of Saudi women. Above all, this emancipation is dependent on women's ability to become a social force that can exert pressure on the state to change its current policies that enforce their subordination. As long as women's participation in the workforce remains limited, and as long as they continue to be consulted by the state only on women's issues, this development is not predicted to occur in the near future
>
> (al-Rasheed, 2015: 312–313).

What all of this means is that almost all girls and young women in the KSA would have been and continue to be exposed to strict gender-role socialisation while growing up. For example, although she made the following observations in the late 1990s, al-Munajjed's comments about the upbringing of women and men remain very relevant today:

> In Saudi Arabia's gender-based system, family organisation represents the core of society. Girls are socialized from their early years to acquire a domestic role that fits their expected gender roles. For a Saudi girl, becoming a mother is the norm, the ultimate aim of her life. She is brought up to believe she should be a 'good mother', and that it is her natural duty to devote her time to her husband and children. Girls' schools institutionalise this mother role ... Children in Saudi Arabia are socialized into family

dependence and obedience to the parents, especially to the father who holds authority over all members of the group ... Men are seen as the 'breadwinners' of the family, women are considered to be responsible for the home, assuming the domestic role of wife and mother. The first responsibilities of a woman are therefore to stay at home to care for the husband and children

(al-Munajjed, 1997: 67–68, 78 and 83).

Hence, as in the UAE and Oman, it would have been normal for almost all Saudi girls and boys to have been taught that men were superior to women during their childhoods. Young boys were taught that they were responsible for the conduct of their wives, sisters and mothers, that they were their natural guardians and protectors and the behaviour of 'their' women would reflect on them throughout their lives. As they grew up and were educated in male- or female-only schools, these beliefs would have been imbued and reinforced. The school system would have directed boys and girls into segregated curricula streams, 'with boys being taught to think about male activities and the jobs they would do in the future, and girls being encouraged to think about the future roles as mothers and housewives and attending courses in home management, sewing, cooking and childcare' (al-Munajjed, 1997: 67). According to Human Rights Watch, the curricula taught at all Saudi schools during the 2000s adhered closely to Article 153 of the Saudi Policy on Education, which states that 'A girl's education aims at giving her the correct Islamic education to enable her to be in life a successful housewife, an exemplary wife and a good mother' (Human Rights Watch, 2008: 14). Furthermore, despite promised reforms from the new (male) Education Minister in 2014, there is still a great emphasis on Islamic religious studies in school curricula which continue to reinforce negative stereotypes about girls and women (Freedom House, 2016b; Khashoggi, 2014).

The evidence and examples presented in Section 6.3 demonstrate that while some women in the KSA have built successful careers over the last two decades, most Saudi women still do not have this opportunity. Traditional cultural and attitudinal stereotypes persist and, as we will see in Chapter 7, they continue to be expressed by most university-educated Saudi men today. Nevertheless, a growing number of educated Saudi women now choose to work and build careers, some have started their own companies, and there are several women in leadership roles in the public and, to a lesser extent, the private sector. Most Saudi fathers support the education of their daughters and some now provide active support and encouragement for them to pursue careers. As more women have entered the KSA labour market and succeeded in their professions and careers, traditional views about the roles of women in KSA society and the workforce have also begun to evolve, but only to a limited extent. However, in Chapter 7, we will see that the gender self-perceptions of young Saudi women and their beliefs about the 'appropriate' roles of women and men in the KSA are changing much more quickly. This is a trend that has also been noticed by Bennoune:

> Despite, or perhaps because of the considerable restrictions imposed on them, Saudi women are very much in the forefront of social and economic change in the kingdom. By dint of their academic, professional and economic successes, they are quietly breaking down their country's pervasive discriminatory policies and social attitudes. They are also challenging the puritanical interpretations of the Wahhabist religious establishment that are used to justify restrictions on women in the first place ...
> [However], given the deeply entrenched religious establishment in the kingdom, women reformers are careful to couch their efforts within an Islamic discourse
>
> *(Bennoune, 2013: 205 and 207).*

This shift in attitudes is also reflected in the interviews conducted with three groups of graduating business and management students at Al Faisal University during 2009–2011. Although they were a self-selecting sample of the more confident and liberal-minded female students at this university, their comments about their country and their hopes for the future clearly signify something of a generational shift in beliefs about the roles that women could play in the KSA in the future. As with their peers in the UAE and Oman, they were all ambitious and fully committed to pursuing careers in their chosen professions, they were all hoping to marry men who would allow them to continue to work and who would provide some support for their careers and most of them planned to delay marriage and pregnancy for a few years while they made some progress in their chosen careers. For example:

> My perspective has changed. When I was a little girl, I had all these Cinderella dreams, to marry a rich, strong, wealthy man, and just be a good mother and wife, all these things. Now, I want to be strong and wealthy and successful for myself. Of course, I also want to be with the right person, and have children … but I want all these other things now. So, I want someone who accepts me, and we would help each other. I want to have a career, not because it might pay a lot of money, or because I get promoted a lot. I will do this because I want to and because I enjoy finance
>
> *(22-year-old finance major).*

> I want to have a career in the future, but you have to be able to manage all three roles: mother, wife and business woman. It's manageable but obviously it depends on the man, the husband. For me, we both have to do this because not working for me is not an option. So, I will be looking for a husband who is willing to compromise. I don't want to get married and just sit at home, have babies, be a mum! I don't want that! I want someone who knows that I have ambitions and goals and who knows that there are things that I want to do with my life and I don't want my life to just revolve around him and what he decides to do. So, for me, you have to find a good partner – someone who's willing to compromise
>
> *(22-year-old management major).*

Nevertheless, they all recognised that further change for women would be slow, and many men (and some women) in the KSA would be resistant to this:

If I was a man, why would I change? Even if they wanted to, the system doesn't allow it. You know that most Saudi men don't have a lot of political power, but they do have some economic power and they have a lot of authority over women. This makes them feel good about themselves and their egos. So they would resist it to the last minute. Power is hard to let go of. But, in 20 years' time, I think things will have changed, because women are changing and they are less willing to accept their traditional roles and discrimination ... I don't want to live in a discriminatory environment, but things will only change if women double their efforts to make the changes. We have to be persistent!

(23-year-old management major).

I think our government is willing to do more, but that is dependent on Saudi society. I think our society is changing, or at least parts of it are. For example, who could have imagined that we would have had women studying with men at the same universities or women in the national assembly!? This was impossible a few years ago but it has happened ... But, I think women are 90 per cent of the problem. They do not do enough to promote their own interests, and a lot of women are happy with the way things are. They do not have independence or their own wealth, but they are very comfortable and they like their lives

(22-year-old accounting major).

They also understood that they were not typical of all young Saudi women. For example:

We may seem like the majority of women, but we're not. We are well-off. If you really open your eyes, there are a lot of Saudi women who do not have the opportunities that we do. It's still very common for women here to be married at sixteen or seventeen, and some of them still marry an older man because of their circumstances. For poorer families, this can help them to raise their status and wealth ... for them that's a way out of poverty.

We can see that we have more options and freedoms now, but they don't have these opportunities, so we are very lucky

(22-year-old finance major).

I remember watching this program on CNN a few months ago and it was all about how women in Saudi Arabia are either oppressed or pampered and, honestly, the first thought that came to my mind was that we are pampered [laughs]! I'm not saying that everything is open and equal for women here and we can't do and say whatever we want, but we are pampered. Everything is handed to us. In our own homes, we are treated as a queen you know. Like, you get driven around and get everything done for you. Maybe it's not a lifestyle that every Saudi woman wants and it's not one that all Saudi women have, but it's definitely not as bad as maybe people in the West think it is. I honestly believe that their opinion of us is too extreme ... we're not oppressed, but I agree that on some levels many things do need to change but I think everyone knows that will only happen very slowly, *shweya-shweya*

(23-year-old finance major).

However, they also felt that there were signs of change in the KSA, and the impetus for further reforms was growing:

30 years ago things were very different. I think even for the very conservative people, it doesn't make sense to go backwards. So, even when some of our *imams* say we are on the wrong path and we need to stop the reforms, it doesn't make sense to most Saudis to do that now, well at least to the people I know. If we were five million people, maybe we could do that but we are now more than 10 million and heading to 20 or 25 million. We are increasing our population, so how can we have a successful economy without more women working? It doesn't make sense ... we have to change because half of our society is women and half of our society is under 25

(22-year-old finance major).

Things could change very quickly. I think that some young women are now unstoppable, and there are so many of them coming through our universities. Can you imagine what would happen if our government then says, 'No, you can't work'. I can't see how this can happen ... We have already seen a lot of changes under King Abdullah*, because he was supportive of greater opportunities for women and so I think we will continue to see more changes, but these will take a long time ... I think 100 per cent we will see this, but while our dreams are high, we have to realistic because of all the uncertainties that there are in our region outside Saudi Arabia. These may slow down this change

(23-year-old management major; *the ruler of the KSA at the time of this interview).

I hope that in 20 years' time with the expected changes in social perceptions resulting from all the factors I have mentioned, that women will be in the driving seat and driving to and from their various employment positions ... Women will work as engineers, architects and scientists and in all the professions that men do ... More women will be business leaders and will be in important positions in our national assembly. Many more graduates will create their own firms and be successful business women. They will work in courts of law and will be judges and lawyers. The permission of a male guardian will be officially overruled, the *wakeel* will be unheard of, and we will be allowed to drive to and from our workplaces, *inshalla*!

(22-year-old marketing major; I had asked her to imagine how she hoped things would be for Saudi women in 20 years' time).

6.6 CONCLUSION

Saudi Arabia: the heart of the Arab and Islamic worlds, the investment powerhouse, and the hub connecting three continents.

'Our vision', from the KSA's *Vision 2030* document,
25 April 2016 (Eye of Riyadh, 2016)

By the will of Allah, the Saudi Economy in 2024 will be a developed, thriving and prosperous economy based on sustainable foundations. It will extend rewarding work opportunities to all citizens, will have a high quality education and training system, excellent health care for all, and will provide the necessary services that will bring about the best conveniences to all citizens ... the Saudi Economy will be a diversified, prosperous, private-sector driven economy, providing job opportunities, quality education, health care and necessary skills to ensure the well-being of all citizens, while safeguarding Islamic values and the Kingdom's cultural heritage.

> The original goals of the KSA's 'Economic Vision 2024' (Kingdom of
> Saudi Arabia Ministry of Economy and Planning, 2005: Section 3.4)

An alternative scenario to the optimistic Economic Vision 2024 is that the KSA will still be a relatively prosperous country in 2024 with adequate, but no longer cost-free education and healthcare. It will, in the absence of significant economic, political and social reforms, be characterised by growing wealth inequalities, rising levels of poverty among its minority cultural/religious groups and the increasing alienation of a significant number of the country's young people. It is unlikely that the KSA will have developed a high-quality education system across the country's primary, secondary and tertiary sectors or the 'necessary skills to ensure the well-being of all its citizens.' It will, in all probability, still be very reliant on its diminishing oil and gas resources and will not have created a fully diversified or a private-sector–driven economy. There will be even higher levels of unemployment among its young people and it will be unable to provide adequate job opportunities for its growing population, particularly for the increasing number of young women and men who will be graduating from the country's universities and vocational colleges. It will, despite growing social divisions, continue to safeguard its 'Islamic values' and the kingdom's cultural heritage as much as it can, because the power of the al-Sauds, the country's ruling-elite and the *ulama* will depend on this. At the same time, more liberal-minded and educated Saudis will be questioning the legitimacy of their country's political and business leadership and the authority of a religious establishment whose most fervent and radical supporters will still be fighting for the remnants of ISIS or other militant Islamic groups that emerge during the 2020s while advocating for the overthrow of the al-Sauds and the creation of a 'pure' Islamic State in the KSA. It will still be a major regional military power and continue to be involved in several military conflicts in the Gulf and broader MENA region.

This alternative scenario may well be much more plausible than the optimistic Economic Vision 2024 document, which had envisaged that the KSA's industrial and manufacturing sectors would contribute 24.9 per cent of the country's GDP by 2024. This document arose out of discussions at the first National Dialogue Forum in 2003, which was established in the aftermath of the 9/11 attacks on New York and increasing internal security threats to discuss economic, social, cultural and religious issues. Meetings of this forum have been held every year since in different cities in the KSA and, in more recent times, these have also been televised. Topics have covered terrorism, religious extremism, religious toleration, education, labour issues, young people and women's rights. The recommendations of the carefully selected professionals and intellectuals who are invited to these forums are compiled and addressed to the king in the belief that these will be used to inform policy makers in the relevant government ministries and agencies (al-Rasheed, 2015: 243). Several of these meetings have dealt with women's issues, and none of them have gone smoothly, with routine verbal clashes between conservatives and traditionalists and those advocating for greater economic opportunities and equality for Saudi women. The problem, as with all the other 'dialogue' initiatives sponsored by the Saudi state, is that:

> These meetings are far from being an independent initiative, organised and run by autonomous civil society associations,

although the government and civil servants in charge of their
organisation have endeavoured to fix them in the public
imagination as free platforms for consultation. The early
enthusiasm surrounding the first meetings gave way to apathy
[and] many soon realised that this dialogue would not produce
serious political change ... Bluntly put, the National Dialogue is
a step towards the modernisation of autocratic rule, without
any serious impact on the course that political reform takes in
Saudi Arabia

(al-Rasheed, 2010: 246).

This is not to dismiss this (and similar forums) out of hand, because it
did represent a small step forward in civic dialogue in the KSA, and
some of its (non-controversial) recommendations have since been
taken on board by policy makers, particularly in the education field.
However, its lack of real power is symptomatic of a much deeper
malaise in the body politic of the KSA and what al-Rasheed has
accurately described as the 'infantile' relationship between the Saudi
people and 'their' state. As she describes this, 'Saudi society remains
weak vis-à-vis the state, which prohibits communal action, with the
exception of that which takes place under government sponsorship
and authorisation ... through paternalism and patronage, it co-opts
groups and creates the semblance of liberalisation' (al-Rasheed, 2010:
251). Consequently, there has never been an open and honest discussion of the existential economic, political and social problems that
the KSA faces, why these are likely to get worse during the remainder
of the 2010s and the 2020s and no acknowledgement of what the
nation needs to do to deal with these before it is too late.

As Hertog has observed, 'the Saudi rentier state has prevented the emergence of independent macro-organisations such
as labour unions or broad parties in Saudi Arabia and has left little
space for independent meso-structures such as professional associations and functional interest groups (consumer protection, sec-
toral business associations, regional interest groups, and so on)'

(Hertog, 2015 : 260). This is, as it is in Oman and to a lesser extent in the UAE, a reflection of the top-down, autocratic political and economic systems of many countries in the MENA region and explains why the Saudi state (even if it wants to) will struggle to implement the economic changes that were proposed by Crown Prince Muhammad at the beginning of 2016. The Saudi state did not emerge organically and incrementally, as it did in Western industrialised societies. Rather, it grew out of the hierarchical power relations that grew up between the al-Sauds, an extremely conservative religious establishment, a very small business caste, an emerging middle class and – at critical junctures – foreign multinational companies. Consequently, much of the national economy is still controlled by the ruling elite that formed around the all-powerful al-Saud family during the 1960s, 1970s and 1980s and one of the pejorative nicknames that Saudis have for this pervasive and very powerful group is *iqta'iyin* (feudal lords). This also means that there has never been any independent oversight or scrutiny of how the country's oil wealth has been allocated to fund the country's massive infrastructure projects, sustain the royal family's opulent standard of living, create a bloated and very inefficient public sector, maintain the country's ever-growing military expenditure (about $57 billion; more than 10% of annual GDP in 2015) or how it has been used to 'buy off' dissent among the Saudi people (Stockholm International Peace Research Institute, 2016).

In addition, the national economy has been almost entirely based on *consumption* over the last forty years rather than on *production*, with, of course, the notable exception of the still very dominant oil and gas sector. Consequently, it is not easy to see how such an autocratic, top-down rentier state with so many vested and entrenched business interests will ever encourage a more open and less restrained 'bottom-up' private sector in which new value-added entrepreneurial small and medium-sized businesses can thrive. The patrimonial and rentier systems first put in place in the 1930s and 1940s and consolidated during the 1970s, 1980s and 1990s are as strong as ever – as is the control that the al-Sauds have over these (al-Rasheed, 2010: 260). These factors may well explain why Moody's was considering a major downgrade of the KSA's Aa3 credit rating in June 2016 (Moody's Investor Services, 2016).

There is little disagreement, at least among foreign observers, that the Saudi Arabian economy requires a significant overhaul but the new regime has shown no interest in political reform, no interest in challenging the vested business interests that have dominated the economy for the last forty years, no interest in creating a bottom-up culture of creativity, innovation and entrepreneurship, little interest in curtailing the suffocating conservative influence of the country's powerful clerics and not enough interest in improving the legal and social rights of Saudi women. Externally, it is now engaged in what will become an increasingly bloody sectarian struggle between Sunni and Shiite Islam, a struggle that it can neither afford nor – more importantly – win. Defence and national security already use up 35.7 per cent of all government revenues and will eat up an increasing share of a shrinking national budget during the rest of this decade and the early 2020s. The collapse in oil prices between 2014 and 2016 means, in the starkest terms, that the Saudi state can no longer afford to sustain and subsidise its growing and economically unproductive population; and, according to *The Economist*, 'Saudi Arabia's public finances are unsustainable for more than a few years' (*The Economist*, 2016c: 17).

The foundations of the 'three compacts' described in Section 5.3 are also showing signs of fragmenting. The enduring but always complicated relationship it has had with the KSA's religious establishment is under stress, because the *ulama* remains resolutely opposed to many of the moderate economic, political, legal, social and educational reforms that are required to steer the Saudi state and economy onto a new path. As we have seen, in common with other oil-rich Gulf States, the al-Sauds have dealt with internal political and social unrest with a combination of iron-fist repression and social largesse, while also regularly dipping into the country's financial reserves to buy off discontent among their population. While the religious, regional, ethnic and tribal conflicts that beset the KSA are nothing new and have been features of Saudi life for centuries, the lack of 'modern' and accountable civil institutions and a complete absence of democratic accountability (as described in Chapter 1) mean that this country will be dealing with these challenges for the foreseeable future. In late April 2016, Deputy Crown Prince Muhammad bin Salman launched the KSA's ambitious Vision 2030 document, a national transformation plan that one commentator described enthusiastically as:

> Astonishing ... a renaissance project built on pragmatic and scientific foundations ... aiming to substitute nationalisation, rentier and top-down [economic] models with a liberal and social approach, a philosophy of rewarding creativity and excellence, and a policy based on citizenship and participation. The new Vision lays the foundations for a historical leap that will no doubt shake up Saudi Arabia and the Arab region
>
> (Dergham, 2016).

However, a less partisan analysis of the text of this document indicates that it while it is strong on generalities it is very weak in describing the detailed policies that might lead to the kind of economic and political reforms that would 'shake up' Saudi Arabia. 'Our vision', this document informs us, 'is a tolerant country with Islam at its constitution and moderation as its methods'. It contains proposals to reform the country's Public Investment Fund, the development of new industrial and special economic zones and the part-privatisation of the KSA's biggest company, Saudi Aramco (although the government will still control 95% of its shares). It describes, as many earlier economic plans have done, the need to 'create a more diverse and sustainable economy', 'unleash the capabilities of our promising economic sectors and privatise some government services', 'create more opportunities for the entrepreneur' and 'improve the business environment, so that our economy grows and flourishes, driving healthier employment opportunities for citizens and long-term prosperity for all.'

This document also promises to 'reduce delays and cut tedious bureaucracy [and] wide ranging transparency and accountability reforms' and to create 'an effective, transparent, accountable, enabling and high-performing government.' It stresses the importance of improving the general health and fitness of Saudis, 'developing our children's characters from an early age by reshaping our academic and educational systems', and 'to also redouble efforts to ensure that the outcomes of our education system are in line with market needs.' The document makes several references to developing the human capital of the KSA, including the importance of 'unlocking the talent, dedication and potential of our young men and women' and, in one of three very minor references to Saudi women, describes them 'as yet another great asset' and the need 'to develop their talents, invest in their productive capabilities and enable them to strengthen their future and contribute to the development of our society and our economy' (Eye of Riyadh, 2016).

However, as noted earlier, systemic economic reforms have been promised by the ruling elite of the KSA many times in the past but have rarely materialised and, to no one's surprise, this document contained no proposals to reform or modernise the kingdom's moribund and repressive political system and its opaque legal system or to restrict the power of the kingdom's ultra-conservative clerics. Many of the economic reforms proposed in the Vision 2030 document should be applauded because, if they are successful, 'the Kingdom could double its GDP and create as many as six million jobs by 2030, enough to employ the sizeable cohort of young Saudi men and women entering the labour force over the next fifteen years' (al-Kibsi et al, 2015: iv). However, Prince Muhammad's very modest goal of increasing female workforce participation from 20 to 30 per cent 'by 2030' will not be enough and, according to *The Economist*, reflects the continuing resistance of the Wahhabist religious establishment to significant changes in the economic and legal rights of women in the kingdom (*The Economist*, 2016k: 41).

There are also understandable doubts about the Saudi government's ability to find the $4 trillion which external commentators say is required to fund the systemic reforms that are the necessary prerequisites to implementing their ambitious economic development strategies. There is even greater scepticism about the willingness of the country's government ministries to embrace and implement the many reforms proposed by Prince Mohammad in April 2016. The KSA public sector has been variously described as 'bloated', 'corrupt', 'deadweight', 'flabby', 'highly centralised', 'hierarchical', 'immobile', 'opaque', 'reactive', 'territorial', 'unaccountable', 'unresponsive', 'vertically divided' and 'weak' (Bertelsmann Stiftung, 2015c: 24–25; Hertog, 2010b: 95–98 and 107; *The Economist*, 2016b and 2016j). As one of these reports has commented:

> The Saudi state suffers from capacity deficiencies due to its comparatively recent emergence, the rentier mentality of many of its bureaucrats, its limited penetration of society from a regulatory perspective, and its own penetration by clientelist networks* in significant parts. This can make consistent implementation of policies difficult … More fundamentally, no one within the Saudi elite seems committed to substantial political change [and] the primary consideration remains regime survival … the large and immovable state apparatus, and the complex structure of political clienteles attached to it and the al-Saud family, limits the pace of any large scale change
>
> *(Bertelsmann Stiftung, 2015c: 21, 22 and 23;*
> **i.e. 'vested business interests').*

The Economist has also observed that 'although there is much flab to cut' in the KSA's public sector:

> That is still a perilous undertaking which means dismantling the system according to which petro-cash, not taxes, pay for free education and health care as well as highly subsidised electricity, water and housing. More than money is at stake: this largesse has

disguised how far the economy is chronically unproductive and dependent on foreign labour. It has been too easy for Saudis to avoid working or to snooze away in government offices

(The Economist, 2016b: 8).

There is also widespread suspicion about the motives of the country's billionaire princes who control many key areas of the national economy and who have, in the past, often disguised their acquisitions of state-owned businesses under the shield of 'privatisation' and 'economic reform'. Although a National Anti-Corruption Commission (*Nazaha*) was established in 2011, and Deputy Crown Prince Mohammad announced in April 2016 that there would be 'zero-tolerance for all levels of corruption' (Eye of Riyadh, 2016), this remains a widespread problem in the KSA. The country was ranked 52/167 countries for corruption in 2015, with a score of 47/100, which may also act as an impediment to economic reform (Transparency International, 2015: 6; a score below 50 signifies that corruption is 'widespread'). In addition, the Heritage Foundation Index of Economic Freedom placed the KSA at 78/178 countries, with low scores for 'rule of law', 'regulatory efficiency', 'investment freedom' and 'financial freedom' (Heritage Foundation, 2016). This perhaps explains why twenty-one of the world's leading banks have established regional offices in Dubai, but not one of these has expressed any interest in doing the same at the $10 billion King Abdullah Financial District in Riyadh, which opened in January 2016 (*The Economist*, 2016f). However, while these factors may well impede significant economic reforms, 'the conjunction of a fall in oil prices, a geopolitical crisis and a hyperactive Deputy Crown Prince afford a once-in-a-generation chance to modernise the country' (*The Economist*, 2016c: 18).

While this may be true, it would also require significant changes to its economic growth model, because 'based on current trends, Saudi Arabia could face a rapid economic deterioration over the next 15 years' (al-Kibsi et al, 2015: i). The KSA certainly has a longer period of time than the UAE and Oman to build a post-hydrocarbon economy and it was the twentieth-largest economy in the world in 2015, but it will have to find new and innovative ways to support its growing and increasingly restive young population quickly rather than pursue old strategies that have largely served the economic interests of its ruling elite and maintained a fragile status quo in the kingdom over the last four decades.

Prince Saud bin Khalid Al Faisal, Deputy Governor of SAGIA, has suggested that 'there is a reason why having vast hydrocarbon resources is also known as the "oil-curse", and while Saudi Arabia is not immune to overdependence on hydrocarbon revenues, the government has been seeking to diversify the Kingdom's economy through various initiatives such as enacting the Foreign Investment Law in 2000 and joining the WTO in 2005' (Vietor and White, 2015: 12). It has also been trying to encourage entrepreneurship through the establishment of financing programs such as the Kafala and Centennial Funds, established in 2005, in addition to numerous small-business incubators and the establishment of the SME Authority in 2016. Unfortunately, there are few visible signs that these initiatives have had much of an impact on the growth of the country's private sector, on business start-up rates among Saudis and the growth of the country's SME sector or if they are encouraging Saudi women and men to leave the security of well-paid and – for now – secure public-sector employment. Indeed, the early indicators do not look promising. The KSA private sector grew, on average, by 7.2 per cent a year between 2010 and 2014, but this fell to 5.2 per cent during 2015 (Oxford Business Group, 2015a: 2).

Moreover, data from the World Bank Knowledge Economy Index, which looks at the extent to which the cultural, legal, business, educational and scientific environments of countries are conducive for sustainable long-term economic development, placed the KSA at 50/146 countries in 2013 (World Bank, 2013: 2), which is a surprisingly high ranking given the very low global ranking of all but one of the country's universities, the absence (until very recently) of well-funded research institutes and very low levels of commercial and industrial innovation in the country. Although the government has established fourteen specialist science research centres at its public universities and plans to increase this to twenty-five by 2020, it will be many years before the fruits of this research become apparent (*Chronicle of Higher Education*, 2010: 4). These realities will make it very difficult for the KSA to manage a rapid and smooth transition from an economy still heavily dependent on oil to one that is diversified and internationally competitive, and this may be further hampered by rapid fluctuations in global oil and gas prices over the next five to ten years.

Of course, if the KSA is to achieve this transition by 2030, Saudi women will have to play a much bigger role in the country's workforce than they currently do. In 2007, the Saudi journalist and activist Samar Fatany, who we first met in Chapter 1, suggested that:

> The untapped potential of Saudi women can propel us ahead but only if we let it. Wise deliberations that do not result in resolution will neither be very wise nor very helpful to our shared economic future. Therefore, it is imperative that we do arrive at a resolution and put a plan into action to help Saudi women overcome their challenges and succeed – both for their nation and for Islam … If we don't make a strong case for change, our society is likely to languish … the message to Saudi women is clear. The barriers to success are coming down; the negative attitudes are changing, and it's time for women to take a leading role in the kingdom's growth and economic development
>
> *(Fatany, 2007b: 16, 21 and 49).*

Unfortunately, while the barriers may have been shaken a little since she wrote these words they are still firmly in place and, nearly a decade on, Saudi women do not play a leading role in the economic development of the KSA. They are not free to participate as equals with men in the public domain, even if they now have more freedom to participate in municipal elections, public events and the media. There is still no independent ministry for women to represent their interests or autonomous women's associations, and there are no signs that the draconian male-guardianship laws will be loosened any time soon. We also noted earlier that the Saudi education system is still not set up to prepare young women or men for suitable employment in the national labour market, and there also are significant misalignments between the curricula delivered at the primary, secondary and tertiary levels and the changing requirements of the country's private sector (al-Kibsi et al, 2015: 10–11). The new Education Minister appointed in 2014 did not have a background in education and those familiar with him and the KSA's education system had little confidence that the religious and KSA–centric 'humanities' components of school and university curricula would be replaced with a greater emphasis on science, technology and mathematics because of resistance from the *ulama* (Freedom House, 2016b; Khashoggi, 2014).

For the reasons outlined in this chapter, it does not appear that the 'new' ruling elite of the KSA understands the crucial role that women could play in the growth and development of the Saudi economy in the future. There were, until very recently, few indications that the country's rulers appreciate the urgent need to encourage more women to join the national workforce and to greatly increase their participation in the nation's private sector. If the KSA decides not to create a more level playing field for women in all sectors of its national labour market, it would be the first country in the world to have offered large numbers of young women the opportunity to graduate from universities and vocational colleges and then refused them the opportunity to work. To those who care about the long-term future of the KSA, it makes no sense – economically, politically, socially or morally – to do this. Involving significantly more Saudi women in the KSA workforce would, of course, necessitate a fundamental shift in cultural attitudes and some reduction in the dominant influence of the country's clerics, and we will return to look at this issue in Chapter 8 and the Postscript to this book. But, as noted at the end of Chapters 3 and 5, many other countries have gone through similar economic and social transformations in recent decades, and how the KSA might be able to do this, if it chooses to, is described in Chapter 9.

7 The Experiences of Women in Public- and Private-Sector Organisations in the Kingdom of Saudi Arabia

7.1 INTRODUCTION

As we saw in Chapter 6, the KSA is one of the most patriarchal and conservative countries in the world, but even here, there are some embryonic signs of change in the roles women play in civic society and in the national labour market. To better understand the extent and depth of this change, we first look at the attitudes Saudis have about women in the workplace, explore their views about the leadership abilities of women and also ask if they believe that more women will become business leaders in the KSA in the future. We evaluate their opinions about the degree of equality that Saudi women have in the national labour market and also describe the entrenched cultural, attitudinal and structural barriers they encounter in the workplace. Next, we focus on an area of the Saudi economy in which women are still noticeably under-represented – the entrepreneurial and small and medium-sized enterprise (SME) sector. We then examine an issue that is of concern to a few Saudi women: how to balance the competing demands of their busy work and home lives. The chapter concludes by evaluating the progress that national women have made in the Saudi labour market and the emergence of a growing number of Saudi women business leaders, and it also draws attention to those sectors where they are still plainly under-represented. In the conclusion, we ask if some very recent initiatives by the Saudi government may mean that women will have a bigger role to play in the KSA's labour market and national economy in the future.

7.2 THE ATTITUDES OF SAUDIS TOWARDS WOMEN IN THE WORKPLACE AND IN LEADERSHIP ROLES

In this section, we look at the opinions that Saudis have about women in the workplace, their attitudes towards female business leaders and their beliefs about the leadership abilities and competencies of Saudi women. The material presented here is based on questionnaire surveys of 133 female and 104 male Saudis.[1] As in Chapters 3 and 5, some of the figures in this section also include comparative data from other surveys that have examined the attitudes of women and men towards women in business leadership roles in the United States. To supplement this survey, face-to-face interviews were conducted with twenty female and fifteen male part-time MBA students and twenty final-year female business and management students at Al Faisal University in Riyadh during 2012–2014.

Our respondents were employed in a variety of organisations in the KSA (twelve public and semi-government organisations and seven private-sector companies). The age profiles of the respondents reflect the very young working population of KSA, with 54.0 per cent of the sample being aged twenty to twenty-nine, 28.3 per cent thirty to thirty-nine, 13.9 per cent forty to forty-nine, and just 3.8 per cent were over fifty years of age. Most of them worked in supervisory or middle-management roles and 30.4 per cent had less than five years' work experience; 30.0 per cent had six to ten years' experience and 23.6 per cent had eleven to fifteen years' work experience. Only 16.0 per cent of these women and men had worked full time for more than fifteen years. The data, presented in Table 7.1, provide a summary of the attitudes that these women and men have about working for a female boss. The results indicate that a majority of Saudi women were comfortable with the prospect of working for a female boss although nearly 30 per cent were only 'sometimes' comfortable, and about 10 per cent were not at all comfortable with this. Almost half of them also believed that it is acceptable for a man to work for a female boss, but more than a quarter were not comfortable with this idea.

One quarter of men did not appear to have difficulties working for a female boss, but two in five were not at all comfortable about this, and close to half of this group did not find the general idea of Saudi men working for a female boss to be acceptable.

These attitudes are symptomatic of the very conservative attitudes that a significant number of Saudi males have about working for female bosses. The comparative data included in Table 7.1 indicates that while these are very similar to those of male managers in the United States in the mid-1960s, there were significant differences between their opinions about working for a woman and those of male executives in the United States in 2005. The difference between the results for Saudi women and American female executives is much smaller and, once again, we have the (as yet unexplained) fact that one in five American female executives still preferred not to work for another woman as recently as 2005, which is – surprisingly – higher than the proportion of Saudi women who believe this. To reiterate the point made in Section 2 of Chapters 3 and 5, it took two generations for largely negative male attitudes to evolve to the point that three quarters of male executives could indicate that they had a favourable attitude towards women in management roles and were also 'comfortable' working for a woman. In the context of the KSA, it is perhaps encouraging that a quarter of these Saudi men do not seem to have difficulties working for a female boss. This, however, is a speculative assumption, because there is no comparative historical data that can be used to evaluate if the attitudes of Saudi men towards female bosses have become more positive over the last ten to fifteen years.

There were also somewhat mixed results when we asked these women and men, 'Do you think that male Saudis still have difficulties accepting decisions made by a female boss?', with most of these women and men indicating that male Saudi employees had some problems dealing with this (Table 7.2).

We then asked a series of questions to elicit their attitudes towards women in leadership roles and as leaders of organisations;

TABLE 7.1 *The attitudes of Saudis towards working for a female boss* (N = 133 *women and* 104 *men*)

Women
'I am comfortable with the idea of working for a female boss'
Always: 32.2
Often: 29.0
Sometimes: 28.0
Rarely: 5.8
Never: 5.0
'The idea that men can work for a female boss is acceptable to me'
Always: 21.9
Often: 27.5
Sometimes: 25.4
Rarely: 17.3
Never: 7.9
Men
'I am comfortable with the idea of working for a female boss'
Always: 6.8
Often: 16.4
Sometimes: 34.6
Rarely: 22.1
Never: 20.1
'The idea that men can work for a female boss is acceptable to me'
Always: 10.6
Often: 17.3
Sometimes: 36.5
Rarely: 20.2
Never: 15.4

Comparative data (*Carlson et al, 2006*)
'I would feel comfortable working for a woman'

	1965	2005
Women	*78.0*	*78.0*
Men	*27.0*	*75.0*

1965, N = 2,000 *American executives*; 2005, N = 286 *executives*;
(*% that agreed with this statement*)

TABLE 7.2 *Do you think that male Saudi employees still have difficulties accepting decisions made by a female boss?*

Women	Men
Always: 14.5	*Always: 14.0*
Often: 24.6	*Often: 32.4*
Sometimes: 37.7	*Sometimes: 39.4*
Rarely: 14.5	*Rarely: 11.2*
Never: 8.7	*Never: 3.0*

and their beliefs about the leadership abilities and competencies of Saudi women (Table 7.3)

As with women in the UAE and Oman, the data clearly indicate that Saudi women had much more confidence in the ability of women to succeed in leadership positions and to be the leaders of organisations when compared to male Saudis. And while half of the women believed that women had the same leadership abilities as men, only one third of Saudi men thought that this was true and a quarter of them did not believe that women have the ability to succeed in leadership positions. Having said this, we noted in Section 2 of Chapters 3 and 5 that the more encouraging data lies in the number of responses in the 'sometimes' and 'maybe' categories in Table 7.3. These suggest, as did the UAE and Oman employee data, that a significant number in both groups are not making generic assumptions about the leadership potential or abilities of all Saudi women. Rather, they are indicating that while some women can be successful in leadership roles, not all women have the 'right stuff' to succeed as leaders. Having said this, while most of these Saudi men were not opposed 'in principle' to women working, most still had major concerns about this. The fifteen university-educated Saudi men that I interviewed during 2012–2014 again fell into three distinct groups, a liberal 'Yes' group ($N = 3$) who were supportive of

TABLE 7.3 *The attitudes of Saudis towards female leaders and their beliefs about the leadership abilities and competencies of Saudi women*

'Do you think that Saudi women can be successful in business leadership positions?'

Women	Men
Always: 14.0	*Always: 11.6*
Often: 32.4	*Often: 13.7*
Sometimes: 39.4	*Sometimes: 34.4*
Rarely: 11.2	*Rarely: 25.2*
Never: 3.0	*Never: 15.1*

'Do you think that it is acceptable for a Saudi woman to be the leader of an organisation?'

Women	Men
Very much so: 54.2	*Very much so: 29.2*
Maybe: 37.4	*Maybe: 57.3*
Never: 8.4	*Never: 13.5*

'Do Saudi women have the same leadership abilities and competencies as men?'

Women	Men
Always: 8.1	*Always: 7.7*
Often: 42.4	*Often: 26.1*
Sometimes: 30.4	*Sometimes: 29.4*
Rarely: 11.2	*Rarely: 21.2*
Never: 7.9	*Never: 15.6*

'Do you think that Saudi women have the ability to succeed in leadership positions?'

Women	Men
Very much so: 64.2	*Very much so: 28.4*
Maybe: 24.4	*Maybe: 47.3*
Never: 11.4	*Never: 24.3*

women's rights, a 'Yes, but …' group who had some reservations about this (N = 5) and a very conservative 'No' group (N = 7) who were strongly opposed to the idea that women should have the right to work and enjoy legal equality with men. The extracts from four of these interviews illustrate the very different attitudes that these men had about working Saudi women and female leaders:

> As I've already mentioned, I was at school in the USA for five years when my father* was posted there and so my views about how women are treated here definitely changed. Also, my father is a very liberal man and he really pushed my sisters to go to university and to have careers ... When I came back here [to begin undergraduate studies at Al Faisal University] I found the views of most of the guys in my year to be like the Middle-Ages in Europe, but I understand this mentality because they didn't know any different, this is what their parents taught them to believe ...
> I think their attitudes about women did change a little when they were at Al Faisal but mine had changed more quickly because I was exposed to different ideas, and I could see that things could be very different for women ... We had a lot of arguments about this issue and I used to tell them that the Prophet himself said that we must change when it is right to do so! It is obvious to me that women have to be given more freedom and they have to be allowed to work in any jobs they choose and so I am for liberalisation. But, I know that most Saudi men do not agree with this and even those who support these ideas know that it will take a long time
>
> (26-year-old male bank employee; middle management; married with two children; studied for an MBA during 2012–2013. *As a military attaché from 2004–2008).

I really, really wish that men would study the life and teachings of the Prophet with much more care. This to me shows how the true religion of Islam has been distorted by some men. There are many *hadiths* which show that the Prophet was gentle with his women and cared about them ... Our *imams* often quote selectively from his teachings, but many of their edicts have nothing to do with the Qur'an – it is more to do with the cultural traditions of this country. For example, they say that this prohibits women from having an education, or driving, or working, or even mingling with men in public, but it doesn't ... None of these prohibitions can be found in our holy book. I am a Muslim and I believe totally in my religion, but I have no issue with Saudi women having more freedom and independence

(34-year-old self-employed IT consultant; married to a doctor; three children; studied for an MBA during 2012–2013).

For me it depends. I think that women can be allowed to work and more Saudi women do work these days, but not if this affects their marriage and their family. These are very important to us and so I do not think that it is right for a woman to work when she has young children, because who will look after them? I know that you have many problems with this in Australia and America and other countries with your high divorce rates and single mothers and we do not want to see these things here ... the family is the most important thing to us and if a woman works this may have many negative effects on her children and husband. My wife has never worked and she does not complain about this

(35-year-old senior manager; public sector; married with four children; studied for an MBA during 2009–2011).

I know that you have discussed these ideas of women's equality in class Dr. Nick, but I can tell you that very few men in this country will agree with these ideas. Here, we believe that the man is the guardian of the women and he is the protector of the family and the children. This is his responsibility. This is our culture and our belief and we do not believe that this is 'wrong', as you have sometimes implied. Why should a woman work? If she has a good husband, there is no need for her to do this ... Women are naturally more emotional than men and tend to be more biased even if they do not want to be this way, women are driven by their emotions and this stops the process of effective decision-making ... Women should not hold any leadership positions in the Cabinet and National Council because they depend too much on their emotions in decision making and men do a better job in using their minds and logic ... Women always ask for equality and justice when they think it might be for their advantage but in the long run, women by nature should be a sister, a wife and a mother. But, just because we say a woman should not work does not mean that we do not respect them or do not care for them, but it is my decision if my wife can work or not ... So, I do not believe that women should work unless they do not have a husband. This is what we believe

(36-year-old senior manager; married with three children; private-sector healthcare company; studied for an MBA during 2011–2012).

These mixed opinions about the 'appropriate' roles of Saudi women are reflected in the data in Table 7.4, which indicate that women were much more optimistic when compared to men about the possibility that the KSA business community will accept more female Saudi executives in the future. However, although the comparative data in Table 7.4 indicate that the beliefs that Saudi women have about this are similar to those of female American executives in 2005 and those of their peers in the UAE and Oman, a significant minority of both women and men were not at all optimistic about this. Male Saudis were much more likely to be neutral about or disagree that this is likely to happen any time soon, and nearly 40 per cent felt that this would never happen. They were also much more pessimistic about the chances of this happening when compared to male executives in the United States in the mid-2000s. But to repeat a point made in Chapters 3 and 5 about the comparative data in Table 7.1, while attitudes towards female business leaders did become more positive in the United States during this period of time, it took nearly two generations for these to evolve to the point that most men believed that there was a greater probability that the US business community would 'wholly accept' female executives.

We then asked these women and men a series of questions about equality of opportunity for Saudi women in the workplace and if they thought that there were still barriers and challenges for Saudi women to overcome in the workplace (Table 7.5).

TABLE 7.4 *Will the Saudi business community ever wholly accept female executives?*

Women	Men
Strongly agree: 17.3	*Strongly agree: 11.9*
Agree: 26.3	*Agree: 16.7*
Neutral: 23.3	*Neutral: 33.4*
Disagree: 21.1	*Disagree: 22.6*
Strongly Disagree: 12.0	*Strongly Disagree: 15.4*

Comparative data (Carlson et al, 2006)
'The business community will never wholly accept female executives'

	1965	2005
Women	*47.0*	*39.0*
Men	*67.0*	*20.0*

1965, N = 2,000 American executives; 2005, N = 286 executives;
(% that agreed with this statement)

TABLE 7.5 *Beliefs about equality of opportunity for Saudi women and the challenges and barriers they encounter in the workplace*

'Is there now full equality of opportunity for Saudi women in the workplace?'

Women	Men
Strongly agree: 3.0	*Strongly agree: 1.9*
Agree: 6.3	*Agree: 10.7*
Neutral: 17.7	*Neutral: 38.4*
Disagree: 42.1	*Disagree: 33.6*
Strongly disagree: 31.1	*Strongly disagree: 15.4*

'Are there still challenges and barriers for Saudi women to overcome in the workplace?'

Women	Men
Strongly agree: 34.6	*Strongly agree: 14.0*
Agree: 37.3	*Agree: 28.7*
Neutral: 21.2	*Neutral: 28.4*
Disagree: 6.1	*Disagree: 18.6*
Strongly disagree: 0.8	*Strongly disagree: 10.3*

It is evident that while these Saudi women knew that there are now more opportunities for gainful employment, particularly in the KSA public sector, only a very small number of them believed that there was equality of opportunity for women in the workplace (9.3%), which is similar to men (12.6%), and it was noticeable that most of this group were public-sector employees. Perhaps surprisingly, more than half of the men agreed with this and more than 40 per cent also believed that there were 'still challenges and barriers for Saudi women to overcome in the workplace', an honest confirmation that there is not equality of opportunity for Saudi women in the workplace. More than 70 per cent of the women agreed with this statement. It was also apparent that both women and men believed that female Saudis are much less likely to be in leadership positions in the private sector in the future when compared to the public sector (Tables 7.6 and 7.7). This indicates that they believed that the barriers to women's career advancement in private-sector organisations were more significant in comparison to those they might encounter in public-sector organisations. However, for the KSA, these results are significant because they suggest that government initiatives to encourage more Saudi women to work in the private sector are likely to flounder unless attitudes towards women who choose to work in

TABLE 7.6 *At this moment in time, do you think that it is easier for Saudi men to become leaders in private-sector organisations than it is for women?*

Women	Men
92.5	*82.7*
(% that agreed with this statement)	
Comparative data (Parker et al, 2015: 32)	
'It is easier for men to get top executive positions in business'	
Women	*Men*
61.0	*74.0*
N = 921 women and 914 men in the United States	
(% that agreed with this statement)	

TABLE 7.7 *Do you think we will see more Saudi women in leadership positions in the public sector and in business organisations in the future?*

In public-sector organisations:	
Women	*Men*
Definitely: 77.4	*Definitely: 47.2*
Maybe: 22.8	*Maybe: 48. 1*
Unlikely: 0.8	*Unlikely: 4.7*
In business organisations:	
Women	*Men*
Definitely: 35.4	*Definitely: 23.1*
Maybe: 62.4	*Maybe: 42.4*
Unlikely: 2.2	*Unlikely: 34.5*

that sector change, and Saudi organisations become more willing to develop younger female employees and promote more of them to leadership positions in the future.

During the interviews with Saudi women I asked them about the attitudes and beliefs that may be holding them back in the workplace. While they acknowledged that there had been changes in Saudi society and the country's labour market over the last ten to fifteen years, all agreed that there were still significant barriers for them to overcome and that the divisions that exist between them and men in the KSA are instilled in boys and girls very early in their lives:

> I think there were a lot of restrictions imposed on us when we were
> growing up. It's hard to explain this in a few words, but our religion
> labels everything. For example, our religion or rather our religious
> traditions did impose a lot of restrictions on women. I think it's
> obvious that we are not as free as men, we are not treated equally,
> which is a big, big issue for me and most of my friends ... When
> I was very young I didn't really notice these things but by the time
> I went to middle and senior school it was obvious that men and
> women were treated differently. For example, I wasn't allowed to
> go to a mixed international school because it would have meant

mixing with boys, so that was frustrating because I'd spent some time in the USA in a mixed private school.* I also saw more differences between how my brothers were treated and how I was when we came back here to live. They were allowed to go to camps and do things that me and my older sisters weren't allowed to do because we were girls. My parents were very traditional in many ways, so while they thought it was very important that I get a good education that was okay, but I was expected to conform to a traditional role in many other ways

*(28-year-old senior HR manager; energy company; studied for an MBA during 2009–2010. *She had spent three years in the United States when her father, a diplomat, had been posted there in the early 2000s.).*

You won't get many people here to talk about this openly, but I believe that most Saudi families are very repressive, for both men and women. One thing you learn when growing up here, although it took me a long time to understand why this happened, is that everything is imposed from above and often with force. So, there was never any question that my father was the head of the family, then came my brothers, then my mother and then me and my sisters. And where did this belief come from? From the father's family, and his father's family and from the society, and the teachers at school and from the *imams* ... It was impossible to question this, but I did as I got older and got into a lot of trouble for being 'rebellious', because this belief was everywhere, it was just the way things were ... It was really only when I went to university and started reading about how women lived in other cultures that I began to see ways in which these beliefs could be questioned and challenged

(34-year-old public-sector HR manager; married with three children; studied for an MBA between 2013–2014).

I think men are also repressed. They are put in this, what's the English word ... straightjacket? When you see Saudi men abroad for the first time, they tend to go wild. They are thrown into another world and they're not ready for it. What's even more annoying is that their families only allowed them to study abroad because they were boys. They might have sisters who were not allowed to do this who were probably just as smart as their brothers or even smarter, but just because they are girls, they aren't allowed to study abroad ... Even today, everything has to be approved by our fathers or husbands, if we can go to university, if we can study abroad or work, everything has to be approved by a man ... Apart from in our families where we do mix, we are segregated at school and boys don't mix with girls. Even at university, men and women don't mix and socialise. And, suddenly it's, 'Now, I have to work with women!' It's very strange for Saudi men and they are not used to this! And, they are definitely not used to a woman being in charge, to be their boss!

(29-year-old single manager at a private-sector
IT company; studied for an MBA from 2013–2015).

Even those women who grew up in families with more liberal social attitudes soon became aware of the restrictions that all women face in Saudi society:

Growing up here, of course, you don't really think about a lot of issues. While growing up, I was happy and proud that I was a Saudi because in many ways there was much less responsibility and we were very protected by our families. In my case, my father actually spent more on my education than he did on my brothers. He paid for me to go to a private school, but my brothers went to public schools. At school, I was always taught by women and they were very good. We also had a very broad curriculum of history, mathematics, geography, biology, most aspects of a good curriculum ... It's only when you go to university and then start working that you realise the limitations. You start to learn that there are some companies that won't hire women, simply because you are a woman. That's what hits you

(25-year-old single women; not employed and
studying full-time for an MBA during 2012–2013).

One of these women also 'bucked the trend' and chose not to marry despite considerable pressure being put on her by her family to do this:

> You may have noticed that on the MBA program, the women who say the most and who are in the most senior positions, most of them are not married. They have made this choice, and they have lost a lot in terms of marriage and so on. You see this. They have made these sacrifices, and they are willing to pay the price and this is why things will change ... When I first started work, some men came to ask for my hand. Some of them said, 'We didn't know she was working in a mixed environment, so we will pull out'. It's like it's an implicit thing that because she works with men she wouldn't make a suitable wife ... because a lot of men still do not think that it is suitable for their wives to work and they prefer to have their wives dependent on them because they believe it will make their lives much easier. So, my work has affected me and it continues to affect me and even today when a man asks for my hand, he asks 'Would you quit your job?' and I always say, *'La'*. I still often get asked, 'You are a Saudi, you come from a good family, why do you need to work here? Don't you want to have kids and a husband?' I get this the whole time! So, I have to be patient with them [laughs]
>
> *(35-year-old single public-sector tourism development manager; studied for an MBA during 2011–2013).*

I also asked these women if they believed that their lack of legal rights and prescribed roles in Saudi society were the result of religious or cultural restrictions. Almost all of them indicated that their culture, not their religion, was to blame for this:

> It's very important to distinguish between our religion and *shari'a* laws ... I respect tradition, and so I'm very comfortable with wearing the *hijab* and *abaya* because that's part of who we are and I respect our religion. I think it is quite wrong to believe that these things are a sign of our oppression; for me this is a personal

choice and it's part of my Islamic identity. What I completely
object to, what I don't respect, are cultural traditions that say
I can't do certain things just because I'm a woman ... For example,
the Qur'an does not say we cannot work, or be doctors, or
engineers, or professors, or drive cars and yet many men will still
say we cannot do these things! If you look at other non-Muslim
groups in the Middle-East, and there are still many of those, you
always find the same family structures, the same attitudes to
women, the same restrictions, same everything – so it cannot just
be Islam that is to blame ... So for me it's not about our religion,
it's about our culture

(24-year-old student; studying full time for an MBA during 2012–2013).

I am speaking personally, but for me it is our culture that holds
women back. I don't mean our religion, Islam, it is Arabic culture
which says that women should be held back. Men here are very
reluctant to do anything that lessens their control over women ...
My own judgment about this is based on one lady in Islam, the
best lady, who is Khadijah, the first wife of the Prophet. All my
life I have looked at her, and I would say that she should be the
role model for all women in Islamic countries. Within my close
circle, I always tease my more conservative friends by saying
'Why don't you take this lady as your role model? Did our
Prophet ever try to prevent his first wife from practicing her
business?' ... The problem is that men, our *imams*, are always
tending, whether they know they are wrong or not, to lead us
away from the real Islam, not only in Saudi Arabia but in many
other Muslim countries

*(41-year-old self-employed business consultant; divorced with three
children; studied for an MBA during 2011–2012).*

I also asked these women about Western feminist ideas and if they
believed these had any relevance in their lives. Without exception,
they felt that while some of the core values and principles of feminism were very applicable to their lives, this was neither a label that

they would be comfortable being associated with nor one that they would make use of in their daily lives, particularly with Saudi men:

> This is difficult to explain ... we don't believe in Western feminism because we are Muslims but I would say that we support many of the goals of the *al-haraka al-nissa'iyya* in countries like Egypt and Morocco ... the problem is that most men here think of Western feminism as being something to do with promiscuity, and also being anti-religious and anti-Muslim, so it has many negative meanings for them ... they think that it is something to do with women who are opposed to men and want to control them and so that is very dangerous in their minds. So, if we are going to change this attitude, it must be from an Islamic perspective because this affects everything, our customs and traditions and how we are described by men. We can only change this within our Islamic beliefs
>
> *(35-year-old HR manager at an energy company; married with two children; studied for an MBA during 2011–2012).*

I am Muslim, a Saudi, Arab, Muslim and these are all important to me. I believe in Islam. But, when I'm talking about Islam, I do not mean that we need an Islamic state, this is not Islam to me and neither is the *al-mutawwa'a*. But, what we do need is for our society to be true to the teachings of the Qur'an ... Whether it's Islam, Christianity or Judaism, men have always found ways to repress women and they have used religion as a way to make sure it would stay like that and that is what I see is happening in my country. It is easy for Westerners to blame what they see as 'our oppression' on our religion, but for me it is our culture that is responsible for this and what people often forget is that while we can't change our religion we can change our culture

(29-year-old public-sector manager; married with two children).

I'm not sure about this. I come from a wealthy family, so I'm privileged in a lot of ways. I have a good job, get driven everywhere and we can afford servants and drivers but that's not true of most

Saudi women, who don't work and are still restricted to their homes. It really depends on how you fit into our society and what family you come from. If you're middle-class or above middle-class that makes a huge difference and where you are in our society really does affect how you think about these things ... I think that we are in a lucky minority and many Saudi women do suffer from some oppression. The vast majority of women from wealthy families are still content to do nothing, not to work, to socialise and go on foreign trips with their friends, so for them Western feminism is not at all relevant in their lives. I wish Westerners could come here and see what a lazy, kick-back life many of these women do have [laughs] ... Women of my generation are very weird. They say they want more independence, but they would still sacrifice this for a good marriage and children because there are many consequences if you do not follow this path

(29-year-old public-sector financial manager; married with one child).

These women and men were also asked about some possible future scenarios for Saudi women in leadership positions in public- and private-sector organisations in 2030 (Table 7.8).

These results add credence to the suggestions made in Chapter 6 about the continuing under-representation of Saudi women in the private sector and their over-representation in public-sector employment. They show that while more than three quarters of women and two in five men believed that there will be more women in public-sector leadership roles by 2030, only 18.8 per cent of these women and 11.5 per cent of the men agreed that Saudi women will hold as many top positions in business organisations as men by 2030. Even those men and women may be over-optimistic about this possibility, given the slow pace at which women have been rising to executive and board-level positions in most non-Islamic countries and the relative lack of women in middle-management roles in the KSA today. The comparative data from Pew Research in Table 7.8 also indicates that there are marked

TABLE 7.8 *Possible scenarios for Saudi women in leadership positions in public and private-sector organisations by 2030*

'By 2030, Saudi men will continue to hold more leadership positions in public-sector organisations than women do'

Women	Men
33.1	62.5

'By 2030, Saudi women will hold as many leadership positions as men in public-sector organisations'

Women	Men
76.9	37.5

'By 2030, Saudi men will continue to hold more of the top positions in business organisations than women'

Women	Men
81.2	88.5

'By 2030, Saudi women will hold as many top positions in business organisations as men'

Women	Men
18.8	11.5

(% that 'strongly agreed' or 'agreed' with each statement)

Comparative data (Parker et al, 2015: 5)

'Men will continue to hold more top executive positions in business in the future'

Women	Men
55.0	52.0

'It's only a matter of time before there are as many women as men in top executive positions in business'

Women	Men
44.0	45.0

N = *921 women and 914 men in the United States*
(*% that agreed with these statements*)

differences between the beliefs that Saudis have about the likelihood that there will be as many women as men in executive positions in business in the future when compared with American men and women in 2015. The latter group is more than twice as likely to believe that this is going to happen in the future when compared to this group of Saudi women and the contrast with what Saudi men believe is likely to happen is even starker.

This suggests that attitudes towards working professional women and women in leadership roles have been evolving at a rather slower pace in the KSA when compared to the UAE and Oman. However, on a more positive note, all of the women I interviewed believed that there would be further changes in Saudi society, even if they did have many doubts about how long this process would take and whether Saudi men would be willing to accommodate the changing aspirations of Saudi women:

> Of course men have to change! The problem is how can you change the way that the majority of men here think! Maybe for 80 or 90 per cent of the men here, that is their mentality. They are very conservative. That is the mentality, so how are you going to change that? How can we change the way they were raised and the way they think? ... I think we have to be the ones who do this, to be assertive and express our opinions honestly, even if it means we get into some trouble. We can't expect things to change unless we are willing to be part of that change – I mean that's what happened in the West isn't it? Women had to fight for their rights and we have to do the same. But, it's so hard. Women here have gone to jail because they drove cars, so what's going to happen if we do fight? We have to be ready to step forward, but there is also the reality of our society which is very conservative ... If I get arrested, that's not a problem for me but the whole family name would be shamed if I get into trouble; 30, 40 or 50 people could be affected if that happens, so we have to be very careful.

Later in the interview, she added:

> We have a verse in the Qur'an which says, 'God will not change people, people must change themselves', so the change first has to come from within. I think women need to change. They should start focusing on themselves first and they should focus on their

rights in Islam. They should focus on the rights they do have in this country and their rights in our society. As long as what I'm doing is not wrong, I should be allowed to do this … As we say in Islam 'Man is the provider' but many more women are working. For them, they need to work even if they have families. And, more women don't want to be dependent on their fathers and husbands … And, if we don't do more, I don't see how we can build a better economy and create more jobs for our people. We cannot have a better future unless we demand this

(37-year-old public-sector finance director; married with two children).

In conclusion, we can say – with some qualifications – that attitudes towards women in the workplace and in leadership roles have changed to a limited degree in the KSA over the last ten to fifteen years and more than half of these women and men agreed that the prospects for working women have generally improved in the KSA over the last ten years. However, it appears that these attitudes are changing more slowly than they did in many Western countries during the 1970s, 1980s and 1990s and when compared to the UAE and Oman over the last two decades. Almost all of these women and men agreed that women still encountered significant barriers in the workplace, particularly in the private sector and most Saudi men still have very conservative attitudes towards the women who work in their organisations. More than two thirds of the female private-sector employees in the sample believed that 'women are not able to progress beyond a certain level in my organisation', while only one in three female public-sector employees agreed with this statement. In addition, as we have seen, very few Saudi women believe that 'there is now full equality of opportunity for women in the workplace' and nearly all of them agreed that 'there are still challenges and barriers for women to overcome in the workplace'. In spite of these difficulties, all of these women were fully committed to their careers and professions, and they work for exactly the same reasons that women in the West, in Oman and in the UAE do. When asked to provide three or four reasons they chose to work, more than four out of five of the group mentioned 'financial independence', two thirds indicated that 'achieving my personal goals in life' was important to them. 'Personal growth and development' were important to more than half of the group, as was an intrinsic interest in their professions and careers.

7.3 FEMALE ENTREPRENEURS AND SMALL BUSINESS OWNERS IN THE KSA

We want to start our own businesses. It's the only way we can gain some independence. We all want to be modern Khadijahs!

An aspiring female Saudi entrepreneur (Coleman, 2010: 204)

We noted in Chapter 5 that women are notably under-represented as both entrepreneurs and SME owners in the nineteen countries of the MENA region. The reports cited in that chapter concluded that levels of female entrepreneurship in the region were well below those of the leading OECD nations, largely because of the low levels of participation of women in the formal economic sphere as both employees and employers. These reports concluded that there were significant gender-specific barriers to women that were preventing more of them from becoming entrepreneurs and SME owners. They also noted that most businesses owned by women in the MENA region tended to be very small, with most female businesses being sole-proprietorship micro-businesses, and between one third and half of those were home-based businesses operating in the informal economy. And, as with Oman and to a lesser extent the UAE, there is a lack of reliable and detailed information on female entrepreneurship and SME ownership in the KSA, and it was not included in the detailed 2015 GEM report on female entrepreneurship (Kelley et al, 2015: 13).

It has also been noted in two studies that Saudi women 'are virtually absent from the body of international literature on female entrepreneurship in the Middle-East and North Africa' (Alturki and Braswell, 2010: 8), and 'not much is known about the roles, characteristics, personal profiles, behaviors and business activities of women ... and the performance of women entrepreneurs in Arab society in general. This is particularly true of the KSA [where] there is virtually no academic literature that addresses women's entrepreneurial behavior and their business activities in the KSA' (Ahmad, 2011a: 123).

Another study noted that the situation regarding women entrepreneurs and business owners 'appears to be omitted', and 'supporting data from the government is either lacking or conflicting' (Minkus-McKenna, 2009: 4 and 10). A study of 202 registered and 62 unregistered women-owned SMEs indicated that while it was difficult to estimate the exact number and size of these enterprises in the KSA, 'the evidence suggests that they account for a small but growing share of total business activity' (Alturki and Braswell, 2010: 8).

We do know that the number of officially registered businesses managed by Saudi women was around 22,500 in 2004. This had grown to 35,400 by 2009 (Minkus-McKenna, 2009: 4) and it appears that the number of companies owned by women may have exceeded 40,000 by 2013; about 7 per cent of the 700,000 SMEs that were officially registered in the KSA (Abu-Sharkh and al-Shubaili, 2013). However, these figures certainly under-estimate the total number of self-employed female Saudis because at least one third of the businesses run by women are not officially registered (al-Kibsi et al, 2015; Sfakianakis, 2014). In addition, because the KSA has not engaged with the ILO's Decent Work Country Programme as Oman and the UAE have done, there is no information available from this reliable source that might enable us to estimate the precise number of female Saudi entrepreneurs and business owners (International Labour Organisation, 2016). Nevertheless, it is reasonable to conclude that while the level of participation by Saudi women in the SME sector has increased a little over the last decade and may be close to 10 per cent of all SMEs if the informal sector is included, it is still very low by international standards. For example, as noted in Chapter 5, the number of SMEs owned by American women exceeded 10 million for the first time in 2015 – nearly 40 per cent of the national total (National Women's Business Council, 2015: 2).

While acknowledging the lack of reliable labour-market data on female entrepreneurship and SME activity in the KSA, the Saudi government has recognised the significant role that the SME sector plays in economic growth in the world's leading economies, and it has been trying to promote the idea of entrepreneurship and small business growth among Saudis since the early 2000s. Conscious of the need to create an environment that would be more conducive to Saudi entrepreneurs, and the enormous challenge of overcoming its entrenched public-sector employment culture, several initiatives have been taken by government organisations and local chambers of industry and commerce to facilitate the development of SMEs. These include:

The Centennial Fund (CF), which was established in 2004 'to be the leading foundation for enabling young people to be successful business owners'. To date, the CF has provided training courses for more than 30,000 Saudis and 'partial or complete' funding for 4,168 projects, of which 21 per cent were headed by Saudi women. However, no information is provided on this organisation's website to indicate how many of these have developed into successful established businesses or what the CF's return on investment in these start-up ventures may have been over the last 13 years (Centennial Fund, 2016).

The Kafala Fund, launched in 2006, is a loan guarantee program to help improve access to bank lending for SMEs and to encourage commercial banks to lend more money to the SME sector. The program guarantees up to 80 per cent of eligible loans to new and existing business, up to a value of SAR 30 million ($8,333,000). Bab Rizk Jameel, launched in 2004, helps young entrepreneurs set up small and micro-enterprises and provides loans of up to SAR 150,000 (Abu-Sharkh and al-Shubaili, 2013: 4–5).

The Saudi Arabian General Investment Authority's (SAGIA) National Competitiveness Centre launched the National Saudi Fast Growth 100 (NSFG 100) program in 2010 to promote entrepreneurship and innovation among the fastest-growing emerging companies in the KSA. It says it has created 35,000 jobs since, and companies involved in this program also serve as business incubators for their employees and have launched forty-one new companies in the past two years (Saudi Fast Growth 100, 2016).

TAQNIA, an organisation owned by the Public Investment Fund, provides start-up capital for local and international R&D projects and, in 2015, was supporting twenty-nine joint technology ventures between local and international companies. TAQNIA also formed a partnership with Riyadh Capital in 2015 to launch the first venture capital fund in the KSA with funds of about $133 million. This will be invested primarily in the country's energy, advanced materials and sustainability sectors (Oxford Business Group, 2015a: 4–5).

The Technovia initiative, launched in 2014, to encourage technology innovation and commercialisation. This is a joint venture with Saudi Aramco, who will provide funding for technology projects, the King Fahd University of Petroleum and Minerals and the King Abdullah University of Science and Technology (Technovia, 2016).

Other incubators, such as the Badir Advanced Manufacturing Incubator, the Riyadh Technology Incubator, Riyadh Techno-Valley and Dharam Techno-Valley have also been created to encourage more industry-driven technology innovation, and MIT's Sloan School of Management runs an annual business plan competition for budding Saudi technology entrepreneurs.

The Aramco Entrepreneurship Centre, established in 2012, which aimed to 'ignite entrepreneurship and help develop local enterprises in the Kingdom of Saudi Arabia'. This has offered courses on entrepreneurship development to some 1,700 young Saudis. However, it has only approved thirty-eight loans and fourteen venture capital investments since 2012 (Aramco Entrepreneurship Centre, 2016).

In addition to these initiatives, several new centres and training programs have also been established in the major cities of the KSA to act as facilitators of female entrepreneurship. These include the Institute of Entrepreneurship in Jeddah, the Prince Sultan Fund for Supporting Women's Small Projects, the al-Sayedah Bint Khuwailid Business Women Centre, the Abdul Latif Jameel community service program which provide job opportunities for women, small loans and training programs; and the King Abdul Aziz Women's Charity Association's al-Barakah Loans Centre which finances projects undertaken by low-income, divorced and widowed Saudi women. The Human Resource Development Fund also supports HR development in companies in most of the Kingdom's regions and has distributed SAR 43,308,000 ($12,030,000) to 301 female- and 460 male-owned businesses (SUSRIS, 2016). New laws that would regularise the status of home-based businesses were also being considered by the government in 2015, which could provide a considerable boost for female Saudi entrepreneurs. In 2015, plans for the creation of an SME Authority were announced and this was established in 2016 (National Women's Business Council, 2015: 2; Oxford Business Group, 2015a: 6).

However, according to one report, the agencies that have been set up to promote and support entrepreneurship 'operate without any coordination' and 'the KSA does not yet have a small-business infrastructure that provides adequate support for female (or male) entrepreneurship activities' (Sfakianakis, 2014). In the 2015 Global Entrepreneurship and Development Institute's Female Entrepreneurship Index the KSA was ranked 49/77 countries for female entrepreneurship, with the highest-ranked MENA countries being the UAE at 27 and Israel at 34. This relatively low ranking was attributed to several factors: the lack of an adequate 'entrepreneurial environment' and 'entrepreneurial eco-system', 'low entrepreneurial aspirations' among Saudi women, significant gender inequalities, difficulties in obtaining first-tier start-up funding, lack of access to technology, a lack of female entrepreneurial role models and inadequate support networks (Terjesen and Lloyd, 2015: 11, 7 and 29). Moreover, the most recent GEM report on the KSA (2010) noted that more than 50 per cent of new business start-ups were not truly creative/innovative ventures, tending to fill small vacant competitive niches in the market and 70 per cent offered the same products or services as existing SMEs. They were predominantly what has been described as 'factor-driven' rather than 'efficiency' or 'innovation' driven firms. The latter type of company is much more prevalent in the world's most innovative countries such as Switzerland, the United Kingdom and the United States (Skoko et al, 2010: 10 and 31).

For example, in the 2013 *Forbes* Middle-East list of sixty-two emerging entrepreneurs and future business leaders in the Middle East, six of these were Saudi women: Nourah Bander Mugaiteeb (Nouryat Centre for Cooking), Sarah al-Otaibi (A Cup of Cake), Lateefa Alwalaan (Yatooq – Arabic Coffee), Hind al-Zahid (Zoha Arabian Trading), Razan Alazzouni (Fashion Designer) and Kholoud Attar (*Design Magazine*) (*Forbes* Middle-East, 2013). In 2015, out of 100 entrepreneurs in the MENA region, there were a total of 14 women and four of these businesses were partnerships between men and women *Forbes* Middle-East, 2015: 44–54). However, almost all of them were 'factor' or 'efficiency' driven firms and none of the new companies created by these women, including those in the KSA, were in the manufacturing sector. They were all service businesses in food and beverage, retail, on-line retail, fashion and design, business services and education, although there were three businesses that could be described as IT service companies. This closely matches the profile of the firms involved in Alturki and Braswell's study of 264 female Saudi business owners (Alturki and Braswell, 2010: 56).

The 2010 GEM report indicated that the KSA scored well in terms of physical and commercial infrastructure, opportunities for start-ups, entrepreneurial motivation, availability of finance and tax policy but poorly in the provision of government support programs, entrepreneurship education, R&D transfer, ease of market entry for new firms, protection of intellectual property and support for female entrepreneurs. It also found that the rate of small business start-ups had 'doubled' between 2009 and 2010 and 'much of this increase can be attributed to large gains among female entrepreneurs', who made up 26 per cent of the KSA's 'nascent entrepreneurial workforce' in 2010 (Skoko et al, 2010: 11–12). However, Saudi women owned only a tiny proportion of new businesses in the KSA in 2010 – less than 2 per cent of the total according to this report – placing the KSA in the bottom fifteen of a group of fifty-four countries in 2010. This report also indicated that while about two thirds of Saudi female entrepreneurs felt that it was socially acceptable for a woman to own a business in the KSA, 60 per cent also felt that it was much harder for a woman to start a new business and nearly half felt that women were not encouraged to do this (Skoko et al, 2010: 65–66). This report concluded that 'women in Saudi Arabia still represent a large untapped source of entrepreneurial potential' and also suggested that much more had to be done 'to unleash this potential by providing better support for women entrepreneurs' (Skoko et al, 2010: 109 and 113).

Another study of female Saudi entrepreneurs in 2010 concluded that while their primary motivations for starting a new business were similar to those of men ('personal achievement', 'independence', 'self-confidence' and 'profit motive'), it also reported that most of these women resented the restrictions imposed on them under the *wakeel* and *mudeer* laws, the lack of information available to help female entrepreneurs, the absence of women-only advisory sections in government ministries, complex paperwork and the lengthy amount of time it took to process business registrations at different government departments (Sadi and al-Ghazali, 2012: 109–110). Officially, the registration process for men and women is the same and the only stipulation is that women must do this through designated women's sections with separate entrances. A qualitative study of nineteen female Saudi entrepreneurs confirmed that female-owned SMEs are heavily concentrated in the service sector and three quarters of these were micro-enterprises.

Three quarters of the women who owned these businesses reported that they had encountered difficulties starting their businesses and mentioned a lack of relevant information, difficulties obtaining start-up finance, complex small-business regulations and policies, bureaucratic registration processes and procedures, restrictions on business interactions with men, lacking small-business management skills and recruiting suitably qualified staff (Ahmad, 2011b: 132, 134 and 135).

The study by Alturki and Braswell of 202 registered and 62 unregistered businesses also identified similar gender-specific barriers in the regulatory environment including a heavy reliance on male relatives to complete the business registration process, limited access to formal (non-family) sources of start-up capital, restricted access to and use of business-support technologies, a lack of government support services, restrictions on mobility outside the KSA and the continuance of the *wakeel* and *mudeer* regulations. It also reported that regulatory changes that had been intended to ease the process of registering female-owned businesses were not being implemented effectively and suggested that as many as one in four small enterprises managed by women were not officially registered. More than 90 per cent of the women in this study had used either personal savings or money from their families to create their businesses, which suggests that women who have access to personal or family wealth were much more likely to use this as their primary source of start-up capital. This report confirmed that almost all women-owned businesses were in the service sector and most were very small, employing six to nineteen staff on average, and only about 20 per cent were involved in trade or business outside the KSA. It also identified one other significant challenge: managing male employees. More than half of the women who had businesses in Riyadh said that they had difficulties with this and only 11.2 per cent of the women in this study indicated that they liked to hire Saudi men as employees (Alturki and Braswell, 2010: 9–10, 20–21, 28 and 59).

A more recent study, of thirty-seven Saudi women entrepreneurs during 2011–2012, observed – as other studies have done – that while research on this group is limited, most commentators on the KSA agree that women 'are clearly under-represented in this sector, representing a significant source of untapped potential for Saudi Arabia' (Lavelle and al-Sheikh, 2013: 3). The authors of this report noted that there are several positive factors that should encourage the development of women's entrepreneurship in the KSA. These include its very young population, public pronouncements about the need to develop the country's SME sector, the growing number of university-educated women entering the labour market, the slowdown in public-sector employment opportunities (which were becoming even more restricted in 2016) and the independent wealth that some Saudi women have. However, they also pointed out the economic, political and cultural barriers that were impeding women's participation in this sector. These included the cultural-religious restrictions described in Chapter 2 and 6 a lack of clear policies and targets for female entrepreneurship from the government, the slowness, complexities and difficulties of licensing start-up companies, restrictions on women's mobility – both domestically and internationally – restricted access to government advisory services, the *wakeel* and *mudeer* requirements and restricted licensing options (Lavelle and al-Sheikh, 2013: 5–6). The last factor refers to a number of business activities that were not available in the official licensing categories and the lack of home-based business licenses. These difficulties have also been highlighted by the World Bank Group, which ranked the KSA 130 out of 189 countries for 'ease of starting a business' in 2016 (a fall from 124/189 in 2015) and also documented the twelve stages and six government ministries that would-be entrepreneurs in the KSA have to deal with in order to register a new business (World Bank, 2016c).

In addition to the challenges associated with business start-ups, ones that are common to all Saudi entrepreneurs, Lavelle and al-Sheikh also noted that 'women face a unique set of gender-specific obstacles that hinder their participation in this sector' and, in something of an understatement, 'All things considered, becoming an entrepreneur is an unlikely consideration for the majority of Saudi women' (Lavelle and al-Sheikh, 2013: 3 and 8; see also Danish and Smith, 2012). Even in family-run businesses, women do not appear to enjoy parity with their male relatives. For example, a study of thirty family-owned enterprises in the KSA, Bahrain, Kuwait and the UAE reported that while one third of these companies have women on their boards of directors, most of the women employed in these businesses do not participate as equals (even when they are, on paper, the owners). More than half of the Saudi women who were interviewed for this study said that they felt excluded from management and decision-making processes and lacked support from male family members to engage as equals in these enterprises. On a more optimistic note, 35 per cent of the women and most of the male interviewees felt that there will be a 'significant increase' in women's employment in family businesses in the future (Majdalani et al, 2015: 8, 10 and 11).

On the basis of the limited information that is available, it is reasonable to conclude that few Saudi women are either self-starting entrepreneurs or own their own businesses, even if a handful do run some very large businesses in the KSA and are extremely wealthy. It is also still difficult for both female and male Saudis to establish new businesses and for smaller entrepreneurs to expand their businesses, because *wasta* is still a very important factor in dealings with the governmental agencies, public-sector bureaucracies and larger companies. Obtaining funding for Saudi start-up companies remains a complex and lengthy process and most commercial banks still prefer to lend to established companies with proven track records. According to one report, commercial loans to SMEs in the KSA represent less than 3 per cent of the approximately $1.1 trillion lent by banks to businesses in 2014 compared to about 25 per cent in OECD countries, and 'despite all the reform attempts of recent years, setting up a business can be relatively cumbersome ... and in such an environment, larger and more powerful players naturally have advantages. This also explains why few new large companies have come into being in recent decades: de facto barriers to entry are fairly high' (Bertelsmann Stiftung, 2015c: 12 and 14). Local 'angel investors' are starting to emerge, but we do not know what impact these may be having on the rate of indigenous business start-ups in the KSA and lending under the KSA's SME Loan Guarantee Program (Kafala) plunged by 76 per cent to SAR 572 million ($153 million) during 2014 as commercial banks tightened lending rules. This, according to Bloomberg, will be 'an obstacle in the country's efforts to diversify the economy away from oil, which brings in about 90 per cent of government revenues' (Bloomberg, 2015).

Case Study

During the first half of 2012, several female part-time MBA students at Al Faisal University were able to facilitate introductions to thirty-seven women entrepreneurs and SME owners based in Riyadh. The owners of these businesses were contacted and twenty-three of them agreed to be interviewed either at their businesses or at Al Faisal University; a number that was later rounded to twenty.[2] It should be noted that, as in Oman, this case study could not be a comprehensive analysis of all female entrepreneurs and SME owners in the KSA. It was an exploratory investigation of the mixed experiences that a small group of Saudi women entrepreneurs had while trying to establish and grow their businesses.

The women in this group ranged in age from twenty-six to fifty-one and, on average, had started their businesses when they were thirty-two years old. Sixteen were married, two were divorced, and two were single. Fifteen of these women had children. Fourteen had university degrees (three of them also had MBAs), and five had college diplomas. All of these women had worked for at least five years prior to establishing their own businesses, fourteen in public-sector organisations and six in the private sector. Three had worked for their families' businesses before creating their own firms, and four indicated that other members of their extended families were also involved in business ventures. Nine of the women had worked in jobs that were related to the businesses they created, and two indicated that these had grown out of hobbies or pastimes that had interested them during their teenage years and twenties. The main sources of financing for their businesses were personal or family savings (thirteen), business loans from a commercial bank (three) and loans from the Kafala Fund (two) and Bab Rizk Jameel (two).

They managed several types of small companies: food and catering (four), retail (four), women's tailoring and fashion (three), women's beauty and hairdressing (three), children's day-care (two), recruitment and HR training (two), fashion design (one) and educational services (one). On average, they had been in business for seven years. The mean number of employees in these businesses was eight; the smallest number of employees was five, and the largest number was thirty-six. None of these businesses were involved in manufacturing, they were all service companies and two had expanded their businesses to the UAE and Bahrain. Sixteen of these women were sole owners of their businesses, two were in partnerships with another woman and two were owned jointly with their husbands. Only two of these women had plans to expand their businesses overseas within the next five years and none were planning to publicly list their companies in the future. When I asked them what were the main reasons they had decided to become entrepreneurs, their answers were very similar to those of female entrepreneurs in Oman. All of them cited 'financial independence' or 'freedom' as being the most important factors, followed by 'dissatisfaction' or 'frustration' with the jobs they had been doing in large public- or private-sector organisations. 'Personal fulfilment' and 'personal growth' came next, followed by 'the challenge of creating my own business' and 'identifying a new market opportunity'.

Eleven of these women acknowledged the support that their families and husbands had given them when establishing their businesses. As this thirty-seven-year-old woman who had established a children's day-care centre in 2010 observed:

My inspiration was my mother who decided to be her own boss
a long time ago, after my father died. I saw the struggle she had
with this when I was a teenager and I thought, 'If she could do that
with all the problems she had, then I could also do this.' She was
one of the first women in Riyadh to own a shop selling women's
fashion lines and she found this very difficult because of the
cultural viewpoint at this time. People just didn't accept that a
woman could start her own company and she was often asked
why her husband allowed this and so she had to explain that it
was her business ... my sisters and brothers often helped out at
the shop and that is where I learned about running a business ...
my mother was of course very supportive of my decision to create
my own company after I graduated from university.

Although the government of the KSA has said on several occasions
that it is striving to make the process of business start-ups easier, the
experiences of the twenty Saudi women entrepreneurs that
I interviewed during 2012–2013 suggested that they faced significant
difficulties in creating new companies. For example:

Without the approval of male guardian it can be very difficult to
start a business in this country. But, my father is a good man and
the only condition he made was that I had to work for him for five
years after I graduated, not because he wanted to restrict my
ambitions but because he wanted me to have some experience of
management before I started my own company ... this also gave
me more experience and confidence ... [Later] he provided some of
the start-up capital and also helped me find a loan from a bank and
from the Kafala Fund, and also with the preparation of all the
forms ... there are many of these for the Ministry of Commerce
and Industry, the Ministry of Labour, for the social insurance
and other matters! Because he had also managed his own
businesses for many years he was very helpful with his advice
and opinions ... the main difficulties I had were not so much to
do with creating the business, the main problems I had were

dealing with some men in other companies that we did business with, and the attitudes of some of the male employees that we first recruited. They were not used to working for a female boss ... gradually, over time we got better at this and most of my employees are now women, with some male expatriates

(32-year-old businesswoman; married, no children; food and catering company established in 2009).

All of these women felt that conservative attitudes in the KSA created problems and difficulties for women entrepreneurs, although these were changing:

There are a lot of limitations and restrictions. Even when I had established my company, I had to appoint a male Saudi manager because this is required if I employ any men, and for some business and legal matters. When we started the company, we felt that some men wouldn't accept female bosses, and wouldn't accept tasks from us or listen to our decisions, and this happened – particularly from Saudi men. So, as far as possible, we only hired women or expatriate male managers and as trainers and so we have much less of a problem with this now ... I must also say this is changing a little. We are now recruiting two or three graduates each year as the business grows and find that this is less of a problem among younger Saudi men who are getting more used to the idea of working for a woman

(39-year-old businesswoman; joint venture recruitment and HR training company established with two women partners in 2008; three children).

La, it is not easy for many women to create their own businesses. But, it is very important to make the difference between the women who are part of the *iqta'iyin* group, who we have discussed, and women like me. If you have their wealth and connections, it is much easier to do this but for me it was much harder and my first husband and family did not support me in this at the beginning ... But, my age and experience did help because I had planned to do this for a long time. I had done my MBA, written a business plan, and also worked out all the financial issues. I think this was a surprise to the two banks that I first contacted for a loan [laughs]. I did not find it hard to get loans, but it took nearly 12 months for me to obtain all the government approvals, to register my company, get the offices fitted out and other matters. This was a very annoying and frustrating experience!

> *(43-year-old businesswoman; catering business established in 2010;*
> *divorced and re-married, three children).*

In my view, it is very difficult for both men and women to create a new business but I agree that it is still harder for women. This is not because we find this process harder, but because there is still this perception that women should not be doing this ... although I have to say that while my husband did not oppose me in this I know that he is not typical of most Saudi men ... I also know, because I have studied this, that women in many other countries have also struggled for their rights and freedoms. So my decision to build my own business was an easy one because I believed I would succeed and it was also for me something I had to do, to say that I am a woman but I will be successful even if some men say I should not do this ... Most of the women I know, some are very conservative, but most want a better lifestyle for themselves and their daughters and so they are also striving for more independence so I think, yes, we are seeing some signs of change ... We want to see this change before our daughters grow up and so we must be successful for them

> *(35-year-old; educational services company created in 2007;*
> *married with two children).*

All of the women who had been in business since the mid-2000s were very critical of the complex bureaucratic processes they had to endure in several different government ministries when setting up their businesses. Among the difficulties they identified were the plethora of forms and certificates that had to be completed, the number of separate licenses they had to obtain and difficulties in complying with the country's strict Saudisation policies after they had opened their businesses. They also commented on the lack of women's entrepreneur networks and general information from government ministries when establishing their businesses, their over-reliance on informal female networks and their own research or on advice from family members who had some experience of creating and managing SMEs. Those who had established businesses during the mid-to-late 2000s were also critical of the bureaucratic hurdles involved in setting up new businesses in the KSA. However, none of these women mentioned that they had major problems balancing their work and family commitments, and only four indicated they had experienced 'some' work–life conflicts. Moreover, all of the women observed that the situation was better for young women entrepreneurs today, and several mentioned that government small-business initiatives described earlier *should* have a beneficial effect on the rate of business start-ups among women in the KSA. For example:

> I think it has become a bit easier for ladies to start their own businesses. The government has talked much more about this issue recently, about the need for more Saudi women and men to start their own businesses and we even have a national Entrepreneurship Week* now. I think there's also been a change among young Saudis because they are more open to the world and they see changes happening in other countries and of course they see more young business men and women with their own eyes ... Many of my friends visit the UAE, and they can see how things are changing for women there – even my brothers are changing their views a little! I think more women do want to start their own businesses now, but there are still many difficulties with this ... For me, the biggest issue is still the male-guardianship law. It doesn't matter what the government says about this, for all practical matters a woman's father or husband is the owner of her business and her finances. He controls this. So if my husband dies,

my father might gain control of my business. Where is the justice
in this situation!?

*(38-year-old businesswoman; women and children's clothing design and
retail-company established in 2009; married with two children;
* this is held in November each year).*

All of these women felt that the support systems that are supposed to
help Saudi women establish small businesses were still 'inadequate'
or 'underdeveloped' during 2012–2013. They also believed that
existing registration and licensing law procedures were still too complex, repetitive and time consuming and that local chambers of commerce and Industry did not really understand the unique problems
faced by female entrepreneurs. All suggested that there should be a
'one-stop' department at the Ministry of Commerce and Industry,
staffed by well-qualified and experienced women that they could
not only go to for advice but also to facilitate the business registration
process. They also said that there was a lack of suitably qualified and
motivated employees to satisfy their human resource needs, citing
both the lower salaries they were able to offer and the longer and
more flexible working hours they required from employees as being
deterrents for many Saudis. And, when I asked these women who
they would least like to employ, all of them replied 'Saudi men',
which confirmed the widespread belief that they do not make the
best employees for Saudi business women.

When I asked these women what else could be done to encourage more Saudi women to become entrepreneurs and SME owners,
they gave very similar answers to female business owners in Oman.
Most of them suggested that public and private universities should
offer more major programs or specialisation courses in innovation,
entrepreneurship and small-business management and also set up
business incubators to encourage more female undergraduates to
become entrepreneurs. The 2010 GEM report on entrepreneurship
in the KSA had noted the need to improve education at secondary
schools, vocational colleges and universities to encourage would-be
entrepreneurs and to provide much better vocational-education

support for both female and male entrepreneurs. The authors of this report commented that the KSA's education system was 'very weak with regards to teaching entrepreneurship, at all levels of schooling [and] almost nothing is done to encourage creativity and new firm creation' (Skoko et al, 2010: 79–80). As regards women, a study cited earlier also observed that the Saudi education system was failing to create the conditions under which women's entrepreneurship can thrive:

> Rather than preparing women for their role as active participants in the Saudi economy, the focus remains on upholding dominant socio-cultural norms that emphasise the role of women as wives and mothers. The curriculum continues to place a strong emphasis on traditional content and teaching methods. This system is failing to foster entrepreneurial qualities, skills and knowledge among Saudi women
>
> *(Lavelle and al-Sheikh, 2013: 3).*

Unfortunately, it appears that this sensible advice has not been heeded by university leaders in the KSA and, at least at the university level, there were no signs of significant change in this domain during 2015–2016. A review of the business and management programs offered by the top ten universities in the KSA during March 2016 showed that only one of these offered an undergraduate major in entrepreneurship (the women-only Effat University).[3] Of the eight universities that offered undergraduate business and management programs, seven provided at least one elective in entrepreneurship, but only one offered an elective course in small business management. Of the six that offered postgraduate degrees, none offered programs in entrepreneurship and small business management although five did offer at least one elective course in these subjects. None of these appeared to offer specialised undergraduate or postgraduate courses in creativity and innovation. While the need to introduce such programs was something that the leadership of Al Faisal University was well aware of when I worked there during 2011–2014 and a new undergraduate major in Human Resource Management (HRM) was created in 2015, there were no major undergraduate or postgraduate programs in innovation, entrepreneurship and small-business management at that university in June 2016.

As in Oman, even if an entrepreneurship/small business management major was to be introduced at the Al Faisal University College of Business (or at other KSA universities) in the near future, it will take some time to 'sell' the idea of entrepreneurship and self-employment to new intakes of Saudi students. This would be followed by a time lag of three to four years before they enter what is likely to be a depressed national labour market in the early 2020s, and it would be several more years before any businesses they create become established. As I did in the UAE and Oman, I often asked final-year undergraduate students at Al Faisal about their entrepreneurial intentions. Routinely, about 15 to 20 per cent of students in each group raised their hands when asked if they were thinking about creating their own businesses. When I then enquired if any of them had started to prepare a business plan, hardly any were ever able to do this. Just one of the twenty female undergraduates I interviewed during 2012–2013 indicated that she was planning to establish her own business.

The findings of this study are very similar to those of other studies on women entrepreneurs and SME owners in the KSA but they also confirm the view that the generic factors that inhibit most Saudi women from becoming entrepreneurs and SME owners are not unique to their country. The traditional gender stereotypes and negative attitudes towards female entrepreneurs and business owners that prevail in all MENA countries, including the UAE and Oman, continue to be prevalent in the KSA. It is also apparent, to repeat a comment made earlier, that while Saudi women are being encouraged by government authorities and the media to become entrepreneurs, there is not a 'female-friendly' small business culture in the KSA. However, the evidence from the interviews with these Saudi women also indicated that families played a pivotally important role in the decisions they made about becoming entrepreneurs and confirmed that not all Saudi fathers and husbands are opposed to women having greater economic independence. Fifteen of these women indicated that their families (and husbands) were very supportive of their decision to become entrepreneurs, while two were neutral and in three cases their families were opposed to this; but they also believed that this level of positive support was not typical of most Saudi families. They also agreed that most Saudi women are still prevented from 'doing their own thing' by their families and/or husbands and believed that there was still some social stigma associated with Saudi women becoming independent entrepreneurs, although all of them felt that this was beginning to diminish. Eight of these women felt that young women were not willing to work hard enough to create new businesses, fourteen of them felt that young Saudi women were still too 'risk averse', and, without exception, they believed that the continuing availability of well-paid and secure employment in the public sector was a major disincentive for most working Saudi women to become entrepreneurs and SME owners.

As noted earlier, while all the women I interviewed were running solvent businesses, all of these were service firms and none of them were in high-value markets. Only four had modest plans to expand their companies within the KSA, and they did not employ many Saudis (in fact, with one exception, most of their employees were expatriates). This confirms the widespread view that much entrepreneurial and small business activity among Saudi nationals in the KSA is not in high-value and high-growth sectors. As noted earlier, the 2010 GEM report indicated that most entrepreneurial activity in the kingdom is 'necessity' and 'efficiency' driven rather than 'innovation' driven. In turn, this reflects the reality that the KSA's economy is still, in many important respects, under-developed and lacks a national culture of entrepreneurship that is supportive of self-sufficiency, personal initiative, autonomy, creativity, innovation and risk taking. There is also no synergy between the government's appeals for younger Saudis to become entrepreneurs and the courses that are currently being offered to their 'best and brightest' at the country's leading universities (Abu-Sharkh and al-Shubaili, 2013: 11; Skoko et al, 2010: 31, 34 and 80).

This evidence indicates that there is a disconnection between government- and state-controlled media rhetoric and the reality of establishing the kind of thriving, high-value entrepreneurial and SME sector that young Saudi women and men will readily participate in. Nevertheless, as Skoko and his colleagues noted in 2010, 'diversification in non-hydrocarbon activities has started, but is relatively modest. Since the oil/gas/hydrocarbon sectors are largely capital intensive, they are not a dynamic source of jobs, at least of the magnitudes currently needed ... Here, small and medium-sized firms can play a leading role in solving the kingdom's employment problems' (Skoko et al, 2010: 44). While there is no doubt that the KSA's SME sector *could* be a powerful driver of economic growth over the next fifteen years, there is considerable scepticism about the government's willingness and, more importantly, its ability to unleash this potential. And, although further research is needed to confirm this, it is reasonable to assume that there is a big gap between 'entrepreneurial intentions' and actually starting a business in the KSA. As in Oman and possibly the UAE, there are probably a significant number of Saudi women who aspire to create new businesses but choose not to because of the barriers and difficulties they are likely to encounter. And, we still know very little about the experiences of women in the many established family-owned businesses of the KSA and if these are markedly different to those of self-starting female entrepreneurs from less privileged backgrounds.

In conclusion, the available evidence suggests that women's nascent entrepreneurship remains a woefully under-utilised source of untapped economic wealth in the KSA and this is a dreadful waste of the entrepreneurial potential of Saudi women. The cultural and socio-political constraints on Saudi women described in Chapter 6 are the primary causes of this, and these continue to stand in the way not only of greater participation by women in the KSA's SME sector but also in the private sector and the nation's broader labour market. In

Chapter 9, we will review some strategies that could be implemented by government and private-sector organisations to increase the participation of Saudi women (and men) in high-value entrepreneurial and SME ventures in the future.

7.4 BALANCING WORK AND FAMILY LIFE

As noted in Chapters 3 and 5, the issues of work–life balance and work–family conflict have been the subject of hundreds of research articles and dozens of books over the last three decades. However, in common with the UAE and Oman, it is only very recently that there has been some public discussion about the impact of rising levels of female employment on family life and the traditional (domestic) roles of Saudi women. Although there are one or two passing references to work–life balance and work–family conflict issues in the few articles that have been written about working Saudi women, no systematic research has been conducted on these issues in the KSA. Hence, as in Oman, this section is among the first to describe the emergence of work–life balance and work–family conflict issues in this country.

The material presented here is based on the results of a questionnaire survey of 107 working Saudi women conducted during April 2013.[4] The demographic profile of this sample reflects the very youthful female Saudi working population of the KSA following the national baby boom of the 1980s and 1990s and growing employment opportunities for Saudi women during the 2000s and 2010s: 19.4 per cent of the sample were aged twenty to twenty-five years, 28.6 per cent twenty-five to thirty, 37.7 per cent thirty to thirty-five, and just 14.3 per cent were older than thirty-five. All of these women were married, and forty-eight had one child, thirty-five had two, twenty-six had three, and ten had four or more children. Of our respondents, 92.5 per cent had husbands who were also working full time or managing their own businesses. They worked in a variety of public (65.5%), semi-government (8.4%) and private-sector organisations (26.1%) and included national and local government employees, airline employees, bank officers and branch managers, human resource managers, import–export managers, seven women working in IT, marketing managers, a few medical professionals, media employees and several teachers and university employees. Most of these women worked in supervisory or middle-management roles, and 35.3 per cent had fewer than five years' work experience; 26.9 per cent had six to ten years' work experience, and 21.8 per cent had eleven to fifteen years' experience. Less than 15.0 per cent of these women had worked for more than fifteen years.

On average, women in the private sector reported that they worked slightly longer weeks than their peers in the public sector (5.3 versus 5.0 days per week) and – as there were with women in the UAE and Oman – noticeable differences in their average daily working hours (Table 7.9).

TABLE 7.9 *Daily hours worked by women in public, semi-government and private-sector organisations in the KSA* (N = 107)

| | Daily average working hours | | | |
	7–8	9–10	11–12	12 or more
Public sector &	71.9	28.1	0.0	0.0
Semi-government				
Private sector	35.6	53.2	11.2	0.0

(*This includes 'time spent on work-related duties while at home' in order to assess the total number of hours engaged in non-family activities by these women each week. Because Saudi women are not allowed to drive, they do have additional time that can be used to deal with work, SMS and email correspondence while travelling to and from their workplaces.*)

In the public-sector sub-sample, a majority of respondents reported being 'neutral' about the amount of time they spend at work, with 53.8 per cent of respondents reporting that they were 'happy' and 26.9 per cent 'very happy' with their working hours. However, more respondents in the private-sector sub-sample felt 'unhappy' or 'very unhappy' about the amount of time they spend at work (43.7 per cent compared to 9.2 per cent among public-sector employees).

Furthermore, 47.4 per cent of the private-sector employees reported that work pressures 'sometimes make me feel very tired', and only 11.8 per cent reported that their work never left them feeling tired. And while 22.2 per cent of public- and semi-government-sector employees indicated that they had 'sometimes' dealt with work during weekends and holidays, this figure rose to 53.5 per cent among those working in the private sector. To better understand how our respondents coped with the competing demands of work and family life, we asked: 'Do you feel that you are able to balance your work responsibilities and family life?' The results are presented in Table 7.10.

TABLE 7.10 *Do you feel that you are able to balance your work responsibilities and family life?*

	Never	*Rarely*	*Sometimes*	*Often*	*Always*
Public sector & semi-government	0.0	2.8	27.1	60.8	9.3
Private sector	0.0	26.1	48.6	21.5	3.8

The responses to this question show that most of the women who work in the public and semi-government sectors felt that they are able to balance their work responsibilities and family lives, although just over one quarter of public and semi-government employees reported that it was sometimes difficult to balance the competing responsibilities of work and family. The situation for those working in the private sector was rather different, with one quarter reporting that they were rarely able to balance the demands of their jobs and families. There was also evidence of some negative spill-over between work and the respondents' leisure time, with noticeable differences in the responses of the private-sector employees when compared to public and semi-government employees (Tables 7.11 and 7.12).

The data also suggested that work responsibilities had few negative effects on the amount of time that our public-sector respondents had to spend with their children. However, once again, the longer working hours required of those working in private-sector companies in the KSA was having a demonstrable effect on the time they could spend with their children during the week and at weekends (Tables 7.13 and 7.14).

TABLE 7.11 *How often do you think about work when you are not actually at work or when travelling to work?*

	Never	Rarely	Sometimes	Often	Always
Public sector & *Semi-government*	0.0	36.5	57.0	6.5	0.0
Private sector	0.0	18.7	53.3	24.3	3.7

TABLE 7.12 *Do you ever miss out on quality time with your families and friends because of work pressures?*

	Never	Rarely	Sometimes	Often	Always
Public sector & *Semi-government*	0.0	47.7	39.2	13.1	0.0
Private sector	0.0	15.7	57.0	27.3	0.0

In order to evaluate how Saudi women coped with the competing demands of work and family, we also asked them about childcare arrangements in their households. The data showed that most working Saudi women – regardless of the employment sector they work in – relied on extended families and older relatives for child care and support or some combination of family support, nannies or servants (Table 7.15). As in the UAE and Oman, this makes childcare a less onerous and expensive proposition for most working Saudi women, and, given the enduring strength of extended family networks in the KSA and limited geographical career mobility among most working Saudi women, this level of family support will likely continue for some time.

TABLE 7.13 *On an average working day, how much time do you have to spend with your children?*

	< 2 hours	2–3 hours	3–4 hours	> 4 hours
Public sector and semi-government	11.3	30.8	49.5	8.4
Private sector	39.3	33.6	25.3	1.8

TABLE 7.14 *During an average weekend, how much time do you spend with your children?*

	< 4 hours	4–5 hours	5–6 hours	> 6 hours
Public sector and semi-government	5.6	21.5	34.5	38.4
Private sector	18.7	32.7	29.9	18.7

TABLE 7.15 *Who – primarily – takes care of your children while you are at work?*

	Spouse	Parents, in-laws or close relatives	Servant or Nanny
Public sector and semi-government	0.0	44.8	55.2
Private sector	0.0	40.2	59.8

Only a small minority of our respondents felt overwhelmed by the competing demands of their home and work lives, but there was evidence of some strains and stresses being created by this for around one in six women who work in the private sector (Table 7.16). These findings confirm the results of other studies on work–life balance and work–family conflict, indicating the existence of a 'high-pressure' sub-group of Saudi women working in the private sector who, at times, were struggling to balance the competing demands of high-pressure jobs and busy family lives.

TABLE 7.16 *What is the impact of home life on your work performance?*

	Public sector and semi-government	Private sector
Impact		
My home life has no impact on my work performance	73.8	43.9
Family responsibilities can reduce the time I have to work on job- related tasks	7.5	21.5
Family responsibilities can distract me from work-tasks	6.5	22.5
Problems at home can make me feel irritable at work	6.5	19.7
At times, work pressures and family responsibilities can overwhelm me	5.7	16.8
(% that 'strongly agreed' or 'agreed' with each statement)		

In the final section of the survey, we examined the work–life balance support provided by our respondents' employers. The data show that work–life balance support in both public- and private-sector organisations in the KSA is virtually non-existent and services or HR policies that are known to help with balancing work and family responsibilities are largely absent (Table 7.17). Today, there are no high-quality day-care systems in the KSA and this remains a significant impediment to some Saudi women entering the national labour force (al-Kibsi et al, 2015: 88).

In an open-ended question, we asked those respondents who had reported conflicts between their jobs and family lives to select five factors that they believed were the greatest hindrance to achieving better work–life balance. In order of importance, these were 'Negative/patriarchal/conservative attitudes of (male) senior managers, bosses or supervisors' (N = 43), 'Inadequate maternity leave provisions' (N = 37), 'Lack of childcare facilities at work' (N = 33)

TABLE 7.17 *Work–life balance support and services provided by respondents' employers*

'Does your company have any specific services or HR policies to help with work–life balance?'

	Yes	No	Not sure/don't know
Public sector and semi-government	*11.2*	*72.0*	*16.8*
Private	*12.2*	*66.4*	*21.4*

'What support does your company provide to help with WLB?'

	Public sector and semi-government	Private sector
Policy		
Flexible starting and finishing times	*39.2*	*22.5*
Option to work part-time or job share	*17.7*	*0.0*
Crèche, day-care or nursery at your workplace	*0.0*	*0.0*
Career breaks or sabbaticals	*11.3*	*0.0*
Parental or family advice	*0.0*	*0.0*
Paid maternity leave*	*100.0*	*100.0*

(*This excludes 'Not sure/don't know' responses. *Based on information provided by three female Saudi MBA students at Al Faisal University, it appears that Saudi women are entitled to maternity leave for a period of four weeks preceding and for six weeks after the birth, and they receive full salary for one year if they have three years' work experience. This can be taken pro-rata, i.e. they can take two years' maternity leave and be paid 50 per cent of their salary for two years. It is not known what discretionary maternity leave/salary may be provided by Saudi private-sector employers or international companies in the KSA*)

'Negative attitudes of family members' ($N = 31$), 'culture and religion' (i.e. social pressures to put family before work and their husband's career) ($N = 19$), and 'technology' (i.e. being accessible 24/7 for work-related matters) ($N = 9$). The final question asked in the questionnaire was, 'Do you think that if employees enjoy a good balance between their work and family lives, then their work performance will improve?' Four out of five of these women replied 'Yes', one in five were 'not sure', and none of them replied 'No'.

In conclusion, work–life balance and work–family conflict were not a perceptible part of mainstream public discourse or media commentary in the KSA when I worked there during 2011–2014. However, as in the corresponding samples in the UAE and Oman, there were consistent differences in the responses of those who worked in the private sector when compared to those in the public sector. Women in the former group reported longer working hours, had less time to spend with their children and families and experienced greater difficulties in balancing work and family commitments. There was also some evidence of work overload and work–family conflict among this group. However, almost all of the women in both groups did have the support of extended families and kin who routinely helped out with childcare or they could afford nannies and, in some cases, servants. This meant that work–family conflict appeared to be a much less significant and stressful issue for Saudi women when compared to most working women in Western societies and a growing number of female professional employees in the UAE.

While it seems likely that most working Saudi women will be able to rely on their extended families or nannies and servants for support with childcare for some time, if their participation rate in the national labour market were to increase significantly over the next five to ten years, then work–life balance and work–family conflict could become more significant issues in the KSA. In turn, this will require a response from both employer organisations and the KSA government if they are not to become impediments to the active participation of more Saudi women in the national labour market in the future. As in the UAE and Oman, most of the women in this study also felt that the organisations they worked for could be more sympathetic to work–life balance and work–family conflict issues, and they too suggested a range of HR initiatives that could be implemented to help with them. Their suggestions are discussed further in Chapter 9.

7.5 CONCLUSION

Saudi Arabia's women represent an untapped and important source of power for the economy. Although incorporating women fully into the labour-market may not be achieved overnight, it can – and must – be achieved if the Kingdom is to transition to a knowledge-based economy. Decision makers at every level of government can no longer avoid the implementation of sweeping reforms in education and labour policies to ensure that women have the opportunity and skills to participate – and succeed – in the economy. Women's employment should be a crucial element in a larger macro-economic policy designed to foster equitable social and economic development.

al-Munajjed (2010a: 13)

We saw in Chapter 6 that while the labour force participation rate of Saudi women has improved over the last decade, this has not matched the increase experienced by women in the UAE. A few Saudi women have moved into senior positions in the public sector, some are now involved in the political administration of the country and there are a few notable examples of high-profile female business leaders. However, they are still under-represented among the ruling political elite and the only female minister in a national cabinet of thirty lost her job in 2015. Most Saudi women do not work, and even those that do are heavily concentrated in the public sector. The traditional view that women 'take care' and men 'take charge' is still deeply embedded in the culture of Saudi society today and many men continue to believe, as their more conservative peers in the UAE and Oman also do, that the most suitable role for women is to be wives and mothers. Furthermore, two 'self-imposed' barriers that were mentioned towards the end of Chapters 3 and 5 affect most Saudi women to a much greater extent than their peers in the UAE. The country's conservative and patriarchal culture and its school system still reinforce the idea that men should be the 'leaders and guardians' and women should be, primarily, the 'loyal followers and supporters' and such deeply entrenched attitudes will take a long time to change. And, as several of the female interviewees attested, it will not be enough for the government to create more opportunities for the country's female citizens: women must grasp whatever opportunities that are presented in the future and push and agitate for more change themselves. There are signs that some Saudi women have been doing this for a while and that a growing number will be doing the same in the future.

One encouraging example of a Saudi woman who has succeeded in achieving her career and life goals is Huda al-Ghoson, and her story also shows that it is possible for any Saudi company to create a more level playing field for female employees if there is active support from the organisation's leadership group. She grew up in the KSA, and both of her parents encouraged her education and, after she graduated from university in the mid-1980s, her mother saw a Saudi Aramco advertisement for graduate positions for both men and women, and she applied for a position with the company. As al-Ghoson observed in 2015, 'this was very rare at the time and reflects Saudi Aramco's early commitment to women in business.' After working in junior roles and then obtaining an MBA in the United States, she became a manager in charge of national and expatriate employees, both male and female. She recalls that:

> This was still unusual and of course came with challenges. For example, in the early 1990s, when I was Aramco's supervisor of housing policy, a Saudi male asked to transfer out of my unit. He told my supervisor that if his family knew that his boss was a woman, it would ridicule his masculinity, and maybe he would be asked to divorce his wife. When my supervisor told me this, I said, 'Absolutely, let the guy move out. I don't want to be responsible for a divorce'
> (al-Ghoson, 2015).

She also remembers that there was some resistance from some female employees who did not want to work for a female boss. Nevertheless, she believes that Saudi women are becoming, 'increasingly accepted in the workplace and in leadership positions as well and today we have more talented, capable, ambitious and educated women than ever before.' However, 'in Saudi Arabia, women, especially if they are married and have children, face the problem managing their personal and work lives. Here we still believe that raising children and running a household is a woman's job. The man does not share these responsibilities. That puts pressure on many women' (al-Ghoson, 2015). More importantly, and we will return to look at this important theme in Chapter 8, al-Ghoson makes the following comments about why companies like Saudi Aramco are employing more Saudi women and how this company is facilitating this:

> Given our strategic goal to become the world's leading integrated energy and chemical company by 2020, we realised that we had to have the right talent. There is a huge shortage of qualified, skilled professionals in our industry. Yet we have a huge pool of untapped talent – women. The number of women in Saudi Aramco had risen, but not quickly enough to meet our goals, so in 2010 we set up two initiatives to expand women's participation. One program, Women in Business, targets younger people starting their careers. The second, Women in Leadership, is for senior employees. In the former, we teach basic soft skills to build character, self-confidence, resilience, tolerance, flexibility, assertiveness, and awareness of how to succeed in a male-dominated business. Some of these women have never worked with men or interacted with them outside their families and don't know how to do so. When such women come to a more open, diverse company, some stumble and feel awkward. Very often, you are the only woman in a room full of men. You find it difficult to speak up or do a presentation. And young women can be invisible: they do their work and share it with others, but if they don't speak up their contribution may not be noticed
>
> (al-Ghoson, 2015).

The purpose of the Women in Business program is 'to raise awareness and train women to speak up, to become visible. We want them to contribute in ways that everyone can see, to ask the boss for meetings where they can give their feedback and opinions, to document their contributions, and to manage their own careers' (al-Ghoson, 2015). The Women in Leadership program aims to develop female middle managers for leadership positions. During the 2000s Saudi Aramco had only three or four women leaders. In 2015, the number was eighty-four, a small number given the size of the company's work-force but a significant increase on just a few years ago. Al-Ghoson recognises that increasing the representation of women in technical fields remains one of the biggest challenges in Saudi Aramco, but she also believes the company will deal with that issue in time. She is also encouraged that numerous companies, government agencies and educational organisations have approached Saudi Aramco to help them launch similar programs for their female employees. The com-pany is also expanding its outreach programs for school and univer-sity students, who are invited to visit the company, hear inspirational speeches and attend short courses which are often delivered by women. It also offers scholarships to young women to pursue STEM studies at universities around the world.

She also believes that it is possible to create more opportunities for women that 'won't affect our Islamic values. It won't demean us, nor will it fundamentally change our traditional ways.' She also observes that 'there is also the economic dimension. Everybody wants to maintain a high standard of living, and many families can't do that with one salary. Two incomes will help families to send their kids to good schools, get good medical care, maintain a good lifestyle, and prosper and grow. Ultimately, a successful Saudi is a happy Saudi, and that will be reflected in the way she cares for her children, her husband, her family and herself' (al-Ghoson, 2015). The examples of successful Saudi women in Chapter 6 and the working women, entre-preneurs and business owners in this chapter also suggest that things may be improving, to some extent, in the KSA. However, the progress of women in the KSA seems to be very much a case of two steps forward, one step back, and there are both positive and negative signals about what might happen to Saudi women during the second half of this decade and the 2020s.

While most well-educated Saudi women would agree that they now have better opportunities to pursue careers and to work, they still believe that there are barriers and impediments to their career progression in organisations, and most women and men remain pessimistic that many Saudi women will ascend to leadership positions in private-sector companies in the future. Most Saudi men continue to have very conservative opinions about working women and question their ability to succeed in leadership roles and as business owners. Saudi women continue to face significant cultural and social barriers which impede their full participation in the national labour market particularly, to repeat the point, in the kinds of jobs and entrepreneurial activities that can generate new and diverse sources of national wealth in the future. It is clear that while some progress has been made over the last decade, it may be a long time before the cultural, attitudinal and structural barriers that hold women back in Saudi society and in the labour market of the KSA are no longer so predominant.

Moreover, for most university-educated Saudi women, the longer working hours, lower salaries and more mixed working environments in most private-sector organisations remain significant deterrents to moving out of public-sector employment. As in the UAE and Oman, the public-sector generally offers better pay, more security, better holiday entitlements and shorter working hours when compared to equivalent jobs in the private sector, particularly for younger employees. However, as we saw in Chapter 6, the KSA public sector is bloated and continues to use up considerable financial resources and the quota system of 'Saudisation', introduced in the late 2000s to compel private-sector companies to employ more Saudis, has not been very successful. These imbalances, combined with the inability of the private sector to create enough new jobs for Saudis, continue to hamper the country's transition to becoming a diversified knowledge-based economy. And, as several of the women featured in this chapter observed, while change has to come from both the top and the bottom of Saudi society they are still not allowed to establish independent organisations to represent their collective interests. This means that it will be a long uphill struggle to improve the legal rights of Saudi women and this will be a slow and incremental process which, for the foreseeable future, can only occur within a rigid Wahhabist theological framework. This, in itself, may impede or even halt the kinds of reforms that would be required to allow more Saudi women to work and pursue any career that they choose to. Consequently, *The Economist* was not alone in being pessimistic about the prospects for Saudi women in the KSA during 2016:

> King Abdullah's reforms seem to be stalling and even going into reverse under his successor, King Salman. His young son Muhammad, who operates most of the levers of power, says he is anxious to increase Saudi productivity, and to lower birth rates by getting women out of the home and into the workplace. But, even he seems nervous about confronting the religious establishment, on whom the al-Saud rulers depend for legitimacy. Many of Abdullah's reformers have been shifted; and a host of hardliners are back. The only female minister, in the Education Ministry, was dismissed soon after Salman took the throne … The talents of women, who already make up the majority of new university graduates will have to be harnessed better. But, for now, even the limited reforms to give women more opportunities have gone into reverse
>
> *(The Economist, 2016g: 45, and 2016m: 9).*

Although the government had made several public pronouncements during the early to mid-2010s about the need to develop new policies and strategies to empower women in the national labour force, there were – to the best of my knowledge – no national programs in place in June 2016 to facilitate the advancement of women in the national labour market. It is also not an encouraging sign when the Saudi Arabian Monetary Agency, which controls the fiscal levers of the national economy, organised a workshop for the leaders of the country's major public- and private-sector organisations to discuss the urgent need for further economic diversification in the KSA and yet chose not to mention the role women should play in this transformation a single time during the entire presentation (Kingdom of Saudi Arabia Monetary Agency, 2014). Having said this, there are some reasons to be mildly optimistic about the future for Saudi women. As Coleman has observed, the status of women in the KSA today has a uniquely 'bi-polar' quality to it:

> Saudi Arabia is a country of contrasts, no more so than with respect to women. Saudi women are internationally recognised doctors. They are prominent business women running international companies. They are Ph.D. economists and scientists. They are deans of colleges and heads of university departments. They are journalists and newscasters. Yet none of these women can drive in their home country or vote in a local election.* Saudi women enjoy fewer legal rights than women in any other country in the world today ... The Saudi state treats women as legal minors their whole lives, requiring a father's, then a husband's permission for many basic activities. Yet despite, or perhaps because of, the considerable restrictions on them, Saudi women are very much at the forefront of social and economic change in the kingdom. By dint of their academic, professional and economic successes, they are quietly breaking down their country's pervasive discriminatory policies and social attitudes. They are also challenging the puritanical interpretations of the Wahhabi religious establishment that are used to justify restrictions on women in the first place
>
> (Coleman, 2010: 205; *at that time).

As al-Rasheed and Azzam have suggested, it is also a myth that all Saudi women are either 'victims' or 'survivors of the oppression they have been subjected to' and an increasing number of Saudi women are – within very constrained circumstances – 'pushing-back', advocating for greater legal rights and demanding that the authorities deal with the most flagrant and violent abuses of women by men (al-Rasheed and Azzam, 2012: 2). It is also now evident that the unsuccessful lobbying for political representation that occurred during the 2000s and the informal (and illegal) women's networks that were created at this time were instrumental in creating a more conducive environment that allowed women to stand in the country's municipal elections at the end of 2015. Similarly, the appointment by Royal Decree of selected women to regional Chambers of Commerce during the 2000s led, a decade later, to some women being elected on their own merits to these bodies (al-Dabbagh, 2009 10–11; *The Economist*, 2016g). And, in a move that was probably as big a surprise to most Saudis as it was to those outside the kingdom, the government announced on 15 April 2016 that the powers of the feared *al-mutawwa'a* were to be curbed. While they can still arrest and detain people, they now have to report any arrests they make to the civilian police. They were also warned about their conduct after numerous complaints to the authorities by Saudi women who had been assaulted and beaten by their officers (Khalaf, 2016). These examples suggest that even in the very conservative and male-dominated culture of the KSA, change is possible, and 'amid the fraught, fragile, extraordinary changes under way in the daily lives of the kingdom's women – multiple generations are now debating what it means to be both truly modern and truly Saudi' (Gorney, 2016: 116).

However, it is also equally plausible to suggest that their situation will not change substantively until the ruling elite of the KSA realise that their survival and the future of their country will depend not only on transformative economic, political and social reforms, but also that this cannot be achieved unless Saudi women are allowed to participate fully in the country's political system and in its labour market, at all levels and in all professions, particularly in the private sector. Until recently, there has been no economic necessity for large numbers of Saudi women to work outside the home but this is not sustainable in the medium-long term. Like Oman, the KSA is at a critical juncture in its evolution as a nation-state and, as noted in the conclusion to Chapter 6, several studies have suggested that the Kingdom has already passed its peak oil production capabilities.

Sooner rather than later, the ruling elite of the KSA will have to acknowledge this reality and accelerate the process of creating an economy that can sustain their country and its people in the future and one of the most important elements of this will be to initiate reforms that will allow more Saudi women to contribute to the economic development of the KSA. With several million expatriate workers on short-term visas in the KSA, there are certainly opportunities for many more women to work, although substantially reducing the size of this workforce is 'the last resort' according to Crown Prince Muhammad bin Salman (*The Economist* Middle East and Africa, 2016).

The Economist has suggested that 'the best hope for women is that the country might rediscover its own traditions', citing a video on social media that showed the king of the KSA holding court in the 1930s while women ride past on horseback bringing their goods to the local market and the annual festival in Jeddah that displays the colourful costumes that Saudi women used to wear before the country's religious zealots decreed that *abayas* should be all black. And, 'most striking of all is the Prophet Muhammad's own requirement that women and men perform the pilgrimage to Mecca together: and that when women go round the *Kaaba*, they show their face. Saudi Arabia's new rulers might take note' (*The Economist*, 2015h: 46). These sentiments are ones that all the Saudi women – and some of the men – I interviewed during 2012–2014 would agree with wholeheartedly. *The Economist*'s gloomy prognosis about the KSA may still prove to be correct and the unanswered question is: Can the KSA hope to build a diversified and internationally competitive economy *without* the participation of significantly more Saudi women in its national workforce? Every report cited in Chapters 1 and 6 that has addressed this question has concluded that this will not be possible. We will re-evaluate this claim and describe the impact that they could have on the development of the KSA's economy in Chapter 8.

8 The Economic Rationale and Business Case for Increasing the Participation of Women in the Economies and Labour Markets of the MENA Region

8.1 INTRODUCTION

In this chapter, we revisit two themes that were first addressed in Chapter 1. We look again at how difficult it will be for the countries of the MENA region to modernise and diversify their national economies (and, if they choose to, reform their moribund rentier political systems) but also why it is essential that they do this. We then explain, in some detail, why women must be allowed to play a bigger role in this process during the 2020s and 2030s. While there are many legal, ethical and moral reasons for doing more to emancipate and empower women in this part of the world, there are now equally well-established, robust and compelling economic and business cases for doing this. Indeed, in an academic career spanning twenty-five years, I cannot recall any other issue over which there is such a degree of unanimity among scholars and other commentators with often very different ideological and economic viewpoints. The economic rationale for increasing the participation of women in regional labour markets is described in Section 8.3, and in Section 8.4 we present the business case for encouraging greater gender diversity in public- and private-sector organisations in the UAE, Oman, the KSA, the other Gulf States and the broader MENA region. As noted in Chapter 1, it is these – more than anything else – which may eventually compel governments in this region to initiate the reforms that would allow many more women to participate as equals with men in their societies, economies and workplaces. The conclusion describes why there is understandable trepidation among most Arab men about the

369

emancipation and empowerment of women, but it also seeks to explain why the countries of the MENA region must embrace the legal, regulatory and labour market reforms that are necessary prerequisites for creating inclusive and gender-diverse workforces in the future.

8.2 THE LIMITS OF GLOBALISATION IN THE MENA REGION

The process of economic and political transformation begins with democracy, but it does not end there. It is time for meritocracy to replace nepotism, corruption and favouritism ... The choice is ours: either become the 350 million people of the cave, ahl-kahf, *or the 350 million people of the cosmos,* ahl-kawn.

Ahmed Zewail, winner of the Nobel Prize for Chemistry in 1999 (2011)

My father rode a camel. I drive a Porsche. My son flies in a private jet. My grandson will own a supersonic plane. But, my great-grandson will be a camel driver.

Arabian Gulf saying from the 1980s

While many commentators have highlighted the enormous economic potential of the MENA region, they have also commented with monotonous regularity on its 'extraordinary talent for disappointment' (*The Economist*, 2015c: 64) and, in his widely cited 2007 book, *The Emerging Markets Century*, Agtmael barely mentions the MENA region preferring instead to focus on what he regarded as the much more promising economic prospects of Asia, Africa and South America (Agtmael, 2007). On first impression, they do not appear to be particularly difficult places in which to conduct business. In 2015, for example, the UAE was ranked thirtieth of eighty-two countries and the KSA forty-first of eighty-two in *The Economist*'s 'Business Environment' rankings (Oman did not appear on this list, and the highest-ranked countries in 2015 were Singapore, Switzerland, Hong Kong, Canada and Australia). However, no MENA countries were ranked in the top twenty, and *The Economist* continues to place the region at the bottom or joint bottom in seven of ten business categories.

It should also be remembered that this ranking, only assesses how easy – or difficult – it is for foreign-owned entities to conduct business and establish new ventures in these countries. It does not measure how easy – or difficult – it is for nationals in these countries to create new businesses and to carry out their daily functions and tasks (*The Economist* Intelligence Unit, 2015a: 1, 2 and 7). Furthermore, while 'talking the innovation talk' and creating some technology parks and technology incubators, most Arab countries are still investing very little in research and development (R&D) or in emerging technology sectors. In fact, with the notable exception of Israel and Morocco, the MENA region has fallen even further behind the world's leading industrial economies on all metrics of innovation and R&D over the last five years (*The Economist*, 2016n: 42).

As we have seen, while several countries in the Arabian Gulf and elsewhere in the region still have ample supplies of oil and gas, these are finite, and even those states with substantial reserves have, at most, a generation to use this wealth to diversify their national economies and greatly improve the per-capita productivity levels of their still-under-developed private sectors.[1] As we have also seen, the Gulf States and broader MENA region are home to rapidly growing, young, educated and – in some cases – very affluent populations. This could lead to the emergence of a large and stable professional middle-class; something that all economists believe has to happen in the region to support sustainable economic development in the future. However, all MENA countries, including the relatively stable countries of the Arabian Gulf, continue to be characterised by systemic structural weaknesses. As we saw in Chapter 1, these include unrepresentative and often oppressive governments, a lack of institutional governance and oversight, the absence of open civic discourse and citizen engagement, the absence of a free and independent press and media, repressive security agencies, often inefficient and overbearing public-sector institutions, widespread corruption, opaque legal processes and a quagmire of complex tribal, ethnic and religious divisions (Foley, 2010; Ulrichsen, 2011). As *The Economist* has observed,

Supposedly, globalisation represents the triumph of the logic of capitalism over the limitations of geography. But, in the Middle-East, the legacy of history is triumphing over the logic of capitalism. Even as governments try to make it easier to do business in the region and even as pockets of it, such as Dubai, profit from globalisation, resurgence of political conflicts and ideological passions is making global firms think twice about investing there ... The Middle-East is divided into mutually hostile groupings. The Sunni-dominated Gulf states will have nothing to do with Shia-dominated Iran. Israel is more or less isolated. There is no pan-regional trade agreement, making it a more fragmented market than, say, South-East Asia.

Western companies face a growing risk of blowback from their behaviour in the Middle-East. Their home governments are cracking down on corruption. For instance, America is imposing more fines under its Foreign Corrupt Practices Act, and Britain has brought in a strengthened Bribery Act. But, it can be hard to square the requirements of these laws with Middle-Eastern traditions of agreeing on deals informally (asking for them to be put in writing may be taken as an insult), and of paying commissions to middle-men ... At home, Western firms are also under unprecedented pressure, from politicians, customers, and even shareholders, to be good corporate citizens. Many are making efforts to ensure, for example, that women have equal career opportunities to men, and that gay couples get the same benefits and treatment as straight ones. But, in much of the Middle-east, local law and culture treats women as second-class citizens and gay people as criminals

(The Economist, 2015c: 64).

A report from Chatham House, an organisation that publishes considered and balanced reports on the economic, political and social development of countries, has described the challenges that face the Arabian Gulf States and – by implication – the broader MENA region in these stark terms:

The current economic bargain between state and citizen in the
Gulf States is unsustainable as they all prepare for a post-oil era,
albeit with greatly differing timescales ... None of these states can
afford to keep increasing public spending in the way to which their
economies and societies have become accustomed in the last
decade of high oil prices ... The declared economic policy visions,
entailing radical revisions of the state are not matched by visions of
the political and social changes that would be required to achieve
these ... These intensifying pressures will not necessarily lead to
revolution, but if the Gulf rulers do not act to accommodate
changing public expectations, more and more republican
revolutionary movements could arise in the coming years ... and
larger regional and international powers could take advantage of
their unaddressed political weaknesses ... Curbing fiscal spending
will be a pressing concern for the next five to ten years, and the
need to diversify away from oil will require long-term
transformations of their economies and education systems
(Kinninmont, 2015: 2 and 4).

Another study that was equally critical of the lack of progress made
by the 'state-capitalist' countries of the GCC towards economic
diversification has concluded that:

They remain in a position where the oil sector continues to
dominate their economies and few of the industries and services
they have established would survive in a post-oil era. So, the GCC
states continue to be in the situation where they sell their
hydrocarbons on the world market and use the proceeds to import
almost all of their living requirements and large parts of their
labour forces. Viewed in this manner, the diversification strategy
has largely failed ... The process up to now has been slow and has
yielded minor results in relation to establishing non-oil economic
activities ... Such reforms necessitate a mature administrative
apparatus, which at present is not found in the GCC countries...
The lessons that emerge from the response to the Arab Spring

uprising, concerning planning, are not encouraging. They suggest that in times of crisis, *ad hoc* measures take precedence over planning and, even more seriously, governments are not only ready to abandon their long-heralded policies of diversification but willing to implement measures that directly contradict them

(Hvidt, 2013: 16, 39 and 43).

The collapse of oil and gas prices during 2014–2016 has meant that average GDP growth across the GCC fell from 4.0 per cent in 2014 to 2.3 per cent in 2015 to less than 1 per cent in 2016, and every country in this group had to draw on significant cash reserves to prop up their economies, maintain their generous welfare systems and complete expensive infrastructure projects. However, even when hydrocarbon prices rise – as they inevitably will – this will not help ensure that these countries move with alacrity to developing diversified economies, with the possible exceptions of the UAE and Qatar, which can be regarded as (relatively) the most 'progressive' countries in the Arabian Gulf. For the best part of four decades, the hydrocarbon-rich countries of the GCC have showered cash and largesse on their national citizens, and they greatly increased their lavish spending on healthcare, education and other subsidies in the aftermath of the 2011 Arab Spring. In 2016, the citizens of the UAE, Oman and the KSA still received free land to build houses on and enjoyed free cradle-to-grave medical care, and there were no income or property taxes. Education costs were still heavily subsidised and included generous grants for undergraduate and postgraduate studies abroad. These subsidies are, as we have seen, an essential part of the implicit social contract that has kept the ruling elites of these three countries in power for decades, and it will be extremely difficult to remove them without provoking some kind of backlash.

All external observers of the MENA region believe that the inexorable regional fall-back from 'peak oil' levels of oil production will mean that such munificence will become increasingly unsustainable in the future. The steep fall in the price of oil and gas during

2014–2016 also served as a reminder to the governments of the GCC and other MENA countries that this bounty will not last forever and what will eventually happen to their economies when they can no longer rely on the revenues these had been generating. On average, 80 per cent of the income of the governments of the GCC was still derived from the refining and sale of hydrocarbons and associated industries and businesses in 2015. In the case of the KSA, as noted in Chapter 6, the country's cash reserves fell from $737 billion in 2014 to $623 billion in December 2015, and at this rate, it could use up all of its financial reserves by 2021 if oil and gas prices were to remain at 2016 levels. Oman has had a growing debt burden since the early 2010s and was expected to issue government bonds to cover revenue shortfalls from its declining oil and gas sector during 2017. The UAE will also suffer from large budget deficits if it cannot further diversify its economy by 2020 and create new sources of state revenue.

Meanwhile, the governments of Europe and North America have been making concerted efforts to reduce their dependence on oil imports from the Gulf and develop new sources of indigenous oil and gas supplies. There is also a collective international aversion to intervene militarily in the region after the bitter experiences of Iraq, Afghanistan, Libya and Syria. Consequently, this period of relative austerity may act as a spur to more significant economic and labour-market reforms. All GCC governments are mulling over plans to increase corporate taxation for foreign companies, raise excise duties and make cutbacks to their highly salaried and bloated public sectors, and they are even considering the possibility of levying income tax on both expatriates and their national citizens, albeit at initially very low levels (al-Khatteeb, 2015: 2; Spindle, 2013). Such short-term and reactive measures, however, will not provide systemic, sustainable or long-term solutions to the economic, political and social challenges which all GCC and MENA countries now confront. As a report cited in Chapter 1 has suggested, 'the best indicator of countries' successful development is no longer sheer gross domestic product growth but rather risk-adjusted, sustainable growth. In order to implement the most effective diversification strategy, nations must first establish strong economic institutions capable of overseeing this process; a truly diversified economy requires institutional regulatory reform and systemic workplace development initiatives' (Shediac et al, 2011: 2).

As noted, the UAE and Qatar now appear have the most sustainable economies and, perhaps not coincidentally, they are also the ones in which women have made the most progress in their national labour markets, and both countries advocate a (comparatively) liberal interpretation of Islam. Kuwait and Bahrain, while still very conservative Islamic countries, appear to be making some progress with their diversification strategies. Oman is likely to face the biggest challenges to the compact it has created between the state and its citizens. The KSA, with a much larger and increasingly restive population, has the highest risk of political and social disorder and will face a very difficult transition to a post-oil economy over the next twenty years. Moreover, every government in the affluent Arabian Gulf States will have to deal with young populations who have skills and knowledge-sets that are unsuited to the changing requirements of their emerging private sectors and, in all likelihood, smaller public sectors during the 2020s. In 2016, more than 80 per cent of the economically active citizens of the UAE, Oman and the KSA still worked in government jobs or in state-owned companies, and, on average, more than 70 per cent of jobs in the private sector were still held by expatriates in these countries (*The Economist*, 2016b: 7). We have also seen that the educational systems of all three countries need major overhauls, particularly at the tertiary level, with a much greater emphasis being placed on courses in business and management, entrepreneurship and innovation and mathematics, science, technology and engineering – not the social sciences, humanities, education and religion.

Even the much-touted potential of the growing and youthful population of the MENA region comes with considerable risks, particularly from the spread of radical Islam in the region among poorer and disenfranchised groups. One report we cited in Chapter 7 identified a 'widespread and simmering discontent' among this demographic. Almost all of the 3,500 women and men who were interviewed for this study in sixteen MENA countries wanted to see significant reforms in their countries, although many were sceptical that 'greater democracy' was the solution to the problems their countries faced. Almost all of them believed that the rise of radical Islam and terrorism were the biggest threats to economic growth and stability in the MENA region, and very few supported ISIS. More than 40 per cent, on average, did not believe that their country was 'heading in the right direction', although this fell to just under 20 per cent in the Gulf States (excluding the KSA). More than 80 per cent were concerned about high levels of unemployment among young people. When asked which country in the MENA region they would most like to live in, the UAE was the top choice for both men and women. This was because they believed that the UAE is 'a country where young Arabs are encouraged to reach their full potential across a range of industries and businesses, from technology start-ups to the arts and finance, in a culture they are familiar with' (ASSDA'A Burson-Marsteller, 2015: 3 and 18). While they were very concerned about the many problems that confront the region they were cautiously optimistic about the future, although this survey was conducted during 2013–2014 before the recent slow-down in the economies of the MENA region.

While the three countries described in this study have – through a combination of generous public-sector employment and welfare provisions combined with overt and covert repression of independent political and civic activity – managed to maintain social stability, there are no guarantees that this can be maintained in the future. It is evident that there is a growing cleavage between the current generation of rulers in the UAE, Oman and the KSA and a rapidly growing and well-educated younger generation, who are beginning to question their countries' traditional ruling arrangements and the social contracts that have held their countries together for the last four decades. Not only are they exposed to a wider range of external influences and alternative sources of information, they have also witnessed the upheavals and changes in other countries in the MENA region. This suggests that if the needs of all of their citizens, including those of women, are not accommodated, it seems very probable that increased civil conflict and social dislocation will be the most likely outcomes in these countries and others in the region in the future. Addressing these needs and providing greater opportunities for them to participate in national economies will be a critically important part of the transition to a more secure future for the countries of the Arabian Gulf and the broader MENA region. Kinninmont has suggested, as many commentators before her have done, that this will require all states in the region to introduce gradual and consensual political and social reforms (including a move to constitutional monarchies); align their economic diversification strategies with more participative political systems; develop stronger and more transparent parliamentary, institutional and judicial systems; encourage better standards of governance; allow peaceful, independent political groups and business associations to emerge and also ensure economic and social inclusion for all their citizens, including women (Kinninmont, 2015 4–5). Hence, while there is no doubt that economic, political and social change will occur in the Arabian Gulf States and the MENA region in the future, what form will these take and how well will they be managed?

All of the reports and studies by academic researchers, NGOs and international consulting and financial companies that are cited in this book are unanimous in their belief that the emancipation of women and their increased involvement in all economic, business and political spheres in Muslim countries is neither an ideological attack nor some kind of 'Western' conspiracy against Islam; it is, rather, an essential prerequisite for an Arabic Renaissance. In their view, the conservative attitudes that continue to hold women back in the MENA region were not and are not mandated by the Qur'an; they are rooted in culture, tradition and custom. And, as all sociologists and historians will attest, this means that they can change and evolve. The key to this transformation will be to find ways of empowering women that do not threaten deeply held religious values in Islamic countries, an issue we will revisit towards the end of this chapter, in Chapter 9 and the Postscript. Moreover, there are good reasons to believe that the economic empowerment and emancipation of women in the Gulf States and the broader MENA region is now, at the very least, *possible*.

8.3 THE RATIONALE FOR INCREASING THE PARTICIPATION OF WOMEN IN THE ECONOMIES OF THE MENA REGION

Evidently, Arab society must find a new equilibrium for men and women based on nominal equality. To achieve this will require making provisions for basic freedoms and constructing a civil society in the broader sense of the term ... Despite the inroads that Arab women have made in political, social and economic fields, the gap between such progress and stereotyped images of women remains enormous. These images invariably confine a woman to the roles of mother, homemaker and housekeeper ... In spite of the many guarantees for the protection of women in the workplace in Arab legislation, various forms of discrimination still persist either because the law explicitly sanctions them or because it fails to intervene to remove them ... It follows that the ultimate objective of the rise of women in the Arab region, and the first organizing principle behind it is for women – all women – to enjoy all components of human rights equally with men.

United Nations (2005: 149, 176, and 187)

Women now constitute about 40 per cent of the global workforce, but there are significant regional disparities in their participation in national economies. In the Gulf States and the MENA region they continue to be under-represented in national labour markets, and there is still an apparent lack of understanding among most regional governments of the enormous contribution they could make to their economies. Paradoxically, the Gulf States that are the richest in oil and gas (Bahrain, Kuwait, the KSA, Qatar and the UAE) had been – at least during the 1990s and 2000s – the most reluctant to extend political suffrage to women, had the smallest number of women in their national parliaments and ruling councils, had the fewest women working in their private and non-oil/gas sectors and offered their women very limited legal rights. Conversely, states with little hydro-carbon wealth such as Lebanon, Morocco and Tunisia tended to have more women elected to national assemblies and more women in the workforce, and they had also granted women more liberal legal rights (Cole, 2014). This has changed to some extent in Bahrain, Kuwait, the KSA, Qatar and the UAE during the 2000s and 2010s, but is this enough to encourage the belief that these countries are committed to creating a more level playing field for women in either the political or economic spheres?

A Booz&Co report, first cited in Chapter 1, has argued that 'the MENA region should remain committed to long-term reform [and] by providing policy stability governments can unleash the region's con-siderable human promise – its increasingly educated and ambitious youth, its budding middle-class and its aspiring women.' However, this report also cautioned that 'it would be unfortunate if Middle-East government leaders, while pursuing appeasement measures and other short-term policies, regressed or relented on the systemic economic reforms that are needed for future growth and success' (Saddi et al, 2012: 1–2). Included in these reforms is the necessity for greater inclusion, 'particularly of those groups … who have thus far been omitted from the development equation. The most prominent and significant of these groups is women … Millions of young women are ready to enter the workforce and their inclusion will probably affect the Middle-East dramatically' (Saddi et al, 2012: 9 and 11). This report – and many other studies – have shown repeatedly that broad-based macro-, meso- and micro-economic diversification will not be possible without increasing the number of women who work in the emerging economies of the MENA region. However, these have also demonstrated that when this is promoted by governments, it has always had a significant impact on national economic performance and growth. It is also, invariably, accompanied by a variety of beneficial socio-economic outcomes for women, because they have more disposable income, greater independence and – over time – enhanced legal rights. Another report, also cited in Chapter 1, has argued persuasively that:

> The women of the Third Billion have the potential to become a tremendous economic force in global markets over the coming decade. The countries and companies that can harness this force and empower women economically – as employees, entrepreneurs, and executives – will gain a clear edge. If the social benefits of economically empowering women is not a sufficient rationale to act, the sheer business opportunities should tip the scale
>
> *(Aguirre et al, 2013: 5).*

This study demonstrated that countries in which women are well integrated into their national labour markets, in which they have advanced in all professional occupations and as business owners, and in which equal opportunity legislation has been enacted are also those where their economic power and social status was the highest. This, over time, has what economists describe as a 'multiplier effect' on emerging economies. As the level of socio-economic development in a given country increases, more women participate in its labour market and attitudes towards women at work, in different professional roles and, eventually, in leadership positions become more positive. This leads in time to further labour-market expansion, increases macro-economic performance and GDP growth and improves general socio-economic indicators, such as disposable wealth, security, health and personal autonomy and freedom for *everyone*, not just women (Aguirre et al, 2013: 2–3). Moreover, because the economic development of all countries is strongly correlated with the level of participation of women in their national labour markets, 'the economic advancement of women doesn't just empower women; it results in greater overall prosperity [and] economically empowering women is the key to greater economic and societal gains' (Dubai Women Establishment, 2009: 39).

We noted in Chapter 1 a report by the McKinsey Global Institute which has examined how economic, legal and social gender inequality is distributed across the world, the impact of this on the national economic performance of ninety-five countries and the inevitable loss of economic performance output that accompanies large gender inequalities (Dobbs et al, 2015). The nine McKinsey analysts who compiled this comprehensive report found that North America and Oceania had the highest gender-parity score of 0.74, Western Europe 0.71, and the nineteen countries of the MENA region had the lowest overall average score of 0.48 (based on fifteen measures, where a score of 1 represents perfect economic, legal and social parity between men and women). For 'labour force participation', 'gender equality in work' and 'leadership positions', the MENA region had scores of 0.32, 0.34 and 0.12, compared to 0.82, 0.74 and 0.72 in North America, Oceania and Europe. In 2015, women contributed about 18 per cent of the cumulative GDPs of MENA countries, and this was even lower in the oil-rich countries of the Arabian Gulf.

The authors of this report believe that there is 'a clear link between gender equality in society and in work ... gender equality in society is correlated with gender equality in work and with economic development [and] higher education ... higher income-parity and better working conditions drive women to assume leadership roles on a par with men, and to move toward realising their full economic potential.' They also found, not surprisingly, that there is 'a strong link between attitudes that limit women's potential and the actual gender equality outcomes in a given region.' More than half of the MENA respondents in this study expressed such attitudes. The report also examined the potential impact of increasing the labour participation rate of women in emerging economies. They concluded that increasing female labour-force participation could boost national economic performance by 85 per cent across the MENA region and, potentially, could add more than 50 per cent to the region's cumulative annual GDP within a decade. However, this would only happen if the labour-force participation rate of women exceeded 50 per cent by 2025 and they were making a significant contribution in the private sectors of these economies (Dobbs et al, 2015, ix, 2–4, 6–7, 11, 14–15, 33 and 47–48).

In a follow-up report, McKinsey has estimated that the national economic benefits of investing in women in emerging economies would be six to eight times higher than the initial spending that would be required to unlock economic opportunities for women (Woetzel et al, 2016: 25). Globally, the world economy could be $US24 trillion richer if the gender gaps in labour-force participation, the hours worked and the productivity of men and women were bridged. This results directly from a number of positive GDP impact indicators. These include having larger indigenous labour forces and a much bigger pool of potential employees to recruit from; fewer skills mismatches and labour shortages; an increase in the general skill levels, aptitudes and quality of employees; a surge in the number of people working in high-productivity and high-value growth sectors and, critically, having significantly more entrepreneurs and SME owners. Their report concluded that 'gender inequality is not only a pressing moral and ethical issue, but it is also a critical economic challenge. The global economy cannot operate at its full potential with constraints holding back a significant proportion of the world's population [and] regions with the largest gaps in gender equality have the largest economic opportunity' (Woetzel et al, 2016: 55).[2]

In its analysis of the global labour-force participation of women, the International Finance Corporation concluded that economic growth in emerging markets means that 'more than ever, firms operating in these are expanding and constantly looking to sharpen their competitive edge and recruit the best talent. Against the backdrop of global increases in women's education levels, employers can no longer afford to ignore women workers. Companies that do not integrate women's employment into their business strategies risk a series of missed opportunities' (International Finance Corporation, 2013b: 5). As Cole has also observed,

> The Arab world suffers from remarkably low female workforce participation, in part because of religious strictures on gender mixing in public and because of low investment rates and high unemployment in general. If transitional governments can stabilise and bring in new investment, and if a new, more open media landscape can allow a challenge to shibboleths such as gender segregation, young women will be able to press for substantial structural change
>
> *(Cole, 2014: 274–275).*

Consequently, all countries in the MENA region and their respective governments are now confronted with an irrefutable economic reality (even those with reasonable oil and gas reserves):

> *There are no examples of advanced, diversified and stable economies that do not permit the active participation of a substantial proportion of women in their labour markets or any that have not removed all barriers to their entry into every profession and occupation.*

Hence, if the nation states of the MENA region are to rise from their generally low positions in the global league table of the world's leading economies and improve on a range of other economic and development indexes, it is no longer reasonable or logical to hold back the rising aspirations and ambitions of their women. Perhaps a measure of the growing international awareness of this economic reality was the decision, ratified unanimously by the members of the G20 at their annual meeting in November 2014, to reduce the global gap between women's and men's labour-force participation rates by 25 per cent before 2025 in order 'to bring 100 million women into the labour force, significantly increase global growth and reduce poverty and inequality' (G20 Watch, 2014: 3).

The impact of initiatives that empower women can have a remarkably quick effect on their participation in national labour markets and economies. For example, women filled 75 per cent of the new jobs created in the European Union between 2000 and 2010. In the United States, just fifteen years after the influential 1995 United States Federal Glass Ceiling Commission (FGCC) report was published, women had become the breadwinners or co-breadwinners in two thirds of all families (up from one third in the early 1990s). By 2010, American women were also responsible for 83 per cent of all consumer purchases, controlled 51 per cent of personal wealth and had more than \$5 trillion a year in consumer spending power, more than the annual GDP of most developed countries (Bennett and Ellison, 2010: 40). They also represented one third of all entrepreneurs and were establishing new businesses at more than double the rate of men. Even with the pay gap between men and women which prevailed at that time, some economists predicted that the average woman in the United States, several European countries and Oceania would not only have achieved pay parity, many could be out-earning the average man by the late 2010s. As Bennet and Ellison noted at this time:

> On a global level, women are the biggest emerging market in the history of the planet – more than twice the size of India and China combined. It's a seismic change, and by all indications it will continue: of the 15 job categories expected to grow the most in the next decade, all but two are filled primarily by women ... But, there are more important implications as well, like the reality that because it is women, not men, who are starting more businesses on their own, it will be women, not men, who will one day employ the majority of workers ... [and] in developing countries, the social effects of women's empowerment are particularly evident, since women reinvest 90 per cent of their income into community and family, compared with 30–40 per cent invested by men
> *(Bennett and Ellison, 2009: 40 and 42).*

Robert Zoellick, the president of the World Bank Group from 2007 to 2012, has described gender equality as 'smart economics' and also pointed to the strong correlation between gender equality and the economic development of all countries (Ernst & Young, 2009: 6). And the World Economic Forum, in an exhaustive analysis of the global competitiveness of 144 countries in 2015, concluded that:

> With respect to labour-markets, raising the share of women in the labour force would greatly strengthen the talent base available in these countries ... the participation and empowerment of women is key to ensuring a large talent pool ... any type of social exclusion that prevents people from fully participating in the labour-market reduces the availability of talent to a country's firms, thereby reducing competitiveness ... a society that does not allow them to access education or to move ahead will not be leveraged for economic advantage and they may leave their home country to pursue opportunities abroad
>
> *(World Economic Forum, 2015a 37, 59 and 65).*

Hence, it is very clear to those who have taken the time to study this evidence that the future economic sustainability of the MENA region will be dependent on the ability of governments to attract more women into their national labour markets and for public- and private-sector organisations to recruit, retain and promote a much larger number of female employees in the future. Those that fail to do this and respond in positive ways to the needs of women employees will lose out, as will the national economies in which they operate.

8.4 THE BUSINESS CASE FOR PROMOTING GENDER DIVERSITY IN THE LABOUR MARKETS OF THE MENA REGION

As a global company, we work in countries with a broad array of laws and regulations. But, regardless of where we operate, we take care to respect the diversity, talents and abilities of all. We define diversity as all the unique characteristics that make up each of us: personality, lifestyle, thought processes, work experience, ethnicity, race, colour,

religion, gender, gender identity, sexual orientation, marital status,
national origin, disability, veteran status or other differences ... Our
core values and guiding principles set the framework for our sectors and
markets to pursue diversity and inclusion with passion and energy,
tailoring our efforts to make them locally relevant.

PepsiCo (2016)

Although we are unlikely to see anything similar to PepsiCo's diversity statement on the 'Vision, mission and values' websites of most indigenous companies in the MENA region in the immediate future, it is emblematic of the sea change that has occurred in the HRM policies and practices of many businesses based in the European Union, North America and Oceania over the last two decades. This came about in response to pro-women legal and regulatory reforms in these regions, the entry of tens of millions of women into their labour forces, changing cultural norms and social attitudes and, more recently, a growing awareness of the business case for promoting gender and other forms of diversity in organisations. The first part of this section presents the generic business case for gender diversity in public- and private-sector organisations, and the second deals with the relationship between the presence of women in executive positions and on boards of directors and corporate performance and profitability. Broadly speaking, three arguments have been presented for promoting gender diversity in public- and private-sector organisations although, in practice, these invariably overlap with each other. These are:

> *The moral/legal case:* 'Because our organisation believes it is the right thing to do and/or employment laws require us to address the issue of gender equality and diversity.'
>
> *The qualitative case:* 'It just makes good intuitive business sense to employ more women and promote gender diversity in our organisation.'
>
> *The quantitative case:* 'Because there is a strong evidential case for employing more women and promoting gender diversity in our organisation.'

The well-established moral and legal cases for the inclusion of women in national labour markets and for promoting gender diversity in organisations were presented in earlier chapters and have also been described in many previous reports on women in the MENA region, most notably in those published by the United Nations over the last two decades. This is not to downplay the importance of these, but the primary purpose of this section is to present the business case for doing this.[3] This begins with a trip back in time to one of the earliest national reports on gender and ethnic inequalities in the labour market of what was then the dominant industrial economy in the world. In 1995, the United States government published its 245-page FGCC report which presented the following bleak national employment statistics in its executive summary: '97 per cent of the senior managers of the Fortune 1000 companies are white; 95 to 97 per cent are male. In the Fortune 2000 industrial and service companies, 5 per cent of senior managers are women and, of that 5 per cent, virtually all are white' (Federal Glass Ceiling Commission, 1995: iii). Of the tiny number of women who were in senior management or leadership positions at this time, most were concentrated in HR and administrative roles and not in operational roles such as production, manufacturing, sales or marketing.

The FGCC commented that 'America's vast human resources are not being fully utilised because of glass-ceiling barriers. Over half of all Masters degrees are now awarded to women, yet 95 per cent of senior level managers of the top Fortune 1000 and 500 service companies are men. Of them, 97 per cent are white' (Federal Glass Ceiling Commission, 1995: iv). The principal causes of these inequities were 'negative stereotypes, prejudice and bias' among white men and the cultural, attitudinal and structural barriers embedded in the working cultures of male-dominated organisations in the mid-1990s. Among the common stereotypes about working women prevalent at this time were 'not wanting to work', 'not being as committed to their careers as men', 'not being tough enough', 'being unwilling to work long or unusual hours', 'being unwilling to relocate', 'unwilling or unable to make decisions', 'too emotional', 'not sufficiently aggressive', 'too aggressive', 'too passive' and 'lacking quantitative skills' (Federal Glass Ceiling Commission, 1995: 27–36). Such attitudes are, of course, still very familiar to the women who have been featured in this study and to all those who work in other countries in the MENA region. What is also remarkable is that despite compelling evidence that linked the promotion of equal opportunities with organisational performance and profitability, during the 1990s, 2000s and early 2010s there were reports almost every month of female employees suing organisations for discrimination and sexual harassment in North America, Europe and Oceania. This, as we will see in Chapter 9, still happens today.

While this report was a damning critique of the ways things were for working women and minority ethnic groups in the United States at this time, an equally important objective of the FGCC was to explain why both public- and private-sector organisations had to start engaging with the issue of employee diversity. It commented that 'this state of affairs is not good for business. Corporate leaders recognise that it is necessary for their businesses to better reflect the market-place and their customers' (Federal Glass Ceiling Commission, 1995: 148). To succeed in an increasingly competitive global business environment they also needed 'to attract and retain the best, most flexible, workers and leaders available, for all levels of their organisations. Narrowing the pool of talent from which they draw is – among other things – a blunder in competitive tactics. Most business leaders know that they simply cannot afford to rely exclusively on white males for positions of leadership' (Federal Glass Ceiling Commission, 1995: iv). Citing several research studies that had been published during the early 1990s, it concluded that there was a growing body of research 'which indicates that shattering the glass ceiling is good for business. Organisations that excel at leveraging diversity (including hiring and promoting minorities and women into senior positions) can experience better financial performance in the long run than those which are not effective in managing diversity' and this, over time, would also have a positive effect on macro-economic growth in the United States (Federal Glass Ceiling Commission, 1995: 14).

Every study and report on gender diversity that has been published since this time has arrived at broadly the same conclusions that the USFGCC did: *gender exclusion is not only ethically and morally indefensible; it has a very negative effect on national economic growth and is an utterly thoughtless strategy for any business organisation.* However, those organisations that have embraced gender diversity have found that this has invariably resulted in several tangible benefits.

It Expands the Organisation's Employee Recruitment Pool by 50 Per Cent

I have stated categorically, many times, that the army has to be an inclusive organisation, in which every soldier, men and women, is able to reach their full potential, and is encouraged to do so. Those who think that it is okay to behave in a way that demeans or exploits their colleagues have no place in this army. On all operations, female soldiers and officers have proven themselves worthy of the best traditions of the Australian Army. They are vital to us, maintaining our capability now, and into the future. If that does not suit you ... then get out.

Former Chief of the Australian Army Lieutenant-General David Morrison
(Australian Broadcasting Corporation News, 2014)

By opening their doors to female employees and promoting inclusive recruitment practices, organisations will have a much bigger pool of candidates to draw on at both the entry level and – over time – for middle- and senior-level positions. In the Arabian Gulf States and the MENA region more women than men now graduate from universities and this pool of female graduates is growing year by year. So any organisation that gains a reputation for being 'women- friendly' will attract the best female university graduates, thereby improving the general quality of their new recruits. And, in the simplest terms, the best and brightest young women are going to be much better long-term recruitment options than young men with average abilities. This then creates a virtuous circle as the organisation attracts the best female recruits and, in turn, they move up the organisational hierarchy into more senior positions. As this organisation gains a reputation for inclusion and promoting gender diversity, the best women will hear about this and want to work for it, including those who may have been overlooked for promotions to more senior positions by their employers simply because they were female. Conversely, talented and ambitious women will not apply for jobs at companies that have reputations for discriminating against women, and *their* best female employee will leave to join organisations where their gender is not an issue; and where judgments about them are based solely on their performance, character and the added value they bring to those organisations.

In every business sector and in all government-controlled organisations, this transition is precisely what did occur in many Western countries during the 1980s, 1990s and 2000s; although this was also accompanied by a long struggle to end discrimination against women in every one of these places, including the United Kingdom, Australia and the United States. There are no examples of organisations or professions in which women did not encounter at least *some* discrimination by men during these decades, and in certain sectors they still do encounter negative attitudes. In the case of the military, for example, the move to recruit women to what had been historically a very male-dominated profession was driven by legal compliance considerations but also by self-interest. The armed services of several Western countries began to recruit more young women in the mid to late 1990s because fewer young men were joining up, and this also enabled them to draw from a much wider pool of recruits. There was also a growing belief in these organisations that women had specific multi-tasking skills to offer, had quicker comprehension and were demonstrating more dexterity and manual agility when compared to men. These were becoming more important skills, as warfare had become more reliant on technology, computerisation, smart weapon systems, robotics and remote warfare capabilities. The trend towards 'smart weapons' and 'engagement at a distance' meant that for most roles, men's superior strength and stamina were no longer relevant employment criteria. Women, the top brass had come to realise, were as capable as men of dealing with the increasingly complex weapons systems and technologies that the military was beginning to use at this time (Garran, 2001a, 2001b; Maddison, 1999).

True to form, the initial response of men in the military to the presence of women was to conclude that they 'are not suited to be warriors', 'not strong or tough enough', 'don't have the instinct to kill' and so forth. In reality, many of these claims turned out to be specious or based on tests that were rigged against women. In one study, Francke showed that physical training courses designed for men ended up breaking many women. When these were changed to suit women's physical development needs, most women were able to get up to the same level as men (Francke, 2001). Bogus data about their alleged lack of resilience in battle zones were also a culprit in fostering negative attitudes towards women. For example, after the First Gulf War in the early 1990s, some senior men in the US military claimed that 'large numbers' of women had been withdrawn from the battlefront because they had fallen pregnant. The army actually sent home 81 women for 'pregnancy-associated diagnoses' and evacuated 207 for 'other injuries'. More than 400 men were also evacuated as a result of non-combat injuries out of a total deployment of more than 20,000 troops. The Navy sent 72 women home out of a total of 2,600 female personnel (Maddison, 1999). Concurrently, evidence had begun to emerge of systemic discrimination against women and of sexual harassment:

> An independent panel has urged the Pentagon to hold Air Force leaders accountable for rapes and assaults of female cadets at the US Air Force Academy, blaming them for a decade of inaction and failure at the service's top school for officer training. The seven member

panel said yesterday that the air force leadership had known at least since 1993 that sexual assaults on cadets was a serious problem at the Colorado school, but failed to take effective action

(Agence France Presse, 2003).

The US defence secretary had appointed this panel in the wake of reports that dozens of female cadets had been sexually assaulted or raped at the school but had been ignored by the academy's leaders and, in some cases, even punished for failing to carry out their duties. From 1 January 1993 through 31 December 2002, there were 142 allegations of sexual assault at the academy, an average of more than fourteen such allegations a year. The US Air Force replaced the academy's superintendent and other top officers soon afterwards in response to this scandal. Tillie Fowler, a former Republican member of Congress from Florida who chaired the panel, praised the 'quick response to the crisis' by US Air Force Secretary James Roche and Chief of Staff General John Jumper, but she said that the problems were 'real and continued to this day' (Agence France Press, 2003). And these were still prevalent nearly a decade later. In 2011 it was reported that:

> Rape within the US military has become so widespread that it is estimated that a female soldier in Iraq was more likely to be attacked by a fellow soldier than killed by enemy fire. So great is the issue that a group of veterans is suing the Pentagon to force reform. The lawsuit, which includes three men and twenty-five women, who claim to have been subjected to sexual assaults while serving in the armed forces, blames former defence secretaries Donald Rumsfeld and Robert Gates for a culture of punishment against those who report sex crimes and a failure to prosecute offenders. Since the lawsuit became public last February, 400 more have come forward. In 2010, 3,158 sexual crimes were reported within the US military … and only 104 convictions were made
>
> *(Broadbent, 2012).*

In 2013, the US Senate Armed Services Committee – now with seven female members – was told by Senator Kirsten Gillibrand that 'sexual assault in the military is undermining the credibility of the greatest military force in the world' and, presumably, acting as something of a deterrent for potential female recruits (Steinhauer, 2013). However, despite continuing problems with sexual harassment and some inequities in promotion prospects, increasing numbers of young women have entered the military in North America, Europe and Oceania in recent years. There are also a growing number of women in the most senior ranks of the armies, navies and air forces of all countries in these regions. Throughout the 2000s and early 2010s they continued to be excluded from a few functions, including most front-line combat roles, but by 2015, the ban on women in these had been lifted in all these countries. In December 2015, the Pentagon announced that all combat roles in the navy, air force and army would be open to women including the all-male Army Rangers and SEALs (*The Economist*, 2015g).

This example is a salutary reminder that even after a substantial number of women have been recruited, on merit, to male-dominated organisations that overt and covert discrimination against them will persist for a long time, and it will usually take a considerable amount of effort and resources to create an inclusive and 'gender-blind' working culture for women. The US military is still working towards achieving this goal. However, public- and private-sector organisations in the MENA region, if they are smart, do not have to repeat all the mistakes made by organisations in Western countries when they first admitted women.

It Enhances the Organisation's Customer and Client Focus

It is important that all businesses are in tune with the people they serve, and gender diversity can help them to be more closely attuned to female customers and clients and to changes in their needs, preferences and expectations. Organisations that are mono-gender (or mono-cultural) cannot be as responsive to their markets as those whose workforce profiles more closely mirror the demographic characteristics of the markets in which they operate. Women, on average, are also involved in 80 per cent of consumer goods purchases in both developed and emerging economies and female employees can help to develop new products and services for those women. Organisations that do not employ women will be less responsive to the needs of female consumers in the markets they operate in, thereby losing out on the 'domestic dollar'. If handled well, this will also enhance the company's reputation among women as an organisation that is good to do business with and may make them more willing to spend money on their products and services (Brush, 2014; Lawson and Gilman, 2009).

One practical illustration of these business realities is the iconic American motorbike company, Harley-Davidson. This had come close to bankruptcy in the early 1980s and then went through a twenty-year period of change and renewal under the leadership of Richard Teerlink and his successors (Teerlink and Ozley, 2000). Although Teerlink retired from the company in 2000, his philosophy of continuous change and learning has continued to underpin the way that Harley-Davidson has planned for its future. In the late 1990s, most of the company's customers were middle-aged men and it was this demographic that had been largely responsible for rescuing Harley-Davidson during the late 1980s and early 1990s, when the company decided to market its leather-jacket image to affluent white-collar, male baby boomers. However, this did not bode well for future sales, because the average age of Harley-Davidson customers was thirty-two in 1990, thirty-eight in 1998 and by 2001 had risen to forty-six and, by the late 2000s, many baby boomers were simply too old to buy new motorcycles. In addition, by the mid-1990s, younger bike-riders who were unaware of iconic road movies like *Easy Rider* – or Harley-Davidson's once youthful and rebellious image – were showing a clear preference for the flashier and cheaper bikes provided in abundance by the Japanese and German firms. In response to these developments, the company started to revamp the range of bikes that it offered. In 1995, the go-ahead was given to start work on a new bike project, which culminated in the launch of the

V-Rod in 2003. It was widely praised by aficionados and commentators alike as being 'revolutionary', 'radical', 'cool beyond words' and 'breath-taking' while remaining true to the history, traditions and spirit of the company (Zackowitz, 2003).

However, this was never going to be enough to increase the company's market share, either in the United States or in emerging foreign markets. Harley-Davidson realised that it needed to appeal to a new demographic: younger women. The company's marketing department had noticed that the number of women attending bike-training courses in the United States had doubled between 1995 and 2005, from less than 20 to more than 40 per cent a year, and yet less than 5 per cent of Harley-Davidson's bikes were being sold to women. Keith Wandell, appointed CEO in 2009, recalls attending a bikers' event in Orlando when 'ten questions were asked and nine of those were from women, and all of them were really asking the same thing: when are you going to design a bike that's more suitable for women riders?' (Clothier, 2010). This question prompted him to immediately announce that the company was going to hire and promote more women in what was still, at that time, a male-dominated company and to start work on a range of lighter bikes for women. This also led to the creation and launch of the *Superlow* in July 2010, designed to appeal to women and first-time riders, and the introduction of a bike customisation program specifically for female riders.

In March 2010, the company held 500 women-only evenings at its dealerships, attracting 27,000 women, of whom 11,000 were in a Harley-Davidson dealership for the first time. It also created a women-specific website a few years ago to attract new women customers and to retain existing ones. By 2012, Harley-Davidson boasted a market share of more than 65 per cent among women in the United States and the proportion of the bikes it sold to this group had risen fivefold to nearly 25 per cent. Women spent more than $300 million on Harley-Davidson bikes in 2015 in the United States, not including riding gear and accessories (Clothier, 2010; Harley-Davidson, 2016; Raval, 2012). The lesson learned from this example is a straightforward but important one for all business organisations. In the words of Jan Plessner, editor of LadyMoto.com and a former Kawasaki public relations manager, 'Other manufacturers will learn from Harley-Davidson's initiatives. Women have for a long time been so absent from advertising campaigns, and now these motor-cycle manufacturers are slowly waking up to this huge untapped market. We will see more from these companies in the next few years' (Raval, 2012). This, it must be emphasised, is just one of hundreds of similar examples of the bottom-line advantages of employing more women and the benefits of gender diversity for companies in non-Islamic countries.[4]

It Increases Employee Engagement, Motivation, Performance and Innovation

There is abundant evidence in the organisational behaviour and occupational psychology literatures which has shown that diversity, combined with a strong sense of inclusiveness, leads to improved employee retention, lower levels of labour turnover and reduced recruitment costs. This, in turn, has positive effects both on individual employee engagement and work effort and, over time, leads to improved organisational and commercial performance. 'Inclusiveness' refers to a situation where people are judged solely on the basis of their work performance and the positive contributions they make to their organisations. A *Harvard Business Review* study of companies that have made significant commitments to gender diversity in recent times describes an inclusive culture as one 'in which employees can contribute to the success of the company as their authentic selves, while the organisation respects and leverages their talents and gives them a sense of connectedness.' One of the twenty-five CEOs who was interviewed for this study believes that in an inclusive culture, 'employees know that irrespective of gender, race, creed, sexual orientation, and physical ability, you can achieve your personal objectives by aligning them with the company's, have a rich career and be valued as an individual' (Groysberg and Connolly, 2013: 72).

It also appears that inclusiveness is strongly correlated with employee engagement and performance. For example, an Australian study of the relationship between gender diversity and employee performance, involving 1,550 employees across three business sectors (manufacturing, retail and healthcare), reported that:

> When [we] modelled the relationship between diversity and inclusion and business performance, we identified an 'uplift' of 80 per cent when both were high ... Employees who perceive their organisation is committed to, and supportive of, diversity and who feel included, are 80 per cent more likely to believe that they are working in a high-performance organisation, in comparison to workplaces perceived as having low commitment and support for diversity and employees not feeling included ... These data lead us to argue that a greater emphasis on diversity and inclusion – and knowing what this means from a practical point of view – is the way forward
>
> *(Swiegers and Toohey, 2012: 2. 'Diversity' was measured by three variables: customer service, innovation and team collaboration, and 'inclusion' was measured by five variables: equity, non-discrimination, uniqueness, decision-making and connectedness).*

This study concluded that 'diversity and high levels of inclusion are needed for top performance' and, critically, that employee engagement and performance was very closely correlated with the level of trust they had in their organisation's recruitment, merit, performance management, staff development and promotion policies. It also showed that 'the behaviours of senior leaders and managers influence employees' perceptions about whether an organisation is authentically committed to, values and supports diversity, and whether they feel included' (Swiegers and Toohey, 2012: 10, 15 and 19). Organisations that have created inclusive working cultures and have put systems in place to get the best out of all of their people have been described as 'high-performance organisations' and 'employers of choice'. These companies have made a real commitment to diversity and to creating both psychological and economic engagement among their female and male employees. These include, among many other examples, Booz&Co, Boston Consulting Group, Cirque du Soleil, Deloitte, DreamWorks Animation, Genentech, Google, W.L. Gore, Mercedes Benz, McKinsey, Morning Star, Patagonia, SAS Institute, Wegmans Food Markets, and all of the 'small giants' in Burlingham's mid-2000s study of exemplary SMEs in the United States.

They have been and continue to be highly innovative, commercially successful and very profitable firms, and many of these companies are also ranked in national surveys of the '100 best companies for women' to work for (*Working Mother*, 2015). These and many other exemplar companies are also regarded as 'employers of choice for women' and characterised by loyal, highly motivated and high-performing employees, with several hundred (or more) recruits applying for every job vacancy in these organisations. There is now abundant evidence in the leadership and people-management literatures to confirm the view that companies that value inclusiveness and place all of their people, including their female employees, at the centre of their organisational and operational policies are more commercially successful over the long term when compared to companies that fail to do this. This indicates that the old saying 'people are our greatest assets' is not just an empty mantra or cliché; it is in fact the main differentiator between flourishing business organisations and those that are less commercially successful over the long term (Burlingham, 2005; Collins, 2001; Corporate Leadership Council, 2004; Hamel, 2011; International Finance Corporation, 2013b: 57–58; Katzenbach, 2000; Martel, 2002; O'Reilly and Pfeffer, 2000; Page, 2007).

Other studies have indicated that gender diversity improves individual and collective decision making and creativity and innovation in organisations, which, in turn, leads to increased sales revenue and market share, more customers and greater relative profits (Barsh and Yee, 2012b, Bourke and Dillon, 2015; Catalyst, 2011, 2004; Curtis et al, 2012; Hewlett et al, 2013; Hunt et al, 2015; Noland et al, 2016; Thomas, 2004). It is now well-established in the organisational research literature that the world's most innovative companies employ the best available talent, regardless of their age, culture or gender, and do not recruit unimaginative 'clones'. For example, one study by the US Centre for Talent Innovation, which involved more than forty companies and 1,800 employees across a broad range of business and industry sectors, looked at the relationship between employee creativity and innovation and two types of diversity: 'inherent diversity' (gender and ethnicity), and 'acquired diversity' (global experience and professional skills). Together these constitute 'two-dimensional diversity' (TDT). This study identified 'a startlingly robust correlation between workforce diversity, innovation and bottom-line growth.' And, those companies 'whose leaders manifest both inherent and acquired diversity (what we term two-dimensional diversity) are measurably more innovative ... employees at these firms are 60 per cent more likely than employees at non-diverse firms to see their ideas developed or prototyped, and 75 per cent more likely to see their innovation actually developed or prototyped.' This study also showed that companies with diverse workforces were 75 per cent more likely to report that they had captured new markets and 45 per cent more likely to say they had increased their market share in the previous twelve months (Centre for Talent Innovation, 2014: i; see also Hewlett et al, 2013). As Leonard and Strauss have suggested, 'to innovate successfully, you must hire, work with and promote people who are unlike you. You need to understand your own preferences and blind spots, so that you can complement your weaknesses and exploit your strengths. The biggest barrier to recognising the contributions of others who are unlike you is your own ego' (Leonard and Strauss, 1999: 66).

Female Leaders May Improve Company Performance and Profitability

The research on the relationship between corporate performance and gender diversity at the executive levels of organisations and on boards of directors is more mixed but, overall, shows that there may well be a positive relationship. For example, a McKinsey study of 366 companies from the United States, the United Kingdom, Canada and Latin America and almost five thousand executives 'found a statistically significant relationship between a more diverse leadership team and better financial performance. The companies in the top quartile of gender diversity were 15 per cent more likely to have financial returns that were above their national industry median ... It should come as no surprise that more diverse companies and institutions are achieving better performance' (Hunt et al, 2015: 1; for ethnic/cultural diversity, the difference was a remarkable 35%). In the United Kingdom, they found that a 10 per cent increase in the number of women in the senior team in companies led to a 3.5 per cent increase in earnings before interest and taxes (EBIT). However, they did note that this relationship only became significant when women constituted at least 22 per cent of the senior management teams of organisations, suggesting that there is a time lag between the recruitment of women to senior positions and enhanced corporate performance.

According to a report by Credit Suisse which involved 2,360 companies, 'while it is difficult to demonstrate definitive proof', companies with one or more women on their boards had delivered 'higher average returns on equity, lower gearing, better average growth and higher price/book value multiples over the course of the last six years [and] enhanced stability in corporate performance and in share price returns ... our results demonstrate superior share price performance for the companies with one or more women on the board.' For companies with market capitalisation values (MCVs) of more than $10 billion, those with one or more women on their boards outperformed those with male-only boards by 26 per cent. For 'small-mid-cap' companies with MCVs of less than $10 billion, the margin was 17 per cent. This report also indicated that return on equity over six years was 16 per cent (compared to 12 per cent among those companies with no female board representation), the price/book value for companies with female board members was on average one third higher than companies with no female board members, and the average capital growth rates for the two groups of companies were 14 per cent and 10 per cent respectively. The authors of this study noted that 'none of our analysis proves causality' and did cite two studies that had shown a negative relationship between female board representation and company performance. However, they believed that their research supports the belief that diversity (broadly defined and properly managed) can significantly improve decision making in organisations, particularly at senior levels, improve corporate governance and social responsibility performance, reduce excessive risk taking and can have a discernible effect on bottom-line results (Curtis et al, 2012: 3, 12, 14–15, and 18–19).

A study of 180 American, British, French and German publicly listed companies in 2012 looked at executive board composition (by gender and ethnic origin), return on equity (ROE) and EBIT. These analysts found that:

> The findings were startlingly consistent: for companies ranking in the top-quartile of executive-board diversity, ROEs were 53 per cent higher, on average, than they were for those in the bottom quartile. At the same time, EBIT margins at the most diverse companies were 14 per cent higher on average, than those of the least diverse companies. The results were similar across all but one of the countries we studied; an exception was ROE performance in France; but even there, EBIT was 50 per cent higher for diverse companies
> *(Barta et al, 2012: 1).*

While also being cautious about identifying a direct causal connection between top-team diversity and the financial performance of these companies, the authors of this study cited several examples of companies who do believe that there is a tangible link. These included a global telecommunications firm, a food company and Adidas, which at this time was aiming to have 35 per cent of senior management positions filled by women in 2015. They concluded by saying that 'while we can't quantify the exact relationship between diversity and performance in such cases, we offer them as part of a growing body of best practices. These successful companies are sim-ultaneously pursuing top-team diversity, ambitious global strategies and strong financial performance' (Barta et al: 3). A parallel study by McKinsey consultants on the impact of gender diversity on corporate performance has observed that 'as the number of women participating in the workforce grows, their potential influence on business is becoming ever more important. Seventy-two per cent of respondents to a recent McKinsey survey believe there is a direct connection between a company's gender diversity and its financial success' (Werner et al, 2010: 1; 772 men and 1,042 women; 85 per cent of the women and 58 per cent of men in this survey, believed there was a connection). They also noted that where gender diversity was a high priority in companies there was also a higher proportion of women in their senior ranks.

The most comprehensive study of this relationship, a meta-analysis of 21,980 firms from 91 countries, concluded – cautiously – that the presence of women in corporate leadership positions 'may' improve the performance of companies, and 'the payoffs of policies that facilitate women rising through the corporate ranks ... could be significant.' Not surprisingly, this report found, considerable vari-ation in female representation across regions and countries, as well as in different sectors of the economy, with almost 60 per cent of these firms having no female board members and half having no female senior executives. It noted that while the evidence for a posi-tive relationship between the number of women in CEO and board roles is 'inconclusive', on average, they neither out-perform nor under-perform male CEOs. While this report did not draw any firm conclusions about the nature of the relationship between the pres-ence of women on corporate boards and company performance, it did find that this was 'positive and statistically significant – that is, the presence of female executives is associated with unusually strong firm performance.' It also found 'a positive correlation between firm performance and the share of women in upper management ... the correlation between women at the C-suite level is demonstrated repeatedly, and the magnitude of the estimated effects is not small.' The firms in their sample that had at least 30 per cent of their senior positions filled by women had, on average, a 6 per cent increase in net profits during the study period compared to an average of 3 per cent for all the companies in their study (Noland et al, 2016: 1, 4, 7, 9 and 15; this study did not include any countries in the MENA region).

The *Financial Times* has concluded that the body of evidence about the benefits of diversity (gender, ethnicity, skills and experience) is 'hard to ignore [and] capital markets and investors now link this to corporate performance.' However, while the business case for diversity may now be proven it seems that action is lagging behind words. They cautioned that there was 'a twist in this evidential tale. Almost all the research on workplace diversity is unanimous on one thing: it can go wrong. Organisations without proper managerial or cultural understanding of diversity can end up with heightened conflict and reduced productivity' (Smedley, 2014: 3). This, as we will see in Chapter 9, is why the process of introducing gender diversity policies to a male-dominated organisation requires a high level of pre-planning, energy and commitment, great care in execution, will always take a long time to implement successfully and, in some sectors, may be very slow (Binham, 2014: 4; see also Bohnet, 2015).

It is early days, but an awareness of the benefits of gender diversity is also beginning to appear on the agendas of some businesses in the Gulf States. A survey of 550 employees in 6 GCC countries reported that 80 per cent of female and 53 per cent of male respondents believed that the presence of women in leadership positions would be a 'very important' driver of organisational effectiveness in the future. Another encouraging indication of changing attitudes towards working women was that 85 per cent of the UAE respondents in this study reported that gender diversity had been on the strategic agenda of their organisations for a few years. For Oman the figure was 75 per cent, and for the KSA, it was just under 50 per cent. The fifty executives who were interviewed for this study in Bahrain, Kuwait, the KSA, Oman, Qatar and the UAE suggested that gender diversity could benefit their organisations in a number of ways. They would be able to recruit from a broader talent pool (and, thereby, employ more country nationals rather than expatriates), and would also benefit from having a greater diversity of perspectives and ideas and more creative and innovative thinking. They also mentioned the 'generally positive effects of gender diversity on team dynamics and decision-making processes.' This report also noted that while a few women leaders could be found in politics, government ministries and in business, 'more work must be done to reach a new status quo in which building diverse leadership teams featuring multiple highly qualified women becomes standard practice ... and to transform the prevailing aspiration on gender diversity from "the first women" to "the norm". ' It concluded that even in the Gulf States 'there is a compelling business case for greater gender diversity in the leadership of organisations. For the economies of the GCC states, leaders have also begun to recognise that realising the full potential of women will be instrumental to achieving their organisations' and countries' ambitions' (Sperling et al, 2014: 3–4, 6, 23 and 28; see also Ellis et al, 2015).

8.5 HOW GENDER DIVERSITY CAN BENEFIT PUBLIC- AND PRIVATE-SECTOR ORGANISATIONS IN THE MENA REGION

Diversity is nothing to do with political correctness. It's all to do with getting the best brains together, and I strongly believe that business leaders who fail to recognise this will inevitably suffer, both commercially and in terms of brand reputation. They'll fail to get the best people, and they'll lack the antennae to reach the full range of potential customers ... there are so many moral and business reasons for making diversity a priority, and I think it's becoming increasingly apparent these days that companies that do diversity the best are also the best performing companies.

Sir Archie Norman, former CEO of ASDA, United Kingdom
(cited by Leighton, 2007: 242)

In theory, the case for employee diversity in business makes good sense. It should mean that businesses that have embraced gender and ethnic diversity are in a stronger position to recruit and retain the best available staff; have employees that are more representative of and in tune with the company's markets, clients and customers; have a broader range of insights and perspectives that will improve problem solving and decision making processes and, ultimately, higher levels of employee motivation, engagement and performance. In practice, however, the relationships between gender diversity and employee/organisational performance are more complicated and nuanced than this, and one of the first phrases that anyone who has studied statistics will hear is that 'correlation does not equal causality' (Vigen, 2015). Some of the studies cited in the last section were cautious about inferring direct causal links between gender diversity at the most senior levels of organisations and corporate performance. While there does not appear to be any indication of a *negative* relationship between these in the most recent studies that have been conducted, and while a positive relationship may well exist, more research is required to confirm this.

This ambiguity is understandable because business performance depends on so many endogenous (internal) and exogenous (external) variables. This makes it very difficult to tease out precise cause-and-effect relationships between input variables such as gender diversity and outcome measures such as organisational performance and profitability or, indeed, identifying the many factors that may ultimately explain why so few companies are able to sustain high performance levels over long periods of time (Rosenzweig, 2007). So it is important to say that there are no guarantees that employing more women will lead, inevitably, to improved organisational efficiency, effectiveness and profitability. Given everything that has preceded this comment, it may appear to be a very contradictory thing to say, and the only way to justify this is with a few illustrative examples.

For the best part of the twentieth century Kodak was the world's biggest manufacturer of photographic equipment, film and developer paper. This company no longer exists because its complacent and out-of-touch male leadership missed the inexorable uptake of digital technologies by consumers and the rise of the Internet in the early to mid-1990s. They were also unable to see that if the company was to survive it would have to make a rapid transition from manufacturing traditional cameras and reloadable film to digital units with digital photographic support. By 2011, the company was bankrupt and engaged in a desperate last-ditch attempt to raise capital to fund new digital and printer businesses by selling off its extensive patent portfolio (Bachelard and Crawford, 2004; Matioli, 2012). Embracing gender diversity in, say, the early 2000s would not have rescued this company from oblivion because it was past saving. It is also highly improbable that employing more women or embracing gender diversity would have helped Apple much during the time when Steve Jobs was not the leader of that company from the mid-1980s to the late 1990s, and the same can be said of Blackberry or Nokia during the 2000s and many other companies that have struggled for survival in recent times. What this means is that if an organisation is already dysfunctional and rapidly losing market share, simply employing more women will neither guarantee greater organisational efficiency and effectiveness nor help a failing company to turn its fortunes around. And, in the absence of good leadership and a high-performance operating culture, simply employing more women will probably have no effect on organisational performance, at least in the short term. Hence, employing more women would have done little to help oil, gas and mining companies cope with low natural resource prices during 2015–2017. However, and this is the key point, it could help all of them become more commercially successful in the future, and we will look at one international mining and resource company's renewed commitment to company-wide gender diversity initiatives in Chapter 9.

What all of the research on the relationship between gender and high-performance companies really provides us with are some very powerful insights into the mind-sets of those organisations that have made this (and all other types of employee diversity) a strategic HR priority and who have – as far as possible – jettisoned all 'irrelevant differences', such as their employees' gender and ethnic origins, from their operational cultures. They are, quite simply, only interested in recruiting *the best employees*, and these days that means attracting the best-qualified and smartest women who will, to repeat a point made earlier, outperform men of average abilities and intelligence. For those who may still be sceptical about the benefits of gender diversity, it is also worth asking why so many Western companies have made this a strategic HRM priority in recent times. They would not be doing this unless they believed it made a tangible and measurable improvement to both employee and organisational performance. For example, the CEOs in the *Harvard Business Review* study cited earlier included Arjay Banga (MasterCard), Paul Black (Merisant), Ken Frazier (Merck), Carlos Ghosn (Nissan), Andrea Jung (Avon), Brian Moynihan (Bank of America), Mikael Ohlsson (IKEA), Ken Powell (General Mills), Jim Rogers (Duke Energy), Barry Salzberg (Deloitte), Randolph Stephenson (AT&T) and Jim Turley (Ernst & Young) (Groysberg and Connolly, 2013). While the significant commitment that these CEOs have made to gender and cultural diversity may have been driven by ethical, moral and altruistic motives, it is also reasonable to assume that none of them would have done this if they had not also believed in the commercial benefits of doing so.

Hence, while a strategic commitment to gender (and ethnic/cultural) diversity may not lead immediately to enhanced organisational and commercial performance, the evidence presented in this chapter indicates that functional companies that have diverse workforces are much more likely to be commercially successful and more profitable than companies with less diverse workforces as measured by a number of well-established quantitative and qualitative organisational performance metrics. All other things being equal, those businesses that employ *the right people*, from the top to the bottom of the organisation, will, given time, perform better than those who choose not to do this. Consequently, employing the best women is likely to be beneficial for any business that has the potential to improve what it is currently doing and to enable it to function more effectively in an increasingly competitive and complex global business environment.

Can these principles and policies be applied in the Gulf States and the MENA region? The answer appears to be yes, but with a few qualifications. A detailed study by the International Finance Corporation of the diversity policies of numerous companies in several dozen emerging economies provides many practical examples of how these have benefited those organisations, leading to increased employee productivity and improved corporate performance. The benefits documented by these firms include an ability to attract a broader range of new employees and an improvement in the quality of new recruits, better customer outreach and greater awareness of potential new markets, reduced labour turnover among women, increased employee motivation, engagement and performance, better decision making, more creative and innovative ideas from employees, improved compliance and risk-management oversight, improved health and safety records, better community outreach and an enhanced company image.

This report also noted that some of the benefits of diversity programs may become apparent quite quickly, such as an improvement in the quality of graduate recruits and lower levels of labour turnover among women. Others are likely to take longer, such as improvements in employee performance, creativity and innovation, macro-organisational performance and bottom-line results and the organisation's image and reputation among women. Nevertheless, in an age when the behaviour of companies is under increasing scrutiny, a demonstrable commitment to women's employment and inclusion 'can help companies to become, "employers of choice", and ensure their long-term access to talent [and] it can also help companies gain access to markets where investors and buyers are influenced by social objectives' (International Finance Corporation, 2013b: 56; see also Kotler and Lee, 2005; McElhaney, 2008: 122–123).

The annual meeting of the World Economic Forum on the Middle-East and North Africa, held in Jordan during May 2015, was notable for the appeals made by the several hundred predominantly male businesspeople who attended this event to their governments. They asked them to resist the spread of militant Islam, to allow more partnerships with foreign companies, to encourage inward investment and business collaborations, to work harder to modernise and diversify their economies and *to encourage more women to work in their home countries* (Reuters, 2015). Other signs of changing attitudes towards working women and female leaders in the MENA region included the creation of the Gender Balance Council in Dubai to promote new strategies for female empowerment chaired by Sheikha Manal Bint Mohammed Bin Rashid al-Maktoum, the daughter of the ruler of Dubai. Dubai also hosted the first Power of Women of Arabia Debate in October 2015, which was co-chaired by the CNN anchor Becky Anderson and Dr Essam Tamimi. The attendees included Raja al-Gurg and Nadine Halabi of the Dubai Women Council; Lana Mamkegh, Lebanon's Minister of Culture; Natasha Ekstedt, Director of Marketing and PR at *Leaders Middle-East* magazine; Dr Amina al-Rustamani, CEO of TECOM investments; and Sheikha Zain al-Sabah, Kuwait's Minister for Youth. There were also representatives from numerous public- and private-sector organisations including the Dubai Chamber of Commerce and Industry, Philips, AIG, the Meera Kaul Foundation, Servcorp and AT Kearney Consulting (Moukhallati, 2016).

On 22 February 2016, Dubai was also host to the first Global Women's Forum to be held in the MENA region. This was attended by Christine Lagarde, the Managing Director of the IMF; Queen Rania of Jordan; Sheik Abdullah bin Zayed, UAE Minister for Foreign Affairs; Reem al-Hashimy, UAE Minister for International Cooperation; Sheikha Lubna al-Qasimi, UAE Minister for Tolerance; Hana al-Rustamani, Head of Consumer Banking at First Gulf Bank; and several other notable local businesspeople, as well as 200 speakers and 2,000 participants drawn from every country in the MENA region and elsewhere. Its purpose is to act as 'a global exchange of ideas related to gender diversity, female engagement and women's contribution to societies' and to 'boost women's influence, design plans to encourage their greater contribution and to promote diversity in the business world' (*Leaders Middle-East*, 2015; Redvers, 2015a). And, in September 2015, the international hotel group Rezidor announced that it had committed to increasing the number of women in leadership roles to 30 per cent, including in its Middle East division. The general manager of the company's Radisson Blue Hotel in Dubai, Maria Tullberg, commented that 'organisations with more women in the team do out-perform companies with less women. They have higher equity, they have higher returns on sales, and they have a higher return on investment capital. So, this is a business issue' (Hoteliermiddleeast.com, 2015). Similar initiatives for female employees in the Middle East operations of the American firm Honeywell were also announced in 2015 (Honeywell, 2015).

Even in Saudi Arabia, there were some signs of changing attitudes in the local business community towards working women with the establishment of the Step Ahead Program by the Saudi recruitment agency Glowork. This is now an annual careers event that connects Saudi women to job opportunities and offers workshops on writing CVs and coaching for interviews. In 2013, forty-five KSA organisations attended this event. In April 2015, more than 300 organisations, many from the private sector, attended sessions in Riyadh, Jeddah and Dammam. As we saw in Chapter 6, women now make up more than half of all university graduates in Saudi Arabia and they represent a woefully under-utilised talent pool that many private-sector companies have yet to engage with. The Saudi companies that will benefit the most from this will be those who are the quickest to implement programs to recruit, develop and retain women, and the example of Huda al-Ghoson and Saudi Aramco in Chapter 7 is a suitable reminder that it is possible for organisations in the KSA to embrace gender diversity if they choose to do so.

A measure of the progress that has been made in attitudes towards female employment in the MENA region, but also a reminder of the work that remains to be done to improve job opportunities for women, can be found in a survey by the recruitment and job agency Bayt.com in 2014. This reported that 72 per cent of 1,453 female respondents from thirteen MENA countries were working in mixed-gender environments, an increase from less than 50 per cent in 2010, although this figure fell to just 31 per cent in the KSA. Less than one in seven of these women were working in 'female-only' work environments, and 15 per cent worked in mixed organisations with separate male/female sections. Only 8 per cent of this group of women indicated that they were 'uncomfortable' working in mixed-gender environments. Most of the women in mixed environments felt they had equal treatment in recruitment and selection, advice and support, working hours and training and development. While almost half felt that their promotion prospects were based entirely on performance on the job, not their gender, about one third felt that they had a lower chance of being promoted than their male colleagues and were treated less favourably than men in terms of career progression (Bayt.com, 2014).

Of course, if these results had been obtained from a sample of American, British or Australian working women in 2014 they would have been regarded, at the very least, as disappointing. They would also have been followed by critical media reports and prompt remedial action by the organisations concerned. However, in the context of the MENA region, they can be regarded as encouraging signs of change. While only one of these women was the CEO of a private-sector firm, 11 per cent of these women worked in senior management or executive positions, and 24 per cent were in middle-management roles. It was also notable that 55 per cent of these women reported that the biggest source of happiness in their lives was 'having a successful career', well ahead of 'spending time with my family' (32%) and 'making money' (30%); and perhaps the most surprising result from this survey was that 67 per cent of these women believed that their country 'has reached the same level of workplace gender equality as Western countries, at least to some extent' (Bayt.com, 2014).

While there will be continuing deliberations about the effects of diversity initiatives on the bottom-line performance of companies, the international consulting firm Deloitte has concluded that debates about the benefits of gender diversity in business organisations 'are over'. For this international consulting business, 'the volatile, uncertain, complex and ambiguous world that all businesses now operate in makes employee diversity an organisational imperative ... making robust decisions and solving complex problems will only be possible if leaders are connected to, and include, diverse points of view. And, in relation to followership, leaders will need to behave highly inclusively, if they are to lead increasingly diverse and dispersed workforces' (Bourke and Dillon, 2015: 6). In comments that are of particular relevance to the countries of the MENA region, this report also underscored the emergent demographic trends that have been highlighted in previous chapters which:

> [W]ill change the workforce profile even more, putting greater pressure on leaders to be highly inclusive to allow individuals to succeed regardless of their irrelevant differences ... Leaders will require greater levels of adaptation of personal behaviours and organisational systems to bring out the best from this diverse talent pool ... Our prediction is that it is only those leaders who understand what it is to be truly inclusive who will be able to adapt and forge the way ahead
>
> *(Bourke and Dillon, 2015: 7, 17 and 36).*

These 'irrelevant differences' have been highlighted throughout this book and we will look at how organisations in the UAE, Oman and the KSA could make them a thing of the past in Chapter 9.

Although there are some encouraging signs of change it will be some time before a significant number of women rise to leadership positions in public- and private-sector organisations in these countries and in the broader MENA region. In part, this is a direct consequence of demographic realities. Most national employees are young and they are concentrated in junior and middle-management positions, and so it will be ten to twenty years before most of them are ready for the challenges associated with leadership roles. It is also important to remember that even the leading industrial economies of the OECD are still 'works in progress' when it comes to the partici-pation of women in their national labour markets and in terms of the number of women in leadership positions in those countries. In the West, while women made major inroads into all professions and occupations during the 1990s and 2000s, most were employed at the lower to middle levels of organisational hierarchies and many of them encountered discrimination at work. During the 2000s, few women made it into leadership positions in North American, European or Oceanic business organisations. In the United States, for example, women occupied 11.9 per cent of CEO positions in the private sector in 2002; in Australia, it was a paltry 1 per cent – down from 2.9 per cent in 2000. Fifty-three per cent of Australia's top 200 companies had no women in executive positions in 2002 compared to 14 per cent of US companies (Casella, 2001). These figures remained static during the 2000s, and the number of women directors in the United States actually declined slightly during the second half of this decade (Fox, 2006; Wittenburg-Cox and Maitland, 2008).

It is true that a small number of women have since become CEOs of some of the largest companies in the world. During 2011, Meg Whitman (former CEO of eBay) was appointed CEO of Hewlett-Packard and Virginia Rometty replaced Sam Palmisano as the first female CEO of IBM. But by May 2012, just seventeen women were CEOs of Fortune 500 companies, although this did represent an increase of more than 100 per cent from the meagre seven who were CEOs in 2003 and, by 2016, nearly 20 per cent of board directors in the United States were women, an increase from 16.9 per cent in 2013 (Catalyst, 2015; Parker et al, 2015: 13). In the UK, the very small number of women applying for executive positions in the private sector during the 2000s prompted the creation of Bird & Co Executive

Board and Mentoring by Kathleen O'Donovan, one of the country's most senior non-executives. Its mission was to coach, mentor and develop 100 women to make them 'board-ready' (Groom, 2009). By mid-2012, one quarter of UK companies had at least 25 per cent female membership on their boards (Dzhambazova, 2012), and the total number of women on the boards of the Financial Times Stock Exchange (FTSE) 100 companies had risen from 12.5 per cent in 2011 to 17.3 per cent in 2013 to nearly 23 per cent by 2016 (Peacock, 2013; Women on Boards, 2016). And, in what may be a sign that female representation on the boards of listed companies in Australia had reached a tipping point, the number of women directors exceeded 22 per cent in 2016 for the first time and 48 per cent of appointees during the first six months of the year were women (Australian Institute of Company Directors, 2016).

In Europe, two studies in the early 2000s revealed that women accounted for only 8 per cent of the top executive jobs in 235 European companies (Barta et al, 2012; Paradise et al, 2012). The relatively small ratio of women sitting on the boards of large firms in the European Union (13.7% in 2012) prompted Viviane Reding, the European Union's Justice Commissioner, to consider legislative action and, possibly, quotas to redress this inequity. Four notable exceptions to this general pattern of low representation were Norway, Finland, France and Sweden where, respectively, 35.5, 29.9, 29.7 and 28.8 per cent of company board positions were occupied by women in 2015. The figures for other countries in the Euro-region in 2015 were Belgium (23.4%), United Kingdom (22.8%), Denmark (21.9%), Netherlands (21.0%), Germany (18.5%), Spain (18.2%) and Switzerland (17.0%) (*The Economist*, 2012: 65). Overall, these data reveal a steady but not spectacular rise in the number of women in senior and board positions in business organisations in many countries over the last decade. There are, however, continuing disparities between men and women in all countries. In Australia, for example, while women constituted one third of managers in seventy-two large private-sector companies in 2015, they only occupied 25 per cent of senior management positions and just 14 per cent of executive-level roles in these organisations. The Workplace Gender Equality Agency, which has collected data from 4,600 Australian companies, believes that both cultural and structural barriers still hold women back and these are a consequence of 'our nation's cultural perceptions of the traditional roles of men and women at work. We have a strong notion of the male breadwinner that flows into workplace cultures' (Desloires et al, 2015: 1).

Even in countries where there is a reasonable degree of parity and equity between women and men, some curious gender discrepancies still persist. For example, while 80 per cent of the 1,835 Americans surveyed by Pew Research in 2015 believed that men and women make equally good leaders, 37 per cent felt that a woman would do a better job as the head of a major hospital or a retail chain (compared to 14% and 15% for men), but for a large bank or financial institution, the figures were 29 and 19 per cent. For a computer software company, the figures were 18 per cent for women and 29 per cent for men, 11 versus 46 per cent for a large oil or gas company and 8 versus 54 per cent for a professional sports team (Parker et al, 2015: 26 and 29). A study of 30,000 employees at 118 companies across 9 industrial sectors found that many organisations still face problems ensuring that women move up the career pipeline, 4 decades after national equal-opportunity laws were first introduced in the United States and many other countries. This report suggested that women 'are less likely to advance than men, hold fewer roles leading to top management positions, and are a century away from gender parity in the C-suite if progress continues at the pace that prevailed between 2012 and 2015' (Krivkovich et al, 2016: 1).

Certain sectors, such as industrial manufacturing, automotive, energy, mining/resources and technology are still unable to attract equal numbers of women for entry-level positions. This is not because any of these organisations discriminate against female applicants – it is a consequence of the low number of women who graduate in STEM disciplines. It does, however, limit the pool of female talent that is available for middle- and senior-management positions. Even in sectors where there is parity in entry-level recruitment between women and men (logistics and transportation, retail and consumer goods, healthcare and pharmaceuticals, hospitality and financial and professional services), there is a noticeable drop-off in the number of women in middle- and senior-management roles. To cite one example, in logistics and transportation, 48 per cent of entry-level employees are women, this falls to 30 per cent at the managerial levels, 21 per cent for senior managers and directors, 22 per cent for VPs, 17 per cent for senior VPs, and 13 per cent at the CEO level. The authors of this report concluded that this can happen because many of these companies preferred to fill vacant senior positions by importing a high percentage of 'lateral hires' or had inadequate succession and leadership development processes in place for their female employees in middle-management positions. This pattern was repeated across all nine industrial sectors, although once women had made it past the senior VP level they were then almost as likely as men to become CEOs (Krivkovich et al, 2016: 4–5 and 6).

Why aren't there more women in senior and executive positions in business in OECD countries? For the 1,835 American men and women surveyed by Pew Research in 2015, the top three reasons were: 'Women are held to a higher standard than men' (for 52% of women and 33% of men), 'Many businesses aren't yet ready to hire women for the top positions' (50%/35%), and 'Family responsibilities don't leave enough time for running a major corporation' (26%/20%). While few of this group believed that gender discrimination was a widespread problem, as many as 77 per cent of women and 63 per cent of men felt that further changes will be required to bring about full gender equality in American workplaces (Parker et al, 2015: 35 and 38). What this comparative information tells us is that even if the business case for gender diversity is now well established and broadly accepted by business organisations in the West, there are few companies in which women have achieved full professional equality with men, and stereotypical attitudes about women's aptitude for senior roles are still prevalent. It also confirms that even if countries in the MENA region were to significantly increase the participation of women in their national labour markets, it will take at least one generation before we see a significant number of women in business leadership roles.

8.6 CONCLUSION

If reform gains any momentum, I suspect it will come from the frustrations within the business community rather than from women or religious dissidents. Only business men have sufficient influence to counterbalance the religious establishment, plus princes invest in companies with increasing frequency.

Macfarquhar (2009: 359)

The evidence presented in this chapter demonstrates that there is a strong economic case for encouraging more women to work in the Arabian Gulf States, the broader MENA region and, indeed, in all emerging economies. The business case for gender diversity is also robust, although there may still be some uncertainties about the cumulative effect that women at the most senior levels have on corporate performance and bottom-line results. It is also significant that I have not come across a single study which has suggested that either the introduction of equal-opportunity legislation at the national level or introducing gender diversity policies at the company level have ever had any *negative* effects on either national economic growth or the performance of individual businesses. It appears then, as Deloitte and many others have suggested, that the debate about the cumulative macro-, meso- and micro-benefits of gender diversity are indeed 'over' and discrimination against women is, quite simply, bad for both national economic development and business performance. However, to reiterate the point, the evidence presented at the end of the preceding section also demonstrates that even in the world's leading industrial economies, systemic gender inequities do persist, particularly at the most senior levels of organisations.

The Arabian Gulf States and the MENA region operate in a global economy, one characterised by increasing job mobility between countries, growing competition in all industrial and business sectors, perpetual change and rapid technological innovation. The management of intellectual capital and knowledge is becoming one of the most important drivers of organisational performance and adaptability in these fast-changing market environments (Avent, 2016: 29–45 and 162–179). And this, in turn, is entirely dependent on the skills, abilities and engagement of employees. While most of the Arabian Gulf States and some other MENA countries still have a hydrocarbon cushion to rely on, this will not last forever and, as we have seen, the 'end of oil' is now firmly on the horizon for all of them. This means that every business operating in this region will have to consider how they are going to recruit and retain the very best talent, regardless of gender and ethnicity, in the future. If they do not, many of them will struggle to survive when the business opportunities and lucrative contracts generated by the region's oil and gas sectors no longer exist (Ellis et al, 2015). And, if they have visionary and forward-thinking leaders, some of them will already be thinking about and planning for this inevitable scenario. These leaders will already understand that the main reason for changing negative attitudes and behaviours towards women is because it will be good for their businesses. They know that this will help them enhance employee performance and enable them to become more responsive to the markets and environments they operate in and, ultimately, this will improve the performance and profitability of their businesses. They will realise that this is true even if they might not consider moral, ethical or legal reasons to be sufficiently important reasons for employing more women and embracing the principle of gender diversity.

However, it is true to say that the majority of the Emirati, Omani and Saudi men that I interviewed between 2008 and 2015 expressed anxiety and uncertainty about what all this might mean for their traditional roles, their families and their societies. Some were genuinely afraid of what they regarded as the 'feminisation' of organisations and the 'emasculation' of their male identities. Being the head of the family and the principal breadwinner is such an integral and deeply ingrained part of the masculine psyche in

Arabic-Muslim cultures that it will take a generation or two before they may become more accepting of less dominant roles (i.e. about the same length of time it has taken for this to happen in many non-Islamic countries). This, however, will not be easy for those men who do change how they think about working women and how they behave towards them, because as Sinclair has suggested:

> When men observe other men leading differently, there is often disbelief, censure, marginalisation, even ridicule. The man trying a new path by, for example, limiting the hours he works, is seen as 'under the thumb' (masculinity compromised by an assertive wife); 'not up to it' (finding an excuse for failure in the big-boy's world); or hopelessly diverted and rendered a limp and impotent SNAG*
>
> (Sinclair, 1998: 74. *Sensitive New Age Guy).

However, if the societal trends that have emerged in the leading Western industrialised countries are repeated in the MENA region over the next two decades, the vast majority of men who live there will not be the sole breadwinners in their families with dependent stay-at-home wives who never work outside the home. Such a scenario would not be feasible in any economy in which most women do work. And it is apparent from the evidence and data presented in earlier chapters that attitudes towards working women are changing, perhaps slowly and not as quickly as many women would hope, but they are clearly evolving, particularly among younger educated Emiratis, Omanis and Saudis and among some local political and business leaders. It is this generational shift that is likely to have the greatest impact on traditional stereotypes about women and, when these do start to change, they can evolve very quickly. The main challenge that still lies ahead is how to create an alternative vision of women:

> [T]hat can co-exist with differing or opposing trends and advance women's position in discourse and practice, not as a result of, but as one of the conditions for building the Islamic society they desire ... Arab society must find a new equilibrium for men and women based on nominal equality [and this] will require making

provisions for basic freedoms and constructing a civil society in the broader sense of the term

(United Nations, 2005: 21, 172).

Consequently, unleashing the full economic potential of women in the MENA region will require strategies that go well beyond what this report described as 'a merely symbolic makeover that permits a few distinguished Arab women to ascend to positions of leadership in state institutions.' Rather, 'this must extend to the empowerment of the broad masses of Arab women in their entirety ... and full opportunities must be given to Arab women for effective participation in all types of human activity outside the family on an equal footing with their male counterparts'. If this does not happen, this report concluded that they would be unable to participate effectively 'in the project for Arab Renaissance ... and achieve the full blossoming of their potential and a better future for all' (United Nations, 2005: 22, 24 and 220). How they can achieve this is described in the next chapter, but a good starting point can be found in a comment made by *The Economist* in 2014:

> Arab Muslims ... need to cast their minds back to the values that once made the Arab world great. Education, which underpinned its supremacy in medicine, mathematics, architecture and astronomy. Trade, which paid for its fabulous metropolises and their spices and silks. And, at its best, the Arab world was a cosmopolitan haven for Jews, Christians and Muslims of many sects, where tolerance fostered creativity and innovation. Pluralism, education, open markets; these were once Arab values and they could be so again ... for a people for whom so much has gone so wrong, such values still make up a vision of a better future
>
> (The Economist, 2014a: 10).

And, to repeat what has become a repetitive mantra in this book, it is not possible to imagine how this can be achieved without the active participation of many women in the nineteen countries of the MENA region in their political systems and, even more importantly, as equals with men in their economies and labour markets. A growing number of educated and liberal-minded women (and some men) no longer accept some of the core assumptions and values of the social and cultural systems they were born into, in particular the still-widespread view that women are somehow 'dangerous' to the established social order and must somehow be 'contained'. These beliefs are mirrored in every study cited in this book, and the message from those is clear: the countries of the Gulf and the broader MENA region must find ways to remove the constraints that are still imposed on women and allow them to make the fullest possible contribution to the growth of their national economies in the future. Having said this, I remain doubtful that we might see job advertisements in the Gulf States and other countries in the MENA region in the near future that contain statements like this:

> The University of Pennsylvania values diversity and seeks talented students, faculty and staff from diverse backgrounds. The University of Pennsylvania does not discriminate on the basis of race, color, sex, sexual orientation, gender identity, religion, creed, national or ethnic origin, citizenship status, age, disability, veteran status, or any other legally protected class status in the administration of its admissions, financial aid, educational, or athletic programs, or other University-administered programs, or in its employment practices ... Diversity is valued at Penn State as a central component of its mission, and helps create an educational and working environment that supports the University's commitment to excellence in teaching, research and scholarship
>
> (University of Pennsylvania, 2015).

However, it is now at least possible and maybe even conceivable that governments and public- and private-sector leaders in the MENA region could address – in more proactive and systemic ways – the issues of women's engagement in their national economies and also embrace the benefits of gender diversity in organisations; and we look at how they might be able to achieve this in Chapter 9.

9 Creating a Level Playing Field for Women in Public- and Private-Sector Organisations in the Arabian Gulf States and the MENA Region

9.1 INTRODUCTION

Having described the economic rationale and business case for the economic empowerment of women in emerging economies, we now turn to look at how women can be encouraged to participate in greater numbers in the national labour markets of the UAE, Oman, the KSA and the broader MENA region. We first focus on generic reforms that should be made to the national laws and regulations that affect women's legal rights and employment opportunities in these countries and the establishment of new ministries for women's economic empowerment and development. We then explain how educational opportunities and capability building for women can be enhanced and present specific policies that could be introduced in schools and universities to encourage more women to work in science, technology and engineering professions. In Section 9.3, we describe the HRM strategies that could be implemented by public- and private-sector organisations in these countries to encourage greater participation by women and the complex process of introducing gender-diversity policies. In Section 9.4, we describe several cost-effective strategies that can be implemented by regional governments to enable more women to become entrepreneurs and business owners. The conclusion asks if these strategies and policies are likely to be embraced by the UAE, Oman, the KSA and other countries in the MENA region in the future.

9.2 THE ROLE OF NATIONAL GOVERNMENTS IN FACILITATING LABOUR MARKET REFORMS

While there is no consensus about minimum expectations for gender-equality in society, clear standards, laws and regulations are needed. Governments can create the right climate through legislation while companies can collaborate with NGOs in advocacy to achieve more gender-friendly laws. The onus is on governments to create strong legal frameworks that protect the rights of women ... and to implement and enforce anti-discrimination legislation. [However] it is important to note that legislation and mandatory policies that create an enabling environment for women do not, on their own, address gender equality issues ... Therefore, the design and implementation of policies should be undertaken carefully.

Dobbs et al (2015: 87)

Many reports and studies have been published over the last two decades that have described the generic institutional, legal and social reforms that would be required to transform the political economies of the nineteen countries of the MENA region. While not downplaying the substance and importance of these, the main purpose of this section is to describe the broad-brush legislative changes that would have to be implemented in order to increase the participation of women in the economies and labour markets of these three countries, ones that could also be put into effect in other stable countries in the Arabian Gulf and the MENA region.[1] While there certainly are differences of emphasis and policy detail in these reports between, for example, neo-liberal free-market proponents and Keynesian economists, the analysts who wrote these are unanimous in their belief that any governments in the MENA region that are genuinely committed to improving the participation of women in their national labour markets will have to implement integrated national action plans that cover four principle domains of change. These are:

*Ratifying and Implementing, without Reservations or
Qualifications, All International Treaties and Conventions
Relating to the Legal Equality of Women*

Perhaps the most important step that governments of the UAE,
Oman, the KSA and other MENA countries could take is to ensure
full compliance with all UN treaties governing the legal rights and
treatment of women. This would be a ground-breaking decision
because it would mean, over a five- to ten-year period, that their
national laws would have to be brought into line with all the requirements of the United Nations CEDAW treaty, in particular the provisions contained in Article 2 which covers the principal of legal
equality for women. This would necessitate major legislative changes
including the creation of 'in-principle' equal-opportunity employment laws that conform to established best international practices
in leading OECD countries, setting time lines and targets for improving their rankings in the WEF's GGG reports and permitting the free
formation of autonomous women's associations and business organisations to help advance their economic, political, legal and social
interests. To facilitate this, the UAE, Oman and the KSA should
consider establishing well-resourced national ministries for women's
economic empowerment and development. These would create integrated five-year plans for increasing the participation rate of women
in their national economies, develop systemic policies to encourage
them to move from public- to private-sector employment and establish better support services and financing systems for female entrepreneurs and SME owners.

These ministries could also draft new policies and laws relating
to women for consideration by their legislatures and also ensure that
existing female employment laws, policies and Royal Decrees are
being applied uniformly across all public- and private-sector organisations. More broadly, they would also work to ensure that women's
rights to credit, land, capital and property are brought into line with
those of men in these countries. Other short-term measures that

could be taken to facilitate women's employment include abolishing the male-guardianship rules for women when they reach the age of eighteen, annulling the requirement to appoint male managers in businesses that employ or serve both men and women, easing hiring restrictions for female-owned businesses in staff positions that require international female (or male) skills and expertise or which cannot be filled by national employees, and easing the restrictions on women's geographical mobility, both domestically and internationally.[2] In the KSA, many women and some men also believe that the archaic ban on women driving must be lifted, although, because of the considerable logistical difficulties involved, this is unlikely to happen any time soon. Other measures that need to be taken in the KSA and Oman include improving the quality and responsiveness of the women's sections at government ministries and launching a nationwide, multi-media campaign to champion the right of women to work and the contribution they could make to the growth and diversification of their national economies.

Ensuring That All Girls and Women Have Full Access to Relevant High-Quality Education and Vocational Training at the Primary, Secondary and Tertiary Levels

Universal education at the primary and secondary levels has been largely achieved in the UAE, Oman and the KSA, but there are still, as we have seen in previous chapters, significant concerns about both the content and relevance of the curricula and the quality and style of teaching in their schools and tertiary sectors. In Oman and the KSA, and to a lesser extent in the UAE, there are still noticeable disparities between the curricula taught in these and the changing requirements of the economies and national labour markets of these countries. To quote from three studies which have been very critical of the general quality of education in MENA countries:

> The quality of education [in MENA countries] is a key challenge to women who aspire to leadership positions ... the Arab educational

system has traditionally placed little value on innovation, critical thinking or problem solving and does not encourage independent thinking or creativity ... There is also a lack of leadership training. Few if any leadership programs for young women exist in the Arab world. The curriculum for girls and boys places heavy emphasis on domestic responsibilities for women and work responsibilities for men and boys

(Dubai Women Establishment, 2009: 57).

Education is still widely seen as involving the acquisition, not of skills that might be put to use in productive work, but of qualifications that will secure entry into the kind of employment that confers upon the holder an appropriate social position. Another is a lack of capacity in crucial technical and scientific fields and a tendency, among many Oman university entrants, to avoid studying the subjects that might prepare them for productive work. These problems are exacerbated by the fact that demand for people with scientific and technical expertise can still often be satisfied by recourse to non-Omani professionals

(Jones and Ridout, 2015: 263).

The government must revamp both the educational and vocational training systems to better prepare women for the labour force – emphasising science, mathematics, foreign languages and information technology – and reduce the influence of harmful stereotypes. It should establish a life-long learning system of training and guidance that promotes entrepreneurship and self-employment, and Saudi workers must have access to professional development in the areas that matter most in a knowledge-based economy

(al-Munajjed, 2010a: 13).

While almost all girls in the UAE, Oman and the KSA attend primary and secondary schools and a growing number are enrolled at university and vocational colleges, further efforts should be made to ensure that more women have the opportunity to attend tertiary institutions and to improve mentoring and networking opportunities for these young women before they enter the labour market. One of the very few Western academics who has looked at leadership education for women in an Arabic context has also suggested that the curricula of all university courses should include a bigger component of critical and creative thinking, involve local female role models, provide more beneficial internship experiences and also teach practical skills and competencies for working in mixed-gender environments (Moore, 2009: 49). Private-sector companies could offer more fast-track graduate trainee scholarships for exceptional women graduates in order to encourage more of them to work in the non-government sector and to mentor them for middle-management and leadership positions in the future. A few local companies already do this. For example, Deloitte Dubai has offered three annual fast-track scholarships for Emirati graduates in finance, accounting and HRM since 2008.

There is also a pressing need for the introduction of major courses in entrepreneurship, innovation and small business management for young women (and men) at local universities. These, as noted in Chapters 5 and 7, are noticeably lacking in Oman and the KSA, and there is still further room for improvement in this domain in the UAE. In order to encourage more women to become entrepreneurs, all relevant courses at public universities in the UAE, Oman and the KSA should encompass a business development component which would cover entrepreneurship, small business management and business leadership skills. Until this happens, it is unlikely that a significant number of young tertiary-educated women in these countries will consider becoming entrepreneurs in the future. There is also a compelling case for involving local female leaders and business owners in the design of these courses and for them to become involved in the delivery of leadership workshops to female *and* male students who, one would hope, would also benefit from greater exposure to indigenous business women.

In order to encourage more women to work in STEM and CSIT professions in the Gulf States and the MENA region, four strategies could be implemented. The first is to ensure that science, technology and mathematics' subjects are well-integrated into all school curricula, particularly in girl-only schools in the UAE, Oman and the KSA. Girls could be more actively exposed to these subjects through activities such as field trips to high-tech and manufacturing companies, visits to appropriate conferences and exhibitions and presentations from women who have built their own technology businesses. One of the very few reports that has looked at the lack of women working in these professions has indicated that many young Emirati women are forced to choose either arts or science streams at the age of fifteen, and 'many choose arts because they perceive it as easier than science, resulting in an oversupply of arts and humanities students, which in turn exacerbates unemployment among nationals later in life', an educational trend that was also very evident in the KSA and Oman (*The Economist Intelligence Unit*, 2014: 12). Science, engineering and IT employers could be encouraged to play a more active role in encouraging Emirati, Omani and Saudi girls to embrace these types of careers by visiting secondary schools, particularly at the critical juncture when students are making choices about the subjects they will be studying in the last two years of their school education and at university.

Second, private-sector engineering and IT companies could offer scholarships and internships for exceptional female students in order to encourage more of them to choose these subjects at universities and vocational colleges. For example, the UAE Petroleum Institute launched its Women in Science and Engineering (WiSE) program in 2006 with 104 students. By 2014, it had more than 500 enrolled female students and more than 200 alumnae. The Dean of Women in Science and Engineering at this university, Nadia M. Alhsani, was one of the first women in the MENA region to be appointed to such a role. The aero structures firm Strata Manufacturing, which supplies Boeing, Airbus and other companies, employs around 600 staff, of whom more than one third are Emiratis and 80 per cent of these are women. They have achieved this, in the face of much early scepticism, by offering more internships to female undergraduates at local universities, recruiting them after they have graduated and creating a supportive and inclusive work environment (Petroleum Institute, 2016; *The Economist* Intelligence Unit, 2014: 13 and 19).

Third, in order to encourage more women to become technology entrepreneurs, all STEM and CSIT courses at public universities and vocational colleges in the Gulf States should include courses on business development. These would cover creativity, innovation and entrepreneurship; and all management and business courses could have a more significant IT component than they currently do. Fourth, women who work in the science, engineering and CSIT sectors and female entrepreneurs should be involved in the design of these courses and also become engaged in some of the teaching, with a strong emphasis being placed on techno-entrepreneurial practice rather than academic theory and textbook-based learning.

Encouraging Greater Participation by Women in Politics and a Greater Say in National Policy Formulation

The opportunities that women have to participate as equals in policy discussions and decisions that affect their lives are still very limited in most MENA countries, and this must change, particularly in the KSA and Oman. Although women are represented in the national assemblies of these countries, they are noticeably underrepresented at the most senior levels of government and as leaders of the major ministries in these countries. This means that there are few women who can advocate for new laws to promote the interests of national women or provide oversight of draft legislation that affect them. In the UAE, there are more women leaders in the country's public sector, and clear signs that women in their national assembly are having more influence on policy decisions that affect Emirati women. There is also some evidence that this is starting to happen (if slowly) in Oman and the KSA, although women outside these elite political forums are still not allowed to form independent networks, associations and organisations to represent their interests. Until more women are voted into office, these countries should consider appointing more women to the Federal Council in the UAE, the Majlis al-Wuzara in Oman and the Shura council in the KSA. We had noted in Chapters 2 and 4 that just one woman was elected to the national legislatures of the UAE and Oman in 2015, and just 1 per cent of these elected to municipal seats in the KSA in 2015 were women. The Oman result was described as 'disappointing' by the Omani human rights advocate Aisha Kharusi, and she believes that the only way to improve their representation in the country's national assembly would be by introducing quotas (Trabelsi, 2015).

This, however, could create a backlash among religious conservatives and so a better long-term option might be to first actively encourage more women to enter politics, second set aside additional resources to help them set up independent electoral offices and third encourage the state-controlled media to help them get their messages across to their supporters and potential voters at future elections. Most of the regional Chambers of Commerce and Industry in these countries now have elected female members, a positive trend that should be further encouraged. There is also a persuasive case for encouraging more women to become Islamic jurists (*faqihat*) and to embrace careers in the legal professions of Oman, the UAE, the KSA and other MENA countries. One noted Islamic legal scholar has argued that:

> The legal system is a product of society. As women leave the home to be educated, take jobs and see the world, the legal system must be re-evaluated. This is the experience worldwide, and it is no different in the Arab world ... The contradictions in books of interpretation and *Hadith* collections, like *Bukhari*, need the close scrutiny of scholars to show the fallibility of such 'sanctified' sources upon which much of the laws discriminating against women are based ... Arab governments should take a direct role in changing these laws
>
> *(Sonbol, 2009: 95–96).*

Female lawyers would be able to provide better representation for women who may be the victims of discriminatory behaviour in the workplace and abuse in the domestic sphere. They could also provide a necessary counter-balance to the very conservative mind-sets of the male-dominated judicial systems of these countries and, perhaps, make full use of *shari'a* principles that could be used as a basis for improving women's economic, legal and social rights. Female lawyers and judges could also review the strict work-segregation laws in the KSA and Oman with a view to modifying or reforming these. In the KSA, women's sections should be established in all regional court-rooms and in the Ministry of Justice in Riyadh in order to ensure that women have equal access to justice and are no longer required to be accompanied by a male relative.

Creating an Environment of Equitable Access to All Forms of Employment

This has not yet transpired in Oman and the KSA, but it has happened to some extent in the UAE. The evidence presented in Chapters 2 through 7 demonstrates that the participation rate of women in the labour markets of Oman and the KSA is very low by international standards, few work in the private sector and only a handful are business leaders, entrepreneurs and self-made business owners. The UAE has made the most progress in these domains, but there is still room for further improvement in that country. In all three countries the absence of laws and regulations that encourage female equality and gender diversity in their national labour markets continue to be major impediments to the equal participation of women in all professions and occupations. This lack of legal equality, as we have seen, also extends into the domestic sphere, restrictions on free movement, the male-guardianship laws, divorce and child-access rights and protection from male harassment and violence.

The governments of these countries could establish task forces, coordinated by their new ministries for women, encompassing the Ministries of Commerce and Industry, Labour and Education, which would develop a strategic policy framework for the advancement of women in their national labour markets. Comprising a balanced mixture of women and men recruited from public- and private-sector organisations, the SME sector, academia and local and international NGOs, these task forces would first gather reliable and detailed workforce statistics on women and then create comprehensive action plans, timetables for their implementation and supervisory frameworks for monitoring progress. These would be comprehensive at the macro-, meso- and micro-levels and would ensure that every aspect of their countries' national labour policies are monitored, evaluated and modified as needed. These bodies would also ensure that compliance with national and international labour treaties is enforced – including conventions on gender equality in the workplace – and would monitor the implementation of these by all public- and private-sector organisations. They could also begin to consider how strict gender segregation laws might be reformed. There is considerable legal ambiguity about these, and the extent to which these are enforced varies from region to region in the UAE, Oman and the KSA and in every other country in the MENA region. Nevertheless, these continue to be major disincentives for firms (including those led by women) to employ more female employees, as this often necessitates the creation of costly female-only facilities and work areas.

In addition to ratifying key international treaties and conventions, such as CEDAW, government ministries in the region could also encourage a more supportive environment for gender diversity by only entering into contracting arrangements with businesses that have non-discriminatory employee policies and fostering business opportunities with female suppliers, contractors and distributors. In Europe, Australia and New Zealand, for example, legislation enacted during the 2000s made it compulsory for all public companies to report on gender diversity in their annual reports and when bidding for commercial contracts with government agencies. They also need to make local business and public leaders more aware of the value of recruiting, retaining and promoting women employees; show support for the right to equal pay for equal work in their public pronouncements and internal employee HRM policies; support the right to equal employment opportunities for women; and also advocate for stronger workplace laws to protect the interests of female employees.

Changing perceptions of the role of women in society and the labour market will also play a critical role in changing negative attitudes towards women in the workplace, and although this is more of an issue in the KSA and Oman, it is still relevant to the UAE. Public awareness and media campaigns should be launched that challenge traditional gender stereotypes of women as mothers and housewives and promote the roles that women should play in the development of their national economies, as well as fostering more awareness of women who have become public- and private-sector leaders and those who have created successful new businesses. This would help promote more positive images and perceptions of women as employees, employers, entrepreneurs and business leaders which, over time, will change negative stereotypes about women in these roles (developed from Barsh and Yee, 2012; Darlberg Global Development Advisors, 2014; Devillard et al, 2012; Dubai Women Establishment, 2009: 77–80; Groysberg and Connolly, 2013; Ibarra et al, 2013; al-Munajjed, 2010a).

9.3 STRATEGIES FOR CREATING GENDER EQUALITY IN THE WORKPLACE

It has been pointed out many times that the process of transforming the lives of women in the MENA region has to be both a top-down and a bottom-up process, and the bottom-up impetus for change is growing year-by-year. Two decades ago, similar pressures for change were emerging in the United Kingdom:

> Since the beginning of the Industrial Revolution women have faced exclusion and organisations have suffered enormously as a result. Strategies to bring women into the centre of the enterprise during the last 15 years have been very successful, but much remains to be done. A younger generation of women are knocking at the door and it is time to take a decisive leap and start using

the knowledge and skill that women have in order to transform
the way that things get done. Women at all levels must take up
this challenge and settle for nothing less than everything in pursuit
of their empowerment

(Simmons, 1996: x).

Towards the end of this pioneering book, Simmons also observed that
'pressure from global marketplaces makes it inevitable that the only
organisations to survive will be those able to harness the intelligence,
creativity and initiative of all their people, and this will only be
possible if people feel that they are at the heart of the business ...
especially those who have been ignored for so long' (Simmons, 1996:
107). These quotes are also accurate descriptions of the situation
facing educated working women in the three Gulf States featured in
this book and in every other country in the MENA region. They too
are now dealing with the same cultural, attitudinal and structural
barriers that women encountered in Western countries during the
1970s, 1980s and 1990s as they entered predominantly male-
dominated public- and private-sector organisations and encountered
discrimination and exclusion. As Simmons also observed at that time:

The main block to establishing an inclusive organisation is the
way that discrimination and prejudice operate to exclude members
of particular groups. In my experience, discriminatory practices
and prejudices towards and individual or group of people, using
the excuse of their gender, race, disability, or any other aspect
of their identity, is the biggest single reason for the waste of
human potential in most enterprises and in society as a whole

(Simmons, 1996: ix).

At different speeds, often with great reluctance and sometimes as the
result of women taking legal action against them for discrimination,
all businesses in the West have woken up to these realities but most
are still dealing with their residual effects today. It is also true that
there remain major doubts about the extent to which countries in the
MENA region and their business and industrial sectors are likely to

accept the idea that more women should work in all professions and occupations. However, if they understand the economic rationale and business case for doing this, they do have one major advantage: they do not have to repeat all the expensive mistakes that countless male-dominated organisations in Western countries made when women did start working in large numbers during the last two decades of the twentieth century. They can also learn three important lessons from their experiences. First, almost every male-dominated organisation will (initially) be very resistant to the idea of gender diversity. Second, overcoming this resistance will require great determination and resilience. Third, every organisation has to move through four evolutionary stages before it can be described as being truly gender inclusive:

Stage 1: Denial

The issue of gender diversity does not register as even a dim blip on the organisation's radar. The absence of women across the organisation and in in senior management positions is not regarded as either a problem or a core business issue. If the organisation is operating in a country that has equal-opportunity legislation, the primary objective will be compliance with this and avoiding any negative consequences of non-compliance. Typical (male) rationalisations for not employing more women during this stage will include: 'We don't employ women here because they don't want to do this kind of work, they are incapable of doing this kind of work, they are less rational than men, not as intelligent, not as strong/tough/resilient as men, they will leave to have babies after we have trained them' and 'they should be at home looking after their children'.

Stage 2: The Problem Is Women

There is some awareness that the employment of women and gender diversity may be issues that the organisation should be considering, but initiatives that go beyond legal compliance are not supported by either senior management or most of the male workforce. Any initiatives that are introduced to support women are *ad hoc* and sporadic. Typical and widespread (male) rationalisations that hold women back at this stage will include: 'Women are incapable of being senior managers because they are less rational than men, not as intelligent, not tough/resilient enough, will leave to have babies after we have trained them and/or not come back after maternity leave'; and 'If women want to get into senior positions, they should manage like men do'. The absence of women in senior positions will be explained away by comments such as, 'Women lack senior management experience so we can't promote them' rather than asking 'Where can we find female employees with the potential to succeed at senior management levels?'

Stage 3: Incremental Adjustment

There is a growing awareness in the organisation that gender and diversity may be HRM issues that need addressing. It will obey the letter if not the spirit of legal regulations covering equal pay and discrimination against women. There is some understanding that diversity could improve employee recruitment, staff retention, employee and organisational performance and the company's image and reputation. Some efforts may be made to promote women's interests by, for example, introducing minimum quotas for women in selection and recruitment procedures. Employee audits may be conducted to assess the extent of the problem and what might be done about it. Typical rationalisations at this stage for not doing more for women will include: 'We operate on meritocratic principles. If they're good enough, they'll get promoted to the top jobs' rather than asking 'Why don't more women apply for senior positions in this organisation?' or 'Why are there so few women in middle-management roles? Or, 'Do our promotion systems discriminate against women or discourage them from applying for senior positions?' Or, 'Well, if they want the top jobs, they can't buzz off at five o'clock to look after the kids' rather than asking 'How can we make our employment policies more family friendly for women *and* men?'

Stage 4: Commitment to an Inclusive Organisational Culture

'Women's issues' have evolved into 'diversity and talent management issues' and this stage also signifies a shift from focusing on equality to an emphasis on parity, where the needs of men and women are seen as being different but of equal importance. The organisation has recognised that it needs to create a working culture that is equitable and inclusive for all employees and every effort is being made to remove any cultural, attitudinal, structural barriers that still hold women back. There is recognition, at the most senior levels, that this will be good for the overall performance, productivity and profitability of the organisation. Specific targets are set for recruiting women and, once they are employed, promoting them within the organisation. Conscious efforts are made to build equity principles into recruitment policies, employee induction processes, staff development and internal promotion policies. Flexible employment policies recognise that employees may have partners and children and strive to be 'family-friendly'. The organisation is creating an inclusive culture in which all employees feel valued and respected; one where they are evaluated and promoted solely on the basis of their performance, not their gender (or ethnic origin).

The only remaining questions that the organisation now needs to ask are: 'Can we say that we truly a gender-diverse and inclusive company and is this commitment fully integrated into our operating culture and HRM policies?' and 'Do able and talented women outside our organisation regard us as a potential employer of choice?' The end objective of this evolutionary stage is to create an organisation that is able to look above and beyond stereotypical attitudes about women (and men), one that is characterised by a culture that is 'capable of harnessing the intelligence, creativity and initiative of people at all levels, especially those who have been traditionally excluded [and which] reaches beyond equality to an organisation where there are no boundaries or limitations placed on anyone' (Simmons, 1996: x; see also, Sinclair, 1998).

It is reasonable to assume that most indigenous public- and private-sector companies in the UAE, Oman and the KSA are at Stages 1 and 2, although a few, as we saw in Chapter 8, are entering Stage 3. However, any organisations that hope to make the transition through Stage 3 to Stage 4 will have to introduce gender-diversity policies. These are described below, and the main elements of this process and the time-line for introducing these, are summarised in Table 9.1.

TABLE 9.1 *Implementing gender diversity policies in organisations*

1. Secure CEO, board and senior management support (3–6 months).
2. Discuss and understand the business case for gender diversity and incorporate this into the organisation's strategic business agenda (6–12 months).
3. Collect gender-disaggregated data on female employees (diagnosis), develop a strategic gender-diversity action plan (prognosis) and set quantitative targets and metrics for women's employment and representation in the organisation (9–12 months).
4. Introduce gender-equality and diversity policies (1–3 years).
5. Concurrent with 4, establish women's development programs, including mentoring systems, management and leadership workshops and introduce HRM programs designed to increase the number of women in senior positions (1–5 years).
6. Build an inclusive working culture that fully incorporates the organisation's gender-diversity objectives (5–10 years).

Committed Leadership Support

All of the studies cited in Chapter 8 have emphasised the vital role that committed leadership plays in championing gender-diversity initiatives, and one of the biggest barriers to successfully implementing these is 'a low level of commitment from the CEO and top management' (Werner et al, 2010: 7). Diversity programs cannot succeed in any organisation unless these have been embraced, endorsed and championed by its leader and the leadership group. In turn, this will require the creation of an executive-level position for gender, diversity and inclusion and a cross-functional change team made up of senior, middle and junior employees. This group must demonstrate that diversity is a *business* priority and courageously model the way through their leadership behaviours and actions and by communicating this message repeatedly in one-to-one dialogues, in informal groups and in formal meetings. If gender diversity is an organisational priority, then it has to be conveyed to all employees in exactly the same way as any other operational or strategic objective. This means that the leader and leadership of the organisation must constantly champion the business benefits of gender diversity and participate in as many planning meetings, information sessions and gender-diversity workshops as they can. And if they are smart, they will present a rationale for gender diversity that appeals to both heads and hearts and explain the personal journey that led them to believe in the importance of gender diversity and inclusiveness. Only when this commitment is visible and unequivocal can change begin to happen and, if they can present a compelling business case for the advantages of gender diversity and lead the way onto this new organisational path, their employees will eventually follow (Kotter and Cohen, 2002; Kouzes and Posner, 2008).

Integrated with Business and Human Resource Management Strategies

Gender diversity should be treated like any other business initiative: as one that requires commitment, adequate resources, a clear value proposition and action plan, specific targets and goals, metrics to monitor progress towards these and ongoing monitoring and evaluation of the change program. The action plan must include strategies and targets for recruiting, developing, mentoring, retaining and promoting women and a clear commitment to gender inclusion at all stages in the employer–employee relationship. Many of the studies cited in Chapter 8 and this chapter show that there is a clear relationship between the detail and rigour of gender-diversity programs and equal-opportunity policies, how well companies monitor the progress they are making towards achieving gender-diversity targets and the successful implementation of these over time. One of the McKinsey studies cited in Chapter 8, for example, concluded that the measure that was likely to have the greatest effect on the successful imple-mentation of gender-diversity initiatives was the 'visible monitoring of gender-diversity programs by the CEO and executive team' (Werner et al, 2010: 6). However, as Barsh and her McKinsey colleagues have observed:

> No two companies will start this journey from the same point. Each company's combination of heritage, location, regulation and aspiration is unique. That said, all companies are on a similar transformation journey. Companies can take a handful of practical steps at any stage: just getting serious about accelerating progress, scaling up successes to move the needle, or embedding the change to sustain the transformation ... Each company's transformation plan depends on its industry context and starting point – but wherever companies are today is a great place to start
>
> *(Barsh and Yee, 2012: 10 and 2).*

Hence, all successful diversity programs begin with a diagnostic stage, followed by a detailed prognosis and then the development of a strategic action plan that is customised to fit the specific oper-ational and HRM requirements of each organization; there is no one-size-fits-all strategy for achieving this. The diagnostic stage is critical, because this provides a clear, evidence-based picture of the status of women in the organisation. This means understanding the gender balance at all levels of the organisation and by function, business unit and region, as well as pay levels, recruitment, selection and retention policies and the number of female employees who are being promoted across the organisation in staff, support and oper-ational line roles. While gender-disaggregated quantitative data is essential, qualitative data that can tap into staff perceptions and concerns about gender-diversity initiatives should also be collected.

It is likely that all companies will have some information about these in their employee records, but this may require additional resources and further work to garner accurate information on how many women apply for jobs or are interviewed for promotions, their pay levels and salary differentials (compared to men), turnover rates, how many are in middle- and senior-management positions, their work engagement and job satisfaction, and so forth.

This information then leads to the prognostic stage and identifying what the gaps and challenges are, the development of strategies to increase the number of female employees, establishing what targets (or quotas) should be set for this and the promotion of women within the organisation, the creation of an action plan and a likely timeline that will be needed to achieve these objectives. Several of the studies cited in Chapter 8 have shown that organisations with clear starting and end points are more successful at implementing diversity initiatives than those who do not establish these at the outset. For example, an organisation with very few female employees might set a target that 20 per cent of all new recruits will be female within three years and 40 per cent within six years. It could also specify that within three to five years, 10 to 20 per cent of these should be ready for promotion into middle-management positions. It might also set targets for appointing more senior women from outside the company to leadership and board roles within, say, five years. This, in turn, enables the organisation to build a female talent pipeline for the future. And, as Barsh and her McKinsey colleagues have suggested, 'If greater representation of women in the talent pipeline promises a competitive advantage, successful leaders will work hard to include them. If greater female representation better serves the company's customers, those leaders will make that happen' (Barsh and Yee, 2012: 8).

Gender-diversity policies will often be regarded as a threat by many men but not all. Successful programs emphasise the common needs of all employees and address the concerns, real or perceived, that some men may have. It can be pointed out, for example, that incumbent men will not have fewer opportunities for promotion, only that more candidates for these positions will be women in the future, and it can be emphasised that there will be no prejudicial changes to existing performance-management policies, mentoring arrangements, career-development opportunities, leadership training and succession-planning systems. This can help to ameliorate perceptions that these new policies are 'only for women' or that women need 'remedial training' and 'extra help' in order to gain promotions or become leaders. One powerful way to sell the idea of gender diversity is through illustrative stories and case studies, particularly those that show how diversity has benefitted every single organisation that has moved in this direction and, of equal importance, the compelling business case for doing this. The views of both men and women, at all levels of the organisation, are important. Male employees should be included in this process, and there should be regular forums in which their concerns can be discussed and addressed.

In this context, one very important decision that will have to be made is whether to introduce quotas for female employees. Advocates of quota systems believe these can create an impetus for change, promote the belief that organisations are serious about diversity initiatives and also encourage women to apply for promotions to middle- and senior-management positions in male-dominated organisations. For example, a recent report on gender inequalities in the United Kingdom's labour market recommended that 'mandatory quotas be introduced to ensure greater gender balance in decision making positions ... Quotas backed by legislation are one of the most effective ways of effecting change; they are more effective than soft company initiatives and help ensure that society and firms reflect diverse ideas and talents' (London School of Economics, 2016: 5 and 21). The United Nations has also advocated for the introduction of quotas for women in all of its Arab Human Development reports because 'it would allow the dismantling of the centuries-old structure of discrimination against women' (United Nations, 2005: 221); and as Noland and her colleagues have suggested:

> If increased gender diversity in corporate leadership contributes to
> firm performance, if quotas have negligible costs, and if the
> presence of women in the C-suite encourages the pipeline effect
> by encouraging more women to pursue these positions ... then
> some kind of quota system may warrant consideration,
> particularly if the dearth of women in these positions at least
> in part, reflects pure discrimination ... Mandating a percentage
> of women on boards for a set number of years, for example,
> could mitigate such biases
>
> (Noland et al, 2016: 16).

An early example of the use of quotas in a business organisation is
Coca-Cola, where former CEO Steve Reinemund implemented hiring
and recruiting policies in 2001 that required half of all new hires to be
either women or recruits from ethnic minorities. A component of
managers' bonuses was calculated by how well they recruited and
retained these groups. By 2005, 25 per cent of the company's employees were women, up from 12 per cent in 1997. There were no women
or employees from minority backgrounds in executive positions in
2000; by 2006 there were six (Yang, 2006: 20). Since this time, many
other businesses have introduced quotas (or 'targets') for female
employees, including the Lloyds Banking Group. In 2014, 28 per cent
of its senior management positions were occupied by women, and
this company has set a target of 40 per cent by 2020. Barclays, another
UK bank, is in the process of increasing the proportion of women in
senior roles from 21 to 28 per cent by 2018 (Financial Times, 2014: 4).
Several European countries have legislated mandatory targets for
women on corporate boards, including Iceland, Norway, Finland,
Sweden, France, Germany and Italy. The German government has
made it mandatory for more than 100 of the country's biggest companies to have a minimum of 30 per cent female representation on
their boards by 2020. All public and private companies above a certain
size now have to set targets for the number of women on their boards
and also publish annual reports on their progress towards meeting
these. In France, similar requirements introduced in the early 2000s

led to a doubling of the number of women on company boards to nearly 30 per cent by 2014. Although there has been opposition to these changes, 'analysis appears to show that quotas work and have been highly successful across Europe. This could result in a quota system being implemented at the EU level' (Barrett, 2014: 6). Advocates of quota systems also suggest that initial targets can be set fairly low and steadily increased over time until a more equitable balance is achieved.

However, opponents of quotas (a group that includes many women in business leadership roles) believe that these are, *ipso facto*, discriminatory and will be viewed in a very negative light by most men and some women. They can also create the perception that recruitment and promotion are not based on merit and also foster the belief that women in senior positions are 'tokens' or 'golden skirts'. One report has suggested that job advertisements that specified 'quotas for women' actually made firms less attractive to both male and female applicants (25% and 13%, respectively) in the belief that 'a gender quota negated the importance of merit'. This, as the authors of this study noted, does not mean that companies should abandon the goal of employee diversity; rather, they need to focus on the 'pull' factors that would encourage talented women to *choose* to work for them rather than another employer and how to create work cultures in which employees are promoted solely on the basis of merit and performance (Shemla and Kreienberg, 2014). And, as the Secretary General of the European Confederation of Directors Associations Beatrice Richez-Baum has observed, 'A more diverse board, including gender diversity, promotes a richer debate in the boardroom. However, women should be chosen because of their qualifications and not because they are women' (Sullivan, 2015).

It is also noteworthy that while most of the ninety-four female Arabic leaders who were interviewed for the Arab Women Leadership Outlook report in 2009 did believe that quotas were appropriate to help increase the current low level of women's participation in their countries' political systems, they were very sceptical about the efficacy of this approach in business organisations in the MENA region. They believed that performance should be the primary criteria for appointing and promoting women, and also felt that positive discrimination and quotas would, on balance, probably do more harm than good in an Arabic-Islamic context (Dubai Women Establishment, 2009: 38). Furthermore, none of the women that I interviewed in the UAE, Oman and the KSA were advocates of gender quotas, believing that this would not be an effective remedial strategy in their countries. But, having looked at both sides of this debate, it is also reasonable to conclude that it would be a pointless exercise for any organisation to introduce gender-diversity policies unless *some* targets for recruiting and promoting female employees, however conservative, are established and achieved. And, if judgments about the hiring and promotion of employees are based entirely on merit and performance, then there is no need for the implementation of rigid gender quotas.

Is Systemic and Systematic

It has been estimated that 90 per cent of Fortune 100 companies in the United States had a chief diversity officer in 2015, all publicly listed companies had policies covering employee diversity, a growing number of companies were publishing diversity data, and the diversity-training business was valued at $8 billion. A single company, Intel, announced in 2015 that it was planning to spend $300 million over three years to improve the gender and ethnic mix of its workforce and to 'improve the inclusiveness of its culture' (McGirt, 2016 49–50). The study of twenty-four pro-diversity CEOs cited in Chapter 8 concluded that companies with the most gender-inclusive cultures had committed leadership support, systematically measured diversity and inclusion, held all managers accountable for diversity, provided leadership development programs for women at all levels, had companywide mentoring programs for female employees, had strong female role models in senior positions and had created a well-resourced senior diversity team headed by a chief diversity officer (Groysberg and Connolly, 2013). This report also suggested that diversity programs must be systemic and systematic if they are to be successful, and meaningful change cannot happen if an organisation simply tinkers with these initiatives and only tries to change a few things. This will require an overhaul of its entire HR strategy and policies, including labour-market outreach, internship policies, recruitment, interviewing and appointment processes, employee performance management, retention and promotion policies, mentoring arrangements, career management and leadership development programs, discretionary pay and rewards for managers and work–family balance policies. It also means that changes will have to be made to the organisation's promotional, marketing, job advertising, Internet, web and social media profiles by, for example, ensuring that 'she/her' appears as often as 'he/him' in these materials and including pictures of female employees and leaders.

One way organisations in the MENA region can learn quickly about gender-diversity initiatives is to learn from best-practice examples in other countries, and there many instances of companies that have decided to consign gender inequality to history. The example which now follows provides several useful insights into how the goal of creating a level playing field for female employees can be fully realised, but it also reinforces the point that this can only happen if the leadership of a business is fully committed to this transformation and understands the importance of embedding these changes in the company's operating culture and HRM policies. This corresponds to Stage 4 in the sequence described earlier and is the most difficult part of this evolutionary process. The example is BHP Billiton, one of the largest mining and resource companies in the world which was, for much of its history, dominated by men. However, in more recent times, it has employed a much larger number of women not only in managerial roles but also in a variety of technical roles in the company's mines – as geologists, engineers, truck drivers – and in other operational roles. BHP Billiton also has the obligatory corporate vision, mission and core values statement on its website and, like many other companies these days, it also has a written commitment to employee diversity:

> Our corporate strategy is based on owning and operating assets diversified by commodity, geography and market. To achieve this, we also need a workforce that reflects diversity in all forms, including gender, skills, experience and ethnicity. Embracing trust, openness, teamwork, diversity and relationships that are mutually beneficial, reflects our core value of Respect and is the focus of our people strategy. In all our efforts, we aim to be inclusive and build pride and loyalty in our workforce
>
> *(BHP Billiton, 2016a).*

This company is also unequivocal about the importance of its equal-opportunity policies:

> Employment, development opportunities and promotion at BHP Billiton are offered and provided on merit. All employees and applicants for employment will be treated and evaluated according to their job related skills, qualifications and abilities. Decisions based on attributes unrelated to job performance, such as race, gender, sexuality or family responsibilities, constitute unlawful discrimination and are prohibited
>
> *(BHP Billiton, 2016b: 14).*

Unfortunately, as many organisations have realised over the last two decades, well-meaning statements about gender diversity contained in policy documents on their websites mean little unless the principles and values they espouse are embedded in their cultures and in the attitudes and work behaviours of all their employees. This, as the CEO of BHP Billiton Andrew Mackenzie admitted in early 2016, had not yet happened in his company. While working for British Petroleum in the 1990s, he had realised that his work environment was characteristic of the Anglo-American resource sector at that time – white, male and heterosexual. After being seconded to the US oil company Amoco, he encountered a company that was making a concerted effort from the top to the bottom to creating a more gender and ethnically diverse workforce, and he also witnessed the beneficial effects of this on the performance of both employees and the company. He recalls that 'if you were an African-American engineer or a woman you would choose Amoco over all the other oil companies, and all the stats showed that. There are a lot of very successful women who started at Amoco because it was a place where they were pulled through' (Maiden, 2016). After he became the CEO of BHP Billiton in May 2013, he soon had to deal with the global commodity price slump during 2014–2015 and the tragic dam breach at the company's Samarco iron ore venture in Brazil. However, his experience at Amoco prompted him to create a group-level Inclusion and Diversity Council in November 2015, a group that he also chairs. While incorporating the heads of the company's main operations, it also includes managers of different ages, levels, gender, ethnicity and sexual orientation.

He is keen to set firm diversity targets because his experience at Amoco taught him that 'whether you like it or not, even if you don't know it, we all have – are guilty of – unconscious bias. You can do it through lots of education, or you can confront it a bit more by having blunt targets' (Maiden, 2016). Mackenzie and his 'Chief People Officer' Athalie Williams believe that this is not simply a 'politically correct' matter of creating 'a diverse workforce'; it is much more about 'tapping the best brains on the planet'. To achieve this means attracting, and retaining, the best young people 'who are at their most productive, their most inspirational, their most quick-witted. We need to be attractive to them by having a modern approach to sexuality, race and inclusion. When they get here there should be absolutely no discrimination and a sense that they can flourish.' The company's workforce is now about 25 per cent female and ethnically diverse, and although the number of female senior executives is just 17 per cent a growing number of women are ready to move into these more senior positions (Maiden, 2016).

In a more localised illustration of these company-wide changes in BHP, when Mike Henry took over as head of marketing for BHP Billiton

in Singapore a few years ago, he was happy with the overall performance of his division but felt that there was much greater untapped
potential because gender and ethnic diversity was minimal. He attributes this to 'unconscious bias, a lack of capability and a lack of real
commitment' (Gray, 2015: 7). To change this, he brought in expert help
from outside the company for advice and also established a new leadership position, a head of diversity and inclusion. He also realised that if
he was going to create a more diverse and gender-balanced marketing
division he would have to model the way towards this objective:

> You need to make it a priority – you need to lead from the front – to
> overcome barriers. You have to make yourself vulnerable in the
> interests of the cause. You need to ensure that the leaders you
> cultivate are equally committed to the cause of leading in that way
> and your ability to rally people to the cause ensures that nothing is
> able to withstand the momentum that you create ... Diversity is
> now the main game. It's strategically important and Andrew
> McKenzie has made it clear that it's part of his leadership agenda
>
> (Gray, 2015: 8).

It took several years to embed these changes in the working culture
and HR processes of this division, but female representation in
BHP's executive marketing team has since grown to 40 per cent.
Since moving to a new role as the president of BHP's coal business,
Henry has boosted the representation of women and employees from
different ethnic backgrounds in that division. For Henry, gender
diversity aligns with his personal beliefs and a sense of fairness and
also with BHP's core values. He has also said that 'I am someone
who is very rational and there is a very strong business case for both
diversity and inclusion. I am someone who has a lot of energy for
excellence, and if you really want to have this as both an individual
and collectively, you have to have an inclusive culture' (Gray, 2015:
9). For the company's CEO, there is also no going back to the old
days: 'We are starting further back than some of the other [business]
sectors – we've got to think creatively. But, we're committed to
doing more and doing it more quickly than we've done. Where we

are today is not acceptable, and we are absolutely committed to shifting the dial' (Maiden, 2016).

Is Measurable and Requires Accountability

As with all organisational activities and processes, gender-diversity programs require monitoring and, when required, adjustments and corrections. This requires metrics for measuring the progress that is being made towards greater diversity, including, for example, indicators for hiring, developing, retaining and promoting women and the inclusion of gender-diversity indicators in performance reviews. There are three principal stages involved in evaluating the introduction of diversity initiatives:

> Establishing base-line employee data, identifying key stakeholders, deciding which employee metrics to use, identifying the resources needed for data collection and establishing and monitoring gender diversity tracking-systems.
>
> Analysing the data and business metrics before and after the introduction of the diversity policies, comparing costs and benefits, monetising diversity outcomes and return-on-investment wherever possible (i.e. the cost of introducing and implementing diversity policies and the quantitative financial gains over time), and getting feedback from key stakeholders on the conclusions and implications of the data analyses.
>
> Documenting the benefits to the organisation and disseminating this information internally and externally. Nearly all organisations have KPIs and/or metrics that can be used to evaluate the monetary value and business benefits of changes that they make to their HRM policies such as the higher quality of new recruits, reduced labour turnover and absenteeism, improved employee retention and performance and productivity gains
>
> *(International Finance Corporation, 2013b: 51).*

At W.L. Gore & Associates, the successful and innovative American manufacturing company that has been featured in several Harvard

Business School case studies, CEO and president Terri Kelly is a firm believer in developing metrics for diversity initiatives:

> At Gore we believe that diversity of all kinds – gender, race, cultural identity – invariably drives better business outcomes from our teams, whether we're working on new products, sales or manufacturing products. Our starting point has been to raise awareness of these benefits. This does not mean, as some of us many have assumed initially that our culture on its own will take care of the problem. We now have tools that help us to view HR and other processes through a diversity lens so that we consider the full range of talented associates* for key positions. It is essential to track and monitor the progress of women as we evaluate our needs for current and future leaders ... I feel that we are at a tipping point and there's a lot of energy and peer-pressure building up to make further progress
>
> *(Barsh and Yee, 2012: 10; * this is Gore's word for 'employees' – many of these are shareholders in the company).*

Accountability means exactly that: it reinforces the message that gender diversity is a priority, and managers will be held accountable for the recruitment, treatment, retention and promotion of women. Clearly defined expectations and targets must be communicated across the organisation and down through all managerial levels to the front line. Goals and timetables should be set and annual progress reports produced, and discretionary incentives and rewards can be linked to managers' performance in meeting desired diversity goals and outcomes. Such metrics help imbed diversity initiatives into the organisation's working culture by integrating targets and measures in the day-to-day operational realities of management, and they also help managers to evaluate the progress they are making with diversity initiatives.

Is Responsive to the Needs of Female Employees

One of the most important tasks for organisations that have introduced gender-diversity initiatives is to create HRM and talent-development systems that will enable them to promote more women into middle- and senior-management positions in the future. As we saw in Chapter 8, this is an issue that many businesses outside the MENA region are still wrestling with. For example, while only twelve of the firms in Barsh and Yee's study of sixty large companies had more than 50 per cent of their most senior positions filled by women, these organisations shared two key characteristics. First, they all had 'fat funnels', which meant that well over 50 per cent of their entry-level recruits were women. As a result, with female-friendly development and training policies, about 40 per cent of their mid-level positions were filled by women. Second, they had companywide HR policies that kept this ratio steady for the most senior positions and had also established mentoring programs to help women grow into these roles (Barsh and Yee, 2012: 4).

A parallel study by another team of McKinsey consultants of 235 European companies has highlighted the manner in which women drop out of consideration for the most senior positions in many companies at the top of the 'talent funnel'. They too identified the two key enablers identified by Barsh and Yee and determined that there was a correlation between the number of women in senior positions in these companies and the rigour of the HR policies that they had put in place to support this. Conversely, those with 'limited diversity practices' had the smallest number of women in senior positions. They concluded that:

> The best performing companies in terms of the proportion of senior positions filled by women ... excel on three particular fronts: they have the highest levels of management commitment, they monitor women's representation carefully, and they seek to address men's mind-sets the better to support gender diversity. Not coincidentally, these companies are those that are the most diligent in driving through their gender diversity programs
> (Devillard et al, 2012: 1; 13–14).

This means that if diversity initiatives are to succeed, it is not enough just to 'hire more women'; organisations must also ensure that adequate mentoring/development and objective performance appraisal systems are established to facilitate their growth and advancement. Mentoring can obviously benefit those who are being mentored, but it can also be of value to male mentors who may not be used to working with capable, ambitious and motivated young women. Despite negative stereotypes about men, most have a paternal and nurturing streak and becoming sponsors of able women may also help in ameliorating the negative attitudes they might have about the abilities of younger female employees. Organisational leaders can also set a positive example for senior and middle managers by becoming sponsors of female employees. For example, Alan Joyce – the CEO of the Australian airline Qantas – realised that if he did not actively and publicly mentor female employees, then his senior managers were unlikely to do so. This led him to audit the amount of time that he was dedicating to this over a six-week period and then increase it. This audit 'was hugely symbolic in its own right and served as a model for other leaders in his organisation' (Bourke and Dillon, 2015: 24).

In many organisations, there will also be a need to create women-only management and leadership-development workshops. The best women's leadership programs do focus on knowledge and skills development, but they also emphasise personal mastery and self-confidence. This encourages women to become responsible and accountable for proactively managing their own careers and to become more comfortable with exercising authority over male employees (Barsh and Yee, 2012 Ibarra et al, 2013). This is clearly something that would be both appropriate and applicable in male-dominated organisations in the MENA region. As we saw in Chapters 6 and 8, this is exactly what Saudi Aramco is doing in the KSA, where the company's Women in Business and Women in Leadership programs were established to develop female middle-managers for leadership positions. Many Saudi companies, government agencies and educational organisations have since approached Saudi Aramco to help them launch similar programs for their female employees.

Addresses Negative Gender Stereotypes

No one likes to believe that they are biased towards those they perceive as being 'different', but we all are to some extent. Most men in patriarchal societies have preconceived notions about the intrinsic natures of women and their 'appropriate' roles in society and the workplace which unconsciously guide their attitudes and behaviours towards female colleagues (the opposite of this is, of course, also true). Given that these biases are deeply ingrained, it requires considerable time and a great deal of effort to change them, as illustrated by the examples of the US military and Harley-Davidson in Chapter 8 and BHP Billiton in this chapter. The good news is that diversity workshops that address these views have been used successfully in thousands of organisations and are, if handled well, a non-threatening way to address negative stereotypes about the competence and capabilities of women. It is, to repeat the point, critical that the leadership group of the organisation is actively involved in these with the diversity team, because this signifies a genuine commitment to gender inclusiveness.[3]

In organisations that have been, historically, very male dominated, it may well be appropriate to call on third-party expertise to advise on the content and delivery of diversity-training workshops. These can include NGOs, advocacy groups, other local companies that have introduced diversity policies and specialist training organisations such as the consulting and training company Borderless. It is equally important that all HR and performance policies are transparent, applied consistently and based on accurate and objective information. It may also be appropriate to introduce an 'employee charter' or 'statement of values' which explicitly describes how all employees should be treated, any behaviours that are considered to be off limits (e.g. sexual or racial discrimination and harassment) and how aggrieved employees make seek redress if they believe they have been the victims of inappropriate conduct.

Recognises the Importance of Work–Family Balance

The emerging field of feminist economics, or 'womenomics', has focused on continuing global gender inequalities, continuing salary differentials between women and men in many occupations, and the perennial lack of women in executive positions in business and political leadership roles. It has also highlighted the covert and subtle forms of discrimination that still prevent women from working and, when they do work, from rising to senior positions in their professions. As *The Economist* has observed:

> When men announce they are about to have a child, they are
> simply congratulated; when women do, they are congratulated and
> then asked what they plan to do about work. Given the strength
> and persistence of societal expectations about women's role in
> parenting, presenting their choices in that regard as purely personal
> is misleading at best, and a sop to sexism at worst ... by leaving
> unpaid work out of the national accounts, the feminist argument
> goes, economists not only diminish women's contribution, but also
> gloss over the staggering inequality in who does it. Of course, in a
> perfectly equal world, men would do much more child-rearing than
> they currently do. In the meantime, it's women who are
> disadvantaged by economists' failure to measure the value of
> parenting properly
>
> *(The Economist, 2016h: 72).*

Women, on average, do about 75 per cent of the world's total unpaid care work. This includes essential tasks such as child care, domestic work, shopping and caring for the elderly. It has been estimated that this is worth about $10 trillion a year to the global economy and is strongly correlated with low female labour-force participation rates across the world (Dobbs et al, 2015: 29). The United Nations has also noted that while women are still underrepresented in the labour markets of the MENA region, those that do work are experiencing an 'imbalanced sharing of care responsibilities that serves to circumscribe [their] options', and if barriers to their full and equal participation in work are to be removed there will also need to be a 'reduction and redistribution of the care burden that they disproportionally carry [and] a move towards a more equitable sharing of the unpaid burden of care work between men and women.' This will require workplace arrangements 'that accommodate flexible schedules, without penalising professional advancement and a shift in mind-sets about gender-specific roles and responsibilities' in order to bring these closer into line with those of the most gender-equal countries in the world (United Nations 2015a: 107–108, 122 and 123).

We noted in Chapters 3, 5 and 7 that work–life conflict (WLC) appears to be largely a problem for the minority of women who work in private-sector organisations in the UAE, Oman and the KSA. However, if much larger numbers of women do enter the labour markets of the Gulf States and the MENA region, if more of them do move to private-sector employment (as their governments would like them to do), if more become entrepreneurs and SME owners and if more dual-career couples do emerge, then both work–life conflict and work–life balance will become more significant concerns in these countries. Another trend that may exacerbate this is the weakening of extended kin networks in the UAE, Oman and the KSA. In many cultures, such as those in Southern Europe, Asia, Latin America, the Pacific Islands and Sub-Saharan Africa, extended families are still commonplace. This, until very recently, was also true of the UAE, Oman and the KSA where it is still normal for three generations of a family to share a single household. While it is true that in this part of the world extended families are still much more commonplace than they are in the West, this has changed with the emergence of a growing number of nuclear families in recent times – ones that consist of a father, mother and their children – who can no longer rely on parents or other close relatives to look after their children while they are at work. Hence, a growing number of younger Arab women, who may be both occupationally and geographically mobile, may no longer be able to rely on extended kin networks to the extent that their parents did.

There is evidence in recent reports on working women in the MENA region that concerns about work–family conflict are growing. For example, a very surprising finding of a 2014 survey of 1,543 working women in 13 MENA countries was that just over half of this group had never been married and, of the 39 per cent who were married, nearly half had no children. This suggests that some professional women are choosing to put their careers before marriage and are choosing either not to have or to delay having children. One third of those who were married with children were not satisfied with the maternity leave benefits that were available to them, and a similar proportion were 'neutral' about these. Just over half of the women in this group also indicated that their decision to have children had negatively affected their career 'at least to some extent' (Bayt.com, 2014). A study of 555 women and men in several MENA countries reported that the biggest obstacles to increasing the number of women in leadership positions in their organisations were 'double-burden syndrome' (i.e. coping with work and family responsibilities), 'a lack of appropriate infrastructure' (i.e. suitable workplace facilities for women) and 'a lack of pro-family public policies or support services' (e.g. adequate and affordable childcare facilities). Conversely, just 12 per cent of this group thought that 'attitudes toward women in the workplace' was a significant obstacle to their career advancement (Ellis et al, 2015: 5).

Of the three countries featured in this study, the UAE has made the most progress in promoting work–life balance and in providing affordable childcare services for working women. In June 2006, the government sector was allowed to set up nurseries in its buildings, but this was not widely implemented because of the lack of space in some government buildings. And, in 2008, a National Corporate Child Care Project was launched by HRH Sheikha Manal Bint Mohammed Bin Rashid al-Maktoum to establish day-care centres in all government departments in Dubai. This initiative aimed 'to improve the standard of child care in Dubai by setting international benchmarks and incorporating local values, traditions and culture' and 'create new employment opportunities for national women by providing appropriate training and employment in the day-care centres.' According to Maitha al-Shamsi, the Managing Director of the Dubai Women Establishment, 'We want to help the working woman find a balance between work and life. Before, once women hit their thirties they would give up work and stay at home looking after the family. Yet today many women want to continue working' (Dubai Women Establishment, 2008a).

The United Nations believes that much greater consideration must be given by all governments and employers in the MENA region to creating family-friendly working arrangements for women to enable them to cope with career breaks to have children and in caring for family dependents. Working women in emerging economies want this flexibility as much as working women in the West do, and this can be offered at little or no cost to employers (International Finance Corporation, 2013a: 42). PepsiCo, for example, already offers female employees in the MENA region flexible starting and finishing times, the option to work from home one day a week, time in lieu (if the employee has worked over a weekend, for example) and part-time and job-sharing options (PepsiCo, 2016). Employer initiatives to assist women by providing a childcare allowance or by providing in-house crèche or nursery facilities are other options. These are increasingly common in US companies (e.g. at the SAS Institute), and female employees can also pay something towards the costs of these services. When 264 Saudi women business owners were asked to identify the most important changes they would like to see in current government regulations and services for women, their first choice – chosen by a third of this group – was 'the provision of subsidised day care services' for their children (Alturki and Braswell, 2010: 34).

To promote better work–life balance policies, the governments of the UAE, Oman and the KSA could perhaps emulate countries like the United Kingdom, Australia and New Zealand, which have promoted the importance of work–life balance by launching a variety of targeted campaigns in recent years. The governments of these countries have created websites to provide information to policy analysts, employees, employers and trade unions on the importance of reducing work–life conflict. In Australia, the Equal Opportunity for Women in the Workplace Agency views paid maternity leave as playing an essential role in helping women and their families enjoy a balanced life and a policy that also has a positive impact on gender equity in the workplace. In addition to this, Australia already recognises the benefits of parental leave by allowing male employees the option of twelve months unpaid parental leave. A Work and Family Unit (WFU) has been established in the Department of Employment and Workplace Relations that provides information and advice to employers and employees on how to improve work–life balance. There are also a variety of resources on the WFU website to assist with work–life harmonisation, and this organization also oversees the annual Family Friendly Employer awards (Equal Opportunity for Women in the Workplace Agency, 2015). Similar initiatives also began in the United Kingdom in the late 1990s (The Work-Life Research Centre, 2000).

There is no logical reason these options could not also be offered to male employees whose partners are having children. The study by the Peterson Institute for International Economics of 21,980 firms in ninety-one countries, cited in Chapter 8, noted that in most societies, 'women are more likely than men to take on the double burden of work and family – and be expected to do so [and] women by and large assume a greater share of child care and household responsibilities' (Noland et al, 2016: 12). However, an interesting conclusion of this study was that while generous maternity leave provision for women is not positively correlated with the number of women in leadership positions, the provision of paternity leave for men is. Consequently, they have suggested that:

> One could argue that countries in which fathers have access to more leave have significantly more women on corporate boards. It stands to reason that policies that allow childcare needs to be met,

but do not place the burden of care explicitly on women, increase the chances that women can build the business acumen and professional contacts necessary to qualify for a corporate board. More gender-neutral family leave (and more supportive childcare institutions generally) would also curtail expectations that young men will necessarily provide greater returns to training and mentoring than young women. This interpretation of results suggests that policies that place a disproportionate burden of childcare on women are one barrier to female corporate advancement

(Noland et al, 2016: 12–13).

Many of the studies cited in Chapter 3 and Chapter 8 have identified work–life balance policies as being an important element of diversity management in organisations. One of these had identified fourteen measures that companies can introduce to recruit, develop, retain and promote women. Four of these are directly related to maintaining a good balance between work and family life: 'options for flexible working', 'support programs and facilities to help reconcile work and family life', 'programs to smooth transitions before, during and after parental leave' and 'performance evaluation systems that neutralise the impact of parental leave' (Werner et al, 2010: 4). These studies have also shown that company-sponsored maternal and paternal leave, flexible working options, access to good-quality child-care (or in-house crèches/nurseries) and the involvement of families in company social activities can all be cost-effective interventions and, when cost savings such as employee attendance, commitment and retention are factored in, can actually save money for companies (Dobbs et al, 2015: 84; International Financial Corporation, 2013b: 15).

The benefits for companies and employees of introducing supportive work–life balance policies have been well documented, and there is every reason to believe that companies in the UAE, Oman and the KSA could also enjoy these. A commitment to work–life balance sends a signal that the organisation is serious about gender diversity and is also a key element of employee inclusiveness. It signifies that the employee has a life both within and outside the organisation and, within reasonable limits, the employer respects this. Hence, private-sector companies in these countries that take the lead in maternity leave, flexi-working, sensitivity to family responsibilities and childcare provision today will also have a competitive advantage in recruiting the best and most talented women tomorrow. However, local companies also need to be aware that introducing work–life policies, like all other aspects of organisational management, will require top-level leadership support and commitment to ensure that they are implemented successfully. The problem for working women in these countries is that the support currently provided by regional governments and most private-sector companies is very limited by international standards and in comparison to most OECD countries. While a few private-sector companies may provide some additional work–life balance support to their employees, most provide no support other than that mandated by law. However, there is nothing – apart from tradition and myopic thinking – that is preventing the governments of the UAE, Oman and the KSA from adopting similar policies and enacting supportive employment legislation that can help women – and men – balance their work and family lives more effectively in the future.[4]

9.4 STRATEGIES TO ENCOURAGE FEMALE ENTREPRENEURSHIP AND BUSINESS OWNERSHIP

There is no doubt that the potential for entrepreneurship and the growth of the SME sectors of all countries in the MENA region is enormous (Mahajan, 2012). A new and younger generation of entrepreneurs is emerging and includes successful start-up companies such as Flat6Labs and Ekshef (Egypt), Oasis500 (Jordan), Cinemoz (Lebanon), Diwanee and SmartAd (UAE), Careem (KSA) and many other examples. In 2015, Seeqnce – a business incubator in Beirut – ran a competition to find 8 winning entries from 433 start-up companies in the MENA region, and new private equity firms such as Abraaj

Capital and Citadel Capital are investing in new high-growth companies. There are also some examples of recently established companies becoming successful global enterprises, such as Emirates Airlines, Etihad and Flydubai in the UAE. However, most Arab companies come in two varieties: 'lumbering giants', predominantly in the oil, gas, construction and financial sectors and 'rickety dwarves', SMEs which lack both the financial and employee resources they need to expand into and compete in a hyper-competitive global economy. In addition, most SMEs in the region are family owned and these are constantly fragmenting because Islamic inheritance law mandates the division of property and business, and *shari'a* laws do not make clear distinctions between corporate and family property. Consequently, it is difficult to see how and where a substantial number of MENA–wide equivalents of companies like Etihad are going to emerge across the region over the next ten to twenty years, because when it comes to establishing and growing new businesses, 'red tape is as abundant as sand' (*The Economist*, 2015b). As the OECD has also noted:

> With only 12 per cent of women running their own businesses, compared to 31 per cent of men, the MENA region has the highest gender gap in the world, as well as a high attrition rate for women-led firms. Enabling women to participate fully in the economy, both as employees and as entrepreneurs, would bring high economic and social returns for MENA societies ... Women's entrepreneurship in the MENA region represents an underutilised reservoir for job creation, economic growth and social cohesion (*Organisation for Economic Cooperation and Development, 2014: 3 and 7*).

The reasons for this gender gap and the additional entry barriers that female entrepreneurs face when creating and growing new firms were explained in Chapters 2 through 7 although, as we saw in Chapters 5 and 7, these barriers are more onerous in the KSA and Oman when compared to the UAE. In this section we describe several generic and country-specific strategies that could be introduced to encourage more women to start their own businesses in these three countries (developed from Alturki and Braswell, 2010; Ernst & Young, 2009; International Finance Corporation, 2013b; Lavelle and al-Shaikh, 2013; MENA-OECD Investment Program, 2009; Organisation for Economic Cooperation and Development, 2014 and 2012; Terjesen and Lloyd, 2015).

Create an Environment That Is More Supportive of Female Entrepreneurship and Business Ownership

The OECD, among others, has indicated in several reports on female entrepreneurship in the emerging economies of the MENA region that all of their governments need to establish 'a business climate that is conducive to increased entrepreneurial activity', 'take action to level the playing field for women entrepreneurs', 'further develop and implement policies and measures aimed at helping women address the specific challenges they face' and 'make adequate human and financial resources available' for them. To date, according to the OECD, 'no MENA government has established a comprehensive policy to tackle the core barriers to developing female entrepreneurship ... and institutional support for women entrepreneurs remains fragmented' (Organisation for Economic Cooperation and Development, 2014: 16). Currently, none of the Gulf States or other countries in the MENA region has a national ministry dedicated to female entrepreneurship and SME ownership, and there is little evidence of coherent national strategies aimed at improving women's access to their small-business sectors. The governments of these countries need to develop clear, systemic and visible policies that support female – and male – entrepreneurship and business ownership in all business and industrial sectors. If the countries in this region still do not recognise and promote the value and importance of female entrepreneurship, then women will continue to have marginal roles in their SME sectors and they will struggle to gain access to the resources they need to establish and grow new businesses.

It is not enough, to reiterate a point made in Chapters 5 and 7, for governments to improve the *supply* side of female entrepreneurship in these countries – which they have done to some extent – they must focus on the *demand* side as well. And, in both domains, it would be sensible to adopt the best-practice principles that are employed in the world's most creative and innovative economies. Under the auspices of their (new) national ministries for Women's Empowerment and Development, a dialogue can be initiated in the KSA, Oman and the UAE,[5] encompassing all relevant government agencies, commercial banks and other support agencies. These could then promote the economic benefits of female entrepreneurship and business ownership as being important building blocks in the development of thriving private sectors and the creation of sustainable economies in the future. It is important that this be articulated primarily as an economic issue rather than a 'gender' or 'social' issue. These organisations, as mentioned, could also send a positive message about female business owners by making a public commitment to sourcing some of their business and services from female-owned companies. Reviews of laws that impede female entrepreneurs and business owners should be initiated and, where needed, new regulations should be introduced that better integrate female entrepreneurs into the national economy. Most entrepreneurs in Oman and the KSA are still heavily reliant on male relatives to help them complete the complex business registration process, which is unnecessary, and the *wakeel/mudeer* requirements in the KSA undermine the freedom that Saudi women have to manage their firms as they would like to and appoint better-qualified female managers of their choice.

In Oman and the KSA, new registration categories need to be created which cover businesses such as beauty salons, fitness and day-care centres and other female-run enterprises which may require categorisation and licensing. Mechanisms should also be put in place to encourage 'informal' female-owned businesses in these countries to register and become part of the formal national economy. Remaining in the informal economy may be a rational choice for some Saudi and Omani women, but it limits their ability to grow and expand micro-businesses and access commercial sources of capital. And, while there is certainly more awareness of successful female Arab entrepreneurs and business owners in the Arabian Gulf States and the MENA region today, greater efforts should be made to publicise the achievements of self-starting female entrepreneurs, organising more local and regional conferences for entrepreneurs and SME owners and promoting the idea of female self-employment at schools and universities. Publications and documentaries that profile successful business women and the contributions they have made to job creation and their national economies could also be produced.

Collect Reliable and Comprehensive Data on Female Entrepreneurs and SME Owners

A specialised department within the new women's ministries (similar to the United States' Government Office of Women's Business Ownership) should be created that will enable the KSA, Oman and the UAE to develop more comprehensive databases on female entrepreneurship and business ownership, particularly in the 'informal' sector, and to provide clarity about what is meant by 'micro', 'small', 'medium-sized' and 'informal' enterprises to enable better planning for these sectors in the future. Comprehensive gender-disaggregated entrepreneurship and SME ownership data should be collected as well as information on the outcomes of SME support provided by government agencies to women and men (i.e. both the ratios of government loans provided to them and the relative amounts of those loans). Follow-up surveys and interviews should be conducted at one, three and five years, and the success/failure-rate of female start-up companies should be monitored and evaluated. Surveys and case studies of female entrepreneurs should also be conducted to better understand the main obstacles and challenges they had encountered when establishing, managing and growing their businesses.

A review of the services currently provided for female entrepreneurs by government agencies in the UAE, Oman and the KSA and the quality and speed of the services provided to women in the female sections of government ministries should also be conducted, although this appears to be less of a problem in the UAE. Wherever possible, bureaucratic red tape and 'administrivia' in company registration processes should be eliminated. Further research should be conducted on laws and bureaucratic regulations that impede women's ability to engage in entrepreneurial and business activities, with recommendations for modifying, reforming or abolishing these (e.g. as noted in Chapters 5 and 7, the male-guardian and male-manager rules, status of ownership rights and restrictions on employing qualified non-national staff). Information could also be gathered to ascertain the reasons so few young Emirati, Omani and Saudi women choose to become entrepreneurs and why they are underrepresented in this sector of their economies, something that could also be done in the UAE. Additional research could be conducted to find out why most Saudi and Omani women still have to rely on personal and family savings to fund business start-ups and why commercial lenders in their countries are still so reluctant to lend money to female entrepreneurs. Over time, summary reports can be provided about the net contribution that the female entrepreneurial/SME sector is making to the growth and diversification of their national economies, and this will enable targeted funding to be provided to those ventures and sectors that are likely to have the biggest job creation and economic impacts in the future. These reports should be made publicly available and open to comment from all interested parties.

Improve Women's Access to Start-Up Finance

While there are variations country by country, the MENA region as a whole has the least-developed capital markets in the world, lags behind many other regions in terms of economic and financial inclusion for women and has the least-developed financial support systems for female entrepreneurs. According to one report on 431 female business owners in the MENA region, 'the overwhelming majority of women who were planning to grow their businesses were unsuccessful in obtaining finance from formal institutions.' Nearly 70 per cent of the women in this study also felt the bank staff they dealt with lacked adequate knowledge and experience to advise female SME owners and were 'ill-equipped to deal with women-owned businesses in the region' (International Finance Corporation, 2013a: 16 and 20). Consequently, it was not surprising to discover that the female entrepreneurs featured in Chapters 5 and 7 had relied primarily on personal or family savings to establish their businesses, although a few did make use of government micro-loans. It is also evident – as was the case in all Western countries until the 1990s – that there was still considerable gender bias against women entrepreneurs in commercial banks in the KSA and Oman, and they were much less likely to be successful in obtaining loans from these sources when compared to men or established businesses. Moreover, government business start-up programs in these countries have typically focused on providing micro-finance for low-income female entrepreneurs and, generally, have not provided additional funding during the growth phase of SMEs.

The strict male-guardianship laws in these countries – and the attitudes of male financiers – mean that most women still do not have equitable access to funding for starting new businesses, and if the experience of women entrepreneurs in Western countries in the 1970s and 1980s is any guide, there is likely to be residual (male) discrimination against female entrepreneurs for some time. Although there is government funding for female start-up businesses, there is an urgent need for improved women-tailored financial advisory services at banks and other commercial lenders and the introduction of internal lending processes that do not discriminate against women. Hence, lending institutions must be encouraged or cajoled into providing more (and larger) loans to female entrepreneurs and established business owners, particularly in the KSA and Oman. Local banks and other financial organisations need to design and implement operational and HR strategies that can better target and attract female entrepreneurs and incorporate international best practices to improve the access that women have to business loans, and as indicated earlier in this chapter, they could then start to measure the tangible business benefits of doing this. They could consider establishing loan packages, products and instruments that are tailored to the specific needs of female entrepreneurs and SME owners, as well as better-targeted information on the range of financing options available to women and advice on preparing good business plans. In addition, these organisations could also offer monthly female-only advisory workshops for would-be female entrepreneurs, perhaps making use of successful business women who had obtained start-up loans from them.[6]

Allow Women to Establish Independent Business Associations

While business women's associations exist in every MENA country, they are all government-controlled and funded organisations. And, while some Chambers of Commerce and Industry in the region now have women's committees, very little is known about how much influence these have on decision-making processes in those organisations, how well they represent the interests of female business owners or how accessible they are to female entrepreneurs and SME owners. Independent associations have played a pivotal role in the success of entrepreneurial initiatives in many other countries, and so female entrepreneurs and business owners in the KSA, Oman and the UAE should be allowed to create autonomous organisations in which they can meet, network, build coalitions and share their experiences, knowledge and best-practice ideas. These would also enable them to better represent their individual and collective interests to government agencies and ministries and help them advocate more effectively for improvements in regulations, laws and policies that affect female company owners across different business and industrial sectors. These organisations would also be free to organise independent forums and symposia and invite local and foreign business women to speak at these. Although there are now award ceremonies for successful Arab women, such as the Top 20 Saudi Business Women Award, more annual awards, business competitions and prizes for female entrepreneurs could be created, particularly for new and younger entrepreneurs in the UAE, Oman and the KSA. These new associations could also consider organising collectively under the institutional framework of the OECD-MENA Women's Business Forum to network, share information and develop international partnerships and collaborative ventures.

Improve Training and Vocational Support for Female Entrepreneurs

There is an urgent need to provide better training and vocational support for female entrepreneurs in the KSA, Oman and – to a lesser extent – the UAE. In 2012, the OECD described these as being 'generally weak in the MENA region and women entrepreneurs apparently make little use of professional advice and counselling services … women more often rely on personal contacts, such as spouses or other family members, when they start businesses, thus missing out on the benefits of entrepreneurship training, information and professional advice' (Organisation for Economic Cooperation and Development, 2012: 18). Capability building is an important aspect of gender equality and female empowerment in general, and this is essential for entrepreneurs and SME owners. Entrepreneurship and business management training can be very effective in building the capacity that women have to create new businesses and, when established, improve the chances that they will survive and grow. A broader range of vocational, women-relevant, part-time/modular courses should be created and offered at vocational colleges, government ministries and university business faculties. These should be delivered by facilitators who have practical knowledge of business start-ups and focus on the skills needed to establish, build and grow new firms and how to integrate information and support technologies into business operations. The International Finance Corporation survey cited earlier indicated that the most useful topics that could be covered if such training courses could be offered were 'general business management skills', 'using financial products and accessing equity capital', 'exporting', 'accounting and financial management', 'selling to large, multi-national corporations' and 'legal advice' (International Finance Corporation, 2013a: ix and 18).

Promote Female Entrepreneurship and Self-Employment at Schools and Universities

Several of the reports cited in Chapters 5 and 7 have called for changes to school curricula to foster more critical, creative and independent thinking and to incorporate the teaching of entrepreneurship and self-employment in schools. We also noted in those chapters that there are hardly any entrepreneurship and small business management programs taught at universities in the KSA, Oman and the UAE, a significant educational deficit also noted in other studies (Jones and Ridout, 2015: 264; Skoko et al, 2010: 107–108 and 110; Sokari et al, 2013: 110–111 and 113–114). All universities in these countries should be encouraged to introduce these as a matter of urgency and, perhaps, create specialised departments and establish more professorial positions in creativity, innovation, entrepreneurship and small business management. New courses and programs that cover these subjects should not be restricted to business and management students but could be included in other undergraduate and postgraduate courses, including design, engineering, information technology and science courses. At schools and universities, female guest speakers should be brought in to talk about their businesses and to promote the idea of self-employment among girls and young women. There is also a pressing need for better incubator support for young women (and men) at universities in the UAE, Oman and the KSA where there are, in almost all cases, no institutional resources to help them transform their business ideas into viable commercial realities and encourage the development of new female-run businesses.

9.5 CONCLUSION

The qualities that are defined as masculine are the same as those defined as the qualities of leadership. There is virtually no overlap between the qualities ascribed to femininity and those to leadership. Yet, in several studies, results show that when you have a critical mass of women in an organisation, you have less corruption. Peru and Mexico have even implemented initiatives based on such thinking. Lest you think that all we aspire to for the world can be accomplished by male dominated organisations, I have only to say to you: Enron, Taliban and Roman Catholic Church.

Kim Cambell, former Prime Minister of Canada (Schlosser, 2002: 70)

A question that will be in the mind of anyone who is familiar with the political, cultural, religious and social characteristics of the nineteen countries of the MENA region is: 'How likely are they to embrace and implement any of the recommendations and proposals contained in this book?' The only reasonable answer that can be given to this question is, 'There is a good chance that they won't – but it is absolutely essential that they do.' For anyone who still has doubts about this, we only have to remind ourselves of the consequences for the economic and political futures of all countries in this region if they choose not to implement at least *some* of them. Even before the precipitous fall in oil and gas prices during 2015–2016, economic growth in the MENA region had decelerated sharply to 2.2 per cent in 2013. Although this increased slightly during 2014, it fell in 2015 and 2016 and is likely to fall further during 2017–2018. Writing before the full impact of the loss of oil and gas revenues became apparent in 2016, the ILO observed that stalled political and economic reform and regional instability 'are likely to result in a sluggish and protracted economic recovery, with unemployment at best stabilising at currently high levels. This situation is likely to fuel social unrest and further instability as a youthful population faces severely limited job opportunities' (International Labour Organisation, 2015: 62 -63). To a considerable degree, the entire MENA region remains an 'oil-driven' economy and the economic fortunes of all countries in this region rise and fall with the price of oil and gas. While resource wealth may provide time, it does not provide solutions and those countries that still have this will have to finally deliver on what they have long promised: economies that are not reliant primarily on declining hydrocarbon resources. And, as every report cited in this book has shown, the diversification and growth of the economies of the UAE, Oman, the KSA and the other countries of the region cannot happen unless many more women become active participants in their labour markets in the future.

However, as noted in earlier chapters, the process of female emancipation and economic empowerment in the West has already taken three generations, and it is far from complete. This indicates that it will not be easy to initiate the legal, regulatory and social changes that would allow this to happen in the MENA region. It is also not a simple task to introduce diversity policies into male-dominated organisations, and the example of BHP Billiton is a salu-tary reminder that most businesses in OECD countries are still striving to make their organisations truly gender inclusive. Hence, governments and companies in the MENA region would have to understand that while this transformation is essential, it will not happen overnight. Changing their national and business cultures will take a long time, and this process will create many new challenges as well as benefits. However, regardless of these difficulties and the overwhelming national economic and business cases for gender equality and inclusiveness, this will only happen when a majority of the citizens of the MENA region decide that their beliefs about the 'appropriate' roles of women in their societies, political systems and workplaces have to change. As Fadl observed more than a decade ago:

> It is not possible to achieve the moral and ethical objectives of the
> Islamic faith without understanding the particular and specific
> demands and challenges of each age. It is also not possible to fulfil
> our obligations as agents of God and discharge the duty to 'enjoin

> the good and forbid the evil' without understanding the shifting
> circumstances and conditions of human beings [and Muslims
> must] try to strike a balance between the necessary flexibility in
> dealing with modernity's unique challenges and the need for
> historical authenticity ... the Islamic tradition must be able to
> engage in new paradigms for the contemporary age
>
> *(Fadl, 2005: 175–176).*

Moreover, as Ali has noted, there is some hope that a more liberal Islamic world-view will emerge in the future because 'today, there is a war within Islam – a war between those who wish to reform (the Modify Muslims or dissidents) and those who wish to turn back to the time of the prophet (the Medina Muslims). The prize over which they fight is the hearts and minds of the largely passive Mecca Muslims. For the moment ...the Medina side seems to be winning.' But she also believes that 'a Muslim reformation is coming' for the simple reason that 'Muslim people are like everyone else in one important respect: most want a better life for themselves and their children and, increasingly, they have good reasons to doubt that Medina Muslims can deliver it' (Ali, 2015: 224 and 226). Ali also makes the extremely important point that the movement to reform Islam should not be viewed in narrowly 'Western' or 'feminist' terms because it is, fundamentally, a question of how the Islamic diaspora, its political and business leaders, and its senior clerics respond and adapt to the inexorable economic, political, demographic, technological and social pressures that are buffeting their societies. As she suggests, 'In order to avoid eventual collapse, even the most revered structures require innovation. Mere restoration is no longer a plausible option for Islam, no matter how much blood the Islamists shed' (Ali, 2015: 235).

While the moral and ethical cases for the emancipation of women are authoritative and compelling, I now believe that it is the economic rationale and business case that are much more likely to have the greatest effect on male attitudes towards women in all the societies of the MENA region. If, or more hopefully when that eventually happens, change could happen relatively quickly. More-over, it appears that the bottom-up pressures for meaningful change in the region are becoming overwhelming, particularly among younger, educated, professional women and men. This rapidly growing group is – in spite of the best efforts of conservative Islamic clerics to control it – exposed to many other cultural and social influences and, as we have seen in earlier chapters, they represent the vanguard of a discern-ible bottom-up movement for economic and social change. We also noted in Chapter 8 that the issue of gender diversity is beginning to appear on the agendas of some businesses and public-sector organisa-tions in the Gulf States, and the policy recommendations contained in the many reports that have described the introduction of gender-diversity initiatives in the MENA region are almost identical to those that can be found in studies of gender-diversity programs in non-Islamic cultures (Ellis et al, 2015: Sperling et al, 2014). Taken together, these pressures and social trends make it inevitable that some changes *must* occur in the role that women play in the political systems and economies of all countries in the MENA region in the future. In the Postscript, we revisit these suggestions in the context of the major regional economic, political and social challenges facing this region first described in Chapter 1.

Postscript: The Implications of this 'Quiet Revolution' for the Future of the Arabian Gulf States and the MENA Region

And among his signs is this: that he created for you mates from among yourselves that ye may dwell in tranquility with them. And, he has put love and mercy between your hearts. Verily in that are signs for those who reflect … Live with them on a footing of kindness and equity.

The Qur'an (al-Roum, 30, verse 20; al-Nisaa', 4, verse 19)

We must recognise the full human equality of all of our people – before God, before the law, and in the councils of government. We must do this, not because it is economically advantageous – although it is; not because the laws of God demand it – although they do; not because people in other lands wish it to be so. We must do it for the single and fundamental reason that it is the right thing to do.

Robert F. Kennedy, 1966 (John F. Kennedy Presidential Library and Museum, 2014)

In this postscript, we turn full circle to revisit the themes and issues raised in Chapter 1 and the suggestions made at the end of Chapter 9. We also ask if the three countries featured in this study, the other Arabian Gulf States and other countries in the MENA region are likely to encourage and support the 'quiet revolution' described in this book and the probable consequences if they fail to do this. It concludes with some quotes from three inspirational young women in the UAE, Oman and the KSA which describe their hopes and dreams for the future.

In the post–9/11 world, there has been much discussion of 'a war' between the 'Christian West' and the 'Islamic World', with conservative commentators portraying this as a defining struggle between two entirely incompatible value-systems and worldviews

(Huntington, 2011). While such ideas may appeal to the likes of Donald Trump, Fox News and right-wing media pundits like Rush Limbaugh (and their counterparts in many other countries), it does not help us to advance reasoned and evidence-based debates about the future of the MENA region. This matters because what does happen in this region during the 2020s will affect the entire world for decades. And, while it is easy for some commentators to blame 'Islam' for all of the problems confronting this part of the world, this is no different to blaming Christianity for colonialism, slavery, anti-Semitism and the repression of women. As *The Economist* has suggested:

> This is partly true, but of little practical help. Which Islam would that be? The head-chopping sort espoused by IS, the revolutionary-state variety that is decaying in Iran or the political version espoused by the besuited leaders of Ennahda in Tunisia, who now call themselves "Muslim Democrats" To demonise Islam is to strengthen the Manichean version of IS. The world should instead recognize the variety of thought within Islam, support moderate trends and challenge the extremists. Without Islam, no solution [to the region's problems] is likely to endure
>
> *(The Economist, 2016l: 9).*

The Economist was absolutely right to say this because the reality – as anyone who has lived and worked in the MENA region for some time soon realises – is far more nuanced and complex than a simplistic 'evil versus good' dichotomy implies. There is, once you get beneath the cultural and religious 'surface' of the countries in this region, a remarkable degree of commonality in the beliefs, hopes, dreams and aspirations of women and men in the UAE, Oman and the KSA and their peer groups in (e.g.) the United States, Canada, the United Kingdom and Australia. Hence, the arguments and policy recommendations presented in this book could only be regarded as misplaced or erroneous *if* the people of the MENA region have needs that are fundamentally different to those who live in other parts of the world. However, the evidence clearly indicates that all human groups and societies have broadly similar hopes and aspirations, including the people of the MENA region. For example, according to a study of 1,450 women and men in Egypt, Morocco and Saudi Arabia:

> Our results show, with minor national variations, that the middle-class in these countries are anxious about core issues such as living standards, inflation and job security. Respondents expressed dissatisfaction with the delivery of public services, including education, healthcare and social security. Perhaps most troubling, many middle-class residents in the region do not believe that their countries offer them opportunities to succeed … As it happens, the dreams of the middle-class in MENA countries are decidedly practical and modest. Principally, they want a safe and secure country, a strong and developing economy, and stability. Beyond that they dream of excellent educational opportunities, for themselves and their children, and enjoying a happy life with family. Material dreams, such as home ownership and financial stability, are on this list as well, but far fewer people focus on this
> (Shediac et al, 2012: 32).

Without knowing which country nationals were being referred to, the hopes and aspirations articulated in the second part of this quote could be those of the citizens of any country. They are also the same as those expressed by all of the women and men that I met in the UAE, Oman and the KSA between 2008 and 2015. They want to live in more open societies. They want growing and sustainable economies that can support them and their families now; ones that can also provide security and good jobs for their children and grandchildren in the future. They all hope for greater freedom of expression and a more active say in how their countries are governed and who rules over them. And, although there was a wide range of opinions about this issue, almost all of the women I met wanted enhanced legal and social rights and the right to work as equals with men in the careers of their choice. Even among the men there were many who also advocated these changes, although they were generally more conservative than the women and most of them had some concerns and worries about what the long-term consequences of these changes might be. Conversely, they did not want greater oppression or to live in fear if they speak out about problems or injustices in their societies that should be addressed. Consequently, the idea that these hopes and aspirations are somehow the result of subversive Western influences or ones that pose a threat to Arabic-Islamic values is both inaccurate and misdirected. However, they certainly pose a very real challenge to the established political and religious elites of the region because, if they are not addressed, the entire MENA region could face an extremely uncertain and dangerous future.

Why do all human beings appear to have broadly similar life needs, regardless of their national, cultural and religious backgrounds? The American psychologist Abraham Maslow, was one of the first researchers to suggest that these are 'hardwired' into all human beings and meaning, motivation and a sense of purpose in life are determined by the extent to which people are able to satisfy a sequence of intrinsic and universal needs. In ascending order, these are:

Physiological needs (food, water, shelter, recreation and sex).
Safety needs (security and protection from external threats).
Social needs (love, affection, friendships and social interaction with other people).
Esteem needs (attention, recognition, respect, achievement, autonomy and status).
Self-actualisation (psychological growth, self-expression, self-fulfilment and the achievement of individual potential).

Maslow argued that all human beings are motivated by a strong desire to satisfy these needs, starting with the lowest and, when their lower-order needs are met, they will actively seek self-actualisation – regardless of the societies they are born into (Maslow, 1954, 1943). Charles Handy has also described how more collectivist societies, such as nomadic African tribes, have cultures that emphasise 'lesser hungers' (safety, security and sustenance) and 'greater hungers' (self-esteem, connections to others and authenticity) for centuries, broadly corresponding to the lower and higher order needs categories described in Maslow's theory (Handy, 1996: 200). These needs are universal, although there are of course distinctive regional and local variations in the economic, political, cultural, legal, social and religious expressions of these. Nevertheless, as an eminent scholar of Islam has also argued in (if he will forgive me for suggesting this) a somewhat complicated way:

> Different cultures produce different modernities. This statement cannot be otherwise than true ... [However it] is far more a question of [their] specific adaptability to the modes and the accelerated pace that the attributions of development require – presupposing that beyond cultural diversity men and women strive for the fulfilment of their personalities based on anthropologically similar, if not equal, universal assumptions for the advantages and sometimes the blessings of individual and collective security, of freedom, and of material well-being for the greatest number possible. The core moment of the ability to produce and reproduce the attributes of modernity leads us into the prerequisites and requirements for the development of humankind – the political, social and cultural environment to discover, to create and to invent ... Modernity is a continuously ongoing universal process of transformation, conversion and change – and all humankind has its role in this endeavor ... That is the inescapable message inherent in the critique presented by the Arab Human Development Report
>
> *(Diner, 2009: 179–180).*

What Diner is saying is very important: all human beings, broadly speaking, have very similar basic needs – for security from threats and violence, freedom to express their opinions and a reasonable standard of living, among other things. And, if history tells us anything, it is in large measure a very long account of the struggles that people have been engaged in for hundreds of years in numerous societies to satisfy these basic human needs. It is also a story of the repeated failures of the ruling elites of many of those societies to respond positively to these in the past and the consequences of their repeated failures to do so. In the words of a respected historian of science:

> People everywhere wish for a better world – a more peaceful and prosperous world, where their children can lead healthy, happy lives and they have long sought the intellectual tools with which to pursue this goal. Religion works best when it emphasises common decency, philosophy when stressing our ignorance, art when exposing us to visions larger than ourselves, history by drawing lessons from the past – but the most effective tools are liberalism and science. [They] have an unequalled capacity for doing good – for reducing cruel ignorance and villainous certitude, encouraging freedom and effective government, promoting human rights, putting food in the mouths of the hungry and attainable prospects in their future. If we use our heads, nourish learning, tend the fires of freedom, and treat one another with justice and compassion, our descendants may say of us that we had the vision to do science, and the courage to live by liberty
> *(Ferris, 2010: 290–291).*

However, on so many levels, this does not appear to be a message that has been heeded by the often corrupt and unrepresentative ruling elites of most of the nineteen countries of the MENA region, and this may explain why they have failed to implement most of the sensible policy recommendations repeated in every United Nations report on the MENA region over the past fifteen years. The Arab Human Development Report of 2005, for example, is no less than a heartfelt appeal for a large-scale transformation of the MENA region. As Diner has noted, 'its diagnosis and its recommendations are so sweeping that it is barely conceivable that the change demanded could proceed without great upheavals. Thus, this document prepared under UN auspices must be considered a revolutionary manifesto' (Diner, 2009: 13). While it may well be 'revolutionary', the most important decision that the rulers of the MENA region now have to make is whether they can continue with economic, political and social policies that will lead to decades of social unrest and, in all probability, further violent upheavals in their societies in the future or will they decide to introduce the reforms that will lead to evolutionary, incremental and peaceful change?

Throughout this book, I have sought to justify two key propositions. The first is that the rentier/clientelist and state-controlled political-economic systems of most nation-states in the MENA region are not viable models for sustainable economic growth and development in the medium- to long-term. With the exception of a few corrupt and despotic resource-rich emerging economies, these have been largely abandoned by the rest of the world. Second, the countries of this region will be unable to build the stable, diversified economies that can sustain them in the future unless they also emancipate and empower their female citizens. This means that the rulers of the MENA region will have to agree on how they can develop their political economies in ways that benefit the vast majority of their populations (not just the entrenched elites), and they must enhance the economic and legal rights of women. To achieve that, they will have to start openly discussing what form of Islam will govern their lives in the future. It is easy to say this, but the rulers and the people of the MENA region are confronted with what appears to be an irreconcilable dilemma. This is encapsulated in a short quote from the Saudi sociologist Khaled al-Dakhil who has said that 'We have a chronic problem of governance that is more than 1,400 years old. Who is the rightful successor to the Prophet? That question is still hanging over our heads' (*The Economist*, 2016m: 5).

While this is true, it is also a historical fact that all religions evolve, as Islam and other monotheistic religions have done over the centuries, and those that stopped evolving in the past did not survive and were eventually superseded by new emergent faiths (Bellah, 2011; Wright, 2009: 328–389). This means that all Muslims (be they Sunnis or Shiites) will eventually have to ask themselves some very difficult questions about their religious beliefs. To this end, the liberal and progressive Islamic scholars cited throughout this book have suggested that contemporary Muslims should focus less on what the Prophet may have said and done in his lifetime and instead ask themselves: *'What would the Prophet do and say if he were alive today?'* Would he, for example, oppose women driving in the KSA, or would he support this? Would he oppose women's right to work and would he prevent them from becoming entrepreneurs or managing their own businesses? Would he oppose *murshida* (female religious guides and preachers) and *tahrir al-mahra* (women's liberation)? Would he support greater *infitah* (openness) in the countries of the MENA region, and would he be opposed to *istid'af* against women (oppressive or abusive behaviour that renders another person powerless)? Would he be opposed to widespread nepotism and corruption? Would he be tolerant of other religious beliefs, or would he seek to repress them?

Would he agree or disagree with the opinions of the Moroccan sociologist Fatima Mernisi, who has asked, 'Why is it that we can find some Muslim men saying that women in Muslim countries cannot be granted full enjoyment of human rights? What grounds do they have for such a claim? None – because they are simply betting on our ignorance of the past, for their argument can never convince anyone with an elementary understanding of Islam's history' (Bennoune, 2013: 32). In other words, literalism and constantly harking back to what the Prophet *may* have believed in the past will inevitably lead to the further fragmentation of the Islamic faith and, perhaps, even destroy it. Although literalist beliefs do provide comfort, focus and purpose for disenfranchised and oppressed groups in this region and many other parts of the world, the increasingly militant, totalitarian and strident demands of Islamic extremists offer no long-term hope for the people of the MENA region or, indeed, the rest of the global Muslim diaspora. Tribalism, religious hatred, the repression of cultural and religious minorities, and the exclusion of women from society cannot be long-term strategies for building stable and modern societies in this or any other part of the world (Manne, 2016).

Having said this, the most significant 'unknown-unknown' concerns the willingness and ability of the governments and societies of the MENA region to change and evolve in the future. This is because:

> It is a region consumed by religious conflicts between groups who claim to be the true adherents of their faith and deep theological schisms between radicals and moderates. Heretics are imprisoned, tortured and slaughtered in their thousands. There are rebellions and civil wars within countries in the region and conflicts between these states are commonplace. The loss of life is devastating and there are thousands of homeless refugees across the entire region. These conflicts are fuelled by despotic and autocratic rulers who have their own economic, military and security agendas, and corruption and nepotism are widespread. Women have very few legal rights and they are, effectively, the chattels and property of men. Hardly any of them work in professional occupations and are almost entirely excluded from participation in their countries' political systems.

This will sound very familiar, and while it could well be an accurate depiction of the MENA region today, it isn't. It is my description of Europe during the first half of the seventeenth century, a period characterised by bloody and brutal warfare between (and among) Protestants and Catholics and the emerging European proto-states of the time. This was also the worst period of continuous armed conflict in this region until the two World Wars of the twentieth century. There are, of course, some important differences between the MENA region today and Europe between 1618 and 1648, but there are also many similarities. And, as noted in Chapter 1, it is a sobering reminder that the relatively stable nation-states of Europe only emerged after a very long period of civil and interstate wars, religious conflicts and the gradual replacement of corrupt, despotic monarchies by quasi-accountable democracies (a process that is still incomplete) and, critically, the gradual separation of the symbiotic relationship between religion and the state. Hence, another question for the people of the Gulf States and the broader MENA region to answer is: Do they really want to repeat all the mistakes that Europe did, before the process of economic, political and social renewal can start in their countries? And, can they also begin to have an open discussion about a reformation of the Islamic faith (Badran, 2009)? Perhaps, as several scholars have suggested, a good starting point for the rulers and the people of the MENA region would be to remind themselves about what made the Islamic Abasid Caliphate of the eighth to thirteenth centuries one of the world's pre-eminent civilisations (al-Khalili; 2012; Lyons, 2010).

At the end of Chapter 9, I suggested that any decisions that are made about the roles of women in MENA societies will ultimately be made by the people who live there, and only they can reverse their civilisational decline. Many young people (the Arab 'Generation Y' or 'Millennials'), who now constitute more than a third of the population of the MENA region, are demanding something different to their parents' generation in terms of employment opportunities, participation in political processes, freedom of expression and *karamah*. Consequently, we must hope that the changes that most of the people of this region yearn for do not happen as a result of revolution and mass protests (although it seems inevitable that these will keep recurring in the absence of fundamental change), but rather by an incremental process of evolution in their societies, cultures, economies, labour markets and workplaces, by the construction of stronger and more representative civic institutions and by emancipating and empowering their female citizens. The history of coups and overthrows of governments in the MENA region since World War II tells us that, on almost every occasion, one form of despotic rule was quickly replaced by another and only on rare occasions have these led to significant political and social reforms. And, at least among the growing educated professional middle classes of the UAE, Oman and the KSA, there is clear evidence of a strong desire for a more gradual process of evolutionary change. Everywhere else in the MENA region, although they may be muted, there are also growing demands for more equitable economic policies, greater government transparency and accountability, a devolution of centralised power, better justice systems, more freedom of speech and enhanced legal rights for women.[1]

Some hopeful recent examples of evolutionary change in the region include a significant event that was barely mentioned by Western or Arabic media agencies: the decision not to enshrine *shari'a* law in Tunisia's new constitution, which was ratified in 2015. This means that edicts by Islamic clerics will not form the primary basis of the country's legal code, which is a remarkable outcome and one that bodes well for the women of that country in the future (*The Economist*, 2016e: 35). In Morocco, after a spate of terrorist attacks in Casablanca in 2003, the state has been incrementally exerting greater control over its clerics. A new school for *imams* was opened in 2015 in Rabat which promotes a more modern and secular form of Islam based on the Maliki school of Islamic theology. It has also initiated a program to train Muslim women as spiritual counsellors and as *murshida* to counter religious radicalism and the messages and edicts propagated by conservative male *imams*. In Tunisia, the country's dictator for twenty-five years, Zein al-Abidine Ben Ali, was removed from office in 2011 after largely peaceful mass protests. In 2015, the country became the first Arab state to be judged 'fully free' by Freedom House and moved up thirty-two places on its international rankings. In 2014, four Nobel Peace Prizes were awarded to the civil-society groups who had overseen the introduction of the country's new democratic constitution (*The Economist*, 2016m: 12).

One of the few scholars who has studied women's political and social movements in the Arab world has observed that many more women have become actively engaged in the changing politics of several countries in the MENA region since the 2011 uprisings. She believes that 'women's power maneuvering within patriarchal and tribal societies has succeeded in constructing new gender practices that challenge the social exclusion and marginalisation of women', and while non-feminist female Islamic leaders rarely question the basis of patriarchy, even they 'have contributed to redefining gender norms in an empowering manner.' While acknowledging the Islamic/secular division among women activists in the region, she sees clear signs of the emergence of a new trend of women's activism 'which may be seen as a new wave of feminism', particularly at the community level (Muhanna-Matar, 2014: 3 and 5). She believes that this is a genuine, grassroots and organic women's movement that will also challenge the hegemony of the small 'co-opted' female elites in MENA countries. While this movement is calling for equal rights, greater opportunities for women to work, political reform, human dignity and justice for both women and men, it is not necessarily calling for a revolution against traditional religious practices and is firmly grounded in Islamic beliefs. She believes that this has a much better chance of gaining traction in the Arabic-Islamic world because it is not advocating or promoting a Western feminist ideology. However, while this 'bargaining with patriarchy' may well be a necessary strategy, its efficacy will depend on its ability to dismantle tribal and patriarchal beliefs. If not, these new women's movements 'will remain hostage to masculinised political agendas ... and the interests of the state's political elites.' However, if successful, it could eventually evolve into a MENA–wide movement for 'Islamic feminism' (Muhanna-Matar, 2014: 10; 16–17). As the United Nations has also suggested:

> The most significant aspect of women's activism in the Arab world today is its transcendence of traditional expectations: it is now a comprehensive position in step with other major changes in Arab societies involving questions of renaissance, development and progress. Arab women have made the project of political and economic reform, and the establishment of a positive interaction with the human rights' system, part of their direct objectives; and this is reflected in the increasing presence of women in the organisations of civil and political society ... Yet, this qualitative

change in Arab thinking should not lead one to neglect ... the large
scale reappearance of traditional perceptions and conservative
views about the role of women in society

(United Nations, 2005: 152–153).

Another point that has been made several times in this book is that
the transition to gender equality in Western societies only started in
comparatively recent times. In every case, this remains a work in
progress and there are no countries where women have achieved
complete economic, legal and social equality with men. It had also
taken a very long time before these principles were widely discussed
in Western countries. In 1792, Mary Wollstonecraft published one of
the earliest works of proto-feminist philosophy, *A Vindication of the
Rights of Woman: With Strictures on Moral and Legal Subjects*. In
this she proposed the radical and dangerous ideas that women
should have the same legal rights as men and should also receive
an education so that they could contribute more to the societies in
which they lived (Wollstonecraft, 1792). Her ideas were, in part, an
outcome of the revolutionary times in which she lived, and these
were a direct consequence of the Europe-wide intellectual renaissance during the fifteenth and sixteenth centuries, the Reformation,
the emergence of Enlightenment thinking during the eighteenth
century and the rise of the first republican and proto-democratic
movements in America, France and the Caribbean at that time.
However, most people at the time dismissed her ideas, and it was
another century before most girls in Western countries had access to
a primary-school education and women were granted the right to
vote (starting with New Zealand in 1893). It was another fifty to
sixty years before they had equal access to higher education and
gender discrimination had been outlawed, and it was not until the
1990s and 2000s that women had gained equal access to all professions and occupations.

We also know that in the very recent past there were considerable national and cultural variations in men's attitudes about
women's capabilities in Western countries, as illustrated in Table P.1.

TABLE P.1 *Beliefs about working women in Europe (1995)*

	Bus/train driver	Surgeon	Barrister*	MP**	Average
Denmark	86	85	82	96	87.25
Netherlands	75	83	75	79	78.00
France	77	70	70	68	71.25
UK	77	70	70	68	71.25
Italy	54	56	55	59	56.00
Ireland	43	51	50	61	51.25

(% of men who believed that a woman was capable of doing these jobs,

* Barrister: senior trial lawyer,

** MP: member of elected national assemblies, Wilson, 1995: 39)

However, it is also apparent that if this survey was to be repeated today these confidence scores would have risen markedly over the last three decades, particularly in the United Kingdom, Ireland and Italy. In Ireland, such attitudes would have changed significantly as the influence of the patriarchal and discredited Roman Catholic Church steadily declined and the country became much more affluent, open and cosmopolitan during the 1990s and 2000s. More importantly, this also tells us that negative attitudes about women's abilities can and do evolve over time and, when they are challenged, they can change very quickly. As many economic historians have also demonstrated, enhanced legal rights for women have invariably followed educational and economic empowerment, and this has *always* led to cultural and attitudinal change in societies. This does not mean that this will happen in the MENA region, because if the necessary reforms are not implemented then the participation of women in their political systems, economies and labour markets will not improve in the future.Having said this, the consequences for the nineteen countries of the MENA region if they do not embrace these changes have been fully articulated in this book. It was also apparent that the young undergraduate women I met, the hundreds of working female MBA students who attended the courses

I taught and most of the other women and men I encountered or interviewed during my time in the UAE, Oman and the KSA knew what their political and business leaders needed to do to ensure their economic well-being, security and prosperity in the future. This book concludes with the thoughts of three final-year female management students from these countries who will, *inshalla*, become leaders in their countries in the future:

> I want us to be more than all the buildings and construction that we see. In my view, I want us to reach beyond all of that and be a country that we are all proud of. A good country is more than money and tourism and business. I want us to have the attitude that we are a country that invests in its people, and that encourages learning and science and research and is tolerant of other people ... I think just focusing on making money will take our country nowhere, we know that we have to build a country that will be strong when we do not have oil which still pays for so many things ... I also want us to keep our Emirati identity and our culture, this is a very important part of it. Nowadays, sometimes it's a real struggle to know who we are because a lot of people are just focused on making money and there are so many foreign workers in our country! So, I think we need to be something more than this ... You once used the phrase, 'gross domestic happiness' in class and I think we need to focus as much on that as we do on our gross domestic product in the future
>
> *(23-year-old finance major, Zayed University, UAE; she hoped to be a successful business-woman and also become a member of the UAE's Federal National Council in the future).*

> I think we have to spend our money more wisely, because everyone knows we cannot rely on our oil-wealth for much longer and Omanis are the future resource of the country. All our other energy resources are going to run out, so we need to invest in our people ... I think there is a perception that the only thing Omanis want to do is make money. But this is not true, we are

not a bank! We have to see our people as the only resource we have for the future, and so we must invest in them ... I also believe that any community or society has to be based on the family. And, I think if we lose this there could be negative effects. There's no doubt that the family is changing, it's not how it used to be 20 or 30 years ago. You have to have happy, stable families and I think in some ways we are losing sight of that ... It is obvious to anyone who thinks about these things that we must change, this is essential I think. *Yanni*, we cannot keep doing the same things that have worked for us in the past. If we do, then there may be big problems for our country in the future

(22-year-old management major, Sultan Qaboos University, Oman; she was planning to study for a PhD in the United States and become a professor and a university provost in the future).

I think we will have a lot of problems because our population is growing so quickly and we will need to create many more jobs for young Saudis in the future ... Obviously, more women have to be allowed to work but we also have to invest much more in education, and even more in creativity and science and building many new businesses ... I think we have done a huge amount in a short time in construction and infrastructure and also education and health and other things like this, but that won't be enough in the future ... More women are working these days but I still don't see a lot of Saudi women who are entrepreneurs and business owners and business leaders and we need to encourage this even more than we do now ... We have to do much better than this because we must change our economy to be less reliant on oil-wealth ... Saudi women have to do better than this and it is my generation that must do this!

(22-year-old marketing major, Al Faisal University, KSA; she was planning to build an IT/marketing/video-game design business after she graduated).

Appendix I Research Methodology

THE BACKGROUND TO THE STUDY

An initial literature review on women in the countries of the MENA region was conducted between October 2007 and June 2009. It soon became apparent that while there were extensive literatures on women in national economies and labour markets, and on business leadership and management practices across many different countries and cultural contexts , almost all Western business and management researchers had treated 'the Arab World' as an essentially monolithic and (implicitly) highly patriarchal entity. For example, the extensive GLOBE leadership studies conducted during the 2000s described countries in the 'Middle East' cluster as having high scores on 'group orientation', 'collectivism', 'hierarchy' and 'masculinity' but lower than average scores for 'future orientation', 'assertiveness' and 'gender egalitarianism' (House et al, 2004; Javidan et al, 2006).

However, in both studies, the 'Middle East' cluster consisted of only five countries: Egypt, Morocco, Qatar, Kuwait and Turkey (which is not, strictly speaking, part of the Middle East) and they did not differentiate between men and women in their analysis of leadership practices in these countries. To make generalisations about business leadership practices in any country in the Arabic world on the basis of this small sample is analogous to involving Estonia, Norway, Poland, Austria and Italy in a cross-cultural study of leadership and management practices in Europe, then making general inferences about these in, say, France and then fashioning broad generalisations about these across all of this region. This would be, to say the least, problematic. Every country in the 'Arabic world' (and, indeed, in Europe) has a distinct history and unique sociological, cultural and religious

492

characteristics, and these have a profound influence on the core beliefs and life experiences of the women (and men) who live in these countries. Hence, while the GLOBE studies were innovative and informative, they did not adequately portray these differences.

Moreover, the limited research literature that was available at this time had not examined the possible consequences of the entry of large numbers of university-educated women into regional labour markets during the 2000s and their emergence as business and political leaders, particularly in the UAE and, to a lesser extent, in Oman, the KSA and other countries in the MENA region. In addition, there was very little research that had looked at the beliefs that Arab women have about their changing roles in society and their experiences in the workplace and in leadership roles. Furthermore, no research had been conducted on the opinions that Arabic men have about the changing roles and growing economic power of women in their societies. Another notable and surprising omission in the literature at this time was the almost complete absence of articles or books written by Western scholars about the personal lives and experiences of women in the MENA region. Not surprisingly, several female Islamic scholars have been very critical of this 'oversight':

> Most western liberals appear to be more uncomfortable with my condemning the ill-treatment of women under Islam than most conservatives are. Rather than standing up for western freedoms and against the totalitarian Islamic belief system, many liberals pretend to shuffle their feet when faced with questions about cultural differences ... Well-meaning westerners, eager to promote respect for minority religions and cultures, ignore practices like forced marriage and confinement in order to 'stop society from stigmatizing Muslims', and they deny countless Muslim girls their right to wrest their freedom from their parents' culture. They fail to live up to the ideals and values of our democratic society, and they harm the very same vulnerable minority whom they seek to protect
> (Ali, 2010: 106 and 164).

To redress these gaps in our understanding of the changing lives of university-educated working professional women in the MENA region, this study set out to understand the historical, sociological, economic, political and cultural characteristics of three countries in the MENA region, explain how Emiratis, Omanis and Saudis interpret and make sense of their lives in these contexts and evaluate what they think about the remarkable changes that have occurred in their countries over the last twenty to thirty years. Consequently, it moves among macro-, meso- and micro-levels of analysis while 'paying tribute to human subjectivity and creativity, showing how individuals respond to social constraints and actively assemble and recreate their social worlds' (Plummer, 1983: 5). As many sociologists have argued, societies do not 'act', *sui generis*, but at every stage in their historical, socio-cultural and economic/technological evolution, they do shape and influence the core beliefs and behaviours of those who live in these social systems. In simpler terms, 'big public issues' and 'small private concerns' have a deeply symbiotic relationship, and the role of this *al-bahith* (researcher) was to try to understand these, explain how they are changing and evolving and anticipate what their consequences might be for these three countries and the MENA region in the future (Berger and Luckmann, 1967; Schutz, 1966; Weber, 1949). Hence, the broad objectives of this study were to:

Make an original contribution to the extensive literatures on women in management and professional roles, female business leaders, cross-cultural aspects of management and leadership and the field of gender studies in an Arabian/Islamic context, within the broader context of the significant economic, political and social challenges that confront the Arabian Gulf States and the MENA region.

Understand how Islamic culture and religious beliefs/practices determine and regulate the legal rights and economic freedoms of women in the UAE, Oman and the KSA.

Examine how Islamic culture and religion shape the personal identities of Emirati, Omani and Saudi women (and men) and how these have influenced their attitudes to the societies they live in and their roles in the workplace.

Describe the cultural, social and attitudinal barriers that these women still encounter in their societies and workplaces in the UAE, Oman and the KSA and how these have affected their lives.

Examine the attitudes of Emiratis, Omanis and Saudis towards female employees and women in leadership positions.

Assess the attitudes that men in these countries have about the growing economic independence of women and female leaders.

Evaluate if women in the UAE, Oman and the KSA are 'deconstructing' their learned gender identities in order to develop the self-belief and self-confidence needed to pursue professional careers and seek leadership positions, particularly in private-sector organisations.

Analyse the experiences of women in specific sectors of the labour markets of the UAE (information technology) and Oman and the KSA (entrepreneurs and SME owners).

Examine how Emirati, Omani and Saudi women deal with work–life balance and work–life conflict.

Describe the national economic case for increasing the participation rate of women in the economies and labour markets of the UAE, Oman and the KSA and other countries in the MENA region.

Describe the business case for gender diversity and creating a more 'level playing field' for women in public and private organisations in these countries and the broader MENA region.

Describe governmental policies that could be implemented to allow more women to join the labour forces of these countries and others in the MENA region, explain how gender-diversity policies can be implemented in organisations and present practical policies that would encourage more women to work in STEM occupations and become entrepreneurs and business owners.

THE RESEARCH STUDIES

In order to address these issues, fourteen research studies were conducted between January 2008 and August 2015:

Pilot Study 1 (January–May 2008): examined the differences in the gender self-attributions and self-perceptions of 144 final-year Zayed University Business Leadership students and 114 female MBA postgraduates at the University of Western Australia.

Pilot Study 2 (January–May 2009): examined the attitudes that fifty women at the College of Business Sciences at Zayed University and fifty male students at the Dubai Men's College had towards women in business leadership roles in the UAE.

Studies 3 through 14 were conducted as follows:

Study 3 (June–December 2009): questionnaire survey of female and male Emirati employees. 816 electronic and 'drop-off' questionnaires were distributed to employees at twelve public-sector and semi-government organisations and nine private-sector companies. After sending two reminders, 337 completed questionnaires had been returned by 1 June 2010. The data from this and subsequent surveys were analysed using SPSSx.

Study 4 (March 2008–November 2010): semi-structured interviews were conducted with twenty working Emirati women and twenty men who were attending the Executive Master of Business Administration (EMBA) program at the Zayed University College of Business Sciences in Abu Dhabi. The questions used during these two to three hour interviews may be obtained from the author on request. I had also hoped to conduct at least ten interviews with older Emirati women (i.e. over sixty-five) who had memories of the Emirates before the 1970s. However, their general lack of English (and my lack of Arabic) meant that I was able to locate just four of these remarkable and resilient women with the help of some female part-time MBA students and undergraduates at Zayed University. A few quotes from these interviews can be found at the beginning of Chapter 2. I was unable to replicate this in either Oman or the KSA.

Study 5 (January–June 2010): case study of Emirati women working in the UAE IT sector. Although we contacted the Abu-Dhabi Women's Society, Dubai Women's Development Society, Dubai Women's Establishment, Dubai Women's Council and the UAE General Women's Union, we were unable to easily identify a sufficiently large number of Emirati women working in IT to conduct a valid questionnaire survey. This led to the pragmatic decision to utilise interviews as the primary data collection method. We located sixteen participants employed in IT during January and February 2010, three

interviewees from a group of Executive MBA students and one from a
group of Masters in International Business students at the College of
Business Sciences, Zayed University. Consequently, twenty interviews
were conducted, lasting from two to three hours, during the first half of
2010. The interview questions used in this study can be found in
Forster and al-Marzouqi (2011).

Study 6 (April–June 2011): examined how working mothers in the UAE
deal with work–life balance and work–life conflict issues and also
evaluated the work–life balance support provided by their employers.
Two online questionnaire surveys were distributed to 400 female
Emirati employees in twenty-one UAE public- and private-sector
organisations. After we sent two reminders, 210 questionnaires had
been returned by the end of June 2011; thirty-seven of these were
incomplete and excluded from the data analysis. The respondents who
were married with children were then identified, leaving
119 questionnaires for data analysis.

Study 7 (February 2012–June 2013): questionnaire survey of female and
male Saudi employees. We distributed 523 electronic questionnaires to
employees in nineteen public- and private-sector organisations. After
we sent three reminders, 237 completed questionnaires had been
returned by 1 June 2013. The questionnaire on work–family balance
issues was distributed and completed by the 133 women who had
returned the first questionnaire; 107 of this group were married with
children.

Study 8 (March 2012–April 2014): interviews were conducted with twenty
female and fifteen male working part-time Executive MBA students at
Al Faisal University in Riyadh during 2012–2014.

Study 9 (May 2012–January 2013): case study of twenty female Saudi
entrepreneurs. Personal introductions to twenty-nine female Saudi
entrepreneurs were provided by MBA students in early 2012. After we
made contact with these women, twenty were selected for interviews,
which were conducted either at the participant's business premises or
at Al Faisal University. The questions addressed during the interviews
may be obtained from the author on request.

Study 10 (March–April 2015): questionnaire survey of female and male
Omani employees. We distributed 500 online questionnaires to female
and male Omani employees at ten public- and six private-sector

organisations. These included staff at several key government and semi-government organisations and employees from banking and finance, tourism, oil and gas, construction and telecommunication companies in the private sector. After we sent three rounds of reminders, 180 completed questionnaires had been returned by early August 2015 (N = 104 women and 76 men). These questionnaires also included a section on work–family balance issues, which was completed by the married women in this sample (N = 91). Follow-up interviews were conducted with ten female and ten male employees from this sample during May through September 2015, either at their workplaces or by video calls from Australia.

Study 11 (April–August 2015): case study of female Omani entrepreneurs. Initial contacts with seventeen female entrepreneurs were provided by five undergraduate management students in March 2015. After we had made contact with them, ten agreed to be interviewed. These were conducted during 2015, comprising four face-to-face interviews conducted in May 2015 at their business premises and video calls with the other six during July and August.

Studies 12 through 14 (January 2009–August 2015): semi-structured interviews with twenty graduating female business and management students at Zayed University during 2009, 2010 and 2011 (*Study 12*); twenty final-year female students at the College of Business, Al Faisal University (*Study 13*) during 2012–2014; and ten final-year female management students at Sultan Qaboos University during April and May 2015 (*Study 14*). The questions addressed during these interviews may be obtained from the author on request.

The interviews conducted in the UAE, Oman and the KSA were analysed by utilising the well-established method of 'thematic clustering' (Husserl, 1931; Hycner, 1985; Kvale, 1983). This process is used to search 'for meaningful segments, cutting, pasting and rearranging until the reduced summary reveals the interpretative truth in the text' (Kvale, 1983: 175), with the original textual data being compared with the research questions being addressed in each of the interview studies. Illustrative thematic quotes that emerged from this process can be found throughout this book.

In addition to this research, I also convened two one-day workshops on Women and Business Leadership at Zayed University in Dubai in 2009 and 2010, one at Al Faisal University in Riyadh in 2012 and one at Sultan Qaboos University during May 2015. From February to June 2015, I was also involved in the delivery of six gender-diversity workshops at two private-sector companies in Dubai. In total, more than 200 women (and about forty men) attended those workshops, and insights from the discussions and debates we had at these are included throughout this book. I also taught more than 300 working female part-time MBA students at Zayed University in Dubai and Al Faisal University in the KSA from 2007 to 2014, sessions that also provided many useful insights into the lives of women in these countries.

APPENDIX 2 Glossary of Phonetic Arabic Words and Phrases

Abaya:	Full-length outer garment worn by women in all Muslim countries when in public and by all expatriate women in the KSA.
Abra:	Boat.
Abu:	Father of.
Ahl al-kitab:	Literally, 'people of the book', that is Muslims, Christians and Jews.
Ahliyya:	Authorisation to act in legal or financial transactions.
Al-bahith:	Researcher.
Al-haraka al-nassa'wiyya:	The (Western) feminist movement.
Al-haraka al-nissa'iyya:	The women's movement in the MENA region.
Al-Jumhuriyyah al-Arabiyyah:	The Arabian Republic, not a likely prospect in the KSA at this time.
Al-mutawwa'a (or al-hay'a):	Originally, religious ritual specialists and teachers from the Najd region of the KSA. This descriptor today means 'volunteers who promote virtue and prevent vice'. The Committee for the Promotion of Virtue and Prohibition of Vice is made up largely of poorly educated men schooled only in Islamic teachings (there are some women employed by this organisation, but I was unable to find out how many). They had, until May 2016, unlimited powers to harass, arrest and imprison without trial anyone they believed

	had violated any aspect of *shari'a* laws. This organisation is not well regarded by educated and liberal-minded Saudis.
Al-mabahith:	Officially known as the General Investigation Directorate, the Saudi Arabian secret police is a department of the Ministry of the Interior (*al-mabahith al-amma*). This well-resourced organisation is all pervasive and one reason the KSA is relatively 'stable' when compared to other MENA countries. There is a Mabahith informant in every mosque in the KSA and, I was told, in every university in the KSA on the lookout for potential 'troublemakers' among students and academic staff.
Al-nahda:	Renaissance or awakening.
Al-sahwa:	The Islamist opposition in the KSA.
Al-taraf:	Literally, paternity or affiliation through the male of the family; also the primary basis of kinship relations within the tribe.
Al-wasatiyya:	The middle path of Islam.
Allahmdulillah:	Thanks be to God.
Albaseeta:	Entrepreneur.
Allah hu-akbar:	God is great.
Almani:	Secular.
Almaniyyun:	Secularists.
Amal maidani:	Civil activism. Something that is not permitted by almost all of the rulers of countries in the MENA region
Asabiyya qabaliyya:	Tribal solidarity.
Barasti:	Traditional mud and palm-fronded dwellings.
Bid'a:	Religious innovation, but can also mean 'heresy' if the 'innovation' challenges Islamic beliefs.

Bin (or ibn):	Son of.
Bint:	Daughter of.
Burqa:	Outer garment that covers a woman's entire face and body.
Caliph:	Commander of the Faith; literally, 'successor', from *kalifah*, the title bestowed on Islamic leaders in the time after the Prophet's death.
Caliphate:	Generic name given to the civilisation that at its height extended from central Spain through North Africa, the modern Middle East and up to the western borders of ancient China.
Dar al-Harb:	The realm where Islam's enemies prevail.
Dar al-Islam:	The realm where Islam prevails.
Dayooth:	Not directly translatable into English. It refers to a man who does not guard the honour of his female relatives or his wife.
Dhow:	Traditional sail-powered fishing, pearling and trading boat.
Diwan:	Royal court; a ruler's group of senior advisers.
Emir:	Ruler, prince (occasionally spelled as *amir*).
Fadila:	Virtue.
Fajr:	Pre-dawn Islamic prayer.
Faqihat:	Female Islamic jurists. There were many examples of these in the early years of Islam and a small but growing number of them in the MENA region today.
Fasl al-dinn wa al-dawla:	The separation of religion from the state, something that appears to be very unlikely to happen in most MENA countries.
Fatwa:	Religious edict issued by Islamic clerics.
Ghulat:	Religious extremists.

Hadith:	Reported sayings and actions of the Prophet that were transmitted aurally until they were compiled and written down some years after his death. These serve as the guide to Islamic beliefs and conduct in conjunction with the Qur'an.
Hajj:	The pilgrimage to Mecca, one that all devout Muslims should make at least once in their lives.
Halal:	'Permissible' or 'lawful'.
Halqat al-elmya:	Literally, 'the circle of education'; traditional teaching method with the teacher sitting on the floor and his pupils sitting in a semi-circle in front of him/her.
Haram:	Forbidden (pronounced with an extended 'a'; with a shortened 'a', this means 'holy place').
Harim:	Alternative spelling of *harem*.
Hay'at kibal al-ulama:	The Committee of Senior Clerics, a group of imams in the KSA who advise both the ruling regime and Saudi citizens on all matters relating to interpretations of the Qur'an, Islam and Shari'a law.
Hisbah:	To do good.
Hizb al-Ghulat:	Literally, 'the fanatic party', a phrase that more moderate/liberal Arabs use to describe Islamic fundamentalists.
Huquq:	Rights.
Ibadi:	Sometimes spelled *Ibadhi*; an offshoot of Sunni Islam, the dominant Islamic faith of Oman.
Iftar:	Breaking of the fast at sunset during Ramadan.
Ihsan:	Physical demonstrations and manifestations of a Muslim's faith.

Ijma:	Consensus of opinion among Islamic scholars. As this book demonstrates, there is a notable lack of consensus among contemporary Islamic theologians about the 'true' meaning of the Qur'an.
Ijtihad:	This is the closest word in Arabic to the English word, 'reform'. Its literal meaning is 'to find out, to follow the truth' or 'independent reasoning'. This is, according to liberal Muslim scholars, permitted when (re) interpreting the 'real' meaning of the Qur'an and *shari'a* laws.
Ikhtilat:	Prohibition on non-related men and women mixing in public spaces. This is rigorously enforced in the KSA but much less so in the UAE and Oman.
Imam:	Islamic teacher, leader and cleric (see also *mufti*).
Iman:	Conscious acceptance of the metaphysical aspects of Islam and an unquestioning belief in the six articles of the faith.
Imara:	Emirate.
Infitah:	Openness.
Inshalla:	'God willing', a phrase all Arabic Muslims use habitually during social interactions.
Intifada:	Uprising, insurrection.
Iqta'iyin:	Feudal lords, a nickname for the al-Sauds and the ruling elite of the KSA.
Ird:	The honour/reputation of women.
Istid'af:	Oppressive or abusive behaviour that renders another person powerless.
Iwah:	Yes.
Jahiliyya:	Ignorance of the true faith.

Jihad:	Holy war.
Kaaba:	The central courtyard of the holy site at Mecca.
Kafir:	Infidel (i.e. anyone who is not a Muslim); from *kufr*, meaning 'blasphemy'.
Karamah:	Dignity, a word often heard during the Arab uprisings during the early 2010s.
Khalifa:	Descendant of Muhammed
Khula:	Divorce.
Khususiya:	The unique Islamic traditions of Saudi Arabia.
La':	No.
La 'illaha illa allah	There is no God but God.
Madrassa:	School. In religious schools, much of the curriculum is still based on rote learning of the Qur'an.
Mahdi:	One who guides.
Mahram:	Male guardian.
Majlis al-Shura:	Consultative Council.
Majlis al-Wuzara:	Council of Ministers.
Moohima:	Professor.
Moqaddas:	Sacred.
Mudeer:	Legal requirement in the KSA for women-owned companies to appoint a male Saudi manager if they employ any men or if they or their company deals with men in external business transactions. This requirement was still being applied when the twenty women I interviewed during 2012–2013 had registered their businesses.
Mufti:	Male religious scholar and interpreter of *shari'a* law (see also *imam*).
Muftia:	Female religious scholar and interpreter of *shari'a* law; not officially recognised by the

entirely male religious establishments of the UAE, Oman and the KSA.

Muhafadhat: Governate; regional administrative division of Oman.

Muhammed rasoolu-allah: Muhammed is the messenger of God.

Mujahid/een: Holy warrior; group of holy warriors defending Islamic communities.

Mukhabaraat: A collective noun, used by people throughout the Arab world to describe the overlapping networks of agencies that monitor them and suppress any dissent or opposition to the ruling elite and/or religious clique or and/or military junta that rules their countries.

Mulhid: Atheist.

Murshida: A religious guide, and the title given to female Islamic preachers in Morocco. The country's ruler, Muhammed VI, had issued a royal decree in 2003 to allow women to be preachers, a move that was vehemently opposed by Islamic clerics in Morocco and others throughout the MENA region. The first class of *murshidat* graduated in 2006. In 2005, Turkey launched a similar program, as did Dubai in 2007. Several Islamic scholars have pointed out that this is a case of 'back to the future' because the tradition of female Islamic preachers and jurists is a very old one, dating back to the time of the Prophet.

Niqab: Veil that covers the face with a small open space for the eyes.

Qadi: Judge.

Qadiyyat al-mara: Women's issues.

Qawwamuna:	Literally 'responsibility'; the role of men (husbands, brothers and fathers) as the 'guardians' of women (wives, sisters and mothers) in Islamic societies.
Qiyas:	Deductions inferred from the deeds and sayings of the Prophet, written down in the *Hadith*.
Qur'an:	The holy book of Islam; usually written as 'Koran' in English. Because the prophet could not read or write, the revelations he is said to have received from God over a period of about twenty-three years were memorised by the *huffaz* (professional remembrancers) and also written down by his secretary, Zaid ibn Thabit. These were compiled into one volume about a year after Mohammed's death in CE 644, but it was many centuries before the 'official' version of the Qur'an that is used by most Muslims today was finally settled.
Ramadan:	Islamic holy month of fasting and prayer. The timing of this is based on a pre-Copernican lunar calendar.
Sa'b al-tasdiq:	Hard to believe; unbelievable.
Shari'a:	Originally, the path or way to a water source; now the canon of civil and criminal law based on the interpretations and rulings of Islamic scholars and jurists.
Sheikh:	Leader (in English, also spelled as *shaikh* and *shaykh*).
Sheikha:	Female leader.
Shia/Shiite:	Minority religious group in the UAE, Oman and the KSA (about two million people who live mainly in the east and south-west of

Saudi Arabia) who Sunnis often refer to as *Rafidah* ('those who reject') and, for Syrian Alowites, *Nusayri*. The Sunni/Shia schism in Islam explains why the KSA, Bahrain and the UAE gave military and financial support to crush the Shiite uprising in Bahrain during 2011 and why there have been violent protests by Shiites in the KSA throughout the 2000s and 2010s; why the KSA, the UAE and Oman hate Iran; and why they also fund and support groups who are fighting Assad in Syria. There are two Shia schools of jurisprudence, *Jafari* and *Zaidi*.

Shirq: Anything outside the prescriptions of Islam. This includes all other religions, atheism, secularism and some well-established bodies of scientific knowledge, such as human evolution. The antonym of this is *tawhid*, an unequivocal belief in the true God.

Shura: Consultation.

Shweya-shweya: Little by little; a phrase used by some of my interviewees when describing the often glacial or non-existent pace of economic, political and social change in their countries.

Souk: Market.

Sukuk: Islamic bond.

Sunnah: Sayings of the Prophet and the body of Islamic customs based on his conduct during his life.

Sunni: Derived from *Ahlus Sunnah*, meaning 'people of the Sunnah'. This is the variant of Islam followed by most of the populations of the UAE, Oman, the KSA and much of the

MENA region. Sunni Islam has four main theological schools: *Hanafi, Hanbali, Maliki* and *Shaifi*

Sura: Verse in the Qur'an.

Tabaruf: Colloquially, 'to display one's charms'.

Tagrib: Westernisation.

Tahrir al-mar'a: Women's liberation.

Takfir: An accusation of apostasy made about another Muslim.

Talib/Taliban: Student(s).

Ulama/ulema: 'Those who possess knowledge'; senior Islamic clerics.

Umm: Mother of.

Umma: The worldwide Islamic community.

Wadi: Water source; oasis.

Wahhabism: Austere and very conservative variant of Islam. This originated during the despotic Omayyad dynasty (661–705 CE). The Omayyads introduced dynastic rule and also decreed that no one could question the decisions made by the ruling Caliph. The Omayyads slaughtered the descendants of Mohammed because they were competitors, creating the schism that led to the emergence of the Shiite sect. Wahhabism was further articulated in the thirteenth-century theological teachings of Ibn Tamiyya and by Muhammad bin Abd al-Wahhab during the eighteenth century. Wahhabists regard Shiites as heretics. For Western readers who may be struggling to understand the obscure theological 'reasons' for the mutual antipathy between Sunnis and

	Shiites (and Alawites), these are similar in kind to the Catholic–Protestant schisms of the sixteenth and seventeenth century in Europe and the decades of mutual antipathy and warfare that ensued. Archaic echoes of this bloody conflict can still be found in places like Northern Ireland and Scotland today. To imagine the nearest Western equivalent to present-day Wahhabists, imagine a merger of zealous English Puritans and the Spanish Inquisition.
Wakeel:	Literally, 'he who can be trusted', and used to describe the role of male 'guardians' in the KSA.
Wallah:	All-purpose exclamation, literally 'I swear to God'; meaning, 'honestly, it's the truth'.
Wasta:	Formally, 'personal connection'. In practice, this means 'influence' and is associated with the return of a favour or the granting of a request to someone who has provided help in the past. This widespread Middle Eastern practice would generally be regarded as 'nepotism', 'cronyism', 'favouritism' or 'corruption' in many other countries.
Yanni:	I mean.
Zlayeb:	Morons; a word used by a few Saudi interviewees to describe the *al-mutawwa'a*.

Notes

1 It has often been said that not all Arabs are Muslims and not all Muslims are Arabs. The meaning of the terms 'Arab' and 'Muslim' also vary from context to context, and can refer to ways of identifying commonalities with other Arabs and also as a means of differentiation from non-Muslims. In practice, these terms are 'simply so intertwined that separating them is almost impossible' (Telhami, 2013: 21), and that is the approach taken in this book. The terms 'Islam' and 'Islamic' are used throughout this book to signify an all-embracing theological worldview that encompasses all aspects of public and private life in Muslim societies. It should, however, also be remembered that there are significant national and local variations in how Islamic beliefs are interpreted, practiced and applied across the MENA region and in other parts of the world.
2 The background to this research and a summary of the 14 studies conducted between 2008 and 2015 in the UAE, Oman and the KSA can be found in Appendix A.

CHAPTER I

1 Please refer to Appendix 2 for a glossary of the Anglicised Arabic words and phrases used throughout this book.
2 Many scholars have written about the reasons why the MENA region and the Ottoman Empire did not readily embrace industrialisation and the scientific revolution of the late eighteenth and nineteenth century; why Islamic cultures have been – and continue to be – unwilling to separate the religious and secular (or sacred' and 'profane) domains of their societies and why much of the Islamic world became locked into a circular paradigm of history – in contrast to a Western linear paradigm of historical and societal evolution. For more information on how these beliefs impeded the economic, political and technological development of the MENA region during the nineteenth and twentieth centuries, why European colonial powers were able to seize control of the MENA region with relative ease, and how this in turn led to the rise of the radical Islamic theologians and the early political movements that were the progenitors

of al Qaeda and ISIS, see Cole (2014: 62–68, 120–125 and 163–165), *The Economist* (2014b), Ferris (2010: 267–279), Holland (2012) and Stark (2014).

3 For anyone who still believes that ISIS and the many terrorist attacks carried out by Muslims in numerous countries during the 2000s and 2010s 'are nothing to do with the Islamic faith', please refer to Ali (2015), Badawy et al (2015), Fadl (2005) and Manne (2016). They are deeply bound up with each other and Aayan Hirsi Ali has described those who still deny this link as 'moral idiots' (Ali, 2015: 232). The same, of course, can also be said of the more zealous adherents of Christianity, Judaism and other religious faiths who have used their beliefs to justify all kinds of barbarous acts against those they have considered to be 'non-believers' or 'heretics' in the past.

4 Unless otherwise indicated, all financial data are in US dollars throughout the book.

CHAPTER 2

1 When Sheik Zayed abolished slavery in 1964, he immediately gave former slaves full legal rights and free blocks of land to enable them to establish homes and businesses. As in the United States, freed slaves often took the names of their former owners. The difference is that the descendants of these 'African Emiratis' now benefit from having some of the most prestigious names in the UAE, their integration into Emirati society was fast and they don't (as far as I was able to ascertain during my time in the UAE) face discrimination from 'indigenous' Emiratis.

2 In an official act of gratitude, the ruler of Dubai, Sheikh Mohammed bin Rashid al-Maktoum, renamed the world's tallest building, the Bur Dubai, the Bur Khalifa in honour of the ruler of Abu Dhabi, Sheikh Khalifa bin Zayed al-Nahyan.

3 The UAE, in common with every other country in the MENA region, has significant environmental problems. In 2008, the World Wildlife Fund estimated that the UAE had the worst per-capita environmental footprint in the world – more than five times greater than the global average (Davidson, 2009: 69). This had improved a little by 2014, when it had the third-worst per capita environmental footprint on the planet (Bertelsmann Stiftung, 2015a: 20). The World Fund for Nature's Living Planet Report, in 2008, reported that the UAE's 'ecological footprint' was 9.5 hectares per person (hpp), slightly higher than the USA's 9.4 hpp. The report commented that if everyone on the planet devoured as many resources as the citizens of the UAE and the United States do, we would need 4.5 Earth-sized planets to achieve this (Krane, 2009: 223–224). The government has been making some efforts to deal with these environmental concerns and has recently signed (but not ratified) several international environmental conventions (World Economic Forum, 2016a: 70).

4 As in Oman and the KSA, this lack of enforceable legal rights extends to the domestic sphere in relation to matters such as inheritance, freedom to choose their place of residence, divorce and child-custody rights, which are still weighted in favour of men; the lack of protection against domestic violence and rape; female circumcision and (male) polygamy. For further information on these issues, please refer to the report by the International Federation for Human Rights (2010), and for some heartrending stories of the (allegedly) routine domestic violence directed at women in countries like Yemen and Saudi Arabia, see Eltahawy (2015). To the best of my knowledge, only one MENA country (Tunisia) has abolished male-guardianship laws and introduced Personal Status protections for women, giving them equal legal rights with men.

5 Several NGOs routinely challenge decisions made by the all-male *ulama* which discriminate against women in Muslim countries. These include Sisters in Islam, established by Zainah Anwar in the mid-1990s in Malaysia: www.sistersinislam.org.my/; and many of the authors cited in this section cite examples of liberal Islamic scholars who have argued passionately for the emancipation of Muslim women in the past and today (e.g. Fadl, 2005: 250–274; al-Munajjed, 1997: 28–32; al-Rasheed, 2016, 2015, 2013 and 2010). For more information on how the often nebulous and contradictory prescriptions about women contained in the Qur'an evolved into strict cultural and legal restrictions, see the United Nations Arab Human Development Report (2005: Chapter 7).

CHAPTER 3

1 Please see Appendix 1 for further information about this study. All the data in the tables in this chapter and subsequent chapters are rounded to one decimal point.

2 This section is based on research first published by Forster and Al Marzouqi (2011).

3 This process is described in more detail in Appendix 1.

4 The 'UAE Ministry of Education Strategy 2010–2020' document indicated that one of its goals for national schools was 'to develop curricula and align with Higher Education and job market requirements' (United Arab Emirates Ministry of Education, 2010: 2). However, this did not explain how this was to be achieved and I could not find any information about what progress, if any, has been made towards this goal since this policy document was published.

5 Additional information on the design of this questionnaire and the distribution of the survey can be found in Appendix 1.

CHAPTER 4

1 It has been noted by several authors (e.g. Limbert, 2010, 167–169) that there are discrepancies in both internal and external estimates of Oman's annual oil production output since 1970. Because of its international reputation for accuracy, the data provided by the United States Energy Information Agency figures is the primary source of the information in this chapter concerning oil and gas production in Oman.

2 The consensus is that Said was not a particularly bad, greedy or malicious leader but was very concerned about how rapid economic modernisation (i.e. 'Westernisation') might affect Oman's cultural and religious traditions and so he adopted isolationist policies for a decade. For a detailed explanation of the reasons for the 1970 coup, the creation of the coalition of Omani and British forces which ensured that Said surrendered without a fight and why the 1960s insurgency by communist insurgents in Dhofar was not finally ended until 1976, see Jones and Ridout (2015: Chapters 5 and 6). It is also worth noting that the national budget of 1972 emphasised the creation of better infrastructure, social welfare and jobs for the people of the troubled region of Dhofar (Jones and Ridout, 2015: 157). For a rich and informative ethnographic study of how one town in Oman, Bahla, has coped with the rapid economic development of the country, see Limbert (2010).

3 Oman has better one of the better environmental records of countries in the GCC and MENA region. It was the first Arab country to become a member of the International Union for the Conservation of Nature (in 1996). The country's first environmental legislation was passed in 1974, and in 1984 Oman became the first Arab country to establish a ministry for the environment. A bi-annual award, the Sultan Qaboos International Prize for Environmental Protection, is presented to a conservation group chosen by UNESCO for its environmental protection work. 'Environment Day' is celebrated each year at schools and universities on 8 January. However, like all MENA countries, Oman does have some significant environmental challenges (Index Mundi, 2015).

4 Although I did not encounter a single Omani who was willing to discuss such a forbidden (*haram*) issue, several expatriates I met in 2015 said that it was widely rumoured that Sultan Qaboos was gay and had bestowed generous endowments on his paramours throughout his reign. To complicate matters, there have been rumours for years about Sultan Qaboos having an illegitimate son although all the Omanis I asked about this thought it was a myth.

5 As in the UAE and the KSA, this lack of legal rights extends to the domestic sphere in relation to matters such as inheritance, freedom to choose their place of residence, marriage, divorce and child-custody rights which are still weighted

in favour of men; the lack of protection against domestic violence and rape (the rape of a spouse is not regarded as a criminal offence); female circumcision and (male) polygamy. Further information on this can be found in the reports by CEDAW (United Nations, 2011) and UNICEF (United Nations Children's Fund, 2014). Hence, the claim made in a well-known tourist guide to Oman suggesting that women 'enjoy equality with their male counterparts in every respect and in every field' is way off the mark (Walker et al, 2010: 176).

6 It is notable that the reports that are most upbeat and optimistic about Oman's economic development and diversification strategies (and, indeed, about the UAE and the KSA) are, without exception, written by consulting firms that also have commercial interests in these countries. The most critical reports, as well as being generally more rigorous and detailed, were written by organisations like the International Labour Organisation and the United Nations or NGOs who have no commercial interests in these countries.

CHAPTER 5

1 Please see Appendix 1 for further information about these studies.

2 Jennings and Brush indicate that the first academic article on women entrepreneurs was by Schwartz (1976). However, this topic was not covered in a special issue of an academic journal until 1997 (in *Entrepreneurship and Regional Development*) and it was 2009 before the *International Journal of Gender and Entrepreneurship* was launched (Jennings and Brush, 2013: 666). It is something of a simplification, but this literature is grounded in three overlapping areas of scholarship: the employment, organisational and occupational psychology literatures; feminist theory and gender studies; and creativity and innovation. It should also be noted that there is no international consensus about what a 'small', 'SME' or a 'large' company is (in terms of the number of staff employed and/or market capitalisation). In some countries, the cut-off point for a 'medium-sized' company is 500 employees, in others 250, 100, 50 and 20. In this chapter and in Chapter 7, a 'small' company is defined as one with 19 or fewer employees, and a 'medium-sized' company is one with 20 to 199 employees, following the current Australian Bureau of Statistics' descriptors (Australian Bureau of Statistics, 2016).

3 Please see Appendix 1 for further information about this study.

4 There had also been some discussions about creating an 'Innovation Centre' at CEPS/SQU during the spring semester 2015, but there was no indication on this university's website (in June 2016) that this had been established.

5 The ten institutions were Sultan Qaboos University, University of Nizwa, Bayan University College, Muscat College, Sohar University, Higher College of

Technology, Dhofar University, Majan University College, Al Musanna College of Technology and Al Buraimi University College (Webometrics, 2016). All of these offer undergraduate and postgraduate business/management degree courses, but none of them were involved in partnerships with any international organisations who promote female entrepreneurship in emerging economies, such as the Goldman Sachs 10,000 Women Initiative (Brush, 2014).

6 Please see Appendix 1 for further information about this study.

CHAPTER 6

1 To say that the political history of the KSA since 1932 has been complex, turbulent and at times very violent would be an understatement. For further information about this, see al-Rasheed (2010), Haykel et al (2015), Lacey (2009 and 2001) and Weston (2008). For additional material on the alliance between the al-Sauds and the Wahhabist *ulama* in the KSA, see Mouline (2015: 48–70) and al-Rasheed (2010: chapters 1–3).

2 The KSA has many serious environmental problems. These include deforestation, desertification, urban, coastal and industrial pollution, marine ecosystem degradation, water shortages and huge amounts of domestic, commercial and industrial waste. There are no recycling systems to deal with any of this waste, although plans were being prepared in 2014 to introduce these. Almost all of the country's aquifers are now completely depleted, and these sources have been largely replaced by energy-intensive desalination plants which supply about 60 per cent of the nation's water. Millions of barrels of oil are burned each day for subsidised domestic, commercial and industrial use, and in 2015, the KSA had the fifth-highest per-capita rate of carbon dioxide emissions in the world. The domination of gas-guzzling private cars and taxis, combined with the absence of an adequate urban public transport infrastructure, also means consistently high exhaust and particulate pollution in all of the KSA's cities and towns (Hussain and Khalil, 2013; al-Suhaimy, 2013; United Nations, 2015a: 250). It is also worth mentioning that I did not see a single solar panel on any domestic or industrial building during the thirty-six months I worked in the KSA, a country which has at least 300 sunny days a year. The country's *Vision 2030* document did dedicate one very short paragraph which mentioned the need 'to safeguard our environment' but contained no specific policy recommendations (Eye of Riyadh, 2016).

3 *The Economist* (2013a: 11) estimated that these cost about $240 billion in 2013, about one third of the revenues generated by the Saudi oil and gas industry. A way to illustrate the individual value of these generous energy subsidies is

with two personal examples. During the three years I worked in the KSA, the combined annual bill for utilities (water, gas and electricity) was about $150 and for nine months of the year the air-conditioning system in my apartment was on most of the time. It cost about $20 to fill the gasoline tank of a Ford Explorer in 2014.

4 In 1992, the Basic Law of the KSA had been amended to limit future successions to the direct male descendants of al-Saud (i.e. sons or grandsons) and, in order to forestall potential conflicts between rival candidates, King Abdullah had also introduced the first set of transparent rules for the selection of an heir in 2006 overseen by the thirty-five all-male members of the Committee of Allegiance (al-Rasheed, 2015: 257–259; Vietor and White, 2015: 4).

5 For more information about the KSA's dismal human rights record and the KSA's Human Rights Commission, see al-Rasheed (2015: 251–253 and 2013), Haidar (2015), Human Rights Watch (2015) and Lacey (2009: 168–169, 256, 272, 313, 317–319 and 334). For anyone who may be unfamiliar with this, arbitrary arrest, imprisonment and torture are commonplace in the KSA; there is no concept of *habeas corpus* in the Saudi legal system and there are no trials by jury. Most court cases are held *in camera*. Amputations of hands for theft still occur, seventy to eighty lashes is considered to be a normal punishment for minor infractions of the law and death by stoning and crucifixion are still permitted under Saudi law. 'Witchcraft' remains a crime in the KSA, punishable by beheading. Homosexuality is punishable by corporal and capital punishments, as are atheism and apostasy.

There are, on average, about seventy executions a year in the KSA, compared to about thirty executions in the United States which has a much larger population, and some of these are still carried out in public places. The state advertised for eight new executioners in early 2016 after beheading more people in the first half of 2015 than it did in all of 2014 and a surge in the beheading of Saudi Shiites. In its advertisement, the Civil Service Ministry said that no qualifications were necessary and that applicants would be exempted from the usual civil service entrance exams. Successful applicants would also be required to carry out amputations ordered by Saudi judges (*The Guardian*, 2015).

To cite just one example of the thousands of Saudis and expatriates who have fallen foul of the Saudi judicial system, a liberal blogger, Raif Badawi, was condemned to ten years in jail and 1,000 lashes in 2014, after a campaign of vilification conducted against him by his psychopathic father and several zealous clerics. The lashes were to be administered each month, fifty strokes at a time, during his sentence. What, you may be wondering, was the dreadful crime that had provoked the ire of those who imposed this sentence? He had mocked some Saudi clerics who had claimed that astronomy provoked skepticism of *shari'a* law and also questioned the rule of the al-Sauds and, as a result, had shown 'disrespect of Islam' and 'signs of apostasy' (Haidar, 2015). Although the floggings were suspended in January 2015 after an international outcry and a personal appeal by President Obama to King Abdullah, he was still imprisoned in December 2016 (Amnesty International, 2016). The KSA has been a signatory to the United Nations Convention against Torture and Other Cruel, Inhuman or Degrading Treatment or Punishment since 1997 and is also a member of the UN's Human Rights Council (Baird, 2016: 12).

Officially, slavery was abolished in 1962, although several human rights and labour organisations have claimed that this still exists in practice for the tens of thousands of exploited and poorly paid indentured domestic workers and labourers in the kingdom. No official government figures are available, but it has been alleged that hundreds of construction workers have been seriously injured while working on unsafe building sites and dozens killed over the last twenty years. At least eleven migrant workers died during the construction of the $10 billion King Abdullah Financial District in Riyadh (Amnesty International, 2014; Chamberlain, 2013; *The Economist*, 2016f).

6 Drawing on some earlier research on the causes of joyriding in Riyadh, Menoret suggests that the hierarchical, authoritarian and patriarchal relationships that are characteristic of many Saudi families produced, 'routine humiliation and violence' with fathers abusing elder sons, who in turn bullied their younger siblings, both male and female; and this cycle of abuse repeats itself generation after generation. This produces a lot of angry young men who know only how to submit to society (and bully and intimidate others, particularly women), or they try to find some way to 'rebel' and joyriding in fast cars was one of the few outlets that young men had to do this in Saudi society. It was also an opportunity for young Saudi men to enage in illicit sexual relationships, which was one of the main reasons why the authorities clamped down hard on joyriding at this time (Menoret, 2014: 182–185).

7 There have been numerous protests against the KSA's arcane ban on female driving since at least 1990 and there are several videos on YouTube that feature Saudi women doing this (YouTube, 2016), or you can do a Google search for Wajiha al-Howayder who has been arrested several times for driving. Lujain al-Hithlul, who attempted to drive from the UAE to the KSA on 1 December 2015, was arrested at the border and kept in prison for 73 days. It has been estimated that approximately 1 million foreign drivers are required to provide transport services for Saudi and expatriate women in the KSA (Bennoune, 2013: 208).

8 The 2008 CEDAW report indicated that the KSA was due to submit its third report on its compliance with its provisions in October 2009 and a fourth report in 2013. However, there is no indication on the United Nations CEDAW website that these reports were submitted or reviewed and I did not receive a reply from this organisation to three emails sent during 2016 asking for information about this.

9 As in the UAE and Oman, this lack of legal rights extends deeply into the domestic sphere in relation to matters such as female inheritance, freedom to choose their place of residence and mobility, marriage, divorce and child-custody rights, the lack of protection against domestic violence and rape (the rape of a spouse is still not considered to be a crime under Saudi law), female circumcision and (male) polygamy (Tucker, 2008). In 2013, a law was passed which made domestic violence a criminal offence, but I was unable find any information about the effectiveness of this or if any Saudi men have since been prosecuted for this. One report, published in 2010, cited some 1500 instances of documented domestic violence but this was certainly just the tip of the proverbial iceberg (National Society for Human Rights 2010: 41–46). For further information on this, please refer to the reports by CEDAW (United Nations, 2007) and Human Rights Watch (2015: 23–33). These are, as far as I know, the most recent reports on the KSA published by these organisations. For more information about the very disturbing and pathological beliefs that conservative male Saudi clerics (and, it would appear, a sizeable number of Saudi men) have about polygamy, violence against women, rape, death by stoning, female genital mutilation and female sexuality, see Ali (2015, 2010 and 2007); al-Rasheed (2015: 297–298), Eltahawy (2015), Fadl (2007: 250–274) and Lacey, (2009: 303–315). For a discussion of these issues in other MENA countries, such as Algeria, Iran, Algeria and Somalia, see Bennoune (2013). Some people may find several of the true stories in Mona Eltahawy's book to be extremely distressing.

10 Although this is a very sad and true story, Lacey (2009: 279) mentions a joke – which I heard several variations of while working in the KSA – about royal female Saudis who might want to marry a non-royal: they must be over forty, physically disabled and have a PhD, preferably all three at the same time. At Al Faisal University, there were two royal princesses in their early thirties who worked in administration and, I was told, were not betrothed because there were no suitable first or second royal male cousins for them to marry. The KSA has the highest rate of marriage between first and second cousins in the world.

CHAPTER 7

1 Please see Appendix 1 for further information about this study.

2 Please see Appendix 1 for further information about this study.

3 The ten institutions were the King Abdullah University of Science and Technology, Ibn Sina National College for Medical Studies, King Abdulaziz University, Prince Mohammed Bin Fahd University, Arab Open University, Effat University, Umm Al Qura University, Al Faisal University, Al Yamamah University and Al Jouf University (Webometrics, 2016). Eight of these offered undergraduate business/management degrees, and six offered postgraduate business/management courses. None of these institutions was a partner with any international organisations that promote female entrepreneurship in emerging economics, such as the Goldman Sachs 10,000 Women Initiative (Brush, 2014). The Saudi Vision 2030 document says that the KSA 'aims to have at least five Saudi Universities ranked in the top 200 universities in international rankings' by 2030, a goal that can only be described as 'very optimistic' (Eye of Riyadh, 2016).

4 Please see Appendix 1 for further information about this study.

CHAPTER 8

1 A measure of how low the per-capita economic performance of two of these countries is can be gauged by the following comparative GDP-to-population statistics from 2014:

Oman population: 4.155 million
GDP in 2014: $US81.80 billion
KSA population: 30.890 million
GDP in 2014: $US753.800 billion
Singapore population: 5.470 million
GDP in 2014: $US307.9 billion
Sweden population: 9.696 million
GDP in 2014: $US571.1 billion
Switzerland population: 8.188 million
GDP in 2014: $US701 billion
(World Bank, 2014)

2 A question that might be asked is whether never-ending economic growth in this or any other part of the world is a rational objective given the well-documented problems of climate change, global warming, environmental degradation and the rapid depletion of the world's natural resources. My answer is that it probably is (given the absence of realistic alternatives) but only with a major commitment to

environmental sustainability and renewable energy. Also, what is being proposed in this chapter should not be regarded as any kind of endorsement for the application of neo-liberal or 'Chicago School' economic policies in the MENA region.

3 The main purpose of this chapter is to document the economic and business benefits of gender equality and diversity, not to describe the benefits of all forms of employee diversity (cultural/ethnic, sexual, skills, experience and so forth). However, the business case for embracing these other forms of diversity is also well established, and many of the employee diversity studies mentioned here and in Chapter 9 describe these.

4 Numerous case-studies of the beneficial effects of employee diversity on employee performance, sales growth and market penetration, customer/client retention and the bottom-line results of companies can be found in the studies by (among others) the Centre for Talent Innovation (2014) and Hewlett et al (2013).

CHAPTER 9

1 Among the studies and reports cited throughout this book, several describe reforms to national legal frameworks, improving legal rights for women and ensuring that they have equal access to justice (e.g. every United Nations reports on the MENA region and the United Nations Economic and Social Commission for Western Asia, 2014a). The latter report covered eight domains: access to equitable and safe employment, education and training, access to and control over economic resources and opportunities, voice in society and influencing policy, freedom from the risk of violence, freedom of movement, access to and control over reproductive health and family formation, and social protection and childcare (United Nations Economic and Social Commission for Western Asia, 2014: 5–6). For a detailed discussion of the range of legal changes that could be introduced for women in Islamic countries, please refer to the United Nations (2009 and 2005) and Dobbs et al (2015: 81–87). For information on what should be done to improve the often abysmal working conditions of the two million-plus female domestic servants who work in the Gulf states, see the United Nations (2015a: 114–116). It should also be remembered that the actions taken by Western countries in recent decades to emancipate and empower women emerged in a largely reactive and *ad hoc* fashion – they were not systematically planned with the future in mind.

2 GCC countries operate a partial regime of free movement for their citizens but not for expatriate workers, who are required to have a sponsoring

employer before they can obtain a residence and work visa, driving licence and so forth. In theory, national women also have the right to move to other GCC countries to work, but this is rare in practice because of the male-guardianship laws (Babar, 2011). In a sign of a possible relaxation of its employment and residence laws, the KSA announced in April 2016 that it would issue 'green card' permanent residence documents to foreigners. However, it was not made clear if this would include female expatriate workers (*The Economist*, 2016k: 40).

3 For a very detailed guide to overcoming entrenched male attitudes and their (inevitable) resistance to their initial shock of working with women, no one has ever bettered the advice provided by Michael Simmons's in his *New Leadership for Women and Men: Building an Inclusive Organisation* (1996). It is also worth mentioning that I was still doing seminars on gender issues in organisations for MBAs in Australia until 2007, and these continued in the UAE and the KSA until 2014. Just *talking* about these issues can be a powerful catalyst for getting men and women to start questioning negative gender perceptions and attitudes. An example I often used during these sessions to illustrate the very shaky foundations of misogynist beliefs was the true story about the female lead violinist, Abbie Conant, who had applied – and failed – to get a position with orchestras *eleven times* (Gladwell, 2006: 245–252).

4 For a very detailed HRM policy document that describes how companies in emerging (and Islamic) economies can introduce diversity programs and how to accurately quantify the costs, outcomes and benefits of these, see the International Finance Corporation (2013a and 2013b).

5 Most of the recommendations in this section are primarily relevant to the KSA and Oman. The UAE is partially excluded from this discussion because several reports have indicated that it has one of the most female-friendly entrepreneurial/SME sectors in the MENA region. In 2015, for example, it was ranked twenty-seventh of seventy-seven countries in the Global Entrepreneurship and Development Institute's Female Entrepreneurship Index. Saudi Arabia was ranked forty-ninth and Oman was not included in this report (Terjesen and Lloyd, 2015: 11). This is not to say that the UAE should not endeavour to further enhance institutional support for female entrepreneurs and business owners. For more information about this see Sokari et al (2013).

6 For a more detailed description of the measures that financial institutions could take to provide better support and advice for female entrepreneurs and SME owners, see the International Finance Corporation (2013a: 25–28) and Alturki and Braswell (2010).

POSTSCRIPT

1 There is only one long-term solution to the apparently intractable conflicts of the MENA region, and that is a political one. For more information on how this might happen, and the parallels between this region today and Europe in the early seventeenth century, see the website of the Forum on Geopolitics at Cambridge University: www.coggs.polis.cam.ac.uk/, and Simms et al (2016). For more information on how numerous apparently dominant and successful civilisations have collapsed in the past, see Diamond (2005).

Bibliography

Following the referencing style used in several Cambridge University Press books on the Middle East and North Africa, the surnames of many Arabic authors in the bibliography ignore the definitive article 'al-'. For example, 'al-Hassan, 1996' can be found under surnames beginning with 'H' or 'al-Kibsi et al, 2015' can be located under surnames beginning with 'K'.

Abdalla, I. 1996. 'Attitudes towards women in the Arabian Gulf region', *Women in Management Review*, 11(1): 29–39.

Abdulrahman, A., Saif, N. Ahmed and Abdulla, S. 2009. 'A comparative analysis of the beliefs that Emiratis have towards the evolving nature of business leadership in the UAE', Final-year Capstone Dissertation, College of Business Sciences, Zayed University, Dubai.

al-Abed, I. 2007. *United Arab Emirates Yearbook 2007*. Dubai: Trident Press.

Abouzied, R. 2008. 'Emirati women an economic force', *The National (Business Section)*, 14 May.

Abu-Sharkh, A. and al-Shubaili, W. 2013. 'The EY G20 entrepreneurship monitor 2013: Saudi Arabia', Ernst & Young, accessed 11 April 2014 from www.ey.com/Publication/vwLUAssets/EY-G20-country-report-2013-Saudi-Arabia/$FILE/EY-G20-country-report-2013-Saudi-Arabia.pdf.

Acemoglu, D. and Robinson, J. 2012. *Why Nations Fail: The Origins of Power, Prosperity and Poverty*. New York: Random House.

Adams, J., King, C., Pendlebury. D, Hook, D. and Wilsdon, J. 2011. 'Exploring the changing landscape of Arabian, Persian and Turkish research', Thomson Reuters Business, accessed 21 April 2012 from http://researchanalytics.thomsonreuters.com/m/pdfs/globalresearchreport-aptme.pdf.

Agence France Presse 2003. 'Panel pins rape scandal on top brass', *The Australian*, 24 September.

Agtmael, A. 2007. *The Emerging Markets Century*. New York: Free Press.

Aguirre, D., Hoteit, L. and Sabbagh, K. 2013. 'How to keep the promise of the third billion: a new index of countries links their future prosperity to raising the status of women', Strategy+Business, 15 October, accessed 8 July 2013 from www.strategy-business.com/article/00137?gko=5d83b.

Ahmad, S. 2012. 'Micro, small and medium sized enterprises development in the Kingdom of Saudi Arabia: problems and constraints', *World Journal of Entrepreneurship, Management and Sustainable Development*, 8(4): 217–232.

——— 2011a. 'Evidence of the characteristics of women entrepreneurs in the Kingdom of Saudi Arabia', *International Journal of Gender and Entrepreneurship*, 3(2): 123–143.

——— 2011b. 'Business women in the Kingdom of Saudi Arabia: characteristics, growth patterns and progression in a regional context', *Equality, Diversity and Inclusion: An International Journal*, 30(7): 610–614.

Ahmed, L. 2011. *A Quiet Revolution? The Veil's Resurgence from the Middle East to America*. New Haven, CT: Yale University Press.

Ahmed, N. 2016. 'Oil on the skids: is the kingdom's oil wealth running out?' *New Internationalist*, March: 22–23.

Al Arabiya News 2014. 'First female lawyer's office opens in Saudi Arabia', *Al Arabiya News*, 3 January, accessed 2 February 2016 from http://english .alarabiya.net/en/News/Middle East/2014/01/03/First-female-lawyer-s-office-opens-in-Saudi-Arabia.html

Aleklett, K., Hook, M., Jakobsson, K., Lardelli, M., Snoden, S. and Soderburgh, B. 2010. 'The peak of the oil age: analysing the world oil production scenario in World Energy Outlook 2008', *Energy Policy*, 38(3): 1398–1414.

Algar, H. 2002. *Wahhabism: A Critical Essay*. New York: Islamic Publications International.

Ali, A. 2004. *Islamic Perspectives on Management and Organization*. Cheltenham, UK: Edward Elgar.

——— 1992. 'Islamic work ethic in Arabia', *Journal of Psychology*, 126(5): 507–520.

Ali, A. H. 2015. *Heretic: Why Islam Needs a Reformation Now*. New York: Harper Collins.

——— 2010. *From Islam to America: A Personal Journey through the Clash of Civilisations*. New York: Free Press.

——— 2007. *Infidel: My Life*. New York: Free Press.

al-Ali, J. 2008. 'Emiratisation: drawing UAE nationals into their surging economy', *International Journal of Sociology and Social Policy*, 28(9–10): 365–379.

al-Ali, N. 2000. *Secularism, Gender and the State in the Middle East: The Egyptian Women's Movement*. Cambridge: Cambridge University Press.

Al Raffd Fund 2015. 'Sultanate of Oman Al Raffd Fund', Al Raffd Fund Oman, accessed 17 March 2015 from http://alraffd.gov.om/?lang=en.

Almasah Capital 2010. 'The Saudi woman: a catalyst for change?' Almasah Capital, Riyadh, accessed 11 October 2012 from http://almasahcapital.com/uploads/ report/pdf/report_30.pdf.

Alsanea, R. 2008. *The Girls of Riyadh*. London: Penguin Books.

Alturki, N. and Braswell, R. 2010. 'Business women in Saudi Arabia: characteristics, challenges and aspirations in a regional context', Monitor Group, accessed 10 March 2013 from www.jeg.org.sa/data/modules/contents/uploads/infopdf/businesswomen.pdf.

Aluwaisheg, A. 2012. 'Will Saudi Arabia become an oil importer by 2030?' *Arab News*, 9 September, accessed 28 January 2016 from www.arabnews.com/will-saudi-arabia-become-oil-importer-2030.

AME Info 2005. 'Raja al-Gurg encourages Arab women to realize their full potential', AME Info, accessed 3 December 2007 from www.ameinfo.com/69312.html.

Amlak Finance 2006. 'Amlak sets the trend for UAE women's leadership', Amlak Finance, accessed 9 March 2008 from www.amlakfinance.com/arabic/index.php?option=com_contentandtask=viewandid=148andItemid=170.

Amnesty International 2016. 'Raif Badawi: Saudi Arabia', Amnesty International, accessed 3 February 2016 from www.amnesty.org.au/activist/individuals-at-risk-case/37643.

—— 2014. 'Migrant workers exploited and abused in Saudi Arabia', Amnesty International, accessed 9 July 2014 from www.amnesty.org.uk/press-releases/india-migrant-workers-exploited-and-abused-saudi-arabia.

Answering-Christianity 2015. 'Is the Koran a scientific miracle?' Accessed 5 June 2015 from www.answering-christianity.com/ac20.htm and www.answering-christianity.com/ac20.htm#links.

Arab News 2016. '350,000 Saudi women are employed in the private sector', *Arab News*, 29 February, accessed 15 March 2016 from www.arabnews.com/saudi-arabia/news/888031.

—— 2014a. 'Kingdom records highest Twitter penetration', *Arab News*, 17 November, accessed 5 March 2015 from www.arabnews.com/news/478691.

—— 2014b. 'Only 5 percent of Saudis study engineering', *Arab News*, 6 April, accessed 5 March 2015 from www.arabnews.com/news/551356.

—— 2014c. '1.7 million firms out of Nitaqat purview', *Arab News*, 3 February, accessed 5 March 2015 from www.arabnews.com/news/519811.

Arabian Business 2014. 'Abu Dhabi Al Jaber Group signs debt restructuring', *Arabian Business*, 16 June, accessed 4 April 2015 from www.arabianbusiness.com/abu-dhabi-s-al-jaber-group-signs-debt-restructuring-554082.html#.ViBHaH4rLI.

Aramco Entrepreneurship Centre 2016. Saudi Aramco, accessed 11 March 2016 from www.saudiaramco.com/en/home/citizenship/economy/aec.html.

al-Ardhi, M. 2015. 'Present accomplishments will drive future success of Oman', *Times of Oman*, 23 May.

al-Arkoubi, K. 2008. *Spiritual Leadership and Identity in Moroccan Business: An Ethnographic Study of Yanna Holding.* Doctoral dissertation, New Mexico State University, 2008.

Armstrong, K. 2000. *Islam: A Short History.* New York: Modern Library.

Ashcraft, C. and Blithe, S. 2009. *Women in IT: The Facts.* Boulder, CO: National Center for Women and Information Technology.

ASSDA'A Burson-Marsteller 2015. 'Arab youth survey 2015', ASSDA'A Burson-Marsteller, accessed 3 February 2016 from www.arabyouthsurvey.com/media/document/2015-AYS-White-Paper-EN.pdf.

Ataya, L. 2010. 'Women in the Middle East workplace: standing tall', Bayt.com, accessed 23 December 2010 from http://blog.bayt.com/2010/06/women-in-the-Middle East-workplace-standing-tall/.

Attas, S. (ed.) 1996. *Islam and the Challenge of Modernity: Historical and Contemporary Contexts.* Kuala Lumpur: International Institute of Islamic Thought and Civilisation.

Australian Broadcasting Corporation 2016. 'Saudi Arabia elects at least 17 women to local councils in historic polls', Australian Broadcasting Corporation, accessed 10 January 2016 from www.abc.net.au/news/2015-12-14/saudi-arabia-elects-women-to-local-councils-first-time-ever/7024862.

Australian Broadcasting Corporation News 2014. 'Army chief lieutenant-general David Morrison labels gender inequalities in militaries a "global disgrace"', Australian Broadcasting Corporation, accessed 15 June 2014 from www.abc.net.au/news/2014-06-14/australia-army-chief-delivers-speech-to-summit-on-wartime-rape/5523942.

Australian Bureau of Statistics 2016. 'Defining small business', Australian Bureau of Statistics, first accessed 14 April 2014 from www.abs.gov.au/AUSSTATS/abs@.nsf/mf/1321.0.

Australian Institute of Company Directors 2016. 'Appointments to ASX Boards', Australian Institute of Company Directors, accessed 22 March 2016 from www.companydirectors.com.au/Director-Resource-Centre/Governance-and-Director-Issues/Board-Diversity/Statistics.

Avent, R. 2016. *The Wealth of Humans: Work and Its Absence in the Twenty-Fist Century.* London: Allen Lane.

Aycan, Z. 2008. 'Cross-cultural perspectives to work-family conflict', in K. Korabik and D. Lero (eds.) *Handbook of Work-Family Conflict*, pp. 359–371. Cambridge: Cambridge University Press.

Aycan, Z., Ayman, R., Bardoel, A., Desai, T., Drach-Zahavy, A., Hammer, L., Huang, T., Korabik, K., Lero, D., Mawardi, A., Poelmans, S., Rajadhyaksha, U., Shafiro, M. and Somech, A. 2004. 'Work-family conflict in cultural context: a ten-country investigation', Paper presented at the *Nineteenth Annual Society for Industrial and Organizational Psychology Conference, Chicago,* April.

Babar, Z. 2011. 'Free mobility within the Gulf Cooperation Council', Georgetown University Center for International and Regional Studies, Occasional Paper No. 8, accessed 14 September 2014 from https://repository.library .georgetown.edu/bitstream/handle/10822/558290/CIRSOccasionalPaper8 ZahraBabar2011.pdf.

Bachelard, M. and Crawford, B. 2004. 'Jobs at Kodak in digital danger', *The Weekend Australian* (Business Section), 26 January.

Badawy, E., Comerford, M. and Welby, P. 2015. 'Inside the jihadi mind: understanding ideology and propaganda', Tony Blair Faith Foundation, accessed 27 November 2015 from http://tonyblairfaithfoundation.org/religion-geopolit ics/reports-analysis/report/inside-jihadi-mind

Badran, M. 2009. *Feminism in Islam: Secular and Religious Convergences.* Oxford: One World Publications.

Baird, V. 2016. 'Our friends: why is the West still cosying up to an ever more repressive Saudi Arabia?' *New Internationalist,* March: 10–14.

Bank Dhofar 2014. 'Bank Dhofar signs an agreement to provide financing options for SME pioneers', Bank Dhofar, 17 September, accessed 15 December 2015 from http://bankdhofar.com/en-GB/News/2/509.aspx.

Barrett, C. 2014. 'Gender quotas feel coercive but appear to work', *Financial Times: The Inclusive Workplace,* 15 May: 2–3.

Barsh, J., Cranston, S. and Craske, J. 2008. 'Centered leadership: how talented women thrive', *McKinsey Quarterly,* September, accessed 30 March 2013 from www.mckinsey.com/global-themes/leadership/centered-leadership-how-talented-women-thrive.

Barsh, J., Devillard, S. and Wang, J. 2012. 'The global gender agenda', *McKinsey Quarterly,* November, accessed 30 March 2013 from www.mckinsey.com/ business-functions/organization/our-insights/the-global-gender-agenda.

Barsh, J. and Yee, J. 2012. 'Unlocking the full potential of women at work', McKinsey and Company, accessed 5 October 2012 from www mckinsey.com/business-func tions/organization/our-insights/unlocking-the-full-potential-of-women-at-work.

Barta, T., Kleiner, M. and Newman, Y. 2012. 'Is there a pay-off for top team diversity?' *McKinsey Quarterly,* April, accessed 11 August 2013 from www .mckinsey.com/business-functions/organization/our-insights/is-there-a-payoff-from-top-team-diversity.

al-Barwani, T. 2011. 'Women, education and the redefinition of empowerment and change in a traditional society', in F. Sadiqi and M. Ennaji (eds.) *Women in the Middle East and North Africa: Agents of Changes,* pp. 215–231.

Bastian, B. 2015. 'Against all odds: women entrepreneurs in the region', *Middle East Business*, 10 March, accessed 11 April 2015 from http://middleeast-business.com/against-all-odds-women-entrepreneurs-in-the-region/.

Bayt.com 2014. 'Women in the Middle East workplace survey 2014', Bayt.com, accessed 17 September 2015 from http://img.b8cdn.com/images/uploads/art icle_docs/bayt_women_workplace_2014_final_23102_EN.pdf.

———— 2010. 'Women in the Middle East workplace survey 2010', Bayt.com, accessed 17 September 2011 from http://bayt.com/en/research-report-7782.

Beblawi, H. 1990. 'The rentier state in the Arab world', in H. Beblawi and L. Giacomo (eds.) *The Arab State*, London: Routledge, pp. 85–98.

Beinhocker, E. 2007. *The Origin of Wealth: Evolution, Complexity and the Radical Remaking of Economics*. London: Random House.

Bellah, R. 2011. *Religion in Human Evolution: From the Palaeolithic to the Axial Age*. Cambridge, MA: Harvard University Press.

Belwal, S., Belwal, R. and al-Saidi, F. 2014. 'Characteristics, motivations and challenges of women entrepreneurs in Oman's Al-Dhahira region', *Journal of Middle East Women's Studies*, 10(2): 135–151.

Benchiba-Savenius, N., Mogielnicki, R., Owens, S. and Scott-Jackson, W. 2016. 'Oman employment report: insights for 2016', Oxford Strategic Consulting Company, accessed 12 May 2016 from www.oxfordstrategicconsulting.com/ wp-content/uploads/2016/01/OxfordStrategicConsulting_OmanEmployment _Jan2016.pdf.

Bennet, J. and Ellison, J. 2010. 'Women will rule the world: men were the main victims of the recession. The recovery will be female', *Newsweek*, 12 July: 38–42.

Bennoune, K. 2013. *Your Fatwa Does Not Apply Here: Untold Stories from the Fight against Muslim Fundamentalism*. New York: W. W. Norton.

Berger, P. and Luckmann, J. 1967. *The Social Construction of Reality*. London: Allen Lane.

Bertelsmann Stiftung 2015a. 'BTI 2015: United Arab Emirates country report', Bertelsmann Stiftung 2015, accessed 12 February 2016 from www .bti-project.org/uploads/tx_itao_download/BTI_2015_United_Arab_Emirates .pdf.

———— 2015b. 'BTI 2015: Oman country report', Bertelsmann Stiftung, accessed 12 October 2015 from www.bti-project.org/uploads/tx_itao_download/BTI_ 2015_Oman.pdf.

———— 2015c. 'BTI 2015: Saudi Arabia country report', Bertelsmann Stiftung, accessed 12 October 2015 from www.bti-project.org/uploads/tx_itao_down load/BTI_2015_Saudi_Arabia_.pdf.

BHP Billiton 2016a. 'About us: our company', BHP Billiton, accessed 22 March 2016 from www.bhpbilliton.com/aboutus/ourcompany.

——— 2016b. 'Working with integrity: code of business conduct', BHP Billiton, accessed 22 March 2016 from www.bhpbilliton.com/~/media/bhp/docu ments/aboutus/ourcompany/code-of-business-conduct/160310_codeofbusi nessconduct_english.pdf?la=en.

Binham, C. 2014. 'Legal laggards begin to master diversity briefs. Law firms: elite cadre double promotion of women but still has a long way to go', *Financial Times: The Inclusive Workplace*, 15 May: 4–5.

Bioenergy Consult 2015. 'Solar energy prospects in Oman', Bioenergy Consult, accessed 4 December 2015 from www.bioenergyconsult.com/solar-oman/.

Bitar, Z. 2010. 'Empowering women in the UAE: government is committed to investing in their skills to boost country's growth', *Gulf News* (Business Section), 23 August.

Bloomberg 2015. 'Saudi banks pull welcome mat for SMEs: lending under the nation's SME program plunges 76%', *Bloomberg*, 26 February, accessed 3 August 2015 from www.bloomberg.com/news/articles/2015-02-26/saudi-banks-pull-welcome-mat-for-smes-seeking-loans-arab-credit.

Bohnet, I. 2015. *What Works: Gender Equality by Design*. Cambridge, MA: Harvard University Press.

Bosma, N., Jones, E. and Levie, J. 2007. 'Global entrepreneurship monitor 2007 executive report', GEM Consortium, accessed 2 August 2008 from http://gemconsortium.org/report/1313078590_GEM_2007_Global_Report.pdf.

Bourke, J. and Dillon, B. 2015. 'Fast forward: leading in a brave new world of diversity', Deloitte and Chartered Accountants Australia and New Zealand, accessed 7 August 2015 from www2.deloitte.com/au/en/pages/human-cap ital/articles/fast-forward-leading-brave-new-world-of-diversity.html.

Broadbent, L. 2012. 'Targeting rape in the US military', *Guardian Weekly*, 13 January: 26–27.

Brulliard, K. 2012. 'After the Arab spring, the struggle continues on a university campus', *Guardian Weekly*, 19 October.

Brush, C. 2014. 'Investing in the power of women: progress report on the Goldman Sachs 10,000 women initiative', Goldman Sachs and Babson College, accessed 19 April 2016 from www.goldmansachs.com/citizenship/10000women/news-and-events/10kw-progress-report/progress-report-full.pdf.

Bryan, R. 2001. 'A man's world: women are breaking down traditional male bastions', *The Australian*, 7 June.

Buckley, G. and Rynhart, G. 2011. 'The Sultanate of Oman. The enabling environment for sustainable enterprises: an "EESE" assessment', International Labour

Office, Geneva, accessed 8 March 2015 from www.ilo.org/wcmsp5/groups/public/-ed_emp/-emp_ent/-ifp_seed/documents/publication/wcms_167007.pdf.

Bugliosi, V. 2008. *The Prosecution of George W. Bush for Murder*. Cambridge, MA: Vanguard Press.

Buhumaid, H., Constantin, M. and Schubert, J. 2016. 'How the UAE government modernized government services', McKinsey & Company, May, accessed 24 May 2016 from www.mckinsey.com/industries/public-sector/our-insights/how-the-uae-government-modernized-citizen-services?cid=other-eml-alt-mip-mck-oth-1605.

Burgot, F. 2003. *Face to Face with Political Islam*. London: Taurus.

Burlingham, B. 2005. *Small Giants: Companies That Choose to Be Great Instead of Big*. New York: Portfolio.

Business in the Community 2015. 'The Times top 50 employers for women 2015', Business in the Community, United Kingdom, accessed 12 January 2016 from http://gender.bitc.org.uk/Awards/TTT502015.

Butler, K. 2008. 'Islam and science: the data gap', *Nature*, 444, 2 November, 26–27, accessed 18 May 2014 from www.nature.com/nature/journal/v444/n7115/full/444026a.html.

Carlson, D., Whitten, D. and Kacmar, M. 2006. 'What men think they know about executive women', *Harvard Business Review*, September: 28.

Carrington, D. 2013. 'Meet Saudi Arabia's first female lawyer', CNN, 29 May, accessed 2 February 2014 from http://edition.cnn.com/2013/05/09/business/saudi-arabia-first-female-lawyer/index.html.

Casella, N. 2001. 'Women in fight to reach top roles', *The Sunday Times* (Western Australia), 11 July.

Catalyst 2015. '2014 Catalyst census: women board directors', Catalyst, accessed 22 March 2016 from www.catalyst.org/knowledge/2014-catalyst-census-women-board-directors.

——— 2011. 'The bottom line: corporate performance and women's representation on boards', Catalyst, accessed 12 April 2012 from www.catalyst.org/knowledge/bottom-line-corporate-performance-and-womens-representation-boards.

——— 2004. 'The bottom line: connecting corporate performance and gender diversity', Catalyst, accessed 21 May 2013 from www.catalyst.org/knowledge/bottom-line-connecting-corporate-performance-and-gender-diversity.

Centennial Fund 2016. 'About the Centennial Fund', The Centennial Fund, Riyadh, KSA, accessed 13 March 2016 from www.tcf.org.sa/en/about-tcf/Pages/default.aspx.

Central Intelligence Agency 2015. 'The world fact-book', United States Central Intelligence Agency, accessed 25 November 2015 www.cia.gov/library/publications/the-world-factbook/geos/mu.html.

Centre for Talent Innovation 2014. 'How diversity drives innovation: a compendium of best practices', Centre for Talent Innovation, accessed 28 March 2015 from www.talentinnovation.org/Research-and-Insights/index.cfm?sorter=All#top.

CEO Middle East 2015. 'Top 100: the world's most powerful Arabic women', *CEO Middle East*, March: 16–61 and 78–79.

———— 2011. 'Interview with Fatima al-Jaber', *CEO Middle East*, February: 20–27.

Chamberlain, G. 2013. 'Saudi Arabia's treatment of foreign workers under fire as Sri Lankan maid is beheaded', *The Guardian*, accessed 9 July 2014 from www.theguardian.com/world/2013/jan/13/saudi-arabia-treatment-foreign-workers.

Chronicle of Higher Education 2010. 'Saudi Arabia's education reforms emphasise training for jobs', *The Chronicle of Higher Education*, 3 October, accessed 28 January 2013 from http://chronicle.com/article/Saudi-Arabias-Education/124771/.

Clothier, M. 2010. 'Motorcycles: Harley shows its feminine side', *Bloomberg Businessweek*, 4–10 October.

Cohoon, J. and Aspray, W. (eds.) 2007. *The State of Social Science Research on Gender and IT Entrepreneurship: A Summary of Research Literature on Women's Entrepreneurship in the Information Technology Field.* National Center for Women and Technology, Entrepreneurial Report Series.

———— (eds.) 2006. *Women and Information Technology: Research on Underrepresentation.* Boston, MA: MIT Press.

Cole, J. 2014. *The New Arabs: How the Millennial Generation Is Changing the Middle East.* New York: Simon and Schuster.

Coleman, I. 2010. *Paradise Beneath Her Feet: How Women Are Transforming the Middle East.* New York: Random House.

Collins, J. 2001. *Good to Great: Why Some Companies Make the Leap and Others Don't.* New York: Harper Business.

Constitute Project 2012. 'United Arab Emirates Constitution with amendments through 2004', Constitute Project, accessed 10 May 2013 from www.constituteproject.org/constitution/United_Arab_Emirates_2004.pdf.

Corby, C. 2015. 'The beat goes on', Deloitte Middle East, accessed 20 December 2015 from www2.deloitte.com/content/dam/Deloitte/xe/Documents/About-Deloitte/mepovdocuments/mepov17/the-beat-goes-on-mepov17.pdf.

Corporate Leadership Council 2004. *Driving Employee Performance and Engagement through Retention: A Quantitative Analysis of the Effectiveness of Employee Engagement Strategies.* Washington, DC: Corporate Executive Board.

Countryeconomy.com 2016. 'United Arab Emirates gross domestic product 2015', Countryeconomy.com, accessed 5 May 2016 from http://countryeconomy .com/gdp/united-arab-emirates.

——— 2015. 'United Arab Emirates gross domestic product 2014', Countryeconomy.com, accessed 26 October 2015 from http://countryeconomy.com/gdp/ united-arab-emirates.

Crabtree, J. and Allam, A. 2014. 'Tata unveils first all-female outsourcing centre in Saudi Arabia, *Financial Times*, 1 April: 7.

Curley, N. 2013. 'What it's like to be a woman entrepreneur in Saudi Arabia', *Wamda Ventures*, 1 July, accessed 11 November 2013 from http://static .wamda.com/web/uploads/resources/UMUC_WP-2009-02.pdf.

Curtis, M., Schmid, C. and Struber, M. 2012. 'Gender diversity and corporate performance', *Credit Suisse Research Institute*, Zurich: Credit Suisse AG, accessed 11 May 2013 from www.credit-suisse.com/newsletter/doc/gender_diversity.pdf.

al-Dabbagh, M. 2009. 'The context for intergroup leadership: women's groups in Saudi Arabia', in T. Pittinsky (ed.) *Crossing the Divide: Intergroup Leadership in a World of Difference*, pp. 171–186. Cambridge, MA: Harvard Business School Publishing.

Danish, A. and Smith, H. 2012. 'Female entrepreneurship in Saudi Arabia: opportunities and challenges', *International Journal of Gender and Entrepreneurship*, 4(3): 216–235.

Darlberg Global Development Advisors 2014. 'The business case for women's economic empowerment: an integrated approach', Oak Foundation, Darlberg Global Development Advisors, International Centre for Research on Women and Witter Ventures, accessed 22 April 2015 from www.icrw.org/sites/ default/files/publications/The%20Business%20Case%20for%20Womens % 20Economic%20Empowerment.pdf.

Davidson, C. 2009. 'Abu Dhabi's new economy: oil, investment and domestic development', *Middle East Policy*, 16(2): 59–79.

——— 2005. *The United Arab Emirates: A Study in Survival*. London: Lynne Rienner Publishers.

Dawkins, R. 2006. *The God Delusion*. New York: Houghton-Mifflin Company.

Dawson, J., Kersley, R. and Natella, S. 2014. 'The CS gender 3000: women in senior management', Credit Suisse Research Institute, Zurich, accessed 29 May 2013 from http://30per centclub.org/wp-content/uploads/2014/10/2014-09- 23_ Research_Institute_Women_in_Business.pdf.

Daya, A. and el-Baltaji, D. 2012. 'Saudi Arabia may become oil importer by 2030, Citigroup says', *Bloomberg*, 4 September, accessed 28 January 2016 from www.bloomberg.com/news/articles/2012-09-04/saudi-arabia-may-become-oil-importer-by-2030-citigroup-says-1-.

De Cremer, E. and Harrison, R. 2015. 'Women on boards – to quota or not to quota? That's the question', *Muscat Daily* (Business Section), 25 May.

Dechant, K. and al-Lamky, A. 2005. 'Towards an understanding of Arab women entrepreneurs in Bahrain and Oman', *Journal of Developmental Entrepreneurship*, 10(2): 123–140.

Dergham, R. 2016. 'Saudi Vision 2030: a quiet pragmatic revolution', *The Huffington Post*, 30 April, accessed 5 May 2016 from www.huffingtonpost.com/raghida-dergham/saudi-vision-2030-a-quiet_b_9814466.html.

Desloires, V., Uther, B. and Yustantio, J. 2015. 'This is the glass ceiling: an early look at the data published by Australia's largest companies shows that women get stuck on the lowest rung of the management ladder', *Boss* (Australian Financial Review), January, accessed 5 February 2015 from www.afr.com/it-pro/new-data-shows-location-of-glass-ceiling-20141009-jy90a.

Devillard, S., Graven, W., Lawson, E., Paradise, R. and Sancier-Sultan, S. 2012. 'Women matter 2012: making the breakthrough', McKinsey and Company, accessed 5 October 2013 from www.mckinsey.de/sites/mck_files/files/mckinsey_women_matter_2012.pdf.

Diamond, J. 2005. *Collapse: How Societies Choose to Fail or Survive*. London: Allen Lane.

———— 1998. *Guns, Germs and Steel: A Short History of Everybody for the last 13,000 Years*. London: Random House.

Dilevko, J. and Harris, R. 1997. 'Information technology and social relations: portrayals of gender roles in high-tech product advertisement', *Journal of the American Society for Information Science*, 44(8): 718–727.

Diner, D. 2009. *Lost in the Sacred: Why the Muslim World Stood Still*. Princeton, NJ: Princeton University Press.

Dobbs, R., Woetzel, J., Madgavkar, A. Elingrud, K., Labaye, E., Devillard, S. Kutcher, E., Manyika, J. and Krishnan, M. 2015. 'The power of parity: how advancing women's equality can add $12 trillion to global growth', McKinsey Global Institute, accessed 9 December 2015 from www.mckinsey.com/global-themes/employment-and-growth/how-advancing-womens-equality-can-add-12-trillion-to-global-growth.

Donaghy, R. 2001. *The Future of Work-Life Balance*, Economic and Social Research Council. Swindon, UK: Economic and Social Research Council.

Dorfman, P. and House, R. 2004. 'Cultural influences on organisational leadership: literature review, theoretical rationale and GLOBE project goals', in R. House, P. Hanges, M. Javidan, P. Dorfman and V. Gupta *Culture, Leadership and Organisations: The GLOBE Study of 62 Societies*, pp. 51–73.

Drago, R. 2007. *Striking a Balance: Work, Family, Life*. Boston, MA: Dollars and Sense.

Dubai Strategic Plan 2015. 'Dubai strategic plan 2015', Dubai eGovernment, accessed 12 July 2008 from http://egov.dubai.ae/opt/CMScontent/Active/Corp/en/Documents/DSPE.pdf.

Dubai Women Establishment 2016. 'Women's forum Dubai 2016', Dubai Women Establishment, accessed 11 March 2016 from www.dwe.gov.ae/women forum2016.aspx.

―――― 2015. 'UAE women statistics', Dubai Women Establishment, accessed 10 December 2015 from www.dwe.gov.ae/stat.aspx.

―――― 2009. *Arab Women: Leadership Outlook 2009–2011*. Dubai: Dubai Women Establishment.

―――― 2008a. 'Dubai Women Establishment launches National Corporate Child Care Project', Dubai Women Establishment, accessed 28 November 2008 from www.dwe.gov.ae/press08_06_08.aspx.

―――― 2008b. 'Female Emirati Employees in Dubai for the year 2008', Dubai Women's Establishment, accessed 28 November 2008, from www.dwe.gov.ae/women_dubai_06.aspx.

―――― 2008c. 'Message from Sheikha Manal', Dubai Women Establishment, accessed 28 November 2008 from www.dwe.gov.ae/index.aspx.

―――― 2008d. 'Reasons behind UAE women's reluctance to participate in activating the country's strategy', Dubai Women Establishment, accessed 28 November 2008 from www.dwe.gov.ae/countrys_strategy.aspx.

Dyes, R. 2009. 'Helping Emirati women join the private sector', *Emirates 247*, accessed 22 December 2010 from www.emirates247.com/2.273/uae-economy/helping-emirati-women-join-the-private-sector-2009-04-29-1.9763.

Dzhambazova, B. 2012. 'Gender gap shrinking on UK firms' boards', *International Herald and Tribune* (Business Section), 2 July.

Ebrahim, S., Khamis, A., Abdulsamad, H. and Mohammed, N. 2008. 'The development of female business leadership in the United Arab Emirates', Final-year Capstone Dissertation, the College of Business Sciences, Zayed University, Dubai.

Elamin, A. and Omair, K. 2010. 'Males' attitudes towards working females in Saudi Arabia', *Personnel Review*, 39(6): 746–766.

Ellis, T., Marcati, C. and Sperling, J. 2015. 'Promoting gender diversity in the Gulf', McKinsey & Company, accessed 21 September 2015 from www.mckinsey.com/business-functions/organisation/our-insights/promoting-gender-diversity-in-the-gulf.

Eltahawy, M. 2015. *Headscarves and Hymens: Why the Middle East Needs a Sexual Revolution.* New York: Farrar, Strauss and Giroux.

Embassy of the United Arab Emirates 2015. 'Women in the UAE', Embassy of the United Arab Emirates, Washington, DC, accessed 10 October 2015 from www.uae-embassy.org/uae/women-uae.

―――― 2009. 'Women in the UAE', Embassy of the United Arab Emirates, Washington, DC, accessed 17 November 2009 from www.uae-embassy.org/uae/women-in-the-uae.

Emiratisation.org 2015. 'Manpower group: helping Emiratis succeed in the world of work', Emiratisation.org, accessed 12 July 2015 from https://emiratisation.org/about-us-2.

Ennis, C. 2015. ' Between trend and necessity: top-down entrepreneurship promotion in Oman and Qatar', *The Muslim World*, 105(1): 116–138.

Ennis, C. and al-Jamali, R. 2014. 'Elusive employment: development planning and labour-market trends in Oman', Chatham House, accessed 5 June 2015 from www.chathamhouse.org/sites/files/chathamhouse/field/field_docu ment/20140916ElusiveEmploymentOmanEnnisJamali.pdf.

Entrepreneurs – SME Asia 2014. 'Oman small business ideas, opportunities and SME organisations', Entrepreneurs – SME Asia, accessed 25 November 2014 from http://entrepreneur-sme.asia/entrepreneurship/Middle East-sme/oman-small-business-ideas/.

Equal Opportunity for Women in the Workplace Agency 2015. 'Facts on work-life balance in Australia', Equal Opportunity for Women in the Workplace Agency, accessed 30 September 2015 from www.eowa.gov.au/About_Equal_Opportun ity/Key_Agenda_Items/Work_Life_Balance/Facts_on_Work_Life_Balance_in_ Australia.asp.

Ernst & Young 2009. 'Scaling up: why women-owned businesses can recharge the global economy', Ernst & Young, accessed 15 March 2013 from www.ey.com/ Publication/vwLUAssets/Scaling_up_-_Why_women-owned_businesses_can_ recharge_the_global_economy/$FILE/.pdf.

Erogul, M. and McCrohan, D. 2008. 'Preliminary investigation of Emirati women entrepreneurs in the UAE', *African Journal of Business Management*, 2(10): October: 177–185.

―――― 2007a. 'Do socio-cultural factors affect female entrepreneurship in the UAE?' *Proceedings of the Cultures and Context Conference*, Aberdeen, United Kingdom, September: 13–15.

―――― 2007b. 'Socio-cultural factors inhibiting female entrepreneurship in the United Arab Emirates', Working Paper, College of Business Sciences, Zayed University, Dubai.

Exelby, J. 2008. 'UAE swears in first woman judge', *Arabian Business*, 8 October, accessed 20 December 2008, from www.arabianbusiness.com/533444-uae-swears-in-first-first-woman-judge.

Eye of Riyadh 2016. 'Full text of Saudi Arabia's Vision 2030', *Eye of Riyadh*, 26 April, accessed 5 May 2016 from www.eyeofriyadh.com/news/details/full-text-of-saudi-arabia-s-vision-2030.

Fadl, K. 2005. *The Great Theft: Wrestling Islam from the Extremists*. New York: Harper-Collins.

Fakhro, M. 1990. *Women at Work in the Gulf*. London: Kegan Paul International.

Farquhar, M. 2015. 'Saudi petrodollars, spiritual capital and the Islamic University of Medina: A Wahhabi missionary project in transnational perspective', *International Journal of Middle East Studies*, 47(4): 701–721.

Fatany, S. 2011a. *Modernizing Saudi Arabia*. Self-published book, available from amazon.com/Modernizing-Saudi-Arabia-Samar-Fatany/dp/1482509989.

——— 2011b. 'Itjihad deserves new consideration', *Arab News*, 6 November.

——— 2007a. 'Saudi Arabia forum on the role of women suggests that empowerment is the key to future economic prosperity', *Arab News*, 24 July.

——— 2007b. *Saudi Women: Towards a New Era*. Ghainaa Publications, accessed 12 November 2014 from http://d1.islamhouse.com/data/en/ih_books/single/en_Women_saudi_Towards_A_New_Era.pdf.

Federal Glass Ceiling Commission 1995. 'Good for business: making full use of the nation's human capital', Washington, DC: U.S. Department of Labor, accessed 19 June 2010 from www.dol.gov/oasam/programs/history/reich/reports/ceiling.pdf.

Federal Statistics and Competiveness Authority 2016. 'Labour force', Federal Statistics and Competiveness Authority UAE, accessed 11 May 2016 from www.fcsa.gov.ae/PublicationEN/tabid/187/Default.aspx.

Ferris, T. 2010. *The Science of Liberty: Democracy, Reason and the Laws of Nature*. New York: Harper Collins.

Fleishman, J. 2011. 'Arabs look to restore hope and reclaim dignity', *Gulf News*, 1 March.

Foley, S. 2010. *The Arab Gulf States: Beyond Oil and Islam*. London: Lynne Reiner.

Forbes Middle East 2015. 'Entrepreneurs shaping Saudi Arabia's future', *Forbes Middle East*, December, accessed 20 January 2016 from www.forbesmiddleeast.com/en/lists/read/2015/entrepreneurs-shaping-saudi-arabia-s/listid/269/.

——— 2013. 'Saudi stimuli: from IT to interiors and energy to education, Saudi self-starters are forces for inspiration in a kingdom full of potential', *Forbes Middle East*, December: 44–54.

Forster, N. 2017. 'Why are there no world-class universities in the Middle East and North Africa?' *Journal of Further and Higher Education*, 41(6), accepted for publication.

——— 2000. *Managing Staff on International Assignments: A Strategic Guide*. London: Financial Times and Prentice-Hall.

——— 1999. 'A case study of women academics' views on equal opportunities, career prospects and work-family conflicts in a British University', *Women in Management Review*, 15(7): 33–46.

Forster, N., Ibrahim, N. and Ebrahim, A. 2014. 'An exploratory study of work-life balance and work-family conflicts in the United Arab Emirates', *Skyline Business Journal*, 9(1): 34–42.

Forster, N. and al-Marzouqi, A. 2011. 'An exploratory study of the under-representation of Emirati women in the United Arab Emirates' information technology sector', *Equality, Diversity and Inclusion: An International Journal*, 30(7): 544–562.

Foust-Cummings, H., Sabattini, L. and Carter, N. 2008. *Women in Technology: Maximizing Talent, Minimizing Barriers*. New York: Catalyst.

Fox, C. 2006. 'Advances continue at an interminably slow pace', *Australian Financial Review*, 12 December.

Francke, L. 2001. *Ground Zero: The Gender Wars in the Military*. London: Simon and Schuster.

Freedom House 2016a. 'Freedom in the world 2016: Middle East and North Africa', Freedom House, accessed 28 January 2016 from www.freedomhouse.org/report/freedom-world/freedom-world-2016.

——— 2016b. 'Saudi Arabia's curriculum of intolerance', Freedom House, accessed 2 February 2016 from www.freedomhouse.org/report/special-reports/saudi-ara bias-curriculum-intolerance.

Fukuyama, F. 2011. *The Origins of Political Order: From Pre-Human Times to the French Revolution*. New York: Farrar, Strauss and Giroux.

G20 Watch 2014. 'G20 leaders' communiqué: Brisbane summit 15–16 November 2014', G20 Watch, accessed 13 February 2016 from www.g20watch.edu.au/sites/default/files/pictures/brisbane_g20_leaders_summit_communique.pdf.

Gallant, M. and Pounder, J. 2008. 'The employment of female nationals in the United Arab Emirates: an analysis of opportunities and barriers', *Education, Business and Society: Contemporary Middle Eastern Issues*, 1(1): 26–33.

Gambles, R., Lewis, S. and Rapoport, R. 2006. *The Myth of Work-Life Balance*. London: John Wiley and Sons Ltd.

Garran, R. 2001a. 'I am woman – show me war', *The Weekend Australian*, 9–10 June.

——— 2001b. 'Tough enough to kill?' *The Australian*, 23 November.

Gelfand, M. and Knight, A. 2003. 'Cross-cultural perspectives on work-family conflict', in S. Poelmans (ed.) *Work and Family: An International Research Perspective* , pp. 401–415.

General Women's Union 2008. 'The development of the progress of women in the UAE', Tanmia Centre for Labor Market Research and Information, accessed 16 June 2009 from http://lib.ohchr.org/HRBodies/UPR/Documents/Session3/AE/UPR_UAE_ANNEX3_E.pdf.

Ghafour, M. 2016. 'Emirati women break with tradition to study in record numbers', *Financial Times*, accessed 24 December 2016 from www.ft.com/content/1f84dbf4-a5ad-11e6-8898-79a99e2a4de6.

al-Ghoson, H. 2015. 'Women leaders in the Gulf: the view from Saudi Aramco', *McKinsey Quarterly*, February, accessed 9 March 2015 from www.mckinsey.com/insights/leading_in_the_21st_century/Women_leaders_in_the_Gulf_The_view_from_Saudi_Aramco?cid=other-eml-alt-mkq-mck-oth-1502.

Gladwell, M. 2006. *Blink: The Power of Thinking without Thinking*. London: Penguin Books.

Gorney, C. 2016. 'The changing face of Saudi women', *National Geographic*, February: 110–133.

Goveas, S. and Aslam, N. 2011. 'The role and contributions of women in the Sultanate of Oman', *International Journal of Business and Management*, 6(3): 232–238.

Gray, J. 2015. 'The age of diversity: global trends demand that leaders build inclusive cultures and exploit group intelligence', *Boss* (Australian Financial Review), June: 7–9.

——— 2011. *Shall the Religious Inherit the Earth? Demography and Politics in the Twenty-First Century*. London: Profile Books.

Greenspan, A. 2000. 'Removing barriers to women essential for economic growth', *The Australian* (Business Section), 28 July.

Groom, B. 2009. 'Too few UK women ready to be directors: report finds lack of experienced candidates', *Gulf News* (Business Section), 27 May.

Groysberg, B. and Connolly, K. 2013. 'Great leaders who make the mix work: twenty-four CEOs on creating diverse and inclusive organisations', *Harvard Business Review*, September: 69–76.

Gulf Business 2013. 'Special country report: Oman', *Gulf Business*, 3 March, accessed 12 December 2014 from www.gulfbusiness.com/articles/industry/special-country-report-oman/.

Gulf News 2015a. 'Plan to empower Emirati women is launched: strategy for 2015–2021 aims to boost their creative inputs in nation building', *Gulf News* (Business Section), 8 March, accessed 21 October 2015 from http:// gulfnews

.com/news/uae/government/national-strategy-to-empower-emirati-women-launched-1.1468122.

—— 2015b. 'UAE gender balance council to be formed', *Gulf News*, 10 February, accessed 27 October 2015 from http://gulfnews.com/news/uae/government/uae-gender-balance-council-to-be-formed-1.1454675.

—— 2015c. 'Museum of the future to harness innovation', *Gulf News* (Business Section), 5 March, accessed 24 April 2015 from http://gulfnews.com/news/uae/government/museum-of-future-to-foster-innovation-in-uae-1.1563238.

—— 2015d. '34,000 enrol in SANAD programme in Oman', *Gulf News*, 4 December, accessed 16 December 2015 from http://gulfnews.com/news/34000-enrol-in-Sanad-program-in-oman.

—— 2010. 'Oman to launch SANAD program for entrepreneurs', *Gulf News*, 2 November, accessed 16 February 2011 from http://gulfnews.com/news/gulf/oman/oman-to-launch-sanad-program-for-entrepreneurs-1.705344.

—— 2008. 'DNRD helps female employees keep balance between work and family life', *Gulf News*, 11 May, accessed 8 December 2010 from http://gulfnews.com/news/uae/general/dnrd-helps-female-employees-keep-balance-between-work-and-family-life-1.104601.

Gulf Talent 2011. 'Recruiting top graduates in Saudi Arabia', GulfTalent.com, accessed 3 April 2012 from www.gulftalent.com/resources/market-research-reports/recruiting-top-graduates-in-saudi-arabia-2011-28.

Haan, H. 2004. 'Small enterprises: women entrepreneurs in the UAE', Tanmia Centre for Labor Market Research and Information, Labor Market Study No. 19, accessed 12 December 2008 from www.zu.ac.ae/infoasis/modules/mod8/Business/documents/SmallEnterpriseReport.pdf.

Haidar, E. 2015. *Raif Badawi: The Voice of Freedom. My Husband, Our Story*. London: Little, Brown.

Hall, C. and Fattah, Z. 2010. 'The real estate busts hits Oman's Blue City', *Bloomberg*, 27 May, accessed 2 October 2014 from www.bloomberg.com/bw/magazine/content/10_23/b4181045692999.htm.

Halpern, D. and Cheung, F. 2008. *Women at the Top: Powerful Leaders Tell Us How to Combine Work and Family*. UK: John Wiley and Sons Ltd.

Hamel, G. 2011. 'First, let's fire all the managers. Morning Star, a leading food processor, demonstrates how to create an organisation that combines managerial discipline and market-centric flexibility without bosses, titles or promotions', *Harvard Business Review*, December: 49–60.

Harley-Davidson 2016. 'Harley Davidson community: women', Harley Davidson, accessed 30 March 2016 from www.harley-davidson.com/content/h-d/en_US/home/community/women-riders/the-right-bike.html.

Handy, C. 1996. *Beyond Certainty*. London: Arrow Books.

Harrison, L. 2006. *The Central Liberal Truth: How Politics Can Change a Culture and Save It from Itself*. Oxford: Oxford University Press.

Harrison, L. and Huntington, S. (eds.) 2000. *Culture Matters: How Values Shape Human Progress*. New York: Basic Books.

al-Harthi, M. 2015. 'Saudis draw up plans for 2020', *Arab News*, 23 December, accessed 5 February 2016 from www.arabnews.com/news/854611.

al-Hashemi, S., Khan, G., al-Abri, S., Rajasekar, J., Shamsudin, F., al-Habsi, N. and Barwani, N. 2013. 'Undergraduate program specialisation proposal', Department of Management, College of Economics and Political Science, Sultan Qaboos University, Muscat, Oman.

al-Hassan, A. 1996. 'Factors behind the decline of Islamic science after the sixteenth-century', accessed 21 April 2014 from www.history-science-technology .com/articles/articles%208.html.

Hawley, D. 1971. *The Trucial States*. New York: Twayne Publishers.

Haykel, B. 2015. 'Afterword', in B. Haykel, T. Hegghamer and S. Lacroix (eds.) *Saudi Arabia in Transition: Insights on Political, Economic and Religious Change*, pp. 332–336.

Haykel, B., Hegghamer, T. and Lacroix, S. (eds.) 2015. *Saudi Arabia in Transition: Insights on Political, Economic and Religious Change*. Cambridge: Cambridge University Press.

Heard-Bey, F. 2005. *From Trucial States to United Arab Emirates*. Dubai: Motivate.

Hegghamer, T. 2010. '"Classical" and "global" jihadism in Saudi Arabia', in B. Haykel, T. Hegghamer and S. Lacroix (eds.) *Saudi Arabia in Transition: Insights on Political, Economic and Religious Change*, pp. 207–230.

Heritage Foundation 2016. '2016 index of economic freedom', Heritage Foundation, Washington, DC, accessed 24 February 2016 from www.heritage .org/index/ranking.

Hertog, S. 2015. 'National cohesion and the political economy of regions in post-World War II Saudi Arabia', in B. Haykel, T. Hegghamer and S. Lacroix (eds.) *Saudi Arabia in Transition: Insights on Political, Economic and Religious Change*, pp. 97–124.

——— 2010a. 'The sociology of the Gulf rentier systems: societies of intermediaries', *Comparative Studies in Society and History*, 52(2): 282–318.

——— 2010b. *Princes, Brokers and Bureaucrats: Oil and the State in Saudi Arabia*. Ithaca, NY: Cornell University Press.

Hewlett, S., Buck-Luce, C., Servon, L., Sherbin, L., Shiller, P. and Sosnovich, E. 2008a. *The Athena Factor: Reversing the Brain Drain in Science, Engineering and Technology*. New York: Centre for Work-Life Policy.

Hewlett, S., Jackson, M., Sherbin, L., Sosnovich, E. and Sumberg, K. 2008b. *The Under-Leveraged Talent Pool: Women Technologists on Wall Street*. New York: Center for Work-Life Policy.

Hewlett, S., Marshall, M. and Sherbin, L. 2013. 'How diversity can drive innovation', *Harvard Business Review*, December: 22–31.

Hewlett, S. and Rashid, R. 2010. 'The battle for female talent in emerging markets', *Harvard Business Review*, May: 101–106.

Hill, A. 2011. 'The top 50 women in world business', *Financial Times Magazine*, 8–9 January: 6–30.

Hitchens, C. 2007. *God Is Not Great: How Religion Poisons Everything*. New York: Warner Books.

Hitti, P. 2002. *A History of the Arabs*. New York: Palgrave Macmillan.

Hofstede, G. 2001. *Culture's Consequences: Comparing Values, Behaviors, Institutions and Organisations across Nations*. Thousand Oaks, CA: Sage Publications.

―――― 1984. *Culture's Consequences: International Differences in Work Related Values*. Thousand Oaks, CA: Sage Publications.

Holdsworth, P. 2010. 'Native workers in the UAE still avoid working in the private sector', Gulfjobmarket.com, accessed 20 March 2011 from http://news .gulfjobsmarket.com/native-workers-in-the-uae-still-avoid-working-in-the-pri vate-sector-7861475-news.

Holland, T. 2012. *In the Shadow of the Sword: The Birth of Islam and the Rise of the Global Arab Empire*. New York: Random House.

Honeywell 2015. 'Honeywell commits to greater female leadership in the Middle East', Honeywell, 14 May, accessed 15 April from www.honeywell.com/news room/news/2015/05/honeywell-commits-to-greater-female-leadership-in-the-Middle East/.

Hoteit, L., Abdulkader, L., Shehadi, R. and Tarazi, K. 2011. 'Educated, ambitious, essential: women will drive the GCC's future', Strategy& Ideation Centre, accessed 19 April 2013 from www.ideationcentre.com/ideation_research/ media/file/Educated-ambitious-essential-women.pdf.

Hoteliermiddleeast.com 2015. 'Rezidor aims for 30% women in leadership by 2016', Hoteliermiddleeast.com, 9 September, accessed 15 April from www .hoteliermiddleeast.com/24717-rezidor-aims-for-30-women-in-leadership-by-2016/.

Hourani, A. 1991. *A History of the Arab Peoples*. London: Faber and Faber.

House, R., Hanges, P., Javidan, M., Dorfman, P. and Gupta, V. 2004. *Culture, Leadership and Organisations: The GLOBE Study of 62 Societies*. Thousand Oaks, CA: Sage Publications.

Human Rights Watch 2016. 'Middle East/North Africa: United Arab Emirates', Human Rights Watch, accessed 25 January 2016 from www.hrw.org/Middle East/n-africa/united-arab-emirates.

———— 2015. 'World report 2015: Saudi Arabia', Human Rights Watch, accessed 25 November 2015 from www.hrw.org/world-report/2015/country-chapters/ saudi-arabia.

———— 2014. 'World report 2014: Oman', Human Rights Watch, accessed 25 November 2015 from www.hrw.org/world-report/2014/country-chapters/ oman.

———— 2008. 'Perpetual minors: human rights abuses stemming from male guard-ianship and sex segregation in Saudi Arabia', Human Rights Watch, accessed 9 April 2012 from www.hrw.org/sites/default/files/reports/saudiarabia0408_1 .pdf.

Hunt, V., Layton, D. and Prince, S. 2015. 'Diversity matters', McKinsey & Com-pany, accessed 21 September 2015 from www.mckinsey.com/business-func tions/organisation/our-insights/why-diversity-matters.

Huntington, S. 2011. *The Clash of Civilisations and the Remaking of the World Order*. London: Simon & Schuster.

Hussain, T. and Khalil, A. 2013. 'Environmental and sustainable development in the Kingdom of Saudi Arabia: current status and future trends', *Journal of Sustainable Development*, 6 (12): 14–30.

Husserl, E. 1931. *Ideas: A General Introduction to Pure Phenomenology*. New York: Humanities Press.

Hvidt, M. 2013. 'Economic diversification in GCC countries: past record and future trends', The London School of Economics Kuwait Program on Development, Globalisation and Governance in the Gulf States, Research Paper No. 27, accessed 9 October 2015 from www.lse.ac.uk/LSEKP.

Hycner, R. 1985. 'Some guidelines for the phenomenological analysis of interview data', *Human Studies*, 8(3): 279–303.

Ibarra, H., Ely, R. and Kolb, D. 2013. 'Women rising: the unseen barriers', *Harvard Business Review*, September: 62–66.

Ibrahim, N. and Ebrahim, A. 2011. 'Emirati women's perceptions of work-family conflicts in the United Arab Emirates', Final-year Capstone Dissertation, College of Business Sciences, Zayed University, Dubai.

Index Mundi 2016. 'Saudi Arabia GDP', Index Mundi, accessed 20 January 2016 from www.indexmundi.com/facts/saudi-arabia/gdp.

———— 2015. 'Oman's environment: current issues', Index Mundi, accessed 12 November 2015 from www.indexmundi.com/oman/environment_cur rent_issues.html.

———— 2013. 'United Arab Emirates Labour Force: labour force, women', Index Mundi, accessed 2 March 2014 from www.indexmundi.com/facts/united-arab-emirates/labor-force.

Inter-Parliamentary Union 2016. 'Women in national parliaments 2015', Inter-Parliamentary Union, accessed 3 February 2016 from www.ipu.org/wmn-e/classif.htm.

International Federation for Human Rights 2010. 'Women's rights in the United Arab Emirates', Note submitted to the Fourth Session of the Committee on the Elimination of Discrimination against Women on the Occasion of its First Examination of the UAE, accessed 12 October 2012 from www.fidh.org/IMG/pdf/UAE_summaryreport_for_CEDAW.pdf/.

International Finance Corporation 2013a. 'Ready for growth: solutions to increase access to finance for women-owned businesses in the Middle East and North Africa', IFC/World Bank Group, accessed 13 January 2016 from www.ifc.org/wps/wcm/connect/156534804f860a72be27fe0098cb14b9/12316-vv-sme-report.pdf?MOD=AJPERES.

———— 2013b. 'Investing in women's employment: good for business, good for development', IFC/World Bank Group, accessed 12 November 2014 from www.ifc.org/wps/wcm/connect/5f6e5580416bb016bfb1bf9e78015671/Investingin WomensEmployment.pdf?MOD=AJPERES.

International Labour Organisation 2016. 'Ratifications for Saudi Arabia', International Labour Organisation, accessed 13 March 2016 from www.ilo.org/dyn/normlex/en/f?p=NORMLEXPUB:11200:0:NO:P11200_COUNTRY_ID:103208.

———— 2015. 'Global employment trends 2014: risk of jobless recovery?' International Labour Office, accessed 8 March 2015 www.ilo.org/wcmsp5/groups/public/–dgreports/–stat/documents/presentation/wcms_314041.pdf.

———— 2010. 'Sultanate of Oman: decent work country program 2010–2013', International Labour Organisation, accessed 21 May 2015 from ww.ilo.org/public/english/bureau/program/dwcp/download/oman.pdf.

International Monetary Fund 2013. 'Report for selected countries and subjects: Saudi Arabia and United Arab Emirates', International Monetary Fund, accessed 20 June 2013 from www.imf.org/external/pubs/ft/weo/2013/01/data/dbcoutm.cfm?SD=1970andED=2013/.

Islam, S. 2014. 'Saudi women: opportunities and challenges in science and technology', *Education Journal*, 3(2): 71–78, accessed 2 February 2016 from http://article.sciencepublishinggroup.com/pdf/10.11648.j.edu.20140302.15.pdf.

Janzen, J. 1986. *Nomads in the Sultanate of Oman: Tradition and Development in Dhofar*. Boulder, CO: Westview Press.

Javidan, M., Dorfman, P., du Luque, M. and House, R. 2006. 'In the eye of the beholder: cross-cultural lessons in leadership from Project GLOBE', *Academy of Management Perspectives*, 20(1): 67–90.

Jennings, J. and Brush, C. 2013. 'Research on women entrepreneurs: challenges to (and from) the broader entrepreneurship literature?', *Academy of Management Annals*, 7(1): 663–715.

Jenson, J. and Rose, C. 2003. 'Women@work: listening to gendered relations of power in teachers' talk about new technologies', *Gender and Education*, 15(2): 169–181.

Jewish Virtual Library 2015. 'Jewish biographies: Nobel Laureates', Jewish Virtual Library, accessed 2 August 2015 from www.jewishvirtuallibrary.org/jsource/loc/loctoc.html.

Jiffry, F. 2014. 'Unemployment rate among Saudi women reaches 34%', *Arab News*, 23 April, accessed 8 December 2014 from www.arabnews.com/news/560096.

John F. Kennedy Presidential Library and Museum 2014. 'Robert F. Kennedy speeches: day of affirmation address, University of Cape Town, South Africa, 6 June, 1966', John F. Kennedy Presidential Library and Museum, accessed 5 June 2014 from www.jfklibrary.org/Research/Research-Aids/Ready-Reference/RFK-Speeches/Day-of-Affirmation-Address-as-delivered.aspx.

Jones, J. and Ridout, N. 2015. *A History of Modern Oman*. Cambridge: Cambridge University Press.

Joplin, J., Shaffer, M., Francesco, A. and Lau, T. 2003. 'The macro environment and work-family conflict: development of a cross-cultural comparative framework', *International Journal of Cross-Cultural Management*, 3(2): 305–328.

Kandaswamy, D. 2003. 'Seven reasons why women in science and technology remain invisible', *About Islam*, accessed 15 January 2010 from http://aboutislam.net/science/faith-science/7-reasons-women-invisible-science/.

Kargwell, S. 2012. 'A comparative study on gender and entrepreneurship development: still a male's world within UAE cultural context', *International Journal of Business and Social Science*, 3(6): 44–55.

Katz, M. 2004. 'Assessing the political stability of Oman', *Middle East Review of International Affairs*, 8(4): 1–10.

Katzenbach, J. 2000. *Peak Performance: Aligning the Hearts and Minds of Your Employees*. Cambridge, MA: Harvard Business School Publishing.

Kaufmann, E. 2010. *Shall the Religious Inherit the Earth? Demography and Politics in the Twenty-First Century*. London: Profile Books.

Kelley, D., Brush, C., Greene, P., Herrington, M., Abdul, A. and Kew, P. 2015. 'Global entrepreneurship monitor special report: women's entrepreneurship',

GEM Consortium, accessed 23 December 2015 from http://gemconsortium .org/gem_2014_womens_report_1447757361.pdf.

Kelly, S. and Breslin, J. (eds.) 2014. *Women's Rights in the Middle East: Progress Amidst Resistance*. New York: Freedom House.

Kepel, G. 2004. *The War for Muslim Minds*. London: Faber and Faber.

Kerr, S. and Clark, P. 2015. 'UAE drops fuel subsidies to boost finances and cut emissions', *Financial Times International*, 22 July, accessed 6 March 2016 from www.ft.com/intl/cms/s/0/18246646-3050-11e5-91ac-a5e17d9b4cff.html#axzz 424q2WgJK.

Khalaf, R. 2016. 'Saudi religious police face pressure', *Financial Times Middle East and North Africa*, accessed 16 May 2016 from www.ft.com/intl/cms/s/0/ 8af9189c-12b8-11dc-a475-000b5df10621.html#axzz48mx2Shkf.

Khaleej Times 2007. 'Dubai hosts the new Arab woman forum on leadership and social responsibility', *Khaleej Times*, accessed 3 December 2008 from www.zawya.com/mena/en/search?query=www.zawya.com/story.cfm/sidZA WYA20070930131228&filter=news.

————— 2007. 'Friendly environment for new start-ups', *Khaleej Times*, accessed 3 December 2007 from http://209.85.135.104/search?q=cache:2fG7FDKVChMJ: www.khaleejtimes.co.ae/ktarchive/301202/finance.htm+Local+businesswoman +asks+job+seekers+to+get+trainingandhl=arandct=clnkandcd=1andgl=ae.

Khalil, A. 2011. 'Protesters are beaten at women's rights rallies', *The Guardian Weekly*, 9 March.

al-Khalili, J. 2012. *Pathfinders: The Golden Age of Arabic Science*. London: Penguin Books.

Khan, Z. 2009. *The Female Commodity*. Dubai: Gulf Business.

Khashoggi, J. 2014. 'Saudi Arabia's education system in the spotlight again', *Al Arabiya*, 9 February, accessed 2 February 2015 from http://english.alarabiya .net/en/views/news/Middle East/2014/02/09/Saudi-Arabia-s-education-system- in-the-spotlight-again.html.

al-Khatteeb, M. 2015. 'Saudi Arabia's economic time bomb', The Brookings Institute, accessed 18 January 2016 from www.brookings.edu/research/opinions/ 2015/12/30-saudi-arabia-economic-time-bomb-alkhatteeb.

Khurana, A. 2012. 'On the fast track: a new cycle of innovation in the Middle East', PwC Middle East Private Sector Innovation Survey 2012, accessed 21 March 2013 from www.pwc.com/m1/en/publications/documents/innovation- survey-report.pdf.

al-Kibsi, G., Woetzel, J., Isherwood, T., Khan, J., Mischke, J. and Hassan, N. 2015. 'Saudi Arabia: the investment and productivity transformation', McKinsey &

Company, accessed 21 September 2015 from www.mckinsey.com/global-themes/employment-and-growth/moving-saudi-arabias-economy-beyond-oil.

Kingdom of Saudi Arabia Central Department of Statistics 2015. 'Labour force survey 2015', Kingdom of Saudi Arabia Central Department of Statistics, accessed 13 October 2015 from www.cdsi.gov.sa/english/index.php?option=com_docman&task=cat_view&gid=296&Itemid=162.

Kingdom of Saudi Arabia Ministry of Commerce and Industry 2011. 'Industrial Clusters', Kingdom of Saudi Arabia Ministry of Commerce and Industry, accessed 21 February 2012 from www.ic.gov.sa/index.php?option=com_content&view=article&id=5&Itemid=105.

Kingdom of Saudi Arabia Ministry of Economy and Planning 2015. 'Objectives of the tenth development plan', Kingdom of Saudi Arabia Ministry of Economy and Planning, accessed 11 May 2016 from www.mep.gov.sa/en/knowledge-resources/.

——— 2010. 'Objectives of the ninth development plan', Kingdom of Saudi Arabia Ministry of Economy and Planning, accessed 22 December 2011 from www.mep.gov.sa/en/knowledge-resources/.

——— 2005. 'Objectives of the eighth development plan', Kingdom of Saudi Arabia Ministry of Economy and Planning, accessed 3 March 2011 from www.mep.gov.sa/en/knowledge-resources/.

Kingdom of Saudi Arabia Ministry of Labour 2013. 'Saudi employment strategy summary', Saudi Arabia Ministry of Labour, accessed 21 December 2014 from www.portal.mol.gov.sa/en/Document%20Library/SummaryOfSaudiEmploymentStrategy.pdf.

Kingdom of Saudi Arabia Monetary Agency 2015. 'Fifty-first annual report', Saudi Arabian Monetary Agency, accessed 10 January 2016 www.sama.gov.sa/en-US/EconomicReports/AnnualReport/5600_R_Annual_En_51_Apx.pdf.

——— 2014. 'Economic diversification of Saudi Arabia: the past, present and the way ahead', Saudi Arabian Monetary Agency, accessed 10 January 2016 from www.sama.gov.sa/ar-sa/EconomicResearch/Quarterly%20Workshops/الثـــــاني20%العـــرض_2014_الثـــاني20%الــــربع.pdf..

——— 2012. 'Forty-eighth annual report', Saudi Arabian Monetary Agency, accessed 10 October 2014 www.sama.gov.sa/en-US/EconomicReports/AnnualReport/5600_R_Annual_En_48_2013_02_19.pdf.

Kinninmont, J. 2015. 'Future trends in the Gulf', Chatham House, accessed 15 December 2015 from www.chathamhouse.org/sites/files/chathamhouse/field/field_document/20150218FutureTrendsGCCExecSumKinninmont.pdf.

Kock, C. and Upitis, R. 1996. 'Is computer time equal for girls? Potential internet inequities', in the *Proceedings of the Sixth Annual Conference of the Internet Society*. Reston, VA: The Internet Society.

Korabik, K., Lero, D. and Ayman, R. 2003. 'A multi-level approach to cross-cultural work-family research: a micro- and macro-perspective', *International Journal of Cross-Cultural Management*, 3(3): 289–303.

Kotler, P. and Lee, N. 2005. *Corporate Social Responsibility: Doing the Most Good for Your Company and Your Cause*. Hoboken, NJ: John Wiley and Sons.

Kotter, J. and Cohen, D. 2002. *The Heart of Change: Real-Life Stories of How People Change Their Organisations*. Cambridge, MA: Harvard Business School Press.

Kouzes, J. and Posner, B. 2008 (fourth edition). *The Leadership Challenge*. San Francisco: Jossey-Bass.

Krane, J. 2009. *City of Gold: Dubai and the Dream of Capitalism*. New York: St. Martin's Press.

Krivkovich, A., Kutcher, E. and Yee, L. 2016. 'Breaking down the gender challenge', *McKinsey Quarterly*, March, accessed 25 March 2016 from www.mckinsey .com/business-functions/organisation/our-insights/breaking-down-the-gender-challenge?cid=mckwomen-eml-alt-mkq-mck-oth-1603.

Kvale, S. 1983. 'The qualitative research interview: a phenomenological and hermeneutical mode of understanding', *Journal of Phenomenological Psychology*, 14(1): 171–196.

Lacey, R. 2009. *Inside the Kingdom: Kings, Clerics, Modernists, Terrorists and the Struggle for Saudi Arabia*. London: Penguin Books.

—— 2001. *The Kingdom: Arabia and the House of Saud*. London: Penguin Books.

al-Lamki, A. 2007. 'Feminizing leadership in Arab societies: the perspectives of Omani female leaders', *Women in Management Review*, 22(1): 49–67.

Lavelle, K. and al-Sheikh, H. 2013. 'Giving voice to women entrepreneurs in Saudi Arabia', Women's Entrepreneurship Initiative and Ashridge Business School, accessed 26 August from www.ashridge.org.uk/insights/blog/april-2013/ unleashing-female-entrepreneurial-talent-in-saudi/.

Lawson, S. and Gilman, D. 2009. 'The power of the purse: global equality and middle-class spending', Goldman Sachs Global Research Institute, accessed 12 April 2014 from www.goldmansachs.com/our-thinking/investing-in-women/bios-pdfs/power-of-purse.pdf.

Leaders Middle East 2015. 'Power women of Arabia debate', *Leaders Middle East*, 7 September, accessed 15 April 2016 from www.leadersme.com/power-women-of-arabia-debate/.

Leighton, A. 2007. *On Leadership: Practical Wisdom from the People Who Know*. London: Random House.

Leonard, D. and Strauss, S. 1999. 'Putting your company's whole brain to work', in *Harvard Business Review on Breakthrough Thinking*, pp. 57–85. Cambridge, MA: Harvard Business School Publishing.

Lewis, S. 2010. *Towards New Conceptions of Work-Life Balance*. London: Routledge.

Lewis, S., Gambles, R. and Rapoport, R. 2007. 'The constraints of a work-balance approach: an international perspective', *International Journal of Human Resource Management*, 18(3): 360–373.

Limbert, M. 2010. *In the Time of Oil: Piety, Memory and Social Life in an Omani Town*. Stanford, CA: Stanford University Press.

London School of Economics 2016. 'Confronting gender inequality: findings of the LSE commission on gender, inequality and power', London School of Economics Gender Institute, accessed 3 May 2016 from www.lse.ac.uk/gender Institute/pdf/Confronting-Inequality.pdf.

Lupart, J. and Cannon, E. 2002. 'Computers and career choices: gender differences in grades seven and ten students', *Gender, Technology and Development*, 6(2): 233–248.

Lyons, J. 2010. *The House of Wisdom: How the Arabs Transformed Western Civilisation*. London: Bloomsbury.

Macfarquhar, N. 2009. *The Media Relations Department of Hezbollah Wishes You a Happy Birthday: Unexpected Encounters in the Changing Middle East*. New York: Perseus Books.

Maddison, S. 1999. 'Right to fight is front line of feminism', *The Weekend Australian*, 9–10 July.

Madichie, N. and Gallant, M. 2012. 'Broken silence: a commentary on women's entrepreneurship in the United Arab Emirates', *Journal of Entrepreneurship and Innovation*, 13(2): 81–92.

Mahajan, V. 2012. *The Arab World Unbound: Tapping into the Power of 350 Million Consumers*. San Francisco, CA: Jossey-Bass.

Maiden, M. 2016. 'BHP boss turns up the gender diversity dial', *The Sydney Morning Herald* (Business Day), 9–10 January.

Majdalani, F., Sfeir, R., Nader, P. and Omair, B. 2015. 'Leveraging an untapped talent pool: how to advance women's role in GCC family businesses', Al Sayedah Khadijah bint Khuwalid Centre and PwC, accessed 2 November 2015 from www.strategyand.pwc.com/global/home/what-we-think/reports-white-papers/article-display/leveraging-untapped-talent-pool.

Manne, R. 2016. 'The mind of Islamic State: an ideology of savagery', *The Monthly*, June: 25–39.

Manning, M. and Haddock, P. 1995. *Leadership Skills for Women*. Menlo Park, CA: Crisp Publications.

Marmenout, M. 2009. 'Breaking gender stereotypes in the Middle East', INSEAD Research on Women-Focused Leadership Development in the Middle East, accessed 15 April 2010 from www.insead.edu/facultyresearch/research/doc.cfm?did=42246.

Martel, L. 2002. *High Performers: How the Best Companies Find Them and Keep Them*. San Francisco: Jossey Bass.

Maslow, A. 1954. *Motivation and Personality*. New York: Harper.

—— 1943. 'A theory of human motivation', *Psychological Review*, 50(3): 370–396.

Masood, E. 2009. *Science and Islam: A History*. New York: Icon.

Mathew, J., Balakrishnan, S. and Salman, T. 2011. 'Oman budget 2011 and eighth five year plan 2011–2015: key analysis and review', United Securities LLC, accessed 26 October 2014 from http://usoman.com.om/UploadFiles/129627953931718750Budget%20and%208th%20Five%20year%20Plan%20Review_18_jan%20_2011.pdf.

Mattioli, D. 2012. 'Kodak's sale of patents faces hurdles', *The Wall Street Journal*, 11 June.

Mazawi, A. 2005. 'The academic profession in a rentier state: the professoriate in Saudi Arabia', *Minerva*, 43(3): 221–244.

McCrohan, D., Erogul, M., Vellinga, N. and Tong, Q. 2009. 'National global entrepreneurship monitor report for the United Arab Emirates', GEM Consortium and the College of Business Sciences, Zayed University, Dubai.

McElhaney, K. 2008. *Just Good Business: A Strategic Guide to Aligning Corporate Social Responsibility and Brand*. San Francisco, CA: Berrett-Koehler.

McElwee, G. and al-Riyami, R. 2003. 'Women entrepreneurs in Oman: some barriers to success', *Career Development International*, 8(7): 595–612.

McGirt, E. 2016. 'Leading while black: an inside look at what's keeping black men out of the executive suite', *Fortune*, 1 February: 47–53.

MENA-OECD Investment Program 2011. 'Note on the establishment of national task forces', The MENA-OECD Women's Business Forum, accessed 16 October 2012 from www.oecd.org/mena/48778046.pdf.

—— 2009. '2009 action plan on fostering women's entrepreneurship and employment in the MENA region', The MENA-OECD Investment Program, accessed 16 October 2012 from www.oecd.org/mena/investment/44092571.pdf.

—— 2007. 'The OECD-MENA Women's Business Forum', The MENA OECD Investment Program, accessed 16 October 2012 from www.oecd.org/mena/investment/44065473.pdf.

MENA Universities Summit 2015. 'MENA universities summit, Qatar, 23–24 February', accessed 22 August 2015 from www.theworldsummitseries.com/ THEMENAUS2015.

Menoret, P. 2014. *Joyriding in Riyadh: Oil, Urbanism and Road Revolt in Saudi Arabia*. Cambridge: Cambridge University Press.

Metcalfe, B. 2006. 'Exploring cultural dimensions of gender and management in the Middle East', *Thunderbird International Business Review*, 48(1): 93–107.

Middle East Online 2015. 'UAE advisory council elects first female speaker', Middle East Online, 11 November, accessed 21 March 2016 from www .Middle East-online.com/english/?id=74076.

Ministry of State for Federal National Council Affairs 2009. *Women in the United Arab Emirates: A Portrait of Progress*. Abu Dhabi: Ministry of State for Federal National Council Affairs.

Minkus-McKenna, D. 2009. 'Women Entrepreneurs in Riyadh, Saudi Arabia', University of Maryland University College, UMUC Working Paper Series No. 2009-02, accessed 8 July 2013 from www.readbag.com/ksu-sa-sites-ksuara bic-research-ncys-documents-r249.

Moghaddam, V. 2013. *Modernising Women: Gender and Social Change in the Middle East*. Boulder Colorado: Lynne Rienner Publishers.

Mohammed, E. 2008. 'UAE's first female judge says she's not afraid of new role', *Gulf News*, accessed December 17 2008 from www.gulfnews.com/nation/Soci ety/10201944.html.

Al Monitor 2015. 'After Qaboos, who will be Oman's next ruler?' *Al Monitor Gulf Pulse*, 25 January, accessed 13 May 2015 from www.al-monitor.com/pulse/ originals/2015/01/oman-abdullah-qaboos-succession-power-yemen.html#.

——— 2014. 'Oman's uncertain future', *Al Monitor Gulf Pulse*, 21 October, accessed 13 May 2015 from www.al-monitor.com/pulse/originals/2014/10/ oman-sultan-qaboos-future-health-iran-saudi-gcc.html#.

Moody's Investor Services 2016. 'Moody's place Saudi Arabia Aa3 rating on review for downgrade', Moody's Investor Services, accessed 1 June 2016 from www .moodys.com/research/Moodys-places-Saudi-Arabias-Aa3-rating-on-review-for- downgrade–PR_344433.

Moore, L. 2011. 'Worldly leadership through local knowledge: discovering the voice of Emirati women business leaders', in S. Turnbull, G. Edwards, D. Jepson and Simpson, P. (eds.) *Worldly Leadership: Alternative Wisdoms for A Complex World*, pp.171–193. London: Palgrave MacMillan.

——— 2009. 'Voices of women leaders in the UAE and Arab region: implications for leadership education and development', in Dubai Women Establishment, *Arab Women: Leadership Outlook 2009–2011*, pp. 48–50.

Moore, L. and Forster, N. 2009. 'An exploratory analysis of cross-cultural differences in sex-typing, gender self-attributes and the emergence of androgynous leadership traits', *Indian Journal of Management*, 2(2): July–December: 4–15.

Morris, I. 2011. *Why the West Rules – for Now: The Patterns of History and What They Reveal about the Future*. London: Profile Books.

Mostafa, M. 2007. 'Attitudes toward women managers who work in Egypt', *Women in Management Review*, 18(2): 252–266.

—— 2005. 'Attitudes toward women managers in the United Arab Emirates', *Journal of Managerial Psychology*, 20(6): 522–540.

Moukhallati, D. 2016. 'World leaders in Dubai for first global women's forum', *The National*, 22 February, accessed 15 April 2016 from www.thenational .ae/uae/education/world-leaders-in-dubai-for-regions-first-global-womens-forum.

Mouline, N. 2015. 'Enforcing and reinforcing the state's Islam: the functioning of the Committee of Senior Scholars', in B. Haykel, T. Hegghamer and S. Lacroix (eds.) *Saudi Arabia in Transition: Insights on Political, Economic and Religious Change*, pp. 48–70.

Mubarak, F. 2007. 'Achievements in the progress of the UAE Women's Federation', accessed 20 April 2009 from www.zaimuae.com/alain/showthread.php?p= 1352727.

Mubarak, S. 2012. 'Women's rights in Oman', *Muscat Daily*, 27 March, accessed 8 May 2015 from www.muscatdaily.com/Archive/Stories-Files/Women-s-Rights-in-Oman.

Muhanna-Matar, A. 2014. 'Redefining women's leadership', London School of Economics Middle East Centre, Paper Series No. 5, accessed 12 June 2015 from www .lse.ac.uk/middleEastCentre/publications/Paper-Series/WomenActivismAMM.pdf.

al-Munajjed, M. 2010a. 'Women's employment in Saudi Arabia: a major challenge', Strategy & Perspectives Series, accessed 29 May 2011 from www.strategyand.pwc.com/media/uploads/Womens_Employment_in_Saudi_ Arabia.pdf.

—— 2010b. *A History of Saudi Arabia*. Cambridge: Cambridge University Press.

—— 1997. *Women in Saudi Arabia Today*. London: Macmillan.

Muscat Daily 2015. 'Applied sciences colleges' board of trustees visits the national business centre', *Muscat Daily*, 17 May, accessed 23 May 2015 from www.muscatdaily.com/Archive/Applied-sciences-colleges-board-of-trustees-visits-the-national-business-centre-2xx5.

—— 2014. 'Entrepreneurs to get a helping hand in Oman', *Muscat Daily*, 17 February, accessed 18 February 2015 from www.muscatdaily.com/Arch ive/Business/Entrepreneurs-set-to-get-a-helping-hand-in-Oman-

———— 2013. 'National Business Centre opened', *Muscat Daily*, 25 November 2013, accessed 18 February 2015 from www.muscatdaily.com/Archive/Oman/National-business-centre-opened-2qct.

Nagraj, A. 2012. 'Who's the boss? GCC women rising up the ranks', *Gulf Business*, 12 October: 45–46.

Nair, M. 2011. 'Gender no bar to business success: given the same support, women can start equally profitable ventures', *Gulf News* (Business Section), 6 June.

Nasdaq 2016. 'Natural gas: US national average natural gas price', Nasdaq, accessed 18 February 2016 from www.nasdaq.com/markets/natural-gas.aspx?timeframe=3y.

Nasr, J. 2009. *The Status of Women under Islamic Law and Modern Islamic Legislation*. Leiden: Brill.

Nasr, J., Khoury, N. and Azzam, H. 2005. *Women, Employment and Development in the Arab World*. Berlin: Mouton.

National Association of Women Business Owners 2015. 'Women business owner statistics', National Association of Women Business Owners USA, accessed 4 November 2015 from www.nawbo.org/resources/women-business-owner-statistics.

National Business Centre 2015. 'National Business Centre Oman', accessed 12 March 2015 from http://om.gew.co/users/mulkie.

National Centre for Statistical Information 2016a. 'Population and development in Oman', NCSI Oman, accessed 11 February 2016 from www.ncsi.gov.om/NCSI_website/PublicationAttachment/PD%202016%20Book.pdf.

———— 2016b. 'Monthly statistical bulletin', NCSI Oman, accessed 11 May 2016 from www.ncsi.gov.om/(Elibrary/LibraryContentDoc/bar_MSB%20April%202016%20_5cab98c9-2c05-4734-a8f4-3dd43235c7e2.pdf.

———— 2015. 'General statistics: manpower', NCSI Oman, accessed 11 November 2015 from www.ncsi.gov.om/Elibrary/Pages/LibraryContentDetails.aspx?ItemID=mAGHspQq%2bSiwh9lrLO8D3Q%3d%3d.

———— 2014. 'Population and development in Oman', NCSI Oman, accessed 11 February 2016 from www.ncsi.gov.om/NCSI_website/PublicationAttachment/PD%202014%20Book.pdf.

National Society for Human Rights 2010. 'Second report on the status of human rights in the Kingdom of Saudi Arabia', National Society for Human Rights Riyadh, accessed 3 February 2016 from http://nshr.org.sa/en/wp-content/uploads/2013/12/91_التقـــرير-الثـــاني-عن-أحوال-حقـوق-الإنسـان-في-المملكـة-العربيـة-السـعودية-1429هـ-2008م-باللغـة-الانجليزيـة.pdf..

National Women's Business Council 2015. '10 million strong: the tipping point for women entrepreneurs', National Women's Business Council, accessed 4 January 2016 from www.nwbc.gov/sites/default/files/NWBC_2015Annual Reportedited.pdf.

New Internationalist 2016. 'Saudi Arabia: the facts', *New Internationalist,* March: 19.

Noland, M., Moran, T. and Kotschwar, B. 2016. 'Is gender diversity profitable? Evidence from a global survey', Peterson Institute for International Economics, Working Paper Series, WP 16–3, accessed 22 March 2016 from www.piie.com/publications/wp/wp16-3.pdf.

Oman Development Bank 2015. 'Oman Development Bank annual report 2014', Oman Development Bank, accessed 5 December 2015 from www.odb.com.om/AnnualReports/ODB-Annual-Report-2014-Eng.pdf.

Omani Women's Association 2016. 'Omani women in Oman', Omani Women's Association, accessed 11 May 2016 from www.owam.net/.

—— 2014. 'The leading role of women', Omani Women's Association, accessed 12 December 2014 from http://new.mosd.gov.om/index.php/en/associations-and-clubs-2/women-associations.

—— 2007. 'Special issue: Omani women', Omani Women's Association, accessed 12 December 2014 from http://new.mosd.gov.om/index.php/en/associations-and-clubs-2/women-associations.

OmanInfo.com 2015a. 'The people of Oman', OmanInfo, accessed 1 December 2014 from www.omaninfo.com/oman/people.asp.

—— 2015b. 'Business in Oman', OmanInfo, accessed 17 March 2015 from www.omaninfo.com/oman/business.asp.

—— 2015c. 'An insight view of Oman's industrial sector', OmanInfo, accessed 17 March 2015 from www.omaninfo.com/industry-commerce/insight-view-oman-industrial-sector.asp.

—— 2015d. 'Mobilising Oman's future', OmanInfo, accessed 17 March 2015 from www.omaninfo.com/infrastructure/mobilising-omans-future.asp.

O'Reilly, C. and Pfeffer, J. 2000. *Hidden Value: How Great Companies Achieve Extraordinary Results with Ordinary People.* Cambridge, MA: Harvard Business School Publishing.

Organisation for Economic Cooperation and Development 2014. 'Women in business: accelerating entrepreneurship in the Middle East and North Africa region', Organisation for Economic Cooperation and Development, accessed 24 April 2016 from www.oecd.org/mena/competitiveness//womeninbusiness2014 acceleratingentrepreneurshipinthemiddleeastandnorthafricaregion.htm.

—— 2012. 'Women in business: policies to support women's entrepreneurship development in the MENA Region', Organisation for Economic Cooperation and Development, accessed 17 April 2015 from www.oecd.org/mena/competitiveness/womeninbusiness-policiestosupportwomensentrepreneurshipdevelopmentinthemenaregion.htm.

———— 2004. 'Women's entrepreneurship issues and policies', *Second OECD Conference of Ministers Responsible for Small and Medium Sized Enterprises*, Istanbul, Turkey, June, accessed 4 May 2008 from www.oecd.org/industry/smes/31919215.pdf.

Oxford Business Group 2015a. 'Saudi Arabia pursues the twin goals of diversification and the knowledge economy', Oxford Business Group, accessed 13 January 2016 from www.oxfordbusinessgroup.com/overview/forward-thinking-pursuing-twin-goals-economic-diversification-and-creation-knowledge-economy.

———— 2015b. 'The Report: Oman 2015', Oxford Business Group, accessed 19 December 2014 from www.oxfordbusinessgroup.com/oman-2015.

———— 2014. 'Oman working to support SME growth', Oxford Business Group, accessed 15 December 2014 from www.oxfordbusinessgroup.com/news/oman-working-support-sme-growth.

Page, S. 2007. *The Difference: How the Power of Diversity Creates Better Groups, Firms, Schools and Societies*. Princeton: Princeton University Press.

Parker, K., Horowitz, J., Wang, W., Brown, A. and Patten, E. 2015. 'Women and leadership. Public says women are equally qualified, but barriers persist', Pew Research Centre, accessed 3 November 2015 from www.pewsocialtrends.org/2015/01/14/women-and-leadership/.

Peacock, L. 2013. 'Reaching the top tier: new study says firms must cast net wider to maintain momentum on female executives', *The Sunday Telegraph* (Business Section), 7 April.

PepsiCo 2016. 'About us: diversity and inclusion', PepsiCo, accessed 12 April 2016 from www.pepsico.com/Purpose/Talent-Sustainability/Diversity-and-Inclusion.

Petroleum Institute 2016. 'About PI: women in science and engineering', The Petroleum Institute, Abu-Dhabi, accessed 27 April 2016 from www.pi.ac.ae/PI_ACA/arz/index.php.

Pichon, E. 2013. 'Women in politics: the United Arab Emirates', European Parliamentary Research Service, accessed 25 April 2015 from www.europarl.europa.eu/eplibrary/UAE.pdf.

Plummer, P. 1983. *Documents of Life*. London: Allen and Unwin.

Poelmans, S. (ed.) 2005. *Work and Family: An International Research Perspective*. London: Lawrence Erlbaum.

Pollard, R. 2013. 'Licensed to practice: Saudi female lawyers to fly solo at last', *Sydney Morning Herald*, 7 October, accessed 2 February 2014 from www.smh.com.au/world/licensed-to-practise-saudi-female-lawyers-to-fly-solo-at-last-20131006–2v2ac.html.

Powell, H. 2009. 'Women of duty: the number of applicants to the Abu Dhabi police has doubled after a recruitment drive started in October', *Gulf News Magazine*, 19 December: 10–17.

Preis, K. and MacCrohan, D. 2006. 'A study of entrepreneurship in the United Arab Emirates', Mohammed Bin Rashid Establishment for Young Business Leaders and the College of Business Sciences, Zayed University, Dubai.

Private Eye 1996. 'Weird world', *Private Eye*, 25 October: 23 (reprint of an article originally published in *Utusan Malaysia*).

Railway Technology Market and Customer Insight 2012. 'Riyadh metro, Saudi Arabia', Railway Technology Market and Customer Insight, accessed 2 February 2016 from www.railway-technology.com/projects/-riyadh-metro-saudi-arabia/.

Rajab, A. and Al Mahrizi 2013. 'Rise in public expenditure to record levels is a major challenge facing the government', *Oman Newspaper* (Economics Section), 27 November: 8–9.

Ramsey, N. and McCorduck, P. 2005. 'Where are the women in information technology?' Anita Borg, accessed 15 January 2010 from www.anitaborg.org/files/abi_wherearethewomen.pdf.

al-Rasheed, M. 2016. 'Saudi activists: who are they and what do they want?' *New Internationalist*, March, 16–18.

——— 2015. 'Caught between religion and state: women in Saudi Arabia', in B. Haykel, T. Hegghamer and S. Lacroix (eds.) *Saudi Arabia in Transition: Insights on Political, Economic and Religious Change*, pp. 292–313.

——— 2013. *A Most Masculine State: Gender, Politics and Religion in Saudi Arabia*. Cambridge: Cambridge University Press.

——— 2010 (second edition). *A History of Saudi Arabia*. Cambridge: Cambridge University Press.

al-Rasheed, M. and Azzam, M. 2012. 'The prospects and limits of women's mobilization in Saudi Arabia', Chatham House, London, accessed 5 June 2015 from www.chathamhouse.org/sites/files/chathamhouse/public/Meetings/Meeting%20Transcripts/090312rasheed.pdf.

Raval, A. 2012. 'New road for a macho brand: Harley-Davidson offers lessons in how traditionally masculine labels can appeal to women', *Financial Times* (Business Life), 23 September.

Reality in Oman 2010. 'Are black Omanis dumb?' Wordpress.com, 31 January 2010, accessed 12 December 2015 from https://realityinoman.wordpress.com/2010/01/31/are-omani-blacks-dumb/.

Redvers, L. 2015a. 'Is Dubai the best place for women in the Middle East?' British Broadcasting Corporation, 9 April, accessed 15 April 2016 from www.bbc.com/capital/story/20150422-which-women-get-ahead-in-dubai.

——— 2015b. 'Women slowly get the keys to the Kingdom: the slow rise of Saudi women', British Broadcasting Corporation, 9 April, accessed 15 April 2016 from www.bbc.com/capital/story/20150408-slow-gains-for-saudi-women.

Reilly, B. 2010. 'Liberal education in the Middle East', in the Middle East Institute *Higher Education and the Middle East: Serving the Knowledge – Based Economy*, pp. 18–20.

Reporters Without Borders 2015a. 'World press freedom index 2015: United Arab Emirates', Reporters Without Borders, accessed 3 February 2016 from https://rsf.org/ranking.

——— 2015b. 'World press freedom index 2015: Saudi Arabia', Reporters without Borders, accessed 3 February 2016 from https://rsf.org/ranking.

——— 2015c. 'World press freedom index 2015: Oman', Reporters without Borders, accessed 3 February 2016 from https://rsf.org/ranking.

Reuters 2015. '"Barbarians at the gate" as Middle East business leaders meet', *Egypt Independent*, 23 May, accessed 15 April 2016 from www.egyptindependent.com/news/barbarians-gate-Middle East-business-leaders-meet.

Rivlin, P. 2009. *Arab Economics in the Twenty-First Century*. Cambridge: Cambridge University Press.

al-Riyami, R., Warren, L. and McElwee, G. 2002. 'Opportunities and challenges for Omani women entrepreneurs', *International Journal of Entrepreneurship and Innovation*, 39(2): 133–144.

Roberts, P. 2005. *The End of Oil: The Decline of the Petroleum Economy and the Rise of a New Energy Order*. London: Bloomsbury Publishing.

Robertson, L. 2002. *The Culture of Islam: Changing Aspects of Contemporary Muslim Life*. Chicago: University of Chicago Press.

Rogan, E. 2015. *The Fall of the Ottomans: The Great War in the Middle East*. New York: Basic Books.

Romani, V. 2009. 'The politics of higher education in the Middle East: problems and prospects', Crown Centre for Middle East Studies, Brandeis University, USA, accessed from www.brandeis.edu/crown/publications/meb/MEB36.pdf.

Rosenzweig, P. 2007. *The Halo Effect … and the Eight Other Delusions That Deceive Managers*. New York: Free Press.

Royal Decree 2004. 'Royal decree 77/2004: promulgating the privatisation law', The Government of Oman, accessed 12 April 2015 from www.edocr.com/doc/8/royal-decree-no-78-2004-regulation-and-privatisation-electricity-and-water-sector-oman.

——— 2003. 'Royal decree 35/2003', The Government of Oman, accessed 12 April 2015 from www.pdo.co.om/hseforcontractors/Environment/Documents/Oman%20Laws/Royal%20Decrees/labour_law.pdf.

Royal Society 2010. *A New Golden Age? The Prospects for Science and Innovation in the Islamic World*. London: The Royal Society.

Sabbagh, K. and al-Munajjed, M. 2011. 'Youth in GCC countries: meeting the challenge', Strategy& Ideation Centre, accessed 24 January 2013 from www.strategyand.pwc.com/reports/youth-countries-meeting-challenge.

Saddi, J., Sabbagh, K. and Shediac, R. 2012. 'Staying on the road to growth: why Middle East leaders must maintain their commitment to economic reform', Strategy& Ideation Centre, accessed 24 January 2013 from www.strategyand.pwc.com/media/uploads/Strategyand_Staying-on-the-Road-to-Growth.pdf.

Sadi, M. and al-Ghazali, B. 2012. 'The dynamics of entrepreneurial motivation among women: a comparative study of business women in Saudi Arabia and Bahrain', *Asian Academy of Management Journal*, 17(1): 97–113.

Sadiqi, F. and Ennaji, M. (eds.) 2010. *Women in the Middle East and North Africa: Agents of Changes*. New York: Routledge.

Saliba, G. 2007. *Islamic Science and the Making of the European Renaissance*. Cambridge, MA: MIT Press.

Salloum, H. 2003. 'Women in the United Arab Emirates', *Contemporary Review*, 283(1651): 101–118.

Samulewicz, D., Vidican, G and Aswad, N. 2010. 'Expanding women's participation in science, technology and engineering: the case of the United Arab Emirates', the *Eighth Triple Helix Conference*, Madrid, October 2010, accessed 13 October 2012 from www.academia.edu/3396532/expanding_womens_participation_in_science_technology_and_engineering_the_case_of_the_United_Arab_Emirates.

SANAD Fund for Supporting and Developing Small Projects 2015. 'The SANAD fund', Ministry of Manpower Oman, accessed 17 March 2015 from www.omaninfo.com/manpower-and-employment/sanad-fund-supporting-and-developing-small-projects-ministry-manpower.asp.

Sandberg, S. 2013. *Lean In: Women, Work and the Will to Lead*. New York: Alfred Knopf.

Sassoon, J. 2004. *Princess: The True Story of Life Inside Saudi Arabia's Royal Family*. London: Bantam Books.

Saudi Fast Growth 100 2016. 'About SFG', Saudi Fast Growth 100, accessed 5 January 2016 from http://saudifastgrowth.com/en-Overview.

Saudi Gazette 2013a. 'Saudi Arabia deports 800,000 illegal foreign workers', *Saudi Gazette*, 22 September, accessed 2 February 2014 from http://english.alarabiya.net/en/views/business/economy/2013/09/22/Saudi-Arabia-deports-800-000-illegal-foreign-workers.html.

—— 2013b. 'Continued growth expected in KSA's construction sector', *Saudi Gazette*, accessed 15 August 2014 from www.saudigazette.com.sa/ news/con tinued-growth-expected-in-ksa-s-construction-sector/237581

Schlosser, J. 2002. 'Why women should rule the world', *Fortune*, 28 October, 70–71.

Schutz, A. 1966. *Collected Papers: The Problems of Social Reality*. The Hague: Martinus Nijhoff.

Schwartz, E. 1976. 'Entrepreneurship: a new female frontier', *Journal of Contemporary Business*, 5(1): 47–76.

Science Citation Index 2015. Thomson Reuters, accessed 3 January 2016 from http:// thomsonreuters.com/en/products-services/scholarly-scientific-research/ scholarly-search-and-discovery/science-citation-index-expanded.html.

Segal, A. 1996. 'Why does the Muslim world lag in science?' *The Middle East Quarterly*, June, 3(2): 61–70.

Sfakianakis, J. 2014. 'How can SME growth in the kingdom be unlocked?' *Arab News*, 9 June, accessed 13 August 2014 from www.arabnews.com/news/ 583846.

al-Shahri, S. 2011. 'Women's rights in Oman', accessed 8 May 2015 from http:// susanalshahri.blogspot.com.au/2012/03/womens-rights-in-oman.html.

Shallal, M. 2011. 'Job satisfaction among women in the United Arab Emirates', *Journal of International Women's Studies*, 12(3): 114–133.

Shediac, R., Bohsali, S. and Samman, H. 2012. 'The bedrock of society: understanding and growing the MENA middle class', Booz & Company Ideation Centre, Abu Dhabi, accessed 11 May 2013 from www.strategyand.pwc.com/ media/uploads/Strategyand_The-Bedrock-of-Society-MENA-Regions-Middle-Class.pdf.

Shediac, R., Moujales, C., Najjar, M. and Ghaleb, J. 2011. 'Resilient, stable, sustainable: the benefits of economic diversification', Booz & Company Ideation Centre, Abu Dhabi, accessed 11 May 2013 from www.strategyand.pwc.com/ media/uploads/Strategyand_Resilient-Stable-Sustainable-The-Benefits-Of-Eco nomic-Diversification.pdf.

Shemla, M. and Kreienberg, A. 2014. 'Gender quotas in hiring drive away both women and men', *Forbes*, 16 October, accessed 3 May 2016 from www.forbes .com/sites/datafreaks/2014/10/16/gender-quotas-in-hiring-drive-away-both-women-and-men/#1f60b51a42a5.

al-Shihri 2012. 'Sheikh Abdul Mohsen al-Obeikan, Saudi King's ultraconservative adviser dismissed over women's rights issue', *The Huffington Post*, 12 July accessed 2 February 2013 from www.huffingtonpost.com/2012/05/12/sheik-abdul-mohsen-al-obeikan-dismissed_n_1511486.html.

Sidani, Y. 2005. 'Women, work and Islam in Arab societies', *Women in Management Review*, 20(7): 498–512.

Simard, C., Davies-Henderson, A., Gilmartin, S., Schiebinger, L. and Whitney, T. 2005. *Climbing the Technical Ladder: Obstacles and Solutions for Mid-Level Women in Technology*. Palo Alto, CA: Anita Borg Institute.

Simmons, M. 2005. *Twilight in the Desert: the Coming Saudi Oil Shock and the World Economy*. London: John Wiley and Sons.

——— 1996. *New Leadership for Women and Men: Building an Inclusive Organisation*. Aldershot: Gower.

Simms, B., Axworthy, M. and Milton, P. 2016. 'Ending the new Thirty Years War. Why the real history of the Peace of Westphalia in 17th century Europe offers a model for bringing stability to the Middle East', *New Statesman*, 22–28 January: 23–27.

Sinclair, A. 1998. *Doing Leadership Differently: Gender, Power and Sexuality in a Changing Business Culture*. Melbourne: Melbourne University Press.

Sinclair, A. and Wilson, C. 2002. *New Faces of Leadership*. Melbourne: Melbourne University Press.

Singer, S., Amaros, J. and Arreola, D. 2014. 'Global entrepreneurship monitor 2014 global report', GEM Consortium, accessed 20 December 2015 from http://gemconsortium.org/report/1425644863_GEM_2014_Global_Report.pdf.

Sisters in Islam 2015. 'Are men and women equal before Allah?' Sisters in Islam, accessed 29 October 2015 from www.sistersinislam.org.my/files/download/are_men_and_women_equal_before_allah.pdf.

Skeet, I. 1992. *Oman: Politics and Development*. London: Macmillan.

Skoko, H., Wright, N. and Santa, R. 2010. 'State of entrepreneurship activities in Saudi Arabia', GEM Consortium, the Centennial Fund, the National Entrepreneurship Centre and the College of Business, Al Faisal University, Riyadh.

Smedley, T. 2014. 'The evidence is growing – there really is a business case for diversity', *Financial Times: The Inclusive Workplace*, 15 May: 2–3.

Smith, L. 2014. 'World Energy day 2014: how much oil is left and how long will it last?' *International Business Times*, 22 October, accessed 19 October 2015 from http://theconversation.com/oil-prices-eventually-the-gulf-states-will-run-out-of-power-35867.

Smith, M. 2013. 'Dubai aims to triple tourism income by 2020', *Reuters*, 4 May, accessed 29 May 2013 from www.reuters.com/article/2013/05/04/us-dubai-tourism-idUSBRE94306P20130504.

Soffan, L. 1980. *The Women of the United Arab Emirates*. New York: Harper and Row.

Sokari, H., Van Horne, C., Zeng-Yu, H. and Awad, M. 2013. 'Entrepreneurship: an Emirati perspective', Research Gate, accessed 11 February 2014 from www.researchgate.net/publication/25798653_Entrepreneurship_an_Emirati_Perspective.

Sonbol, A. 2009. 'Religion and women's rights', in Dubai Women Establishment *Arab Women: Leadership Outlook 2009–2011*, pp. 95–96.

Sperling, J., Marcati, C., Rennie, M. and Ellis, T. 2014. 'GCC women in leadership – from the first to the norm', McKinsey & Company, accessed 21 September 2015 from www.mckinsey.com/global-locations/europe-and-middleeast/ Middle East/en/gcc-women-in-leadership.

Spindle, B. 2013. 'Break-even oil price bogeyman stalks Gulf economies', *Wall Street Journal*, 28 May, accessed 11 April 2015 from http://blogs.wsj.com/middleeast/ 2013/05/28/break-even-oil-price-bogeyman-stalks-gulf-economies/.

Stark, R. 2014. *How the West Won: The Neglected Story of the Triumph of Modernity*. Wilmington, DE: ISI Books.

Steinhauer, J. 2013. 'Seven women on Senate panel step to the fore: on sexual assault issues they take lead on Senate Armed Services Committee', *International Herald and Tribune*, 3 June.

Stewart, C. 2002. 'It's Amanda's world', *The Weekend Australian*, 1–2 July.

Stockholm International Peace Research Institute 2016. 'Military spending and arms procurement in the Middle East', Stockholm International Peace Research Institute, accessed 28 January 2016 from www.sipri.org/publica tions/test/trends/gulf.

Strolla, A. and Peri, P. 2013. 'Oman 2020 vision', Deloitte Middle East, accessed 12 December 2014 from www2.deloitte.com/content/dam/Deloitte/ xe/Documents/About-Deloitte/mepovdocuments/mepov12/dtme_mepov12_ Oman2020vision.pdf.

al-Suhaimy, U. 2013. 'Saudi Arabia: the desalination nation. Facing acute water supply pressures, Saudi Arabia is planning huge investments in water desalin- ation systems', *Asharq Al Awsat*, 2 July, accessed 21 January 2016 from http:// english.aawsat.com/2013/07/article55308131/the-desalination-nation.

Sullivan, R. 2015. 'Can gender quotas get more women into boardrooms?' *Bloom- berg*, 2 July, accessed 22 January 2016 from www.bloomberg.com/news/art icles/2015-07-01/can-gender-quotas-get-more-women-into-boardrooms-.

Sultan Qaboos Cultural Centre 2014. 'Women of Oman: changing roles and transnational influence', *Arabian Peninsula International Conference 2014*, Kennesaw State University, November, accessed 27 May 2015 from http://dga.kennesaw.edu/yearof/arabianpeninsula/docs/yoap_conference_ overview.pdf.

Sultanate of Oman 1996. 'Sultanate of Oman: the basic statute of the state', Ministry of Legal Affairs, Oman, accessed 12 December 2014 from www.mola .gov.om/eng/basicstatute.aspx.

———— 1995. 'The vision for Oman's economy: Oman 2020', The Sultanate of Oman, accessed 12 December 2014 from http://ebookmarket.org/pdf/chap ter-no6-the-vision-for-omans-economy-oman-51952086.pdf.

SUSRIS 2016.'Human resources development fund', SUSRIS, accessed 5 January 2016 from http://susris.com/glossary/human-resources-development-fund-hrdfhadaf/.

Sussmuth-Dykerhoff, C., Wang, J. and Chen, J. 2012. 'Women matter: harnessing female talent to raise corporate performance', McKinsey & Company, accessed 11 July 2014 from www.leadershipforwomen.com.au/globalize/ women-matter-an-asian-perspective-harnessing-female-talent-to-raise-corpor ate-performance.

Swiegers, G. and Toohey, K. 2012. 'Waiter, is that inclusion in my soup? A new recipe to improve business performance', Deloitte Australia and the Victorian Equal Opportunity and Human Rights Commission, accessed 24 March 2014 from www2.deloitte.com/content/dam/Deloitte/au/Documents/human-cap ital/deloitte-au-hc-diversity-inclusion-soup-0513.pdf.

Tainter, J. 2006. *The Collapse of Complex Societies*. Cambridge: Cambridge University Press.

Takatuf HR Academy 2015. 'Takatuf Oman', Takatuf HR Academy, accessed 17 March 2015 from www.takatuf.om/en/about.html.

Talei, R. 2010. 'Oman', in S. Kelly and J. Breslin (eds.) *Women's Rights in the Middle East: Progress Amidst Resistance*, pp. 337–358.

Technovia 2016. 'About us', Technovia, accessed 5 January 2016 from http:// technoviainc.com/about.php.

Technical and Vocational Training Corporation 2016. 'Foundation and develop-ment of the TVTC', Technical and Vocational Training Corporation Saudi Arabia, accessed 2 February 2016 from www.tvtc.gov.sa/English/AboutUs/ Pages/default.aspx.

Teerlink, R. and Ozley, L. 2000. *More than a Motorcycle: The Leadership Journey at Harley-Davidson*. Cambridge, MA: Harvard Business School Press.

Telhami, S. 2013. *The World through Arab Eyes*. New York: Basic Books.

Terjesen, S. and Lloyd, A. 2015. 'The 2015 female entrepreneurship index: analys-ing the conditions that foster high-potential entrepreneurship in 77 countries', Global Entrepreneurship and Development Institute, accessed 17 December 2015 from http://thegedi.org/female-entrepreneurship-index-2015-report/.

The Economist 2016a. 'Low and behold. Another year of low prices will create strains in the world economy', *The Economist*, 2 January: 9–10.

————— 2016b. 'The Saudi blueprint. The desert kingdom is striving to dominate the region and modernise its economy at the same time', *The Economist*, 9 January: 7–8.

————— 2016c. 'Young prince in a hurry. Muhammad bin Salman gambles on intervention abroad and radical economic change at home. But forget about democracy', *The Economist*, 9 January: 16–18.

————— 2016d. 'Saudi Aramco. Sale of the century?' *The Economist*, 9 January: 18–19.

————— 2016e. 'The Arab winter. Five years after a wave of uprisings, the Arab world is worse off than ever. But, its people understand their predicament better', *The Economist*, 9 January: 9–10.

————— 2016f. 'Saudi Arabia's financial hub: castles in the air. If you build it they may not come', *The Economist*, 9 February: 40.

————— 2016g. 'Women in Saudi Arabia. One step forward, one step back', *The Economist*, 12 March: 45.

————— 2016h. 'A proper reckoning. Feminist economics deserves recognition as a distinct branch of the discipline', *The Economist*, 12 March: 72.

————— 2016i. 'Oil and the Gulf states: after the party', *The Economist*, 26 March: 43–44.

————— 2016j. 'The new oil order. An impetuous prince is rattling the Middle East, but may also bring bold reform', *The Economist*, 23 April: 12.

————— 2016k. 'Saudi Arabia's post-oil future: bold promises from a young prince. But they will be hard to keep', *The Economist*, 30 April: 40–41.

————— 2016l. 'The war within. Europe and America made mistakes, but the misery of the Arab world is caused mainly by its own failures', *The Economist*, 14 May: 9–10.

————— 2016m. 'Special report: the Arab world', *The Economist*, 14 May.

————— 2016n. 'Innovation in the Arab world. From zero to not much more', *The Economist*, 4 June: 42.

————— 2015a. 'Political rights in the Gulf: creeping consultation. Gulf citizens are getting more chances to votes', *The Economist*, 12 September: 48–49.

————— 2015b. 'The other Arab spring. Entrepreneurs in the Arab world are leaping into action', *The Economist*, 11 August: 58.

————— 2015c. 'Beware of sandstorms. The Middle East is a reminder to business of globalisation's limits', *The Economist*, 20 June: 64.

————— 2015d. 'Saudi Arabia's gerontocracy: ail the king. Generational change looms', *The Economist*, 10 January: 41.

————— 2015e. 'Rise of the gulf: soaring ambition. Economic and political influence are shifting to the Gulf. Can it last?' *The Economist*, 10 January: 42.

————— 2015f. 'Tax in the Gulf: filling a hole. Oil-rich states need to find new ways to balance their budgets', *The Economist*, 10 January: 61–62.

———— 2015g. 'America's Amazons. The law now makes women more or less equal in the armed forces. But, how much can they really do?' *The Economist*, 16 May: 35–36.

———— 2014a. 'The tragedy of the Arabs. A civilisation that used to lead the world is in ruins – and only the locals can rebuild it', *The Economist*, 5 July: 9–10.

———— 2014b. 'Tethered by history. The failures of the Arab spring were a long time in the making', *The Economist*, 5 July: 21–23.

———— 2013a. 'Special report: the Arab Spring', *The Economist*, 13 July.

———— 2013b. 'Islam and science. The road to renewal', *The Economist*, 26 January: 50–51.

———— 2012. 'Waving a big stick. Quotas for women on boards in the European Union are moving a little closer', *The Economist*, 10 March: 65.

———— 2009. 'A second life. Abu Dhabi rescues Dubai after all', *The Economist*, 19 December: 119–120.

———— 2002. 'Self-doomed to failure. An unsparing new report by Arab scholars explains why their region lags behind much of the world', *The Economist*, 6 July: 24–26.

The Economist Intelligence Unit 2015a. 'Business environment rankings. Which country is best to do business in?' The Economist Intelligence Unit, accessed 12 October from www.eiu.com/sites/default/files/business_environment_rankings.pdf.

———— 2015b. 'Democracy index 2015: democracy in age of anxiety', The Economist Intelligence Unit, accessed 28 January 2016 from www.eiu.com/public/topical_report.aspx?campaignid=DemocracyIndex2015.

———— 2014. 'UAE economic vision: women in science, technology and engineering', *The Economist* Intelligence Unit, accessed 24 July 2015 from www.economistinsights.com/sites/default/files/ENGLISH%20UAE%20Vision%20Women%20FULL%20-%20WEB_0.pdf.

The Economist Middle East and Africa 2016. 'Transcript: interview with Muhammad bin Salman', *The Economist*, accessed 5 February 2016 from www.economist.com/saudi_interview?fsrc=scn/tw/te/bl/ed/transcriptinterviewwithmuhammadbinsalman.

———— 2014. 'The Saudi royal family: palace coup', *The Economist*, accessed 14 January 2016 from www.economist.com/blogs/pomegranate/2014/03/saudi-royal-family.

The Financial Forecast Centre 2015. 'Crude oil price forecast 2015–2016', The Financial Forecast Centre, accessed 8 February 2016 from www.forecasts.org/oil.htm.

The Guardian 2015. 'Saudi Arabia advertises for 8 new executioners as beheading rate soars', *The Guardian*, 18 May, accessed 3 February 2016 from www.theguardian.com/world/2015/may/18/saudi-arabia-advertises-eight-new-executioners-beheadings-soar.

———— 2010. 'WikiLeaks cables portray Saudi Arabia as a cash machine for terrorists', *The Guardian*, accessed 21 April 2013 from www.theguardian.com/world/2010/dec/05/wikileaks-cables-saudi-terrorist-funding.

The Koran 2003 (eleventh edition). *Penguin Classics Series*. London: Penguin Books.

The Middle East Institute 2010. 'Higher education and the Middle-East: serving the knowledge-based economy', The Middle East Institute, Washington, DC, accessed 11 May 2013 from www.mideasti.org/sites/default/files/publica tions/Education%20VP.pdf

The Ministry of Education 2010. 'Emirates education strategy 2010–2020', UAE Ministry of Education, Abu Dhabi, accessed 13 October 2015 from http://planipolis.iiep.unesco.orgupload/United%20Arab%20Emirates/United%20Arab%20Emirates_Strategy_2010-2020.df.

The National 2014. 'Emirati woman who reached for the skies', *The National*, 10 June, accessed 23 June 2014 from www.thenational.ae/uae/government/emirati-woman-who-reached-for-the-skies.

The Public Establishment for Industrial Estates 2015a. 'Corporate Objectives', PEIE, accessed 21 March 2015 from www.peie.om/ABOUT-PEIE/Corporate-Objectives.

———— 2015b. 'About PEIE', The Public Establishment for Industrial Estates, accessed 21 March 2015 from www.peie.om/ESTATES/About-Industrial-Estate.

The Week Oman 2014a. 'Omani women play larger roles in public and private sectors', *The Week Oman*, 13 March, Issue 572: 4.

———— 2014b. 'Taste of sweet success: Etab al Zadjali has high hopes for Oman entrepreneurs', *The Week Oman*, 13 March, Issue 572: 10.

The Work-Life Research Centre 2000. *The Work-Life Manual: Gaining a Competitive Edge by Balancing the Demands of Employees' Work and Home Lives*. London: The Industrial Society.

Thomas, D. 2004. 'Diversity as Strategy', *Harvard Business Review*, September: 98–108.

Times Higher Education 2016. 'World university rankings', *Times Higher Education*, accessed 2 October 2016 from www.timeshighereducation.com/world-university-rankings/2016/world-ranking#!/page/0/length/25/sort_by/rank/sort_order/asc/cols/stats.

———— 2015. 'World university rankings', *Times Higher Education*, accessed 3 February 2016 from www.timeshighereducation.co.uk/world-university-rankings/2014–2015/world-rankings/.

Times of Oman 2015a. 'Mega solar project in Oman to draw oil from ground', *Times of Oman*, 6 June, accessed 4 December 2014 from www.timesofoman.com/article/35420/Oman/Mega-solar-power-project-in-Oman-to-draw-oil-from-grounds.

———— 2015b. 'Oman National Youth Commission unveils plans', *Times of Oman*, 12 May, accessed 4 December 2014 from www.timesofoman.com/article/51990/Oman/Oman-National-Youth-Commission-unveils-plans.

———— 2015c. 'National Business Centre, Oman Oil to expand business incubator', *Times of Oman*, 28 January, accessed 21 March 2015 from www.timesofoman.com/article/46920/Business/National-Business-Centre-Oman-Oil-to-expand-business-incubator-.

Trabelsi, M. 2015. 'One woman elected in Oman's Shura Council', International Knowledge Network of Women in Politics, accessed 11 January 2016 from http://iknowpolitics.org/en/news/world-news/one-woman-elected-oman%E2%80%99s-shura-council.

Trade Arabia 2010.'Women's forum explores work-life balance', *Trade Arabia*, 13 January, accessed 21 July 2012 from balance www.tradearabia.com/news/media_173183.html.

Trading Economics 2016.'Oman economic forecast 2016–2020',Trading Economics, accessed 11 May 2015 from www.tradingeconomics.com/oman/forecast.

Transparency International 2016. 'Corruption perceptions index 2015', Transparency International, accessed 12 January 2016 from www.transparency.org/cpi2015#downloads.

———— 2015. 'Corruption perceptions index 2014', Transparency International, accessed 12 January 2016 from www.transparency.org/cpi2014/results.

Tucker, J. 2008. *Women, Family and Gender in Islamic Law*. Cambridge: Cambridge University Press.

Ulrichsen, K. 2011. *Insecure Gulf: The End of Certainty and the Transition to the Post-Oil Era*. London: Hurst.

United Arab Emirates Cabinet 2014. 'The national strategy for innovation', United Arab Emirates Cabinet, accessed 8 March 2015 from http://uaecabinet.ae/en/the-national-strategy-for-innovation.

———— 2013. 'UAE Government Strategy Document 2013', Abu-Dhabi Government, United Arab Emirates, accessed 19 January 2014 from www.uaecabinet.ae/English/Documents/PMO%20Strategy2013DocEngFinV2.pdf.

———— 2008. 'UAE Government Strategy Document 2008', Abu-Dhabi Government, United Arab Emirates, accessed 4 April 2010 from www.uaecabinet.ae/English/ Documents/PMO%20Strategy2008DocEngFinV2.pdf.

United Arab Emirates Government 2014. 'Vision 2021', Government of the United Arab Emirates, accessed 6 March 2015 from www.vision2021.ae/en.

United Arab Emirates Ministry of Education 2010. 'UAE Ministry of Education Strategy 2010–2020', United Arab Emirates Ministry of Education, accessed 11 November 2015 from www.moe.gov.ae/Arabic/Docs/MOE%20_Strategy.pdf.

United Arab Emirates National Bureau of Statistics 2016. 'The UAE in figures 2014', United Arab Emirates National Bureau of Statistics, accessed from www.uaestatistics.gov.ae/EnglishHome/ReportsByDepartmentEnglish/tabid/ 104/Default.aspx?MenuId=1&NDId=446.

United Nations 2016. 'United Nations human development report 2015: statistical tables', United Nations, accessed 2 January 2016 from http://hdr.undp.org/en.

———— 2015a. 'United Nations human development report 2014', United Nations Development Program, accessed 16 December 2015 from http://hdr.undp.org/ en/2015-report/download.

———— 2015b. 'Convention on the elimination of all forms of discrimination against women', United Nations, accessed 14 September 2015 from www.un .org/womenwatch/daw/cedaw/text/econvention.html.

———— 2014. 'United Nations gender related development index', United Nations Development Program, accessed 14 September 2005 from http://hdr.undp.org/ en/content/gender-development-index-gdi.

———— 2011. 'Concluding observations of the committee on the elimination of all forms of discrimination against women: Oman', United Nations, accessed 14 January 2015 from www2.ohchr.org/english/bodies/cedaw/docs/co/ CEDAW-C-OMN-CO-1.pdf.

———— 2010a. 'United Nations human development report 2010', United Nations Development Program, accessed 19 February 2011 from http://hdr.undp.org/ en/2010-report/download.

———— 2010b. 'Strengthening of national capacities for national development strategies and their management: an evaluation of UNDP's contribution. Country Study – Saudi Arabia', United Nations Development Program, accessed 17 October 2012 from http://web.undp.org/evaluation/documents/thematic/ cd/Saudi-Arabia.pdf.

———— 2009. 'The Arab human development report 2009: challenges to human security in the Arab countries', United Nations Development Program, accessed 3 May 2014 from www.arab-hdr.org/publications/other/ahdr/ahdr2009e.

—— 2008. 'Concluding comments of the committee on the elimination of discrimination against women: Saudi Arabia', United Nations, accessed 14 January 2012 from www.ohchr.org/english/bodies/cedaw/docs/CEDAW.C.SAU.CO.2_en.pdf.

—— 2007. 'Consideration of reports submitted by states parties under article 18 of the convention on the elimination of all forms of discrimination against women. Combined initial and second periodic reports of states parties. Saudi Arabia', United Nations, accessed 14 January 2012 from http://daccess-dds-ny.un.org/doc/UNDOC/GEN/N07/296/67/PDF/N0729667.pdf?OpenElement.

—— 2005. 'The Arab human development report 2005: towards the rise of women in the Arab world', United Nations Development Program, accessed 3 May 2014 from www.arab-hdr.org/publications/other/ahdr/ahdr2005e.pdf.

—— 2004. 'The Arab human development report 2004: towards freedom in the Arab world', United Nations Development Program, accessed 3 May 2014 from www.arab-hdr.org/publications/other/ahdr/ahdr2004e.pdf.

United Nations Children's Fund 2014. 'MENA gender equality profile: girls and women in the Middle East and North Africa, Oman', UNICEF, accessed 25 November 2014 from www.unicef.org/gender/files/Oman-Gender-Equality-Profile-2011.pdf.

United Nations Economic and Social Commission for Western Asia 2015. 'Demographic profile of Oman', United Nations, accessed 4 January 2016 from www.escwa.un.org/popin/members/oman.pdf.

—— 2014a. 'Status of Arab women report. Access to justice for women and girls in the Arab region: from ratification to implementation of international instruments', United Nations, accessed 14 January 2016 from www.unescwa.org/sites/www.unescwa.org/files/publications/files/e_escwa_ecw_15_1_e.pdf.

—— 2014b. 'Demographic profile of Saudi Arabia', United Nations, accessed 14 April 2015 from www.escwa.un.org/popin/members/saudi_arabia.pdf.

United Nations Educational, Scientific and Cultural Organisation 2014. 'Entrepreneurship education, Oman', United Nations, accessed 25 November 2014 from www.unevoc.unesco.org/fileadmin/user_upload/pubs/Entrepreneurship%20education%20-%20Oman.pdf.

United States Energy Information Agency 2015a. 'Country analysis brief: United Arab Emirates', United States Energy Information Agency, accessed 25 November 2015 from www.eia.gov/beta/international/analysis_includes/countries_long/United_Arab_Emirates/uae.pdf.

—— 2015b. 'Country analysis brief: Oman', United States Energy Information Agency, accessed 25 November 2015 from www.eia.gov/beta/international/analysis_includes/countries_long/Oman/oman.pdf.

———— 2015c. 'Country analysis brief: Saudi Arabia', United States Energy Information Agency, accessed 25 November 2015 from www.eia.gov/beta/international/analysis_includes/countries_long/Saudi_Arabia/saudi_arabia.pdf.

University of Pennsylvania 2015. 'Affirmative action policy', accessed 24 May 2014 from www.upenn.edu/affirm-action/eoaa.html.

Vassiliev, A. 1998. *The History of Saudi Arabia*. London: Saqi.

Vidal, J. 2011. 'How much oil does Saudi Arabia actually have?' *The Guardian*, 16 February, accessed 28 January 2016 from www.theguardian.com/environment/blog/2011/feb/15/oil-saudi-arabia-reserves.

Vietor, R. and White, H. 2015. 'Saudi Arabia: finding stability after the Arab Spring', Harvard Business School Case Study 9-714-053, accessed 30 November 2015 from https://hbr.org/search?search_type=search-all&term=Case+Study+9-714-053.

Vigen, T. 2015. *Spurious Correlations: Correlation Does Not Equal Causation*. New York: Hachette Books.

Visa Reporter 2014. 'Oman exempts SMEs from ban on recruitment', Visa Reporter, 15 December, accessed 20 December 2015 from www.visareporter.com/news-article/oman-exempts-smes-from-ban-on-recruitment.

Wadud, A. 2006. *Inside the Gender Jihad: Women's Reform in Islam*. Oxford: One World Publications.

Walker, J. Butler, S., Schulte-Peevers, A. and Shearer, I. 2010. *Oman, UAE and the Arabian Peninsula*. London: Lonely Planet Publications.

Walters, T., Walters, L. and Barwind, J. 2010. 'Tertiary education in the Arabian Gulf: a colossal wreck, remaining boundless and bare?', in The Middle East Institute *Higher Education and the Middle East: Serving the Knowledge – Based Economy*, pp. 18–20.

Weber, M. 1949. *The Methodology of the Social Sciences*. London: Allen and Unwin.

Webometrics 2016. 'Ranking web of universities', Webometrics, accessed 22 January 2016 from www.webometrics.info/en/Asia/Oman%20.

———— 2015. 'Countries arranged by number of universities in top ranks', Webometrics, accessed 17 May 2015 from www.webometrics.info/en/node.54.

Wenar, L. 2016. *Blood Oil: Tyrants, Violence and the Rules That Run the World*. Oxford: Oxford University Press.

Werner, C., Devillard, S., Sancier-Sultan, S. and Desvaux, G. 2010. 'McKinsey global survey results: moving women to the top', McKinsey & Company, accessed 21 April 2012 from www.mckinsey.com/business-functions/organisation/our-insights/moving-women-to-the-top-mckinsey-global-survey-results.

Weston, M. 2008. *Prophets and Princes: Saudi Arabia from Muhammed to the Present*. Hoboken, NJ: John Wiley and Sons.

White, B., Cox, C. and Cooper, C. 1994. *Women's Career Development: A Study of High Flyers*. Oxford: Blackwell.

Wikan, U. 1982. *Behind the Veil in Arabia: Women in Oman*. Chicago: University of Chicago Press.

Wikipedia 2016. 'Emirati parliamentary election 2015', accessed 8 March 2016 from https://en.wikipedia.org/wiki/Emirati_parliamentary_election,_2015.

––––––– 2015. 'List of universities and colleges by country: the Arab world', accessed 8 March 2015 from http://en.wikipedia.org/wiki/Lists_of_universities_and_colleges_by_country#The_Arab_World.

––––––– 2014. 'Cabinet of Oman', accessed 4 December 2014 from https://en.wikipedia.org/wiki/Cabinet_of_Oman.

Willoughby, J. 2008. 'Let a thousand models bloom: forging alliances with western universities and the making of a new higher education system in the Gulf', Working Paper Series No. 2008-1, American University Washington, Department of Economics, accessed 14 April 2013 from http://w.american.edu/cas/economics/repec/amu/workingpapers/2008-01.pdf.

Wilson, F. 1995. *Organisational Behavior and Gender*. London: McGraw-Hill.

Withnall, A. 2014. 'Saudi cleric issues religious edict banning all-you-can-eat buffets', *The Independent*, 18 March, accessed 22 July 2014 from www.independent.co.uk/news/world/Middle East/saudi-cleric-issues-religious-edict-banning-all-you-can-eat-buffets-9200111.html.

Wittenburg-Cox, A. and Maitland, A. 2008. *Why Women Mean Business: Understanding the Emergence of Our Next Economic Revolution*. London: Jossey-Bass.

Woetzel, J., Madgavkar, A., Manyika, J. Ellingrud, K., Hunt, V. and Krishnan, M. 2016. 'Realising gender equality's $12 trillion economic opportunity', McKinsey Global Institute, accessed 18 May 2016 from www.mckinsey.com/global-themes/employment-and-growth/realizing-gender-equalitys-12-trillion-economic-opportunity?cid=other-eml-alt-mgi-mck-oth-1605.

Wollstonecraft, M. 1792. *A Vindication of the Rights of Woman: With Strictures on Moral and Legal Subjects*, accessed 29 March 2015 from www.earlymodern texts.com/assets/pdfs/wollstonecraft1792_2.pdf.

Women on Boards 2016. 'Success stories', Women on Boards (Australia), accessed 18 May 2016 from https://womenonboards.net/en-AU/About-Us/Success-Stories-On-Board#2016.

Women's Entrepreneurship Day 2014 'Women's entrepreneurship day Oman', Oman Entrepreneurs, accessed 12 March 2015 from www.omanentrepreneurs.com/about.html.

Working Mother 2015. '2015 Working Mother: 100 best companies', *Working Mother Magazine*, accessed 12 April 2014 from www.workingmother.com/2015-working-mother-100-best-companies.

World Bank 2016a. 'Doing business: ease of doing business in the United Arab Emirates', World Bank Group, accessed 12 January 2015 from www.doing business.org/data/exploreeconomies/unitedarabemirates/.

────── 2016b. 'Doing business: ease of doing business in Oman', World Bank Group, accessed 15 March 2016 from www.doingbusiness.org/data/exploreeco nomies/oman.

────── 2016c. 'Doing business: ease of doing business in Saudi Arabia', World Bank Group, accessed 15 March 2016 from www.doingbusiness.org/data/exploreeco nomies/saudi-arabia.

────── 2015. 'GDP per capita: Saudi Arabia', World Bank Group, accessed 7 Febru ary 2016 from data.worldbank.org/indicator/NY.GDP.PCAP.CD/countries/SA?display=graph.

────── 2014. 'Data by country 2014', World Bank Group, accessed 23 March 2016 from data.worldbank.org/country/switzerland.

────── 2013. 'Knowledge economy index 2012', World Bank Group, accessed 2 November 2014 from siteresources.worldbank.org/INTUNIKAM/Resources/2012.pdf.

────── 2012. 'Middle East and North Africa: overview', World Bank Group, accessed 9 May 2012 from www.worldbank.org/en/region/mena/overview#1.

────── 1994. 'Document on the Sultanate of Oman: sustainable growth and eco nomic development', World Bank Group, Report no. 12199-OM, accessed 24 March 2014 from http://documents.worldbank.org/curated/en/1994/05/698315/oman-sustainable-growth-economic-diversification.

World Economic Forum 2015a. 'The global competiveness report', World Eco nomic Forum, accessed 6 April 2016 from www.weforum.org/reports/global-competitiveness-report-2014–2015.

────── 2015b. 'Global gender gap report 2015', World Economic Forum, accessed 29 December 2015 from www3.weforum.org/docs/WEF_GenderGap_Report_2015.pdf.

────── 2013. 'Global gender gap report 2013', World Economic Forum, accessed 24 March 2014 from www3.weforum.org/docs/WEF_GenderGap_Report_2013.pdf.

────── 2011. 'Global gender gap report 2011', World Economic Forum, accessed 4 December 2013 from www3.weforum.org/docs/WEF_GenderGap_Report_2011.pdf.

——— 2010. 'Global gender gap report 2010', World Economic Forum, accessed 4 January 2011 from www3.weforum.org/docs/WEF_GenderGap_Report_2010.pdf.

——— 2007. 'Global gender gap report 2007', World Economic Forum, accessed 16 February 2008 from www3.weforum.org/docs/WEF_GenderGap_Report_2007.pdf.

World Population Review 2016. 'United Arab Emirates population 2015', World Population Review, accessed 10 May 2016 from http://worldpopulation review.com/countries/united-arab-emirates-population/.

World Trade Organisation 2005. 'Accessions: Saudi Arabia', World Trade Organisation, accessed 2 February 2016 from www.wto.org/english/thewto_e/acc_e/a1_arabie_saoudite_e.htm.

Wright, R. 2009. *The Evolution of God.* London: Little, Brown and Company.

Xie, Y. and Popina, E. 2015. 'Saudi Arabia credit rating cut after oil prices sink', *Bloomberg,* accessed 4 February 2016 from www.bloomberg.com/news/art icles/2015-10-30/saudi-arabia-cut-to-a-from-aa-by-s-p-after-oil-prices-plunge.

Yamani, M. 2008. *Polygamy and Law in Contemporary Saudi Arabia.* Reading, UK: Ithaca.

Yang, J. 2006. 'Pepsi's diversity push pays off', *Fortune,* 4 September: 20.

Yang, N. 2005. 'Individualism-collectivism and work-family interface: a Sino-US comparison', in S. Poelmans (ed.) *Work and Family: An International Research Perspective,* pp. 287–319.

Yaseen, Z. 2013. 'Women entrepreneurs: challenges and opportunities in the Arab world, UAE case', *Business and Entrepreneurship Journal,* 2(1), 43–48.

Yousef, D. 2010. 'Industry ventures get low priority: high start-up costs and lack of technology limit Emirati participation', *Gulf News* (Business Section), 14 July.

YouTube 2016. 'Women drivers in Saudi Arabia', YouTube, accessed 3 February 2016 from www.youtube.com/results?search_query=women+drivers+in+saudi+arabia.

Zackowitz, M. 2003. 'Harley's mid-life crisis', *National Geographic,* August: 4–5.

Zakaria, F. 2004. *The Future of Freedom: Illiberal Democracy at Home and Abroad.* London: W. W. Norton and Company Ltd.

Zewail, A. 2011. 'A scientific revolution: the Arab Spring puts the Middle East in a position to become a scientific powerhouse, but it needs help from the west', *New Scientist,* 23 April: 26.

Index